FUNDAMENTALS
Cognition

Is it possible to learn something without being aware of it?
How does emotion influence the way we think?
How can we improve our memory?

Fundamentals of Cognition, third edition, provides a basic, reader-friendly introduction to the key cognitive processes we use to interact successfully with the world around us. Our abilities in attention, perception, learning, memory, language, problem solving, thinking, and reasoning are all vitally important in enabling us to cope with everyday life. Understanding these processes through the study of cognitive psychology is essential for understanding human behaviour.

This edition has been thoroughly updated and revised with an emphasis on making it even more accessible to introductory-level students. Bringing on board Professor Marc Brysbaert, a world-leading researcher in the psychology of language, as co-author, this new edition includes:

- developed and extended research activities and "In the Real World" case studies to make it easy for students to engage with the material;
- new real-world topics such as discussions of attention-deficit/hyperactivity disorder, the reading problems of individuals with dyslexia, why magic tricks work, and why we cannot remember the Apple logo accurately;
- a supporting companion website containing multiple choice questions, flashcards, sample essay answers, instructor resources, and more.

The book provides a perfect balance between traditional approaches to cognition and cutting-edge cognitive neuroscience and cognitive neuropsychology. Covering all the key topics within cognition, this comprehensive overview is essential reading for all students of cognitive psychology and related areas such as clinical psychology.

Michael W. Eysenck is Professor Emeritus in Psychology at Royal Holloway, University of London, and is also a Professorial Fellow at Roehampton University, UK. He is the best-selling author of a range of textbooks, including *Cognitive Psychology: A Student's Handbook*, *Memory* (with Alan Baddeley and Michael Anderson), and *Fundamentals of Psychology*.

Marc Brysbaert is Professor of Psychology at Ghent University, Belgium. He has authored a number of textbooks and is Editor of the *Quarterly Journal of Experimental Psychology*.

FUNDAMENTALS OF
Cognition

Third edition

Michael W. Eysenck and
Marc Brysbaert

Routledge
Taylor & Francis Group

LONDON AND NEW YORK

Third edition published 2018
by Routledge
2 Park Square, Milton Park, Abingdon, Oxon, OX14 4RN

and by Routledge
711 Third Avenue, New York, NY 10017

Routledge is an imprint of the Taylor & Francis Group, an informa business

100791544X

First edition published by Psychology Press 2006

Second edition published by Psychology Press 2012

British Library Cataloguing-in-Publication Data
A catalogue record for this book is available from the British Library

Library of Congress Cataloging-in-Publication Data
Names: Eysenck, Michael W., author. | Brysbaert, Marc, author.
Title: Fundamentals of cognition / Michael W. Eysenck and Marc Brysbaert.
Description: Third Edition. | New York : Routledge, 2018. | Revised edition
    of Fundamentals of cognition, 2012. | Includes bibliographical references
    and index.
Identifiers: LCCN 2017052947 | ISBN 9781138670433 (hardback : alk.
    paper) | ISBN 9781138670457 (pbk. : alk. paper) | ISBN 9781315617633
    (ebook)
Subjects: LCSH: Cognition.
Classification: LCC BF311 .E938 2018 | DDC 153—dc23
LC record available at https://lccn.loc.gov/2017052947

ISBN: 978-1-138-67043-3 (hbk)
ISBN: 978-1-138-67045-7 (pbk)
ISBN: 978-1-315-61763-3 (ebk)

Typeset in Sabon
by Apex CoVantage, LLC

Printed in Great Britain
by Bell & Bain Ltd, Glasgow

Visit the companion website: www.routledge.com/cw/eysenck

Contents

Preface

Cognitive psychology is concerned with the processes that allow us to make sense of the world around us and to make sensible decisions about how to cope with everyday life. As such, it is of huge importance within psychology as a whole. The advances made by cognitive psychologists have permeated most of the rest of psychology – areas such as abnormal psychology and social psychology have been transformed by the cognitive approach. As cognitive psychologists, we may be biased. However, we genuinely believe cognitive psychology is at the heart of psychology.

The Chinese have a saying, "May you live in interesting times." For cognitive psychologists, these are indisputably very interesting times. One important reason is that there has been a substantial increase in research showing the relevance of the cognitive approach to the real world. Examples discussed in this book include the following: security scanning at airports, why fingerprinting experts make mistakes, the misinterpretations of patients with anxiety disorders, the fallibility of eyewitness testimony, why our reasoning is often apparently very illogical, and what CAPTCHAS (distorted images of connected characters you have to make sense of to access certain websites) tell us about perception.

Another important reason why cognitive psychology has become increasingly interesting is that technological advances now permit us to observe the brain in action in great detail. You have undoubtedly seen the fruits of such research in the brightly colored pictures of the brain to be found within the covers of numerous magazines. In this book, there is much coverage of the exciting discoveries based on brain imaging.

We would like to express our gratitude to all those who helped in the preparation of this book. They include Ceri Griffiths, Amy Welmers, and Marie Louise Roberts. Finally, the first author owes a huge debt of gratitude to his wife, Christine, who devoted hundreds of hours to tracking down important articles to be discussed in this book. Although the second author had to track down his own articles, there is no doubt the book would have taken much longer to write without his wife's support, too. The book is deservedly dedicated to them.

Michael W. Eysenck and Marc Brysbaert

To Christine and Elise, with love

Don't become a mere recorder of facts, but try to penetrate the mystery of their origin.

Ivan Pavlov (1849–1936)

Chapter 1

Contents

What is cognitive psychology?

INTRODUCTION

There is more general interest than ever in understanding the mysteries of the human brain and the mind. So far as the media are concerned, numerous television programs, movies, and books are devoted to the more dramatic aspects of the brain and its workings. You must have seen pretty colored pictures of the brain in magazines, revealing which parts of the brain are most active when people are engaged in various tasks. So far as science is concerned, there has been an explosion of research on the brain by scientists from several disciplines including cognitive psychologists, cognitive neuroscientists, biologists, and so on.

How does all of this relate to cognitive psychology? **Cognitive psychology** is concerned with the processes involved in acquiring, storing, and transforming information. Let's make that more concrete by focusing on what you are currently doing. In the next paragraph, the italicized words indicate some of the main aspects of human cognition.

Learning objectives

After studying Chapter 1, you should be able to:

- Define "cognitive psychology" and identify which types of mental processes are studied in cognitive psychology.
- Explain why introspection is not a good method for understanding these mental processes.
- Discuss the advantages and disadvantages of the behaviorist approach to studying human cognition.
- Describe the uses and limitations of the four main methods/ approaches used in cognitive psychology – experimental cognitive psychology; cognitive neuroscience; cognitive neuropsychology; and computational cognitive science.
- Define, compare, and contrast "bottom-up" and "top-down" processes.
- Define, compare, and contrast "serial" and "parallel" processes.

Key term

Cognitive psychology: studies the processes involved in acquiring, storing, and transforming information.

You are using *visual perception* to take in information from the printed page, and hopefully you are *attending* to the content of this book. As a result, *learning* is taking place. In order for this to happen, you must possess good *language skills* – you wouldn't learn much if you tried to read a textbook written in an unfamiliar language! Your reading benefits from having *stored knowledge* relevant to the material in this book. There may also be an element of *problem solving* as you relate what is in the book to the possibly conflicting information you learned previously. Finally, the acid test of whether your learning has been effective and has led to *long-term memory* comes when you are tested on your knowledge of the material contained in this book.

The italicized words in the previous paragraph form the basis of much of the coverage of cognitive psychology in this book. If you look at the titles of the various chapters, you may feel cognitive psychology can be neatly divided up into various categories (e.g., attention; perception; language). However, it is important to realize that all the categories *interact* with each other. For example, language isn't totally irrelevant to the other categories. Much of what we learn and remember is language-based, and language is heavily involved in most of our thinking and reasoning.

In the Real World 1.1 *Remembering what we have seen*

As we will see throughout this book, cognitive psychology is very relevant to everyday life. For example, consider how often we talk about things we experienced. This can be to friends, but also, sometimes, when we are asked to make an official statement of what we witnessed. How accurate are these memories? How detailed? Do we inadvertently tell lies because our memories fail us?

First, the good news. We have a reasonably good gist of many things we have seen. Brady et al. (2008) presented 2,500 photographs of everyday objects to participants at a speed of one picture per 3 seconds (the whole experiment lasted more than 5 hours) and afterwards asked the participants which photos they had seen. On each trial, the participants saw two photographs next to each other: one that had been seen and a new one. The participants' task was to indicate which picture they had seen before. In one-third of the trials the task was made rather easy by using photos of new objects that had not been presented before. In another one-third, a new exemplar of an object that had been seen was shown (e.g., a new hammer). Finally, the remaining foil photos consisted of the same object but taken from a different angle. To their surprise, the researchers observed that the participants were good not only on trials with new objects (92% correct) but also on trials with new exemplars (88%) and on trials with the same exemplars photographed from a different angle (87% correct). So, we are quite good at remembering what we have seen in a series of 2,500 photographs presented one after the other in the past 5 hours.

However, how detailed are our long-term memories for things we have seen some time ago? Blake et al. (2015) asked 85 students to draw the Apple logo (try it before reading on!). This is a very simple stimulus encountered many times. In addition, half of the participants were avid Apple users. When asked beforehand how confident the participants felt that they would be able to draw the logo, most of them indicated they were fairly sure their rendition would be correct. Still, only one of the 85 participants drew an accurate picture of the logo! (Are you happy with the picture you drew?)

An obvious criticism against the finding is that the participants knew the logo well but were just bad at drawing. Therefore, in a second study, Blake et al. presented the participants with an array of logos to select from (as shown in Figure 1.1).

In the recognition task, less than half of the participants gave the correct answer! In later studies with more options to choose from, the percentage

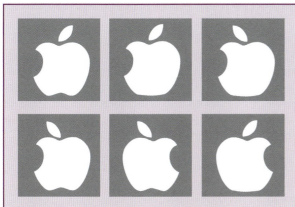

Figure 1.1   Is the real Apple logo present in the line-up? Can you find the Apple logo among the alternatives? The answer is given at the end of this chapter.
Source: From Blake et al. (2015).

even dropped to 25%. How is this possible for a simple stimulus we have seen thousands of times? The authors ventured that in our long-term memory we do not store visual information in a form more detailed than needed for daily interactions. For the Apple logo, it is enough to know that it consists of a white apple against a grey background (mostly). We usually don't need more information (unless we are asked to take part in the experiment of Blake et al.). So, there is no need to invest memory capacity in storing more details.

Needless to say, Blake et al.'s (2015) findings have implications for eyewitness testimony. To what extent can people identify a perpetrator better within a line-up of similar-looking persons than they can identify the correct Apple logo among a set of lures? How much detail do we store in our memory when confronted with an incident? Only research in cognitive psychology can tell us how accurate eyewitness testimony is and which aspects of the procedure improve or deteriorate performance (for a first pointer to this literature, see Clark, 2012).

Research Activity 1.1 *How much do you know about human memory and cognition?*

In the real-world example, we saw that participants remembered much less of the Apple logo than they thought. So, how good is our knowledge of our own memory performance? How does it live up to the data collected in cognitive psychology? Answer the quiz below with yes or no. "Yes" means there is more evidence in favor of this statement than against it; "no" implies there is more evidence against it. How good is your score? Is there scope for improvement? If there is, the present textbook (in particular, Chapters 4 and 5) will help you.

1. Being a genius is due to hard work more than to innate talent.
2. Visual memory is like a video camera.
3. Memory performance is better when you devote part of your preparation time to testing yourself rather than reading and re-reading the material.
4. People do not have personal memories of events that happened in the first three years of their life.
5. Memory is better for exciting events.
6. If you are the victim of a violent crime, your memory for the perpetrator's face is perfect.
7. Only a few individuals have bad memory.
8. When there is a gun present, victims are better at remembering the details of the event.
9. Memory performance for an exam is worse if you learn all the information on a single day than if you spend the same time learning over several days.
10. We do not forget the source of our knowledge.
11. People do not have memories of things that never actually happened.
12. We can typically remember things that we did not attend to.
13. Memories recalled under hypnosis are not better than memories retrieved without hypnosis.
14. Accurate memories of childhood sexual abuse usually arise years after the abuse.
15. The questions asked to an eyewitness may change the actual memories of the eyewitness.

Source: Partly based on Chaplin & Shaw, 2016.

Answer key: 1.Y 2.N 3.Y 4.Y 5.N 6.N 7.N 8.N 9.Y 10.N 11.N 12.N 13.Y 14.N 15.Y

HISTORY OF COGNITIVE PSYCHOLOGY

We can date the origins of cognitive psychology to the ancient Greek philosopher Aristotle (384–322 BC), who was perhaps the cleverest person that ever lived. He was interested in several topics relevant to psychology, including imagery and learning (Leahey, 2012). For example, Aristotle argued that people, events, and things tend to be linked and remembered on the basis of three laws of association: contiguity or closeness; similarity; and contrast. For instance, seeing Donna can make us think of Jack for three reasons:

1. We've previously seen Donna and Jack together (law of contiguity).
2. Donna and Jack resemble each other (law of similarity).
3. Donna and Jack are very different (law of contrast).

INTROSPECTION

Aristotle thought that introspection (the systematic investigation of one's own thoughts) was the only way of studying thinking. Two thousand years later, there was still much enthusiasm for using introspection. Oswald Külpe (1862–1915) founded the Würzburg School, which was dedicated to the use of introspection. Participants focused on a complex stimulus (e.g., a logical problem), after which they reported their conscious thoughts during the task. This revealed that people consciously think about sensations, feelings, images, conscious mental sets, and thoughts.

Introspection is still important in contemporary psychology (e.g., when we are answering a questionnaire or thinking about our feelings, we make use of introspection), but it is no longer a popular way of studying human cognition. *Why* is that? One problem is that it isn't possible to check the accuracy of the conscious thoughts people claim to have. Külpe argued that people sometimes have "imageless thoughts," whereas another prominent psychologist (E.B. Titchener) claimed that *all* thoughts have images. This controversy couldn't be resolved on the basis of introspection, because introspective evidence is unverifiable.

Another major problem with introspection was pointed out even before the Würzburg School had been set up. According to the British scientist Francis Galton (1883), the position of consciousness "appears to be that of a helpless spectator of but a minute fraction of automatic brain work." As we will see in this book, many processes must happen rapidly and in parallel for us to have good performance. Thinking that we can grasp all these fast and automatic processes with our limited conscious capacity is an illusion.

Our behavior is often influenced by processes occurring *outside* of consciousness (see also Chapter 3). Nisbett and Wilson (1977) discussed an experiment in which participants were presented with a horizontal array of essentially identical stockings. They decided which pair was best and then indicated why they had chosen that particular pair. Participants typically justified their choices by claiming the chosen pair was slightly superior in color or texture. This introspective evidence was well wide of the mark. In fact, most participants chose the right-most pair – their choices were actually influenced by relative spatial position. However, even when they were specifically asked whether the position of the selected pair of stockings in the array might have influenced their choice, they vehemently denied it. Even the authors were at a loss to explain why in this particular study the participants tended to select the stockings to the right, independent of which stockings hung there. They ventured that "subjects carried into the judgment task the consumer's habit of 'shopping around', holding off on choice of early-seen garments on the left in favor of later-seen garments on the right" (p. 244).

Some motivational processes are also outside conscious awareness. Pessiglione et al. (2007) gave participants the task of squeezing a handgrip to earn money. Immediately before each trial, the money that could be earned was indicated by a £1 (about $1.25) or 1 pence (about 1.25 cents) coin presented on the screen. The coin was clearly visible or it was subliminal (below the level of conscious awareness). Participants squeezed harder on high-reward trials even when the reward wasn't consciously visible, and there was more activation in brain areas associated with reward processing. Thus, motivation can be influenced by unconscious processes.

In sum, there are four major problems with relying heavily on introspective evidence:

1. We are largely unaware of many of the processes influencing our motivation and behavior. We are generally consciously aware of the *outcome* of our cognitive processes rather than those *processes* themselves (Valentine, 1992). For example, what is the name of the person who became American President after George W. Bush? We imagine you rapidly thought of Barack Obama, but without any clear idea of how you produced the right answer.
2. Our reports of our conscious experience may be distorted (deliberately or otherwise). For example, we may pretend to have more positive thoughts about someone than is actually the case.
3. There is a delay between having a conscious experience and reporting its existence. As a result, we may sometimes forget part of our conscious experience before reporting it (Lamme, 2003).
4. Introspection has no way of ascertaining what is going on when two (groups of) persons differ in their introspection.

BEHAVIORISM
The dominant approach to psychology throughout most of the first half of the 20th century was behaviorism. Behaviorism started in the United States in 1913. Its central figure was John Watson (1878–1958), who was determined to make psychology an experimental science. He argued that psychology could not be a science as long as it relied on introspection. The only way forward was to carry out well-controlled behavioral experiments under laboratory conditions.

According to Watson, psychologists should focus on observable stimuli (aspects of the immediate situation) and observable responses (behavior produced by the participants in an experiment). Learning occurs when an association is formed between a stimulus and a response. Terms referring to mental events can't be verified by reference to observable behavior, and so should be abandoned. Watson (1913, p. 165) wanted behaviorism to be an approach that would "never use the terms consciousness, mental states, mind, content, introspectively verifiable, and the like."

Key term

Behaviorism: an approach to psychology that emphasizes a rigorous experimental approach and the role of conditioning in learning.

It is helpful in understanding Watson's approach to focus on one of his key assumptions: "The behaviorist . . . recognizes no dividing line between man and brute" (Watson, 1913, p. 158). This is an important assumption, because you can't obtain introspective evidence from other species, nor can you study their mental states. Watson had spent several years prior to 1913 involved in animal research. He found he could conduct proper experiments on other species with no reliance on introspection.

The American psychologist Burrhus Frederic Skinner (1904–1990) was the most influential behaviorist of all. He focused on operant conditioning, a form of learning in which behavior is controlled by its consequences. We learn to produce responses followed by reward or positive reinforcement and to avoid producing responses followed by unpleasant or aversive consequences. Operant conditioning is important, but it fails to account for complex human cognition (e.g., problem solving; reasoning; creativity).

Skinner agreed with Watson that the behaviorists' emphasis on *external* stimuli and responses should be accompanied by a virtual ignoring of *internal* mental and physiological processes. This had bizarre consequences. As Murphy and Kovach (1972) pointed out, "It is for the behaviorist no more intelligible to say that we think with the brain than to say that we walk with the spinal cord."

Not all behaviorists agreed with Watson and Skinner that internal processes and structures should be ignored. A prominent opponent of that position was Tolman (1948). He carried out studies in which rats learned to run through a maze to a goal box containing food. When he blocked off the path the rats had learned to use, they rapidly selected an alternative path leading in the right general direction. This suggested the rats had an internal cognitive map indicating the approximate layout of the maze and were not simply learning a sequence of responses.

Evaluation

+ The behaviorists argued that it was desirable for psychology to become a fully fledged science.

+ Their claim that the careful observation of behavior in controlled settings under experimental conditions is of fundamental importance is still valid a century later (Fuchs & Milar, 2003).

− The behaviorists understated the impact of internal factors (e.g., past experience; goals) on behavior. Skinner argued that our behavior is controlled by *current* rewards and punishments. If that were the case, we would be like weather vanes blown about by changes in the rewards and/ or punishments in the environment (Bandura, 1977).

− Most human behavior doesn't simply involve learning to associate certain stimuli with certain responses. For example, when we speak, we generally plan what we are going to say several words ahead of the words we are uttering. This involves complex internal processes that are neither stimuli nor responses.

COGNITIVE PSYCHOLOGY

Cognitive psychology, with its emphasis on understanding *internal* processes and structures, is very different from behaviorism. Indeed, it is common to talk about the "cognitive revolution" that overthrew behaviorism (e.g., Hobbs & Burman, 2009). However, we mustn't exaggerate the differences. Both approaches attached great importance to the use of a scientific approach and the experimental method. In addition, we have seen that some behaviorists (e.g., Tolman) were interested in internal processes. Thus, what happened as behaviorism gave way to cognitive psychology was "rapid, evolutionary change" (Leahey, 1992) rather than a revolutionary change.

It is almost as pointless to ask "When did cognitive psychology start?" as it is to inquire "How long is a piece of string?" The reality is that several psychologists made early contributions to cognitive psychology, but their efforts were mostly unsystematic and uncoordinated.

Many of the pioneers in cognitive psychology focused on memory. For example, Hermann Ebbinghaus (1850–1909) carried out numerous well-controlled studies of forgetting (Zangwill, 2004). He used nonsense syllables (e.g., KEB) designed to lack meaning so that he could obtain a relatively "pure" measure of forgetting. In fact, some meaning can be attached to almost any nonsense syllable (e.g., KEB might remind you of kebab). In spite of that, Ebbinghaus (1885) established that forgetting is especially rapid shortly after learning, with the rate of forgetting decreasing after that (Chapter 5).

Hugo Münsterberg (1863–1916) was interested in eyewitness testimony and wrote a book about it (*On the Witness Stand*, 1908). In this book he discusses one of the earliest experiments in cognitive psychology. A fake murder was staged during a lecture. A student drew a revolver and a second student rushed at him. Professor von Liszt stepped between them, and the revolver went off. The students who witnessed this event made many errors in recalling the event, including adding nonexistent elements.

The English psychologist Sir Frederic Bartlett (1886–1969) made an outstanding contribution to memory research (Pickford & Gregory, 2004). In his book *Remembering: An Experimental and Social Study* (1932), Bartlett argued that human memory is an active process (see also Henderson, 1903). We recall events so as to make them *consistent* with our preexisting knowledge and experience. This will often lead to systematic errors and distortions in memory (see Chapter 5).

Towards the end of the 19th century, there was rapid economic development in North America. The construction of a national railroad system meant that people were traveling more, and it became increasingly important to improve communication systems. These developments led Bryan and Harter (1897, 1899) to study learning in Morse code telegraph operators working for Western Union. Not surprisingly, they found that these operators became increasingly efficient at both receiving and sending messages in Morse code. More importantly, the operators' ability to receive messages showed some periods of rapid improvement with other periods of no improvement (plateaus) in-between. The operators initially became skilled at identifying individual letters. After that, they required a period of learning before mastering the ability to identify syllables and whole words.

The American William James (1842–1910) was possibly the most influential early contributor to cognitive psychology (Hunter, 2004). His greatest contributions came in his book *Principles of Psychology* (1890), which

Key terms

Bottom-up processing:
processing that is
determined directly by
environmental stimuli
rather than by the
individual's knowledge
and expectations.

Serial processing:
this involves only one
process occurring at
any given moment; that
process is completed
before the next one
starts; see **parallel
processing**.

Top-down processing:
stimulus processing
that is determined by
expectations, memory,
and knowledge rather
than directly by the
stimulus.

contains numerous fascinating insights into a host of topics including consciousness, attention, emotion, memory, and reasoning. William James argued that we are shaped as individuals by our actions and habits. In his own words, "Sow an action, and you reap a habit; sow a habit, and you reap a character; sow a character, and you reap a destiny" (quoted in Hunter, 2004, p. 493).

The year 1956 was of critical importance in the emergence of cognitive psychology (Thagard, 2005). During this year, several researchers who were to become highly influential cognitive psychologists made major contributions. At a meeting at the Massachusetts Institute of Technology, Noam Chomsky gave a paper on his theory of language; George Miller presented a paper on short-term memory (Miller, 1956); and Newell and Simon discussed their approach to problem solving (Newell et al., 1958). In addition, the first systematic attempt to consider concept formation from a cognitive perspective was reported (Bruner et al., 1956).

INFORMATION-PROCESSING APPROACH

At one time, most cognitive psychologists subscribed to the information-processing approach. A version of this approach popular about 45 years ago is shown in Figure 1.2. A stimulus (an environmental event such as a problem or a task) is presented. This stimulus causes various internal cognitive processes to occur, which finally lead to the desired response or answer. Processing directly affected by the stimulus input is often described as **bottom-up processing**. It was typically assumed that only one process occurs at any moment in time. This is known as **serial processing** – it means that one process is completed before the next one starts.

We can see more clearly what was involved in the information-processing approach by considering the model of human memory put forward by Richard Atkinson and Richard Shiffrin (1968; see Figure 1.3 and Chapter 4). They argued that we possess a separate sensory store for each of the sense modalities (e.g., vision; hearing).

With our limited processing capacity, there is generally too much information in the sensory stores for us to attend to all of it. Accordingly, we attend to only *some* of the available information, which then proceeds to the short-term store. This store has limited capacity, and information doesn't remain in it for long. However, if we rehearse (say over to ourselves) information in the short-term store, some of it will be transferred to the long-term store.

Top-down processing

The initial information-processing approach provided a drastic *oversimplification* of a complex reality. It is nearly always the case that processing is not exclusively bottom-up but also involves top-down processing. **Top-down processing** is processing influenced by the individual's expectations and knowledge rather than simply by the stimulus itself. Look at the triangle shown in Figure 1.4 and read what it says. Unless you are familiar with the trick, you probably read it as "Paris in the spring." If so, look again, and you will see the word "the" is repeated. Your expectation that it was the well-known phrase (top-down processing) dominated the information actually available from the stimulus (bottom-up processing).

Top-down processes are also prominent in memory and, therefore, had to be added to the bottom-up processing in Atkinson and Shiffrin's (1968)

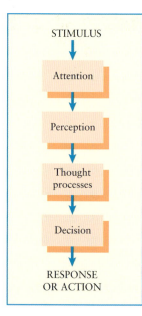

Figure 1.2 An early version of the information-processing approach.

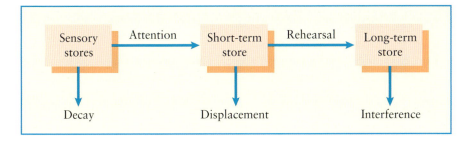

Figure 1.3 The multistore model of memory.

multistore model of Figure 1.3. Here are just two examples. First, if attentional processes determine which fraction of the information available in the sensory stores enters short-term memory, then top-down processes such as our goals and expectations are likely to influence what we attend to. So, they must be added to the model.

Second, let's focus on the notion that information enters the short-term store *before* the long-term store. Suppose you see the word "yacht" and start rehearsing it in the short-term store. How do you know it has an odd pronunciation? You must have obtained its pronunciation from long-term memory *before* rehearsing it. Thus, we seem to need an arrow pointing from the long-term store to the short-term store to explain what is happening. This is another example of top-down processes needed to understand memory functioning.

Mitterer and de Ruiter (2008) showed that top-down processes influence perception as well. Objects that can be almost any color (e.g., socks) were presented in an ambiguous hue intermediate between yellow and orange. The object was more likely to be perceived as orange when observers had previously seen an "orange" object (e.g., goldfish; carrot) in the same hue than when they had seen a "yellow" object (e.g., lemon; banana) in that hue. Thus, color perception depends in part on top-down processes based on world knowledge.

Clearly, cognition involves both bottom-up and top-down processing. This is called *interactive processing*. Information coming from the senses (bottom-up) is combined with expectations on the basis of the context (top-down) to optimize processing efficiency. Figure 1.5 gives another example of how the perception of a stimulus depends on the context in which it is seen.

Figure 1.4 Demonstration of top-down processing.

Figure 1.5 Another demonstration of top-down processing.

Parallel processing

Another limitation of the traditional information-processing approach was the assumption that processing is necessarily serial. In numerous situations, some of the processes involved in a cognitive task occur at the same time – this is **parallel processing**. As we will see repeatedly in this book, several different brain areas are usually active at the same time when someone performs a complex task. That is what we would expect if most processing is parallel rather than serial. We are particularly likely to use parallel processing when performing a much-practiced task, which is what we do most of the time. For example, someone taking their first driving lesson finds it almost impossible to steer accurately and to pay attention to other road users at the same time. In contrast, an experienced driver finds it easy and can even hold a conversation as well.

Key term

Parallel processing:
two or more processes occurring simultaneously; see **serial processing**.

> ## Section summary
>
> ### Introspection
> - Introspection was much used to study thinking before the advent of behaviorism. It is limited because many cognitive processes occur below the level of conscious awareness, and conscious reports are sometimes distorted.
>
> ### Behaviorism
> - Behaviorism (dominant in the first half of the 20th century) emphasized a scientific approach based on observable stimuli and responses. It was limited because it exaggerated the importance of current rewards and punishments as factors influencing behavior and minimized the importance of goals and past experience.
>
> ### Cognitive psychology
> - Cognitive psychology extended behaviorism by focusing on *internal* processes and structures as well as *external* stimuli and responses. There were many early pioneers in cognitive psychology, of whom William James probably had the greatest long-term impact.
> - In the 1950s and 1960s, cognitive psychologists put forward information-processing theories that emphasized bottom-up, serial processes. Such theories were oversimplified and were gradually replaced by theories that recognized the importance of top-down and parallel processes.

CONTEMPORARY COGNITIVE PSYCHOLOGY

We discuss up-to-date theory and research in cognitive psychology throughout this book. One of cognitive psychology's most distinctive features is the use of several approaches to increase our understanding of human cognition. There are four major approaches, each with its own strengths:

1. *Experimental cognitive psychology*: This approach involves carrying out experiments on healthy individuals (often psychology undergraduates). Behavioral evidence (e.g., participants' level of performance) is used to shed light on internal cognitive processes.
2. *Cognitive neuroscience*: This approach also involves carrying out experiments. However, it extends experimental cognitive psychology by using evidence from brain activity (as well as from behavior) to understand human cognition.
3. *Cognitive neuropsychology*: This approach also involves carrying out experiments. Although the participants are brain-damaged patients, it is hoped the findings will increase our understanding of cognition in healthy individuals as well. Cognitive neuropsychology was originally closely linked to cognitive psychology, but it has recently also become linked to cognitive neuroscience.
4. *Computational cognitive science*: This approach involves developing computer models based in part on experimental findings to explain human cognition.

Is one of these approaches better than any of the others? The answer is "no." Each approach has its own strengths and weaknesses (see following sections). As a result, researchers increasingly use two or more of these approaches to shed as much light as possible on the complexities of human cognition. Hence the dividing lines among these four approaches are becoming increasingly blurred.

EXPERIMENTAL COGNITIVE PSYCHOLOGY

For many decades, nearly all research in cognitive psychology involved carrying out experiments on healthy individuals under laboratory conditions. Such experiments are typically tightly controlled and "scientific." Researchers have shown great ingenuity in designing experiments to reveal the processes involved in attention, perception, learning, memory, and so on. As a result, the findings of experimental cognitive psychologists have played a major role in the development and subsequent testing of most theories in cognitive psychology.

Experimental cognitive psychologists typically obtain measures of the speed and accuracy of task performance. They want to use such behavioral measures to draw *inferences* about the internal processes involved in human cognition. Following we consider one example of this kind of approach.

An important phenomenon in cognitive psychology is the **Stroop effect** (Stroop, 1935). Participants name the colors in which words or letter strings appear (see Research Activity 1.2). Performance is fast and accurate when words congruent with the colors (e.g., BLUE printed in blue; RED printed in red) or neutral letter strings (e.g., FPRSM) are used. However, participants are much slower when words incongruent with the colors (e.g., BLUE printed in red) are used – this is the Stroop effect (MacLeod, 2015).

Why does the Stroop effect occur? We are so familiar with reading words that time-consuming conflict resolution is needed on incongruent trials. However, an additional mechanism is also involved. Kane and Engle (2003) compared performance on incongruent trials when 75% of the total trials were congruent and when 0% were congruent. They argued that it would be much harder to maintain the task goal ("Ignore the word and respond to the color") in the former condition because the correct response could be produced on most trials by simply reading the word. As predicted, the error rate was much higher in the 75% condition than the 0% condition (14% vs. 3%).

Key term
Stroop effect: the finding that naming the colors in which words are printed takes longer when the words are conflicting color words (e.g., the word RED printed in green).

Research Activity 1.2 *Are you susceptible to the Stroop effect?*

In the following task, you have to say the colors of the stimuli as fast as possible. If you make a mistake to a stimulus, you have to say that stimulus again. Measure the time you need for each column. If you need more time in column 4, you show a Stroop effect. Do you also need more time to read column 5 than column 4, as suggested by the research of Kane and Engle (2003) discussed in the main text?

Column 1	Column 2	Column 3	Column 4	Column 5
▬ (black)	NEST	BLACK	YELLOW	YELLOW
▬ (purple)	CHAOS	YELLOW	RED	RED
▬ (maroon)	OVEN	RED	BLUE	RED
▬ (teal)	TENNIS	GREEN	BLACK	BLACK
▬ (blue)	RING	BLUE	GREEN	GREEN
▬ (maroon)	OVEN	RED	BLUE	BLUE
▬ (blue)	RING	BLUE	GREEN	GREEN
▬ (purple)	CHAOS	YELLOW	RED	RED
▬ (black)	NEST	BLACK	YELLOW	BLACK
▬ (blue)	RING	BLUE	GREEN	GREEN
▬ (teal)	TENNIS	GREEN	BLACK	BLACK
▬ (purple)	CHAOS	YELLOW	RED	RED
▬ (blue)	RING	BLUE	GREEN	GREEN
▬ (purple)	CHAOS	YELLOW	RED	YELLOW
▬ (maroon)	OVEN	RED	BLUE	BLUE
▬ (teal)	TENNIS	GREEN	BLACK	BLACK
▬ (black)	NEST	BLACK	YELLOW	YELLOW
▬ (maroon)	OVEN	RED	BLUE	RED
▬ (teal)	TENNIS	GREEN	BLACK	BLACK
▬ (blue)	CHAOS	BLUE	GREEN	GREEN

We will see the huge contribution experimental cognitive psychology has made to our understanding of human cognition throughout this book. However, a concern is that how people behave in the laboratory may differ from how they behave in everyday life. In other words, laboratory research may be low in **ecological validity** – the extent to which the findings of laboratory studies are applicable to everyday life.

Two points need to be made here. First, it is far better to carry out well-controlled experiments under laboratory conditions than poorly controlled experiments under naturalistic conditions. It is precisely because it is considerably easier for researchers to exercise experimental control in the laboratory that so much research is laboratory-based. Second, there are very few studies showing that fundamental processes found in the lab differ from those used in everyday life. Research in cognitive psychology often has direct real-world applicability. Such research is highlighted in nearly every chapter of this book.

COGNITIVE NEUROSCIENCE

Much can be discovered about human cognition by obtaining behavioral evidence. However, what is exciting about **cognitive neuroscience** is that it provides us with information about brain activity during performance of cognitive tasks as well as behavioral evidence. As we will see, much research in cognitive neuroscience involves the use of various brain-imaging techniques while participants perform a cognitive task.

| Key terms

Ecological validity: the extent to which research findings (especially laboratory ones) can be generalized to the real world.

Cognitive neuroscience: an approach that aims to understand human cognition by combining information from brain activity and behavior.

Carving up the brain in different areas

To understand research involving functional neuroimaging, we must consider how the brain is organized and how the different areas are described. There are various ways of describing specific brain areas. We will discuss two of the main ones as follows.

First, the cerebral cortex is divided into four main divisions or lobes (see Figure 1.6). There are four lobes in the left and the right brain hemisphere: frontal, parietal, temporal, and occipital. The frontal lobes are divided from the parietal lobes by the central sulcus (sulcus means furrow or groove); the lateral fissure separates the temporal lobes from the parietal and frontal lobes; and the parieto-occipital sulcus and pre-occipital notch divide the occipital lobes from the parietal and temporal lobes. The main gyri (or ridges; gyrus is the singular) within the cerebral cortex are shown in Figure 1.6. Notice that, because we have two brain halves (left and right), the lobes exist in pairs (e.g., the left and the right frontal lobe).

Researchers use various terms to describe more precisely the brain area(s) activated during the performance of a given task:

- *dorsal*: superior or toward the top
- *ventral*: inferior or toward the bottom
- *anterior*: toward the front
- *posterior*: toward the back
- *lateral*: situated at the side
- *medial*: situated in the middle

Second, the German neurologist Korbinian Brodmann (1868–1918) produced a map of the brain based on variations in the cellular structure of the tissues (see Figure 1.7). Many (but not all) of the areas identified by Brodmann

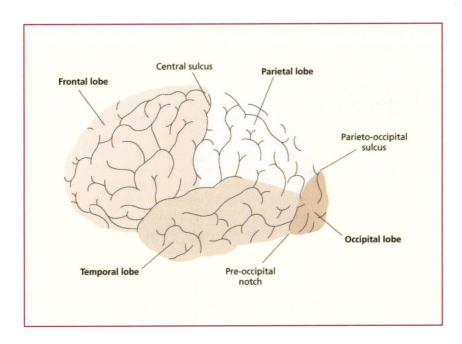

Figure 1.6 The four lobes, or divisions, of the cerebral cortex in the left hemisphere.

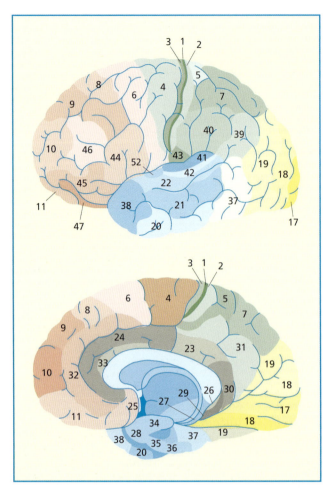

Figure 1.7   The Brodmann areas of the brain on the lateral (top) and medial (bottom) surfaces.

correspond to functionally distinct areas. We will often refer to areas such as BA17, which simply means Brodmann Area 17.

The brain is more than the cerebrum

Thus far we have discussed the cerebrum, the large rounded structure that makes the visible part of the brain and consists of grooves and ridges. Underneath the cerebrum, in the middle of the head, there are a number of small structures, called subcortical structures (the cerebrum is also called the cortex, although technically speaking the cortex is only the outer, grey layer of the cerebrum; hence the word *subcortical*: under the cortex).

Three subcortical structures will be important for the rest of the book: the hippocampus, the amygdala, and the thalamus (Figure 1.8).

The **hippocampus** is a subcortical structure particularly important for memory encoding and spatial knowledge (e.g., orienting yourself and finding a way to a target). With some imagination, it looks like a seahorse (hence its name). There is one part on the left side of the brain and one on the right.

The **amygdala** consists of a left and a right structure in front of the hippocampus. This structure is particularly active in situations that provoke fear and that are emotionally arousing. There is evidence that stimuli (in particular dangerous ones) can directly activate the amygdala without elaboration by the cortex.

The **thalamus** is at the very center of the brain and functions as the brain's relay station connecting the various parts (although there are also many direct connections between different parts of the brain). It is a structure involved in regulating the state of consciousness (e.g., asleep, awake, in coma).

Dramatic technological advances in recent years mean we now have many ways of obtaining detailed information about what the brain is doing when we perform tasks. We can work out *where* and *when* in the brain activity occurs. In the following sections, we describe two widespread techniques: one primarily meant to investigate where the processing is taking place and the other to investigate when it occurs.

Functional magnetic resonance imaging (fMRI)

In magnetic resonance imaging (MRI), radio waves are used to excite atoms in the brain. This produces magnetic changes detected by a very large magnet (weighing up to 11 tons) surrounding the patient (Figure 1.9). These changes are then interpreted by a computer and turned into a very precise three-dimensional picture. MRI scans can be obtained from numerous different angles but only tell us about the *structure* of the brain rather than about its *functions*.

Cognitive neuroscientists are generally more interested in brain functions than brain structure. Happily, MRI technology can provide functional information in the form of **functional magnetic resonance imaging (fMRI)**. What is measured in fMRI is based on assessing brain areas in which there is an accumulation of oxygenated red blood cells suggestive of activity. Technically, this is the BOLD (blood oxygen level–dependent) signal. Changes in the BOLD signal produced by increased neural activity take some time, so the temporal resolution of fMRI is about 2 or 3 seconds. However, its spatial resolution is very good (approximately 2–3 mm).

Using fMRI, Carter et al. (1998) examined which brain areas are involved in error detection and correction. People often make a wrong response and have to rapidly correct the mistake. To investigate the issue, the authors asked participants to take place in a scanner and to press one button whenever the letter X was preceded by the letter A and another button on all other trials. This procedure is error-prone, and Carter et al. compared the brain activity on trials with and without an erroneous response. As can be seen in Figure 1.10, a small area in the dorsomedial frontal lobe became active after the participants made an error. Later studies showed that this area has close connections to other areas in the frontal lobes and the rest of the brain involved in cognitive action control. Cojan et al. (2015) further observed reduced activation in this region in individuals susceptible to hypnosis and ventured that differences in

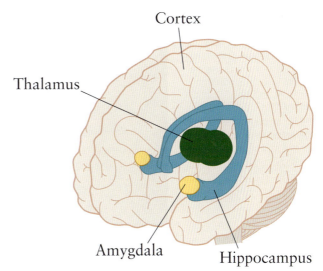

Figure 1.8 Three important subcortical structures: the hippocampus, the amygdala, and the thalamus.

Key term

Functional magnetic resonance imaging (fMRI):
a brain-imaging technique based on imaging blood oxygenation using an MRI scanner; it has very good spatial resolution and reasonable temporal resolution.

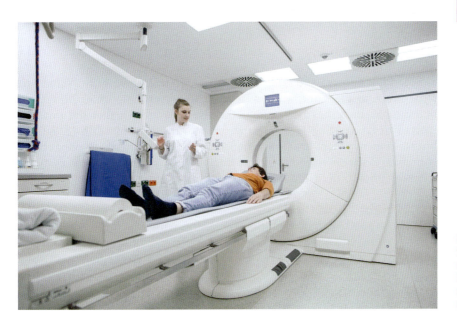

Figure 1.9 Scanner used to measure the BOLD responses on which fMRI is based.
Source: © Westend61 GmbH/Alamy.

Figure 1.10 Part of the brain that becomes active after we notice we have made a mistake. The area is situated in the dorsomedial frontal lobe (in Brodmann areas 24 and 32).
Source: From Carter et al. (1998), with permission from the American Association for the Advancement of Science.

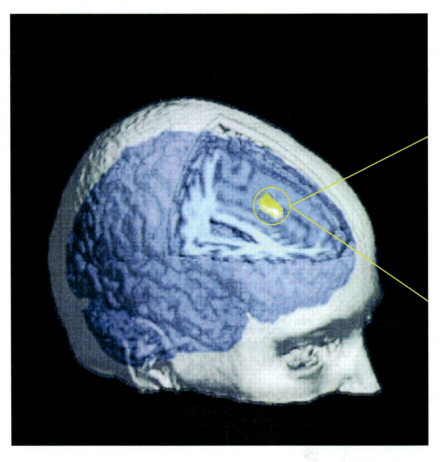

error monitoring may be one reason why some people are easier to hypnotize than others.

Why is fMRI information useful? First, it allows us to work out the order in which different parts of the brain become active when someone is performing a task. This may provide valuable insights into the processes involved in task performance.

Second, it allows us to find out whether two tasks involve the same parts of the brain in the same way, or whether there are important differences. For example, there has been some controversy as to whether the processes involved in recognizing faces are the same as those involved in recognizing objects. Evidence from brain-imaging studies indicates that somewhat different brain areas are involved, which strongly suggests that the processes used in face recognition differ from those used in object recognition.

Event-related potentials

fMRI has a good spatial resolution (precision with which the area of brain activity can be measured) but a limited temporal resolution (precision with which the timing of brain activity can be assessed). Basic cognitive processes last less than one second and, therefore, must be measured with a resolution of one millisecond (one-thousandth of a second; usually abbreviated as ms). Such precision can be achieved with an electroencephalogram (EEG). An EEG is based on recordings of electrical brain activity measured at the surface of the scalp (Figure 1.11). Very small changes in electrical activity within the brain are picked up by scalp electrodes. However, spontaneous or background brain activity sometimes obscures the impact of stimulus processing on the EEG recording. This problem can be solved by presenting the same type of stimulus several times. After that, the segment of EEG following each stimulus is extracted and lined up with respect to the time of stimulus onset. These EEG segments are then simply averaged to produce a single waveform. This method produces event-related potentials (ERPs) from EEG recordings and allows us to distinguish genuine effects of stimulation from background brain activity.

Key term

Event-related potentials (ERPs): the pattern of electroencephalograph (EEG) activity obtained by averaging the brain responses to the same stimulus (or similar stimuli) presented repeatedly.

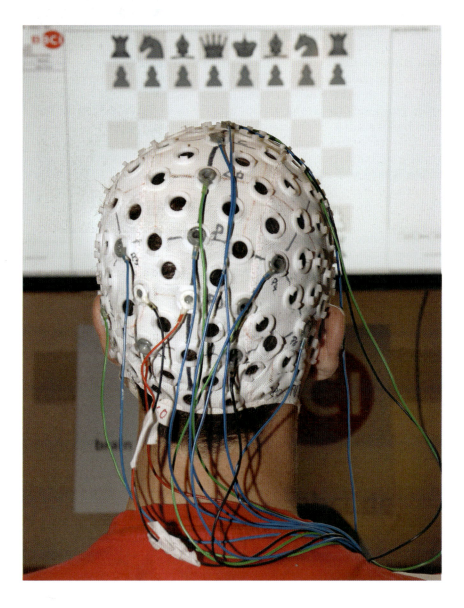

Figure 1.11 A cap with electrodes is placed on the head to measure the EEG signal from the brain. By repeatedly presenting the same stimulus, the researchers can extract the ERP signal from the EEG recordings.
Source: © dpa picture alliance archive/Alamy.

An interesting application of ERP was published by Lorist et al. (2005). They wondered whether the error-related signal observed by Carter et al. (1998) would be visible in the EEG signal. The authors presented the letters H and S on a computer screen. Participants had to press a button with the left hand when the letter H was presented and with the right hand when the letter S was presented. Occasionally, participants made an error. Lorist et al. (2005) compared the ERP signal on correct and incorrect trials. In addition, they compared the signal at the beginning of the 2-hour session and at the end of the session. As can be seen in Figure 1.12, there was a major difference between both types of trials. Whereas the signal on correct trials was rather flat, it first became negative and then positive on incorrect trials. The effect was stronger at the beginning of the session than at the end. Apparently, fatigue and/or habituation made error detection less sharp towards the end of the session. Importantly, the conclusions could be derived directly from the EEG signal. The researchers did not have to ask the participants whether they responded differently to correct and incorrect trials, or whether they were more attentive in the beginning of the session than at the end.

ERPs have poor spatial resolution but their temporal resolution is excellent. Indeed, they can indicate when a given process occurred to within a few milliseconds. However, there are limitations with the use of ERPs. Remember that a given stimulus needs to be presented several times in order to produce consistent ERPs. That works well when participants process the stimulus in the same way on each trial, but it is inappropriate when processing differs over trials. For example, it may take some time to work out the anagram BLTTOE the first time you see it, but it is likely to involve far less processing on subsequent trials.

Evaluation

ERPs and brain-imaging techniques provide useful information about the timing and location of brain activation during performance on an enormous

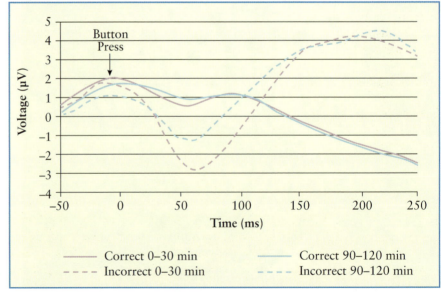

Figure 1.12   Difference in ERP signal after a mistake compared to after a correct response in the first 30 mins and the last 30 mins of a two-hour experiment.
Source: Based on Lorist et al. (2005).

range of cognitive tasks. Such information (when combined with behavioral evidence) has proved of much value in increasing our understanding of human cognition. We will consider numerous examples in the course of this book. However, brain-imaging techniques don't provide a magical solution. The crucial point is that it is often hard to *interpret* the findings from brain-imaging studies. We will consider four reasons why that is the case.

First, when researchers argue that a given brain region is active during the performance of a task, they mean it is active relative to some baseline. What is an appropriate baseline? We might argue that the resting state (e.g., participant sits with his/her eyes shut) is a suitable baseline condition. However, the brain is very active even in the resting state, and performing a task increases brain activity by 5% or less. Indeed, the brain is very active even when someone is in a coma, under anesthesia, or in slow-wave sleep (Boly et al., 2008). Thus, most brain activity we observe reflects basic brain functioning. Furthermore, researchers are particularly attentive to *increased* brain activity as a result of task performance reflecting task demands. In fact, however, there is often *decreased* brain activity in some brain regions (Raichle, 2010). Decreased activity is especially likely when the current task requires considerable effort, and so there is reduced ability to engage in task-unrelated processing. The take-home message is that brain functioning is much more complex than often assumed.

Second, brain-imaging techniques only indicate there are *associations* between patterns of brain activation and behavior. For example, performance on a reasoning task may be associated with activation of the prefrontal cortex at the front of the brain. Such associations are hard to interpret. We can't be certain that involvement of the prefrontal cortex is necessary or essential for performance of the task. Perhaps anxiety caused by thoughts of possible failure on the reasoning task causes activation of that brain area?

Third, most brain-imaging research is based on the assumption of **functional specialization** – the notion that each brain region is specialized for a different function. In fact, matters are often much more complex. The performance of a given task is often associated with activity in several brain regions at the same time, and this activity is often integrated and coordinated. It is harder to identify brain networks involving coordinated brain activity than to pinpoint specific regions active during task performance (Ramsey et al., 2010).

Fourth, knowing when and where in the brain processing takes place does not answer the most important question of "how" the processing is done. An answer to the last question requires a detailed theory of how the task is performed and which processes are involved.

COGNITIVE NEUROPSYCHOLOGY

Sadly, millions of people around the world have a **lesion** – structural damage to the brain caused by injury or disease. As a result, they have problems with cognitive processing. Psychologists discovered that they can learn useful aspects about the workings of the brain by studying its malfunctioning. This research made much progress after the World Wars, because in these wars many soldiers (and civilians) had small brain lesions caused by bullets hitting the brain.

Key terms

Functional specialization:
the assumption (only partially correct) that cognitive functions (e.g., color processing; face processing) occur in specific brain regions.

Lesion:
a structural alteration within the brain caused by disease or injury.

Key terms

Modularity:
the assumption that
the cognitive system
consists of several
fairly independent or
separate modules or
processors, each of which
is specialized for a given
type of processing (e.g.,
face processing).

Dissociation:
as applied to brain-
damaged patients, intact
performance on one task
but severely impaired
performance on a
different task.

Numerous fascinating conditions produced by brain damage are considered in this book. Here we will mention just two. First, there is blindsight,
a puzzling condition discussed more fully in Chapter 2. Patients with blindsight deny they can see objects presented to the "blind" parts of their visual
field, and so we might assume they have *no* perceptual abilities in those areas.
However, their performance is reasonably good when they guess whether a
stimulus is in one of two locations, or whether a stimulus is present or absent!
Thus, various visual processes can operate with some efficiency in the absence
of any conscious experience of seeing.

Second, there is prosopagnosia or face blindness (see Chapter 2 for
a detailed account). Patients with this condition suffer much embarrass-
ment because they can't recognize faces. As a result, they are in constant
danger of ignoring close friends or colleagues. Intriguingly, the perceptual
impairment is not general, and so the problem is *not* simply one of poor
eyesight. Prosopagnosics are reasonably good at recognizing most objects
other than faces, suggesting that part of the brain is specialized for face
recognition.

Major assumptions

Here we discuss some of the main theoretical assumptions of cognitive neuropsychology (Coltheart, 2001). One such assumption is that of **modularity**,
meaning that the cognitive system consists of numerous modules or processors operating relatively independently of each other. It is assumed
these modules respond to only *one* particular class of stimuli. For example, there may be a face-recognition module responding only when a face
is presented.

There is some support for the modularity assumption. For example, consider the processing of visual stimuli. It has been documented that different
aspects of visual stimuli (e.g., color; form; motion) are processed in different,
specific brain areas. On the other hand, the existence of top-down influences
and interactive processing, discussed above, suggest that very few brain systems function completely independently. They are always embedded in larger
networks.

Another important assumption is that the way the modules or processors
are organized is very similar across people. If this assumption is correct, then
we can generalize the information obtained from one brain-damaged patient
to draw conclusions about the organization of brain systems in other people.
If the assumption is incorrect, then the findings from a single brain-damaged
patient won't generalize.

A final important assumption is that of subtractivity. The basic idea is that
brain damage impairs one or more modules but can't lead to the development
of any new ones or to the use of new processing strategies. As a result, the
contribution of brain areas to a particular function may be underestimated
if the patient manages to perform reasonably well on the basis of alternative
strategies.

One way cognitive neuropsychologists understand how the cognitive
system works is by searching for dissociations. A **dissociation** occurs when
a patient performs at the same level as healthy individuals on one task but
is severely impaired on a second one. For example, patients with amnesia (a

condition associated with severe memory problems) perform very poorly on some tasks involving long-term memory. However, they perform as well as healthy individuals on tasks involving short-term memory (see Chapters 4 and 5).

The above findings suggest that long-term memory and short-term memory involve separate memory systems. Alternatively, it could be argued that brain damage reduces the ability to perform difficult (but not easy) tasks, and that long-term memory tasks are more difficult than short-term memory ones. To avoid this problem, cognitive neuropsychologists are particularly interested in a double dissociation. If they have a patient performing at the healthy level on task X but impaired on task Y, then they search another patient with the opposite pattern. Applied to the example of short-term and long-term memory, if neuropsychologists can also find patients with very poor performance on most short-term memory tasks but intact long-term memory, then they have much stronger evidence for separate short-term and long-term memory systems, as we will see in Chapter 4.

An important issue cognitive neuropsychologists have addressed is that of whether to focus on individuals or groups in their research. In research on healthy individuals, we can have more confidence in our findings if they are based on fairly large groups of participants. However, the group-based approach is problematical when applied to brain-damaged patients because patients with apparently the same condition typically differ in the pattern of impairment. Indeed, every patient can be regarded as unique, just as all snow-flakes are different from each other (Caramazza & Coltheart, 2006). As a result, neuropsychological data must be integrated in wider research lines, involving both impaired and healthy people. Neuropsychological findings based on a single patient are particularly worthwhile when they test cognitive theories developed on the basis of group data. Similarly, if the performance of a patient leads to a new theory, predictions of this theory must be tested on new groups of healthy participants.

Transcranial magnetic stimulation (TMS)

The ideal kind of lesion for researchers seeking to understand human cognition would, first, be small and would affect only *one* brain system. Second, it would last only briefly, so that it is easy to compare performance with that module when it is functioning and not functioning. Third, the researcher should be able to decide precisely *which* brain area is to receive a brief lesion.

It may sound impossible to achieve the above ideal, but the technique we are about to discuss comes close to doing so. It does *not* involve brain-damaged patients. However, it resembles traditional cognitive neuropsychology in that the emphasis is on patterns of performance resulting from inactivation of various brain areas.

In transcranial magnetic stimulation (TMS), a coil (often in the shape of a figure of eight) is placed close to the participant's head. Then, a very brief (less than 1 ms) but large magnetic pulse of current is run through it. This causes a short-lived magnetic field producing electrical stimulation of the brain. This generally leads to inhibited processing activity in the affected area (often about 1 cm³ in extent). In practice, several magnetic pulses are usually administered in a fairly short period of time; this is repetitive transcranial magnetic stimulation (rTMS).

Why are TMS and rTMS useful? If TMS applied to a particular brain area leads to impaired task performance, we can conclude that brain area is necessary for task performance. Conversely, if TMS has *no* effect on task performance, then the brain area affected by it isn't needed to perform the task effectively. For instance, Desmurget et al. (1999) observed that participants were poorer at correcting their arm movement when they were pointing to a moving target after TMS to their posterior parietal cortex (i.e., the upper part at the rear of the brain). On the basis of this finding, the authors hypothesized that by building an internal representation of the hand location, the posterior parietal cortex computes a dynamic motor error signal used by the motor cortex to correct the ongoing trajectory (the parietal cortex is known to play a major role in the direction of attention and the localization of stimuli in the environment). What is most exciting about TMS is that it can reveal that activity in a particular brain area is *necessary* for normal levels of performance on some task. So, the study of Desmurget et al. showed that not only the motor cortex and the frontal cognitive control systems are needed for correct arm movements but also the posterior parietal cortex.

A limitation with TMS is that it isn't clear exactly how much cortical area it affects or what its effects are on the brain. It mostly *reduces* activation in the brain areas affected (inhibitory effect), which fits with the notion that its effects resemble those of a temporary lesion. However, TMS can also *increase* brain activation (excitatory effect), especially shortly after administration (Bolognini & Ro, 2010). In either case, it is assumed that disruptive effects of TMS on a cognitive task indicate that the brain area affected is required for effective performance of that task (Ziemann, 2010).

Evaluation

+ Cognitive neuropsychology and TMS both permit the identification of brain areas necessary for the performance of a given task (Fellows et al., 2005).

+ TMS is a flexible technique that can be used to disrupt activity of numerous brain areas.

+ Double dissociations with brain-damaged patients provide strong evidence for various major processing modules.

− It would be relatively easy to interpret findings from patients if the brain damage were limited to a *single* module. In fact, however, much brain activity is interactive (involving several modules), and brain damage often affects several brain systems, which complicates the interpretation of findings.

− TMS can only be applied to surface structures of the brain, and it is hard to know how much of the brain is affected.

− The effects of TMS on the brain are complex. It generally produces inhibitory effects but can also produce excitatory effects.

COMPUTATIONAL COGNITIVE SCIENCE

Another way to study cognition is by constructing artificial systems doing some of the same things as brains – this is computational cognitive science. Let's start by distinguishing between computational modeling and artificial intelligence. **Computational modeling** involves programming computers to model (or mimic) some aspects of human cognitive functioning. In contrast, artificial intelligence involves constructing computer systems that produce intelligent outcomes, but the processes involved are typically very different from those used by humans.

Artificial intelligence was used to construct a chess program known as Deep Blue that in 1997 beat the then–World Champion, Garry Kasparov, in the second of two matches. It did so by considering 200 million chess positions per second, which is radically different from the approach adopted by human chess players.

We will focus on computational modeling rather than artificial intelligence because it is of more direct relevance to understanding human cognition. Our coverage of computational modeling will be fairly brief because computational models require good mathematical knowledge. Indeed, computational models are usually built by psychologists with a strong interest in mathematics and computer programming or by engineers with a strong interest in psychological processes (and in robots).

Computational cognitive scientists often rely on one or more previous relevant theories or models when developing their own computational models. What is the point of taking an existing theory and implementing it as a program? One important reason is that theories only expressed verbally often contain hidden assumptions or vague terms. This is much less likely to happen with a computer program because *all* the details need to be spelled out.

Let's consider a concrete example. In Chapter 2 we will discuss various steps involved in visual perception. However, it rapidly became clear that such verbal expressions did not suffice to make a computer see and understand visual stimuli. As it happened, it took cognitive scientists and engineers about five decades to develop systems that approached the perceptual capacities of humans and animals. Indeed, the best test to determine whether a website is contacted by a person or by a spam robot is to present a distorted picture and to ask what it represents. Humans are very good at this, but web crawlers are not yet. Such a test is known as a *CAPTCHA test* ("Completely Automated Public Turing test to tell Computers and Humans Apart"). Figure 1.13 shows an example of such a test. Needless to say, CAPTCHA tests are currently seen by many computational modelers as a challenge to solve, so that in the future computational models will not only be able to perceive these complex visual stimuli as well as we can, but they will also make the current CAPTCHA tests obsolete.

Arguably the most ambitious computational model is the *Adaptive Control of Thought – Rational (ACT-R) model* built by John Anderson. The model is ambitious because it aims to be potentially applicable to all different human functions. This contrasts with most theories in cognitive psychology and with most existing computational models, which tend to be very limited in

Key term
Computational modeling: this involves constructing computer programs that will simulate or mimic some aspects of human cognitive functioning.

Figure 1.13 Example of a CAPTCHA test. Humans are still better than computers at identifying what is shown visually. So, this test can be used to stop spam robots from accessing webpages.

Figure 1.14   The main modules of the ACT-R (Adaptive Control of Thought – Rational) cognitive architecture with their locations within the brain. VLPFC = ventrolateral prefrontal cortex. There are four main modules, plus a visual module for perception and a manual module for action.
Source: Reprinted from Anderson et al. (2008), Copyright © 2008, with permission from Elsevier.

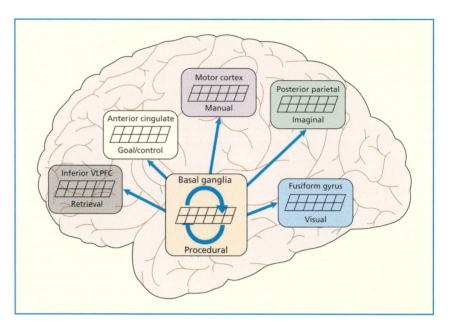

their application. For example, there are theories and computational models concerned with short-term memory (see Chapter 4) or with reading written words (see Chapter 8). Although these theories and models are extremely useful to understand how very specific functions can be achieved, they tell us little about the overall structure of the human cognitive system.

John Anderson has produced several versions of his approach. We discuss the one put forward by Anderson et al. (2008). It is based on the assumption that the cognitive system consists of several modules, each performing its own specialized operations fairly independently of the other modules. Here are four of the main modules, each of which can be used across numerous tasks:

1. *Retrieval module*: Maintains the retrieval cues needed to access stored information.
2. *Goal module*: Keeps track of an individual's intentions and controls information processing.
3. *Imaginal module*: Changes problem representations to facilitate problem solution.
4. *Procedural module*: Uses various rules to determine what action will be taken next; it also communicates with the other modules.

What is especially exciting about Anderson et al.'s (2008) version of ACT-R is that it combines computational cognitive science with cognitive neuroscience. What that means in practice is that Anderson identified the brain areas associated with each module of the program (see Figure 1.14).

Connectionism

Over the past 35 years or so, there has been much interest in connectionist networks to simulate human performance. This interest started with books by Rumelhart et al. (1986) and by McClelland et al. (1986). **Connectionist networks** make use of elementary units or nodes connected together in various structures or layers (Figure 1.15).

There are many types of connectionist models based on the basic architecture shown in Figure 1.15. We will focus here on *two* key features on which connectionist networks differ: (1) whether their representations are localist or distributed, and (2) whether the models can learn new information.

The first key feature is whether the nodes in the model represent meaningful stimuli, as in Figure 1.15, where each input and output node represents a number, or whether the information is distributed across all the nodes of a layer. In the latter scheme, the number 1 would not activate one node in the input and output layer but would activate all the nodes to a certain extent. The number 2 would also activate all the nodes, but in a slightly different way, so that it can be discerned from the number 1, and so on. The former type of representation is called *localist* representations (because information can be localized in a few nodes), and the latter type is called *distributed* representations (because the information is distributed across the entire layer of the network).

Distributed representation are harder to imagine, but they have the great advantage that the network can process new stimuli resembling previously learned stimuli (i.e., the network can *generalize* to new stimuli). This is an interesting aspect because it mimics an important feature of human learning (we do not learn everything at once). Localist models tend to be end-state models; that is, models that contain all the required information and that are fully trained. Distributed models, in contrast, tend to be learning models. For this reason, models with distributed representations may be the future of computational modeling, even though they are more difficult to understand and to integrate in general architectures such as ACT-R. Because localist models are easier to understand, most of the models discussed in this book will be of this type, such as the reading model of Coltheart et al. (2001) and the models of word meaning, discussed in Chapters 6 and 8. If mathematics is your forte, just know that there is an exciting realm of distributed models out there to be discovered.

Key term

Connectionist networks: these consist of units or nodes that are connected in various layers with no direct connection from stimulus to response.

Figure 1.15 Architecture of a basic connectionist network. In such a network, a layer of nodes (brain cells?) codes the input. The activation caused by the input spreads to a layer of hidden nodes and from there to a layer of output nodes. Such a three-layer network can learn many correspondences between input and output. For instance, the model depicted in the figure can learn simple additions. If input node 1 is active, then output node 1 will become active. If input nodes 1 and 2 are active, then output node 3 will become active. If all input nodes are active, then output node 10 will become active, and so on. The model learns which output is expected on the basis of the input by adjusting the weights of the connections between the nodes each time the wrong output is produced (backward propagation of errors).
Source: From Brysbaert (2016), with permission from Academia Press.

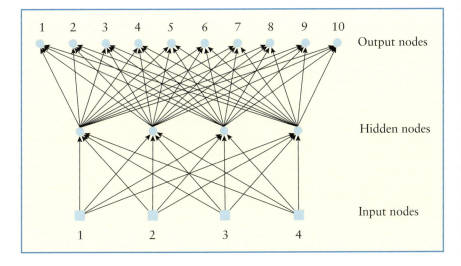

Evaluation

+ The greatest strength of computational models is that the underlying theoretical assumptions are spelled out with precision. This is typically *not* the case with traditional theories expressed purely in verbal terms.

+ Some computational models (e.g., ACT-R; Anderson et al., 2008) are much more comprehensive in scope than most traditional models and theories.

+ The combining of computational cognitive science and cognitive neuroscience (e.g., ACT-R, Anderson et al., 2008) is an exciting development.

+ Connectionist models can learn many correspondences between input and output in a biologically plausible way. They can learn these correspondences to a level that closely approximates that of humans and show processing preferences and difficulties also observed in humans. As such, they are a good model of how we learn information and represent it.

− Building computational models requires skills few people associate with psychologists. As a result, only researchers with strong programming skills and mathematical insight are versatile with them.

− Computational models deemphasize motivational and emotional factors. As the British psychologist Stewart Sutherland said jokingly, he would believe that computers are like humans if one tried to run away with his wife.

COMBINING APPROACHES

We can see the usefulness of combining information from the four perspectives. As we said before, the understanding of a phenomenon becomes much more detailed if one tries to build a computer model that achieves performance similar to humans. Next, we consider a concrete example of how experimental cognitive psychology, cognitive neuroscience, and cognitive neuropsychology strengthen each other. For many years, there has been controversy concerning the relationship between visual perception and visual imagery (see Eysenck & Keane, 2015, for a detailed discussion). Stephen Kosslyn and his colleagues (e.g., Kosslyn & Thompson, 2003) argue that visual imagery typically involves the same processes as visual perception. In contrast, Pylyshyn (e.g., 2003) argues that visual imagery doesn't involve the same processes as visual perception, but instead depends on abstract forms of thinking and knowledge.

If Kosslyn is right, we can make three major predictions. First, people should scan visual images in a similar way to visual arrays (behavioral evidence). Second, the brain areas activated during visual imagery should overlap considerably with those activated during visual perception (brain-imaging evidence). Third, brain-damaged patients with severely impaired visual perception should also have impaired visual imagery, and vice versa (cognitive neuropsychological evidence).

Borst and Kosslyn (2008) compared visual perception with visual imagery. In the perception condition, participants scanned over dots visible in front of them. In the imagery condition, they scanned over dots they imagined. As the distance to be scanned increased, there was a similar increase in scanning time in the two conditions.

The early stages of visual perception involve regions in the occipital area at the back of the brain (BA17 and BA18). If visual imagery tasks produce activation in BA17 and BA18, Kosslyn's theoretical approach receives support but Pylyshyn's does not. In fact, visual imagery is often associated with much activation in BA17 and BA18 (Kosslyn & Thompson, 2003). More generally, visual imagery is typically associated with activation in about two-thirds of the brain areas activated during visual perception (Kosslyn, 2004).

The notion that visual imagery involves many of the same processes as visual perception can also be tested by using repeated transcranial magnetic stimulation (rTMS). If BA17 is necessary for visual imagery, then magnetic stimulation applied to it should impair performance on a visual imagery task. Precisely that finding was reported by Kosslyn et al. (1999).

Many brain-damaged patients with impaired visual imagery also have impaired visual perception, and vice versa (Bartolomeo, 2002). Such patients provide further support for Kosslyn's theory.

In sum, three different kinds of evidence all suggest there are major similarities between visual perception and visual imagery. The totality of the evidence provides much more support for Kosslyn's theory than could be obtained from one kind of evidence on its own. At the same time, the evidence from brain-damaged patients suggests there are important differences between perception and imagery as well. For example, some patients have been reported with intact visual imagery but impaired visual perception (Bridge et al., 2012). We can use behavioral and brain-imaging evidence to further investigate why these patients show a dissociation between visual perception and imagery.

COMBINING FINDINGS FROM EXPERIMENTS

The research literature in psychology consists of literally millions of experiments and studies (as textbook writers discover to their cost!). There are often hundreds of published articles on very narrow and specific research topics. How can we make sense of the multitude of findings? An increasingly influential answer is to use meta-analyses. A **meta-analysis** involves combining the data from a large number of similar studies into one very large analysis. Numerous meta-analyses are discussed throughout this book because they have the great advantage of providing a coherent overall picture of research on any given topic.

What are the potential problems with meta-analyses? Sharpe (1997) identified three:

1. *The "Apples and Oranges" problem*: Studies that aren't very similar to each other may nevertheless be included within a single meta-analysis.
2. *The "File Drawer" problem*: It is generally harder for researchers to publish studies with nonsignificant findings. Because meta-analyses often ignore unpublished findings, the studies included may not be representative of the studies on a given topic.
3. *The "Garbage in – Garbage out" problem*: Many psychologists carrying out meta-analyses include all the relevant studies they can find. This

Key term
Meta-analysis: a form of statistical analysis based on combining the findings from numerous studies on a given issue.

means that very poor and inadequate studies are often included along with high-quality ones.

Note that these three problems are identified as *potential* problems. Cognitive psychologists and neuroscientists have become increasingly sophisticated in the ways they carry out meta-analyses, as a result of which there are now fewer problems than in the past. The "Apples and Oranges" and "Garbage in – Garbage out" problems can be greatly reduced by setting up precise criteria that have to be met for any given study to be included in the meta-analysis. There are mechanisms for estimating the extent of any "File Drawer" problem. For example, it can be reduced by asking researchers in the area of the meta-analysis to supply their unpublished data.

Section summary

Experimental cognitive psychology
- Experimental cognitive psychologists carry out well-controlled laboratory studies on healthy individuals. They use behavioral measures to draw inferences about the internal processes involved in cognition. Some of this research possesses only limited ecological validity.

Cognitive neuroscience
- Much research in cognitive neuroscience involves assessing brain activity as well as behavior during task performance. Various techniques (e.g., fMRI, ERP) allow us to work out *where* and *when* in the brain activity is occurring. These techniques reveal associations between patterns of brain activity and behavior, but they don't establish that any given brain area is *essential* for task performance.

Cognitive neuropsychology
- Cognitive neuropsychology involves studying the performance of brain-damaged patients on cognitive tasks to increase our understanding of cognition in healthy individuals. Strong evidence for the existence of separate modules or processors comes from double dissociations – some patients are impaired on task X but not task Y, and others show the opposite pattern.
- Brain damage is often so extensive that it is difficult to interpret the findings. However, it is possible to disrupt the functioning of a small brain area very briefly using transcranial magnetic stimulation (TMS).

Computational cognitive science
- Computational modeling has been used to develop explicit models of human cognition including cognitive architectures. Connectionist models are able to learn and are based on the assumption that there is considerable parallel processing.

Combining approaches
- It is valuable to combine information from different approaches. For example, converging evidence from experimental cognitive psychology, cognitive neuroscience, and cognitive neuropsychology indicates there are major

similarities between visual perception and visual imagery. Some interesting differences have also been discovered (e.g., Bridge et al., 2012).

Combining findings
- It is possible to make more coherent sense of the large research literature by carrying out meta-analyses combining numerous findings into a single statistical analysis. Meta-analyses can be misleading because of the Apples and Oranges, File Drawer, and Garbage in – Garbage out problems. However, all of these problems can be reduced or eliminated.

STRUCTURE OF THE BOOK

Human cognition involves numerous processes, most of which interact with each other in complex ways. The existence of such complex interactions poses a challenge for textbook writers. For example, Chapter 8 of this book is devoted to language, but it would be ludicrous to argue that language is totally irrelevant to the processes discussed in the other chapters. Much of the information we learn and remember is language-based, and language is heavily involved in most of our thinking and reasoning. Nevertheless, only the topics considered in the language chapter focus *directly* on attempts to understand the nature of language itself.

CHAPTER BY CHAPTER

Chapter 2 is concerned with perception and especially with the processes that enable us to make sense of the visual stimuli we encounter.

Chapter 3 is concerned with attention and consciousness, which both share close links with perception. What we perceive and are consciously aware of at any given moment tends to be those aspects of the environment to which we are directing our attention. Chapter 3 also focuses on multitasking, which has become increasingly important in our 24/7 lifestyles.

Memory is of vital importance within human cognition. Without memory, we wouldn't be able to make any sense of our environment, to use language, or to engage in problem solving and reasoning. More generally, we wouldn't benefit from experience. Chapters 4, 5, and 6 are devoted to human memory. Chapter 4 focuses on short-term memory, which involves retaining information for a few seconds. Short-term memory is essential to us in several ways. It allows us to retain information about some aspects of a problem while focusing on other aspects. It also allows us to remember what a speaker said at the start of a sentence as he/she moves toward the end of it.

Long-term memory is the subject matter of Chapter 5. Our long-term memories are remarkably diverse. They encompass personal memories of events in which we have been involved, general knowledge, and knowledge of how to perform many skills.

Chapter 6 is concerned with general knowledge. We use semantic memory to store a huge amount of information about the world, and the ways such information is stored are discussed in detail.

Chapter 7 is concerned with everyday memory. This includes our autobiographical memories for the important events of our lives, eyewitness testimony, and our ability to remember to perform actions (e.g., meeting a friend) at the appropriate time.

Chapter 8 focuses on our use of language and deals with both language production and language perception in written and spoken modality. It also includes information about language disorders and applied aspects of language research.

Chapter 9 has problem solving and expertise as its central focus. The issues discussed include the processes we use to solve complex problems, the nature of scientific discovery, and what is involved in developing a high level of expertise.

Chapter 10 is devoted to decision making and reasoning, both of which are of major importance in our everyday lives. A common theme is that people surprisingly often make use of simple rules of thumb when engaged in decision making or reasoning.

Chapter 11 deals with cognition and emotion. How we interpret the present situation helps to determine our emotional state. In addition, our current emotional state or mood (e.g., anxious; depressed; happy) has systematic effects on memory, judgment, decision making, and reasoning.

In sum, this book covers all the main areas within human cognition, with an emphasis on the everyday relevance of the topics discussed. Throughout the book, we will use information from behavioral research, brain-imaging research, and research on brain-damaged patients to try to build up a reasonably complete understanding of human cognition.

Essay questions

1. What are the major highlights in the development of cognitive psychology?
2. Why is the information-processing approach of the 1960s no longer highly regarded?
3. Describe the major approaches to understanding human cognition.
4. Why has there been a dramatic increase in research within cognitive neuroscience? What are the limitations with this approach?

Further reading

- Andrewes, D. (2015). *Neuropsychology: From theory to practice* (2nd ed.). Psychology Press. This book describes how neuropsychological research has contributed to our understanding of perception, attention, memory, and reading.
- Brysbaert, M., & Rastle, K. (2013). *Historical and conceptual issues in psychology* (2nd ed.). Pearson Education. This textbook discusses the origins of psychological research and the changes in society that made the research possible.
- Eysenck, M. W., & Keane, M. T. (2015). *Cognitive psychology: A student's handbook* (7th ed.). Routledge. Chapter 1 of this textbook contains a detailed account of the major approaches to human cognition.

- Gazzaniga, M. S., Ivry, R. B., & Mangun, G. R. (2013). *Cognitive neuroscience: The biology of the mind* (4th ed.). Norton & Company. Michael Gazzaniga and his coauthors provide a comprehensive and up-to-date account of research in cognitive neuroscience.

Chapter Solution

Figure 1.1 shows an example of some of the stimuli used in the recognition task of Blake et al. (2015). In the actual task, participants were asked to select the correct logo (not shown here) among eight options, which included the correct logo as well as other lures that had altered features. The correct logo resembles the bottom middle panel of Figure 1.1 with the leaf mirrored. Notice that the absence of the critical stimulus is a real possibility in person line-ups, as the real perpetrator is not present if the target suspect is innocent.

REFERENCES

Anderson, J. R., Fincham, J. M., Qin, Y., & Stocco, A. (2008). A central circuit of the mind. *Trends in Cognitive Sciences*, *12*, 136–143.

Atkinson, R. C., & Shiffrin, R. M. (1968). Human memory: A proposed system and its control processes. In K. W. Spence & J. T. Spence (Eds.), *The psychology of learning and motivation* (Vol. 2). London, UK: Academic Press.

Bandura, A. (1977). *Social learning theory*. Englewood Cliffs, NJ: Prentice Hall.

Bartlett, F. C. (1932). *Remembering: An experimental and social study*. Cambridge, UK: Cambridge University Press.

Bartolomeo, P. (2002). The relationship between visual perception and visual mental imagery: A reappraisal of the neuropsychological evidence. *Cortex*, *38*, 357–378.

Blake, A. B., Nazarian, M., & Castel, A. D. (2015). The Apple of the mind's eye: Everyday attention, metamemory, and reconstructive memory for the Apple logo. *The Quarterly Journal of Experimental Psychology*, *68*(5), 858–865.

Bolognini, N., & Ro, T. (2010). Transcranial magnetic stimulation: Disrupting neural activity to alter and assess brain function. *Journal of Neuroscience*, *30*, 9647–9650.

Boly, M., Phillips, C., Tschibanda, L., Vanhaudenhuyse, A., Schabus, M., Dange-Vu, T. T., et al. (2008). Intrinsic brain activity in altered states of consciousness: How conscious is the default mode of brain function? *Annals of the New York Academy of Sciences*, *1129*, 119–129.

Borst, G., & Kosslyn, S. M. (2008). Visual mental imagery and visual perception: Structural equivalence revealed by scanning processes. *Memory & Cognition*, *36*, 849–862.

Brady, T. F., Konkle, T., Alvarez, G. A., & Oliva, A. (2008). Visual long-term memory has a massive storage capacity for object details. *Proceedings of the National Academy of Sciences*, *105*(38), 14325–14329.

Bridge, H., Harrold, S., Holmes, E.A., Stokes, M., & Kennard, C. (2012). Vivid visual mental imagery in the absence of the primary visual cortex. *Journal of Neurology*, *259*, 1062–1070.

Bruner, J. S., Goodnow, J. J., & Austin, G. A. (1956). *A study of thinking*. New York, NY: Wiley.

Bryan, W. L., & Harter, N. (1897). Studies in the physiology and psychology of the telegraphic language. *Psychological Review*, *4*, 27–53.

Bryan, W. L., & Harter, N. (1899). Studies on the telegraphic language. The acquisition of a hierarchy of habits. *Psychological Review*, *6*, 345–375.

Brysbaert, M. (2016). *Psychologie*. Ghent, Belgium: Academia Press.

Caramazza, A., & Coltheart, M. (2006). Cognitive neuropsychology twenty years on. *Cognitive Neuropsychology, 23*, 3–12.

Carter, C. S., Braver, T. S., Barch, D. M., Botvinick, M. M., Noll, D., & Cohen, J. D. (1998). Anterior cingulate cortex, error detection, and the online monitoring of performance. *Science, 280*(5364), 747–749.

Chaplin, C., & Shaw, J. (2016). Confidently wrong: Police endorsement of psycho-legal misconceptions. *Journal of Police and Criminal Psychology, 31*(3), 208–216.

Clark, S. E. (2012). Costs and benefits of eyewitness identification reform: Psychological science and public policy. *Perspectives on Psychological Science, 7*(3), 238–259.

Cojan, Y., Piguet, C., & Vuilleumier, P. (2015). What makes your brain suggestible? Hypnotizability is associated with differential brain activity during attention outside hypnosis. *NeuroImage, 117*, 367–374.

Coltheart, M. (2001). *Assumptions and methods in cognitive neuropsychology.* Hove, UK: Psychology Press.

Coltheart, M., Rastle, K., Perry, C., Langdon, R., & Ziegler, J. (2001). The DRC model: A model of visual word recognition and reading aloud. *Psychological Review, 108*, 204–258.

Desmurget, M., Epstein, C. M., Turner, R. S., Prablanc, C., Alexander, G. E., & Grafton, S. T. (1999). Role of the posterior parietal cortex in updating reaching movements to a visual target. *Nature Neuroscience, 2*(6), 563–567.

Ebbinghaus, H. (1885/1913). *Über das Gedächtnis.* Leipzig, Germany: Dunker [translated by H. Ruyer & C. E. Bussenius]. New York, NY: Teachers College, Columbia University.

Eysenck, M., & Keane, M. (2015). *Cognitive psychology: A student's handbook.* London: Psychology Press.

Fellows, L. K., Heberlein, A. S., Morales, D. A., Shivde, G., Waller, S., & Wu, D. H. (2005). Method matters: An empirical study of impact in cognitive neuroscience. *Journal of Cognitive Neuroscience, 17*, 850–858.

Fuchs, A. H., & Milar, K. J. (2003). Psychology as a science. In D. F. Freedheim (Ed.), *Handbook of psychology (Vol. 1: The history of psychology)* (pp. 1–26). Hoboken, NJ: Wiley.

Galton, F. (1983). *Enquiries into human faculty and its development.* London: J. M. Dent & Co.

Henderson, E. N. (1903). A study of memory for connected trains of thought. *The Psychological Review, Series of Monograph Supplements, V* (6), (Whole No. 23, p. 93). New York: Palgrave Macmillan.

Hobbs, S., & Burman, J. T. (2009). Is the 'cognitive revolution' a myth? *The Psychologist, 22*, 812–814.

Hunter, I. M. L. (2004). James, William. In R. L. Gregory (Ed.), *The Oxford companion to the mind* (2nd ed., pp. 610–612). New York, NY: Oxford University Press.

Kane, M. J., & Engle, R. W. (2003). Working-memory capacity and the control of attention: The contribution of goal neglect, response competition, and task set to Stroop interference. *Journal of Experimental Psychology: General, 132*, 47–70.

Kosslyn, S. M. (2004). Mental imagery: Depictive accounts. In R. L. Gregory (Ed.), *The Oxford companion to the mind* (pp. 585–587). New York, NY: Oxford University Press.

Kosslyn, S. M., Pascual-Leone, A., Felician, O., Camposano, S., Keenan, J. P., Thompson, W. L., et al. (1999). The role of Area 17 in visual imagery: Convergent evidence from PET and rTMS. *Science, 284*, 167–170.

Kosslyn, S. M., & Thompson, W. L. (2003). When is early visual cortex activated during visual mental imagery? *Psychological Bulletin, 129*, 723–746.

Lamme, V. A. F. (2003). Why visual attention and awareness are different. *Trends in Cognitive Sciences, 7*, 12–18.

Leahey, T. H. (1992). The mythical revolutions of American psychology. *American Psychologist*, 47(2), 308–318.

Leahey, T. M. (2012). *History of psychology: From antiquity to modernity* (7th ed.). London: Routledge.

Lorist, M. M., Boksem, M. A., & Ridderinkhof, K. R. (2005). Impaired cognitive control and reduced cingulate activity during mental fatigue. *Cognitive Brain Research*, 24(2), 199–205.

Macleod, C. M. (2015). Attention: Beyond Stroop's (1935) effect. In M. W. Eysenck & D. Groome (Eds.), *Classic studies in cognitive psychology*. London: Sage.

McClelland, J. L., & Elman, J. L. (1986). The TRACE model of speech perception. *Cognitive Psychology*, 18, 1–86.

Miller, G. A. (1956). The magical number seven, plus or minus two: Some limits on our capacity for processing information. *Psychological Review*, 63, 81–97.

Mitterer, H., & de Ruiter, J. P. (2008). Recalibrating color categories using world knowledge. *Psychological Science*, 19, 629–634.

Murphy, G., & Kovach, J. K. (1972). *Historical introduction to modern psychology*. London, UK: Routledge & Kegan Paul.

Newell, A., Shaw, J. C., & Simon, H. A. (1958). Elements of a theory of human problem solving. *Psychological Review*, 65, 151–166.

Nisbett, R. E., & Wilson, T. D. (1977). Telling more than we can know: Verbal reports on mental processes. *Psychological Review*, 84, 231–259.

Pessiglione, M., Schmidt, L., Draganski, B., Kalisch, R., Lau, H., Dolan, R. J., & Frith, C. D. (2007). How the brain translates money into force: A neuroimaging study of subliminal motivation. *Science*, 316, 904–906.

Pickford, R. W., & Gregory, R. L. (2004). Bartlett, Sir Frederic Charles. In R. L. Gregory (Ed.), *The Oxford companion to the mind* (2nd ed., pp. 86–87). New York, NY: Oxford University Press.

Pylyshyn, Z. (2003). Return of the mental image: Are there really pictures in the brain? *Trends in Cognitive Sciences*, 7, 113–118.

Raichle, M. E. (2010). Two views of brain function. *Trends in Cognitive Sciences*, 14, 180–190.

Ramsey, J. D., Hanson, S. J., Hanson, C., Halchenko, Y. O., Pokdrack, R. A., & Glymour, C. (2010). Six problems for causal inference from fMRI. *NeuroImage*, 49, 1545–1558.

Rumelhart, D. E., McClelland, J. L., & the PDP Research Group (1986). *Parallel distributed processing, Vol. 1: Foundations*. Cambridge, MA: MIT Press.

Sharpe, D. (1997). Of apples and oranges, file drawers and garbage: Why validity issues in meta-analysis will not go away. *Clinical Psychology Review*, 17, 881–901.

Stroop, J. R. (1935). Studies of interference in serial verbal reactions. *Journal of Experimental Psychology: General*, 106, 404–426.

Thagard, P. (2005). How to be a successful scientist. *Scientific and Technological Thinking*, 159–171.

Tolman, E. C. (1948). Cognitive maps in rats and men. *Psychological Review*, 55, 189–208.

Valentine, E. R. (1992). *Conceptual issues in psychology* (2nd ed.). London, UK: Routledge.

Watson, J. B. (1913). Psychology as the behaviorist views it. *Psychological Review*, 20, 158–177.

Zangwill, O. L. (2004). Ebbinghaus. In R. L. Gregory (Ed.), *The Oxford companion to the mind* (2nd ed., p. 276). New York, NY: Oxford University Press.

Ziemann, U. (2010). TMS in cognitive neuroscience: Virtual lesion and beyond. *Cortex*, 46, 124–127.

Chapter 2

Contents

Visual perception

INTRODUCTION

What do we mean by "perception"? According to Sekuler and Blake (2002, p. 621), it is "the acquisition and processing of sensory information in order to see, hear, taste, or feel objects in the world; it also guides an organism's actions with respect to those objects."

Traditionally, five senses are identified for our interactions with the outside world: vision, hearing, taste, smell, and touch. The description of these five senses goes back to the Greek philosopher Aristotle. In addition, we have senses that inform us about our body. They are related to the perception of pain, temperature, balance, the position of our body parts (known as kinesthesia), and the status of our internal organs (stomach, heart, bladder). Each sense has its own receptors, nerves, and brain tissue. Loss of any of them leads to a serious handicap.

In this chapter, we will limit ourselves to the sense people find the most dominant, vision, because otherwise the chapter would be too long. If you are interested in the other senses, there are several good books available, such as Goldstein (2014), Harris (2014), Wolfe et al. (2014), or Yantis and Abrams (2016). Some aspects of auditory perception will be discussed in Chapter 3 (the role of attention in auditory perception) and Chapter 8 (speech perception).

Visual perception is of enormous importance in our everyday lives. It allows us to move around freely, to recognize people, to read magazines and books, to admire the wonders of nature, and to watch movies and television. It is very important for visual perception to be accurate – if we misperceive how close cars are as we cross the road, the consequences can be fatal. As a result, far more of the human cortex is devoted to vision than to any other sensory modality.

Several important questions concerning visual perception are discussed in this chapter. In a world of overlapping objects, how do we decide where one object ends and another begins? How do we make sense of ambiguous two-dimensional stimuli (e.g., handwriting)? How do we decide whether the object in front of us is a cat or a dog? How do we recognize individual faces given that most faces are broadly similar (e.g., they have two eyes, a nose, a mouth, and so on)? Why are we susceptible to many visual illusions in the laboratory when our everyday visual perception is so accurate? Why do we often fail to detect changes in our visual environment? Is vision possible in the absence of conscious awareness?

Learning objectives

After studying Chapter 2, you should be able to:

- Understand the difference between sensation and perception.
- Explain how the two visual systems reconcile differences between perception and reality (optical illusions) so that our actions achieve their goal.
- Explain what change blindness phenomena tell us about human attention and perception.
- Define face recognition, and describe what studies of prosopagnosic patients find concerning where and how face recognition occurs in the brain.
- Define perceptual organization, pattern recognition, and object recognition, and describe the theories that account for each of these processes.

FROM SENSATION TO PERCEPTION

SENSATION VS. PERCEPTION

To understand perception, it is important that we make a distinction between perception and sensation. **Sensation** refers to intake of information by means of receptors and the translation of this information to signals that the brain can process as images, sounds, smells, tastes, and so on. For instance, the receptors at the back of your eyes detect that some parts of Figure 2.1 are black and others white. This information is transmitted to your brain, where it is processed, so that you consciously experience the distinction between the black and the white parts. However, this is not perception as we know it. **Perception** also involves the interpretation and understanding of sensations. If all you saw in the world around you were colored patches, you would be at a loss to move around and to interact with the environment. To understand what we mean, look at Figure 2.3. Now look back at Figure 2.1. Has it changed?

The difference between Figures 2.1 and 2.3 illustrates the transition from sensation to perception. Normally, this transition is so smooth and fast that you don't notice it. All you experience is the perception itself. However, by degrading a stimulus, it is possible to make the transition hard enough for you to experience it. As we will see later in this chapter, because of brain injury some patients can no longer make the transition from sensation to perception. To them, the visual world looks like Figure 2.1 and not like Figure 2.3!

Figure 2.1 Visual sensations Your eyes and brain inform you that some parts of this figure are black and others are white. These are sensations, but not yet perception, because perception involves the interpretation and the understanding of the sensations. To understand what we mean, look at Figure 2.3.
Source: From Brysbaert (2016), with permission from Academia Press.

Using illusions to discover underlying processes

Another way to study the transition from sensation to perception is by means of *visual illusions*. In an **illusion** you experience (perceive) something else than what is physically presented. Psychologists are interested in illusions, because they reveal the processes involved in perception. Usually perception is so fast and accurate that we cannot break it down into its components. Illusions give us a rare glimpse of what is going on. Look at Figure 2.2. What do you perceive? Do you also see some disks that seem to bulge out and others that seem to pull back? Now turn your book upside down. Do the same disks bulge out? What is happening here?

To understand the illusion of Figure 2.2, it is important to keep in mind that the input your brain receives is sensory input coming from a flat page. Some parts of Figure 2.2 are darker than others, and receptors in your eyes convey this information to you. However, your brain does not simply record the sensations. It tries to interpret them. For a start, it will assume that very few objects in the world are flat. So, it will try to project depth in the flat stimulus that comes from the back of your eyes (notice that all information coming from the eyes is two-dimensional, as the eyes do not register how far the light has travelled before it reaches them). A second assumption the brain seems to make is that light usually comes from above. Adding these two assumptions together allows the brain to interpret the sensations coming from Figure 2.2 as a figure with bulging disks on the diagonals and receding disks in-between. If the light comes from above, then a bulging disk will look brighter at the top than at the bottom and the other way around for a receding disk. When the figure is turned upside-down, the same assumptions will lead to the perception of receding disks on the diagonals and bulging disks in-between. Importantly, none of this information is given in the stimulus reaching the brain. It is projected by the brain upon the incoming sensations. However, if the brain did not do this automatically, it would not be able to see depth in a photograph or even in the real world, given that all light stimuli are projected on the two-dimensional back of the eyes. So, our brain "sees" depth in Figure 2.2, because it automatically applies the processes it uses to "see" depth in the stimuli coming from the eyes.

Perception as an active interface between reality and action

Figures 2.1 and 2.2 together illustrate that perception involves more than the passive registration of sensations. It requires the active regrouping and restructuring of the input on the basis of innate structures and previous experiences. For this reason, Hoffman et al. (2015) argued that we should not compare perception with stimulus recording (filming). It is more informative to compare perception to the interface software provides us with in computers. Files as such do not exist in the computer; they cannot be dragged from one folder to another, and they do not have names and icons. All that happens in the computer consists of thousands of bits turned on and off. The software allows us to interpret these large-scale, minute changes as meaningful input requiring appropriate actions. Similarly, the information reaching the brain from the eyes does not consist of forms, colors, and movements. It consists of millions of cells firing at a particular rate. Our brain translates this input into a code we can work with.

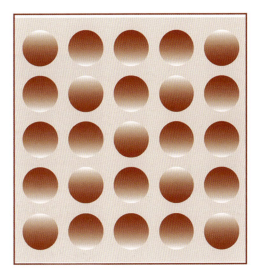

Figure 2.2 A disk illusion Do you also see the disks on the diagonal bulging out? And the ones in-between pulling back like cavities? Now turn your book upside down. What do you see now? See the text for an explanation.
Source: From Brysbaert (2016), with permission from Academia Press.

Figure 2.3   From sensation to perception
It is possible to interpret the black parts of Figure 2.1 as a cowboy riding a horse. This interpretation illustrates the transition from sensation to perception. Normally, the transition happens so fast that you are not aware of it. Only when the stimulus is degraded enough do you experience the interpretation part. Now look back at Figure 2.1: Is it still possible to see the black patches without seeing the cowboy in them? Your perceptual system has changed and learned how to see the "real" stimulus in Figure 2.1.
Source: From Brysbaert (2016), with permission from Academia Press.

Section summary

- Perception is more than the passive registration of sensory input. It involves interpretation of the most likely stimulus on the basis of the sensory input and previous experiences. This can be illustrated with degraded stimuli and visual illusions.

PERCEPTUAL ORGANIZATION

One of the main challenges the perceiving brain has to solve is to decide which parts of the environment go together and which belong to different objects. It is fairly easy to work this out if the objects are spread out in space against a uniform, bland background. However, most of the time our visual environment is complex and confusing, with many objects overlapping others against quite complex backgrounds. As a result, it is often difficult to achieve perceptual segregation of visual objects, as computer programmers found out when they wanted to give robots human-like vision.

The first systematic attempt to study perceptual segregation (and the perceptual organization to which it gives rise) was made by the *Gestalt psychologists*. They were German psychologists (including Koffka, Köhler, and Wertheimer), most of whom emigrated to the United States before the Second World War. Gestalt psychologists were named as such, because they claimed that the percept (the Gestalt, which is the German word for "figure") was more than the sum of the parts (as indeed we saw above: perception is more than the sum of sensations). Their fundamental principle was the **law of Prägnanz**, according to which we typically perceive the simplest possible organization.

THE GESTALT LAWS

The Gestalt psychologists put forward several other laws, but most of them are examples of the law of Prägnanz (see Figure 2.4).

The fact that three horizontal arrays of dots rather than vertical groups are seen in Figure 2.4(a) indicates that visual elements tend to be grouped together if they are close to each other (the law of *proximity*).

Figure 2.4(b) shows the law of *similarity*, which states that elements will be grouped together perceptually if they are similar. Vertical columns rather than horizontal rows are seen because the elements in the vertical column are the same, whereas those in the horizontal rows are not.

We see two lines crossing in Figure 2.4(c) because, according to the law of *good continuation*, we group together those elements requiring the fewest changes or interruptions in straight or smoothly curving lines. Finally, Figure 2.4(d) shows the law of *closure*, according to which missing parts of a figure are filled in to complete the figure. Thus, a circle is seen even though it is actually incomplete.

Kubovy and van den Berg (2008) confirmed the importance of grouping by proximity and of grouping by similarity. They also found that the *combined* effects on grouping of proximity and similarity were equal to the sum of their separate effects.

Key term

Law of Prägnanz:
the notion that the simplest possible organization of the visual environment is what is perceived; proposed by the Gestalt psychologists.

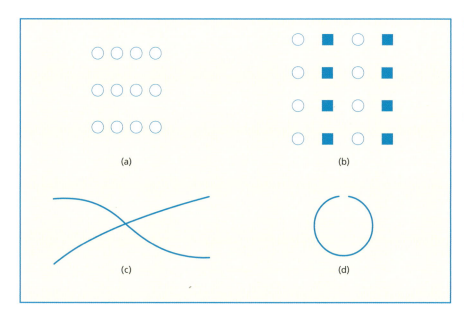

Figure 2.4 Examples of the Gestalt laws of perceptual organization: (a) the law of proximity; (b) the law of similarity; (c) the law of good continuation; (d) the law of closure.

Research Activity 2.1 *Gestalt laws in conflict*

Look at the three displays in Figure 2.5 and decide how you would group the stimuli in each case. You can then compare your judgments with those obtained by Quinlan and Wilton (1998) in a study using very similar stimuli. In their study, about half the participants grouped the stimuli in (a) by proximity or closeness and half by similarity of shape. In (b) and (c), most participants grouped by similarity of color rather than by similarity of shape or proximity.

This Research Activity focuses on what happens when different laws of organization are in conflict, an issue deemphasized by the Gestaltists. According to Quinlan and Wilton (1998), the visual elements in a display are initially grouped or clustered on the basis of proximity or closeness. However, when grouping based on proximity produces mismatches both within and between clusters (b and c), then observers favor grouping on the basis of similarity of color rather than proximity.

Figure 2.5 (a) Display involving a conflict between proximity (two groups of four figures) and similarity (triangles vs. squares); (b) display with a conflict between proximity and color; (c) a different display with a conflict between shape and color. Source: All adapted from Quinlan and Wilton (1998).

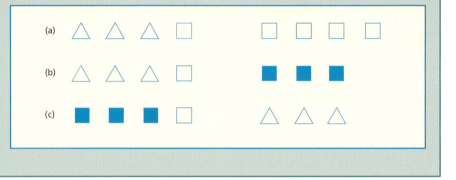

FIGURE-GROUND SEGREGATION

The Gestalt psychologists emphasized that perceptual organization results in **figure-ground organization**. One part of the visual field is identified as the figure, whereas the rest is less important and forms the ground. The Gestaltists claimed that the figure is perceived as having distinct form or shape, whereas the ground lacks form. In addition, the figure is perceived in front of the ground, and the contour separating the figure from the ground belongs to the figure. Check the validity of these claims by looking at the faces-goblet illusion (see Figure 2.6).

There is more attention to (and processing of) the figure than of the ground. Weisstein and Wong (1986) flashed vertical lines and slightly tilted lines onto the faces-goblet illusion, and observers decided whether the line was vertical. Performance was much better when the line was presented to what the observers perceived as the figure rather than to the ground.

Key term

Figure-ground organization: the division of the visual environment into a figure (having a distinct form) and ground (lacking a distinct form); the contour between figure and ground appears to belong to the figure, which stands out from the ground.

FINDINGS

The Gestaltists used artificial figures, and it is important to see whether their findings apply to more realistic stimuli. Elder and Goldberg (2002) presented observers with pictures of natural objects. Proximity or closeness was a very powerful cue when deciding which contours belonged to which objects. In addition, the cue of good continuation made a positive contribution.

Many Gestaltists put little emphasis on past knowledge and experience in the figure-ground segregation (Wagemans et al., 2012a, 2012b). However, if you look back at Figure 2.1, you will see that your past experience with the figure has a big influence on your figure-ground segregation.

The Gestaltists further assumed that figure-ground segregation occurs very *early* in visual processing and so always precedes object recognition. These assumptions were tested by Grill-Spector and Kanwisher (2005). Photographs were presented for between 17 ms and 167 ms followed by a mask of random squares (see also Glossary on *masking*). On some trials, participants performed an object detection task based on deciding whether the photograph contained an object. This was done to assess figure-ground segregation. On other trials, participants carried out an object categorization task (e.g., deciding whether the photograph showed an object from a given category such as "car"). Surprisingly, reaction times and error rates on the two tasks were extremely similar, suggesting that object recognition happened together with figure-ground segregation and, therefore, that both processes were closely related to each other.

In another experiment, Grill-Spector and Kanwisher (2005) asked participants to perform the object detection and categorization tasks on each trial. When the object was not detected, categorization performance was at chance level; when the object was not categorized accurately, detection performance was at chance.

These findings imply that the processes involved in figure-ground segregation are the same as those involved in object recognition. However, that isn't always the case. Mack et al. (2008) also compared performance on object detection (i.e., is an object there?) and object categorization (i.e., what object is it?), but they used conditions in which objects were inverted or degraded to make object categorization harder. In those conditions, object categorization performance was significantly worse than that for object detection. Thus, object categorization is more complex and can involve somewhat different processes from those involved in object detection, suggesting that the Gestalt psychologists were right in postulating figure-ground separation as a separate step *before* object identification.

Figure 2.6 An ambiguous drawing that can be seen either as two faces or as a goblet. Interestingly, nobody spontaneously mentions seeing two faces kissing a goblet. If the faces are seen as the figure, then the goblet becomes the ground, and vice versa. This illustrates the figure-ground segregation made by the visual system.

Evaluation

- (+) The Gestaltists correctly argued for the importance of organization in visual perception.

- (+) The Gestaltists discovered several important aspects of perceptual organization, most of which are relevant with natural scenes.

- (−) The Gestaltists deemphasized the role of experience and knowledge in perceptual organization.

- (−) The Gestaltists may have been wrong to argue that figure-ground segregation always occurs before object recognition.

- (−) The Gestaltists made beautiful demonstrations of how perception is more than the sum of sensations but failed to explain the underlying processes.

Section summary

- Perceptual organization is needed to determine which parts of the visual input go together and which parts belong to different objects.
- According to the Gestalt psychologists, we typically perceive the simplest possible organization when presented with a visual display. They correctly

argued that factors such as proximity and similarity were important, but they didn't focus on what happens when such factors conflict.
- The Gestaltists identified figure-ground segregation as central to perceptual organization, but they largely ignored the role of past experience in determining the form it takes. The Gestaltists provided useful descriptions of perceptual phenomena but had less success in explaining the phenomena.

PATTERN RECOGNITION

Once the figure has been segregated from the background, it must be recognized. Pattern recognition refers to the identification of two-dimensional patterns. This is achieved by matching the input to category information stored in memory. Categorization is important, because pattern recognition involves matching the stimulus to a category of objects (recognizing an object as "a" newspaper) rather than a single, specific object ("the" newspaper I read yesterday).

A key issue in pattern recognition is *flexibility*. It is important that the input need not fully match the stored category information. For example, we can recognize the letter "A" rapidly and accurately across large variations in orientation, typeface, size, and writing style. Similarly, we can recognize a face at various distances, orientations, and covered to various extents. Or we can identify an animal we have never seen before as a dog or a bird. Some of the processes involved in pattern recognition are discussed in this section.

In theory, pattern recognition can be based on two types of information. On the one hand, stimuli may be stored in memory as whole percepts (Gestalts); on the other hand, they may be stored as lists of features. The former are called template theories, the latter feature theories. Although templates and feature lists are often presented as rival theories, years of research have convinced most scholars that both types of information are used to store information about stimuli in memory.

TEMPLATE THEORIES

According to template theories, we have *templates* (forms or patterns stored in long-term memory) corresponding to each of the visual patterns we know. A pattern is recognized on the basis of which template provides the closest match to the stimulus input. This kind of theory is simple. However, it isn't very realistic in view of the enormous variations in visual stimuli allegedly matching the same template.

A modest improvement to the basic template theory is to assume that the visual stimulus undergoes a normalization process. This process produces an internal representation of the visual stimulus in a standard position (e.g., upright), size, and so on *before* the search for a matching template begins. However, it is improbable it would consistently produce matching with the appropriate template.

Another way of improving template theory would be to assume that there is more than one template for each stimulus (e.g., a face in frontal view, in profile view, midway in-between, and so on). This would permit accurate matching of stimulus and template across a wider range of stimuli, but at the cost of making the theory more complex.

In sum, template theories are ill-equipped to account for the flexibility shown by people when recognizing patterns. The limitations of template theories are especially obvious when the stimulus belongs to a category that can take many different forms (e.g., letters written in different cases and fonts). On the other hand, template theory offers a good explanation for the fast recognition of well-known stimuli. One of the reasons why we become more efficient in processing familiar visual input may be that we develop templates for this input (Goldstone, 1998).

FEATURE THEORIES

According to feature theories, a pattern consists of a set of features or attributes (Jain & Duin, 2004). For example, feature theorists might argue that the key features of the capital letter "A" are two straight lines and a connected cross-bar. This kind of theoretical approach has the advantage that visual stimuli varying greatly in size, orientation, and minor details can be identified as instances of the same pattern.

The feature-theory approach has been supported by studies of visual search in which a target letter has to be identified as rapidly as possible. Neisser (1964) compared the time taken to detect the letter "Z" when the distractor letters consisted of straight lines (e.g., W, V) or contained rounded features (e.g., O, G) (see Figure 2.7). Performance was faster in the latter condition because the distractors shared fewer features with the target letter Z.

Most feature theories assume that pattern recognition involves local processing followed by more global or general processing to integrate information from the features. However, global processing can *precede* more specific processing. Navon (1977) presented observers with stimuli such as the one shown in Figure 2.8. In one experiment, observers decided whether the large letter was an "H" or an "S"; on other trials, they decided whether the small letters were Hs or Ss.

What did Navon (1977) find? Performance speed with the small letters was greatly slowed when the large letter differed from the small letters. In contrast, decision speed with the large letter was *not* influenced by the nature of the small letters. Thus, as Navon expressed it, we often see the forest (global structure) before the trees (features) rather than the other way around.

Dalrymple et al. (2009) repeated Navon's study but manipulated the size of the small letters and the distance between them. When the small letters

LIST 1	LIST 2
IMVXEW	ODUGQR
WVMEIX	GRODUQ
VXWIEM	DUROQG
MIEWVX	RGOUDQ
WEIMXV	RQGOUD
IWVXEM	UGQDRO
IXEZVW	GUQZOR
VWEMXI	ODGRUQ
MIVEWX	DRUQGO
WXEIMV	UQGORD

Figure 2.7   How many letters Z do you find? Illustrative lists to study letter search: the distractors in List 2 share fewer features with the target letter Z than do the distractors in List 1. As a result, it is easier to find the letter Z in List 2 than in List 1.

```
        S                    S
        S                    S
        S                    S
        S                    S
        S                    S
        SSSSSSSSSSSSS
        S                    S
        S                    S
        S                    S
        S                    S
        S                    S
```

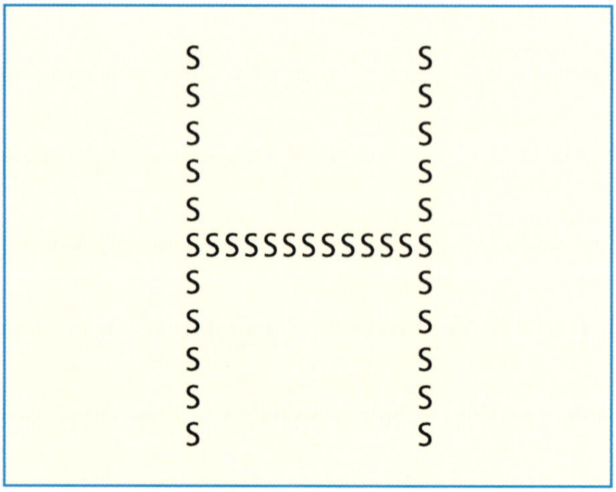

Figure 2.8 The kind of stimulus used by Navon (1977) to demonstrate the importance of global features in perception.

were very small and close together, Navon's pattern was replicated. However, when the small letters were larger and spread out, processing was faster at the level of the small letters than the large letter. In this condition, it was harder to identify the large letter. So, the level processed first depends on the ease with which the features can be discerned. Attention allocation (which part of the visual stimulus is attended to) is another factor influencing whether global processing precedes local processing (Wagemans et al., 2012a, 2012b).

Feature detectors

If the presentation of a visual stimulus leads initially to processing of its basic features, we might be able to identify cells in the brain involved in such processing. Relevant evidence was obtained in the Nobel prize-winning research of Hubel and Wiesel (1962). They studied cells in parts of the occipital cortex (at the back of the brain) associated with the early stages of visual processing.

Hubel and Wiesel discovered two types of neurons in the primary visual cortex: simple cells and complex cells. Simple cells have "on" and "off" regions with each region being rectangular in shape. These stimuli respond most to dark bars in a light field, light bars in a dark field, or straight edges between areas of light and dark. Any given simple cell only responds to stimuli of a particular orientation at a particular position in the visual field.

Complex cells differ from simple cells in that they respond to the presence of features independent of their position in the visual field and to combinations of features. There are many more complex cells than simple cells, distributed over various layers of increasing complexity. At the end, the complex cells feed into cells that fire when the feature combination corresponds to a previously encountered part of a meaningful object. All these types of cell are involved in the transition from feature detection to object perception and can be integrated in a computer model capable of recognizing simple objects from camera input (Figure 2.9).

TOP-DOWN PROCESSES

The object superiority effect

Feature theories of pattern recognition emphasize bottom-up processes: from simple features to meaningful objects. Stimulus features play an important role in pattern recognition. However, feature theories neglect the importance of context and expectations. Weisstein and Harris (1974) used a task involving detection of a line embedded in a briefly flashed three-dimensional form or in a less coherent form.

According to feature theorists, the target line should *always* activate the same feature detectors. As a result, the coherence of the form in which it is embedded shouldn't affect detection. In fact, however, target detection was best when the target line was part of a three-dimensional, meaningful form. Weisstein and Harris called this the object superiority effect. This effect

| Key term

Object superiority effect:
the finding that a feature is easier to process when it is part of a meaningful object than when it is part of an unknown form.

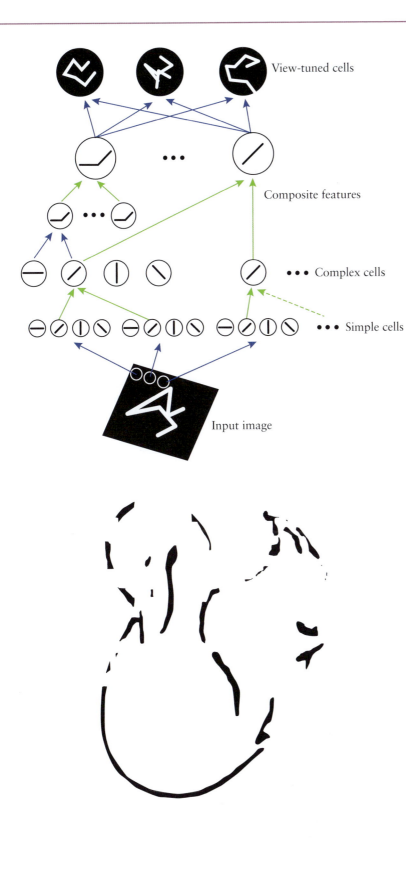

View-tuned cells

Composite features

Complex cells

Simple cells

Input image

Figure 2.9   From features to objects
Hubel and Wiesel discovered that the visual cortex contains simple cells responding to bars with a particular orientation at a particular position in the visual field. It also contains layers of complex cells responding to features independent of their specific position in the visual field and to combinations of features. These layers can be implemented in a computer program to simulate the recognition of simple objects from visual input. The blue arrows represent logical AND operations; the green arrows are logical OR operations.
Source: Koch & Poggio, 1999. Reprinted by permission of Macmillan Publishers Ltd.

Figure 2.10   What is this? Like in Figure 2.1 the transition from sensation to perception has been made difficult by degrading the stimulus. Is the interpretation easier if you know that this object is usually encountered near a pond? And what would you conclude if you knew that this object is often seen under a pine tree? Indeed, depending on the interpretation, the input agrees both with a duck looking to the left or a squirrel looking to the right. Top-down influences speed up the interpretation and may help to disambiguate uncertainties.
Source: From Brysbaert and Rastle (2014), with permission from Pearson Education Press.

Figure 2.11   Another example of top-down influences on perception As in Figure 2.10, the interpretation of the ambiguous stimulus is affected by the context in which it is seen.

THE LAND OF

occurs because the context provides useful information concerning the target stimulus.

Top-down processes also play a role in disambiguating the perceptual input. Remember that in real life, features may belong to different objects with different interpretations and that the brain has to figure out which parts belong together and how to interpret them. Have a look at Figure 2.10. What do you see? Because the stimulus is degraded, perception is more effortful than usual but still reflects the processes normally taking place.

In the Real World 2.1 *Fingerprinting*

Pattern-recognition techniques are extremely important in the real world. For example, finger-printing assists in the identification of criminals. The criminal's fingerprint (the latent print) provides a pattern that is matched against stored fingerprint records.

How does fingerprint identification work in criminal cases? It involves computer systems and human experts working together. Automatic fin-gerprint identification systems (AFIS) scan through huge databases (e.g., the FBI has the fingerprints of over 100 million persons). This produces a small number of possible matches to the fingerprint(s) obtained from the scene of the crime ranked in terms of similarity to the criminal's fingerprint. Experts then decide whether any fingerprint in the database matches the criminal's.

AFIS focuses on features at two levels (Jain et al., 2010). At a general level, there are three basic fingerprint patterns: loop; arch; whorl (circle), with about two-thirds of individuals having the loop pattern (see Figure 2.12).

Fingerprints also contain more specific features. We have patterns of ridges and valleys known as friction ridges on our hands. Of particular impor-tance are minutiae points – locations where a fric-tion ridge ends abruptly or a ridge divides into two or more ridges. There are typically between 20 and 70 minutiae points in a fingerprint, and this infor-mation is stored in a database (Jain et al., 2010). The expert is provided with information about feature or minutiae similarity from AFIS but also makes use of microfeatures (e.g., sweat pores; the width of particular ridges) (Dror & Mnookin, 2010).

Figure 2.12   The loop pattern (found in 60–65% of individuals) involves ridges curving back (left); the whorl pattern (30–35%) involves central ridges turning through at least one complete turn (center); the arch pattern (5%) involves ridges running across the pattern with no backward turn (right).

even though it is probably more accurate than any other identification method except DNA (Spinney, 2010). Decide whether the two fingerprints shown in Figure 2.13 come from the same person. Four fingerprinting experts decided both fingerprints came from the same person – namely, the bomber involved in the terrorist attack on Madrid on 11 March 2004. In fact, the fingerprints come from two different individuals. The top one is from the Madrid bomber, but the bottom one comes from Brandon Mayfield, an Oregon lawyer who was falsely arrested.

Fingerprint misidentification is common in the laboratory. Langenburg et al. (2009) studied the effects of context (e.g., alleged conclusions of an internationally respected expert) on fingerprint identification. Experts and non-experts were both influenced by contextual (top-down) information, but non-experts were more influenced. Dror and Rosenthal (2008) presented five experts with pairs of fingerprints they had judged as matching or not matching several years earlier. About 10% of the time, their two judgments differed.

Why do experts make mistakes in fingerprint identification? First, their judgments are influenced by irrelevant and misleading information (Langenburg et al., 2009). Cole (2005) reviewed real-life cases involving fingerprint misidentification by experts. In more than 50% of the cases, the original expert misidentification was confirmed by one or more additional experts.

Dror et al. (2006) asked experts to judge whether two fingerprints matched, having told them incorrectly that the prints were the ones mistakenly matched by the FBI as the Madrid bomber. Unknown to these experts, they had judged these fingerprints to be a clear and definite match several years earlier. However, when provided with misleading information about the Madrid bomber, 60% of the experts now judged the prints to be definite non-matches! Thus, top-down processes triggered by contextual information can distort fingerprint identification.

Second, a criminal's fingerprints can now be compared against hugely more stored prints than was previously possible. This greatly increases the chances of discovering an incorrect print extremely similar to that of the criminal. As a result, experts should require more evidence of similarity before deciding they have found a match (Dror & Mnookin,

Figure 2.13 The FBI's mistaken identification of the Madrid bomber. The fingerprint from the crime scene is at the top. The fingerprint of the innocent suspect (positively identified by various fingerprint experts) is at the bottom.
Source: From Dror et al., 2006. Copyright © 2006, with permission from Elsevier.

Do you share the common belief that fingerprint identification is almost infallible? In fact you shouldn't,

2010). However, that isn't happening. Charlton et al. (2010) found that fingerprint experts had a strong desire to resolve cases (especially major crimes), which can increase misidentifications.

Other evidence thankfully indicates that experts are less likely than inexperienced novices to make false identifications. Thompson et al. (2014) carried out a study on experts and novices using genuine crime scene prints. Both groups responded "match" accurately on approximately 70% of trials on which there was a genuine match. However, there was a substantial difference in the false-alarm rate. Novices incorrectly responded "match" when the two prints were similar but did not match on 57% of trials compared to only 2% for experts. These findings indicate that experts have much better discrimination than novices. They also have a much more conservative response bias than novices, meaning that they are more reluctant to respond "match." Still, they are not infallible.

In sum, fingerprint identification depends heavily on comparing features at different levels of specificity (bottom-up processing). Errors occur because experts are influenced by misleading contextual information (top-down processing) and because the degree of similarity they require before deciding they have found a match is insufficiently stringent.

In sum, pattern recognition doesn't depend solely on bottom-up processing involving features or other aspects of visual stimuli. Top-down processes are also involved. We will see more evidence for the importance of top-down processes in object recognition in the next section.

Section summary

Template theories
• Template theories assume we recognize a visual stimulus by matching it to the template or stored pattern it most resembles. Such theories can't easily account for human flexibility in pattern recognition but may provide an explanation for the extremely fast recognition of complex, familiar stimuli.

Feature theories
• Some feature theories assume that pattern recognition involves specific feature processing followed by more global or general processing. However, global processing can precede more specific processing. In addition, feature theories deemphasize the effects of context and expectations.

Top-down processes
• The object superiority effect and the interpretation of ambiguous stimuli require top-down processes.

Fingerprinting
• Fingerprint identification involves experts using information about feature or minutiae similarity plus various microfeatures (e.g., sweat pores). Experts make mistakes because their judgments are influenced by irrelevant and misleading information. In addition, their criteria for accepting similar fingerprints as matching are sometimes insufficiently stringent when they are highly motivated to resolve a criminal case.

VISUAL OBJECT RECOGNITION

Perceptual organization and pattern recognition can be illustrated with different types of stimuli, which are thought to involve both general and stimulus-specific processes. For instance, the recognition of written words and digits involves processes that are unique to the translation of visual squiggles into spoken word forms and meanings. These will be discussed in Chapter 8. Here we review some of the research related to the recognition of objects and faces. We start with visual object recognition.

RECOGNITION-BY-COMPONENTS THEORY

What processes are involved in object recognition? An influential answer was provided by Irving Biederman (1987) in his recognition-by-components theory. He argued that the visual perception of objects starts with edge extraction. Edges correspond to differences in surface characteristics such as luminance, texture, or color, providing a line drawing description of the object.

The next step is to decide which edges belong together and which do not. This is done by trying to combine edges into basic shapes or components known as **geons** (geometric ions). Examples of geons are blocks, cylinders, spheres, arcs, and wedges, as shown in Figure 2.14.

How many geons are there? According to Biederman (1987), there are about 36 different geons. That may sound suspiciously few to provide descriptions of all the objects we can recognize and identify. However, we can identity enormous numbers of spoken English words even though there are only about 44 phonemes (basic sounds) in the English language. This is because they can be arranged in almost limitless combinations.

The same is true of geons – the reason for the richness of the object descriptions provided by geons stems from the different possible spatial relationships among them. For example, a cup can be described by an arc connected to the side of a cylinder. A pail can be described by the same two geons but with the arc connected to the top of the cylinder.

Figure 2.14 Some examples of Biederman's geons (left-hand side) and how they can be used to define objects (right-hand side).

According to Biederman, geons form the building blocks on which object recognition is based, and geon-based information about common objects is stored in long-term memory. As a result, object recognition depends crucially on the identification of geons. Of major importance, an object's geons can be identified from numerous viewpoints. Thus, object recognition should generally be easy unless one or more geons are hidden from view. In other words, it is viewpoint-invariant.

The assumption that object recognition is viewpoint-invariant was tested by Biederman and Gerhardstein (1993). They made use of the fact that naming an object is faster when the object has been named before than when it is named for the first time, a phenomenon known as repetition priming. Biederman and Gerhardstein examined whether repetition priming was limited to pictures of objects that looked exactly the same or whether it would generalize to pictures of the same objects taken from different angles. The latter is what the authors found. Object naming was facilitated as much by two different views of an object as by two identical views, even when there was an angular difference of 135 degrees between the views. These findings suggest that object recognition is viewpoint-invariant, although later research has shown that this is only part of the story, as we will see later.

We are most sensitive to those visual features of an object that is directly relevant to identifying its geons. *How* have we developed this sensitivity? Could it be that our everyday experience with simple manufactured objects (e.g., cylinders; funnels; spherical objects; bricks) is of central importance? In fact, there is evidence against this explanation. Consider the Himba, a semi-nomadic people in Northwestern Namibia. They have very little exposure to manufactured objects. In spite of that, they are as sensitive to geon-relevant information as individuals living in the developed world (Lescroart et al., 2010). What seems to matter is exposure to a great variety of naturally occurring objects in the world around us.

How do we recognize objects when only some of the relevant visual information is available? According to Biederman (1987), the concavities (hollows) in an object's contour provide especially useful information. He obtained support for this view in an experiment in which observers were presented with degraded line drawings of objects (see Figure 2.15). Object recognition was much harder to achieve when parts of the contour providing information about concavities were omitted than when other parts of the contour were deleted. Webster (2015) reviews evidence that breaking up contours is one of the techniques animals use in camouflage.

Recognition-by-components theory strongly emphasizes bottom-up processes in object recognition. However, top-down processes depending on factors such as expectation and knowledge are also important, especially when object recognition is difficult. For example, Viggiano et al. (2008) found that observers relied more on top-down processes when animal photographs were blurred than when they weren't blurred. This happened because there was less information for bottom-up processes to make use of with the blurred photographs.

Another limitation of the theory is that it accounts only for fairly unsubtle perceptual discriminations. It explains in part how we decide whether the animal in front of us is a dog or a cat, but not how we decide whether it is a particular breed of dog or cat, or whether the dog is *our* dog.

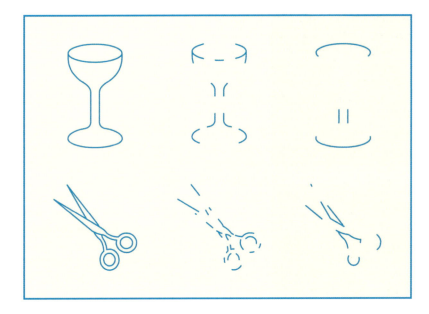

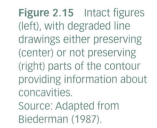

Figure 2.15 Intact figures (left), with degraded line drawings either preserving (center) or not preserving (right) parts of the contour providing information about concavities.
Source: Adapted from Biederman (1987).

Evaluation

+ It is plausible that geons or geon-like components are involved in object recognition.

+ The identification of concavities is of major importance in object recognition.

− The theory only accounts for fairly unsubtle perceptual discriminations. For example, it allows us to decide whether an animal is a dog or a cat, but not whether it is our dog or cat.

− It is assumed within the theory that objects consist of invariant geons. However, object recognition is actually much more flexible than that. For example, the shapes of some objects (e.g., clouds) are so variable that they don't have identifiable geons.

− The theory is based on the assumption that the processes in object recognition are viewpoint-invariant. We will shortly see that this is often not the case.

− As the theory assumes, bottom-up processes are very important in object recognition. However, top-down processes are also important when object recognition is difficult.

DOES VIEWPOINT AFFECT OBJECT RECOGNITION?

Form a visual image of a bicycle. Your image probably involved a side view in which the two wheels of the bicycle can be seen clearly. We can use this example to discuss an important controversy. Suppose some people were presented with a picture of a bicycle shown in the typical view as in your visual image,

a

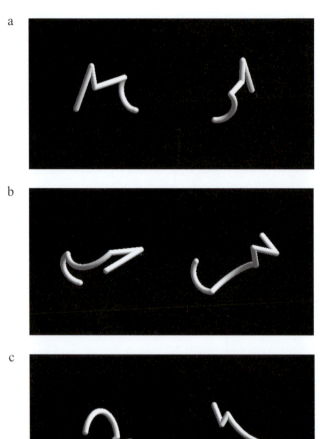

b

c

Figure 2.16 Example images of a "same" (a) and two "different" pairs of stimulus objects (b and c). The time it took participants to indicate that two images differed was less when one of the images had an extra feature (b) than when they had the same number of features but one of them differed (c). In addition, it took participants more time when the viewpoint of the second image differed much from that of the first image.
Source: From Foster and Gilson (2002), with permission from The Royal Society London.

whereas other people were presented with a picture of the same bicycle viewed end-on or from above. Both groups are instructed to identify the object as rapidly as possible. Would the group given the typical view of a bicycle perform this task faster than the other group?

Biederman (1987) claimed that object recognition is equally rapid and easy regardless of the angle from which an object is viewed as long as the same number of geons are visible to the observer. In other words, he assumed that object recognition is viewpoint-invariant. As we have just seen, Biederman and Gerhardstein (1993) obtained evidence supporting that assumption. However, other theorists (e.g., Friedman et al., 2005) argue that object recognition is generally faster and easier when objects are seen from certain angles (especially those with which we are most familiar). Such theorists favor the view that object recognition is viewpoint-dependent.

Evidence that the two kinds of information can be used at the same time in object recognition was reported by Foster and Gilson (2002). Observers saw pairs of simple three-dimensional objects formed from connected cylinders (see Figure 2.16). Their task was to decide whether the two images showed the same object or two different objects. When the two objects were different, they could differ in terms of a viewpoint-invariant feature (e.g., number of parts) and/or various viewpoint-dependent features (e.g., the curvature of one of the parts). Foster and Gilson's (2002) key finding was that observers used both kinds of information. Performance was better when the two objects had different parts, but in addition performance depended on how strongly the viewpoints of the figures matched each other. This suggests that we make use of all available information in object recognition rather than confining ourselves to only some of the information. Object recognition involves both viewpoint-dependent and viewpoint-invariant representations.

You may have noticed that viewpoint-invariant representations follow from feature-list theories of pattern recognition and that viewpoint-dependent representations are more in line with template theories. The fact that evidence for both is found suggests that both feature lists and templates are involved in object recognition.

According to Tarr and Bülthoff (1995), viewpoint-invariant mechanisms are typically used when object recognition involves making easy discriminations (e.g., categorizing stimuli as cars or bicycles). In contrast, viewpoint-dependent mechanisms are more important when the task requires difficult within-category discriminations or identifications (e.g., between different makes of car; between faces). Evidence consistent with this approach was reported by Tarr et al. (1998). They considered recognition of the same three-dimensional objects under various conditions. Performance was close to viewpoint-invariant when the object recognition task was easy, but it was viewpoint-dependent when the task was difficult.

A similar conclusion was reached by Milivojevic (2012) after reviewing the behavioral research in this area. Object recognition is typically not influenced by the object's orientation when *categorization* is required. Thus, it appears to be largely viewpoint-invariant with categorization. In contrast, object recognition is significantly slower when an object's orientation differs from its canonical or typical viewpoint when *identification* is required. Thus, it is viewer-centered with identification.

Cognitive neuroscience

The notion that object recognition involves both viewpoint-invariant and viewpoint-dependent aspects has received further support from research in cognitive neuroscience. Visual processing proceeds through several areas in the occipital lobe at the back of the brain and finishes up in the inferotemporal cortex, which is of crucial importance in visual object recognition (Peissig & Tarr, 2007).

Suppose we consider neuronal activity in the inferotemporal cortex while observers are presented with objects having various angles, sizes, and so on. Neurons vary in invariance or tolerance (Ison & Quiroga, 2008). Neurons responding almost equally strongly to a given object regardless of its orientation, size, and so on possess high invariance or tolerance. In contrast, neurons responding most strongly to an object in a specific orientation or size have low invariance. Viewpoint-invariant theories would expect to find many cells of the former type, whereas viewpoint-dependent theories would predict many cells of the latter type.

As it happens, both types of neurons are prominent in the inferotemporal cortex, with more viewpoint-dependent cells in the posterior part of the inferotemproal cortex (close to the visual cortex) and more viewpoint-invariant cells in the anterior part. Thus, the findings from cognitive neuroscience support the conclusion that object perception involves both viewpoint-dependent and viewpoint-invariant aspects. A way to implement this in a computer program would be to add a layer of viewpoint-independent cells at the top of Figure 2.9.

DISORDERS OF OBJECT RECOGNITION

Insights into the processes involved in object recognition have been obtained by studying brain-damaged patients having deficient object recognition. Such patients suffer from *visual agnosia*. This is a condition in which there are great problems in recognizing visual objects even though visual sensations still reach the brain and the person still possesses much knowledge about the object (e.g., they can describe its shape and its use or they can recognize the object from touch).

There are substantial differences among patients with visual agnosia in the specific problems they have with object recognition. Historically, much importance was attached to a distinction between two forms of impairment in object recognition:

1. **Apperceptive agnosia**: Object recognition is impaired because of deficits in perceptual processing.
2. **Associative agnosia**: Perceptual processes are essentially intact, but there are difficulties in accessing relevant knowledge about objects from long-term memory on the basis of visual input.

According to this view, the problems with object recognition occur at an *earlier* stage of processing in apperceptive agnosia than in associative agnosia. Apperceptive agnosia refers to the impossibility to go from sensation to perception, whereas associative agnosia is related to problems in activating the meaning of the input even though the pattern has been recognized.

How can we distinguish between apperceptive agnosia and associative agnosia? One way is to assess patients' ability to copy objects they can't recognize. Patients who can copy objects are said to have associative agnosia, whereas those who can't have apperceptive agnosia. For example, Riddoch et al. (2008) studied a patient (SA), a hospital clerical worker. She had great difficulties in shape discrimination (e.g., discriminating between rectangles and squares) and in copying complex drawings. This is a typical case of apperceptive agnosia.

However, other patients with apperceptive agnosia seem to have problems at a later stage of processing. Consider HJA, a male patient. He performed well on tasks involving shape discrimination and copying drawings, but he found it very hard to integrate visual information (Riddoch et al., 2008). In his own words, "I have come to cope with recognizing many common objects, if they are standing alone. When objects are placed together, though, I have more difficulties. To recognize one sausage on its own is far from picking one out from a dish of cold foods in a salad" (Humphreys & Riddoch, 1987). This still seems to be apperceptive agnosia, even though the patient is able to copy and even recognize simple, individual drawings.

Foulsham et al. (2009) studied another patient (CH, a 63-year-old woman) apparently suffering from apperceptive agnosia. She had to decide whether a piece of fruit was present in photographs of everyday scenes, a task on which her performance was poor. Inspection of CH's eye movements revealed, however, that she failed to focus on areas most likely to contain a piece of fruit. She couldn't use top-down knowledge

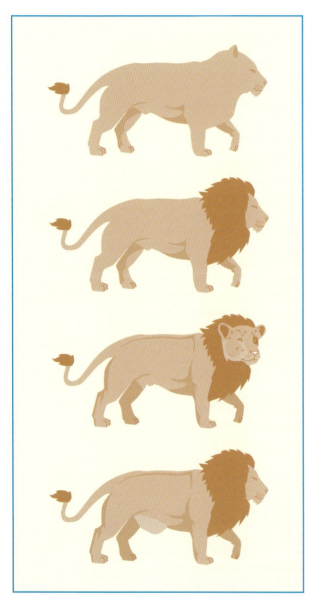

Figure 2.17 Examples of animal stimuli (from top to bottom): with a part missing, the intact animal, with a part substituted, and with a part added.
Source: From Fery and Morais (2003), with permission from Taylor & Francis.

of the structure of visual scenes to guide her eye movements. Given this observation, how sure can we be that the perception problems were due to the transition of sensation to perception and not to the failure of using top-down information to guide the information take-up?

In addition, associative agnosia seems to come in various degrees of severity and clarity. Anaki et al. (2007) reported an ideal example. They studied DBO, a 72-year-old man with associative agnosia who had very poor ability to access stored information about objects. For example, he found it very hard to name famous faces or to realize there was a connection between two famous faces. However, his perceptual processing seemed intact (e.g., he had intact immediate recognition memory for faces).

Another patient with relatively pure associative agnosia is DJ (Fery & Morais, 2003). He recognized only 16% of common objects presented visually, indicating he couldn't easily access stored information about the forms and shapes of objects. In spite of DJ's problems, several processes relating to object recognition seemed essentially intact. He was correct on 93% of trials on a hard animal-decision task requiring a decision as to which one out of various drawings was an animal. On this task, the non-animals were actual animals with one part added, deleted, or substituted (see Figure 2.17).

On the other hand, in many cases there is no clear-cut decision between apperceptive agnosia and associative agnosia. Many patients with associative agnosia have subtle deficiencies in visual perception that may not always be captured by standard neuropsychological tests (Delvenne et al., 2004), in line with the idea the object recognition involves more than two steps and that problems can be situated at any of these stages.

In sum, research on brain-damaged patients has indicated that although the distinction between apperceptive and associative agnosia is meaningful, it underestimates the number of stages involved in object recognition (Riddoch & Humphreys, 2001). A better understanding is possible by using a more detailed model of visual perception, starting from sensations up to how memories of familiar objects support perception by means of top-down influences.

Section summary

Recognition-by-components theory

- According to Biederman's theory, object recognition involves the identification of an object's geons (basic shapes). It is also assumed within the theory that object recognition is viewpoint-invariant and that concavities facilitate geon identification. The theory minimizes the importance of top-down processes and only accounts for unsubtle perceptual discriminations.

Does viewpoint affect object recognition?

- Viewpoint-invariant mechanisms are typically used when object recognition is easy, whereas viewpoint-dependent mechanisms are used when it is difficult. Consistent with this view, some neurons in the inferotemporal cortex are sensitive to an object's orientation whereas others are not. Viewpoint-dependent and viewpoint-invariant mechanisms are often used jointly to facilitate object recognition.

> **Disorders of object recognition**
> • Research on patients with visual agnosia suggests that object recognition involves several processing stages. Some patients have impaired processing at an early stage (form and shape discrimination). Others have impaired processing at the next stage (integration of visual information). Still other patients have problems with accessing stored knowledge about objects. Patients can also have problems in accessing knowledge about the structure of visual scenes to guide their eye movements.

FACE RECOGNITION

Recognizing faces is of enormous importance in our lives. We can sometimes identify people from their physique, the way they walk, or their mannerisms. Most of the time, however, we simply look at their faces. Form a visual image of someone important in your life. Your image probably contains fairly detailed information about their face and its special features.

In view of its great importance, we would expect face recognition to occur rapidly because of the huge amount of practice we have had in recognizing faces. Hsiao and Cottrell (2008) carried out a study on face recognition in which observers were allowed one, two, three, or unlimited eye fixations on each face. Face-recognition performance was above chance even with only one fixation, and was as good with two fixations as with three or unlimited fixations. The fixations are predominantly on the eyes and the nose. Figure 2.18 shows the distribution of first fixations when European students decide as rapidly as possible whether faces are European or Asian. As you can see, most first fixations fall on the eyes and the nose, with more fixations on the eyes for European faces than for Asian faces.

FACE RECOGNITION BY EYEWITNESSES

Face recognition plays a crucial role in many court cases. Hundreds (perhaps thousands) of innocent people have been locked up in prison because eyewitnesses mistakenly claimed to recognize them as the person who committed a crime. We know this because DNA has shown conclusively that the person found guilty of a crime didn't commit it (see Chapter 6).

Why do eyewitnesses sometimes identify the wrong person? The most important reason is that although face recognition is rapid, it is also difficult, certainly for the recognition of unfamiliar faces. In one study (Davis & Valentine, 2009), participants watched moving video images resembling those captured by closed-circuit television (CCTV). The participants decided whether individuals physically present were the same as those shown in the video images. Participants made many errors even when high-quality close-up images were used.

Kemp et al. (1997) provided college students with credit cards containing their photograph. The students were told to buy some goods in a supermarket and then present their photo ID to the cashier. When the students used the correct card, the cashier accepted it 93% of the time. However, when students

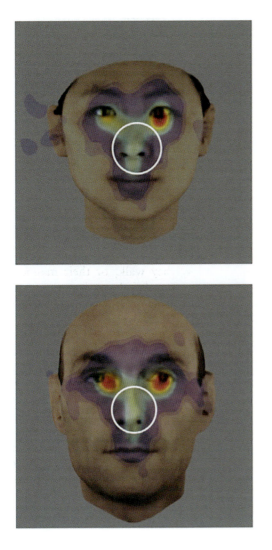

Figure 2.18   Where do we look at when we categorize faces?
When European participants were asked to decide whether faces were European or Asian, they looked predominantly at the eyes and the nose. The eyes were fixated more often when the face was of their own race than when it was of the other race.
Source: Brielmann et al. (2014). Reprinted with permission from Elsevier.

Most fixations

Least fixations

presented the card of someone else who looked similar to them, the cashier accepted the incorrect card 64% of the time!

Burton (2013) argued that face perception is so difficult because there is much variability in the appearance of a face. You can see this in Figure 2.19. How many different people do you see in the pictures?

Students asked to count the number of different persons in Figure 2.19 gave numbers between 3 and 16 (with an average of 7.5). In reality, all pictures were taken from only two individuals. This illustrates the large within-person variability in appearance. Burton (2013) further argued that we are blind to this variability, because we easily recognize familiar people even under extremely degraded circumstances. If we were colleagues of the two persons in the pictures, we would immediately recognize them in every picture. However, we fail to do so for unfamiliar faces. According to Burton (2013), this difference in recognition performance is due to the fact that we have seen a familiar face many times under various circumstances. As a result, we have somehow stored the variability present in the appearance as part of our memory of

Figure 2.19 How many different people do you see?
When students were asked to count the number of different people shown in the photographs, they counted an average of 7.5 different individuals, whereas in reality all pictures were taken from only two! This shows the enormous variability present in images of faces.
Source: Jenkins et al. (2011). Reprinted with permission from Elsevier.

that person's face (see previous section for the discussion of viewpoint-dependent and viewpoint-invariant memories in visual perception). Because we do not have the same experience with a new face, we can only recognize the face when the viewing conditions are very similar to the ones we originally experienced. Therefore, it is very easy for us to recognize a photograph of a previously seen unfamiliar face when exactly the same photo is used in the recognition phase, but not when a different photo is shown taken from the same person a few hours later.

FACE VS. OBJECT RECOGNITION

Does face recognition involve different processes from object recognition? Most of the evidence supports the notion that faces are processed differently from other objects. We will start by considering research on healthy individuals followed by findings from brain-damaged patients. Finally, we consider theoretical approaches to understanding face recognition.

Holistic processing

How does face recognition differ from the recognition of other objects? An important part of the answer is that face recognition involves more **holistic processing** (combining or integrating information across the whole object). Information about specific features of a face can be unreliable because different

> **Key terms**
>
> **Holistic processing:**
> processing that involves *integrating* information from an entire object (especially faces).

individuals share similar facial features (e.g., eye color) or because an individual's features can change (e.g., skin shade; mouth shape). This makes it desirable for us to process faces holistically.

In the **part-whole effect**, memory for a face part is more accurate when it is presented within the whole face rather than on its own. Farah (1994) studied this effect (see also Tanaka & Simonyi, 2016). Participants were presented with drawings of faces or houses and associated a name with each face and each house. After that, they were presented with whole faces and houses or with only a single feature (e.g., mouth; front door). Recognition performance for face parts was much better when the whole face was presented rather than only a single feature. This is the part-whole effect. In contrast, recognition performance for house features was very similar in whole- and single-feature conditions.

Research Activity 2.2 *Composite face illusion*

You can obtain a sense of another illusion (the composite face illusion) found with faces but not with other objects by looking at Figure 2.20. First look at the top row and ask yourself whether the top halves of the faces (above the white line) are the same or different. Then look at the bottom row and perform exactly the same task.

In fact, the top halves are identical in both rows. However, you probably took longer and/or made the wrong decision with respect to the top row. The difference between the two rows is that the bottom halves differ in the top row but are identical in the bottom row. The top halves look slightly different in the top row because it is natural to integrate information from both half faces in a holistic way.

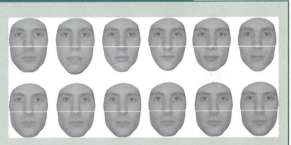

Figure 2.20 The composite face illusion. All the top halves of the faces are identical. However, when aligned with distinct bottom halves (see top row), they appear slightly different. This occurs because faces are perceived as an integrated whole. When the top halves of the faces are aligned with identical bottom parts (bottom row), it is more obvious that the top halves are the same.
Source: From Kuefner et al. (2010). Reprinted with permission from Elsevier.

Research Activity 2.2 gave you some insight into the *composite face illusion*. In this illusion, participants are presented with composite faces (two half faces of different individuals), and these two half faces are aligned or misaligned along the horizontal axis. Performance on tasks requiring perception of only one half face is impaired when the half faces are aligned compared to when they are misaligned (e.g., Young et al., 1987). This composite illusion is typically not found with non-face objects (McKone et al., 2007), suggesting there is less holistic processing with objects.

The fact that faces are processed holistically is also illustrated by the fact that we find it much more difficult to recognize faces shown upside down or even to notice that something is wrong with these faces, as illustrated in Figure 2.21. This is called the **face inversion effect**.

FACE BLINDNESS: PROSOPAGNOSIA

If face processing differs substantially from object processing, we might expect to find some brain-damaged individuals with severely impaired face

Figure 2.21 What is wrong with these faces? Turn the book upside down to see. Source: From Brysbaert (2016), with permission from Academia Press.

recognition but not object recognition. Such individuals exist. They suffer from a condition known as **prosopagnosia** (pros-uh-pag-NO-see-uh), coming from the Greek words meaning "face" and "without knowledge."

Patients with prosopagnosia (often referred to as face blindness) have enormous problems with faces. JK, a woman in her early 30s, described an embarrassing incident caused by her prosopagnosia: "I went to the wrong baby at my son's daycare and only realized that he was not my son when the entire daycare staff looked at me in horrified disbelief" (Duchaine & Nakayama, 2006, p. 166).

Some (but by no means all) prosopagnosics have very good object recognition. Duchaine (2006) studied a prosopagnosic called Edward, a 53-year-old married man with two PhDs, who did very poorly on several tests of face memory. In contrast, he performed slightly better than healthy controls on most memory tasks involving non-face objects, even when the task involved recognizing individual members within categories.

Why do prosopagnosics have very poor face recognition but reasonable object recognition? One explanation is that they have suffered damage to a part of the brain that is specialized for processing faces. Another possibility is that face recognition is simply much harder than object recognition. Face recognition involves distinguishing among members of the same category (i.e., faces), whereas object recognition generally only involves identifying the relevant category (e.g., cat; car). However, the findings of Duchaine (2006) cast doubt on that explanation.

We would have strong evidence that face recognition involves different processes from object recognition if we discovered patients with intact face recognition but impaired object recognition (see double dissociation, discussed in Chapter 1). Moscovitch et al. (1997) studied CK, a man with impaired object recognition. He performed as well as controls on face-recognition tasks regardless of whether the face was a photograph, a caricature, or a cartoon, provided it was upright and the internal features were in the correct locations.

In sum, while most prosopagnosics have somewhat deficient object recognition, others have essentially intact object recognition even with difficult face recognition. Surprisingly, a few individuals have reasonably intact face recognition in spite of severe problems with object recognition. These findings suggest that different processes (and brain areas) underlie face and object recognition.

Interestingly, prosopagnosia is not only observed after brain damage. Some 2% of the general population has very bad face recognition skills, sometimes referred to as *developmental prosopagnosia* (Bate & Tree, 2017). There are various tests on the internet to find out whether you are among these people (type the words *test developmental prosopagnosia* in your search engine).

FUSIFORM FACE AREA

Which brain region is specialized for face processing? The **fusiform face area** in the inferotemporal cortex has (as its name strongly implies!) been identified as such a brain region (see Kanwisher & Yovel, 2006, for a review). This area (shown in Figure 2.22) is frequently damaged in patients with prosopagnosia (Barton et al., 2002).

The fusiform face area typically responds at least twice as strongly to faces as to other objects in brain-imaging studies (McKone et al., 2007). Downing

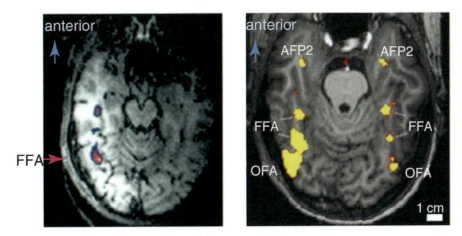

Figure 2.22 The fusiform face area (FFA) is situated at the lower rear end of the brain (in the temporal lobe) and contains two separate components. It forms a ventral network together with two anterior face patches (AFP1 and AFP2) and the occipital face area (OFA).
Source: From Weiner & Grill-Spector (2012). Reprinted with permission from Elsevier.

et al. (2006) presented participants with faces, scenes, and 18 object categories (e.g., tools, fruits, vegetables). The fusiform face area responded significantly more strongly to faces than to any other stimulus category.

An alternative hypothesis was put forward by Gauthier and Tarr (2002). According to them, face perception differs from many other forms of object processing, because we have far more expertise in recognizing individual faces than individual members of other categories. This is called the *expertise hypothesis*. Evidence for this position was found by presenting pictures of birds or cars to keen bird watchers and car experts. These individuals also showed enhanced activity in the fusiform face area when presented with pictures of their expertise. According to Gauthier and Tarr (2002), the fusiform face area is *not* specific to face processing but is used for processing *any* object category for which the observer possesses special knowledge.

It may be possible to reconcile the expertise hypothesis with the idea of face-specific brain tissue, if evidence were obtained that the fusiform area contains several subcomponents each responsible for a different stimulus type. Such evidence was reported by Grill-Spector et al. (2006), who presented observers with faces and three categories of objects (animals, cars, and abstract sculptures). The authors used brain scans with a higher resolution than had been done before, and found that different voxels (representing small volume elements in the brain) in the fusiform face area were selectively activated by the various categories. The average number of voxels selective to faces was 155 compared to 104 (animals), 63 (cars), and 63 (sculptures).

The picture is further complicated by the finding that the fusiform area is not the only area involved in face recognition. Rather, it is part of a more extended network of brain areas, involving not only parts of the temporal cortex but also areas in the occipital cortex and the frontal cortex (Weiner & Grill-Spector, 2012).

In sum, the fusiform face area is definitely involved in face processing and face recognition, but the notion that the processing is *localized* in this area is incorrect. What is more likely is that face processing involves a brain network including the fusiform area. It is also important to note that the fusiform area is activated when individuals are processing other types of objects, in particular if they have expertise with these objects.

THEORIES OF FACE RECOGNITION

Several theories of face recognition have been put forward. We discuss the two best known.

The Bruce and Young model

The most influential theory of face recognition is that of Bruce and Young (1986). According to that theory, when we look at a familiar face, we first access familiarity information followed by personal information (e.g., the person's occupation), followed by the person's name.

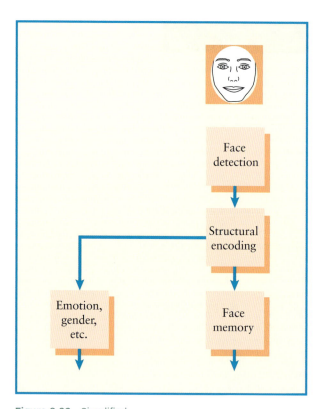

A modified (and simplified) version of that theory was proposed by Duchaine and Nakayama (2006), and will be discussed here (see Figure 2.23). Initially, observers decide whether the stimulus they are looking at is a face (face detection). This is followed by processing of the face's structure (structural encoding), which is then matched to a memory representation (face memory). The structural encoding of the face can also be used for recognition of facial expression and gender discrimination.

We will consider three major assumptions of the theoretical approach. First, the initial stage of processing involves deciding whether the stimulus at which we are looking is a face (face detection). Earlier we discussed a prosopagnosic who had extremely poor face recognition. In spite of his problems with later stages of face processing, he detected faces as rapidly as healthy individuals (Duchaine, 2006).

Second, *separate* processing routes are involved in the processing of facial identity (who is the person? face memory) and facial expression (what is he/she feeling?). It follows that some individuals should show good performance on facial identity but poor performance on identifying facial expression, whereas others should show the opposite pattern. These two patterns were reported by Young et al. (1993). Humphreys et al. (2007) also reported clear evidence from three individuals with prosopagnosia. All three had poor ability to recognize faces, but their ability to recognize facial expressions (even the most subtle ones) was comparable to that of healthy individuals.

Third, it is assumed that we retrieve personal information about a person *before* recalling their name. The person's name can *only* be recalled provided that some other information about him/her has already been recalled. Young et al. (1985) asked people to keep a diary record of problems they experienced in face recognition. There were 1,008 incidents in total, but people *never* reported putting a name to a face while knowing nothing else about that person. In contrast, there were 190 occasions on which someone remembered a reasonable amount of information about a person but not their name.

In spite of Young et al.'s (1985) findings, the assumption that the processing of names *always* occurs after the processing of personal information

Figure 2.23 Simplified version of the Bruce and Young (1986) model of face recognition. Face detection is followed by processing of the face's structure, which is then matched to a memory representation (face memory). The perceptual representation of the face can also be used for recognition of facial expression and gender discrimination.
Source: From Duchaine and Nakayama (2006). Reprinted with permission from Elsevier.

(e.g., occupation) is too rigid. Brédart et al. (2005) found that members of a Cognitive Science Department could name the faces of their close colleagues faster than they could retrieve personal information about them. This occurred because the participants had been exposed so often to the names of their colleagues.

In sum, there is good support for the various processing components identified within the theoretical approach initiated by Bruce and Young (1986). More specifically, it is valuable to distinguish between the processing of facial identity and facial expression. It is typically harder to retrieve someone's name than to retrieve personal information about them. However, this isn't always the case.

The face-space model

Valentine (1991; see also Valentine et al., 2016) proposed a model of how faces are stored in memory. According to the *face-space model*, memories for faces can be thought of as places in a multidimensional space. Each dimension represents a characteristic of a face; for instance, distance between the eyes, length-width ratio of the face, position of the eyes, length of the nose, position of the mouth, and so on. The values on the dimensions together determine the place of the face in the face-space (see Figure 2.24 for an example with three dimensions).

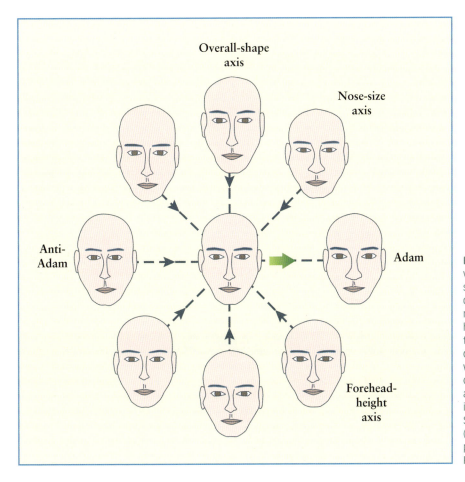

Figure 2.24 Simplified version of the face-space model with three dimensions (overall shape, nose size, and forehead height). Most faces are in the typical range and are difficult to distinguish. Faces with extreme values on one or more dimensions are easier to memorize and identify correctly.
Source: From Hulbert (2001). Reprinted with permission from Macmillan Publishers Ltd.

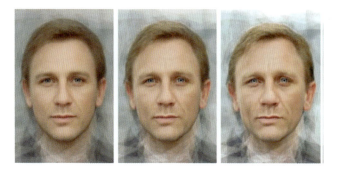

Figure 2.25   The face-space model predicts that the actor Daniel Craig (middle picture) will be easier to recognize if the values on the dimensions are shifted away from the mean value (right picture) than if they are shifted towards the mean value (left picture). This is because the face-space is more densely populated in the typical range than it is on the extremes.
Source: From Hancock, P. J., & Little, A. (2011). Reprinted with permission from SAGE Publications.

For each dimension, many faces have values in the average (typical) range. This part of the face-space is densely populated. Some faces, however, have extreme values on one or more dimensions. They are in an area of the space where few other faces are to be found (because few faces have such extreme characteristics).

The face-space model has made a number of interesting, successful predictions. One of them is that it is more difficult to memorize typical faces with average values on the dimensions than faces with extreme values on one or more dimensions. Another prediction is that faces are easier to recognize when their deviances from the mean are exaggerated. These are so-called caricature faces. In contrast, faces are more difficult to recognize if the features are shifted towards the mean value. An example of this is shown in Figure 2.25.

SUPER-RECOGNIZERS

We saw earlier that some individuals have extremely poor face-recognition ability. There is also evidence for individuals having exceptional face-recognition ability. Russell et al. (2009) identified four individuals who claimed to have significantly better than average face-recognition ability. For example, one of them said, "It doesn't matter how many years pass, if I've seen your face before I will be able to recall it. It only happens with faces" (Russell et al., 2009, p. 253).

All four individuals performed at a very high level on several tasks involving face recognition. For example, one task involved identifying famous people when shown photographs of them before they were famous (often when they were children). Russell et al. (2009) called these individuals "super-recognizers."

Genetic factors probably help to explain the existence of super-recognizers. Wilmer et al. (2010) studied face recognition in identical twins (who share 100% of their genes) and fraternal twins (who share 50% of their human-specific genes). The face-recognition performance of identical twins was much more similar than that of fraternal twins. This finding suggests that genetic factors influence face-recognition ability.

Several studies have shown that extraverts are better than introverts at recognizing faces. According to Lander and Poyarekar (2015), this is because extraverts are more interested in people and, therefore, practice more in recognizing faces. So, both genetic factors and practice make some people better than others at recognizing faces.

Section summary

Face vs. object recognition
- Phenomena such as the part-whole effect and the composite illusion indicate that face recognition involves holistic processing to a greater extent

than does object recognition. However, it has been argued that these phenomena simply reflect our expertise with faces.

Face blindness

- Many patients with prosopagnosia or face blindness have essentially intact object recognition. Other patients have deficient object recognition but intact face recognition. This double dissociation suggests that face recognition involves different processes from object recognition.

Fusiform face area

- The fusiform face area has been identified as being of special importance for face processing. Supporting evidence comes from prosopagnosics, who generally have damage to this area. Brain-imaging studies on healthy individuals indicate that the area is used in expert object recognition as well as face recognition and that the area is part of a wider face recognition network.

Theories of face recognition

- Bruce and Young (1986) and Duchaine and Nakayama (2006) argued that several different processes are involved in face recognition. There is reasonable evidence for processing components including face detection, facial identity, and facial expression. Names are generally (but not always) retrieved more slowly than other kinds of personal information.
- The face-space model of Valentine (1991) argues that memory of faces can be thought of as a multidimensional space in which each dimension represents a typical face characteristic. Most faces have values in a typical range, and they are difficult to keep apart. Faces with more extreme values are situated in empty parts of the space and are easier to memorize and identify. Faces are also easier to recognize when their deviations from the mean are slightly exaggerated (caricature faces).

Super-recognizers

- Super-recognizers have exceptional face-recognition ability. Twin studies indicate that genetic factors strongly influence face-recognition ability, which may help to account for the existence of super-recognizers.

PERCEPTION AND ACTION

The visual system is of great value in allowing us to construct an internal model of the world around us. When we look around us, we are generally very confident that what we see corresponds precisely to what is actually there. Indeed, the human species would have become extinct a very long time ago if we perceived the environment inaccurately! If we thought the edge of a precipice was farther away than was actually the case, our lives would be in danger. In spite of these arguments in favor of accurate visual perception, psychologists have found we are subject to numerous visual illusions, two more of which are discussed in Research Activity 2.3.

Research Activity 2.3 *Visual illusions*

Look at the two figures in Figure 2.26(a) and decide which of the two vertical lines is longer. Nearly everyone says the vertical line on the left looks longer than the one on the right. In fact, they are the same length, as can be confirmed by using a ruler (this is the Müller-Lyer illusion).

Now look at the two horizontal lines in Figure 2.26(b) and decide which is larger. Most people say the upper line is longer than the lower line, but they are in fact the same size (this is the Ponzo illusion).

These are just two out of literally hundreds of visual illusions. How can we explain them? Perhaps we treat two-dimensional illusion figures as if they were three-dimensional (Gregory, 1973). For example, the two skewed lines in the Ponzo illusion look like railway lines or the edges of a road receding into the distance. As a result, the upper line can be seen as farther away from us than the lower line. If it were a three-dimensional scene, then the upper line would be larger than the lower line.

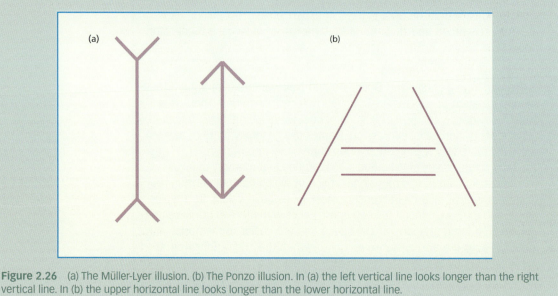

Figure 2.26   (a) The Müller-Lyer illusion. (b) The Ponzo illusion. In (a) the left vertical line looks longer than the right vertical line. In (b) the upper horizontal line looks longer than the lower horizontal line.

The existence of the Müller-Lyer, Ponzo, and other illusions leaves us with an intriguing paradox. How has the human species survived given that our visual perceptual processes are apparently so prone to error? Part of the answer is that most visual illusions involve artificial figures, to which the usual perceptual processes are applied (as discussed in relation to Figure 2.2).

However, this argument does not account for all illusions. For example, you can show the Müller-Lyer illusion with real three-dimensional objects (DeLucia & Hochberg, 1991). Place three open books in a line so the ones on

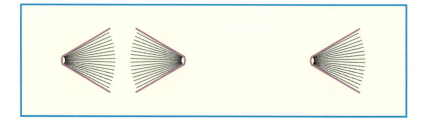

Figure 2.27   The spine of the middle book is closer to the spine of which other book? Now check your answer with a ruler.

the left and the right are open to the right and the middle one is open to the left (see Figure 2.27). The spine of the book in the middle should be the same distance from the spines of each of the other two books. However, the distance between the spine of the middle book and that of the book on the right looks longer.

TWO VISUAL SYSTEMS: PERCEPTION AND ACTION

We turn now to an alternative explanation of the paradox that visual perception seems very accurate in everyday life but can be error-prone in the laboratory. According to Milner and Goodale (1998, 2008), we have *two* visual systems. There is a vision-for-perception system used to identify objects (e.g., to decide whether we are confronted by a cat or a buffalo). This system is used when we look at visual illusions.

There is also a vision-for-action system used for visually guided action. This system provides accurate information about our position with respect to objects. It is the system we generally use when avoiding a speeding car or grasping an object.

The notion of two partially independent visual systems has received support from studies in cognitive neuroscience (Gazzaniga et al., 2009). There is a "what" or ventral pathway going to the inferotemporal cortex (see Figure 2.28) corresponding to the vision-for-perception system.

There is also a "where" or "how" pathway (the dorsal pathway) going to the parietal cortex (Figure 2.28) correspond-ing to the vision-for-action system. Note, however, that these two pathways aren't sep-arated neatly and tidily, and there is consider-able interchange of information between them (Zanon et al., 2010; de Haan & Cowey, 2011).

We can relate Milner and Goodale's (1998, 2008) theoretical approach to visual illusions. Suppose people were presented with three-dimensional versions of a visual illusion such as the Müller-Lyer. It would be expected that the illusion would be present if they were asked which line was longer, because that would involve the vision-for-perception sys-tem. However, the illusion should be reduced in size or disappear if people pointed at the end of one of the two figures, because that would involve the vision-for-action system.

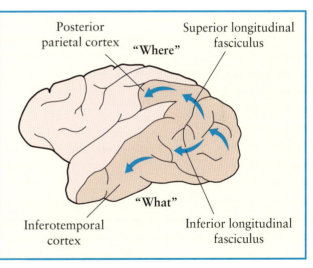

Figure 2.28   The ventral (what) and dorsal (where or how) pathways involved in vision having their origins in primary visual cortex (V1). Source: Adapted from Gazzaniga, Ivry, and Mangun (2009). Copyright © 1998 by W. W. Norton & Company, Inc. Reprinted with permission from W. W. Norton & Company, Inc.

Findings

These predictions have been supported in several studies. Bruno et al. (2008) reviewed 33 studies involving the Müller-Lyer or related illusions in which the observers *pointed* rapidly at one of the figures. The mean illusion effect was 5.5%. In other studies using standard procedures (e.g., verbal estimations of length), the mean illusion effect was 22.4%. Thus, the mean illusion effect was four times greater with the vision-for-perception system than with the vision-for-action system.

Another study involved the hollow-face illusion. The hollow-face illusion is one of the most powerful illusions. In this illusion, a realistic hollow mask looks like a normal face (see Figure 2.29; visit the website: www.richardgregory.org/experiments). In a study by Króliczak et al. (2006), a target (a small magnet) was placed on the face mask or on a normal face. Here are two of the tasks:

1. Draw the target position (using the vision-for-perception system).
2. Make a fast flicking finger movement to the target (using the vision-for-action system).

There was a strong illusion effect when observers drew the target position. In contrast, observers' performance was very accurate (i.e., illusion-free) when they made a flicking movement. These findings were as predicted theoretically.

There was also a third condition in which observers made a slow pointing finger movement to the target. Performance might have been expected to be accurate in this condition because it involved use of the vision-for-action system. In fact, however, the illusory effect was fairly strong. Why was this? According to Króliczak et al. (2006), actions involve the vision-for-perception system as well as the vision-for-action system when they are preceded by conscious cognitive processes.

More evidence that the vision-for-perception system can influence our actions was shown by Creem and Proffitt (2001). They distinguished between *effective* and *appropriate* grasping. For example, we can grasp a toothbrush effectively by its bristles, but appropriate grasping involves picking it up by the handle. Creem and Proffitt's key assumption was that appropriate grasping involves accessing stored knowledge about the object. As a result, appropriate grasping requires use of the vision-for-perception system.

Creem and Proffitt (2001) tested this hypothesis by asking people to pick up various objects with handles (e.g., toothbrush; hammer; knife). The handle always pointed away from the participant, and the measure of interest was the percentage of occasions on which the objects were grasped appropriately. Participants' ability to grasp objects appropriately was greatly impaired when

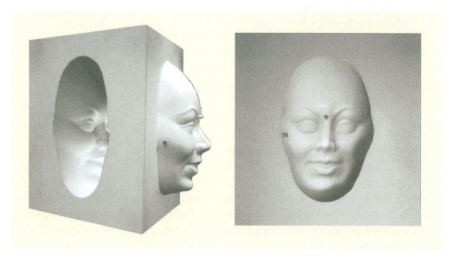

Figure 2.29 Left: normal and hollow faces with small target magnets on the forehead and cheek of the normal face; right: front view of the hollow mask that appears as an illusory face projecting forwards.
Source: Reprinted from Króliczak et al. (2006). Copyright © 2006, with permission from Elsevier.

they performed a learning task involving retrieving words from long-term memory at the same time. These findings suggest that retrieval of knowledge (using the vision-for-perception system) is necessary for appropriate grasping.

Evaluation

+ The notion that there are fairly separate vision-for-perception and vision-for-action systems is very influential.

+ Findings showing that action-based performance (e.g., pointing; grasping) often reduces or eliminates visual illusory effects are consistent with the existence of two visual systems (Stottinger et al., 2010).

− The two visual systems typically *interact* with each other. However, the emphasis within the theory is on their *separate* contributions to vision and action.

− Actions are influenced by the vision-for-perception system more than was implied by early versions of the theory. Actions are most likely to be influenced by the vision-for-perception system when they aren't automatic but instead are based on conscious cognitive processes (Milner & Goodale, 2008).

Section summary

- It has been claimed that many visual illusions occur because we treat two-dimensional figures as if they were three-dimensional. However, this doesn't explain why the Müller-Lyer illusion can be found with three-dimensional objects.

Two visual systems: Perception and action
- Much evidence suggests the existence of two partially independent systems specialized for perception and for action. According to Milner and Goodale, the vision-for-perception system is much more susceptible than the vision-for-action system to visual illusions. This prediction has been supported many times. However, the vision-for-perception system influences actions when they are based on conscious cognitive processes. More generally, the two systems often interact with each other rather than functioning separately, although precisely how they interact remains unclear.

IN SIGHT BUT OUT OF MIND

Have a look around you (go on!). We imagine you have the strong impression of seeing a vivid and detailed picture of the visual scene in front of your eyes. In fact, however, many psychologists argue that we are deluding ourselves.

INATTENTIONAL BLINDNESS
Suppose you are watching a video in which students are passing a ball to each other. At some point a woman in a gorilla suit walks right into the camera shot, looks at the camera, thumps her chest, and then walks off (see Figure 2.30).

Figure 2.30 Frame showing a woman in a gorilla suit in the middle of a game of passing the ball. There are two teams: a black one and a white one. Participants are asked to count the number of times the ball is passed by one team.
Source: From Simons and Chabris (1999), with permission from Dan Simons (www.dansimons.com).

Altogether she is on the screen for 9 seconds. We are sure you feel it is absolutely certain that you would spot the woman dressed up as a gorilla almost immediately. Simons and Chabris (1999) carried out an experiment along the lines just described (see the video at www.simonslab.com/videos.html). What percentage of their participants do you think failed to spot the gorilla? Think about your answer before reading on.

It seems probable that practically no one would fail to spot a "gorilla" taking 9 seconds to stroll across a scene. In fact, the findings were *very* surprising: 50% of observers didn't notice the woman's presence at all!

How was it possible that so many observers failed to see the gorilla? Simons and Chabris (1999) hypothesized that one factor involved was the fact that the participants were looking at two teams passing a ball: a white team and a black team. In the experiment described, the participants were asked to count the passes of the team dressed in white. So, they had to ignore the students dressed in black. As the gorilla was black too, this might explain the blindness.

To test the hypothesis, Simons and Chabris (1999) ran a further experiment in which observers counted the passes made by either members of the team dressed in white or the team dressed in black. As before, the gorilla's presence was detected by only 42% of observers when the attended team was the one dressed in white. However, the gorilla's presence was detected by 83% of observers when the attended team was dressed in black. So, an unexpected object (i.e., the gorilla) attracts more attention and is more likely to be detected when it is *similar* to task-relevant stimuli. When it is different from the task-relevant stimuli, it tends to be ignored.

The observation that we can be blind to something major happening before our eyes because it is not in the center of our attention is called **inattentional blindness**. The existence of inattentional blindness is sobering, because it illustrates how much information we are likely to miss when we are walking or driving through a street.

CHANGE BLINDNESS

Inattentional blindness is not the only situation in which we miss important information. Simons and Levin (1998) carried out a study in which people walking across a college campus were asked for directions by a stranger. About 10 or 15 seconds into the discussion, two men carrying a wooden door passed between the stranger and the participants. While that was happening, the stranger was substituted with a man of different height, build, and voice wearing different clothes. However, half the participants failed to realize their conversational partner had changed! You can see this video on the following website: www.dansimons.com (The "Door" Study).

The failure to detect that an object has moved, changed, or disappeared (e.g., one stranger being replaced with a different one) is called **change blindness**.

It occurs under many different situations. We saw the example of vision being blocked by a door for a few seconds. More surprisingly, change blindness already happens when the image flickers for less than a second, or when some mud splashes appear on the screen for half a second. It further occurs when there is a film cut and the viewpoint of a scene changes. It even happens when we are making an eye movement! When the left and the right images of Figure 2.31 were swapped during an eye movement while the participants were looking at the photos, few participants noticed the change in the photo.

Further of interest is that we seem to greatly underestimate our proneness to change blindness. Levin et al. (2002) showed observers videos involving two people having a conversation in a restaurant. The participants were warned beforehand that in one video the plates on their table would change from red to white and in another a scarf worn by one of them would disappear. After showing the videos, Levin et al. asked their participants whether they thought they would have noticed the changes if they hadn't been forewarned about

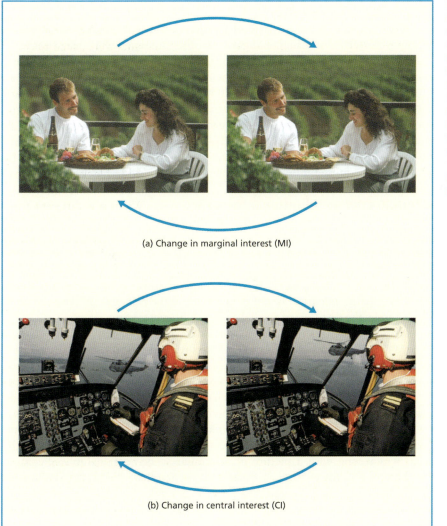

(a) Change in marginal interest (MI)

(b) Change in central interest (CI)

Figure 2.31 (a) The object that is changed (the railing) undergoes a shift in location comparable to that of the object that is changed (the helicopter) in (b). However, the change is much easier to see in (b) because the changed object is more important.
Source: From Rensink et al. (1997). Copyright © 1997 by SAGE. Reprinted by permission of SAGE Publications.

them. Forty-six percent claimed they would have noticed the change in the color of the plates, and 78% the disappearing scarf. As a matter of fact, the videos had previously been used by Levin and Simons (1997), who found that no observers detected any of the changes without forewarning! Levin et al. used the term *change blindness blindness* to describe our wildly optimistic beliefs about our ability to detect visual changes.

Change blindness is important in the real world. For example, an Airbus AT320–111 coming in to land at Strasbourg, France in 1992 mysteriously crashed into a mountain a considerable distance short of the runway. The most likely explanation is that the pilot didn't notice an important signal change on the visual display in front of him. Galpin et al. (2009) found that drivers and nondrivers viewing a complex driving-related scene showed much evidence of change blindness for central items that seemed relatively unimportant.

On a more positive note, change blindness is a blessing for magicians. Most magic tricks involve misdirection – the spectators' attention is drawn away from some action crucial to the success of the trick. When this is done skillfully, spectators fail to see how the magician is doing his/her tricks while thinking they have seen everything that is going on.

Movie makers are also grateful for the existence of change blindness. It means we rarely spot visual changes when the same scene has been shot more than once with parts of each shot being combined in the final version. In *Basic Instinct*, there is a famous scene in which Sharon Stone crosses her legs to reveal her lack of underwear. During that scene, the cigarette she was holding suddenly disappears and then reappears. In the movie *Diamonds Are Forever*, James Bond tilts his car on two wheels to drive through an alleyway. As he enters the alleyway, the car is balanced on its right wheels, but when it emerges on the other side, it is miraculously on its left wheels! You can see more examples at: www.jonhs.com/moviegoofs.

When is change blindness found?

The extent to which we show change blindness depends on several factors. You can (hopefully!) see the effects of one of these factors if you look at Figure 2.31 and try to spot the difference between the pictures. Rensink et al. (1997) found that observers took an average of 10.4 seconds to spot the difference between the first pair of pictures but only 2.6 seconds with the second pair of pictures. This discrepancy occurred because the height of the railing is of marginal interest, whereas the position of the helicopter is of central interest.

In studies such as those of Simons and Chabris (1999) and Simons and Levin (1998), observers were not told beforehand to expect a change in the visual display (incidental approach). Observers are much more likely to detect a change when told in advance to expect one (intentional approach). Beck et al. (2007) found that observers detected visual changes 90% of the time using the intentional approach but only 40% using the incidental approach.

Substantial evidence for change blindness can be found even with the intentional approach. Rosielle and Scaggs (2008) asked students to identify what was wrong with a picture of a familiar scene on their college campus (see Figure 2.32 for examples). Nearly all the students (97%) rated the scene as familiar, but only 20% detected the change. Such findings indicate that our long-term memory for complex scenes can be much less impressive than we believe to be the case (also see the Apple logo example in Chapter 1).

Original scene   Altered scene

Figure 2.32   Examples of the original and altered versions of the photographs. Source: From Rosielle and Scaggs (2008), with permission from Taylor & Francis.

Hollingworth and Henderson (2002) studied the role of attention in change blindness. They recorded eye movements while observers looked at a visual scene (e.g., kitchen; living room) for several seconds. It was assumed that the object fixated at any given moment was being attended. There were two kinds of changes that could occur to each visual scene:

- *Type change*, in which an object was replaced by an object from a different category (e.g., a plate was replaced by a bowl)
- *Token change*, in which an object was replaced by an object from the same category (e.g., a plate was replaced by a different plate)

There were two main findings (see Figure 2.33). First, changes were much more likely to be detected when the changed object had received attention (been fixated) before the change occurred. Second, change detection was much better when there was a change in the type of object rather than merely swapping one member of a category for another (token change).

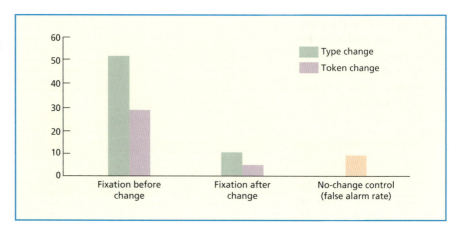

Figure 2.33 Percentage of correct change detection as a function of form of change (type vs. token) and time of fixation (before vs. after change); also false alarm rate when there was no change.
Source: From Hollingworth and Henderson (2002). Reprinted with permission from the American Psychological Association.

WHAT CAUSES CHANGE BLINDNESS?

It has generally been assumed that change blindness (and its opposite, change detection) depends on attentional processes. Thus, we detect changes when we are attending to an object that changes, and we show change blindness when not attending to that object (Rensink, 2002). This approach received support from the finding that observers are more likely to detect changes in an object when it is fixated prior to the change (Hollingworth & Henderson, 2002).

This approach assumes that our visual perception of unattended objects is very incomplete, but other explanations are possible (Simons & Rensink, 2005). Perhaps we initially form detailed and complete representations, but these representations decay rapidly or are overwritten by a subsequent stimulus (Lamme, 2003). That would be consistent with our subjective impression that we briefly have access to reasonably complete information about the visual scene in front of us.

Support was reported by Landman et al. (2003). Observers were presented with an array of eight rectangles (some horizontal and the others vertical), followed 1600 ms later by a second array of eight rectangles. The observers' task was to decide whether any of the rectangles had changed orientation from horizontal to vertical or vice versa. There was very little change blindness provided the observers' attention was directed to the rectangle that might change within 900 ms of the offset of the first array. Thus, we have access to fairly complete information about a visual scene for almost 1 second provided no other visual stimulus is presented.

In an interesting review article, Jensen et al. (2011) enumerated the processes required for successful performance in change blindness tasks. There are *five* of them:

1. Attention must be paid to the change location.
2. The pre-change visual stimulus at the change location must be encoded into memory.
3. The post-change visual stimulus at the change location must be encoded into memory.
4. The pre- and post-change representations must be compared.
5. The discrepancy between the pre- and post-change representations must be recognized at the conscious level.

When looked at in this way, perhaps it is not surprising we are so prone to change blindness. According to Fischer and Whitney (2014), change blindness occurs because we sacrifice perceptual accuracy to some extent, so that we can have continuous, stable perception of our visual environment. If we were hyperattentive to all minute changes in the sensory input, we would be constantly distracted. This is another, interesting element for the explanation of change blindness.

Section summary

Inattentional blindness
- Research has shown that we notice much less of our visual environment than we think we do. Major events can remain unnoticed if our attention is directed at some other event nearby.

Change blindness
- There is much evidence that most people are very susceptible to change blindness. Our optimistic belief about our ability to detect visual changes is known as change blindness blindness.

When is change blindness found?
- Change blindness is less likely to occur when observers expect a change compared to when they aren't forewarned of a change. It also tends to occur less when the changed object is important for the ongoing action, when the changed object resembles task-relevant stimuli, and when it has been fixated prior to the change.

What causes change blindness?
- Change blindness is due in part to our inability to retain detailed information about a visual scene for more than a very short period of time, after which it will be overwritten by new information. It is also due in part to failures of attention.

DOES PERCEPTION REQUIRE CONSCIOUS AWARENESS?

Can we perceive aspects of the visual world without any conscious awareness that we are doing so? In other words, is there such a thing as unconscious perception or subliminal perception (i.e., perception occurring even though the stimulus is below the threshold of conscious awareness; *limen* is the Latin word for *threshold*)? Common sense suggests that the answer is "No." However, there is good evidence that the correct answer is "Yes."

The case for subliminal perception apparently received support from the notorious "research" carried out in 1957 by James Vicary, who was a struggling market researcher. He claimed to have flashed the words HUNGRY? EAT POPCORN and DRINK COCA-COLA for 1/300th of a second (well below the threshold of conscious awareness) numerous times during showings of a movie called *Picnic* at a cinema in Fort Lee, New Jersey. Vicary claimed there was an increase of 18% in the cinema sales of Coca-Cola and a 58%

Key term

Subliminal perception: perceptual processing occurring below the level of conscious awareness that can nevertheless influence behavior.

increase in popcorn sales. The study received a lot of attention, also in popular media. Alas, Vicary admitted in 1962 that it was a hoax.

In the last decades it has become clear, however, that unconscious perception exists but does not have the strong effects Vicary attributed to it (see, e.g., Smarandescu & Shimp, 2015). In what follows, we consider two main strands of research on subliminal perception. First, we discuss studies on individuals with normal vision presented with stimuli they can't see consciously. Second, we discuss studies on brain-damaged patients denying conscious awareness of visual stimuli presented to parts of their visual field. In spite of that, they are often able to detect and localize visual stimuli presented to the "blind" region.

PERCEPTION WITHOUT AWARENESS

There are three main ways we can present individuals having intact vision with visual stimuli below the level of conscious awareness. First, we can present stimuli that are very weak or faint. Second, we can present stimuli very briefly. Third, we can use masking – the target stimulus is immediately followed by a masking stimulus that inhibits processing of the target stimulus.

How do we decide whether an observer is consciously aware of a given visual stimulus? Merikle et al. (2001) distinguished two approaches:

1. *Subjective threshold*: This is defined by an individual's failure to report conscious awareness of a stimulus; it is the most obvious measure to use.
2. *Objective threshold*: This is defined by an individual's inability to make an accurate forced-choice decision about a stimulus (e.g., guess at above-chance level whether it is a word).

In practice, observers often show "awareness" of a stimulus assessed by the objective threshold even when the stimulus doesn't exceed the subjective threshold. What should we do in such circumstances? Some psychologists argue that the objective threshold is more valid than a reliance on observers' possibly inaccurate or biased reports of their conscious experience. Others, however, argue that subjective thresholds are better, because conscious experience requires subjective awareness. Unconscious influence takes place when you fail to notice the stimulus but still are influenced by it. What is clear is that evidence for subliminal or unconscious perception based on the objective threshold is stronger than evidence based on the subjective threshold.

Findings

Naccache et al. (2002) asked participants to decide rapidly whether a clearly visible target digit was smaller or larger than 5. Unknown to them, an invisible masked digit was presented for 29 ms immediately before the target. The masked digit was congruent with the target (both digits on the same side of 5) or incongruent.

There was no evidence of conscious perception of the masked digits. No participants reported seeing any of them (subjective measure). In addition, their performance when guessing whether the masked digit was below or above 5 was at chance level (objective measure). However, performance with the target digits was faster on congruent than on incongruent trials, indicating that unconscious perceptual processing of the masked digits had occurred.

Jiang et al. (2006) presented pairs of pictures followed by a mask making them invisible to observers (based on the objective threshold). One picture was an intact picture of a nude male or female and the other was a scrambled version. These subliminal pictures influenced participants' attentional processes, as measured by asking them to do a difficult visual discrimination task at the place where the nude picture had been presented or the scrambled picture. Participants were more accurate when the discrimination stimulus appeared at the position of the nude prime. The attention of heterosexual males was attracted more to intact pictures of invisible female nudes, and that of heterosexual females more to invisible male nudes. These findings indicate there was some perceptual processing of the invisible sexual stimuli.

It is generally assumed that information perceived without awareness can only *control* our responses via direct stimulus-response associations, unlike information perceived with awareness. In the latter case, we can manipulate the information and associate stimuli with many different responses. If so, there should be situations in which perceiving with or without awareness has very different effects on behavior.

Persaud and McLeod (2008) found supporting evidence in a study in which they presented the letter 'b' or 'h' for 10 ms (short interval) or 15 ms (long interval). In the key condition, participants were told to respond with the letter that had *not* been presented. With the longer presentation interval, participants responded correctly with the nonpresented letter on 83% of trials. This suggests there was some conscious awareness of the stimulus in that condition. With the short presentation interval, however, participants responded correctly on only 43% of trials (significantly below chance). Thus, there was some processing of the stimulus, but participants lacked awareness of that processing, so that they could not link the stimuli to the required responses.

How much visual processing occurs below the level of conscious awareness? In one study (Rees, 2007), activation was assessed in brain areas associated with face processing or with object processing while pictures of invisible faces or houses were presented. The identity of the picture (face vs. house) could be predicted with almost 90% accuracy by studying patterns of brain activation. Thus, even stimuli that can't be perceived consciously can be processed reasonably thoroughly by the visual system.

There is also evidence that some patients with prosopagnosia can identify faces at a subconscious level. This evidence comes from the *galvanic skin response*. When a person becomes aroused through activation of the sympathetic nervous system, this can be measured at the level of the skin. It forms the basis of the lie detector, which measures the person's arousal when confronted with a (threatening) question. The skin response also changes when in a lab we suddenly see a photo of a familiar person amid a series of unknown persons (because the recognition of the photograph increases our arousal). Tranel and Damasio (1985) examined two patients with prosopagnosia. Each patient was shown a series of photographs. Most of the photos were from unknown people. Some, however, were from well-known persons (e.g., the patient's spouse). When asked to indicate which persons they recognized, the patients were very poor. However, they both showed normal skin responses when a photo of a familiar person appeared.

BLINDSIGHT

Several British soldiers in the First World War who were blinded by gunshot wounds that had destroyed their primary visual cortex (V1) were treated by a captain in the Royal Army Medical Corps called George Riddoch. These soldiers could perceive motion in those parts of the visual field in which they claimed to be blind (Riddoch, 1917)!

Many years later, Larry Weiskrantz (2004) at the University of Oxford studied a similar phenomenon. He described brain-damaged patients with some visual perception in the absence of any conscious awareness as having blindsight, which neatly captures the paradoxical nature of their condition.

Most patients with blindsight have extensive damage to V1. However, their loss of visual awareness in the blind field is probably not due directly to the V1 damage. Damage to V1 has knock-on effects throughout the visual system, leading to greatly reduced activation of subsequent visual processing areas (Silvanto, 2008).

Findings

One of the most thoroughly studied blindsight patients is DB. He began to experience increasingly frequent very severe migraines. As a result, he had a brain operation that destroyed the right half of his primary visual cortex (V1). DB showed some perceptual skills including an ability to detect whether a visual stimulus had been presented to the blind area in the left half of his visual field and to identify its location. However, he reported no conscious experience in his blind field. According to Weiskrantz et al. (1974, p. 721), "When he was shown a video film of his reaching and judging orientation of lines [by presenting it to his intact visual field], he was openly astonished."

Another much-studied blindsight patient is GY. He has extensive damage to V1 in the left hemisphere and a smaller area of damage in the right parietal area caused by a car accident at the age of eight. As a result, he couldn't see anything consciously in the right half of his visual field. In a study by Persaud and Cowey (2008), GY was presented briefly with a stimulus in the upper or lower part of his visual field, either in the normal, left half or in the blind, right half. On some trials (inclusion trials), he was told to report the part of the visual field to which the stimulus had been presented. On other trials (exclusion trials), GY was told to report the *opposite* of the stimulus's actual location (e.g., "Up" when it was in the lower part). In the blind half, GY tended to respond with the real rather than the opposite location on exclusion trials as well as inclusion trials. This suggests he had access to location information but lacked any conscious awareness of that information. In contrast, in the normal left half of the visual field, he was able to perform well on both inclusion and exclusion trials, indicating he had conscious access to location information in that part of the visual field.

Other research on patients with blindsight has focused on whether they can discriminate between emotional stimuli presented below the level of conscious awareness. This effect (known as affective blindsight) has been obtained in several studies (e.g., Tamietto & de Gelder, 2008), and is discussed in Chapter 11.

Issues

There is much evidence suggesting that blindsight is a genuine phenomenon. However, there are various reasons why it is sometimes hard to interpret the evidence. The main problem is how to be sure that the patients have no conscious perception in the blind part of their visual field. It is well-known that blindsight patients differ in how much conscious perception they possess (Danckert & Rossetti, 2005). Weiskrantz (2004) used the term blindsight Type 1 to describe patients with no conscious awareness. He used the term blindsight Type 2 to describe those patients with awareness that something was happening. An example of Type 2 blindsight was found in patient EY. He "sensed a definite pinpoint of light," although "it does not actually look like a light. It looks like nothing at all" (Weiskrantz, 1980). Cowey (2010, p. 20) further pointed out that: "Subjects are too seldom asked to describe exactly what they mean when they say they are 'aware'." Blindsight patients may have more conscious perception when the definition of awareness is lenient than when it is stringent (Overgaard et al., 2008).

EVALUATION

All in all, very few cognitive researchers doubt that perception without awareness exists (for reviews, see Eysenck & Keane, 2015, Chapter 16; Van den Bussche et al., 2009). However, it does not have the strong, long-term consequences Vicary attributed to it. Unconscious perception has a negative connotation in popular media, because it suggests that people can be influenced against their will. Partly this is because our society remains strongly influenced by the psychoanalytically inspired idea of a dark, sexually laden unconsciousness that constantly attempts to take over our functioning and must be kept under control by the ego. Another reason why unconscious perception is given mythical status is that it seems to undermine our rationality. A person no longer in control of his or her actions is a derailed person.

In contrast, the view coming from cognitive research is that of unconscious perception very similar and even inferior to conscious perception. All effects shown with unconscious perception can also be obtained (and often more convincingly) with conscious perception. In addition, unconscious perception is limited to the processing of simple stimuli and the activation of directly related responses, as we saw above. For more complex processing and indirect responses, we require access to consciously perceived stimuli.

In the cognitive view, perception largely operates unconsciously, outside awareness, and informs us about the environment. We can only process a small part of this information consciously. For this to happen, we must focus our attention on the stimulus and give it access to our working memory, as we will see in the coming chapters. The rest of the information only interests us if it has consequences for our survival (e.g., the detection of threat) and when it is important to continue our current activity. In both situations it is to our advantage if our brain automatically processes the incoming sensory input and provides our working memory with meaningful end products.

An analogy sometimes used in this respect is that of a theater or global workspace (Baars & Franklin, 2007; Dehaene & Changeux, 2011). According to this view, human information processing involves numerous special-purpose unconscious processors operating in parallel. These processors are distributed in numerous brain areas with each processor carrying out specialized functions (e.g., color processing, motion processing). This processing is very similar regardless of whether a stimulus is or is not consciously perceived.

Consciousness:
information of which we
are aware at any given
moment; it is associated
with perceiving the
environment, thinking
about events and issues
not related to the here-
and-now, understanding
what other people are
thinking, and controlling
our actions.

Information enters **consciousness** when data from several special-purpose processors must be *integrated*. This evokes widespread brain activation, with a combination of bottom-up processing and top-down control procedures igniting synchronized activity across large parts of the brain. The end result is that information in consciousness is globally available to all the special-purpose processors, which can make use of it to optimize their functioning, just like all support teams in a theater must have access to what is happening on stage, in order to synchronize their activities.

According to the global space view, perception largely occurs outside awareness, and we are only aware of the end products when they matter to us. If this were not the case, our perception would be much more limited.

Section summary

Unconscious perception
- Awareness of a visual stimulus can be assessed by using a subjective or an objective threshold (the latter is more stringent). There is evidence for unconscious perception using behavioral data and the objective threshold. Studies using brain-imaging data suggest there can be substantial processing of visual stimuli in the absence of conscious awareness.
- Unconscious processing is the default processing of the perceptual system according to the global space model. It informs the conscious part of our processing about meaningful events in the environment.

Blindsight
- Blindsight patients show some ability to indicate the location and movement of visual stimuli they deny seeing. Some of these patients also demonstrate affective blindsight. However, the use of sensitive methods to assess conscious awareness suggests that some blindsight patients may still have degraded conscious vision in their "blind" area.

Essay questions

1. Describe and discuss the difference between sensation and perception. Link it to visual agnosia.
2. "Face recognition involves different processes from object recognition." Discuss.
3. What factors determine whether or not we experience change blindness?
4. Is all perception conscious? Give evidence-based arguments for the position you take.

Further reading

- Bruce, V., & Yougn, A.W. (2012). *Face perception*. Oxford, UK: Psychology Press. Provides an up-to-date review of research on face perception.
- Cowey, A. (2010). The blindsight saga. *Experimental Brain Research, 200,* 3–24. Alan Cowey provides an excellent overview of theory and research on blindsight.

- Dror, I. E., & Mnookin, J. L. (2010). The use of technology in human expert domains: Challenges and risks arising from the use of automated fingerprint identification systems in forensic science. *Law, Probability and Risk*, *9*, 47–67. This article indicates clearly the limitations associated with current systems of fingerprint identification.
- Eysenck, M., & Keane, M. (2015). *Cognitive psychology: A student's handbook*. London: Psychology Press. This textbook discusses perception in more detail and contains a full chapter on consciousness.
- Harris, J. (2014). *Sensation and perception*. London: Sage Publishing. A book dealing in much more detail with sensation and perception. Includes chapters on the senses not covered here.
- McKone, E., Kanwisher, N., & Duchaine, B. C. (2007). Can generic expertise explain special processing for faces? *Trends in Cognitive Sciences*, *11*, 8–15. Three experts present an excellent account of our understanding of the processes involved in face recognition.
- Milner, A. D., & Goodale, M. A. (2008). Two visual systems re-viewed. *Neuropsychologia*, *46*, 774–785. David Milner and Melvyn Goodale discuss and evaluate their very influential theory based on the notion that there are two visual systems.
- Peissig, J. J., & Tarr, M. J. (2007). Visual object recognition: Do we know more now than we did 20 years ago? *Annual Review of Psychology*, *58*, 75–96. Provides a good overview of developments in our understanding of object recognition.

REFERENCES

Aleman, A., Schutter, D. L. G., Ramsey, N. F., van Honk, J., Kessels, R. P. C., Hoogduin, J. M., et al. (2002). Functional anatomy of top-down visuospatial processing in the human brain: Evidence from rTMS. *Cognitive Brain Research*, *14*, 300–302.

Anaki, D., & Bentin, S. (2009). Familiarity effects on categorization levels of faces and objects. *Cognition*, *111*, 144–149.

Anaki, D., Kaufman, Y., Freedman, M., & Moscovitch, M. (2007). Associative (prosop)agnosia without (apparent) perceptual deficits: A case-study. *Neuropsychologia*, *45*, 1658–1671.

Baars, B. J., & Franklin, S. (2007). An architectural model of conscious and unconscious brain functions: Global workspace theory and IDA. *Neural Networks*, *20*(9), 955–961.

Bartolomeo, P. (2002). The relationship between visual perception and visual mental imagery: A reappraisal of the neuropsychological evidence. *Cortex*, *38*, 357–378.

Bartolomeo, P. (2008). The neural correlates of visual mental imagery: An ongoing debate. *Cortex*, *44*, 107–108.

Barton, J. J. S., Press, D. Z., Keenan, J. P., & O'Connor, M. (2002). Topographic organization of human visual areas in the absence of input from primary cortex. *Journal of Neuroscience*, *19*, 3619–2627.

Bate, S., & Tree, J. J. (2017). The definition and diagnosis of developmental prosopagnosia. *Quarterly Journal of Experimental Psychology*, *70*, 193–200.

Beck, M. R., Levin, D. T., & Angelone, B. (2007). Change blindness blindness: Beliefs about the roles of intention and scene complexity in change blindness. *Consciousness and Cognition*, *16*, 31–51.

Biederman, I. (1987). Recognition-by-components: A theory of human image understanding. *Psychological Review, 94*, 115–147.

Biederman, I., & Gerhardstein, P. C. (1993). Recognizing depth-rotated objects: Evidence for 3-D viewpoint invariance. *Journal of Experimental Psychology: Human Perception & Performance, 19*, 1162–1182.

Brédart, S., Brennen, T., Delchambre, M., McNeill, A., & Burton, A. M. (2005). Naming very familiar people: When retrieving names is faster than retrieving semantic biographical information. *British Journal of Psychology, 96*, 205–214.

Brielmann, A. A., Bülthoff, I., & Armann, R. (2014). Looking at faces from different angles: Europeans fixate different features in Asian and Caucasian faces. *Vision Research, 100*, 105–112.

Bruce, V., & Young, A. W. (1986). Understanding face recognition. *British Journal of Psychology, 77*, 305–327.

Bruno, N., Bernadis, P., & Gentilucci, M. (2008). Visually guided pointing, the Müller-Lyer illusion, and the functional interpretation of the dorsal–ventral split: Conclusions from 33 independent studies. *Neuroscience and Biobehavioral Reviews, 32*, 423–437.

Brysbaert, M. (2016). *Psychologie*. Ghent, Belgium: Academia Press.

Brysbaert, M., & Rastle, K. (2014). *Historical and conceptual issues in psychology* (2nd ed.). Harlow: Pearson Education.

Burton, A.M. (2013). Why has research in face recognition progressed so slowly? The importance of variability. *The Quarterly Journal of Experimental Psychology, 66*(8), 1467–1485.

Calderwood, L., & Burton, A. M. (2006). Children and adults recall the names of highly familiar faces faster than semantic information. *British Journal of Psychology, 97*(4), 441–454.

Charlton, D., Fraser-Mackenzie, P. A. F., & Dror, I. E. (2010). Emotional experiences and motivating factors associated with fingerprint analysis. *Journal of Forensic Sciences, 55*, 385–393.

Cherney, I. D. (2008). Mom, let me play more computer games: They improve my mental rotation skills. *Sex Roles, 59*, 776–786.

Cole, S. A. (2005). More than zero: Accounting for error in latent fingerprinting identification. *Journal of Criminal Law & Criminology, 95*, 985–1078.

Cowey, A. (2010). The blindsight saga. *Experimental Brain Research, 200*, 3–24.

Creem, S. H., & Proffitt, D. R. (2001). Grasping objects by their handles: A necessary interaction between cognition and action. *Journal of Experimental Psychology: Human Perception & Performance, 27*, 218–228.

Dalrymple, K. A., Kingstone, A., & Handy, T. C. (2009). Event-related potential evidence for a dual-locus model of global/local processing. *Cognitive Neuropsychology, 26*, 456–470.

Danckert, J., & Rossetti, Y. (2005). Blindsight in action: What can the different subtypes of blindsight tell us about the control of visually guided actions? *Neuroscience and Biobehavioral Reviews, 29*, 1035–1046.

Davis, J. P., & Valentine, T. (2009). CCTV on trial: Matching video images with the defendant in the dock. *Applied Cognitive Psychology, 23*, 482–505.

de Haan, E. H. F., & Cowey, A. (2011). On the usefulness of "what"and "where"pathways in vision. *Trends in Cognitive Sciences, 15*(10), 460–466.

Dehaene, S., & Changeux, J. P. (2011). Experimental and theoretical approaches to conscious processing. *Neuron, 70*(2), 200–227.

DeLucia, P. R., & Hochberg, J. (1991). Geometrical illusions in solid objects under ordinary viewing conditions. *Perception & Psychophysics, 50*, 547–554.

Delvenne, J. F., Seron, X., Coyette, F., & Rossion, B. (2004). Evidence for perceptual deficits in associative visual (prosop)agnosia: A single-case study. *Neuropsychologia, 42*, 597–612.

Downing, P. E., Chan, A. W. Y., Peelen, M. V., Dodds, C. M., & Kanwisher, N. (2006). Domain specificity in visual cortex. *Cerebral Cortex*, 16, 1453–1461.

Dror, I. E., & Mnookin, J. L. (2010). The use of technology in human expert domains: Challenges and risks arising from the use of automated fingerprint identification systems in forensic science. *Law, Probability and Risk*, 9, 47–67.

Dror, I. E., & Rosenthal, R. (2008). Meta-analytically quantifying the reliability and bias ability of forensic experts. *Journal of Forensic Sciences*, 53, 900–903.

Dror, I. E., Charlton, D., & Péron, A. E. (2006). Contextual information renders experts vulnerable to making erroneous identifications. *Forensic Science International*, 156, 74–78.

Duchaine, B. (2006). Prosopagnosia as an impairment to face-specific mechanisms: Elimination of the alternative hypotheses in a developmental case. *Cognitive Neuropsychology*, 23, 714–747.

Duchaine, B., & Nakayama, K. (2006). Developmental prosopagnosia: A window to context-specific face processing. *Current Opinion in Neurobiology*, 16, 166–173.

Elder, J. H., & Goldberg, R. M. (2002). Ecological statistics of Gestalt laws for the perceptual organization of contours. *Journal of Vision*, 2, 324–353.

Eysenck, M., & Keane, M. (2015). *Cognitive psychology: A student's handbook*. London: Psychology Press.

Farah, M. J. (1994). Specialization within visual object recognition: Clues from prosopagnosia and alexia. In M. J. Farah & G. Ratcliff (Eds.), *The neuropsychology of high-level vision: Collected tutorial essays*. Hillsdale, NJ: Lawrence Erlbaum Associates.

Farivar, R. (2009). Dorsal–ventral integration in object recognition. *Brain Research Reviews*, 62, 144–153.

Fery, P., & Morais, J. (2003). A case study of visual agnosia without perceptual processing or structural descriptions' impairment. *Cognitive Neuropsychology*, 20, 595–618.

ffytche, D. H., Howard, R. J., Brammer, M. J., David, A., Woodruff, P., & Williams, S. (1998). The anatomy of conscious vision: An fMRI study of visual hallucinations. *Nature Neuroscience*, 1, 738–742.

Fields, A. W., & Shelton, A. L. (2006). Individual skill differences and large-scale environmental learning. *Journal of Experimental Psychology: Learning, Memory, and Cognition*, 32, 506–515.

Fischer, J., & Whitney, D. (2014). Serial dependence in visual perception. *Nature Neuroscience*, 17(5), 738–743.

Foster, D. H., & Gilson, S. J. (2002). Recognizing novel three-dimensional objects by summing signals from parts and views. *Proceedings of the Royal Society of London B: Biological Sciences*, 257, 115–121.

Foulsham, T., B arton, J. J. S., Kingstone, A., Dewhurst, R., & Underwood, G. (2009). Fixation and saliency during search of natural scenes: The case of visual agnosia. *Neuropsychologia*, 47, 1994–2003.

Friedman, A., Spetch, M. L., & Ferrey, A. (2005). Recognition by humans and pigeons of novel views of 3-D objects and their photographs. *Journal of Experimental Psychology: General*, 134, 149–162.

Galpin, A., Underwood, G., & Crundall, D. (2009). Change blindness in driving scenes. *Transportation Research Part F: Traffic Psychology and Behavior*, 12, 179–185.

Gauthier, I., & Tarr, M. J. (2002). Unraveling mechanisms for expert object recognition: Bridging brain activity and behavior. *Journal of Experimental Psychology: Human Perception and Performance*, 28, 431–446.

Gazzaniga, M. S., Ivry, R. B., & Mangun, G. R. (2009). *Cognitive neuroscience: The biology of the mind* (2nd ed.). New York, NY: W. W. Norton.

Goldenburg, G., Müllbacher, W., & Nowak, A. (1995). Imagery without perception: A case study of anosognosia for cortical blindness. *Neuropsychologia*, 33, 1373–1382.

Goldstein, E. B. (2014). *Sensation and perception* (9th ed.). Belmont, CA: Wadsworth.

Goldstone, R. L. (1998). Perceptual learning. *Annual Review of Psychology, 49*(1), 585–612.

Gregory, R. L. (1973). The confounded eye. In R. L. Gregory & E. H. Gombrich (Eds.), *Illusion in nature and art*. London, UK: Duckworth.

Grill-Spector, K., & Kanwisher, N. (2005). Visual recognition: As soon as you know it is there, you know what it is. *Psychological Science, 16*, 152–160.

Grill-Spector, K., Sayres, R., & Ress, D. (2006). High-resolution imaging reveals highly selective nonface clusters in the fusiform face area. *Nature Neuroscience, 9*, 1177–1185.

Harris, I. M., & Miniussi, C. (2003). Parietal lobe contribution to mental rotation demonstrated with rTMS. *Journal of Cognitive Neuroscience, 15*, 315–323.

Harvey, L. O. (1986). Visual memory: What is remembered? In F. Klix & H. Hagendorf (Eds.), *Human memory and cognitive capabilities*. The Hague, The Netherlands: Elsevier.

Henderson, E. N. (1903). A study of memory for connected trains of thought. *The Psychological Review, Series of Monograph Supplements, V*(6), (Whole No. 23, p. 93). New York: Palgrave Macmillan.

Hoffman, D. D., Singh, M., & Prakash, C. (2015). The interface theory of perception. *Psychonomic Bulletin & Review, 22*(6), 1480–1506.

Hollingworth, A., & Henderson, J. M. (2002). Accurate visual memory for previously attended objects in natural scenes. *Journal of Experimental Psychology: Human Perception & Performance, 28*, 113–136.

Hsiao, J. H. W., & Cottrell, G. (2008). Two fixations suffice in face recognition. *Psychological Science, 19*, 998–1006.

Hubel, D. H., & Wiesel, T. N. (1962). Receptive fields, binocular interaction and functional architecture in the cat's visual cortex. *Journal of Physiology, 160*, 106–154.

Hulbert, A. (2001). Trading faces. *Nature Neuroscience, 4*, 3–5. doi:10.1038/82877

Humphreys, G. W., & Riddoch, M. J. (1987). *To see but not to see: A case study of visual agnosia*. Hove, UK: Psychology Press.

Humphreys, G. W., Avidan, G., & Behrmann, M. (2007). A detailed investigation of facial expression processing in congenital prosopagnosia as compared to acquired prosopagnosia. *Experimental Brain Research, 176*, 356–373.

Hyde, J. S. (2005). The gender similarities hypothesis. *American Psychologist, 60*, 581–592.

Ison, M. J., & Quiroga, R. Q. (2008). Selectivity and invariance for visual object recognition. *Frontiers in Bioscience, 13*, 4889–4903.

Jain, A. K., & Duin, R. P. W. (2004). Pattern recognition. In R. L. Gregory (Ed.), *The Oxford companion to the mind* (pp. 698–703). New York, NY: Oxford University Press.

Jain, A. K., Feng, J. J., & Nandakumar, K. (2010). Fingerprint matching. *Computer, 43*, 36–44.

James, W. (1890). *Principles of psychology*. New York, NY: Holt.

Jenkins, R., White, D., Van Montfort, X., & Burton, A. M. (2011). Variability in photos of the same face. *Cognition, 121*(3), 313–323.

Jensen, M. S., Yao, R., Street, W. N., & Simons, D. J. (2011). Change blindness and inattentional blindness. *Wiley Interdisciplinary Reviews: Cognitive Science, 2*(5), 529–546.

Jiang, Y., Costello, P., Fang, F., Huang, M., & He, S. (2006). A gender- and sexual orientation-dependent spatial attentional effect of invisible images. *Proceedings of the National Academy of Sciences of the United States of America, 103*, 17048–17052.

Kanwisher, N., & Yovel, G. (2006). The fusiform face area: A cortical region specialized for the perception of faces. *Philosophical Transactions of the Royal Society B: Biological Sciences, 361*, 2109–2128.

Kemp, R., Towell, N., & Pike, G. (1997). When seeing should not be believing: Photographs, credit cards and fraud. *Applied Cognitive Psychology*, *11*, 211–222.

Klein, L., Dubois, J., Mangin, J.-F., Kherif, F., Flandin, G., Poline, J.-B., et al. (2004). Retinopic organization of visual mental images as revealed by functional magnetic resonance imaging. *Cognitive Brain Research*, *22*, 26–31.

Koch, C., & Poggio, T. (1999). Predicting the visual world: silence is golden. *Nature Neuroscience*, *2*, 9–10.

Kornilova, L. N. (1997). Vestibular function and sensory interaction in altered gravity. *Advances in Space Biological Medicine*, *6*, 275–313.

Kosslyn, S. M. (1994). *Image and brain: The resolution of the imagery debate.* Cambridge, MA: MIT Press.

Kosslyn, S. M. (2005). Mental images and the brain. *Cognitive Neuropsychology*, *22*, 333–347.

Kosslyn, S. M., & Thompson, W. L. (2003). When is early visual cortex activated during visual mental imagery? *Psychological Bulletin*, *129*, 723–746.

Kosslyn, S. M., Pascual-Leone, A., Felician, O., Camposano, S., Keenan, J. P., Thompson, W. L., et al. (1999). The role of Area 17 in visual imagery: Convergent evidence from PET and rTMS. *Science*, *284*, 167–170.

Króliczak, G., Heard, P., Goodale, M. A., & Gregory, R. L. (2006). Dissociation of perception and action unmasked by the hollow-face illusion. *Brain Research*, *1080*, 9–16.

Kubovy, M., & van den Berg, M. (2008). The whole is greater than the sum of its parts: A probabilistic model of grouping by proximity and similarity in regular patterns. *Psychological Review*, *115*, 131–154.

Kuefner, D., Jacques, C., Prieto, E. A., & Rossion, B. (2010). Electrophysiological correlates of the composite face illusion: Disentangling perceptual and decisional components of holistic face processing in the human brain. *Brain and Cognition*, *74*, 225–238.

Lamme, V. A. F. (2003). Why visual attention and awareness are different. *Trends in Cognitive Sciences*, *7*, 12–18.

Lander, K., & Poyarekar, S. (2015). Famous face recognition, face matching, and extraversion. *The Quarterly Journal of Experimental Psychology*, *68*(9), 1769–1776.

Landman, R., Spekreijse, H., & Lamme, V. A. F. (2003). Large capacity storage of integrated objects before change blindness. *Vision Research*, *43*, 149–164.

Langenburg, G., Champod, C., & Wertheim, P. (2009). Testing for potential contextual bias during the verification stage of the ACE-V methodology when conducting fingerprint comparisons. *Journal of Forensic Sciences*, *54*, 571–582.

Lee, S.H., Lee, A. C. H., Graham, K. S., Simons, J. S., Hodges, J. R., Owen, A. M., & Patterson, K. (2002). Regional brain activations differ for semantic features but not for categories. *NeuroReport*, *13*, 1497–1501.

Lescroart, M. D., Biederman, I., Yue, X. M., & Davidoff, J. (2010). A cross-cultural study of the representation of shape: Sensitivity to generalized cone dimensions. *Visual Cognition*, *18*, 50–66.

Levin, D. T., & Simons, D. J. (1997). Failure to detect changes to attended objects in motion pictures. *Psychonomic Bulletin and Review*, *4*, 501–506.

Lippa, R. A., Collaer, M. L., & Peters, M. (2010). Sex differences in mental rotation and line angle judgments are positively associated with gender equality and economic development across 53 nations. *Archives of Sexual Behavior*, *39*, 990–997.

Loverock, D. S. (2007). Object superiority as a function of object coherence and task difficulty. *American Journal of Psychology*, *120*, 565–591.

Mack, M. L., Gauthier, I., Sadr, J., & Palmeri, T. J. (2008). Object detection and basic-level categorization: Sometimes you know it is there before you know what it is. *Psychonomic Bulletin & Review*, *15*, 28–35.

McKone, E., Kanwisher, N., & Duchaine, B. C. (2007). Can generic expertise explain special processing for faces? *Trends in Cognitive Sciences*, *11*, 8–15.

Menchaca-Brandan, M. A., Liu, A. M., Oman, C. M., & Natapoff, A. (2007). Influence of perspective-taking and mental rotation abilities in space teleoperation. *Proceedings of the 2007 ACM Conference on human–robot interaction*. Washington, DC, March 9–11, pp. 271–278.

Merikle, P. M., Smilek, D., & Eastwood, J. D. (2001). Perception without awareness: Perspectives from cognitive psychology. *Cognition*, *79*, 115–134.

Milivojevic, B. (2012). Object recognition can be viewpoint dependent or invariant – it's just a matter of time and task. *Frontiers in Computational Neuroscience*, *6*, article 27.

Milner, A. D., & Goodale, M. A. (1998). The visual brain in action. *Psyche*, *4*, 1–14.

Milner, A. D., & Goodale, M. A. (2008). Two visual systems re-viewed. *Neuropsychologia*, *46*, 774–785.

Moè, A. (2009). Are males always better than females in mental rotation? Exploring a gender belief explanation. *Learning and Individual Differences*, *19*, 21–27.

Moro, V., Berlucchi, G., Lerch, J., Tomaiuolo, F., & Aglioti, S. M. (2008). Selective deficit of mental visual imagery with intact primary visual cortex and visual perception. *Cortex*, *44*, 109–118.

Moscovitch, M., Winocur, G., & Behrmann, M. (1997). What is special about face recognition? Nineteen experiments on a person with visual object agnosia but normal face recognition. *Journal of Cognitive Neuroscience*, *9*, 555–604.

Moulton, S. T., & Kosslyn, S. M. (2009). Imagining predictions: Mental imagery as mental emulation. *Philosophical Transactions of the Royal Society B: Biological Sciences*, *364*, 1273–1280.

Naccache, L., Blandin, E., & Dehaene, S. (2002). Unconscious masked priming depends on temporal attention. *Psychological Science*, *13*, 416–424.

Navon, D. (1977). Forest before trees: The precedence of global features in visual perception. *Cognitive Psychology*, *9*, 353–383.

Neisser, U. (1964). Visual search. *Scientific American*, *210*, 94–102.

Overgaard, M., Fehl, K., Mouridsen, K., Bergholt, B., & Cleermans, K. (2008). Seeing without seeing? Degraded conscious vision in a blindsight patient. *PLoS One*, *3*, e3028.

Patterson, K., Nestor, P. J., & Rogers, T. T. (2007). Where do you know what you know? The representation of semantic knowledge in the human brain. *Nature Reviews Neuroscience*, *8*, 976–987.

Pearson, J., Clifford, C. W. G., & Tong, F. (2008). The functional impact of mental imagery on conscious perception. *Current Biology*, *18*, 982–986.

Peissig, J. J., & Tarr, M. J. (2007). Visual object recognition: Do we know more now than we did 20 years ago? *Annual Review of Psychology*, *58*, 75–96.

Persaud, N., & Cowey, A. (2008). Blindsight is unlike normal conscious vision: Evidence from an exclusion task. *Consciousness and Cognition*, *17*, 1050–1055.

Persaud, N., & McLeod, P. (2008). Wagering demonstrates subconscious processing in a binary exclusion task. *Consciousness and Cognition*, *17*, 565–575.

Quinlan, P. T., & Wilton, R. N. (1998). Grouping by proximity or similarity? Competition between the Gestalt principles in vision. *Perception*, *27*, 417–430.

Rees, G. (2007). Neural correlates of the contents of visual awareness in humans. *Philosophical Transactions of the Royal Society B: Biological Sciences*, *362*, 877–886.

Rensink, R. A. (2002). Change detection. *Annual Review of Psychology*, *53*, 245–277.

Rensink, R. A., O'Regan, J. K., & Clark, J. J. (1997). To see or not to see: The need for attention to perceive changes in scenes. *Psychological Science*, *8*, 368–373.

Riddoch, G. (1917). Dissociations of visual perception due to occipital injuries, with especial reference to appreciation of movement. *Brain*, *40*, 15–57.

Riddoch, M. J., & Humphreys, G. W. (2001). Object recognition. In B. Rapp (Ed.), *The handbook of cognitive neuropsychology: What deficits reveal about the human mind*. Hove, UK: Psychology Press.

Riddoch, M. J., Humphreys, G. W., Akhtar, N., Allen, H., Bracewell, R. M., & Scholfield, A. J. (2008). A tale of two agnosias: Distinctions between form and integrative agnosia. *Cognitive Neuropsychology, 25*, 56–92.

Rosielle, L. J., & Scaggs, W. J. (2008). What if they knocked down the library and nobody noticed? The failure to detect large changes to familiar scenes. *Memory, 16*, 115–124.

Russell, R., Duchaine, B., & Nakayama, K. (2009). Super-recognizers: People with extraordinary face recognition ability. *Psychonomic Bulletin & Review, 16*, 252–257.

Santhouse, A. M., Howard, R. J., & ffytche, D. H. (2000). Visual hallucinatory syndromes and the anatomy of the visual brain. *Brain, 123*, 2055–2064.

Schenk, T., & McIntosh, R. D. (2010). Do we have independent visual streams for perception and action? *Cognitive Neuroscience, 1*, 52–62.

Schwarzkopf, D. S., Zhang, J. X., & Kourtzi, Z. (2009). Flexible learning of natural statistics in the human brain. *Journal of Neurophysiology, 102*, 1854–1867.

Sekuler, R., & Blake, R. (2002). *Perception*. New York: McGraw-Hill.

Shepard, R. N., & Metzler, J. (1971). Mental rotation of three-dimensional objects. *Science, 171*, 701–703.

Silvanto, J. (2008). A re-evaluation of blindsight and the role of striate cortex (V1) in visual awareness. *Neuropsychologia, 46*, 2869–2871.

Silverman, I., Choi, J., & Peters, M. (2007). The hunter-gatherer theory of sex differences in spatial abilities: Data from 40 countries. *Archives of Sexual Behavior, 36*, 261–268.

Simons, D. J., & Chabris, F. (1999). Gorillas in our midst: Sustained inattentional blindness for dynamic events. *Perception, 28*, 1059–1074.

Simons, D. J., & Levin, D. T. (1998). Failure to detect changes to people during a real-world interaction. *Psychonomic Bulletin & Review, 5*, 644–649.

Simons, D. J., & Rensink, R. A. (2005). Change blindness: Past, present, and future. *Trends in Cognitive Sciences, 9*, 16–20.

Slezak, P. (1991). Can images be rotated and inspected? A test of the pictorial medium theory. *Program of the Thirteenth Annual Conference of the Cognitive Science Society*, Chicago, IL, pp. 55–60.

Slezak, P. (1995). The "philosophical" case against visual imagery. In T. Caelli, P. Slezak, & R. Clark (Eds.), *Perspectives in cognitive science: Theories, experiments and foundations* (pp. 237–271). New York, NY: Ablex.

Smarandescu, L., & Shimp, T. A. (2015). Drink coca-cola, eat popcorn, and choose powerade: testing the limits of subliminal persuasion. *Marketing Letters, 26*(4), 715–726.

Spinney, L. (2010). The fine print. *Nature, 464*, 344–346.

Stottinger, E., Soder, K., Pfusterschmied, J., Wagner, H., & Perner, J. (2010). Division of labor within the visual system: Fact or fiction? Which kind of evidence is appropriate to clarify this debate? *Experimental Brain Research, 202*, 79–88.

Tamietto, M., & de Gelder, B. (2008). Affective blindsight in the intact brain: Neural interhemispheric summation for unseen fearful expressions. *Neuropsychologia, 46*, 820–828.

Tanaka, J. W., & Simonyi, D. (2016). The "parts and wholes" of face recognition: A review of the literature. *The Quarterly Journal of Experimental Psychology, 69*(10), 1876–1889.

Tarr, M. J., & Bülthoff, H. H. (1995). Is human object recognition better described by geon structural descriptions or by multiple views? Comment on Biederman and Gerhardstein (1993). *Journal of Experimental Psychology: Human Perception & Performance, 21*, 1494–1505.

Tarr, M. J., Williams, P., Hayward, W. G., & Gauthier, I. (1998). Three-dimensional object recognition is viewpoint-dependent. *Nature Neuroscience, 1*, 195–206.

Terlecki, M. S., & Newcombe, N. S. (2005). How important is the digital divide? The relation of computer and videogame usage to gender differences in mental rotation ability. *Sex Roles, 53*, 433–441.

Thompson, M. B., Tangen, J. M. & McCarthy, D. J. (2014). Human matching performance of genuine crime scene latent fingerprints. *Law and Human Behavior, 38*, 84–93.

Thompson, V. A., Evans, J. St. B. T., & Handley, S. J. (2005). Persuading and dissuading by conditional argument. *Journal of Memory & Language, 53*, 238–257.

Thompson, W. L., Slotnick, S. D., Burrage, M. S., & Kosslyn, S. M. (2009). Two forms of spatial imagery: Neuroimaging evidence. *Psychological Science, 20*, 1245–1253.

Tranel, D., & Damasio, A. R. (1985). Knowledge without awareness: An autonomic index of facial recognition by prosopagnosics. *Science, 228*(4706), 1453–1454.

Valentine, T. (1991). A unified account of the effects of distinctiveness, inversion and race in face recognition. *Quarterly Journal of Experimental Psychology, 43A*, 161–204.

Valentine, T., Lewis, M. B., & Hills, P. J. (2016). Face-space: A unifying concept in face recognition research. *The Quarterly Journal of Experimental Psychology, 69*(10), 1996–2019.

Van den Bussche, E., Van den Noortgate, W., & Reynvoet, B. (2009). Mechanisms of masked priming: a meta-analysis. *Psychological Bulletin, 135*(3), 452–477.

Viggiano, M. P., Giovannelli, F., Borgheresi, A., Feurra, M., Berardi, N., Pizzorusso, T., et al. (2008). Disruption of the prefrontal cortex by rTMS produces a category-specific enhancement of the reaction times during visual object identification. *Neuropsychologia, 46*, 2725–2731.

Wagemans, J., Elder, J. H., Kubovy, M., Palmer, S. E., Peterson, M. A., Singh, M., & von der Heydt, R. (2012a). A century of Gestalt psychology in visual perception: I. Perceptual grouping and figure-ground organization. *Psychological Bulletin, 138*(6), 1172–1217.

Wagemans, J., Feldman, J., Gepshtein, S., Kimchi, R., Pomerantz, J. R., van der Helm, P. A., & van Leeuwen, C. (2012b). A century of Gestalt psychology in visual perception: II. Conceptual and theoretical foundations. *Psychological Bulletin, 138*(6), 1218–1252.

Ward, J. (2010). *The student's guide to cognitive neuroscience* (2nd ed.). Hove, UK: Psychology Press.

Webster, R. J. (2015). Does disruptive camouflage conceal edges and features? *Current Zoology, 61*(4), 708–717.

Weiner, K. S., & Grill-Spector, K. (2012). The improbable simplicity of the fusiform face area. *Trends in Cognitive Sciences, 16*(5), 251–254.

Weiskrantz, L. (1980). Varieties of residual experience. *Quarterly Journal of Experimental Psychology, 32*, 365–386.

Weiskrantz, L. (2004). Blindsight. In R. L. Gregory (Ed.), *Oxford companion to the mind*. Oxford, UK: Oxford University Press.

Weiskrantz, L., Warrington, E. K., Sanders, M. D., & Marshall, J. (1974). Visual capacity in the hemianopic field following a restricted occipital ablation. *Brain, 97*, 709–728.

Weiskrantz, L., Warrington, E. K., Sanders, M. D., & Marshall, J. (1974). Visual capacity in the hemianopic field following a restricted occipital ablation. *Brain, 97*, 709–728.

Weisstein, N., & Wong, E. (1986). Figure-ground organization and the spatial and temporal responses of the visual system. In E. C. Schwab & H. C. Nusbaum

(Eds.), *Pattern recognition by humans and machines* (Vol. 2). New York, NY: Academic Press.

Wilmer, J. B., Germine, L., Chabris, C. F., Chatterjee, G., Williams, M., Loken, E., et al. (2010). Human face recognition ability is specific and highly heritable. *Proceedings of the National Academy of Sciences of the United States of America, 107*, 5238–5241.

Weisstein, N., & Harris, C. S. (1974). Visual detection of line segments–Object superiority effect. *Science, 186*, 752–755.

Wolfe, J. M., et al. (2014). Sensation & perception (4th ed.). Sunderland, MA: Sinauer Associates, Inc.

Yantis, S., & Abrams, R. A. (2016). *Sensation and perception* (2nd ed.). Macmillan Learning.

Young, A. W., Hay, D. C., & Ellis, A. W. (1985). The faces that launched a thousand slips: Everyday difficulties and errors in recognizing people. *British Journal of Psychology, 76*, 495–523.

Young, A. W., Hellawell, D., & Hay, D. C. (1987). Configurational information in face perception. *Perception, 16*, 747–759.

Young, A. W., Newcombe, F., de Haan, E. H. F., Small, M., & Hay, D. C. (1993). Face perception after brain injury: Selective impairments affecting identity and expression. *Brain, 116*, 941–959.

Zacks, J. M. (2008). Neuroimaging studies of mental rotation: A meta-analysis and review. *Journal of Cognitive Neuroscience, 20*, 1–19.

Zago, S., Corti, S., Bersano, A., Baron, P., Conti, G., Ballabio, E., et al. (2010). A cortically blind patient with preserved visual imagery. *Cognitive and Behavioral Neurology, 23*, 44–48.

Zanon, M., Busan, P., Monti, F., Pizzolato, G., & Battaglini, P. P. (2010). Cortical connections between dorsal and ventral visual streams in humans: Evidence by TNS/EEG co-registration. *Brain Topography, 22*, 307–317.

Chapter 3

Contents

Attention and performance

3

INTRODUCTION

Attention is absolutely invaluable in everyday life. We use attention to avoid being hit by cars as we cross the road, to search for missing objects, and to perform two tasks at the same time. In Chapter 2 we saw that inattention can result in us missing important information or substantial stimulus changes in front of our eyes.

Attention generally refers to selectivity of processing, as was emphasized by the American psychologist William James (1890, pp. 403–404) more than a century ago:

Attention is . . . the taking into possession of the mind, in clear and vivid form, of one out of what seem several simultaneously possible objects or trains of thought. Focalization, concentration, of consciousness are of its essence.

Learning objectives

After studying Chapter 3, you should be able to:

- Explain how visual attention differs from visual perception.
- Explain how bottleneck theories attempt to account for people's limited attentional resources.
- Answer the question posed by the authors – "spotlight, zoom lens, or split?" – and explain which is the best analogy for human attentional processes.
- Define cross-modal attention, and describe the kinds of illusion that cross-modal attention makes possible.
- Explain disorders of attention and how they inform us about how attentional processes work in the brain.
- Compare and contrast goal-directed (top-down) and stimulus-driven (bottom-up) attentional systems.
- Identify conditions under which multitasking and task-switching are least costly in terms of cognitive resources.
- Compare and contrast controlled and automatic processes.
- Explain how attention and consciousness relate to each other.

James (1890) distinguished between "active" and "passive" modes of attention. Attention is active when controlled in a top-down way by the individual's goals or expectations. It is passive when controlled in a bottom-up way by external stimuli (e.g., loud noise). This distinction remains important (Yantis, 2008).

There is another important distinction between selective and divided attention. Selective attention (or focused attention) is studied by presenting people with two or more stimulus inputs at the same time and instructing them to respond to only one. Work on selective attention tells us how effectively we can select certain inputs rather than others. It also allows us to study the nature of the selection process and the fate of unattended stimuli.

One way we use selective attention in everyday life is when we search the environment for a given object. For example, we may look out of a window trying to see where our cat is or we may look at a bookshelf for a particular book. This involves visual search and selective attention. Visual search generally involves memory as well as focused attention, because we want to avoid re-attending to stimuli that were already rejected as non-targets. Geyer et al. (2007) studied eye movements on a visual search task. They found that observers rarely fixated on previously inspected stimuli.

Divided attention is also studied by presenting at least two stimulus inputs at the same time. However, the instructions indicate that individuals must attend (and respond) to *all* stimulus inputs. Divided attention is also known as multitasking, a skill that is increasingly important in today's 24/7 world. Studies of divided attention or multitasking provide useful information about an individual's processing limitations. They also tell us about attentional mechanisms and their capacity.

SELECTIVE AUDITORY ATTENTION

Many years ago, the British scientist Colin Cherry became fascinated by the "cocktail party" problem – how can we follow just one conversation when several people are talking at once? Cherry (1953) found that this ability involved using physical differences (e.g., sex of speaker; voice intensity; speaker location) to maintain attention to a chosen auditory message. When Cherry presented two messages in the same voice to both ears at once (thus eliminating these physical differences), listeners found it hard to separate out the two messages on the basis of meaning differences alone.

Cherry (1953) also used the shadowing task. Shadowing involves people repeating back out loud the auditory message presented to one ear while a second auditory message is played to the other ear. Very little information seemed to be extracted from the second or non-attended message. Listeners seldom noticed when that message was spoken in a foreign language or reversed (backwards) speech. In contrast, physical changes (e.g., a pure tone) were nearly always detected. The conclusion that unattended information receives practically no processing was supported by Moray (1959). He found there was very little memory for unattended words presented 35 times each.

WHERE IS THE BOTTLENECK?

How can we explain our surprisingly limited ability to extract information from two auditory messages presented at the same time? Many psychologists

(Broadbent, 1958; Treisman, 1960; Deutsch & Deutsch, 1963) argued we have a processing bottleneck. Just as a bottleneck in the road (e.g., where it is especially narrow) can cause traffic congestion, so a bottleneck in the processing system can seriously limit our ability to process two or more simultaneous inputs.

Where is the bottleneck located? Several answers were suggested. At one extreme was Broadbent (1958). He argued there is a filter (bottleneck) *early* in processing that allows information from one input or message through it on the basis of its physical characteristics. The other input remains briefly in a sensory buffer and is rejected unless attended to rapidly.

Broadbent's (1958) *early selection theory* about auditory attention was influenced by studies in which two simultaneous auditory inputs were presented, one to each ear. On this dichotic listening task, three digits were presented to one ear at the same time as three different digits were presented to the other ear. Listeners were asked to report all the digits. Most recalled the digits ear by ear rather than pair by pair. Thus, if 496 were presented to one ear and 852 to the other ear, recall would be 496 852 rather than 48 95 62. This suggested that the digits on one ear (e.g., 562) were stored briefly while those on the other ear (e.g., 496) were processed.

Gray and Wedderburn (1960) repeated Broadbent's (1958) dichotic task, but presented the stimulus "Who 6 there?" to one ear as "4 goes 1" to the other ear. The preferred order of report now was *not* ear by ear. Instead it was determined by meaning (e.g., "Who goes there?" followed by "4 6 1"). These findings are inconsistent with Broadbent's emphasis on selection by physical features only.

Treisman (1964) argued that the location of the bottleneck is more *flexible* than Broadbent had suggested. She proposed an *attenuation theory*, according to which listeners start with processing based on physical cues, syllable pattern, and specific words and move on to processes based on grammatical structure and meaning. If there is insufficient processing capacity to permit full stimulus analysis, later processes are omitted.

At the other extreme from Broadbent (1958) were Deutsch and Deutsch (1963). They argued that *all* stimuli are fully analyzed, with the most important or relevant stimulus determining the response. This *late selection theory* places the bottleneck in processing very close to the response end of the processing system.

Most evidence indicates that unattended stimuli are *not* fully analyzed. Treisman and Riley (1969) asked participants to shadow one of two auditory messages (sequences of digits). The participants were also told to stop shadowing and to tap whenever they detected a letter in either message stream. According to Deutsch and Deutsch (1963), if there is complete perceptual analysis of all stimuli, letter detection should have been equally good in both messages. However, many more target letters were detected in the shadowed message (76%) than in the ignored message (33%). In contrast, all letters in both messages were detected when they were spoken by a different voice (e.g., a female voice saying the letter while a male voice said the digits), in line with Broadbent's suggestion that sudden physical changes in the stimulus were not stopped by the filter.

RECENT DEVELOPMENTS

The opposing theories of selective auditory attention were put forward about 50 years ago. In the years since, it has become clear that Broadbent's early filter model is likely to be wrong. This agrees with what we saw in Chapter 2, where we learned that perceptual processes are largely automatic and unconscious. So, many more stimuli are processed to some extent than we are aware of. Whether this means that they are fully processed, as argued by Deutsch and Deutsch, is less likely.

Taking all evidence into account, it looks like Treisman's attenuation theory is the most promising, but it still requires more refinement to specify what the attenuation consists of and how it is achieved. The lack of detail is felt most strongly in the field of artificial intelligence. It proves very difficult to devise automatic speech recognition systems that can accurately separate out one voice from several speaking at the same time (Shen et al., 2008). How do humans manage to do this and so solve the cocktail party problem?

We now know that the attentional system makes use of a multitude of sophisticated processes, some involving bottom-up processes that help to segregate the different input sources and others involving top-down processes to decrease the impact of non-attended stimuli. According to Corbetta and colleagues (Corbetta et al., 2008; Corbetta & Shulman, 2011), a distinction must be made between two attentional systems in our brains. First, there is a goal-directed attentional system influenced by expectations, knowledge, and current intentions. This system makes use of top-down processes. Second, there is a stimulus-driven attentional system which uses bottom-up information. This system takes effect when an unexpected and potentially important stimulus occurs (e.g., a noise to your left side). It has a "circuit-breaking" function, meaning that attention is redirected from its current focus.

Bottom-up processes

As far as the bottom-up system is concerned, in most early work on the shadowing task, the two messages were rather similar (i.e., auditorily presented verbal messages). This high similarity produced interference and made it harder to process the various inputs. There is less evidence of a bottleneck when an auditory stimulus is combined with a visual task. In one study (Kunar et al., 2008), listeners heard words over a telephone and shadowed each word. At the same time, they performed a visual task involving multiple object tracking. The shadowing task didn't interfere with the object-tracking task, indicating that two dissimilar inputs can be processed more fully than was assumed by Broadbent.

Shamma et al. (2011) pointed out that the sound features of a given source will typically all be present when the source is active and absent when it is silent. They refer to this tendency as *temporal coherence*. If listeners can identify at least one distinctive feature of the target voice, they can then distinguish its other sound features via temporal coherence. As a result, it will be easier to segregate input with distinct features than input with similar features. For example, it will be easier to segregate the input from children's voices when listening to a man than when listening to another child.

Cherry (1953) showed that location is an important bottom-up signal as well. Horton et al. (2013) looked at its effects on brain activity. Listeners heard separate speech messages presented to each ear with instruction to attend to the left or right ear. There was greater brain activity associated with the attended message in several brain areas (starting around 50 ms after stimulus presentation). Of most importance, the difference occurred because there was *enhancement* of the attended message combined with *suppression* of the unattended message.

Top-down processes

There are many cases in which temporal coherence and other bottom-up cues are insufficient to produce sound segregation. In such cases, top-down processes can be used. These processes are possible because of the existence of extensive descending pathways from the auditory cortex to brain areas involved in early auditory processing (Robinson & McAlpine, 2009).

Top-down factors depend on listeners' knowledge and/or expectations, and these have been shown to facilitate the segregation of speech messages. For instance, it is easier to perceive a target message accurately if the words form sentences rather than consisting of random sequences of words (McDermott, 2009).

Familiarity with the target voice is also important. Accuracy of perceiving what one speaker is saying in the context of several other voices is higher if listeners have previously listened to the speaker's voice in isolation (McDermott, 2009).

Marozeau et al. (2010) considered the effects of top-down factors on the ability to follow a melody in the presence of irrelevant notes. Musicians performed better than non-musicians, showing the influence of expertise and knowledge on sound segregation.

Golumbic et al. (2013) pointed out that people at actual cocktail parties can potentially use *visual* information to follow what a given speaker is saying (see also the McGurk effect in Chapter 8). Participants heard two simultaneous messages (one in a male voice and the other in a female voice), having been instructed which voice to attend to. Processing of the attended message was enhanced when participants could see a movie of the speaker talking while listening to the message. This probably occurred because the visual input made it easier to attend to the speaker's message.

Section summary

- It is much easier to separate out two auditory messages on the basis of physical differences than differences in meaning. It has been argued that a bottleneck limits our ability to process two simultaneous auditory messages.
- Two early theories stated that the bottleneck occurred either very early in the processing (at the level of sensations) or very late (after the stimulus was fully processed). Recent evidence suggests that neither of these extreme theories captures the full complexity.
- Current evidence suggests that both bottom-up and top-down processes are involved in selective auditory attention. Bottom-up processes help to segregate the attended message from the remaining messages; there is less evidence of a bottleneck when two simultaneous messages clearly

differ from each other. Top-down processes within the auditory system further enhance the processing of the attended stimulus. Inhibitory processes reduce the brain activity associated with the irrelevant auditory stimuli.

SELECTIVE VISUAL ATTENTION

Over the past 30 years or so, researchers have increasingly studied visual rather than auditory attention. Why is this? One reason is that vision is probably our most important sense modality, with more of the cortex devoted to it than to any other sense. Another reason is that humans make finer distinctions between locations in the visual field than in the auditory surroundings. Finally, it is easier to control the presentation times of visual than of auditory stimuli.

POSNER'S PARADIGM

Michael Posner and colleagues (1978, 1980) developed the first influential paradigm to study selective visual attention. It is illustrated in Figure 3.1.

In Posner's study, participants were sitting in front of a screen. On each trial, at the center of the screen a fixation stimulus was shown (e.g., a ● sign). The participants were asked to look at the fixation stimulus and to keep their eyes on that location (this was checked). After a random time interval, a light flash would appear to the left or to the right of the fixation stimulus. Participants had to press a key as soon as they detected the light flash. On some trials, the fixation sign was replaced by an arrow pointing to the left or to the right one second before the light flash appeared. If an arrow was presented, on 80% of the trials the light flash would appear on the side to which the arrow pointed. These were called valid trials. On 20% of the trials, the light flash would appear on the other side (invalid trials). If a + sign appeared, then the light flash appeared on half of the trials to the left and on half of the trials to the right (neutral trials).

Posner and colleagues noticed that participants were faster to react on valid trials than on neutral trials and were slower to react on invalid trials than on neutral trials, indicating that participants could shift their attention without moving their eyes. Indeed, subsequent research established that people cannot move their eyes without first shifting their visual attention. Attention goes first, followed by the eyes (Deubel & Schneider, 1996). The fact that visual attention can shift without moving the eyes is called **covert attention**.

Posner (1980) further discovered that there are two ways to redirect attention. One makes use of arrows, as described above. In this case, attention is driven top-down by the participant's intentions. Posner called this *endogenous* attention control. Another way to have the attention shifted is by presenting a salient stimulus in the periphery. Then, the attention seems to be captured bottom-up by the new stimulus, a phenomenon Posner called *exogenous* attention control.

Posner's pioneering work was followed by thousands of experiments trying to understand the details of covert attention allocation and the remit of endogenous and exogenous attention control. We discuss some of the findings in the following section.

| Key term

Covert attention:
attention to an object in
the absence of an eye
movement towards it.

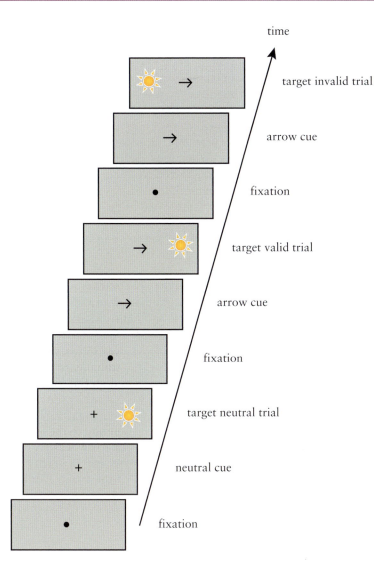

Figure 3.1 Posner's paradigm.
In this figure, three trials are shown on a timeline. The first is a neutral trial, the second is a valid trial, and the third is an invalid trial (in the real experiment, trials were presented in random order). At the beginning of a trial, participants are asked to look at the fixation stimulus in the middle. After about 1 second, the fixation stimulus is replaced by a cue, which is either a plus sign or an arrow pointing to the left or to the right. If the cue is neutral (+), 1 second after the cue, a light flash is presented either to the left or to the right (50% chance each), and the participant has to press a key as soon as they see the flash. If the cue is an arrow, in 80% of the trials the light flash will appear where the cue is pointing to (valid trial), and in 20% the light flash will appear on the other side (invalid trial). Participants are fastest on valid trials and slowest on invalid trials, even if they do not move their eyes. This shows that participants can shift their visual attention without moving their eyes.
Source: Based on Posner (1980).

SPOTLIGHT, ZOOM LENS, OR SPLIT?

Posner's (1980) findings suggest that visual attention works like a spotlight. A spotlight illuminates a relatively small area and can be redirected to focus on any given object. Little can be seen outside its beam. Applied to Posner's paradigm, the central arrow made the participants shift their attention spotlight to the place where the light flash was most likely to appear.

Other psychologists, however, have compared visual attention to a zoom lens (e.g., Eriksen & St. James, 1986). They argued that we can increase or decrease the area of focal attention at will, just as a zoom lens can be moved in or out to alter the visual area it covers. This certainly makes sense. For example, when driving a car, it is mostly desirable to attend to as much of the visual field as possible to anticipate danger. However, when we spot a potential hazard, we focus on it to avoid having a crash.

Support for the zoom-lens theory was reported by Müller et al. (2003). Observers initially saw an array of four squares and were cued to focus their attention on one given square, two given squares, or all four squares. After that, four objects were presented (one in each square), and observers decided whether a target object (e.g., a white circle) was present in one of the cued squares. According to the zoom-lens theory, we would expect targets to be detected fastest when the attended region was small (i.e., only one square). Detection times should be slowest when the attended region included all four squares. Both findings were obtained.

The zoom-lens theory sounds plausible. However, we can use visual attention even more flexibly than was assumed by that theory. Suppose you were asked to report the identity of two digits that would probably be presented to locations a little way apart (see Figure 3.2; Awh & Pashler, 2000). Suppose also that on some trials one digit was presented in the space between the two cued locations. According to zoom-lens theory, the area of maximal attention should include the two cued locations *and* the space in-between. As a result, detection of a digit presented in the middle should have been very good. In fact, it was poor.

Awh and Pashler's (2000) findings show **split attention**, in which attention is directed to two regions of space not adjacent to each other. This suggests that attention can resemble a double spotlight. Additional evidence for

Figure 3.2 (a) Shaded areas indicate the cued locations; the near and far locations are not cued. (b) Probability of target detection at valid (left or right) and invalid (near or far) locations.
Source: Based on information in Awh and Pashler (2000).

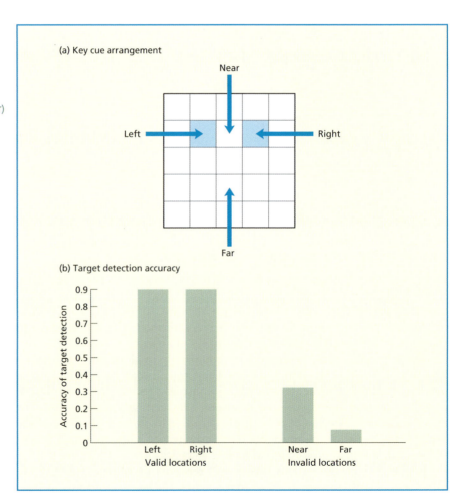

(a) Key cue arrangement

Near

Left

Right

Far

(b) Target detection accuracy

Accuracy of target detection

Left   Right
Valid locations

Near   Far
Invalid locations

multiple spotlights was reported by Morawetz et al. (2007). Stimuli were presented to five locations at the same time. One location was in the center of the visual field, and the other four were in the four corners. When the observers were told to attend to the upper-left and bottom-right locations only, there were peaks of brain activation in brain areas corresponding to these locations. Of most interest here, there was much less brain activation in the area between those locations, including the center of the visual field. Thus, attention can be split with nothing in the middle.

WHAT IS SELECTED?

The spotlight and the zoom-lens models imply that we selectively attend to an area or region of space. This is space-based attention. Alternatively, we may attend to a given object; this is object-based attention. Object-based attention seems likely since visual perception is mainly concerned with objects of interest to us (Chapter 2). Support for that viewpoint was discussed by Henderson and Hollingworth (1999). They reviewed research showing that eye movements as observers viewed natural scenes were directed almost exclusively to objects.

Egly et al. (1994) devised a popular method for comparing object-based and space-based attention (see Figure 3.3). Participants were asked to fixate between two vertical rectangles. The task was to detect a target stimulus as rapidly as possible. As in Posner's paradigm, a cue was presented shortly before the target, indicating the most likely position of the target (valid trial). Of key importance, invalid cues were in the *same* rectangle as the target (within-object cues) or at the same distance from the fixation location in the *other* rectangle (between-object cues). As expected on the basis of Posner's findings, target detection was faster on valid trials than on invalid ones. However, target detection was faster on invalid trials when the cue was in the same object rather than a different one. This suggests that attention is at least partially object-based.

Object-based attention was also demonstrated in an fMRI study by O'Craven et al. (1999). They presented participants with two stimuli (a face and a house) transparently overlapping at the same location with instructions to attend to one of them. Brain areas associated with face processing were more activated when the face was attended to than when the house was. In similar fashion, brain areas associated with house processing were more activated when the house was attended to. Thus, attention was object-based rather than solely space-based.

Further research has clarified that our processing system is so flexible we can attend to an area of space *or* a given object. Participants can strategically

Figure 3.3 Stimuli adapted from Egly et al. (1994). Participants were asked to fixate the + sign in the middle. Two rectangles were shown to the left and to the right. A cue indicated the most likely location of a subsequent target (as shown in the middle panel). The target could appear at the cued location (right panel), at the uncued end of the cued rectangle (location *d*) or at the uncued equidistant end of the uncued rectangle (location *a*). Performance was better at location *d* than at location *a*, suggesting that attention is not purely space-based.

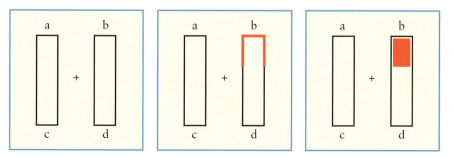

direct their attention to spaces or objects (Shomstein, 2012). This agrees with the findings discussed previously showing visual attention can resemble a spotlight, a zoom lens, or multiple spotlights.

WHAT HAPPENS TO UNATTENDED STIMULI?

As we would expect, unattended visual stimuli are processed less thoroughly than attended ones. Martinez et al. (1999) compared event-related potentials (ERPs; see Glossary) to attended and unattended visual displays. The ERPs to attended visual stimuli were comparable to those to unattended visual stimuli up to 50–55 ms after stimulus onset. After that, however, the ERPs to attended stimuli were greater than those to unattended stimuli. Thus, attention influences all but the very early stages of processing (see also Figure 3.12 for comparable findings with stimuli that are attended to and processed with or without awareness).

We can find out more about the fate of unattended visual stimuli by considering brain-damaged patients. Of particular interest are patients with **neglect**. Most of these patients have damage to the right hemisphere (often caused by stroke) and little awareness of visual stimuli presented to the left side of the visual field. This occurs because of the nature of the visual system – information from the left side of the visual field proceeds to the right hemisphere of the brain. When neglect patients draw an object or copy a drawing, they typically leave out most of the details from the left side of it (see Figure 3.4).

Patients with neglect typically fail to attend to stimuli presented to the left side of the visual field and have no conscious awareness of them (Danckert & Ferber, 2006; Chokron et al., 2008). However, such stimuli receive some processing. Vuilleumier et al. (2002) presented two pictures simultaneously, one to the left visual field and the other to the right visual field. Neglect patients couldn't report the picture presented to the left visual field. After that phase

Figure 3.4 Left is a copying task in which a patient with unilateral neglect distorted or ignored the left side of the figures to be copied (shown on the left). Right is a clock-drawing task in which the patient was given a clock face and told to insert the numbers into it.
Source: Reprinted from Danckert and Ferber (2006), Copyright © 2006, with permission from Elsevier.

of the experiment, the patients identified degraded pictures. They performed better on old pictures that had been presented to the left visual field than on new pictures. Thus, the old pictures had received some processing during the first phase of the experiment.

Vuilleumier et al. (2008) assessed brain activity to see whether neglect patients processed task-irrelevant checkerboard stimuli. When the overall attentional load was low, neglect patients showed increased brain activity to these stimuli even when they were presented to the "blind" left visual field. Thus, visual stimuli that weren't consciously perceived nevertheless received some processing.

Distraction effects

The fact that unattended stimuli receive some processing means they can distract us. To some extent this is good, because it is important for our survival that we remain vigilant for possible threats in the environment. Arguably this is the main reason why some salient stimuli can catch our attention bottom-up, irrespective of the top-down control we are exerting at that moment. However, as we all know to our cost, distraction is not limited to life-threatening stimuli. It is often difficult to avoid attending to (and processing) mundane stimuli irrelevant to our current task. In the real world, we are often distracted by stimuli irrelevant to our current task. For example, more than 10% of drivers hospitalized after car accidents reported they had been distracted by irrelevant stimuli such as a person outside the car or an insect inside it (McEvoy et al., 2007). What factors determine how distracted we are by task-irrelevant stimuli?

One factor is anxiety – individuals with anxious personalities are more distractible than those with non-anxious personalities (Eysenck et al., 2007). Consider a study by Calvo and Eysenck (1996) in which individuals who were high and low in test anxiety (susceptibility to anxiety in test situations) were compared. The participants' task was to read a text for understanding so they could answer questions on a subsequent comprehension task. The participants read the text without interference or an unrelated story was presented over headphones during reading (distraction condition). The comprehension performance of the high-anxious participants was impaired by distraction, whereas distraction had no effect on the low-anxious ones.

Along the same lines, Forster and Lavie (2016) argued that distractibility can be considered as a personality trait, with some people being worse at maintaining attentional focus than others. To measure the degree of distractibility in healthy individuals, the authors made use of a symptom checklist designed to assess ADHD (attention-deficit/hyperactivity disorder; see Figure 3.9).

Another factor determining the distraction power of unattended stimuli is how relevant they are to the current task goals. Sometimes, this factor can even override the effects of salience and distinctiveness. Consider a study by Folk et al. (1992) in which they used apparently salient distractors (having an abrupt onset) and less salient distractors (defined by color). When the observers looked for abrupt-onset targets, abrupt-onset distractors captured attention but color distractors did not. In contrast, when the observers looked for color targets, color distractors captured attention but abrupt-onset distractors did not. Thus, distraction effects were determined by the *relevance* of the distractors to the current task rather than by their salience (see also the findings related to inattentional blindness in Chapter 2).

Forster and Lavie (2008) argued that the extent to which we are distracted by totally irrelevant stimuli depends on the demands of the current task. Tasks vary in terms of perceptual load: some tasks (high load) require nearly all our perceptual capacity whereas others (low load) do not. Forster and Lavie predicted that people would be less susceptible to distraction while performing a high-load task than a low-load one – a high-load task leaves little spare capacity for processing distracting stimuli. If you are a car driver, you will probably agree you are more likely to be distracted while driving along an empty highway than when weaving in and out of heavy traffic.

Forster and Lavie (2008) presented six letters in a circle and participants decided which target letter (X or N) was present. The five non-target letters resembled the target letter more closely in shape in the high-load condition than in the low-load condition. On some trials, a picture of a cartoon character (e.g., Mickey Mouse; Superman; Spongebob Squarepants) was presented as a distractor. These distractors interfered with task performance only under low-load conditions.

So far we have focused on distraction by *external* stimuli. However, we can also be distracted by *internal* stimuli (e.g., task-irrelevant thoughts or "mind wandering"). Participants have significantly fewer task-irrelevant thoughts while performing a high-load task than a low-load task (Forster & Lavie, 2009).

In sum, the extent to which attention is diverted to task-irrelevant stimuli depends on several factors. Anxious individuals are more easily distracted than non-anxious ones, distractors that are task-relevant are more disruptive than those that are not, and distraction is greater when the ongoing task is a low-load one. Finally, task-irrelevant stimuli close in space to task stimuli are more distracting than those farther away (Khetrapal, 2010). In addition, researchers are still trying to fully understand the underlying processes. For instance, with respect to perceptual load, there is discussion whether it should be explained on the basis of limited attentional resources (as Lavie and colleagues argue) or whether it can be explained on the basis of a simple bottom-up effect due to the fact that the perceptual features differ in the high and low load conditions (Benoni et al., 2014).

CROSS-MODAL EFFECTS

So far we have considered processes involved in visual attention when we are presented *only* with visual stimuli. In the real world, however, we very often encounter visual and auditory stimuli at the same time or visual and tactile stimuli.

What happens in such circumstances? One possibility is that attentional processes in each sensory modality (e.g., vision; hearing) operate *independently* of those in all other modalities. In fact, that is incorrect. We typically combine or integrate information from different sense modalities at the same time – this is **cross-modal attention**.

Knoeferle et al. (2016) showed participants pictures of products commonly found in a supermarket. Each picture contained four products, and participants had to indicate whether a target picture was present or not (very similar to the S-search task illustrated in Research Activity 3.1). For instance, participants had to indicate whether there was a bag of crisps in the picture

| Key term

Cross-modal attention: the coordination of attention across two or more sense modalities (e.g., vision and hearing).

or not. On some trials, a congruent sound was presented together with the picture (the crunching of potato chips). On other trials, an incongruent sound was presented. This was the sound associated with one of the other products in the picture (e.g., the sound of uncorking a champagne bottle when such a bottle was shown as one of the distractors in the picture). Knoeferle et al. (2016) observed that participants found the target item faster when it was accompanied by its own, congruent sound than when it was combined with an incongruent sound. Thus, visual selective attention is supported by a congruent sound and hindered by an incongruent sound, in line with what is predicted by cross-modal attention.

Ventriloquist illusion

What happens when there is a *conflict* between simultaneous visual and auditory stimuli? We will focus on the ventriloquist illusion. In this illusion, which anyone who has been to the movies or watched TV will have experienced, sounds are misperceived as coming from their apparent visual source. Ventriloquists try to speak without moving their lips while manipulating the mouth movements of a dummy. It seems as if the dummy rather than the ventriloquist is speaking.

Something similar happens at the movies. We look at the actors and actresses on the screen and see their lips moving. The sounds of their voices are actually coming from loudspeakers to the side of the screen, but we hear those voices coming from their mouths.

Certain conditions need to be satisfied for the ventriloquist illusion to occur (Recanzone & Sutter, 2008). First, the visual and auditory stimuli must occur close together in time. Second, the sound must match *expectations* raised by the visual stimulus (e.g., high-pitched sound apparently coming from a small object). Third, the sources of the visual and auditory stimuli should be close together in space.

Why does vision capture sound in the ventriloquist illusion? The main reason is that the visual modality typically provides more precise information about spatial location. However, when visual stimuli are severely blurred and poorly localized, sound captures vision (Alais & Burr, 2004). Thus, we combine visual and auditory information, effectively attaching more weight to the more informative sense modality.

Rubber hand, body swap, and Barbie doll illusions

In the ventriloquist illusion, people mistakenly attach too much importance to visual information when it conflicts with auditory information. There are several other illusions that depend on an over-reliance on visual information. In this section we will briefly consider some illusions that depend on *integrating* information from the visual and tactile (touch) modalities.

One such illusion is the rubber hand illusion (Botvinick & Cohen, 1998; Tsakiris & Haggard, 2005; Kalckert & Ehrsson, 2014). In this illusion, the participant sees a rubber hand that appears to extend from his/her arm while their real hand is hidden from view. Then the rubber hand and the real hand are both stroked at the same time. Most participants perceive that the rubber hand is their own hand. This illusion occurs because we place more reliance on vision than on tactile sensations.

The body swap illusion, which also depends on integrating information from vision and touch, is more dramatic. What happens here is that the

Key term

Body size effect: an extension of the **body swap illusion** in which the size of the body mistakenly perceived to be one's own influences the perceived size of objects in the environment.

participant and the experimenter squeeze each other's hands repeatedly. The participant wears a head-mounted display, which shows the images coming from two cameras on the experimenter's head, so that the participant sees what is happening from the viewpoint of the experimenters' eyes (Petkova & Ehrsson, 2008).

What do participants experience in this situation? The participants perceive that the stimulation caused by squeezing hands originates in the experimenter's hand rather than their own! Petkova and Ehrsson (2008) explored this illusion further by moving a knife close to the hand of the participant or the experimenter. The participants showed a greater emotional response when the knife was close to the experimenter's hand than when it was close to their own hand.

Why does the body swap illusion occur? Of major importance, we have all spent a lifetime seeing the world from the first-person perspective. We also place special emphasis on vision as a reliable source of information. As a result, we can even experience ourselves in someone else's body when viewing the world from their viewpoint.

Van der Hoort et al. (2011) extended the body swap illusion. Participants equipped with head-mounted displays connected to closed-caption TV cameras saw the environment from the viewpoint of a doll. When the participant's body and the doll's body were touched simultaneously, the participant experienced the doll's body as his/her own. The doll varied in size in different conditions. When the doll was small, other objects were perceived as larger and farther away than when the doll was large. This is the **body size effect**. In one of their experiments, van der Hoort et al. used a Barbie doll (see Figure 3.5), so the body size effect could also be described as the Barbie doll illusion.

Figure 3.5 This shows what participants in the Barbie doll experiment could see. From the viewpoint of a small doll, objects such as a hand look much larger than when seen from the viewpoint of a large doll. This exemplifies the body size effect.
Source: From Van der Hoort et al. (2011), with permission from the Public Library of Science.

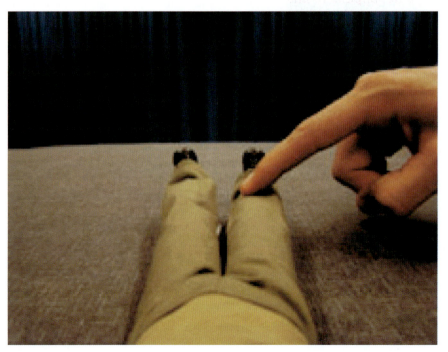

Why does the body size effect occur? As with the body swap illusion, it depends in large measure on our lifelong experience of seeing everything from the perspective of our own body combined with our general reliance on the visual modality. Note that this illusion is not solely based on visual information; only when visual information from the perspective of the doll is combined with the appropriate touch information is the effect found.

Conclusions

In sum, we generally regard vision as providing us with valid information about the environment. The extent of our reliance on the visual modality can be tested by setting up situations in which the visual input provides misleading information. When that is done, people often continue to rely on visual information, and this leads to various illusions. This reliance on visual information can lead people to experience another person's body (or even a doll's body) as their own when visual information is combined with touch information.

Section summary

Spotlight, zoom lens, or split?
- Visual attention can be allocated quite flexibly. In the Posner paradigm, it resembles a spotlight. However, it can also function as a zoom lens, depending on the area that must be covered. In specific circumstances it can even be directed to two non-adjacent regions of space, as illustrated by the existence of split attention.
- In addition to space-based allocation, attention can also be directed to specific objects, as illustrated by a study in which participants had to attend to overlapping houses and faces.

What happens to unattended stimuli?
- There is reduced processing of unattended visual stimuli compared to attended ones. Neglect patients show some processing of stimuli of which they have no conscious awareness.
- Task-irrelevant stimuli resembling task-relevant stimuli are most likely to capture attention. Anxious individuals are more likely than non-anxious ones to attend to distracting stimuli. People are less susceptible to distraction while performing tasks high in perceptual load.

Cross-modal attention: Ventriloquist illusion
- In cross-modal attention, attentional processes are coordinated across two or more sensory modalities. In the ventriloquist illusion, sounds are misperceived as coming from their apparent visual source. Vision captures sound because the visual modality typically provides more precise information about spatial locations. Over-reliance on visual information also plays a major role in explaining various illusions involving vision and touch (rubber hand illusion; body swap illusion; Barbie doll illusion).

VISUAL SEARCH

Visual attention is needed for visual search. We spend much of our time searching for various objects. For example, we look at the mess on our desk for a crucial piece of paper or try to spot a friend in a large group. The processes involved in such activities have been examined in studies on visual search in which a specified target must be detected as rapidly as possible.

Some visual searches are much more efficient than others. Usually, these are searches in which targets differ from distractors on a salient characteristic. For instance, Calvo and Marrero (2009) observed that their participants could detect happy faces faster than angry or sad ones. Further examination revealed that this was because in happy faces the teeth were visible, and these served as a very efficient search cue.

Also, a moving target is conspicuous. Suppose you want to attract the attention of a friend sitting across the room at a party. You could try waving your hand or arms on the assumption that moving objects are especially easy to detect. Royden et al. (2001) found that observers indeed rapidly detected a moving target among stationary distractors. In contrast, it took much longer to detect a stationary target among moving distractors.

In the Real World 3.1 *Security checks*

Airport security checks have become more thorough in the years since 9/11. When your luggage is X-rayed, an airport security screener sits by the X-ray machine searching for illegal and dangerous items (see Figure 3.6). How effective is this type of visual search? Training ensures that it is reasonably effective. However, mistakes do occur. Israel is well known for the thoroughness of its security checks. Nevertheless, on November 17, 2002, a man slipped through security at Ben Gurion airport in Tel Aviv with a pocketknife. He then tried to storm the cockpit of El Al flight 581 en route to Istanbul.

There are two major reasons why it is hard for airport security screeners to detect dangerous items. First, security screeners are looking for a wide range of different objects including knives, guns, and improvised explosive devices. This poses special problems. In one study (Menneer et al., 2009), observers detected two categories of objects: metal threats and improvised explosive devices. Some observers looked for both categories of object on each trial (dual-target search), whereas others looked for only a single category (single-target search). The ability to detect target objects was significantly worse with dual-target search than with single-target search.

A major problem with dual-target search in the experiment above was that the two target categories didn't share any obvious features (e.g., color; shape). When the two categories shared a feature (color), target detection was comparable in the dual-target and single-target conditions (Menneer et al., 2009). Finding a match between stored representations of targets and the stimuli presented is easier for security screeners when there is

Figure 3.6 See if you can spot the dangerous weapon. It is located a little above the center of the picture. Its blade and shaft are dark blue and the handle is orange. Source: From McCarley et al. (2004). Reprinted with permission from SAGE Publications.

reasonable overlap between the stored representations for different target categories.

Second, illegal and dangerous items are (thankfully!) present in only a minute fraction of passengers' luggage. The rarity of targets may make it hard for airport security screeners to detect them. Wolfe et al. (2007) addressed that issue. Observers looked at X-ray images of packed bags, and the targets were weapons (knives or guns). When targets appeared on 50% of trials, 80% were detected. When targets appeared on 2% of the trials, the detection rate was only 54%.

Why was performance so poor when targets were rare? It was *not* due to a lack of attention. Instead it was due to excessive caution about reporting a target because each target was so unexpected.

What can be done to improve the performance of security screeners? First, sophisticated training schemes have been set up. Koller et al. (2009) studied airport security screeners who had been doing the job for an average of 3 years. Some received a computer-based training system (X-Ray Tutor). This system starts with threat items presented in easy views and moves on progressively to threat items presented in harder views with part of their shape obscured. Performance feedback was provided on each trial.

Training produced a substantial improvement in detection performance: more so with improvised explosive devices than with guns or knives. It requires more training to detect improvised explosive devices because they are less familiar and have more variable shapes than guns or knives. Training improves the ability to recognize targets. However, it doesn't reduce the number of eye movements before target fixation (McCarley et al., 2004).

Second, security screening could take account of Menneer et al.'s (2009) findings. Security screeners could specialize in searching for categories of threat items sharing features. However, that would necessitate having two or more screeners inspect each bag, which would increase costs.

Third, security screening at airports already takes account of the impaired performance with rare targets in a simple way. The number of threat targets is increased artificially by including some "test bags" containing such items. Schwark et al. (2012) further reported that false feedback about supposedly missed items makes security staff more likely to report suspicious cases. This increased the number of false alarms due to the shifted criterion but – importantly – also made the staff more successful in detecting targets.

FEATURE INTEGRATION THEORY

What determines how long it takes to find ordinary, non-threatening targets? One important factor was identified by Treisman and Gelade (1980) (see Research Activity 3.1).

In Treisman and Gelade's (1980) research, observers detected a target in a visual display of between one and 30 items. The target was defined by a single feature (a red letter or an S) or by a combination or conjunction of features (a red letter S). In the latter case, when the target was a red letter S, all non-targets shared one feature with it (they were the red letter T or the blue letter S).

Research Activity 3.1 *Single features vs. combinations of features*

Below are two arrays consisting of some 40 letters each. Your task is to find the red S as rapidly as possible.

What you probably found was that you detected the target item much faster in the left array than in the right array. Why is it so much easier to find the target in the left array than in the right one? The answer to that question can be found by returning to the main text.

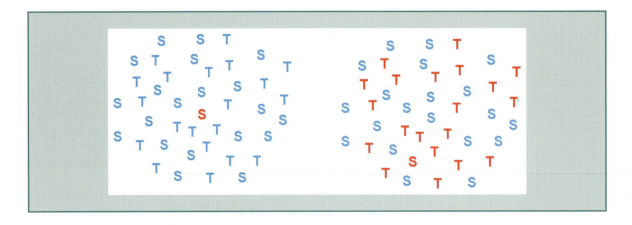

The findings are shown in Figure 3.7. When the target was defined by a single feature, observers detected the target about as quickly regardless of the number of distractors. In contrast, observers found it much harder when the target was defined by a *combination* (or conjunction) of two features. In this condition, performance was considerably slower when there were many distractors than when there were few or none. It also took much longer to decide that a target wasn't present than that it was present – you have to inspect *all* the items to decide that a target isn't present, but not to decide that one is present.

Why is visual search so much faster when the target is defined by a single feature? According to Treisman and Gelade's (1980) feature integration theory, a visual stimulus is a combination of features (see feature theory in Chapter 2). Each feature (form, color, . . .) can be processed independently. So, targets defined by a single feature "pop out" effortlessly regardless of the number of distractors. This suggests that comparisons within a single feature can be done in parallel (processing many stimuli at once). In contrast, when stimulus recognition requires the combination of two or more features, attention

Figure 3.7 Performance speed on a detection task as a function of target definition (conjunctive vs. single feature), display size, and presence (positive trials) or absence (negative trials) of a target.
Source: Adapted from Treisman and Gelade (1980).

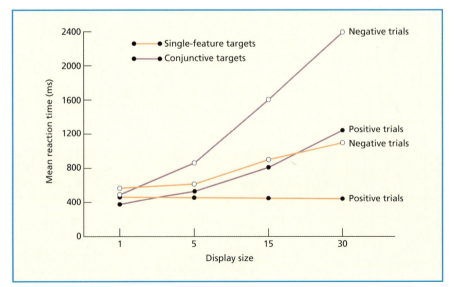

is needed to combine the features, and this can only be done serially, item by item, which is time-consuming.

How do we integrate the features with targets defined by a combination of features? According to the theory, selective or focused attention provides the "glue" allowing us to form unitary objects from the available features. In the absence of focused attention, features from different objects may be combined at random, thus producing an **illusory conjunction**. Friedman-Hill et al. (1995) studied a brain-damaged patient who had problems focusing his attention accurately on object locations. As predicted, he produced many illusory conjunctions in which the shape of one stimulus was combined with the color of another. Illusory conjunction can also be obtained in healthy participants when the stimuli are presented very briefly. For instance, Treisman and Schmidt (1982) presented participants with stimuli like this 6TSN4, presented for 200 ms. Participants first had to report the digits and then the letters in their colors. Many errors concerned illusory conjunctions, such as participants saying they saw a blue T and a red S.

<aside>
Key term

Illusory conjunction: mistakenly combining features from two different stimuli to perceive an object that isn't present.
</aside>

Limitations and theoretical developments

Feature integration theory has been highly influential (Quinlan, 2003). However, the approach is limited. Of major importance, the speed of visual search doesn't depend only on the target characteristics emphasized by Treisman and Gelade (1980). Duncan and Humphreys (1989, 1992) identified two additional factors. First, there is *similarity* among the distractors. Search is faster when the distractors are very similar to each other (Humphreys et al., 1985).

Second, there is the similarity between the target and the distractors. The number of distractors has a large effect on time to detect targets defined by a single feature when targets *resemble* distractors (Duncan & Humphreys, 1989). Visual search for targets defined by more than one feature is typically limited to those distractors sharing at least one of the target's features. For example, if looking for a blue circle in a display containing blue triangles, red circles, and red triangles, you would ignore red triangles.

Wolfe (e.g., 2007) explained these findings. According to him, the initial processing of basic features (e.g., color) produces an activation map, with every item in the visual display having its own level of activation. Suppose someone is searching for red, horizontal objects. Attention is then directed towards items on the basis of their level of activation starting with those most activated. This assumption explains why search times are longer when some distractors share one or more features with targets (e.g., Duncan & Humphreys, 1989).

Wolfe's approach is a useful development of the original version of feature integration theory. A central problem with the initial feature integration theory was that targets in large displays are typically detected faster than predicted. The activation-map notion shows how visual search can be made more efficient by ignoring stimuli not sharing any features with the target.

Rosenholtz et al. (2012a, 2012b) pointed to another overlooked aspect in visual search tasks. In these tasks, the stimuli cover a large part of the visual field. However, it is well documented that visual acuity rapidly decreases outside the fixation location. As a result, you see much less detail in peripheral vision than in central vision. You can easily experience this yourself. Hold up your hand and look at your fingers. Now move your hand to the right, while your gaze remains fixed. Very rapidly, you can no longer clearly distinguish your fingers. What is the relevance of this to visual search? Rosenholtz and colleagues argued that visual search is easy when the information in peripheral vision is sufficient to detect the target and direct your attention (and eyes) towards it, but hard when such information is insufficient. Combinations of features usually require more detailed vision than the detection of single features and, therefore, you need to move your eyes more often to see such combinations. This takes time. A similar claim was made by Hulleman and Olivers (2017), who argued that all visual search data can be simulated if one assumes parallel processing within fixations but different sizes of visual field depending on the detail that must be processed. Clearly this is a worthwhile topic to follow in the literature to come!

Top-down processes

Finally, in most research on visual search, the target is equally likely to appear anywhere within the visual display, so search is essentially *random*. This is very different from the typical state of affairs in the real world. Suppose you are outside in the garden looking for your cat. Your visual search would be *selective*, ignoring the sky and focusing mostly on the ground (and perhaps the trees). Thus, your search would involve top-down processes based on your knowledge of where cats are most likely to be found.

Ehinger et al. (2009) studied top-down processes in visual search. They obtained eye fixations of observers searching for a person in numerous real-world outdoor scenes. Observers typically fixated the regions of each scene most likely to be relevant (e.g., sidewalks) and ignored irrelevant regions (e.g., sky; trees) (see Figure 3.8). Observers also fixated locations very different from neighboring regions and areas containing visual features characteristic of a human figure.

Figure 3.8 The first three eye fixations made by observers searching for pedestrians. As can be seen, the great majority of their fixations were on regions in which pedestrians would most likely be found. Observers' fixations were much more similar in the photo on this page than in the photo on the next page, because there are fewer likely regions in the photo on this page.
Source: From Ehinger et al. (2009), with permission from Taylor & Francis.

Figure 3.8 Continued

There is another way in which top-down processes influence visual search. Bird and car experts searched for car and bird photographs among photographs of real objects (Hershler & Hochstein, 2009). Experts exhibited better visual search performance when searching for targets relevant to their expertise. This occurred because experts scanned a larger region of visual space during each eye fixation when searching for expert-relevant targets.

Evaluation

- Feature integration theory showed that the processes involved in visual search depend on the nature and complexity of the target.

- Research has indicated that a problem faced by security screeners is that the rarity of dangerous targets (e.g., bombs) makes them excessively cautious about reporting such targets.

- Feature integration theory omitted several important factors in visual search, such as the similarity among distractors and the similarity between the target and the distractors. Research also overlooked the fact that we have sharp vision only in a small region around the fixation location.

- In most research on visual search, the location of the target is random. This is very different from the real world, in which we can typically predict to some extent where a target (e.g., missing cat) is likely to be found.

> ## Section summary
>
> - Visual attention is needed for visual search. Some visual searches are more efficient than others.
>
> ### Security checks
> - It is harder for airport security screeners to detect dangerous objects if such objects are presented only rarely and the screeners are searching for several types of object. Training (including feedback) improves the ability to recognize target objects but doesn't improve the effectiveness of scanning. Increasing the number of threat targets artificially by using "test bags" can improve the effectiveness of security screening.
>
> ### Feature integration theory
> - Observers generally find it easier to detect targets defined by a single feature than those defined by a combination of two features. The similarity among the distractors and the similarity between the target and the distractors also influence the speed of visual search, as does the level of visual detail needed to distinguish the target from the distractors.
>
> ### Top-down processes
> - In the real world, top-down processes influence visual search and make it selective. Our environmental knowledge allows us to search for targets where they are most likely to be found. Experts' visual search is faster for targets related to their area of expertise than for other targets.

DISORDERS OF ATTENTION

We can learn much about attentional processes by studying brain-damaged individuals suffering from various attentional disorders. We first consider two of the main attentional disorders resulting from brain injury: neglect and extinction. Then we discuss ADHD, which is a developmental disorder.

NEGLECT AND EXTINCTION

Neglect was introduced earlier in this chapter. According to Driver and Vuilleumier (2001, p. 40):

> *Neglect patients often behave as if half of their world no longer exists. In daily life, they may be oblivious to objects and people on the neglected side of the room, eat from only one side of their plate . . . and make-up or shave only one side of their face.*

The attentional problems of neglect patients can be seen clearly when they copy drawings of objects. They typically leave out most of the details from the left side of such drawings, as shown in Figure 3.4.

Neglect patients in particular ignore information in their affected side of the visual field when other information is presented in their good side. This is called extinction. **Extinction** involves the inability to detect a visual stimulus on the side opposite to the brain damage (contralesional side) when a second visual stimulus is present on the same side as the brain damage (ipsilesional side). Extinction is a serious condition because we are typically confronted by

Key term
Extinction: a disorder of visual attention in which a stimulus presented to the side opposite the brain damage is not detected when another stimulus is presented at the same time to the same side as the brain damage.

multiple stimuli at the same time in everyday life. It is generally assumed that extinction depends on a *competition* mechanism (Marzi et al., 2001): stimuli presented on the contralesional side compete unsuccessfully for attention with those presented on the other side.

Explaining neglect and extinction: the two attentional systems

How can we explain neglect? To answer that question, it is helpful to make use of the distinction between the two attentional systems made by Corbetta and colleagues (Corbetta et al., 2008; Corbetta & Shulman, 2011), discussed previously. According to these authors, there are two attentional systems in our brains. One is goal-directed and makes use of top-down processes; the other is stimulus-driven and uses bottom-up processes to redirect attention from its current focus to an important event in the environment.

Bartolomeo and Chokron (2002) argued that neglect patients have suffered damage to the stimulus-driven system, but their goal-directed system is reasonably intact. Evidence that the attentional performance of neglect patients improves when they can use the goal-directed system was reported by Smania et al. (1998). They compared the time taken to detect stimuli when the side of the visual field to which they were presented was predictable (permitting use of the goal-directed system) and when it was random (*not* permitting use of that system). Neglect patients responded faster in both the attended and unattended (neglect) fields when the side to which stimuli would be presented was predictable. Thus, they made some use of the goal-directed system.

Bonato (2012) argued that neglect patients in addition have reduced attentional resources, so that the stimulus-driven attention system cannot break through. He concluded this from a study in which neglect patients had to detect stimuli in their affected left visual field. Sometimes this was done while performing another, attentionally demanding task at the same time. Healthy participants performed the task almost perfectly with or without the additional task. In contrast, neglect patients' ability to detect targets was markedly worse in the presence of the additional task. This is as predicted on the assumption that neglect patients have limited attentional resources and as a result are less sensitive to information coming from the stimulus-driven attentional system.

Reducing neglect and extinction

There have been various attempts to reduce the attentional problems of patients suffering from neglect. One approach has involved training patients to make more use of top-down control by providing detailed and explicit information about the locations of stimuli. This approach has had limited success (Parton et al., 2004).

A more efficient procedure is to enhance the alertness of the patients to the affected visual field via training. Thimm et al. (2009) found that such training could reduce the severity of the neglect.

When neglect patients who are in the dark are asked to point straight ahead, they typically point several degrees off to the right. Rossetti et al. (1998) wondered whether it would be useful to correct this error by having neglect patients wear prisms shifting the visual field 10 degrees to the right. After wearing a prism for some time, patients in the dark pointed almost directly

Key term

ADHD: a developmental disorder characterized by an attention deficit, hyperactivity, and impulsivity.

ahead. They also included more detail on the left side of their drawings of a daisy for some time after prism removal. Indeed, prism adaptation is effective for several weeks after prism removal (Chokron et al., 2007).

Why does prism adaptation have such beneficial effects? Nijboer et al. (2008) found prism-adaptation training made it easier for neglect patients to use goal-directed processes to shift attention leftwards voluntarily. This voluntary attentional shift compensated for their habitual rightward bias. In contrast, prism-adaptation training had no effect on the stimulus-driven attention system.

ADHD

Attention-deficit/hyperactivity disorder (**ADHD**) is a developmental disorder characterized by an attention deficit, hyperactivity, and impulsivity (Aguiar et al., 2010). It is one of the most common developmental disorders, with an estimated prevalence of 5% among children between 5 and 12 years old. The assessment is made two to four times more often with boys than with girls, possibly because the hyperactivity and impulsivity components are less visible in girls.

Although ADHD is often considered a childhood psychiatric disorder, it has been shown to persist in adulthood and old age (Semeijn et al., 2016). Figure 3.9 lists the main attention-related symptoms used for assessment.

ADHD has a genetic component, as 30% of the parents of children with ADHD also have the disorder, and siblings often report milder symptoms. Environmental factors that have been proposed include negative experiences during pregnancy (use of tobacco, alcohol and drugs, stress, preterm birth) and problems during birth.

Answer the following questions with Yes/No

- Do you often fail to pay close attention to details, or make careless mistakes in school-work, work, or during other activities?
- Do you often have diffi culty sustaining attention in tasks or play?
- Do you often not seem to listen when spoken to?
- Do you often not follow through on instructions and fail to finish schoolwork, chores, or duties in the workplace?
- Do you often have diffi culty organizing tasks and activities?
- Do you often avoid engaging in tasks that require sustained mental effort (such as school or homework)?
- Do you often lose things necessary for tasks or activities?
- Are you easily distracted by extraneous stimuli?
- Are you often forgetful in daily activities?

Figure 3.9 Attention-related symptoms of ADHD. Source: From Semeijn et al. (2016), with permission from Springer.

Individuals with ADHD have difficulties allocating attention to relevant stimuli in the environment and, in particular, maintaining attention. They start many things but complete few. The problem is not primarily that these individuals have too much energy, but that they have difficulty inhibiting distractors and keeping control over what they are doing. As a result, they are more easily distracted and more impulsive. This may explain why the most effective medication for the condition is a stimulant, increasing brain activity (alertness) rather than reducing it. Indeed, the surprising effect of the drug was not discovered deliberately but as a lucky side-effect of a study in which the drug was tried out to treat headaches in a school for children with behavioral problems (Strohl, 2011).

Section summary

- Neglect involves a lack of awareness of contralesional stimuli. Extinction is similar except that this lack of awareness occurs mostly in the presence of an ipsilesional stimulus. Extinction depends on a competition mechanism – stimuli in the contralesional field compete unsuccessfully with those in the ipsilateral field.

Explaining neglect: Two attentional systems
- We have goal-directed and stimulus-driven attentional systems. Information from these two systems is combined in posterior parietal cortex (an area typically damaged in neglect patients). The stimulus-driven attentional system is particularly affected in neglect patients, together with a decrease in attentional resources.

Reducing neglect
- The symptoms of neglect can be reduced somewhat by training designed to increase patients' alertness to the neglected visual field. Prism adaptation also improves patients' ability to shift their attention leftwards voluntarily.

ADHD
- The main attention-related symptoms of ADHD point to increased distractibility, making it difficult for those affected to keep on task.

MULTITASKING

Thus far we have talked about selective attention. As indicated in the introduction, attention is also involved when we try to do several tasks at the same time, a situation known as **multitasking**. Then we require divided attention.

In common with most people, your life is probably becoming busier and busier. In our hectic 24/7 lives, there is an increased tendency for people to try to do two things at once. Examples include holding a conversation on a cell or mobile phone while driving and chatting with friends while watching

Key term

Multitasking:
performing two or more tasks during the same period of time.

television. A survey in 2003 by ComPsych revealed that 54% of workers read emails while on the phone and 11% write to-do lists during meetings. These numbers have increased since. Rideout et al. (2010) found that a majority of teenagers multitask "most" or "some" of the time while listening to music (73% of respondents), while watching TV (68%), while using a computer (66%), and while reading (53%).

If you are one of those people that engage in multitasking most of the time, you should perhaps take heed of a study by Ophir et al. (2009). They used a questionnaire to identify individuals who engage in high and low levels of multitasking. These two groups were given various tasks. On one task, an array of rectangles was presented twice, and participants decided whether the target rectangle had changed orientation. This was done with or without distraction. Distraction adversely affected the performance of the high multitaskers but not of the low multitaskers. The former group was also at a disadvantage when they had to switch between classifying numbers and letters.

What do these findings mean? According to Ophir et al. (2009), those who attend to several media simultaneously develop "breadth-based cognitive control." In other words, they aren't *selective* or discriminating in their allocation of attention. That makes it hard for them to avoid being distracted and to switch attention efficiently. In contrast, low multitaskers are more likely to have top-down attentional control. Note that we can't be sure that high levels of multitasking are responsible for unselective attention, because all that has been found is an *association* between those two measures.

At the same time, there may be some disadvantages in being a low multitasker. Such individuals may be so focused on the immediate task that they ignore other potentially useful information (Lin, 2009). This may make them less creative and adaptive in real life. Indeed, Cardoso-Leite et al. (2016) reported that participants with intermediate levels of media multitasking performed better than both light and heavy media multitaskers. Intermediate users were users who indicated that they combined two tasks "a little of the time" or "some of the time."

Burgess (2015) notes that there is some ambiguity in how multitasking is defined. Most people understand it as *concurrent multitasking*, a situation in which more than one action is executed simultaneously (e.g., driving while speaking). However, most of the time this is not what happens when persons "are doing several tasks at once" (e.g., cooking while preparing the house for a visit and keeping an eye on the smartphone). Then, they pursue multiple task goals by rapidly alternating between tasks, a situation Burgess describes as *serial multitasking*. In such a situation, attention has more to do with task switching (and keeping track of the various goals) than with divided attention across multiple tasks running in parallel.

HOW EFFICIENT IS MULTITASKING?

How efficient (or otherwise!) are we at juggling two or more tasks? The fact that most of us often engage in multitasking suggests that we believe ourselves capable of performing two tasks simultaneously. We multitask because we think it will save us precious time compared to the traditional approach of doing one thing at a time. If that isn't the case, we are simply wasting time and incurring higher stress levels by continuing to engage in multitasking.

Most evidence points to efficiency *costs* during multitasking. For example, while reading a passage from a textbook, students who were simultaneously chatting via instant-messaging took roughly 21% more time compared to those who were not multitasking. Watching television while doing academic work has been found to harm performance on both reading comprehension and memory tasks. Multitasking has also been shown to impair the processing and verification of written information (references for these observations can be found in Wang & Tchernev, 2012).

According to Wang and Tchernev (2012), people are not enticed to multitasking because it is more efficient, but because it fulfills their emotional needs. They asked students at specific moments to write down three sets of information: (1) all the activities going on (including media activities and non-media activities), (2) the needs the participants had at that moment, and (3) how well the needs were being served by the activities. A distinction was made between cognitive needs (information, study/work), emotional needs (fun/entertainment, to relax/kill time), social needs (personal, professional), and habitual needs (habits/background noise).

Wang and Tchernev (2012) found that people engaged in multitasking out of cognitive needs but did not find those needs met by their behavior (in line with the efficiency costs of multitasking). In contrast, multitasking was very gratifying for the emotional needs (fun/entertainment, relax/kill time), even though these were not actively sought at that moment. So, multitasking had the interesting "byproduct" of being emotionally gratifying. This, according to the authors, is the real reason why more and more people find themselves engaged in multitasking. The authors also found that habits play an important role in media multitasking. Once a person is used to combining certain activities, it is difficult to break the habit.

There is a common belief that women are better than men at multitasking. This belief may owe something to the fact that women engage in more multitasking than men do. Floro and Miles (2001) studied two-adult Australian households. Women involved in child care were much more likely than men to multitask (e.g., doing household work and job-related work at the same time). However, Rubinstein et al. (2001) found no gender differences in multitasking performance in a series of experiments in which participants switched rapidly between different tasks.

What are the advantages and disadvantages of concurrent versus serial multitasking? Lehle et al. (2009) trained people to engage in either serial or parallel processing when performing two tasks together. Those using serial processing performed better than those using parallel processing. However, they found the tasks more effortful.

In the Real World 3.2 *Can we think and drive?*

In everyday life, an issue of great importance is whether the ability to drive a car safely is impaired when the driver uses a cell or mobile phone (for a good review article, see Strayer et al., 2011). More than 40 countries have passed laws restricting the use of handheld cell phones by drivers (although hands-free phones are sometimes allowed). These restrictions have led millions of irate motorists to complain that their civil liberties have been infringed.

What does the evidence show? Redelmeier and Tibshirani (1997) studied the cell-phone records of 699 drivers who had been involved in a car accident. The likelihood of an accident was 4.3 times greater when drivers used a cell phone (whether handheld or hands-free).

Many experimental studies have considered the effects of using cell phones on simulated driving performance. Caird et al. (2008) reviewed the findings from 33 studies. Reaction times to events (e.g., onset of brake lights on the car in front) increased by 250 ms compared to no-phone control conditions. The figure was similar whether drivers were using handheld or hands-free cell phones and was larger when drivers were talking rather than listening.

The slowing of 250 ms may sound trivial, but it translates into travelling an extra 18 feet (5.5 m) before stopping for a motorist doing 50 mph (80 kph). This could mean the difference between stopping just short of a child in the road and killing that child.

Caird et al. (2008) found that drivers had little awareness of the negative impact of using cell phones – they didn't slow down or keep a greater distance behind the car in front. The drivers in these studies knew they were being observed and so probably tried to perform as well as possible. This suggests that the adverse effects of using cell phones may be even greater in real life.

On the other hand, traffic accidents have not increased spectacularly since the introduction of cell phones, and legislation to ban cell phones does not lead to sudden, remarkable decreases in the number of accidents. For instance, Kolko (2009) found that the introduction of laws against the use of hands-free cell phones only reduced traffic fatalities when the weather was bad or the roads were wet.

To get a better picture of the consequences of cell phone use in naturalistic circumstances, Farmer et al. (2015) analyzed the day-to-day driving behavior of 105 volunteer subjects over a period of 1 year. In-vehicle video was used to classify driver behavior. The proportion of driving time spent using a cell phone was estimated for each 3-month period and correlated with overall crash and near-crash rates for each period. Thus, it was possible to test whether changes in an individual driver's cell phone use over time were associated with changes in overall near-crash/crash risk.

What were the results? Drivers in the study spent 11.7% of their driving time interacting with a cell phone, primarily talking on the phone (6.5%) or simply holding the phone in their hand or lap (3.7%). The risk of a near-crash/crash event was approximately 17% higher when the driver was interacting with a cell phone, due primarily to actions of reaching for/answering/dialing, which nearly tripled risk (relative risk = 2.8). However, the amount of driving time spent interacting with a cell phone did not affect a driver's overall near-crash/crash risk. Another observation was that most drivers slowed down when making a phone call. Vehicle speeds during a call on average were 5–6 mph lower than speeds at other times.

There is also evidence for individual differences in the degree to which people are able to combine using a cell phone and driving. Watson and Strayer (2010) had participants perform a simulated driving task on its own or while performing a complex working memory task presented over a cell phone. Of 200 participants, there were five whose driving performance was unaffected by the additional task. The high level of performance of these "supertaskers" on both tasks suggests that they were not overloaded by the double task situation.

Is it as dangerous for drivers to converse with their passenger as it is for them to converse on a cell phone? Drews et al. (2008) found that conversations using a cell phone were associated with more driving errors. Drivers were better able to converse with a passenger and drive safely because their conversations became less complex as the difficulty of the driving conditions increased.

In sum, it is surprisingly hard to perform two tasks at once even when they are very different (verbal vs. visual processing). This suggests that performing two tasks together can overload some limited-capacity resource such as attention. The impact may be bigger for some persons than for others.

The adverse effects of cell-phone use are *not* limited to drivers. As you may have noticed, people using a cell phone while walking along often seem fairly oblivious to their surroundings. Hyman et al. (2009) carried out an amusing study in which students walking across Western Washington University's Red Square were exposed to a unicycling clown. Of those walking on their own, 51% noticed the clown, compared to only 25% of those using cell phones. Cell-phone use even affected the apparently very simple task of walking – students using cell phones walked more slowly, weaved about more, and changed direction more often than other walkers. Thus, cell-phone use is so demanding of processing resources that it disrupts our perception of the environment and our walking ability.

The multiple resources model

Wickens (2008) developed a *multiple resources model* to predict how much interference two tasks will produce in a multitask situation. The model assumes that the brain has separate attentional resources and that the cost of task combination depends on the degree to which the tasks address the same resources. Three distinctions are particularly relevant:

1. *Stages of processing*: Perceptual and cognitive tasks use different resources from those underlying the selection and execution of action. So, it is less costly to combine a perceptual with a response execution task than to combine two perceptual tasks or two action tasks.
2. *Codes of processing*: Spatial activity uses different resources than does verbal/linguistic activity (see also the working memory model in Chapter 4). So, it is less costly to combine a spatial task with a linguistic task than to combine two spatial or two linguistic tasks.
3. *Modalities*: Auditory perception uses different resources than does visual perception. So, it is less costly to combine an auditory and a visual task than to combine two tasks within each modality.

Wickins (2008) developed a computational model that makes it possible to estimate the multitasking cost for a wide variety of task combinations. This predicts reasonably well costs observed in real life.

PRACTICE AND DUAL-TASK PERFORMANCE

Everyone knows the saying, "Practice makes perfect." Evidence apparently supporting this saying was reported by Spelke et al. (1976). Two students (Diane and John) received 5 hours' training a week for 3 months on various tasks. Their first task was to read short stories for comprehension while writing down words to dictation. Initially they found it very hard to combine these tasks, and their reading speed and handwriting both suffered severely. After 6 weeks of training, however, Diane and John could read as rapidly and with as much comprehension when taking dictation as when only reading. In addition, the quality of their handwriting had improved.

Spelke et al. (1976) were still not satisfied with the students' performance. For example, Diane and John could recall only 35 out of the thousands of words they had written down at dictation. Even when 20 successive dictated words came from the same category (e.g., four-footed animals), the students

were unaware of that. With further training, however, they could write down
the names of the categories to which the dictated words belonged while maintaining normal reading speed and comprehension.

So, practice can have a dramatic effect on people's ability to perform two
tasks at the same time. It has often been assumed that this happens because
practice allows some processing activities to become automatic. In a classic
line of research, Shiffrin and Schneider (1977) and Schneider and Shiffrin
(1977) made a distinction between controlled and automatic processes:

- **Controlled processes** are of limited capacity, require attention, and can be
  used flexibly in changing conditions; serial processing is involved.
- **Automatic processes** have no capacity limitations, don't require attention,
  and are very hard to modify once learned; parallel processing is involved.

Shiffrin and Schneider (1977) used a task in which participants memorized
up to four letters (the memory set) and were then shown a visual display containing up to four letters. Their task was to decide rapidly whether one of the
letters in the visual display was the same as any of the letters in the memory
set. The crucial manipulation was the type of mapping used:

1. *Consistent mapping*: Only consonants were used as members of the memory set, and only numbers were used as distractors in the visual display (or
   vice versa). Example: H B K D (memory set) followed by 4 3 B 7 (visual
   display) requires a "Yes" response.
2. *Varied mapping*: A mixture of numbers and consonants formed the memory set and provided distractors in the visual display. Example: H 4 B 3
   (memory set) followed by 2 J 7 C (visual display) requires a "No" response.

What do you think happened? You may have guessed correctly that consistent
mapping led to faster performance than varied mapping. However, the actual
difference may be even greater than you thought (see Figure 3.10). According

Figure 3.10 Response
times on a decision task as
a function of memory-set
size, display-set size, and
consistent versus varied
mapping.
Source: Data from Shiffrin
and Schneider (1977).

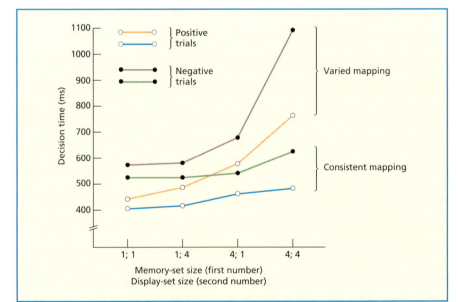

to Shiffrin and Schneider (1977), the participants performed well with consistent mapping because they used automatic processes operating at the same time (parallel processing). These automatic processes have evolved through years of practice in distinguishing between numbers and letters.

In contrast, performance with varied mapping required controlled processes of limited capacity and requiring attention. In this condition, participants compared each item in the memory set with every item in the visual display one at a time (serial processing) until a match was found or every comparison had been made.

Stronger evidence that automatic processes develop with practice was provided in another experiment by Shiffrin and Schneider (1977). They used consistent mapping with the consonants B to L forming one set and the consonants Q to Z forming the other set. As before, items from only one set were always used in the construction of the memory set, and the distractors in the visual display were all selected from the other set. There was a dramatic improvement in performance speed over 2,100 trials, apparently reflecting the development of automatic processes.

So far it has appeared that automatic processes are more useful than controlled ones. However, automatic processes suffer from the serious limitation that they are *inflexible* whereas controlled processes are not. Shiffrin and Schneider (1977) showed this in the second part of the experiment discussed previously. The initial 2,100 trials with one consistent mapping were followed by 2,100 trials with the reverse consistent mapping. Thus, the items in the memory set were now always drawn from the consonants Q to Z if they had previously been drawn from the set B to L. It took nearly 1,000 trials before performance recovered to the level at the very start of the experiment!

DOES PRACTICE MAKE PERFECT?

We have seen that practice can produce very large improvements in performance. However, there are typically *some* interference effects in dual-task performance even after substantial amounts of practice. For example, look back at Figure 3.10. If performance were totally automatic in the consistent mapping condition, response speed should have been unaffected by the number of items in the memory set and the visual display. In fact, however, performance became slower as the number of items increased.

Some theorists (e.g., Levy et al., 2006) argue that we will *always* find evidence of interference in dual-task performance if sensitive techniques are used. One such technique involves two presented stimuli (e.g., two lights) each associated with a different response (e.g., pressing different buttons). The participants must respond to each stimulus as rapidly as possible. When the second stimulus is presented very shortly after the first, there is generally a marked slowing of the response to the second stimulus. This is the **psychological refractory period (PRP) effect**.

The PRP effect does *not* occur simply because people aren't used to responding to two immediately successive stimuli. Pashler (1993) found that the effect was still observable after more than 10,000 practice trials.

On the other hand, Greenwald (2003) reported an absence of a PRP effect when he used very simple tasks. One task involved vocal responses to auditory stimuli: saying "A" or "B" in response to hearing those letter names. The

Key term
Psychological refractory period (PRP) effect: the slowing of the response to the second of two stimuli when they are presented close together in time.

other task involved moving a joystick to the left to an arrow pointing left and to the right to a right-pointing arrow. There was no PRP effect. Why was that? Both tasks used by Greenwald had a very *direct* relationship between stimuli and responses (e.g., saying "A" when you hear "A"), which minimized the involvement of attentional processes.

How can we explain the various findings in this area? The starting point is to reject the assumption made by Shiffrin and Schneider (1977) that there is a clear-cut distinction between automatic and controlled processes. A more plausible perspective was provided by Moors and de Houwer (2006). They identified four key features of automaticity:

1. Unconscious: lack of conscious awareness of the process
2. Efficient: using very little attentional capacity
3. Fast
4. Goal-unrelated: uninfluenced by the individual's current goals

None of these four features is all-or-none. For example, a process can be fairly fast or slow, and it can be moderately efficient or inefficient. The evidence also indicates that the four features of automaticity aren't always found together. Thus, there is no firm dividing line between automaticity and nonautomaticity or controlled processing.

What predictions follow from this approach? Two tasks should be performed together reasonably well if both possess in reasonable measure the four features of automaticity. Conversely, multitasking should be very poor if the two tasks lack most of those features. The evidence reviewed by Moors and de Houwer (2006) is consistent with those predictions.

Section summary

- Individuals who engage in much multitasking find it hard to allocate their attention selectively and are distractible. It has proved hard to obtain evidence of gender differences in multitasking.

Can we think and drive?
- Cell phones (handheld or hands-free) generally impair driving performance, especially in adverse driving conditions. Impaired attentional control and limited processing capacity are responsible. There are a few "supertaskers" with a high overall level of performance whose driving is unaffected by using a cell phone.

Practice and dual-task performance
- Dual-task performance often improves substantially with practice. There is evidence that this happens because some processing activities become relatively automatic through practice. However, automatic processes suffer from the limitation that they are inflexible and hard to alter.

Does practice make perfect?
- There is nearly always some evidence of interference in dual-task performance even after extensive practice. However, that isn't the case when

there are very direct relationships between stimuli and responses. Most findings on dual-task performance can be explained by assuming that processes vary in the extent to which they are automatic. The major features of automaticity are as follows: unconscious, efficient, fast, and goal-unrelated.

ATTENTION AND CONSCIOUSNESS

In the current and the previous chapter, we have seen various examples of stimuli being processed without us being aware of it. In Chapter 2, we saw that this can be expected from the *global workspace model* (see also later section). Human information processing involves numerous special-purpose processors operating in parallel, and their data only need to enter consciousness when they must be combined with data from other processors or when we must respond to the information at once. In such a model, it is better not to place the filter very early, before the information is processed, but later, so that the input entering consciousness has already been handled.

Unconscious processing also helps to better gauge the importance of unattended information. Indeed, we saw that attention is a continuous balance between remaining goal-directed (top-down) and being alert to important events in the environment (bottom-up). In this section we describe the relationship between attention and consciousness in more detail.

CONSCIOUSNESS

The topic of consciousness is one of the most fascinating in the whole of cognitive psychology. There has recently been a substantial increase in research on consciousness. Before discussing it, we must consider what is meant by "consciousness." It can be defined as: "The normal mental condition of the waking state of humans, characterized by the experience of perceptions, thoughts, feelings, awareness of the external world, and often in humans . . . self-awareness" (Colman, 2015, p. 161).

Steven Pinker (1997) argued that we need to consider three issues when trying to understand consciousness:

1. *Sentience*: This is our subjective experience or awareness, which is only available to the individual having the experience.
2. *Access to information*: This relates to our ability to report the content of our subjective experience without being able to report on the processes producing that experience.
3. *Self-knowledge*: This is our ability to have conscious awareness of ourselves.

When talking about consciousness, it is also good to make a distinction between *state of consciousness* (e.g., coma, vegetative state, etc.) and *contents of consciousness* (e.g., consciously experienced qualities of stimuli). The former is a background state which allows the actual contents of awareness to be experienced. Most of the research on (visual) consciousness focuses on the contents.

There are various ways to assess conscious awareness. With respect to visual consciousness, much use has been made of behavioral measures. We can ask people to provide verbal reports of their visual experience or to make a yes/no decision concerning the presence of a target object.

With some brain-damaged patients, this is hard to do. For example, consider patients with locked-in syndrome, who generally possess full conscious awareness but are almost totally paralyzed. The most famous case of locked-in syndrome was Jean-Dominique Bauby, who was a French journalist. Amazingly, he managed to write a book about himself solely by blinking his left eyelid to choose the next letter in the text (Bauby, 1997). Bauby's book was called *The Diving Bell and the Butterfly*, and it was later turned into a successful movie.

It is possible to gain a deeper understanding of consciousness by identifying its major neural correlates. This involves obtaining behavioral measures of conscious awareness and then relating them to the associated patterns of brain activity. It is sometimes impossible to obtain behavioral measures of consciousness. It can then be very useful to obtain brain-imaging data (see In the Real World 3.3).

In the Real World 3.3 *The vegetative state*

Some unfortunate patients with severe brain damage are in a vegetative state. The vegetative state is defined by an apparent lack of awareness and a failure to respond to all external stimuli. The behavioral evidence obtained from patients in that state strongly suggests they totally lack conscious awareness.

Owen et al. (2006) studied a 23-year-old woman who was in the vegetative state as a result of a very serious road accident in July 2005. This woman showed no behavioral responsiveness to stimulation. She was asked to imagine playing a game of tennis or visiting the rooms of her house starting from the front door. These two tasks were associated with different patterns of brain activity. For example, activation in the supplementary motor area was found only when she imagined playing tennis. Of key importance, the patterns of brain activity were very similar to those shown by healthy participants.

Owen et al. (2006) also presented the patient with sentences containing ambiguous words (italicized) (e.g., "The *creak* came from a *beam* in the ceiling"). She showed greater brain activation in areas involved in processing meaning with ambiguous than with unambiguous words. Thus,

brain activity probably provided a more valid assessment of the presence of conscious experience than did behavioral measures. Coleman et al. (2009) studied 41 brain-damaged patients, many of whom were in the vegetative state. None showed any signs of consciousness when behavioral measures were used. However, functional magnetic resonance imaging (fMRI; see Glossary) revealed that two patients in the vegetative state showed evidence of speech comprehension. Of interest, the amount of speech processing indicated by fMRI was strongly associated with the amount of behavioral recovery 6 months later. Thus, brain imaging can sometimes provide a more sensitive measure of conscious awareness than behavioral measures can.

In sum, the findings from patients in the vegetative state are dramatic. Until recently, it had always been assumed that such patients lacked all conscious awareness of themselves and of the environment around them. This assumption has been seriously challenged by the brain-imaging findings suggesting that some 15% of the patients in a vegetative state have a limited form of awareness (Kondziella et al., 2016).

THE RELATIONSHIP BETWEEN ATTENTION AND CONSCIOUSNESS

What is the relationship between consciousness and attention? It seems reasonable to assume they are closely related. Baars (1997) invited us to consider sentences such as, "We look in order to see" or "We listen in order to hear." He argued that looking or listening involves using attention to select an event, whereas seeing or hearing involves conscious awareness of the selected event. Thus, attention is like choosing a television channel and consciousness resembles the picture on the screen.

There is often a close relationship between attention and consciousness. However, that isn't always the case (Koch & Tsuchiya, 2007; Lamme, 2003). For example, attention can influence behavior in the absence of consciousness. As we saw in Chapter 2, Jiang et al. (2006) presented pictures of male and female nudes that were invisible to the participants. In spite of their invisibility, these pictures influenced participants' attentional processes, as measured by their performance on a subsequent discrimination task. Heterosexual males attended to invisible female nudes, whereas heterosexual females attended to invisible male nudes. Gay males had a tendency to attend to the location of nude males, and gay/bisexual females' attentional preferences were between those of heterosexual males and females.

How can unseen emotional stimuli influence attention? Relevant evidence was reported by Troiani et al. (2014). Unseen fearful faces produced increased amygdala activation (associated with emotional processing), which was associated with activation of brain areas associated with an attentional network.

Cohen et al. (2012) provided a sketch-map of what is involved in the relationship between consciousness and attention. According to them, attention is always required for conscious experience, which can be reported by the participant. In contrast, unconscious processing (as measured with brain activity) can be based on both attended and unattended input. Not everyone agrees with the latter statement, however. According to some authors, unconscious processing also requires attention. They focus on exogenous attention capture during search. Sometimes this capture is not observed when the distractor is incompatible with the ongoing search, as we saw earlier when we discussed the experiment of Folk et al. (1992), in which participants either paid attention to the sudden onset of stimuli or to the color. A similar phenomenon was reported by Dalton and Lavie (2007) in the auditory domain: Participants were distracted by an irrelevant high-pitch tone when they were waiting for targets of a particular pitch but not when they were waiting for targets formed by a combination of pitch and duration.

Other authors examined unconscious priming. Priming refers to the observation that processing of a stimulus is facilitated if before the same or a related stimulus was presented. As we saw in Chapter 2, Naccache et al. (2002) asked participants to indicate whether digits were larger or smaller than 5. Unknown to the participants, immediately before the target an invisible prime number was presented that could either be congruent or incongruent with the target digit. Participants were faster when the prime and the target were congruent (e.g., 1 and 4) than when they were incongruent (1 and 6), even though they had no conscious awareness of the prime. However, such priming only occurred when the participants were encouraged to focus their attention to

Key term
Priming: facilitated processing of (and response to) a target stimulus because the same or a related stimulus was presented before; see also **repetition priming** and **semantic priming**.

the screen when the prime was presented. When the participants were led to expect that the target would appear only a second later, there was no priming anymore. Similarly, Lachter et al. (2004) found no priming when attention was caught away from the place of the subliminal prime when it appeared. In contrast, Xiao and Yamauchi (2015) reported that subliminal priming was reduced in the absence of attention but not completely absent.

All in all, it is clear that attention considerably improves the processing of information, also unconscious processing. It is less clear, however, to what extent unconscious processing is possible in the absence of attentional resources.

CONTROLLING ACTIONS: UNCONSCIOUS PROCESSING AND FREE WILL

The existence of unconscious processing also begs the question "*What* controls our actions?" To most of us, it feels as if we form a conscious intention (e.g., "I think I'll get myself a coffee"), which is then followed by us finding ourselves in a café drinking a cup of coffee. In other words, our actions are driven by conscious intentions or free will. This view has been challenged by several theorists.

Wegner (2003) argued that what we have is the *illusion* of conscious or free will. Our actions are actually caused by unconscious processes (e.g., a feeling of thirst). However, we draw the mistaken inference that our actions are determined by our conscious intentions.

If Wegner is right, we should make mistakes such as assuming we didn't cause something to happen even though we did. Support for this prediction comes from the unlikely source of the spiritualist movement that swept through 19th-century Europe and America. Advocates of spiritualism believed that spirits of the dead could convey messages and even move tables. Several people would sit around a table with their hands resting on the top and pressing down on it. After a while, the table would start to vibrate and eventually it would move. The sitters firmly believed they hadn't caused the table to move and that spirits were responsible.

The sitters' beliefs were refuted by the English scientist Michael Faraday. He constructed a table with two tops divided by ball bearings, but the sitters thought it was just an ordinary table. Faraday stuck pieces of paper onto the *upper* table-top, and asked the sitters to put their hands on the piece of card in front of them. The key finding was that the upper table-top moved *before* the lower table-top. Thus, the sitters were moving the table rather than the table (possibly via spirits) moving their fingers. That means that sitters' conscious experience that their actions didn't cause the table to move was mistaken.

What causes us to assume (sometimes mistakenly) that our conscious thoughts have caused our actions? According to Wegner (2003; see also White, 2009), three principles are involved. First, we regard our thoughts as causing our actions when they occur just beforehand (priority principle). Second, thoughts *consistent* with the actions that follow are more likely to be regarded as being causally responsible than inconsistent ones (consistency principle). Third, thoughts not accompanied by obvious alternative causes of action are more likely to be perceived as causing those actions (exclusivity principle).

Evidence that these principles are important was reported by Wegner and Wheatley (1999). They used a 12-cm square board mounted onto a computer

Key term

Free will:
the notion that we freely or voluntarily choose what to do from a number of possibilities; this notion has been challenged by those who claim that non-conscious processes determine our actions.

mouse. There were two participants at a time, both of whom placed their fingers on the side of the board closest to them. When they moved the board, this caused a cursor to move over a screen showing numerous pictures of small objects. The participants were asked to move the mouse in slow, sweeping circles. Both participants wore headphones. They were told that every 30 seconds or so they would hear music and had to stop the cursor at that moment and indicate the extent to which they had consciously intended the cursor to stop where it did. While they were moving the cursor, they would be hearing distractor words, which were different for both participants.

One participant was genuine, but the other was a confederate working for the experimenter. The genuine participant thought the other participant heard a similar series of different distractor words through the headphones. In fact, however, the confederate was receiving instructions to make certain movements. On some trials, the confederate was told to stop on a given object (e.g., cat), and the experiment was set up in such a way that the genuine participant heard the word "cat" 30 seconds before, 5 seconds before, 1 second before, or 1 second after the confederate stopped the cursor.

Genuine participants wrongly believed they had caused the cursor to stop where it did when they heard the name of the object on which it stopped 1 or 5 seconds before the stop. Thus, the participants mistakenly inferred that their conscious intention had caused the action when it had not. This mistaken belief can be explained by the principles of priority, consistency, and exclusivity.

Wegner and other researchers have carried out several similar studies to that of Wegner and Wheatley (1999) in the years since, and have generally obtained similar findings (Nahmias, 2005). There are some limitations with these studies, however. First, the findings are often not especially strong (Nahmias, 2005). For example, only just over 60% of participants in the study by Wegner and Wheatley (1999) believed their conscious intention caused the cursor to stop even when all three principles applied.

Second, most studies have involved very artificial set-ups designed to make it hard for participants to realize their conscious intentions hadn't caused certain actions. By analogy, no one would say visual perception is hopelessly fallible because we make mistakes when identifying objects in a thick fog!

Neuroscientific evidence

Libet et al. (1983) provided neuroscientific evidence against our conviction that conscious intentions determine our actions. Participants were asked to bend their wrist and fingers at a time of their choosing. The time at which they were consciously aware of the intention to perform the movement and the moment at which the hand muscles were activated were recorded. In addition, the researchers recorded the readiness potential in the brain – this is thought to reflect pre-planning of a bodily movement.

What did Libet et al. (1983) find? Figure 3.11 gives a schematic overview of the findings. The readiness potential started to increase about 1 second *before* participants reported conscious awareness of the intention to bend the wrist and fingers. Thus, some preparation of a forthcoming action occurred *before* the individual was consciously aware of what he/she was going to do.

On some trials, participants were told to veto the action they had decided to make. Now the change in readiness potential coincided with the conscious

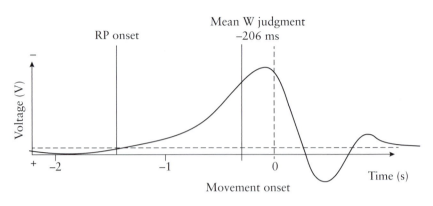

Figure 3.11 Schematic results of Libet's findings. Neural preparation in the motor areas of the brain can begin over 1 s before movement onset. The conscious experience of intending the movement (Mean W judgment), by contrast, begins much later, on average 206 ms before movement onset. As causes necessarily precede effects, conscious intention cannot be the cause of the neural processes that lead to action.
Source: From Haggard (2005).

intention, leading Libet et al. (1983) to conclude that the decision to veto an action was based on a conscious intention, unlike the decision to make an action. We may not have free will but perhaps we have free won't! Several studies have used variations on Libet's experimental approach. Most of the findings were consistent with those of Libet and colleagues (Banks & Pockett, 2007; Banks & Isham, 2009).

Evidence for an even longer unconscious preparation time was reported by Soon et al. (2008). They focused on activation in brain areas (e.g., prefrontal cortex) associated with decision processes. Participants decided whether to make a response with their left or right index finger. The decision that participants were going to make could be predicted from brain activity in parts of the prefrontal and parietal cortex up to 7 seconds before they were consciously aware of their decision! In addition, activity in motor areas 5 seconds before conscious awareness of participants' decisions predicted the timing of their responses. On the negative side, the prediction accuracy was only 55–60%, not impressively better than the chance level of 50%.

Intentional action typically depends on three different decisions: deciding *what* action to produce; deciding *when* to produce it; and deciding *whether* to produce it. This led Brass and Haggard (2008) to propose the what, when, and whether (WWW) model of intentional action, in which different brain areas are involved in the three different decisions. The study by Soon et al. (2008) suggested that the prefrontal and parietal cortex are involved in *what* decisions and motor areas in *when* decisions.

What can we conclude from the various findings? According to John-Dylan Haynes (one of the researchers in the Soon et al., 2008 study) in a press release: "Your decisions are strongly prepared by brain activity. By the time consciousness kicks in, most of the work has already been done."

On the face of it, it looks as if we often make decisions without being consciously aware of having done so. That led Greene and Cohen (2004) to doubt whether we should hold individuals personally responsible for their actions – "I didn't do it, it was my brain!"

There are various reasons for disagreeing with this viewpoint. First, it is based on the misleading assumption that an individual's personal identity and his/her brain are completely separate (Kaliski, 2009). Second, research has focused on *what* and *when* decisions regarding the performance of *trivial* actions. Such research may be of little relevance to real-life situations in which we decide whether to perform some significant action. We probably make most use of our sense of personal responsibility when making *whether* decisions. Suppose a violent criminal wields a knife in his left hand to murder someone at three o'clock in the afternoon. The *whether* decision was probably preceded by a conscious intention even if the *what* (left hand or right hand?) and *when* (now or later?) decisions were not.

Evaluation

(+) There is evidence (Libet et al., 1983; Soon et al., 2008) that some decisions are largely prepared by brain activity occurring before there is conscious awareness of having made a decision.

(+) Our reliance on the priority, consistency, and exclusivity principles can lead us to believe mistakenly that our conscious thoughts have caused our actions.

(−) Much of the research is rather artificial and may not be of direct relevance to everyday decision making.

(−) Decisions about what action to produce and when to produce it may be mostly prepared within the brain prior to conscious awareness. However, it is less clear that the same is true of decisions concerning whether to perform an action.

MORE ON BRAIN AND CONSCIOUSNESS

We have seen that EEG data helped a lot to shed light on various aspects of attention and consciousness (see the findings of Libet). Also other neuroscientific and neuropsychological findings have been used to address the questions of which brain structures are critical for the state of consciousness and what are the differences between contents of consciousness accompanied by conscious awareness or not. Koch et al. (2016) provide an interesting review of the findings, which suggests that no single brain area is necessary for being conscious, but that several areas are involved.

The state of consciousness depends critically on the brainstem reticular formation, parts of the thalamus, and perhaps parts of the cortex surrounding the thalamus. They provide the background conditions for full consciousness. By serving as activating influences and cortical hubs, they enable effective interactions among the cortical areas that directly contribute conscious content.

Conscious content itself depends primarily on a hot zone at the back of the brain on the borders between the temporal, the parietal, and the occipital lobes. This is particularly true for conscious perception of visual stimuli. There may be some contribution from one or two areas in the frontal lobes as well. For instance, Lamme and Roelfsema (2000) hypothesized that visual perception remains unconscious as long as it is limited to a forward sweep of activation from the primary visual cortex to the temporal cortex, but that it becomes conscious when higher areas start providing feedback to the lower areas. This produces synchronicity long enough for conscious experience. Some of the higher areas are likely to include the frontal lobes as well (Bar et al., 2006).

Finally, when perception is combined with action, an extensive network of frontal and parietal regions becomes active, needed for the allocation of attention, task execution, monitoring, and reporting of the stimulus.

A model sometimes used to understand brain activity in conscious and unconscious processing is the *global workspace theory*, first mentioned in Chapter 2 (e.g., Baars & Franklin, 2007). The model assumes that the early stages of information processing involve many special-purpose processors carrying out specialized functions (e.g., color processing; motion processing) in relative isolation from each other. These processors are located in numerous brain areas and are generally not associated with conscious awareness. Consciousness begins when information from several special-purpose processors is integrated (as also hypothesized by Lamme and Roelfsema, 2000). The role of consciousness is to make the information available to the full brain, so that they can synchronize their functioning with the ongoing action.

Findings

There is experimental support for all of the hypotheses mentioned. For example, Dehaene et al. (2001) tested the notion that unconscious processing is limited mainly to special-purpose processors. In one condition, words were presented on their own and could be perceived consciously. The other condition involved **masking** – a second stimulus (mask) disrupts the processing of a first stimulus presented very shortly beforehand. The words couldn't be perceived consciously in the masking condition.

There was widespread activation in the visual cortex, parietal cortex, and prefrontal cortex when the words were perceived consciously (and the participants arguably activated an action schema, such as naming the word). In contrast, activation was largely confined to the visual cortex in the masking condition, and there was no detectable activation in the parietal or prefrontal areas.

Koivisto et al. (2016) presented EEG evidence. They dissociated potential electrophysiological correlates of visual awareness from those occurring during response selection and thus related to action execution. The participants performed two GO-NOGO conditions. In such conditions, they must respond (by pressing a key) to one type of stimulus and withhold a response to another type of stimulus. In the aware-GO condition the participants were asked to respond when they were aware of the stimulus and to withhold responding when they were unaware of it. The stimuli were line patterns that were absent, clearly present, or masked so that they were visible only half of the time. In the unaware-GO condition the participants withheld responding when they were aware and responded when they were not aware of the stimulus. Thus, ERPs could be measured to aware and unaware trials when responding was required and when not required.

Figure 3.12 shows the results. There were two time periods in which the brain response on the aware trials differed from the unaware trials. The first was an early negative response around 200 ms (called N200). It was found on all aware trials: the electric signal went more negative when the participants consciously saw the stimulus, independent of whether they had to respond or not. The signal was limited to the occipital cortex and some of the surrounding parietal cortex.

The second time period started around 300 ms and resulted in a positive deflection of the brain signal (called P3 or sometimes P300). It not only differed between the aware and unaware trials but depended on responding: it was greater when awareness was mapped to a GO-response than when it was not. In addition, the signal was spread all over the brain, in line with the proposed fronto-parietal network becoming active when conscious perception is combined with action.

Limitation

To fully understand the ways in which cognitive neuroscience has helped to shed light on the various aspects of consciousness, it is important that we keep in mind that research has focused excessively on conscious awareness of perceptual stimuli (in particular visual stimuli) and is thus narrow. An important challenge for future research will be to determine to what extent the processes involved in self-awareness resemble those involved in the perception of stimuli.

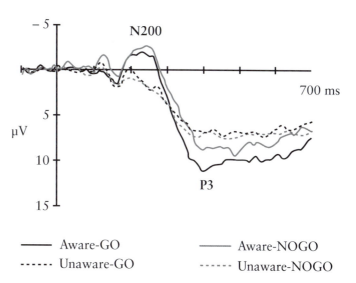

Figure 3.12 Event-related potential (ERP) waveforms in the four conditions of Koivisto et al. (2016). First, there is a negative deflection when the stimulus is consciously perceived (N200), followed by a positive deflection (P3). The latter was larger in the aware GO-trials than in the aware NOGO trials. Notice that in this figure, negative is going up and positive is going down (which is different from Figure 1.10). The present way of presenting ERP data is the one used in most publications.
Source: From Koivisto et al. (2016).

Section summary

The vegetative state
- Behavioral evidence from patients in the vegetative state strongly suggests that they have no conscious awareness. However, brain-imaging research indicates that a few vegetative-state patients have some ability to comprehend speech and may thus have limited conscious awareness.

The relationship between attention and consciousness
- There are often close links between focused attention and conscious awareness, with the former preceding the latter. However, attention can influence behavior in the absence of consciousness, and according to many authors unconscious processing is not possible in the complete absence of attention.

Controlling actions: Unconscious processing and free will
- People sometimes have the mistaken belief that their conscious thoughts have caused their actions. The decision someone will make can be predicted on the basis of their brain activity several seconds before they are consciously aware of having made a decision. However, such research has focused on *what* and *when* decisions concerning different actions and has ignored the more important *whether* decisions.

Brain and consciousness

- The early stages of information processing involve specialized processors that aren't associated with conscious awareness. Consciousness is associated with the subsequent integration of information from these processors. The coupling of perception and action involves the activation of an extensive network of brain areas in the frontal and the parietal lobes.

Essay questions

1. How do we manage to attend to one auditory message in the presence of other, distracting auditory messages?
2. It has been claimed that visual attention resembles a spotlight or a zoom lens. How valid are these claims?
3. What has been discovered about visual search? What advice can psychologists give to those involved in airport security checks?
4. Does practice make perfect? If not, why not?
5. How desirable is it to prohibit the use of cell phones by drivers?
6. How have ERP studies and brain-imaging research increased our understanding of human consciousness?

Further reading

- Chokron, S., Bartolomeo, P., & Sieroff, E. (2008). Unilateral spatial neglect: 30 years of research, discoveries, hope, and (especially) questions. *Revue Neurologique, 164*, S134–S142. This paper provides an excellent account of research on neglect and the relevance of such research to our understanding of attentional processes.
- Fawcett, J.M., Risko, E.G., & Kingstone, A. (2015). *The handbook of attention*. Cambridge, MA: The MIT Press. This book edited by Fawcett et al. consists of 28 chapters by leading experts in the field of attention. Further of interest is that they all make an effort to link the findings from the lab to real-world situations.
- Moors, A., & De Houwer, J. (2006). Automaticity: A theoretical and conceptual analysis. *Psychological Bulletin, 132*, 297–326. The main issues and controversies surrounding the topic of automaticity are discussed at length in this excellent article.
- Nobre, A.C., & Kastner, S. (Eds.) (2014). *The Oxford handbook of attention*. Oxford: Oxford University Press. An edited volume with chapters from all the big authors. Contains 1,200 extra pages of information on the topics covered in this chapter.
- Rayner, K. (2009). Eye movements and attention in reading, scene perception, and visual search. *Quarterly Journal of Experimental Psychology, 62*, 1457–1506. Keith Rayner discusses in detail the role of attentional processes in several important activities such as reading and visual search.
- Salvucci, D. D., & Taatgen, N.A. (2011). *The multitasking mind*. New York, NY: Oxford University Press. The authors put forward a theory of multitasking and consider how we can overcome the disadvantages associated with multitasking.

REFERENCES

Aguiar, A., Eubig, P. A., & Schantz, S. L. (2010). Attention deficit/hyperactivity disorder: A focused overview for children's environmental health researchers. *Environmental Health Perspectives*, 118(12), 1646–1653.

Alais, D., & Burr, D. (2004). The ventriloquist effect results from near-optimal bimodal integration. *Current Biology*, 14, 257–262.

Awh, E., & Pashler, H. (2000). Evidence for split attentional loci. *Journal of Experimental Psychology: Human Perception and Performance*, 26, 834–846.

Baars, B. J. (1997). Consciousness versus attention, perception, and working memory. *Consciousness and Cognition*, 5, 363–371.

Baars, B. J., & Franklin, S. (2007). An architectural model of conscious and unconscious brain functions: Global Workspace Theory and IDA. *Neural Networks*, 20, 955–961.

Banks, W. P., & Isham, E. A. (2009). We infer rather than perceive the moment we decided to act. *Psychological Science*, 20, 17–21.

Banks, W. P., & Pockett, S. (2007). Benjamin Libet's work on the neuroscience of free will. In M. Velmans & S. Schinder (Eds.), *Blackwell companion to consciousness* (pp. 657–670). Malden, MA: Blackwell.

Bartolomeo, P., & Chokron, S. (2002). Orienting of attention in left unilateral neglect. *Neuroscience and Biobehavioral Reviews*, 26, 217–234.

Bauby, J.-D. (1997). *The diving bell and the butterfly*. New York, NY: Knopf.

Benoni, H., Zivony, A., & Tsal, Y. (2014). Attentional sets influence perceptual load effects, but not dilution effects. *The Quarterly Journal of Experimental Psychology*, 67(4), 785–792.

Botvinick, M., & Cohen, J. (1998). Rubber hands "feel" touch that eyes see. *Nature*, 391: 756.

Brass, M., & Haggard, P. (2008). The what, when, and whether model of intentional action. *The Neuroscientist*, 14, 319–325.

Broadbent, D. E. (1958). *Perception and communication*. Oxford, UK: Pergamon.

Burgess, P. W. (2015). Serial versus concurrent multitasking: From lab to life. In J. M. Fawcett, E. F. Risko, & A. Kingstone (Eds.), *The handbook of attention* (pp. 443–462). Cambridge, MA: The MIT Press.

Caird, J. K., Willness, C. R., Steel, P., & Scialfa, C. (2008). A meta-analysis of the effects of cell phones on driver performance. *Accident Analysis and Prevention*, 40, 1282–1293.

Calvo, M. G., & Eysenck, M. W. (1996). Phonological working memory and reading in test anxiety. *Memory*, 4, 289–305.

Calvo, M. G., & Marrero, H. (2009). Visual search of emotional faces: The role of affective content and featural distinctiveness. *Cognition & Emotion*, 23, 782–806.

Cardoso-Leite, P., Kludt, R., Vignola, G., Ma, W. J., Green, C. S., & Bavelier, D. (2016). Technology consumption and cognitive control: Contrasting action video game experience with media multitasking. *Attention, Perception, & Psychophysics*, 78(1), 218–241.

Cherry, E. C. (1953). Some experiments on the recognition of speech with one and two ears. *Journal of the Acoustical Society of America*, 25, 975–979.

Chokron, S., Dupierrix, E., Tabert, M., & Bartolomeo, P. (2007). Experimental remission of unilateral spatial neglect. *Neuropsychologia*, 45, 3127–3148.

Coleman, M. R., Davis, M. H., Rodd, J. M., Robson, T., Ali, A., Owen, A. M., & Pickard, J. D. (2009). Towards the routine use of brain imaging to aid the clinical diagnosis of disorders of consciousness. *Brain*, 132, 2541–2552.

Colman, A. M. (2015). *A dictionary of psychology* (4th ed.). Oxford: Oxford University Press.

Corbetta, M., & Shulman, G.L. (2011). Spatial neglect and attention networks. *Annual Review of Neuroscience*, 34, 569–599.

Corbetta, M., Patel, G., & Shulman, G. L. (2008). The re-orienting system of the human brain: From environment to theory of mind. *Neuron, 58*, 306–324.

Dalton, P., & Lavie, N. (2007). Overriding auditory attentional capture. *Perception & Osychophysics, 69*(2), 162–171.

Danckert, J., & Ferber, S. (2006). Revisiting unilateral neglect. *Neuropsychologia, 44*, 987–1006.

Dehaene, S., Naccache, L., Cohen, L., Le Bihan, D., Mangin, J., Poline, J., et al. (2001). Cerebral mechanisms of word masking and unconscious repetition priming. *Nature Neuroscience, 4*, 752–758.

Deubel, H., & Schneider, W. X. (1996). Saccade target selection and object recognition: Evidence for a common attentional mechanism. *Vision Research, 36*(12), 1827–1837.

Deutsch, J. A., & Deutsch, D. (1963). Attention: Some theoretical considerations. *Psychological Review, 93*, 283–321.

Drews, F. A., Pasupathi, M., & Strayer, D. L. (2008). Passenger and cell phone conversations in simulated driving. *Journal of Experimental Psychology: Applied, 14*, 392–400.

Driver, J., & Vuilleumier, P. (2001). Perceptual awareness and its loss in unilateral neglect and extinction. *Cognition, 79*, 39–88.

Egly, R., Driver, J., & Rafal, R. D. (1994). Shifting visual attention between objects and locations: Evidence from normal and parietal lesion subjects. *Journal of Experimental Psychology: General, 123*, 161–177.

Ehinger, K. A., Hidalgo-Sotelo, B., Torralba, A., & Oliva, A. (2009). Modelling search for people in 900 scenes: A combined source model of eye guidance. *Visual Cognition, 17*, 945–978.

Eriksen, C. W., & St. James, J. D. (1986). Visual attention within and around the field of focal attention: A zoom lens model. *Perception & Psychophysics, 40*, 225–240.

Eysenck, M. W., Derakshan, N., Santos, R., & Calvo, M. G. (2007). Anxiety and cognitive performance: Attentional control theory. *Emotion, 7*, 336–353.

Floro, M., & Miles, M. (2001). *Time use and overlapping activities – Evidence from Australia* (SPRC Discussion Paper No. 93). Sydney, Australia: Social Policy Research Center.

Folk, C. L., Remington, R. W., & Johnston, J. C. (1992). Involuntary covert orienting is contingent on attentional control settings. *Journal of Experimental Psychology: Human Perception and Performance, 18*, 1030–1044.

Folk, C. L., Remington, R. W., & Johnston, J. C. (1992). Involuntary covert orienting is contingent on attentional control settings. *Journal of Experimental Psychology: Human Perception and Performance, 18*, 1030–1044.

Forster, S., & Lavie, N. (2008). Failures to ignore entirely irrelevant distractors: The role of load. *Journal of Experimental Psychology: Applied, 14*, 73–83.

Forster, S., & Lavie, N. (2009). Harnessing the wandering mind: The role of perceptual load. *Cognition, 111*, 345–355.

Forster, S., & Lavie, N. (2016). Establishing the attention-distractibility trait. *Psychological Science, 27*(2), 203–212.

Friedman-Hill, S. R., Robertson, L. C., & Treisman, A. (1995). Parietal contributions to visual feature binding: Evidence from a patient with bilateral lesions. *Science, 269*, 853–855.

Geyer, T., von Mühlenen, A., & Müller, H. J. (2007). What do eye movements reveal about the role of memory in visual search? *Quarterly Journal of Experimental Psychology, 60*, 924–935.

Golumbic, E. Z., Cogan, G. B., Schroeder, C. E., & Poeppel, D. (2013). Visual input enhances selective speech envelope tracking in auditory cortex at a "cocktail party". *Journal of Neuroscience, 33*, 1417–1426.

Gray, J. A., & Wedderburn, A. A. (1960). Grouping strategies with simultaneous stimuli. *Quarterly Journal of Experimental Psychology*, *12*, 180–184.

Greene, J., & Cohen, J. (2004). For the law, neuroscience changes nothing and everything. *Philosophical Transactions of the Royal Society London B: Biological Sciences*, *359*, 1775–1785.

Greenwald, A. G. (2003). On doing two things at once: III. Confirmation of perfect timesharing when simultaneous tasks are ideomotor compatible. *Journal of Experimental Psychology: Human Perception and Performance*, *29*, 859–868.

Henderson, J. M., & Hollingworth, A. (1999). High-level scene perception. *Annual Review of Psychology*, *50*, 243–271.

Herschler, O., & Hochstein, S. (2009). The importance of being expert: Top-down attentional control in visual search with photographs. *Attention, Perception & Psychophysics*, *71*, 1478–1486.

Hulleman, J., & Olivers, C. N. L. (2017). The impending demise of the item in visual search. *Behavioral and Brain Sciences*, *40*(1), 1–20.

Humphreys, G. W., Riddoch, M. J., & Quinlan, P. T. (1985). Interactive processes in perceptual organization: Evidence from visual agnosia. In M. I. Posner & O. S. M. Morin (Eds.), *Attention and performance* (Vol. XI). Hillsdale, NJ: Lawrence Erlbaum.

Hyman, I., Boss, S., Wise, B., McKenzie, K., & Caggiano, J. (2009). Did you see the unicycling clown? Inattentional blindness while walking and talking on a cell phone. *Applied Cognitive Psychology*, *24*, 597–607.

James, W. (1890). *Principles of psychology*. New York, NY: Holt.

Jiang, Y., Costello, P., Fang, F., Huang, M., & He, S. (2006). A gender- and sexual orientation-dependent spatial attentional effect of invisible images. *Proceedings of the National Academy of Sciences of the United States of America*, *103*, 17048–17052.

Kalckert, A., & Ehrsson, H. H. (2014). The spatial distance rule in the moving and classical rubber hand illusions. *Consciousness and Cognition*, *30*, 118–132.

Kaliski, S. Z. (2009). 'My brain made me do it!' – How neuroscience may change the insanity defense. *South African Journal of Psychiatry*, *15*, 4–6.

Khetrapal, N. (2010). Load theory of selective attention and the role of perceptual load: Is it time for revision? *European Journal of Cognitive Psychology*, *22*, 149–156.

Knoeferle, K. M., Knoeferle, P., Velasco, C., & Spence, C. (2016). Multisensory brand search: How the meaning of sounds guides consumers' visual attention. *Journal of Experimental Psychology: Applied*, *22*(2), 196–210.

Koch, C., & Tsuchiya, N. (2007). Attention and consciousness: Two distinct brain processes. *Trends in Cognitive Sciences*, *11*, 16–22.

Koch, C., Massimini, M., Boly, M., & Tononi, G. (2016). Neural correlates of consciousness: progress and problems. *Nature Reviews Neuroscience*, *17*(5), 307–321.

Koivisto, M., Salminen-Vaparanta, N., Grassini, S., & Revonsuo, A. (2016). Subjective visual awareness emerges prior to P3. *European Journal of Neuroscience*, *43*(12), 1601–1611.

Kolko, J. D. (2009). The effects of mobile phones and hands-free laws on traffic fatalities. *Berkeley Electronic Journal of Economic Analysis & Policy*, *9*, No. 10.

Koller, S. M., Drury, C. G., & Schwaninger, A. (2009). Change of search time and non-search time in X-ray baggage screening due to training. *Ergonomics*, *52*, 644–656.

Kondziella, D., Friberg, C. K., Frokjaer, V. G., Fabricius, M., & Møller, K. (2016). Preserved consciousness in vegetative and minimal conscious states: systematic review and meta-analysis. *Journal of Neurology, Neurosurgery & Psychiatry*, *87*, 485–492.

Kunar, M. A., Carter, R., Cohen, M., & Horowitz, T. S. (2008). Telephone conversation impairs sustained visual attention via a central bottleneck. *Psychonomic Bulletin & Review*, *15*, 1135–1140.

Lachter, J., Forster, K. I., & Ruthruff, E. (2004). Forty-five years after Broadbent (1958): Still no identification without attention. *Psychological Review*, *111*(4), 880–913.

Lamme, V. A. F. (2003). Why visual attention and awareness are different. *Trends in Cognitive Sciences*, *7*, 12–18.

Lamme, V. A., & Roelfsema, P. R. (2000). The distinct modes of vision offered by feedforward and recurrent processing. *Trends in Neurosciences*, *23*(11), 571–579.

Lehle, C., Steinhauser, M., & Hubner, R. (2009). Serial or parallel processing in dual tasks: what is more effortful? *Psychophysiology*, *46*, 502–509.

Levy, J., Pashler, H., & Boer, E. (2006). Central interference in driving: Is there any stopping the psychological refractory period? *Psychological Science*, *17*, 228–235.

Libet, B., Gleason, C. A., Wright, E. W., & Pearl, D. K. (1983). Time of conscious intention to act in relation to onset of cerebral activity (readiness potential): The unconscious initiation of a freely voluntary act. *Brain*, *106*, 623–642.

Lin, L. (2009). Breadth-biased versus focused cognitive control in media multitasking behaviors. *Proceedings of the National Association of Sciences of the United States of America*, *106*, 15521–15522.

Marozeau, J., Innes-Brown, H., Grayden, D. B., Burkitt, A. N., & Blamey, P. J. (2010). The effect of visual cues on auditory stream segregation in musicians and non-musicians. *Public Library of Science One*, *5*, e11297.

Martinez, A., Anllo-Vento, L., Sereno, M. I., Frank, L. R., Buxton, R. B., Dubowitz, D. J., et al. (1999). Involvement of striate and extrastriate visual cortical areas in spatial attention. *Nature Neuroscience*, *4*, 364–369.

Marzi, C. A., Girelli, M., Natale, E., & Miniussi, C. (2001). What exactly is extinguished in unilateral visual extinction? *Neuropsychologia*, *39*, 1354–1366.

McCarley, J. S., Kramer, A. F., Wickens, C. D., & Boot, W. R. (2004). Visual skills in airport-security screening. *Psychological Science*, *15*, 302–306.

McEvoy, S. P., Stevenson, M. R., & Woodward, M. (2007). The contribution of passengers versus mobile use to motor vehicle crashes resulting in hospital attendance. *Accident Analysis and Prevention*, *39*, 1170–1176.

Menneer, T., Cave, K. R., & Donnelly, N. (2009). The cost of search for multiple targets: Effects of practice and target similarity. *Journal of Experimental Psychology: Applied*, *15*, 125–139.

Moors, A., & de Houwer, J. (2006). Automaticity: A theoretical and conceptual analysis. *Psychological Bulletin*, *132*, 297–326.

Morawetz, C., Holz, P., Baudewig, J., Treue, S., & Dechent, P. (2007). Split of attentional resources in human visual cortex. *Visual Neuroscience*, *24*, 817–826.

Moray, N. (1959). Attention in dichotic listening: Affective cues and the influence of instructions. *Quarterly Journal of Experimental Psychology*, *11*, 56–60.

Müller, N. G., Bartelt, O. A., Donner, T. H., Villringer, A., & Brandt, S. A. (2003). A physiological correlate of the "zoom lens" of visual attention. *Journal of Neuroscience*, *23*, 3561–2565.

Naccache, L., Blandin, E., & Dehaene, S. (2002). Unconscious masked priming depends on temporal attention. *Psychological Science*, *13*, 416–424.

Nahmias, E. (2005). Agency, authorship, and illusion. *Consciousness and Cognition*, *14*, 771–785.

Nijboer, T. C. W., McIntosh, R. D., Nys, G. M. S., Dijkerman, H. C., & Milner, A. D. (2008). Prism adaptation improves voluntary but not automatic orienting in neglect. *NeuroReport*, *19*, 293–298.

O'Craven, K., Downing, P., & Kanwisher, N. (1999). fMRI evidence for objects as the units of attentional selection. *Nature*, *401*, 584–587.

Ophir, E., Nass, C., & Wagner, A. D. (2009). Cognitive control in media multitaskers. *Proceedings of the National Association of Sciences, 106*, 15583–15587.

Owen, A. M., Coleman, M. R., Boly, M., Davis, M. H., Laureys, S., & Pickard, J. D. (2006). Detecting awareness in the vegetative state. *Science, 313*, 1402.

Parton, A., Mulhotra, P., & Husain, M. (2004). Hemispatial neglect. *Journal of Neurology, Neurosurgery and Psychiatry, 75*, 13–21.

Pashler, H. (1993). Dual-task interference and elementary mental mechanisms. In D. E. Meyer & S. Kornblum (Eds.), *Attention and performance* (Vol. XIV). London, UK: MIT Press.

Petkova, V. I., & Ehrsson, H. H. (2008). If I were you: Perceptual illusion of body swapping. *PLoS One, 3*, e3832.

Pinker, S. (1997). *How the mind works*. New York, NY: W. W. Norton.

Posner, M. I. (1980). Orienting of attention: The VIIth Sir Frederic Bartlett lecture. *Quarterly Journal of Experimental Psychology, 32A*, 3–25.

Quinlan, P. T. (2003). Visual feature integration theory: Past, present, and future. *Psychological Bulletin, 129*, 643–673.

Recanzone, G. H., & Sutter, M. L. (2008). The biological basis of audition. *Annual Review of Psychology, 59*, 119–142.

Redelmeier, D. A., & Tibshirani, R. J. (1997). Association between cellular-telephone calls and motor vehicle collisions. *New England Journal of Medicine, 336*, 453–458.

Rideout, V. J., Foehr, U. G., & Roberts, D. F. (2010). *Generation M2: Media in the lives of 8- to 18-year-olds*. Menlo Park, CA: Henry J. Kaiser Family Foundation.

Robinson, B. L., & McAlpine, D. (2009). Gain control mechanisms in the auditory pathway. *Current Opinion in Neurobiology, 19*, 402–407.

Rosenholtz, R., Huang, J., Raj, A., Balas, B. J., & Ilie, L. (2012a). A summary statistic representation in peripheral vision explains visual search. *Journal of Vision, 12*(4), 1–17.

Rosenholtz, R., Huang, J., & Ehinger, K. A. (2012b). Rethinking the role of top-down attention in vision: Effects attributable to a lossy representation in peripheral vision. Frontiers in Psychology, 3:13.

Rossetti, Y., Rode, G., Pisella, L., Boisson, D., & Perenin, M. T. (1998). Prism adaptation to a rightward optical deviation rehabilitates left hemispatial neglect. *Nature, 395*, 166–169.

Royden, C. S., Wolfe, J. M., & Klempen, N. (2001). Visual search asymmetries in motion and optic flow fields. *Perception & Psychophysics, 63*, 436–444.

Rubinstein, J. S., Meyer, D. E., & Evans, J. E. (2001). Executive control of cognitive processes in task switching. *Journal of Experimental Psychology: Human Perception and Performance, 27*, 763–797.

Schneider, W., & Shiffrin, R. M. (1977). Controlled and automatic human information processing: I. Detection, search, and attention. *Psychological Review, 84*, 1–66.

Schwark, J., Sandry, J., MacDonald, J., & Dolgov, I. (2012). False feedback increases detection of low-prevalence targets in visual search. *Attention, Perception, & Psychophysics, 74*(8), 1583–1589.

Semeijn, E. J., Comijs, H. C., de Vet, H. C. W., Kooij, J. J. S., Michielsen, M., Beekman, A. T. F., & Deeg, D. J. H. (2016). Lifetime stability of ADHD symptoms in older adults. *ADHD Attention Deficit and Hyperactivity Disorders, 8*(1), 13–20.

Shamma, S. A., Elhilali, M., & Micheyl, C. (2011). Temporal coherence and attention in auditory scene analysis. *Trends in Neurosciences, 34*, 114–123.

Shen, W., Olive, J., & Jones, D. (2008). Two protocols comparing human and machine phonetic discrimination performance in conversational speech. Interspeech, 1630–1633.

Shiffrin, R. M., & Schneider, W. (1977). Controlled and automatic human information processing: II. Perceptual learning, automatic attending, and a general theory. *Psychological Review*, *84*, 127–190.

Shomstein, S. (2012). Cognitive functions of the posterior parietal cortex: top-down and bottom-up attentional control. *Frontiers in Integrative Neuroscience*, *6*, 38.

Smania, N., Martini, M. C., Gambina, G., Tomelleri, G., Palamara, A., Natale, E., et al. (1998). The spatial distribution of visual attention in hemineglect and extinction patients. *Brain*, *121*, 1759–1770.

Soon, C. S., Brass, M., Heinze, H. J., & Haynes, J. D. (2008). Unconscious determinants of free decisions in the human brain. *Nature Neuroscience*, *10*, 257–261.

Spelke, E. S., Hirst, W. C., & Neisser, U. (1976). Skills of divided attention. *Cognition*, *4*, 215–230.

Strayer, D. L., Watson, J. M., & Drews, F. A. (2011). Cognitive distraction while multitasking in the automobile. *Psychology of Learning and Motivation*, *54*, 29–58.

Strohl, M. P. (2011). Bradley's Benzedrine studies on children with behavioral disorders. *Yale Journal of Biology and Medicine*, *84*(1), 27–33.

Thimm, M., Fink, G. R., Küst, J., Karbe, H., Willmes, K., & Sturm, W. (2009). Recovery from hemineglect: Differential neurobiological effects of optokinetic stimulation and alertness training. *Cortex*, *45*, 850–862.

Treisman, A. M. (1960). Contextual cues in selective attention. *Quarterly Journal of Experimental Psychology*, *12*, 242–248.

Treisman, A. M. (1964). Verbal cues, language, and meaning in selective attention. *American Journal of Psychology*, *77*, 206–219.

Treisman, A. M., & Gelade, G. (1980). A feature integration theory of attention. *Cognitive Psychology*, *12*, 97–136.

Treisman, A. M., & Riley, J. G. A. (1969). Is selective attention selective perception or selective response? A further test. *Journal of Experimental Psychology*, *79*, 27–34.

Treisman, A., & Schmidt, H. (1982). Illusory conjunctions in the perception of objects. *Cognitive Psychology*, *14*(1), 107–141.

Troiani, V., Price, E. T., & Schultz, R. T. (2014). Unseen fearful faces promote amygdala guidance of attention. *Social, Cognitive, and Affective Neuroscience*, *9*, 133–140.

Tsakiris, M., & Haggard, P. (2005). The rubber hand illusion revisited: Visuotactile integration and self-attribution. *Journal of Experimental Psychology: Human Perception and Performance*, *31*(1), 80–91.

Van der Hoort, B., Guterstam, A., & Ehrsson, H. (2011). Being Barbie: The size of one's own body determines the perceived size of the world. *PLoS One*, *6*(5), e20195.

Vuilleumier, P., Schwartz, S., Clark, K., Husain, M., & Driver, J. (2002). Testing memory for unseen visual stimuli in patients with extinction and spatial neglect. *Journal of Cognitive Neuroscience*, *14*, 875–886.

Vuilleumier, P., Schwartz, S., Verdon, V., Maravita, A., Hutton, C., Husain, M., et al. (2008). Abnormal attentional modulation of retinotopic cortex in parietal patients with spatial neglect. *Current Biology*, *18*, 1525–1529.

Wang, Z., & Tchernev, J. M. (2012). The "myth" of media multitasking: Reciprocal dynamics of media multitasking, personal needs, and gratifications. *Journal of Communication*, *62*(3), 493–513.

Watson, J. M., & Strayer, D. L. (2010). Supertaskers: Profiles in extraordinary multitasking ability. *Psychonomic Bulletin & Review*, *17*, 479–485.

Wegner, D. M. (2003). The mind's best trick: How we experience conscious will. *Trends in Cognitive Sciences*, *7*, 65–69.

Wegner, D. M., & Wheatley, T. (1999). Apparent mental causation: Sources of the experience of will. *American Psychologist*, 54, 480–492.

White, P. A. (2009). Property transmission: An explanatory account of the role of similarity information in causal inference. *Psychological Bulletin*, 135, 774–793.

Wickens, C. D. (2008). Multiple resources and mental workload. *Human Factors: The Journal of the Human Factors and Ergonomics Society*, 50(3), 449–455.

Wolfe, J. M. (2007). Guided search 4.0: Current progress with a model of visual search. In W. Gray (Ed.), *Integrated models of cognitive systems* (pp. 99–119). New York, NY: Oxford University Press.

Wolfe, J. M., Horowitz, T. S., Van-Wert, M. J., Kenner, N M., Place, S. S., & Kibbi, N. (2007). Low target prevalence is a stubborn source of errors in visual search tasks. *Journal of Experimental Psychology: General*, 136, 623–638.

Xiao, K., & Yamauchi, T. (2015). Subliminal semantic priming in near absence of attention: A cursor motion study. *Consciousness and Cognition*, 38, 88–98.

Yantis, S. (2008). The neural basis of selective attention: Cortical sources and targets of attentional modulation. *Current Directions in Psychological Science*, 17, 86–90.

Chapter 4

Contents

Short-term and working memory

4

INTRODUCTION

How important is memory? Imagine if we were without it. We would be unable to talk, read, or write, because we would remember nothing about language. We would have extremely limited personalities because we would have no recollection of the events of our lives and thus no sense of self. We would even not know what to do next, because we would have no recollection of where we come from and what we planned to do. In sum, we would have the same lack of knowledge as newborn babies.

We use memory for numerous purposes throughout every single day of our lives. It allows us to keep track of conversations, to answer questions in examinations, to make sense of what we read, to recognize people's faces, and to understand what we read in books and see on television.

The wonders of human memory are discussed in this chapter and the following three. At the most general level, this chapter is concerned with short-term memory, whereas Chapters 5 to 7 deal with long-term memory. In these chapters the emphasis is on how we can make sense of the incredible richness of human memory. Our memory ranges from detailed personal memories of previous holidays to knowledge of how to ride a bicycle or play the piano.

Learning objectives

After studying Chapter 4, you should be able to:

- Define, compare, and contrast short-term memory and working memory.
- Explain what is meant by the "seven, plus or minus two" capacity of short-term memory.
- Explain how the recency effect informs us of the capacity and duration of short-term memory.

- Provide examples of how working memory capacity is measured.
- Describe the unitary-store approach to short-term memory.
- Describe the components of Baddeley's working memory model, and explain how working memory processes happen according to this model.
- Discuss the implications of having higher or lower working memory capacity.

Let's return to the content of this chapter. In everyday language, the term "short-term memory" refers to our memory over a period up to several hours or days after learning. In contrast, psychologists use the term to refer to memory over a much shorter period (a few seconds). For example, we might use short-term memory to briefly remember the number needed to open a combination lock or to make a phone call. Short-term memory can be contrasted with long-term memory, which refers to memory over periods of time ranging between several seconds and a lifetime.

In the first part of the chapter, we focus on the traditional approach to short-term memory. It was regarded as a *store* that could hold a limited amount of information for a brief period of time. Within that approach, it is important to establish the capacity of short-term memory, its duration, and its relationship to long-term memory.

Later in the chapter, we consider the contemporary approach based on working memory. The basic idea underlying the transition from short-term memory to working memory is that in everyday life we need memory for more than simply storing information for a short or long term. For example, suppose you have to write an essay in psychology. In such a situation, you not only need to keep in mind what you have just written (short term) and what you have learned about the topic (long term) but also think of what to write in the next sentence. The term "working memory" describes a system that combines processing (e.g., what will I write next?) with short-term storage (e.g., what have I just written?).

The easiest way to understand the distinction between working memory and long-term memory is to think of a computer. A computer contains two types of memory. The first is the information stored on the hard disk, which is intended for long-term use. The second type is the information used by the central processor while running the commands given by the user. Often the information must be stored very briefly, to be used again as soon as an ongoing operation is finished. This part of the memory system changes constantly, and we refer to it as the random access memory (RAM). Indeed, when you think of buying a new computer, two aspects you will take into account are the size of the hard disk (which determines how much information you can store on your computer) and the size of the RAM (which determines how fast your computer runs). Working memory can be compared to the random access memory used by the central processor for its operations.

SHORT-TERM MEMORY

Research on short-term memory flourished after the publication of Atkinson and Shiffrin's (1968) influential model of memory, which we briefly introduced

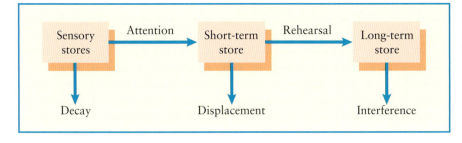

Figure 4.1 The multistore model of memory proposed by Atkinson and Shiffrin (1968).

in Chapter 1 (Figure 1.3) and which is repeated here for your convenience (Figure 4.1).

THE ATKINSON AND SHIFFRIN MODEL OF MEMORY

Atkinson and Shiffrin (1968) made a distinction among three types of memory: (1) the sensory memories, (2) short-term memory, and (3) long-term memory.

The sensory memories

Atkinson and Shiffrin (1968) assumed that stimulation from the environment is initially retained in sensory stores. These stores are sense-specific, meaning there is a separate store for each sensory modality. When we see a stimulus in the environment, information about it is held briefly in the visual sensory store (iconic store). When we hear a stimulus, information about it is held briefly in the auditory sensory store (echoic store). Touch information is briefly retained in the haptic store, and so on. The sensory stores have a large capacity (because they contain the full percept with all its details) but decay rapidly, within less than 1 second for the iconic store and after a few seconds in the echoic store. (The faster decay time in the iconic store has been related to the fact that we can easily relook at something we've forgotten.)

Atkinson and Shiffrin's ideas of sensory memories were based on a classic experiment of Sperling (1960). Sperling presented an array with 12 capital letters to his participants for a very short period of time (50 ms). The letters formed three rows of four letters (Figure 4.2). In a first experiment, Sperling asked the participants to name as many letters from the array as they could. Participants could name some four letters on average.

Sperling reasoned that there could be two origins of this small number: either the iconic memory has a limited capacity or information in it decays rapidly, so that it is lost as soon as the participants have named a few letters. To decide between these possibilities, he introduced another experiment in which he presented tones of different pitch together with the stimulus. When a high tone was heard, participants had to name the first row of letters. When a middle tone was heard, participants had to name the second row of letters, and when a low tone was heard, participants had to name the third row. Sperling discovered that under these conditions participants were nearly flawless. In addition, when in a third experiment he presented the tone 1 second after the array, participants' performance was reduced to the level without a tone. This strongly suggested that the iconic memory had a very high storage capacity, but that information in it decayed rapidly (i.e., within 1 second).

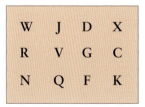

Figure 4.2 An example of the stimuli used by Sperling (1960) to measure the capacity of the visual sensory memory or the iconic memory.

The role of short-term memory

In Atkinson and Shiffrin's model, only a fraction of the information in the sensory stores is transferred to the short-term store. The latter store has a very limited capacity (see following section), so that much information is lost in the transition. Atkinson and Shiffrin here basically followed Broadbent's (1958) early selection model, discussed in Chapter 3: information not attended to was not processed any further and completely disregarded.

Because of the limited capacity of short-term memory, information had to be transferred to long-term memory before it got displaced by new information coming in. Chances of successful transfer, according to Atkinson and Shiffrin, depended on the degree of rehearsal that was possible. Rehearsal refers to the subvocal reiteration of verbal material.

Limitations

Atkinson and Shiffrin's model was tremendously important in the decades following its publication, because it was the main source of hypotheses in memory research. Even today, the distinction among sensory stores, short-term memory, and long-term memory is very useful. However, the limits of the model gradually became clear, so that nowadays the exact model is no longer believed in. We give five examples of what had to be changed in the model.

First, as we have seen, Atkinson and Shiffrin believed that information not in the focus of attention was completely lost because of decay, as argued in Broadbent's (1958) early section model of attention. The fact that Broadbent's model is no longer believed to be correct is a first limitation of Atkinson and Shiffrin's model. Unattended information can still be processed even if we are unaware of it.

A second limitation of Atkinson and Shiffrin's model is that information must first go through short-term memory before it can access long-term memory. This is at odds with much of what we discussed in perception (Chapter 2). There we saw how stimuli activate a host of interacting, unconscious top-down and bottom-up processes leading to a conscious percept that is more than the sum of the sensations. Such processing is not possible without connections between the sensory stores and long-term memory. We must not forget that in Sperling's (1960) study the participants saw arrays of *meaningful letters*, not arrays of line segments.

Third, short-term memory in Atkinson and Shiffrin's model consisted of a storage facility of limited capacity. As we saw earlier, most of our conscious thoughts involve processing of stimuli (e.g., writing words) in addition to short-term storage of information.

Fourth, Atkinson and Shiffrin saw long-term memory as a unitary store. In Chapters 5–7 we will see evidence for different types of long-term memory.

Finally, Atkinson and Shiffrin saw rehearsal as the only mechanism to transfer information from short-term memory to long-term memory. Information that could be rehearsed a few times was more likely to be transferred than information that was presented too rapidly to be rehearsed. Research, however, has indicated that rehearsal is one of the least efficient methods to encode information in long-term memory (see following section).

Still, Atkinson and Shiffrin's model is an interesting entry to memory research, because many of the experimental findings inspired by the model still form the basis of current models of memory.

SHORT-TERM MEMORY CAPACITY

If we think of short-term memory as a limited-capacity store that holds information briefly, then the most obvious question is "how many items of information can we keep in the store?" Another question is, "How long does information stay in short-term memory?" We consider answers to those questions in the following sections.

The first findings

Already before Atkinson and Shiffrin (1968) it was known that the capacity of short-term storage was limited. Atkinson and Shiffrin summarized the evidence and put it into a coherent model.

Jacobs (1887) was the first person to use an experimental approach to measure the capacity of short-term memory. He presented participants with a random sequence of digits or letters at a presentation rate of one item per second, after which they repeated the items back in the same order. **Memory span** was the longest sequence of items recalled accurately at least 50% of the time. Jacobs (1887) observed a mean digit span of 9.3 items (meaning that most participants could repeat 9–10 digits) and an average letter span of 7.3 items.

Note that memory span involves presenting items in a *random* order. Performance would obviously be much higher if the items formed a meaningful sequence such as PSYCHOLOGY or EXPERIMENT. George Miller (1956) took account of this point. He argued that the capacity of short-term memory is "seven, plus or minus two." By this, he meant that healthy adults have a short-term memory span between five and nine items (as we will see later, there are reliable differences among individuals). Miller argued that the same span size is found whether the units are numbers, letters, or words. He claimed that we should focus on **chunks** (integrated pieces of information). What forms a chunk depends on your personal experience. For example, "IBM" is *one* chunk for those familiar with the computer company but *three* letter chunks for everyone else.

Not all chunks lead to equal spans

Shortly after the publication of Miller (1956), various authors argued that short-term memory span is not the same for all types of chunks. Jacobs (1887) already reported a longer span for digits (9.3 items) than for letters (7.3 items). One explanation for this difference is that digits are easy to group into larger chunks. For instance, the digits 2 and 4 can be regrouped into the number 24, and the digits 2, 0, 1, 9 can be regrouped into the year 2019. Indeed, many people group the digits of a telephone number into three or four chunks if they have to keep the number in short-term memory.

Rechunking is not the only reason for differences in span size. Simon (1974) found that the span in chunks was less with larger chunks than with smaller ones. He studied memory span for words, two-word phrases, and eight-word phrases, arguing that each phrase formed a chunk. The number of chunks recalled fell from six or seven with unrelated words to four with two-word phrases and three with eight-word phrases. Later research confirmed that there is a **word-length effect** in short-term memory span. This is the finding that word span (number of words recalled immediately in the correct order) is greater for short words than for long ones (see Research Activity 4.1; Mueller et al., 2003).

Pronunciation time explains some cross-cultural differences in digit span. Chinese Mandarin speakers have a greater digit span than English speakers (Chen et al., 2009). This difference correlates with the fact that digits in spoken Mandarin take less time to pronounce than digits in spoken English. Differences in pronunciation times also explain why memory spans are shorter in Welsh than in English (Ellis & Hennelly, 1980): numbers have longer names in Welsh than in English. The word-length effect suggests that the capacity of short-term memory for words depends on phonological information and not on visual letter information.

Further evidence that the short-term memory span for verbal stimuli depends on speech-based information is the **phonological similarity effect**. This effect refers to the observation that recall performance is worse when the words are phonologically similar (i.e., have similar sounds) than when they are phonologically dissimilar. For example, FEE, HE, PEA, KEY, ME, and SKI form a list of phonologically similar words, whereas BAY, HOE, IT, ODD, SHY, and UP form a list of phonologically dissimilar words. Using those lists, Larsen et al. (2000) found that the ability to recall the words in order was 25% worse with the phonologically similar list.

Research Activity 4.1 *Word length and recall*

Write each of the following words on a separate piece of paper and make two piles, one for each list. Then say five words from List A to a friend at one word per second, after which they try to recall the words in the correct order. After that, do the same with List B. Next present six words from List A, and then six from List B. Work out the maximum number of words your friend can remember correctly in order from each list.

LIST A	LIST B
cult	advantage
dare	behavior
fate	circumstance
guess	defiance
hint	fantasy
mood	interim
oath	misery
plea	narrowness
rush	occasion
truce	protocol
verb	ridicule
zeal	upheaval

The words are taken from a paper by Mueller et al. (2003). Their participants had an average span of 6.7 with List A words and of 5.1 with List B words. *Why* was there this difference? The words in List A took 418 ms on average to say compared to 672 ms for those on the right. Thus, the number of items that can be stored in short-term memory depends in part on the time required to pronounce each one.

Cowan's 4 ± 1 estimate of short-term memory capacity

Cowan (2001) argued that Miller's (1956) memory span of 7 ± 2 chunks was an overestimate. This number is found only when further chunking is possible or when people have enough time to transfer information from short-term memory to long-term memory, from which it can be recalled. When these two factors are eliminated, Cowan (2001) argued that the true capacity of short-term memory is four chunks (plus or minus one). Cowan et al. (2005) used the running memory task – a series of digits ended at an unpredictable point, with the participants' task being to recall the items from the end of the list. The digits were presented very rapidly to prevent transfer to long-term memory, and the mean number of items recalled was 3.9.

Chekaf et al. (2016) presented participants with sequences of pictures that were easy to chunk (e.g., ▲▲ ▲ △△△) or that were difficult to chunk (e.g., ▲ △△ ▲▲ △). Depending on the sequence, one to eight stimuli were displayed serially in the center of a computer screen at intervals of one per second. At the end of the series, participants had to click the correct sequence with the mouse on a pad containing all the pictures used. Chekaf et al. (2016) obtained memory spans of three items for the sequences that were difficult to chunk and four to five items for the sequences that were easy to chunk.

Recency

There is another way to work out the capacity of short-term memory. Suppose we present a list of unrelated words and then ask our participants to provide free recall (producing as many words as possible in any order). The recency effect refers to the finding that the last few items in a list are usually much better remembered in immediate recall than those from the middle of the list. Counting backwards for 10 seconds between the end of list presentation and start of recall mainly reduces memory performance for the last two or three items (Glanzer & Cunitz, 1966; see Figure 4.3).

One interpretation of the recency effect (there are others) is that the last items of the series are still in the short-term store and, therefore, are especially

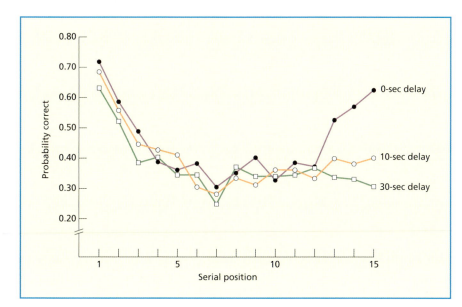

Figure 4.3 Free recall as a function of the item's position in the series and the duration of the task between encoding and recall.
Source: Adapted from Glanzer and Cunitz (1966).

vulnerable to a task intervening between encoding and recall (Farrell, 2010). The fact that the estimate of short-term memory capacity is lower on the basis of the recency effect (two to three items) than Cowan's number (four items) can be understood by the loss of information while the participants are saying aloud the words they remember.

Support for the notion that the recency effect consists of items in short-term memory comes from research on patients with amnesia (see Chapter 5). This is a condition involving severe impairment of long-term memory but not of short-term memory. As predicted, amnesic patients have as large a recency effect as healthy individuals in spite of having poor long-term memory for the rest of the items (Carlesimo et al., 1996).

Age differences

Something else Jacobs (1887) discovered in his first studies on short-term memory span was that the span increased during secondary school years. The memory span for meaningless syllables (like *dak-mul-tak-hin-roz*) was 5.3 for 11-year-olds versus 6.1 for 18-year-olds. Gathercole et al. (2004) confirmed that short-term memory span increases from the age of 4 till the age of 14, while Park et al. (2002) reported a decrease in span between 25 and 85 years old. So, short-term memory capacity is maximal when people are between 18 and 30 years old.

DURATION

In a classic study, Peterson and Peterson (1959) studied the duration of short-term memory. Participants had to remember a three-consonant item (e.g., X R Q) while counting backwards by threes followed by recall of the consonants in the correct order. Memory performance reduced to about 50% after 6 seconds, and forgetting was almost complete after 18 seconds (see Figure 4.4).

Why is forgetting so rapid? There are two main classes of explanation (Jonides et al., 2008). First, there may be *decay* over time caused by various physiological processes. Second, there may be *interference* from items on previous trials and/or interference from the task (i.e., counting backwards) during the retention interval.

Evidence that much forgetting from short-term memory is due to interference was reported by Keppel and Underwood (1962) using the Peterson-Peterson task. There was only minimal forgetting on the very first trial, with forgetting increasing steadily over the following three or four trials. These findings suggested that forgetting of any letter sequence was due to interference from previous letter sequences, a phenomenon known as proactive interference (see Chapter 5).

Nairne et al. (1999) argued that the rate of forgetting observed by Peterson and Peterson (1959) was especially rapid for two reasons. First, they used all the consonants repeatedly. This may have caused considerable proactive interference, as suggested by Keppel and Underwood (1962). Second, the memory task was difficult because participants had to remember the items *and* the presentation order.

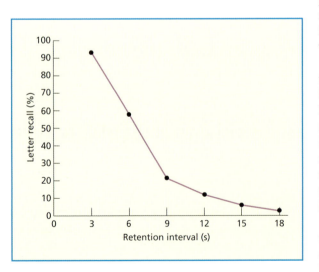

Figure 4.4 Forgetting over time in short-term memory. Source: Data from Peterson and Peterson (1959).

Nairne et al. (1999) presented different words on each trial to reduce interference and tested memory *only* for order information. Participants first saw a sequence of five words presented at a rate of one word per second. Then they had to read aloud digits as an interpolated task (to prevent rehearsal), after which they were shown the five words again in a random order and had to put them in the correct order. Under these circumstances there was remarkably little forgetting even after an interval of 96 seconds. This finding suggests that forgetting in short-term memory is due to interference rather than decay. Otherwise, one would have to explain why decay sometimes can take more than a minute.

Berman et al. (2009) also found that interference is more important than decay. On each trial, participants saw a display with four words for two seconds. Following a three-second blank delay (retention interval), the participants saw a probe word and had to indicate whether the probe word was part of the set to be retained or not. On half of the no-trials, the probe word was one of the words shown on the previous trial. Previous research had indicated that participants take longer to reject such probe words and also make more errors, arguably because the words from the previous trial still linger in short-term memory. To measure decay, Berman et al. (2009) manipulated the interval between trials from 1 second to 13 seconds. Based on the research of Peterson and Peterson (Figure 4.4), the information of the previous trial should have decayed after 13 seconds. This was not what Berman et al. (2009) found. There was as much interference from the previous trial when the inter-trial interval lasted 13 seconds as when it was only one second.

In sum, there is surprisingly little evidence that information in short-term memory is lost because it decays. Rather, such forgetting is due mostly to interference. On the other hand, after a review of the literature, Ricker et al. (2016) concluded that although interference explains many findings of forgetting in short-term memory, it seems unavoidable that some element of decay is present as well. One of the studies they referred to was by Ricker and Cowan (2010), who asked participants to retain three difficult-to-name, unfamiliar characters (such as Ж, Λ, ₡). Such characters were used to avoid rehearsal. Participants saw the characters for 750 ms, followed by a mask. After a variable interval of 1.5, 3, or 6 seconds, they were shown a probe character and had to indicate whether the probe character was in the original set or not. No characters were repeated between trials. There were three blocks of trials, in which the retention interval between encoding and testing was manipulated. In the first block, participants had nothing to do (no load). In the second block, they heard spoken digits which they had to repeat (low load condition). In the third block, they heard spoken digits which they had to subtract (high load condition).

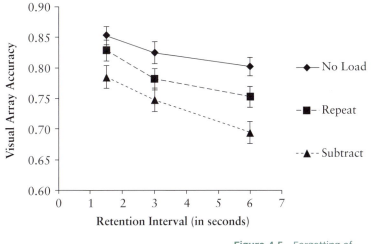

Figure 4.5 Forgetting of unnamable characters over time in short-term memory. Source: Data from Ricker and Cowan (2010).

As can be seen in Figure 4.5, Ricker and Cowan (2010) observed decreased performance for longer retention intervals and also in the no load condition where there was no interference possible. According to them, this was clear evidence of decay, which could not be explained on the basis of interference. They argued that one of the main limitations of short-term memory, apart from its reduced capacity, is its ephemerality, the fact that information is so rapidly lost if it is not refreshed. Notice that Ricker and Cowan (2010) found evidence not only for decay but also for interference, as retrieval was much lower in the repeat and subtract conditions than in the no load condition.

SHORT-TERM VS. LONG-TERM MEMORY

Atkinson and Shiffrin (1968) made a clear distinction between short-term memory and long-term memory, a distinction that is still upheld by most theorists. There are several reasons to make such a distinction. For example, there are enormous differences in capacity: a few items for short-term memory vs. essentially unlimited capacity for long-term memory. There are also massive differences in duration: a few seconds for short-term memory vs. periods of time up to several decades for long-term memory.

Findings suggesting that short-term and long-term memory are separate

Some of the most convincing evidence that short-term and long-term memory are separate comes from research on brain-damaged patients. If there are separate short-term and long-term memory systems located in different brain regions, then we should find brain-damaged patients who have impaired long-term memory but intact short-term memory. In addition, we should find other patients who have impaired short-term memory but intact long-term memory (see *double dissociation* in Chapter 1).

Patients suffering from amnesia nearly all have enormous problems with some aspects of long-term memory (see Chapter 5). For present purposes, note that the overwhelming majority have essentially intact short-term memory. In a review of 147 amnesic patients, Spiers et al. (2001) concluded that *none* had a significant problem with short-term memory.

A few brain-damaged patients have also been reported with impaired short-term memory but intact long-term memory. For example, consider KF, who suffered brain damage after a motorcycle accident. He had no problem with long-term learning and recall, but his digit span was greatly impaired (Shallice & Warrington, 1970). Later research, however, indicated that KF's problems with short-term memory were less widespread than initially assumed. His forgetting of visual stimuli and of meaningful sounds (e.g., telephones ringing) was much less than his forgetting of auditorily presented letters, words, and digits (Shallice & Warrington, 1974). Nevertheless, KF's problems with short-term memory contrasted sharply with his good long-term memory.

How important is rehearsal for the transition from short-term memory to long-term memory?

Long-term storage of information, according to Atkinson and Shiffrin (1968), depended on rehearsal. It was assumed that there is a direct relationship between the amount of rehearsal in the short-term store and the strength of the stored memory trace.

One of the arguments of Atkinson and Shiffrin is shown in Figure 4.3, which we used to illustrate the recency effect. In this figure you see that not only the last items were remembered well (the ones still in short-term memory) but also the first items. This effect is called the *primacy effect*. In addition, the primacy effect survived the introduction of the interpolated task (counting downwards). According to Atkinson and Shiffrin, the primacy effect could be understood if one accepted that the first items (presented before the short-term memory buffer was full) had been transferred to long-term memory. In their view this occurred because the participants were able to rehearse the first presented items a few times.

Later research has questioned Atkinson and Shiffrin's account of the primacy effect, because rote rehearsal is a very inefficient memory encoding strategy (see Oberauer (2003) and Lewandowsky and Oberauer (2015) if you are interested). Already in 1973, Craik and Watkins argued that *elaborative rehearsal* is more efficient than *maintenance rehearsal* to transfer information from short-term memory to long-term memory. Elaborative rehearsal refers to adding organization and meaningfulness to input in short-term memory by linking the new information to information already stored in long-term memory. This aspect will be discussed in more detail in Chapter 5.

Evaluation: Atkinson and Shiffrin's model of memory

- (+) The distinction among three kinds of memory store (sensory stores; short-term memory; and long-term memory) is supported by the evidence.

- (+) The three kinds of store differ from each other in several ways. For example, short-term memory has very limited capacity and short temporal duration, whereas long-term memory has essentially unlimited capacity and some information lasts a lifetime.

- (+) The evidence from brain-damaged patients supports the notion that short-term memory and long-term memory involve different brain areas (see Chapter 5).

- (−) The conceptions of short-term memory and long-term memory are *oversimplified*. As we will see shortly, Baddeley and Hitch's (1974) working memory model replaced the concept of a single short-term store with a working memory system consisting of three different components (later raised to four). In similar fashion, Atkinson and Shiffrin's (1968) notion of a *single* long-term memory system has been discarded because the evidence indicates that there are several long-term memory systems (see Chapter 5).

- (−) Atkinson and Shiffrin (1968) argued that information is in short-term memory *before* long-term memory. In fact, the information processed in short-term memory *must* have already made contact with information in long-term memory. For example, we can only rehearse "IBM" as a single chunk in short-term memory by using relevant information stored in long-term memory. Thus, processing in short-term memory occurs *after* long-term memory has been accessed.

- (−) Atkinson and Shiffrin (1968) assumed that rehearsal is of central importance when we store information in long-term memory. We do sometimes use rehearsal to promote effective learning, but it is not involved in establishing most of our long-term memories.

| Section summary

Short-term memory capacity
- Span measures suggest that the capacity of short-term memory is about seven chunks when people have to repeat series of words or digits. It is somewhat lower with words having long pronunciation times or sounding the same, suggesting that the information retained in short-term memory is phonological information.
- When attempts are made to eliminate the effects of rehearsal and long-term memory on short-term memory, its capacity reduces to four chunks. In similar fashion, the capacity of short-term memory based on the recency effect is closer to four than to seven chunks.

Short-term memory duration
- Information in short-term memory is generally forgotten within a few seconds. This is mostly due to interference rather than decay.

Short-term memory vs. long-term memory
- Evidence from brain-damaged patients suggests that there are separate short-term and long-term memory systems. In Atkinson and Shiffrin's influential multistore model, information is in short-term memory before long-term memory, and rehearsal in short-term memory strongly influences long-term memory. Both of these assumptions have been questioned.

WORKING MEMORY

Research on short-term memory was very much inspired by the serial recall task, introduced by Jacobs (1887). This focus on the serial recall task seemed to suggest that short-term memory is only important to remember a telephone number or a person's name for the few seconds required to write them down.

In 1974, two British psychologists (Alan Baddeley and Graham Hitch) came up with an alternative answer. They argued that we generally use short-term memory when engaged in the performance of complex tasks. With such tasks, you have to carry out various processes to complete the task. However, you also have to briefly store information about the outcome of early processes in short-term memory as you move on to later processes.

Suppose you were given the addition problem 13 + 18 + 24. You would probably add 13 and 18 and keep the answer (31) in short-term memory. You would then add 24 to 31 and produce the correct answer of 55.

Baddeley and Hitch (1974) argued that we should replace the notion of short-term memory with that of working memory. Working memory refers to a system combining processing and short-term memory functions. Baddeley and Hitch's crucial insight was that short-term memory is essential in the performance of numerous tasks that aren't explicitly memory tasks.

Think back to Atkinson and Shiffrin's (1968) theory of memory, in which the importance of verbal rehearsal in short-term memory was emphasized. Baddeley and Hitch (1974) accepted that verbal rehearsal is important. However, they argued that other kinds of information can also be stored in short-term memory. For example, suppose you are driving along focusing on

| Key term

Working memory: a system that can briefly store information while other information is processed.

steering the car, avoiding pedestrians, and keeping a safe distance behind the car in front of you. In addition, you may be storing relevant visual and spatial information (e.g., width of the road; the distance of the car behind you). Thus, short-term (or working) memory involves spatial and visual processes as well as verbal ones.

THE BADDELEY AND HITCH WORKING MEMORY MODEL

Baddeley and Hitch (1974) proposed the original version of the working memory model. We will focus on the most recent version (Baddeley, 2012) consisting of four components (see Figure 4.6):

- **Central executive:** This is a limited-capacity processing system acting as an attentional controller. It is the "boss" of the working memory system and controls what happens within the other components, which are sometimes called *slave systems*. It can process information from any sensory modality (e.g., visual, auditory) but has no storage capacity.
- **Phonological loop:** Component of working memory that stores a limited number of sounds for a limited period of time. It is involved in the processing and brief storage of phonological (speech-based) information.
- **Visuo-spatial sketchpad:** Component of working memory that is used to process visual and spatial information and to store this information briefly.
- **Episodic buffer:** This is a storage system that can hold information from the phonological loop, the visuo-spatial sketchpad, and long-term memory.

You are probably thinking that the working memory model seems rather complicated, but the basic ideas are straightforward. When we carry out a task, we use verbal processing (phonological loop), visual processing, or spatial processing (visuo-spatial sketchpad). Performing the task successfully requires that we attend to relevant information and use verbal, visual, and spatial processes effectively (central executive). During the performance of a task, we often need a general storage system combining and integrating information from the other components and from long-term memory (episodic buffer).

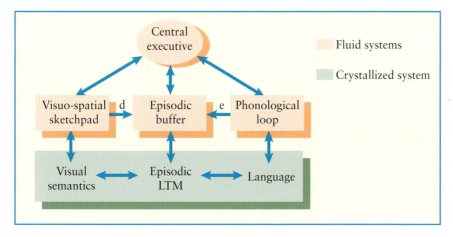

Figure 4.6 The Baddeley (2000) version of the four components of the working memory system, including the connections among them. Working memory involves fluid systems (processing), whereas crystallized systems refer to stored knowledge in long-term memory (see also discussion in the Working Memory Capacity section for the distinction between fluid intelligence and crystallized intelligence).

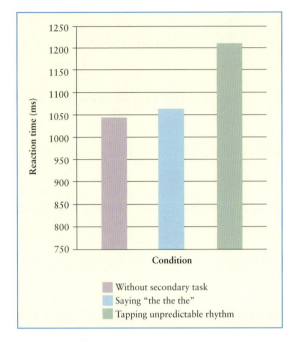

Figure 4.7 Effects of secondary tasks on the time needed to verify one-digit addition problems.
Source: Adapted from De Rammelaere et al. (2001).

It is assumed that all four components of working memory have limited capacity. It is also assumed that each component can function fairly independently of the others. These two assumptions allow us to predict whether or not two tasks can be performed successfully at the same time:

• If two tasks use the *same* component of working memory, they can't be performed successfully together. This is because that component's limited capacity will be exceeded.
• If two tasks involve *different* components, it should be possible to perform them as well together as separately.

We can see how this works in practice by considering which components of working memory are involved in simple calculations. De Rammelaere et al. (2001) asked university students to decide whether one-digit additions were correct or not (e.g. 2 + 3 = 5? or 2 + 4 = 8?). In one condition, the participants performed the task without any secondary task. In a second condition, they performed the task while saying aloud "the the the" all the time. There is good evidence that this task (called articulatory suppression) interferes with rehearsal in the phonological loop. Finally, in the third condition, the participants were asked to tap an unpredictable "rhythm" on the zero key of the numeric keypad. Such an unpredictable, random pattern requires input from the central executive, to make sure that the same sequence is not repeated over and over again.

What did De Rammelaere et al. (2001) find? Figure 4.7 shows the results. The participants solved the additions as easily when they were saying "the the the" as when they could devote their entire resources to the task. This suggests that the phonological loop is not needed for one-digit additions. In contrast, performance was worse when the participants were tapping an unpredictable rhythm, indicating that the central executive was involved. The authors argued that their results agreed with the hypothesis that simple additions are solved by looking up the correct answer stored in long-term memory (for which the central executive is needed).

For more complex problems (e.g., 36 + 47 = 85?) and in young children, performance is also hindered when the phonological loop is loaded (DeStefano & LeFevre, 2004), suggesting that under these circumstances support from the phonological loop is needed for good performance (e.g., to briefly store interim solutions and to do subvocal counting).

In the Real World 4.1 *Simultaneous interpreting*

Millions of people around the world have jobs that place considerable demands on working memory (e.g., air traffic controller; Nolan, 2010). One such job is that of simultaneous interpreter or translator. As we might expect, those inexperienced in simultaneous interpreting find it exceptionally demanding (Christoffels et al., 2006).

What makes simultaneous translation so demanding? Simultaneous interpreters have to, at the same time, comprehend what is said in one language, translate from that language into a second language, and speak in that second language. Other demanding aspects of simultaneous interpretation are less obvious (Albir & Alves, 2009). For example, the interpreter's background knowledge is generally weaker than the speaker's. In addition, he/she has to start translating the auditory message without knowing in detail what the speaker will say next.

Most skills required for simultaneous translation involve the central executive. Attentional control is a major function of the central executive, and attentional control is needed to switch attention appropriately among cognitive processes involved in simultaneous translation.

Simultaneous interpreters generally show "translation asymmetry" – they find it harder to translate from their dominant language into their weaker language than the other way around. Rinne et al. (2000) found that simultaneous interpreting mostly involved the left hemisphere, especially parts of the prefrontal cortex associated with semantic processing and verbal working memory. Of most importance, there was more brain activation when the interpreters translated into their weaker language, suggesting that this imposes high demands on working memory.

It is not always advantageous to use one's dominant language, especially if the switch from a weaker language is unexpected. Philipp et al. (2007) gave individuals fluent in German, English, and French the task of naming digits. Naming times were much longer immediately after they shifted from one of their nondominant languages (English or French) into their dominant language (German). Before the shift, participants had to inhibit their dominant language, and it took time to overcome this inhibition when shifting. Language switching involves several brain areas associated with cognitive control (e.g., inhibitory processes), and such

control involves the central executive (Abutalebi & Green, 2008).

Do simultaneous interpreters have superior working memory to other people? This issue was addressed by Christoffels et al. (2006) in a study of bilingual individuals whose native language was Dutch and whose second language was English. Some were simultaneous interpreters with an average of 16 years of experience, whereas others were teachers of English.

Christoffels et al. (2006) used various tasks to assess working memory capacity. One was a reading-span task in which participants read sentences and then recalled the last word in each sentence. There was also a speaking-span task in which participants were presented with several words and then produced aloud a sentence for each word they remembered. These tasks were performed in both Dutch and English. The interpreters performed better than the teachers on both tasks and in both languages. These findings suggest that excellent working memory ability is a real advantage if you want to be a successful interpreter. However, it is possible in addition that becoming an interpreter helps to develop working memory abilities.

When we listen to a speaker, we can use the phonological loop to store some of the information briefly and so make comprehension easier. In contrast, simultaneous interpreters generally talk almost continuously. As a result, they have little or no access to the phonological loop to aid comprehension. The ability to overcome this problem is important in simultaneous interpretation.

Christoffels (2006) asked participants to listen to stories while saying the Dutch words for *dog, cat,* and *mouse* repeatedly. High levels of subsequent recall for the stories were associated with good simultaneous interpreting performance. Thus, the ability to understand spoken language without using the phonological loop is advantageous for simultaneous interpreting.

In sum, several findings indicate that simultaneous translation relies heavily on the working memory system.

PHONOLOGICAL LOOP

Baddeley and Hitch (1974) classified all existing research on the short-term memory store within Atkinson and Shiffrin's model as related to the phonological loop. They made a distinction between two components:

- a passive *phonological store* directly concerned with speech perception
- an *articulatory control process* needed for maintenance rehearsal and speech production

What use is the phonological loop? We have seen it is useful for remembering a series of unrelated chunks in the correct order. However, that isn't a skill we need very often. Are there other uses? To find out, Baddeley and colleagues studied a brain-damaged individual with a very impaired phonological loop. Patient PV (a native Italian speaker) was a woman who suffered a left hemisphere stroke at the age of 26. As a result, she had a selective impairment of auditory memory span, with a digit span of only two items but good long-term memory. Somewhat surprisingly, PV coped very well with everyday life, including running a shop and raising a family.

One function of the phonological loop that Baddeley and colleagues expected was assistance in understanding sentences. Indeed, to interpret sentences, relationships must be established between words that are sometimes quite far apart. Surprisingly, patient PV did not show many problems understanding spoken sentences, unless they were very long and syntactically complex (Vallar & Baddeley, 1984), indicating that the contribution of the phonological loop to sentence processing in daily life is limited.

Another function of the phonological loop could be related to the acquisition of words. Before meanings are known, words consist of series of unrelated syllables, certainly when they are long words. Suppose someone tells you about "witenagemot." They excitedly tell you that it was a council of powerful nobles who convened to advise and appoint kings in medieval England, and that the word was used by JK Rowling as inspiration to coin the name of the high court in the Harry Potter books, "Wizengamot" (a blend of "wizarding" and "witenagemot"). For you to learn the new word, you have to connect the new knowledge to the ordered sequence of syllables *wit·e·na·ge·mot* stored in the phonological loop. The reason why PV did not show difficulties in language understanding was that she already had acquired the words she needed in her daily life before she suffered the stroke.

On the basis of this reasoning, Baddeley et al. (1988) predicted that PV would have difficulties learning new words. Indeed, she performed as well as healthy participants when learning to associate pairs of unrelated words in Italian. However, her performance was dramatically inferior to that of healthy controls when learning to associate Russian words with their Italian translations. Indeed, she showed no learning at all over 10 trials!

The notion that the phonological loop is useful when learning new words received further support from Papagno et al. (1991). Native Italian speakers learned pairs of Italian words and pairs of Italian-Russian words. Articulatory suppression (repeating an irrelevant sound) greatly slowed down the learning of foreign vocabulary. However, it had little effect on the learning of pairs of Italian words. Thus, the negative effects of articulatory suppression on learning were limited to new words.

Andersson (2010) studied language comprehension in Swedish children. Phonological loop processes predicted the children's comprehension performance when reading a text in their foreign language (English) but not in their native language (Swedish). Why was this the case? An efficient phonological loop is more important when reading in a foreign language because of the greater difficulty in working out how to pronounce the words.

So, one of the reasons why we need a phonological loop is that otherwise we would not be able to learn new words initially consisting of arbitrary sequences of unrelated sounds and syllables. Young children learn several new words per day, and even adults learn a new word every other day (Brysbaert et al., 2016).

VISUO-SPATIAL SKETCHPAD

The phonological loop is a slave system to temporarily hold verbal data while processing information. Baddeley and Hitch (1974) postulated that there would be a similar slave system for visual and spatial data: a visuo-spatial sketchpad. In line with the phonological loop, Logie (1995) hypothesized that the visuo-spatial sketchpad would consist of two components:

- a passive *visual cache*, which stores information about visual forms and their location
- an *inner scribe*, which refreshes the information in the visual cache and transfers information from the cache to the central executive

The visuo-spatial sketchpad is used for the temporary storage and manipulation of visual patterns and spatial movement. In essence, visual processing involves remembering *what* and spatial processing involves remembering *where*. The visuo-spatial sketchpad is very useful in everyday life – we use it to find the route when moving from one place to another (Logie & Della Sala, 2005) or when watching television (Toms et al., 1994).

We also use the visuo-spatial sketchpad when playing computer games. Logie et al. (1989) studied performance on a complex computer game called *Space Fortress*, which involves maneuvering a space ship around a computer screen. Performance on *Space Fortress* was severely impaired early in training when participants had to perform an additional visuo-spatial task at the same time, but less so thereafter. Thus, the visuo-spatial sketchpad was used throughout training on *Space Fortress*, but its involvement decreased with practice.

Logie et al. (2000) wondered whether the visuo-spatial sketchpad also contributed to performance in the word span task. Remember that previous research showed the influence of word length and phonological similarity in this task (which was the reason why Baddeley and Hitch equated the existing short-term memory research with the *phonological* loop). Logie et al. presented series of words on a computer screen shown at a rate of one per second, and they asked participants to recall them. All words were phonologically similar, but one group was also orthographically similar (fly, ply, cry, dry, try, shy), whereas the other group was orthographically dissimilar (guy, thai, sigh, lie, pi, rye). Logie et al. found that performance was better with the second group of words than with the first group, suggesting that the visual information contained in the spellings of the words contributes to good performance in a word span task with visually presented words.

What is the capacity of the visuo-spatial sketchpad? There are good reasons to think it can hold about four items (Vogel et al., 2001; Xu & Chun, 2009). Vogel et al. (2001) presented a display of between 3 and 12 objects. After 900 ms, a second display (identical to the first or with one object changed) was presented. Participants' ability to decide whether the two displays were identical was almost perfect with four objects. Performance declined progressively as the number of items in the display increased above four.

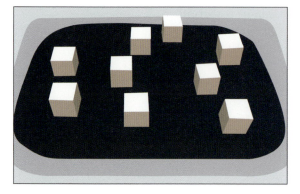

Figure 4.8 The Corsi blocks test.

Another test often used to measure the capacity of the visuo-spatial sketchpad is the **Corsi blocks test**. In this test, the participants are shown some blocks on a table (as in Figure 4.8). The experimenter touches the blocks in a particular sequence, which the participant must repeat. The test starts with a sequence of two blocks, and the length is increased until the participant makes mistakes. The memory span is defined as the longest sequence the participant can indicate with less than 50% mistakes. Capitani et al. (1991) compared the performance of men and women in the general population: men had a Corsi span of 5.2 blocks, whereas women had a span of 4.9. The difference was significant. Vandierendonck et al. (2004) tested university undergraduates and reported a Corsi span of 6.0 blocks, which was not significantly reduced under articulatory suppression, when the participants continuously had to say "the the the," in line with the idea that the visuo-spatial sketchpad and the phonological loop are two independent slave systems.

A single system?

The $64,000 question concerning the visuo-spatial sketchpad is as follows: are visual and spatial processing combined in a *single* system? Much evidence indicates that there are important differences between them. For example, blind people are generally good at using spatial information to move around even though they can't engage in visual processing. Indeed, Fortin et al. (2008) actually found that blind individuals were *better* than sighted ones at learning routes through human-size mazes.

Blind individuals probably performed so well in the study by Fortin et al. (2008) because of their extensive practice in spatial processing. Support for that interpretation comes from another finding reported by Fortin et al. – the hippocampus (see Glossary) was larger in the blind than in the sighted participants. The relevance of this is that the hippocampus is involved in spatial processing.

Further evidence that the visuo-spatial sketchpad consists of *separate* spatial and visual components was reported by Klauer and Zhao (2004). There were two main tasks. One was a spatial task (memory for dot locations) and the other a visual task (memory for Chinese characters). Sometimes the main task was performed with a color discrimination task to provide visual interference. At other times, it was performed with a movement discrimination task to provide spatial interference.

What would we predict if there were separate spatial and visual components? First, the spatial interference task should disrupt performance more on the spatial main task than on the visual main task. Second, the visual interference task should disrupt performance more on the visual main task than on the spatial main task. Both of these predictions were confirmed (see Figure 4.9).

Studies in cognitive neuroscience also indicate that visual and spatial processing involve different brain regions. Smith and Jonides (1997) carried out an ingenious study in which two visual stimuli were presented together followed by a probe stimulus. Participants decided whether the probe was in the

Key term

Corsi blocks test: a test with blocks that must be pointed to according to predefined sequences; used to measure the capacity of the visuo-spatial sketchpad.

same location as one of the initial stimuli (spatial task) or had the same form (visual task). Even though the stimuli were identical in the two tasks, there were clear differences in patterns of brain activation. There was more activity in the *right* hemisphere during the spatial task than the visual task. However, there was more activity in the *left* hemisphere during the visual task than the spatial one.

Zimmer (2008) reviewed findings on the brain areas associated with visual and spatial processing. Areas within the occipital and temporal lobes were activated during visual imagery tasks. In contrast, areas within the parietal cortex (especially the intraparietal sulcus) were activated during spatial imagery tasks.

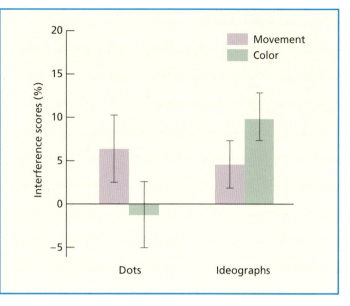

Figure 4.9   Amount of interference on a spatial task (dots) and a visual task (Chinese ideographs) as a function of secondary task (spatial: movement vs. visual: color discrimination).
Source: From Klauer and Zhao (2004). Reprinted with permission from the American Psychological Association.

CENTRAL EXECUTIVE

The central executive (which resembles an attentional system) is the most important and versatile component of the working memory system (it is also the least understood; Logie, 2016). It is involved in processes such as planning and coordination, but it doesn't store information. The central executive is also involved in inhibitory processes that prevent our attention to a task being distracted by irrelevant stimuli such as the sound of a television (Miyake et al., 2000; Friedman & Miyake, 2004). Every time we engage in any complex cognitive activity, such as reading a text or solving a problem, we make extensive use of the central executive.

Parts of the prefrontal cortex are much involved in the functions of the central executive. Mottaghy (2006) reviewed studies using repetitive transcranial magnetic stimulation to disrupt activity within the dorsolateral prefrontal cortex. Performance on many complex cognitive tasks was impaired by this manipulation, indicating that the dorsolateral prefrontal cortex is of importance in central executive functioning. However, it is *not* the only area involved. Patients with damage to the prefrontal cortex don't always show executive deficits, and some patients with no damage to the prefrontal cortex nevertheless have executive deficits (Andrés, 2003).

Executive functions

As can be guessed on the basis of its name, the central executive controls the so-called executive functions. **Executive functions** refer to a set of cognitive skills needed to control and coordinate our cognitive abilities and behaviors. These functions are essential for *goal-directed behavior*. They include the following skills:

- activating a goal and keeping it active,
- selecting the right information and actions to achieve the goal,

Key term

Executive functions: set of cognitive skills used to control and coordinate cognitive abilities and behaviors.

- suppressing irrelevant information and actions,
- taking into account the context in which the task must be performed and specific requirements because of the context,
- detecting errors and correcting them.

Miyake et al. (2000) argued that the executive skills can be grouped under three functions:

1. mental set shifting (shifting between tasks, e.g., by deactivating the present goal and activating a new goal),
2. updating and monitoring of working memory representations (needed to achieve the goal),
3. inhibition of irrelevant dominant or prepotent responses (in order not to be distracted from the goal and its achievement).

We can gain some understanding of the importance of executive functions in our everyday lives by studying brain-damaged patients whose central executive is impaired. Such individuals suffer from **dysexecutive syndrome** (Baddeley, 2007), which involves problems with planning, organizing, monitoring behavior, and initiating behavior. Patients with dysexecutive syndrome typically have damage within the prefrontal cortex, but some have damage to posterior (mainly parietal) regions (Andrés, 2003). Unsurprisingly, sufferers from dysexecutive syndrome have great problems in holding down a job and functioning adequately in everyday life (Chamberlain, 2003).

Executive functions are also impaired in several groups of patients. Heinrichs and Zakzanis (1998), for instance, reported that persons with schizophrenia have diminished executive functions. Willcutt et al. (2005) reported the same for people with ADHD (see Glossary).

The notion of a dysexecutive syndrome implies that brain damage to the frontal lobes typically impairs *all* central executive functions. That is often the case with patients having widespread damage to the frontal lobes, but is *not* true of patients with more specific brain damage. Stuss and Alexander (2007) argued that the three major executive processes outlined by Miyake et al. (2000) are based in different parts of the frontal lobes, although they used slightly different names for the processes:

- *Task setting*: This involves relatively simple planning of the upcoming task.
- *Monitoring*: This involves checking that the current task is being performed adequately.
- *Energization*: This involves sustained attention or concentration.

Many patients with specific brain damage have problems largely limited to one of these processes. Problems with task setting were associated with damage to the left lateral frontal region, problems with monitoring with damage to the right lateral frontal region, and problems with energization with damage to the superior medial region of the frontal cortex.

In sum, the central executive consists of various functions, three of which are task setting, monitoring, and energization (or inhibition of interference). Note, however, that many complex cognitive tasks require all three functions at different stages of task performance.

EPISODIC BUFFER

As we have seen, the central executive plays a major role in the processing of many different kinds of information. However, it doesn't possess any storage capacity. That led Baddeley (2000) to add a fourth component to his theory. The episodic buffer is a limited-capacity storage system used to briefly store information from the phonological loop, the visuo-spatial sketchpad, and long-term memory (Repovš & Baddeley, 2006).

According to Baddeley (2007), the complexities of integrating several different kinds of information mean there are close links between the episodic buffer and the central executive. If so, we would expect to find prefrontal activation on tasks involving the episodic buffer. This is because the prefrontal cortex is typically activated during tasks requiring the central executive.

The usefulness of the episodic buffer can be seen in a study by Baddeley and Wilson (2002) on immediate recall of prose. It used to be argued that good immediate prose recall involves the ability to store relevant information in long-term memory. According to this position, amnesic patients with very impaired long-term memory should have very poor immediate prose recall.

In contrast, Baddeley and Wilson argued that the ability to show good immediate recall of prose depends on two factors: (1) the capacity of the episodic buffer and (2) an efficiently functioning central executive creating and maintaining information in the buffer. It follows that even severely amnesic patients should have good immediate prose recall provided their central executive is efficient. As predicted, immediate prose recall was much better in amnesics having little deficit in executive functioning than in those with a severe executive deficit.

Darling and Havelka (2010) asked participants to recall random digits in the correct order. The digits were presented visually all to the same location, or arranged along a horizontal line, or on a keypad resembling the layout on a cell or mobile phone. It was assumed that performance would be best in the keypad condition. In that condition, visual information (digits) and spatial information based on the familiar keypad layout could be integrated in the episodic buffer. As predicted, serial recall was best in the keypad condition.

In sum, the episodic buffer helps to provide the "glue" to integrate information within working memory. As such, it fulfills a valuable function. As yet, however, we lack a detailed account of how this integration process works.

UNITARY-STORE ALTERNATIVE

In recent years, various theorists (e.g., Cowan, 2001; Postle, 2006; Jonides et al., 2008) have argued that the separation between working memory and long-term memory is misguided and should be replaced by a unitary-store model. The basic assumption in this model is that working memory is simply the part of long-term memory activated at any given moment. Thus, whereas Baddeley and Hitch's model emphasizes the *differences* between working memory and long-term memory, advocates of the unitary-store approach emphasize the *similarities*.

Short-term memory is long-term memory that is attended to

Processing within working memory is often heavily influenced by information from long-term memory. For instance, Ruchkin et al. (1999) reported that semantic [meaning] information from long-term memory affects processing in a typical short-term memory task. They presented verbal stimuli aurally, followed by serial recall. Some of the stimuli were existing words; others were sound sequences sounding like words but not part of the vocabulary (these are so-called pseudowords, like "koor" or "deeph"). If participants had processed only information about the sounds of the stimuli in the phonological loop (or short-term memory), brain activity would have been very similar for words and pseudowords. In fact, there was much more brain activity associated with words than with pseudowords. This suggests that semantic information from long-term memory was processed when the words were presented.

According to the unitary-store idea, there is no separation between working memory and long-term memory. The basic hypothesis is that short-term memory (or working memory) consists of long-term memory representations in the focus of attention. This is how Postle (2006, p. 29) formulates it:

The view that will be advanced here is that working memory functions are produced when attention is directed to systems that have evolved to accomplish sensory-, representation-, or action-related functions. From this perspective, working memory may simply be a property that emerges from a nervous system that is capable of representing many different kinds of information, and that is endowed with flexibly deployable attention.

The main reasons why authors no longer feel happy about the Baddeley and Hitch model of working memory are that (1) there do not seem to be brain areas specifically dedicated to working memory, and (2) the brain areas activated in working memory tasks strongly resemble those related to the type of information processed. The latter is a problem, according to Postle (2006), because it means that the working memory model should be subdivided into an ever increasing number of subcomponents.

We already discussed the evidence suggesting that the visuospatial sketchpad should be divided into a visual part and a spatial part. Other extra independent slave systems that would be required, according to Postle (2006), are:

- for egocentric vs. allocentric spatial working memory (i.e., space related to oneself vs. space related to other points of view),
- for various types of visual stimuli,
- for various aspects of language processing,
- for loudness, pitch, and location of auditory stimuli,
- for tactile and olfactory stimuli.

Given that all these stimuli would seem to require a further fractioning of the working memory model, it becomes doubtful whether the model still is realistic. One of the attractions of the Baddeley and Hitch model was that it could be separated into a *small* number of distinct parts.

Ma et al. (2014) pointed to another shortcoming of multistore models. These models assume that short-term memory is based on a system with a limited number of slots (be they 7±2 in Miller's view or 4±1 in Cowan's). Items in such slots are either present or absent and do not compete with each other until the store is filled. These predictions do not agree with empirical findings suggesting that the capacity of working memory is smaller for items encoded with high precision and larger for items encoded with less precision.

In addition, in many short-term memory tasks not all items are encoded with the same precision. Some are more salient and goal-relevant than others, and they seem to be encoded with more precision. Such a resource-limited view of working memory (rather than a slot-limited view) is more in line with a unitary approach than with a multiple components approach.

Challenges

A weakness of the unitary approach is that thus far no clear model has been proposed with a status similar to that of Baddeley and Hitch's working memory model. Up to now, the account mainly consisted of pointing to problems with the working memory model, without offering a detailed alternative.

One challenge the unitary approach will have to overcome is to explain why most amnesic patients have intact short-term memory in spite of severe problems with long-term memory. Jonides et al. (2008) argued that this pattern emerged because the short-term memory tasks used in the studies were too easy. They claimed that amnesic patients *would* show impaired short-term memory if the memory task were sufficiently complex.

Shrager et al. (2008) tested the prediction using various tasks in which memory was assessed after a short retention interval. Amnesic patients were significantly impaired compared to healthy controls on some tasks but not on others. However, the memory tasks on which amnesic patients performed poorly all involved long-term memory as well as short-term memory. As a result, Shrager et al. concluded that short-term memory processes are intact in amnesic patients. The patients only show impaired performance when so-called short-term memory tasks actually depend on long-term memory.

A second challenge for the unitary-store approach is to explain the processing component of working memory. Remember that working memory is more than short-term storage or activation of information. Baddeley (2007), for example, argued that the unitary account must be able to explain how people can generate novel visual images to stimuli in short-term memory (Logie & van der Meulen, 2009), and how they can also generate solutions to arithmetic problems that are not stored in long-term memory. According to Baddeley (2007), the processing component of working memory requires a system that does not coincide with memory traces activated in long-term memory.

Section summary

Working memory model
• According to Baddeley, the working memory system consists of a central executive, phonological loop, visuo-spatial sketchpad, and episodic buffer. All of these components have limited capacity but can function fairly independently of each other.

Simultaneous interpreting
• Simultaneous interpreting makes substantial demands on working memory because it involves several different processes in rapid succession. Switching from one language to another requires inhibitory control processes, and it is more demanding to translate from the dominant language into the

weaker one. Simultaneous interpreters tend to have greater working memory capacity than other people.

Phonological loop
- The involvement of the phonological loop in short-term memory is shown by the phonological similarity and word-length effects. The phonological loop is very useful when learning and comprehending new words or a foreign language.

Visuo-spatial sketchpad
- The visuo-spatial sketchpad is used when moving from one place to another and when playing computer games. It consists of separate visual and spatial components involving different brain areas.
- A test often used to measure the capacity of the visuo-spatial sketchpad is the Corsi blocks test.

Central executive
- The central executive is an attention-like system used with numerous complex cognitive tasks. Patients with dysexecutive syndrome have extensive damage to the prefrontal cortex and other areas. This causes severely impaired executive functions and major disruptions to their everyday lives. Task setting, monitoring, and energization/inhibition of interference are three of the main functions of the central executive.

Episodic buffer
- The episodic buffer is used to integrate and briefly store information from long-term memory and the other working memory components. It is an important component of the working memory system, but its workings remain somewhat unclear.

Unitary-store approach
- According to unitary-store theorists, the information in working memory is the fraction of long-term memory currently activated. One problem with this theory is that amnesic patients have intact short-term memory in spite of having very poor long-term memory. Another challenge is to explain how we can manipulate information in working memory in complex ways involving more than the mere activation of information in long-term memory.

WORKING MEMORY CAPACITY

So far we have focused mainly on the theoretical approach to working memory pioneered by Baddeley and Hitch (1974). Of central importance within that approach is the notion that the working memory system consists of four somewhat separate components.

Research on working memory received extra impetus, when it was discovered that individuals differ in their working memory capacity and that these differences correlate with intelligence.

Again, the origin of the discovery goes back to Jacobs (1887), who reported that the short-term memory span was longer in the high-achieving children of a class than in the low-achieving children. This observation was incorporated (though not acknowledged!) in the first intelligence test published in France by Binet and Simon (1907) and in many intelligence tests since. Most often, the digit span test is used.

The observation that short-term memory capacity correlates with intellectual functioning makes sense if we assume that short-term memory is used while we are processing information. Some individuals are better at storing and remembering this information and can function at a higher level.

Working memory is more than short-term memory, however. It does not rely solely on the passive maintenance of verbal information (the task of the phonological loop). It also involves the manipulation of information and the need to retain information while processing other information. *How* can we assess such working memory capacity?

MEASURING WORKING MEMORY CAPACITY

One of the first ways to make a more dynamic version of the memory span task was to ask participants to recall the items in a different order than the one in which the items were presented. An often used test is the *reverse digit span test*. Participants have to repeat the sequence of digits in the reverse order. For example, after hearing the sequence 6-1-5-8-3, you would have to say 3-8-5-1-6. In general, the reverse digit span test correlates slightly more with other measures of intelligence than the original digit span test (e.g., Woods et al., 2011).

A major breakthrough in measuring working memory capacity was devised by Daneman and Carpenter (1980). People are asked to read several sentences for comprehension (processing task) and then to recall the final word of each sentence (storage task). The largest number of sentences from which an individual can recall the final words more than 50% of the time is his/her reading span. An individual's reading span is taken as a measure of his/her working memory capacity.

Daneman and Carpenter assumed the processes used in comprehending the sentences require a smaller proportion of the available working memory capacity of those with a large capacity. As a result, these people have more capacity available for retaining the last words of the sentences. In line with their hypothesis, Daneman and Carpenter observed that participants with a high reading span answered more questions correctly after reading a text than participants with a low reading span. In contrast, there was a much smaller difference in text comprehension between participants with a high short-term memory word span and participants with a low span.

Various other ways of assessing working memory capacity have been devised. Turner and Engle (1989), for instance, presented participants with a series of items such as "IS (4 × 2) − 3 = 5? E." The participants had to answer each arithmetical question and remember the letter. Again the number of items per sequence is varied, and the average number of items from which an individual can recall the words is defined as the operation span. The operation and reading span of individuals look very similar and measure the same construct of working memory capacity (Unsworth et al., 2014). On average, participants can remember some five words or letters.

Key terms

Reading span:
the greatest number of sentences read for comprehension for which an individual can recall all the final words more than 50% of the time.

Operation span:
the maximum number of items (arithmetical questions + words) for which an individual can recall all the last words.

Key term

Correlation coefficient: statistical measure to indicate how two variables are related; goes from -1.0 to +1.0. Positive values mean that both variables vary in the same direction (when one increases, the other increases as well); negative values mean that both variables vary in opposite directions (when one increases, the other decreases). The closer the values are to +1.0 or -1.0, the stronger the correlation, the better we can predict one variable on the basis of the other. Values around 0 indicate that the variables are independent; it is not possible to predict one on the basis of the other.

WORKING MEMORY CAPACITY AND INTELLIGENCE

Individuals high in working memory capacity perform most intelligence-related tasks better than those of low capacity. In the previous section we saw that students with a high working memory capacity remembered more from a text they just read than students with a low working memory capacity.

The degree of correspondence between two test scores is usually expressed as a **correlation coefficient**. A correlation coefficient varies between -1.0 and +1.0. A correlation of +1.0 means that two variables differ in the same direction and that you can perfectly predict one variable if you know the other. A correlation of -1.0 also means that you can perfectly predict one variable if you know the other, but now the variables move in opposite directions (when one goes up, the other goes down). A correlation of 0.0 means the two variables are not related to each other and you cannot better predict one if you know the other.

Rephrased into correlation coefficients, Daneman and Carpenter obtained a correlation of +0.7 between the reading span of their participants and knowledge about facts after reading a text. In contrast, they obtained a much lower correlation of +0.4 between the short-term memory word span of their participants and knowledge about facts after reading. So, a person's performance on the text comprehension task could better be predicted on the basis of the reading span task than on the basis of the short-term memory word span task. Unsworth et al. (2014) observed a correlation of +0.72 between the reading span and the operation span of their participants.

How strong is the relationship between working memory capacity and general intelligence? Conway et al. (2003) reviewed the relevant research. The typical correlation between working memory capacity and general intelligence was moderately high ($r = +0.5$ to $r = +0.6$). Thus, individuals with greater working memory capacity are generally more intelligent than those with smaller capacity (see also Redick et al., 2012), but it is not the case that all persons with an operation span of 6 score higher on an intelligence test than all persons with an operation span of 4 (for this to be the case, the correlation should have been higher).

Fluid intelligence vs. crystallized intelligence

A distinction often made in intelligence research is between fluid intelligence and crystallized intelligence. *Fluid intelligence* involves a rapid understanding and manipulation of novel information and is used in tasks such as reasoning and math problem solving. *Crystallized intelligence* depends on knowledge and expertise stored in long-term memory and is typically assessed with vocabulary tests or tests about general knowledge.

As can be expected, Unsworth (2010) found that working memory was more strongly related to fluid intelligence ($r = +0.53$) than to crystallized intelligence ($r = 0.18$). Working memory capacity has more impact on processing new information than on retrieving stored information from long-term memory.

In general, fluid memory decreases as people get older (because their thinking becomes slower), whereas crystallized intelligence stays the same and in some areas even increases (because older people have more information stored in long-term memory). If working memory capacity is involved in fluid intelligence, we would expect to see a decrease in working memory spans as people get older. Sylvain-Roy et al. (2014) indeed reported that older adults (on average 70 years) performed worse than younger adults (24 years on average) on a reading span task.

CAN WORKING MEMORY CAPACITY BE TRAINED?

A correlation of +0.6 between working memory capacity and fluid intelligence tells us that both variables are correlated, but not what causes the correlation. We don't really know whether having high working memory capacity causes a high level of intelligence or whether a high level of intelligence produces high working memory capacity. In addition, it is possible that a third variable causes the correlation, just like a third variable causes the positive correlation between the number of ice creams sold at the beach and the number of people that need to be saved from drowning (people do not need to be saved because they ate ice cream, nor do people need ice cream because they have been saved, but on warm days there are many people on the beach eating ice cream and occasionally in need of help). Correlations tell us that there is a relationship, but they do not inform us about the nature of the relationship.

One way in which we would have more evidence that differences in working memory capacity *cause* differences in intelligence is if working memory training had a positive effect on intelligence. If we can increase working memory capacity by training people on working memory tasks, and if this has a positive effect on their intellectual functioning, then we would feel surer that high working memory capacity causes a high level of intelligence. In addition, it would have important societal value if we could boost the intelligence of people by giving them a working memory training program.

The first results were promising: people trained on working memory tasks became better at these tasks and seemed to perform better on intelligence tests as well (Jaeggi et al., 2008; Holmes et al., 2009). However, recent reviews are more critical. Training working memory tasks improves performance on the tasks trained but does not generalize well to other working memory tasks or fluid intelligence tasks (Shipstead et al., 2012; Au et al., 2015).

At present, it is not clear to what extent the limited impact of working memory training is due to the fact that working memory capacity cannot be increased by training (e.g., because it is constrained by biological factors) or to the fact that differences in working memory capacity do not cause differences in fluid intelligence, even though both variables are correlated (just like at sea you would not decrease the number of people that need to be saved by no longer selling ice creams). It is a much researched topic, however. So, you may want to search for papers on the issue that have been published in the past year!

Section summary

Measuring working memory capacity
- Measures of working memory capacity require processing and brief storage of information. Two measures often used are the reading span and the operation span.

Working memory capacity and intelligence

- People scoring high on reading span tests and operation span tests often have higher intelligence scores (especially on tests for fluid intelligence).

Can working memory capacity be trained?

- Researchers are investigating whether it is possible to boost intelligence by training working memory. At first, the data looked promising, but more recent evaluations are more pessimistic. It is not clear whether the small effect is because working memory capacity cannot be increased via training or because working memory capacity does not have a causal influence on intelligence.

Essay questions

1. How can we assess the capacity of short-term memory?
2. Describe the theoretical approach to working memory proposed by Baddeley and Hitch.
3. In what ways is the central executive the most important component of the working memory system?
4. How separate are visual and spatial processes within the visuo-spatial sketchpad?
5. What are some of the main cognitive differences between individuals who are high and low in working memory capacity?

Further reading

- Baddeley, A. (2012). Working memory: theories, models, and controversies. *Annual Review of Psychology*, *63*, 1–29. In this article, Baddeley describes some of the more recent developments in his working memory model. Presents interesting (but more complicated) updates to the current chapter.
- Baddeley, A., Eysenck, M. W., & Anderson, M. C. (2015). *Memory* (2nd ed.). New York, NY: Psychology Press. Chapters 3 and 4 of this textbook provide detailed coverage of short-term memory and working memory.
- Cowan, N. (2005). *Working memory capacity*. Hove, UK: Psychology Press. The various theoretical perspectives on working memory capacity are discussed at length by Nelson Cowan.
- Jonides, J., Lewis, R. L., Nee, D. E., Lustig, C. A., Berman, M. G., & Moore, K. S. (2008). The mind and brain of short-term memory. *Annual Review of Psychology*, *59*, 193–224. The authors discuss short-term memory at length and compare the multistore and unitary-store models.
- Unsworth, N., Fukuda, K., Awh, E., & Vogel, E. K. (2014). Working memory and fluid intelligence: Capacity, attention control, and secondary memory retrieval. *Cognitive Psychology*, *71*, 1–26. In this article, Nash Unsworth and colleagues put forward a model to link individual differences in working memory capacity to differences in fluid intelligence.

REFERENCES

Abutalebi, J., & Green, D. W. (2008). Control mechanisms in bilingual language production: Neural evidence from language switching studies. *Language and Cognitive Processes*, 23, 557–582.

Albir, A. H., & Alves, F. (2009). Translation as a cognitive activity. In J. Munday (Ed.), *The Routledge companion to translation studies*. London, UK: Routledge.

Andersson, U. (2010). The contribution of working memory capacity to foreign language comprehension in children. *Memory*, 18, 456–472.

Andrés, P. (2003). Frontal cortex as the central executive of working memory: Time to revise our view. *Cortex*, 39, 871–895.

Atkinson, R. C., & Shiffrin, R. M. (1968). Human memory: A proposed system and its control processes. In K. W. Spence & J. T. Spence (Eds.), *The psychology of learning and motivation* (Vol. 2). London, UK: Academic Press.

Au, J., Sheehan, E., Tsai, N., Duncan, G. J., Buschkuehl, M., & Jaeggi, S. M. (2015). Improving fluid intelligence with training on working memory: A meta-analysis. *Psychonomic Bulletin & Review*, 22(2), 366–377.

Baddeley, A. D. (2000). The episodic buffer: A new component of working memory? *Trends in Cognitive Sciences*, 4, 417–423.

Baddeley, A. D. (2007). *Working memory, thought and action*. Oxford, UK: Oxford University Press.

Baddeley, A. (2012). Working memory: Theories, models, and controversies. *Annual Review of Psychology*, 63, 1–29.

Baddeley, A. D., Papagno, C., & Vallar, G. (1988). When long-term learning depends on short-term storage. *Journal of Memory and Language*, 27, 586–595.

Berman, M. G., Jonides, J., & Lewis, R. L. (2009). In search of decay in verbal short-term memory. *Journal of Experimental Psychology: Learning, Memory, & Cognition*, 35, 317–333.

Binet, A., & Simon, T. (1907). Le développement de l'intelligence chez les enfants. *L'Année Psychologique*, 14, 1–94.

Broadbent, D. E. (1958). *Perception and communication*. Oxford, UK: Pergamon.

Brysbaert, M., Stevens, S., Mandera, P., & Keuleers, E. (2016). How many words do we know? Practical estimates of vocabulary size dependent on word definition, the degree of language input and the participant's age. *Frontiers in Psychology*, 7:1116.

Capitani, E., Laiacona, M., & Ciceri, E. (1991). Sex differences in spatial memory: A reanalysis of block tapping long-term memory according to the short-term memory level. *The Italian Journal of Neurological Sciences*, 12(4), 461–466.

Carlesimo, G. A., Marfia, G. A., Loasses, A., & Caltagirone, C. (1996). Perceptual and conceptual components in implicit and explicit stem completion. *Neuropsychologia*, 34, 785–792.

Chamberlain, E. (2003). Review of "Behavioral assessment of the dysexecutive syndrome (BADS)." *Journal of Occupational Psychology*, 5, 33–37.

Chekaf, M., Cowan, N., & Mathy, F. (2016). Chunk formation in immediate memory and how it relates to data compression. *Cognition*, 155, 96–107.

Chen, Z., & Cowan, N. (2009). Core verbal working memory capacity: The limit in words retained without covert articulation. *Quarterly Journal of Experimental Psychology*, 62, 1420–1429.

Christoffels, I. K. (2006). Listening while talking: The retention of prose under articulatory suppression in relation to simultaneous interpreting. *European Journal of Cognitive Psychology*, 18, 206–220.

Christoffels, I. K., de Groot, A. M. B., & Kroll, J. F. (2006). Memory and language skills in simultaneous interpreters: The role of expertise and language proficiency. *Journal of Memory and Language*, 54, 324–345.

Conway, A. R. A., Kane, M. J., & Engle, R. W. (2003). Working memory capacity and its relation to general intelligence. *Trends in Cognitive Sciences*, 7, 547–552.

Cowan, N. (2001). The magical number 4 in short-term memory: A reconsideration of mental storage capacity. *Behavioral and Brain Sciences*, 24(1), 87–114.

Cowan, N., Elliott, E. M., Saults, J. S., Morey, C. C., Mattox, S., Hismjatullina, A., & Conway, A. R. A. (2005). On the capacity of attention: Its estimation and its role in working memory and cognitive aptitudes. *Cognitive Psychology*, 51, 42–100.

Craik, F. I. M., & Watkins, M. J. (1973). The role of rehearsal in short-term memory. *Journal of Verbal Learning and Verbal Behavior*, 12(6), 599–607.

Daneman, M., & Carpenter, P. A. (1980). Individual differences in working memory and reading. *Journal of Verbal Learning and Verbal Behavior*, 19, 450–466.

Darling, S., & Havelka, J. (2010). Visuo-spatial bootstrapping: Evidence for binding of verbal and spatial information in working memory. *Quarterly Journal of Experimental Psychology*, 63, 239–245.

De Rammelaere, S., Stuyven, E., & Vandierendonck, A. (2001). Verifying simple arithmetic sums and products: Are the phonological loop and the central executive involved? *Memory & Cognition*, 29(2), 267–273.

DeStefano, D., & LeFevre, J. A. (2004). The role of working memory in mental arithmetic. *European Journal of Cognitive Psychology*, 16(3), 353–386.

Ellis, N. C., & Hennelly, R. A. (1980). A bilingual word-length effect: Implications for intelligence testing and the relative ease of mental calculation in Welsh and English. *British Journal of Psychology*, 71(1), 43–51.

Farrell, S. (2010). Dissociating conditional recency in immediate and delayed free recall: A challenge for unitary models of recency. *Journal of Experimental Psychology: Learning, Memory & Cognition*, 36, 324–347.

Fortin, M., Voss, P., Lord, C., Lassande, M., Pruessner, J., Saint-Arnour, D., et al. (2008). Wayfinding in the blind: Large hippocampal volume and supranormal spatial navigation. *Brain*, 131, 2995–3005.

Friedman, N. P., & Miyake, A. (2004). The relations among inhibition and interference control functions: A latent variable analysis. *Journal of Experimental Psychology: General*, 133, 101–135.

Gathercole, S. E., Pickering, S. J., Ambridge, B., & Wearing, H. (2004). The structure of working memory from 4 to 15 years of age. *Developmental Psychology*, 40(2), 177–190.

Glanzer, M., & Cunitz, A. R. (1966). Two storage mechanisms in free recall. *Journal of Verbal Learning and Verbal Behavior*, 5, 351–360.

Heinrichs, R. W., & Zakzanis, K. K. (1998). Neurocognitive deficit in schizophrenia: A quantitative review of the evidence. *Neuropsychology*, 12(3), 426–445.

Holmes, J., Gathercole, S. E., & Dunning, D. L. (2009). Adaptive training leads to sustained enhancement of poor working memory in children. *Developmental Science*, 12(4), F9–F15.

Jacobs, J. (1887). Experiments in "prehension." *Mind*, 12, 75–79.

Jaeggi, S. M., Buschkuehl, M., Jonides, J., & Perrig, W. J. (2008). Improving fluid intelligence with training on working memory. *Proceedings of the National Academy of Sciences*, 105(19), 6829–6833.

Jonides, M. G., Lewis, R. L., Nee, D. E., Lustig, C. A., Berman, M. G., & Moore, K. S. (2008). The mind and brain of short-term memory. *Annual Review of Psychology*, 59, 193–224.

Keppel, G., & Underwood, B. J. (1962). Proactive inhibition in short-term retention of single items. *Journal of Verbal Learning and Verbal Behavior*, 1, 153–161.

Klauer, K. C., & Zhao, Z. (2004). Double dissociations in visual and spatial short-term memory. *Journal of Experimental Psychology: General*, 133, 355–381.

Larsen, J. D., Baddeley, A., & Andrade, J. (2000). Phonological similarity and the irrelevant speech effect: Implications for models of short-term memory. *Memory*, *8*, 145–157.

Lewandowsky, S., & Oberauer, K. (2015). Rehearsal in serial recall: An unworkable solution to the nonexistent problem of decay. *Psychological Review*, *122*(4), 674–699.

Logie, R. H. (1995). *Visuo-spatial working-memory*. Hillsdale, NJ: Lawrence Erlbaum.

Logie, R. H. (2016). Retiring the central executive. *The Quarterly Journal of Experimental Psychology*, *69*(10), 2093–2109.

Logie, R. H., & Della Sala, S. (2005). *Disorders of visuo-spatial working memory*. New York, NY: Cambridge University Press.

Logie, R. H., & van der Meulen, M. (2009). Fragmenting and integrating visuo-spatial working memory. In J. R. Brockmole (Ed.), *Representing the visual world in memory*. Hove, UK: Psychology Press.

Logie, R. H., Del Sala, S., Wynn, V., & Baddeley, A. D. (2000). Visual similarity effects in immediate verbal serial recall. *The Quarterly Journal of Experimental Psychology: Section A*, *53*(3), 626–646.

Logie, R. H., Baddeley, A. D., Mane, A., Donchin, E., & Sheptak, R. (1989). Working memory and the analysis of a complex skill by secondary task methodology. *Acta Psychologica*, *71*, 53–87.

Ma, W. J., Husain, M., & Bays, P. M. (2014). Changing concepts of working memory. *Nature Neuroscience*, *17*(3), 347–356.

Miller, G. A. (1956). The magical number seven, plus or minus two: Some limits on our capacity for processing information. *Psychological Review*, *63*, 81–97.

Miyake, A., Friedman, N. P., Emerson, M. J., Witzki, A. H., Howerter, A., & Wager, T. (2000). The unity and diversity of executive functions and their contributions to complex "frontal lobe" tasks: A latent variable analysis. *Cognitive Psychology*, *41*, 49–100.

Mottaghy, F. M. (2006). Interfering with working memory in humans. *Neuroscience*, *139*, 85–90.

Mueller, S. T., Seymour, T. L., Kieras, D. E., & Meyer, D. E. (2003). Theoretical implications of articulatory duration, phonological similarity, and phonological complexity in verbal working memory. *Journal of Experimental Psychology: Learning, Memory & Cognition*, *29*, 1353–1380.

Nairne, J. S., Whiteman, H. L., & Kelley, M. R. (1999). Short-term forgetting of order under conditions of reduced interference. *Quarterly Journal of Experimental Psychology*, *52A*, 241–251.

Nolan, M. S. (2010). *Fundamentals of air traffic control* (5th ed.). Florence, KY: Delmar Cengage Learning.

Oberauer, K. (2003). Understanding serial position curves in short-term recognition and recall. *Journal of Memory and Language*, *49*(4), 469–483.

Papagno, C., Valentine, T., & Baddeley, A. D. (1991). Phonological short-term memory and foreign language vocabulary learning. *Journal of Memory and Language*, *30*, 331–347.

Park, D. C., Lautenschlager, G., Hedden, T., Davidson, N. S., Smith, A. D., & Smith, P. K. (2002). Models of visuospatial and verbal memory across the adult life span. *Psychology and Aging*, *17*(2), 299–320.

Peterson, L. R., & Peterson, M. J. (1959). Short-term retention of individual verbal items. *Journal of Experimental Psychology*, *58*, 193–198.

Philipp, A. M., Gade, M., & Koch, I. (2007). Inhibitory processes in language switching: Evidence from switching language-defined response sets. *European Journal of Cognitive Psychology*, *19*, 395–416.

Postle, B. R. (2006). Working memory as an emergent property of the mind and brain. *Neuroscience, 139*(1), 23–38.

Redick, T. S., Broadway, J. M., Meier, M. E., Kuriakose, P. S., Unsworth, N., Kane, M. J., & Engle, R. W. (2012). Measuring working memory capacity with automated complex span tasks. *European Journal of Psychological Assessment, 28*, 164–171.

Repovš, G., & Baddeley, A. (2006). The multi-component model of working memory: Explorations in experimental cognitive psychology. *Neuroscience, 139*, 5–21.

Ricker, T. J., & Cowan, N. (2010). Loss of visual working memory within seconds: The combined use of refreshable and non-refreshable features. *Journal of Experimental Psychology: Learning, Memory, and Cognition, 36*(6), 1355–1368.

Ricker, T. J., Vergauwe, E., & Cowan, N. (2016). Decay theory of immediate memory: From Brown (1958) to today (2014). *The Quarterly Journal of Experimental Psychology, 69*(10), 1969–1995.

Rinne, J. O., Tommola, J., Laine, M., Krause, B. J., Schmidt, D., Kaasinen, V., et al. (2000). The translating brain: Cerebral activation patterns during simultaneous interpreting. *Neuroscience Letters, 294*, 85–88.

Ruchkin, D. S., Berndt, R. S., Johnson, R., Grafman, J., Ritter, W., & Canoune, H. L. (1999). Lexical contributions to retention of verbal information in working memory. *Journal of Memory and Language, 41*, 345–364.

Shallice, T., & Warrington, E. K. (1970). Independent functioning of verbal memory stores: A neuropsychological study. *Quarterly Journal of Experimental Psychology, 22*, 261–273.

Shallice, T., & Warrington, E. K. (1974). The dissociation between long-term retention of meaningful sounds and verbal material. *Neuropsychologia, 12*, 553–555.

Shipstead, Z., Redick, T. S., & Engle, R. W. (2012). Is working memory training effective? *Psychological Bulletin, 138*(4), 628–654.

Shrager, Y., Levy, D. A., Hopkins, R. O., & Squire, L. R. (2008). Working memory and the organization of brain systems. *Journal of Neuroscience, 28*, 4818–4822.

Simon, H. A. (1974). How big is a chunk? *Science, 183*, 482–488.

Smith, E. E., & Jonides, J. (1997). Working memory: A view from neuroimaging. *Cognitive Psychology, 33*, 5–42.

Sperling, G. (1960). The information that is available in brief visual presentations. *Psychological Monographs, 74*(498), 1–29.

Spiers, H. J., Maguire, E. A., & Burgess, N. (2001). Hippocampal amnesia. *Neurocase, 7*, 357–382.

Stuss, D. T., & Alexander, M. P. (2007). Is there a dysexecutive syndrome? *Philosophical Transactions of the Royal Society B: Biological Sciences, 362*, 901–1015.

Sylvain-Roy, S., Lungu, O., & Belleville, S. (2014). Normal aging of the attentional control functions that underlie working memory. *The Journals of Gerontology Series B: Psychological Sciences and Social Sciences, 70*, 698–708.

Toms, M., Morris, N., & Foley, P. (1994). Characteristics of visual interference with visuospatial working memory. *British Journal of Psychology, 85*, 131–144.

Turner, M. L., & Engle, R. W. (1989). Is working memory capacity task dependent? *Journal of Memory and Language, 28*, 127–154.

Unsworth, N. (2010). On the division of working memory and long-term memory and their relation to intelligence: A latent variable approach. *Acta Psychologica, 134*(1), 16–28.

Unsworth, N., Fukuda, K., Awh, E., & Vogel, E. K. (2014). Working memory and fluid intelligence: Capacity, attention control, and secondary memory retrieval. *Cognitive Psychology, 71*, 1–26.

Vallar, G., & Baddeley, A. D. (1984). Phonological short-term store, phonological processing and sentence comprehension: A neuropsychological case study. *Cognitive Neuropsychology, 1*(2), 121–141.

Vandierendonck, A., Kemps, E., Fastame, M. C., & Szmalec, A. (2004). Working memory components of the Corsi blocks task. *British Journal of Psychology, 95*(1), 57–79.

Vogel, E. K., Woodman, G. F., & Luck, S. J. (2001). Storage of features, conjunctions, and objects in visual working memory. *Journal of Experimental Psychology: Human Perception and Performance, 27*, 92–114.

Willcutt, E. G., Doyle, A. E., Nigg, J. T., Faraone, S. V., & Pennington, B. F. (2005). Validity of the executive function theory of attention-deficit/hyperactivity disorder: A meta-analytic review. *Biological Psychiatry, 57*(11), 1336–1346.

Woods, D. L., Kishiyama, M. M., Yund, E. W., Herron, T. J., Edwards, B., Poliva, O., . . . Reed, B. (2011). Improving digit span assessment of short-term verbal memory. *Journal of Clinical and Experimental Neuropsychology, 33*(1), 101–111.

Xu, Y., & Chun, M. M. (2009). Selecting and perceiving multiple visual objects. *Trends in Cognitive Sciences, 13*, 167–174.

Zimmer, H. D. (2008). Visual and spatial working memory: From boxes to networks. *Neuroscience and Biobehavioral Reviews, 32*, 1373–1395.

Chapter 5

Contents

Learning and long-term memory

INTRODUCTION

Learning and memory are two of the most important topics within cognitive psychology. Why is that the case? If we were unable to learn, we wouldn't have any information available to remember. In the absence of both learning and memory, our lives would be devoid of meaning. The devastating effects associated with the progressive destruction of the human memory system can be seen in patients suffering from Alzheimer's disease.

Learning and memory are closely connected. Learning involves the accumulation of knowledge or skills and would be impossible in the absence of memory. In similar fashion, memory would be impossible in the absence of learning, because we can only remember things we have learned previously.

We start with learning and will see that there is a distinction between two types of learning.

Learning objectives

After studying Chapter 5, you should be able to:
- Define long-term memory (contrasted with short-term memory).
- Define, compare, and contrast implicit learning and explicit learning.
- Define, compare, and contrast declarative memory and non-declarative (implicit) memory.
- Define, compare, and contrast episodic memory and semantic memory.
- Define, compare, and contrast recognition and recall.
- Discuss a number of factors affecting explicit learning, such as level-of-processing theory, distinctiveness, and the testing effect.
- Describe anterograde amnesia, and indicate how the study of amnesic patients has increased our understanding of long-term memory.
- Explain how proactive and retroactive interference affect forgetting.
- Explain the importance of consolidation and reconsolidation.

IMPLICIT VS. EXPLICIT LEARNING

When we think of learning, we spontaneously think of intentional learning, learning that is goal directed and motivated by the intention to retain the information. This is the type of learning you do when you are studying for an exam. However, much more learning is incidental learning, learning that takes place without any intent to learn. It is the type of learning that makes it easy for you to find your way in your house and your town, that makes you recognize faces you've encountered a few times before, that makes you avoid danger, that helps you remember what you did this morning, that made you learn to speak your mother tongue, and so on.

Whereas intentional learning always is conscious learning, there is some evidence that we can incidentally learn without being aware of what we learned. On the face of it, that sounds improbable. Why would we want to acquire information without any conscious awareness? It would seem pointless and wasteful. In most incidental learning situations, we are aware that we are processing information. If we don't realize that we have learned something, how can we make use of the knowledge? But then again, given that we learn so much about our environment, do we really need our consciousness to learn it all? When we sleep in a new bed (or suddenly have a partner in our bed), at first the situation feels uneasy, but the body adapts rapidly. Do we really need consciousness for such learning?

Learning in the absence of conscious awareness of what has been learned is called implicit learning. Implicit learning can be contrasted with explicit learning, which entails conscious awareness of what has been learned.

Learning may involve the acquisition of verbal information (like in studying), but it may also involve knowledge of associations between behaviors and changes in the environment. The latter is typically studied in paradigms of classical conditioning and operant conditioning.

Classical conditioning leads to the learning of associations between stimuli in the environment and positive or negative consequences for us. The prototypical example is Pavlov's dog, which learned to salivate upon hearing a bell announcing the delivery of food. According to Pavlov (1927), the initially neutral stimulus (the bell sound) automatically elicited the reflexive behavior after it had been presented a number of times immediately before the delivery of food. According to cognitive psychologists (Rescorla & Wagner, 1972), what the dog learned was the fact that the bell sound predicted the delivery of food.

Operant conditioning results in behavioral changes as a consequence of whether the behavior is rewarded or punished. Behavior increases in frequency when it is followed by a reward, whereas it decreases in frequency if followed by a punishment. The prototypical example here is the rat in a Skinner box, which learns to press on a lever in order to obtain food but not to press on the lever if the behavior is followed by an electrical shock. The associations between behaviors and changes in the environment need not be experienced at first hand.

Humans and animals can also learn by watching others. Such learning is called *observational learning*.

ASSESSING IMPLICIT LEARNING

The most commonly used implicit learning task is the **serial reaction time task**. On each trial, a stimulus appears at one of several locations on a computer screen. Participants respond as rapidly as possible with the response key corresponding to its location. There is a complex repeating sequence over trials, but participants aren't told this.

Towards the end of the experiment, there is a block of trials conforming to a novel sequence, but this information isn't given to the participants. Participants speed up during the course of the experiment but respond more slowly during the novel sequence (see Shanks, 2005, for a review).

Figure 5.1 shows the results of a typical experiment. In this experiment, participants had to put their index fingers and middle fingers on four keys of a computer keyboard. On the screen were four squares. When the leftmost square lit up, the participants had to press the leftmost key with the left middle finger; when the second square lit up, they had to press the second key with the left index finger, and so on. Unknown to the participants, half of them got repetitions of the sequence 342312143241 (1 = the leftmost square/key, 4 = the rightmost square/key). The other half received repetitions of the sequence 341243142132. There were 15 blocks of 96 trials, always with the same sequence, except for block 13, when participants got the sequence of the other group. The graph shows a clear learning effect across blocks, as

Key term

Serial reaction time task: one of the main tasks used to study implicit learning. Participants have to press keys related to a series of lights appearing on a computer screen. Unknown to the participants, the series consists of a complex sequence that is repeated over and over again but that is too difficult to grasp consciously.

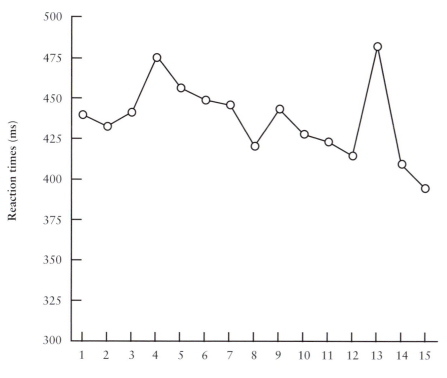

Figure 5.1 Implicit learning. Participants responded faster as more blocks containing the systematic but complex trial sequence were presented, indicating that the participants learned the sequence. When another sequence was used (in block 13), reaction times increased.
Source: From Destrebecqz & Cleeremans (2001). Reprinted with permission from Springer.

Training blocks

the reaction times became shorter, except for block 13 when the unfamiliar sequence was presented. Importantly, the participants were not aware of the systematicity in the sequence.

A point of contention among researchers is *how* we can be sure that people's learning is implicit. When questioned, participants usually show no conscious awareness there was a repeating sequence or pattern in the stimuli presented to them. However, many researchers think this criterion is not sufficient, because of what Shanks and St. John (1994) called the "retrospective problem." That problem occurs when people are consciously aware of what they are learning at the time but have forgotten about it by the time they are asked about their conscious awareness at the end of the experiment.

People may also have partial knowledge, which they find difficult to articulate. Consider a study by Wilkinson and Shanks (2004) on the serial reaction time task as illustrated in Figure 5.1. The participants showed clear evidence of sequence learning. This was followed by a test of explicit learning. Participants were either told to guess the next location in the sequence (inclusion condition) or to avoid guessing the next location (exclusion condition).

If sequence knowledge is wholly implicit and unavailable to consciousness, then performance shouldn't differ in the inclusion and exclusion conditions. In fact, however, participants' predictions in the inclusion condition were significantly more in line with the learned sequence than were their predictions in the exclusion condition, indicating the existence of some conscious knowledge. Thus, some explicit knowledge was acquired.

Because it is so difficult to be sure that learning in the serial reaction time task is entirely implicit on the basis of knowledge assessment (Pothos, 2007), researchers have looked at other evidence indicating that implicit and explicit learning are different forms of learning.

SPECIFIC CHARACTERISTICS OF IMPLICIT AND EXPLICIT LEARNING

Implicit learning would be different from explicit learning if it is affected by other variables. Reber (1993) identified five major differences:

1. *Robustness*: Implicit systems are relatively unaffected by disorders (e.g., amnesia) affecting explicit systems.
2. *Age independence*: Implicit learning is less influenced by age or developmental level.
3. *Low variability*: There are smaller individual differences in implicit learning than in explicit learning.
4. *IQ independence*: Performance on implicit tasks is less affected by IQ than is performance on explicit tasks.
5. *Commonality of process*: Implicit systems are common to most species, whereas explicit systems are not.

Relatively little research is of direct relevance to the third or fifth differences identified by Reber (1993). As a result, we will focus on the other three differences.

There is much evidence supporting the robustness difference between explicit and implicit learning identified by Reber (1993). As is discussed in the next section, amnesic patients have severe problems with explicit memory, but their implicit learning and memory are often well preserved.

Howard and Howard (1992) obtained evidence supporting the age independence of implicit memory. Young and older adults performed an implicit learning task (the serial reaction time task of Figure 5.1). An asterisk appeared in one of four positions on a screen, and participants pressed the corresponding key as soon as possible. Both groups of participants showed comparable learning of the repeating sequence. There was also a test of explicit learning on which participants predicted where the asterisk would appear next. The younger group performed significantly better than the older group on the explicit task. This illustrates the discrepancy between implicit learning (no age difference) and explicit learning (age difference). Later studies, however, indicated that although the decline in performance on implicit learning tasks is small in older adults, it is not completely absent (Howard, Jr. & Howard, 2013; Seaman et al., 2013). Still, it is much smaller than the decline in explicit learning tasks.

Evidence supporting the IQ independence was reported by Gebauer and Mackintosh (2007). They used various implicit learning tasks (e.g., serial reaction time) given with standard implicit instructions or with explicit instructions indicating that rules were to be discovered. Intelligence was positively associated with performance when explicit instructions were given but not when implicit instructions were used. Kaufman et al. (2010) found that intelligence correlated +0.44 with explicit learning but only +0.16 with implicit learning (see Chapter 4 for the interpretation of correlation coefficients). Janacsek and Nemeth (2013) reviewed research on working memory capacity (which, as we have seen in Chapter 4, correlates with intelligence) and learning. There typically is a relationship between working memory capacity and explicit learning but not with implicit learning. These findings support Reber's (1993) fourth difference.

In the Real World 5.1 *Skilled typists and implicit learning*

Millions of people have highly developed word processing skills. However, do they also know where the letters are on the keyboard? Before reading on, try to complete the keyboard given in Figure 5.2.

How well did you do? You can find the answers at the end of the chapter.

Snyder et al. (2014) studied college typists with a mean of 11.4 years of typing expertise. In the

Figure 5.2 Fill in the missing letters.
To see how well you did, find the solution at the end of the chapter.
Source: From Snyder et al. (2014).

first experiment, the participants were presented with a blank keyboard, as shown in Figure 5.2, and instructed to write the letters in their correct locations. The performance was rather poor: participants located only 14.9 (57%) of the letters correctly.

In a second experiment, performance was even worse when participants were asked to indicate the positions of the letter and at the same time were prevented from making use of spontaneous finger movements because they had to continuously press a simple sequence of keys.

Given that all typists could type fluently without looking at the keyboard, their bad performance on the letter position task illustrates that the memory for key presses is not the same as the memory for key positions (see procedural memory later in this chapter). Apparently, the implicit learning of key presses is different from the explicit learning of letter positions on a keyboard.

Key term

Striatum:
subcortical structure situated between the cerebral hemispheres and the brainstem that plays a crucial role in implicit learning. Is part of the basal ganglia.

NEUROSCIENTIFIC EVIDENCE

Further evidence for a difference between implicit and explicit learning would be found if different brain areas were involved in both types of learning.

Brain imaging

Conscious awareness is most consistently associated with activation of the dorsolateral prefrontal cortex and the anterior cingulate, two structures in the frontal lobes (Dehaene et al., 2001; see Figure 5.3). Accordingly, these areas should be more active during explicit than implicit learning. Furthermore, explicit learning depends on the hippocampus (Figure 1.8) and the surrounding medial temporal lobes. These too should be active during explicit learning. In contrast, the striatum has been linked to implicit learning. The **striatum** is a subcortical structure, located between the cerebral hemispheres and the upper region of the brainstem, as shown in Figure 5.3. It is part of the basal ganglia, a collection of nuclei at the base of the cerebral hemispheres.

The available brain imaging data are largely in line with these predictions. At the same time, the critical brain areas for implicit learning are often active in explicit learning tasks as well, and vice versa (Shanks, 2010; Gheysen & Fias, 2012; Yang & Li, 2012). A possible interpretation is that learning always involves a mixture of implicit and explicit learning, with the relative weights depending on the task.

Figure 5.3 Brain structures involved in explicit and implicit learning
This figure shows you the outside of the left hemisphere (left) and the inside of the right hemisphere (right). The dorsolateral prefrontal cortex, the anterior cingulate, the hippocampus, and the surrounding temporal cortex are essential for explicit learning; the striatum plays a critical role in implicit learning.

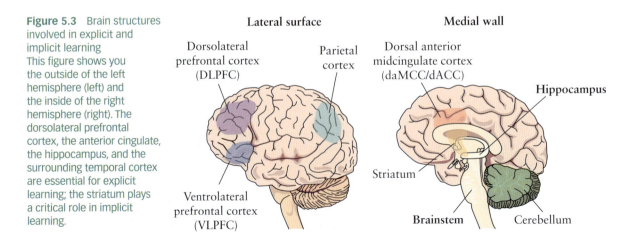

Brain damage

If explicit and implicit learning are controlled by different brain areas, then we should be able to find a double dissociation in brain-damaged patients (Chapter 1): some patients should have poor explicit learning but normal implicit learning, and vice versa.

If the striatum is critical for implicit learning but not for explicit learning, then patients with damage to this structure should have impaired implicit learning but intact explicit learning. Patients with Parkinson's disease (the symptoms of which include limb tremor and muscle rigidity) have damage to these structures, and so should have poor implicit learning. A meta-analysis by Clark et al. (2014) confirmed that these patients are indeed deficient on tasks of implicit learning, but that the deficiency is not as strong as would be expected. Furthermore, it is not present in all patients (see also Gheysen & Fias, 2012). At the same time, patients with Parkinson's disease are to some extent impaired on explicit learning as well, especially when the learning is complex (Vingerhoets et al., 2005; Wilkinson et al., 2009). This points to the possibility that implicit and explicit learning are not completely separated, or that most learning is a combination of both processes.

If explicit learning depends substantially on the hippocampus and the surrounding medial temporal lobes, then patients with damage to that area should have impaired explicit learning but good implicit learning. The most famous amnesia patient is H.M. (1926–2008; for a detailed description, see Corkin, 2013). At the age of 27, he underwent brain surgery in an attempt to treat his epilepsy. The hippocampus and the surrounding brain tissue were removed (this happened in 1953, in the early days of brain surgery when much less was known about the workings of the brain and how to limit the impact of brain surgery). When he woke up, he recognized his family but was unable to learn new information. He never recognized the doctors and the nurses, even though he met them repeatedly. He could have a normal conversation with someone as long as the person was present, but he would not recognize them if they left and came back a few minutes later. This is a typical example of anterograde amnesia, as we will see later in this chapter, the inability to learn and remember information acquired after the event that caused the amnesia. H.M. had retained the skills and the knowledge he possessed before the operation, but he was not able to acquire new explicit information. He kept on assuming that Truman was president of the United States (because Truman had been president before the operation) and never learned the names of the following presidents (Eisenhower, Kennedy, . . .).

During his life, H.M. was tested hundreds of times, but he didn't manage to achieve any new explicit learning (he even didn't realize he was asked to do the same tests over and over again, which was a great help for the researchers, as he started each test session with the same new enthusiasm for the "new" task he was asked to do). It didn't matter whether the stimuli were words, pictures, sounds, faces, personal experiences, or important events happening in the world. H.M. couldn't retain any of them. It also didn't matter whether the questions involved uncued memories or cued memories, whether they were simple yes/no questions or multiple-choice questions, and whether they had been asked several times before. H.M.'s performance remained abysmal.

In 1962 a breakthrough was realized in the research on H.M. (for a review, see Milner, 2005). The psychologist who had examined H.M. since 1955, Brenda Milner, asked him to trace a star viewed through a mirror (Figure 5.4).

Figure 5.4 Mirror drawing and the discovery of implicit learning.
When the amnesia patient H.M. was asked on three consecutive days to trace a star he saw in a mirror, each day he thought he had never done such a task before. Still, the number of errors he made decreased consistently, until he was nearly flawless on day 3. This showed that he had learned how to move his hands when seeing them through a mirror, without being aware of it.

As you can easily experience yourself, such mirror drawing is difficult, and in the beginning you make many errors. As you repeat the task, however, performance improves. Milner asked H.M. to do the task repeatedly on three consecutive days. Each day H.M. started the task in the conviction that he had never done the task before, but his performance improved in very much the same way as that of control participants without amnesia, as is shown in Figure 5.4. This was the first experimental evidence for the existence of implicit learning (which subsequently became a very important research topic, as we saw earlier).

The existence of implicit learning explains some observations in H.M.'s life. Moving houses was a disaster for him, because he was completely lost in the new environment. Still, after some time he developed a sense of familiarity with the new surroundings and the new people he encountered. He was even able to eventually draw a rough floor plan of the house he lived in. He could not formulate this knowledge explicitly, but it helped him to get on in life.

CONCLUSIONS

There is good evidence that implicit and explicit learning are two different types of learning. They are affected by different factors and they involve different brain regions, so that patients can have a much larger deficit in one than in the other.

At the same time, it is clear that a lot of learning involves both implicit and explicit aspects. Indeed, psychologists have been unable to devise tasks that uniquely measure one or the other component. Also in brain imaging studies it has not (yet?) been possible to find tasks that result in brain activity limited to the structures supposed to play a critical role in explicit learning (the hippocampus and the medial temporal lobes) or implicit learning (the striatum and the basal ganglia). This may be because learning always involves a combination of explicit and implicit learning (Sun et al., 2009), particularly when such learning is examined in laboratory circumstances and participants are alert to everything that is happening around them. If pure implicit learning exists, maybe we will only find it in circumstances when participants are not motivated to acquire information?

Section summary

Types of learning
- A distinction is made between intentional learning and incidental learning, based on whether the participant has the goal to learn. Another distinction is made between explicit and implicit learning, based on whether the participant is consciously aware of what they are learning. Intentional learning is always explicit; incidental learning often is explicit as well (people are aware that they are processing information), but can be implicit.

Assessing implicit learning
- The most commonly used implicit learning task involves serial reaction time. In this task, performance improves without people being able to

explain why. However, psychologists disagree to what extent the learning really is unconscious. When more sensitive and detailed tests are used, participants are usually able to show some explicit knowledge of what has been learned.

- In the next section we will see that the word-fragment task is another much-used task to measure implicit learning.

Specific characteristics of implicit learning

- Other evidence that implicit learning differs from explicit learning comes from the findings that implicit learning is more robust and less affected by age and IQ.

Brain evidence

- Brain imaging studies showed that explicit learning mainly involves two areas in the frontal lobes and the hippocampus plus the surrounding medial temporal lobes. Implicit learning relies more on activity in the striatum. At the same time, most tasks seem to involve all brain areas, suggesting that in many situations explicit and implicit learning go together.
- Patients with damage to the striatum generally show greater impairment of implicit than explicit learning, but they also have some deficiency in explicit learning. Patients with damage to the hippocampus and the surrounding medial temporal lobes, such as H.M., typically suffer more on explicit learning than implicit learning.

Conclusions

- All in all, there is good evidence that implicit learning is not the same as explicit learning. However, it is likely that most learning is a mixture of implicit and explicit aspects.

VARIABLES AFFECTING EXPLICIT LEARNING

In the coming chapters on long-term memory we will mainly deal with intentional, explicit learning: participants are presented with stimulus materials they have to memorize, and their subsequent performance is probed. Many of the examples will involve verbal materials, as these are easier to test.

LEVELS OF PROCESSING

What determines how well we remember information over the long term? A very influential answer was proposed by Craik and Lockhart (1972). They argued in their **levels-of-processing theory** that what is crucial is how we process the information during learning. There are various levels of processing ranging from shallow or physical analysis of a stimulus (e.g., detecting specific letters in words) to deep or semantic analysis. The greater the extent to which *meaning* is processed, the deeper the level of processing.

Craik and Lockhart's (1972) main theoretical assumptions were as follows:

- The level or depth of processing of a stimulus has a large effect on its memorability.

Key term
Levels-of-processing theory: this is the assumption that learning and long-term memory will be better the more deeply the *meaning* of the stimulus materials is processed.

- Deeper levels of analysis produce more elaborate, longer lasting, and stronger memory traces than shallow levels of analysis.

Craik and Lockhart (1972) disagreed with Atkinson and Shiffrin's (1968) assumption that rehearsal always improves long-term memory. They argued that rehearsal consisting simply of repeating previous analyses (maintenance rehearsal) doesn't enhance long-term memory, an argument that was recently repeated and substantiated by Lewandowsky and Oberauer (2015).

> **Key term**
>
> **Self-reference effect:** enhanced long-term memory for information if it is related to the self at the time of learning.

Evidence

Numerous studies support the main assumptions of the levels-of-processing approach. Craik and Tulving (1975) compared recognition performance as a function of the task performed at learning:

- *Shallow grapheme task*: Decide whether each word is in uppercase or lowercase letters.
- *Intermediate phoneme task*: Decide whether each word rhymes with a target word.
- *Deep semantic*: Decide whether each word fits a sentence containing a blank.

Depth of processing had impressive effects on memory performance, as can be seen in Figure 5.5. Performance in the deep semantic condition was nearly three times higher than with shallow processing.

Craik and Tulving (1975) argued that *elaboration* of processing (i.e., the amount of processing of a given kind) is important in addition to processing depth. They used the deep semantic task discussed earlier and varied elaboration by using simple sentence frames (e.g., "She cooked the ___") and complex ones (e.g., "The great bird swooped down and carried off the struggling ___"). Cued recall was twice as high for words accompanying complex sentences, showing that memory is better following more elaborate processing.

The levels-of-processing account may also explain why we are especially likely to remember information that relates to ourselves. In the initial study, Rogers et al. (1977) found that asking participants to decide whether words applied to themselves led to better recall than having them process words in terms of their meaning. This is known as the **self-reference effect**.

Figure 5.5 Evidence for the levels-of-processing theory. Participants saw a series of 60 words. For 20 randomly chosen words the participants were asked to indicate whether the word was printed in uppercase letters; for 20 other words they had to decide whether it rhymed with a new word; and for 20 of the words they had to decide whether it belonged to a certain semantic category. Unexpectedly, at the end of the series the experimenters presented a new list of 180 words (120 new and 60 old) and asked the participants to indicate which words had been in the initial list. As the figure shows, the participants were close to chance (33%) for the words on which they had done the letter type task and remembered nearly all the words on which they had done the semantic task.
Source: From Craik and Tulving (1975). Reprinted with permission from the American Psychological Association.

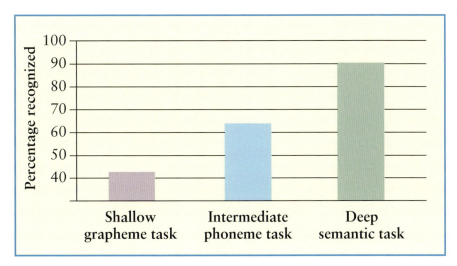

Key term

Word-fragment task:
a task often used to measure implicit learning, which is not based on motoric responses. Participants get a word fragment and are asked to complete the word. Performance is much better if participants in a previous part of the study saw the words, even when they are not aware of the overlap between both parts of the study.

Symons and Johnson (1997) combined the findings from 129 studies on the self-reference effect in a meta-analysis. On average, long-term memory was better when learning occurred under self-reference conditions than any other, perhaps because self-reference encourages deeper semantic processing.

Related to the self-reference effect, Nairne et al. (2007) reported that we are also more likely to remember information we perceive as important for our survival. Students were asked to evaluate a list of 30 nouns (such as truck, mountain, book, shoes, car, sword). The first group of students was asked to imagine they were stranded in the grasslands of a foreign land, and they had to rate how useful each item from the list would be for their survival. A second group of students was asked to imagine that they were planning to move to a new home in a foreign land. Over the next few months, they would need to locate and purchase a new home and transport their belongings. The students were asked to rate how relevant each item from the list would be to accomplish the task. Finally, a third group of students was asked to rate how pleasant the things were that the words referred to. After the rating task and a short distraction task, the students were unexpectedly asked to write down all the words they remembered from the list (incidental learning). As can be seen in Figure 5.6, students in the survival condition recalled more words than students in the other two conditions.

Levels of processing and implicit learning?

Challis et al. (1996) investigated whether the levels of processing was limited to explicit learning. They used various tests of explicit and implicit learning. One test of implicit learning was the **word-fragment task**. In this test, participants see a word with missing letters (e.g., c _ p _ e _) and are asked to complete the word (see Research Activity 5.1). Importantly, performance is easier if participants in an unrelated task before have seen a candidate word. So, participants who a few minutes before have seen the word "copies" are more likely to give this completion. Participants who saw the word "cypher" are more likely to return this answer. This is even true for patients with amnesia (Warrington & Weiskrantz, 1968), in line with the evidence we saw before that amnesics are much less deficient in implicit learning than explicit learning.

The findings of Challis et al. (1996) were clear-cut. There was a strong effect of processing depth and self-reference on performance of all the explicit memory tests (e.g., recognition memory; free recall). In contrast, there were no such effects on the word-fragment task.

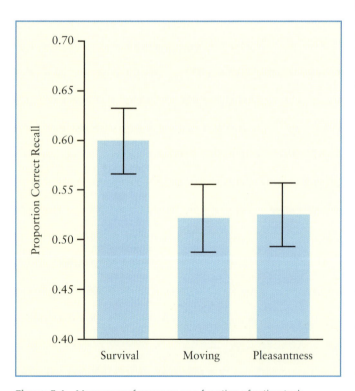

Figure 5.6 Memory performance as a function of rating task.
Source: From Nairne et al. (2007). Reprinted with permission from the American Psychological Association.

Research Activity 5.1 *Do the word-fragment task*

This Research Activity should be carried out with a friend. Read Passage A and then turn your mind to something else for a few minutes. Finally, have a look at the word fragments below. Try to fill in the missing letters to form complete words. Simply write down the first appropriate word that comes to mind. Then ask a friend to read Passage B, to do something else for a few minutes, and then to fill in the missing letters to form complete words.

Passage A
Tom was a bashful young man who had recently arrived in the country. Every day he left his house and headed for his office. There he had a cup of coffee every morning, using a spoon to stir the sugar in. Occasionally, he would consult an almanac. After work, he walked to the station through a meadow. When the sun was shining, he would see his shadow as he walked.

Passage B
Lucy is much affected by climate, having a preference for the summer. She likes to wear a purple skirt as she goes to work in a large factory. On the way to work, she passes a zoo. Her favorite animals in the zoo are a giraffe and a spider. When Lucy returns home in the evening, she likes to play the violin while letting her cigarette burn in the ashtray.

Word fragments

al _ _ n _ c	_ _ ht _ ay
b _ sh _ u _	_ l _ m _ te
_ _ u _ t _ y	f _ _ t _ ry
of _ _ c _	_ urp _ _
_ p _ on	su _ m _ _
_ h _ do _	_ io _ _ n
h _ us _	_ _ r _ f _ e
_ e _ d _ w	_ p _ d _ r

The word fragments in the left column can all form words contained in Passage A. Those in the right column can all form words from Passage B. Due to implicit learning, chances are high that you performed better on the left column, whereas your friend performed better on the right column.

Limitations

Morris et al. (1977) argued that not so much depth of processing was important for learning but the degree to which the stored information matched the subsequent memory test. Their study repeated Craik and Tulving's (1975) learning phase: participants had to answer phoneme-related or meaning-related questions to words they were presented with. However, the subsequent memory test could be of two types:

1. The standard recognition test of Craik and Tulving, in which participants had to indicate the target words among distractors

Key terms

Transfer-appropriate processing:
this is the notion that long-term memory will be greatest when the processing at the time of retrieval is very similar to the processing at the time of learning.

Distinctiveness:
this characterizes memory traces that are distinct or different from other memory traces stored in long-term memory; it leads to enhanced memory.

2. A new rhyming recognition test, in which participants selected words that rhymed with the target words from the learning list (these were different from the words used in the learning list)

With the standard recognition test, Morris et al. (1977) replicated the finding of Craik and Tulving (1975): participants recognized more words from the deep semantic condition than from the intermediate phoneme condition. However, with the rhyming recognition test, participants recognized more words from the intermediate phoneme condition than from the deep semantic condition. This disproved the notion that deep processing always enhances long-term memory. Morris et al. (1977) explained these findings in terms of **transfer-appropriate processing**. Whether what we have learned leads to good performance on a subsequent memory test depends on the *relevance* of that information (and its associated processing) to the memory test. For the rhyming recognition test, storing phoneme information was more relevant than storing semantic information.

Another limitation of the levels-of-processing theory is that many of the findings discussed below were not predicted by the theory. This is because the theory is focused too much on semantic elaboration. As a result, it has not resulted in a richness of paradigms to investigate learning and memory. Most studies were variants of Craik and Tulving's (1975) original studies.

DISTINCTIVENESS

Another factor important in determining learning and long-term memory is distinctiveness (Hunt, 2006). **Distinctiveness** means that a memory trace differs from other memory traces because it was processed differently at the time of learning. There is much evidence that distinctive memories are generally better remembered than are non-distinctive ones (see Research Activity 5.2).

Research Activity 5.2 *Distinctiveness and long-term memory*

Below are two lists of 10 words:

CHAIR	CAT
PIANO	DOG
CLOCK	GIRAFFE
TELEPHONE	MOUSE
CUSHION	CUSHION
LAMB	LAMB
STOVE	MONKEY
MIRROR	BEAVER
RADIO	TURTLE
BOOKCASE	TIGER

Ask a few friends to read the first list, and then ask them to write down as many words as they remember. Ask some other friends to read the second list and ask them to write them down as well. Now, compare the likelihood that the words "cushion" and "lamb" are among the words remembered. Chances are high that the word "lamb" is remembered more often in List 1 than in List 2 and that the reverse is true for the word "cushion".

Why is this so? The word lamb is the only animal in the first list, whereas there are eight other animals in the second list. Similarly, the word cushion is the odd one out in List 2 but not in List 1. Distinctiveness leads to better learning and memory.

Are the effects of distinctiveness separate from those of processing depth? There is much evidence that they can be. For example, Eysenck and Eysenck (1980) studied long-term memory for distinctive memory traces receiving only shallow processing. They used nouns that aren't pronounced in line with the rules of pronunciation (e.g., comb has a silent "b"; yacht has a silent "ch"). In one condition, participants said these nouns in a distinctive way by pronouncing them in line with their spelling (e.g., pronouncing the "b" in comb and the "ch" in yacht). Thus, the processing was shallow (i.e., phonemic) but the memory traces were distinctive. As predicted, recognition memory was as good in this condition as in a deep processing condition involving processing the meanings of the nouns.

Additional evidence was reported by Kirchhoff et al. (2005). Some words (e.g., onyx; abyss) are high in orthographic distinctiveness because the pattern of letters is unusual. Kirchhoff et al. (2005) found that orthographic distinctiveness and deep or semantic processing made separate contributions to enhancing learning.

Why are distinctive memories so well remembered? Two factors are at play. First, in order to retrieve a stored memory trace, it is necessary to have good memory cues. For instance, you will remember much more of your last holidays if you return to the place of your holidays than if you try to remember as much as possible in a college room, because there are many more helpful memory cues at the place of your holidays. Distinct stimuli usually have strong, unique memory cues. For instance, the cue "animal" is a unique cue in List 1 of Research Activity 5.2, but not in List 2. Therefore, you are more likely to remember "lamb" in List 1 than in List 2 ("There was an animal in the list; oh yes, it was lamb").

The second reason why distinctiveness helps learning and memory is that distinct stimuli are less subject to interference. Later in the chapter, we will see that much forgetting is due to interference – our long-term memory for what we have learned can be distorted or interfered with by information we learned beforehand or afterwards. That is especially so when the other information is *similar* to what we are trying to remember. Distinctive memory traces are easier to remember because they are *dissimilar* to other memory traces and so are less liable to interference (Eysenck, 1979).

THE TESTING EFFECT

Answer the following question: imagine you are reading a textbook for an upcoming exam. After you have read the chapter one time, would you rather:

A. Go back and restudy the entire chapter or parts of the chapter?
B. Try to recall material from the chapter (without the possibility of restudying the material)?
C. Use some other study technique?

Karpicke et al. (2009) found that 57% of their students gave answer A, 21% gave answer C, and only 18% gave answer B. What is interesting about this pattern of responses is that the least frequent answer (B) is actually the most effective one in terms of promoting good long-term memory!

The available research provides convincing evidence for the **testing effect**: long-term retention of material is better when memory is tested during the

Key term
Testing effect: the finding that long-term memory is enhanced when some of the learning period is devoted to retrieving the to-be-remembered information.

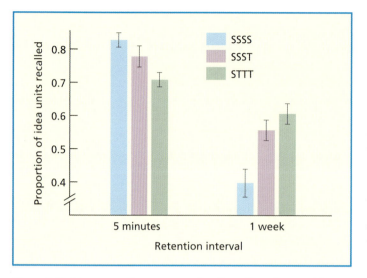

Figure 5.7   Memory performance as a function of learning conditions (S=study; T=test).
Source: From Roediger (2008). Reprinted with permission of Annual Review of Psychology, © by Annual Reviews.

time of learning. Bangert-Drowns et al. (1991) reviewed the findings from 35 classroom studies. A significant testing effect was found in 83% of these studies, and the magnitude of the effect tended to increase as the number of testing occasions went up (see also Rowland, 2014, for a more recent meta-analysis confirming the findings).

One of the most thorough studies on the testing effect was run by Roediger and Karpicke (2006). Students read a prose passage covering a general scientific topic and memorized it in one of three conditions:

1. Repeated study: The passage was read four times and there was no test.
2. Single test: The passage was read three times and then students recalled as much as possible from it.
3. Repeated test: The passage was read once and then students recalled as much as possible on three occasions.

Finally, memory for the passage was tested after 5 minutes or 1 week.

The findings are shown in Figure 5.7. Repeated study was the most effective strategy when the final test was given 5 minutes after learning. However, there was a dramatic reversal in the findings when the final test occurred after 1 week. There was a very strong testing effect – average recall was 50% higher in the repeated test condition than the repeated study condition! That could make the difference between doing very well on an examination and failing it.

Students in the repeated study condition predicted they would recall more of the prose passage than did those in the repeated test condition. This helps to explain why many students mistakenly devote little or no time to testing themselves when preparing themselves for an examination.

How can we explain the findings? Many people feel reassured if they find it easy to retrieve material they have been learning. However, only effortful or demanding retrieval improves long-term memory (Bjork & Bjork, 1992). For example, Metcalfe and Kornell (2007) studied the learning of foreign vocabulary (e.g., house – maison). During learning the French word was presented at the same time as the English word or there was a short delay. Subsequent long-term memory was much better when there was a short delay, because it allowed the participants to engage in effortful retrieval.

Section Summary

Levels-of-processing theory
• According to levels-of-processing theory, deep or semantic processing enhances learning and long-term memory. Deep processing generally

improves performance especially if learners process words in relation to themselves. However, long-term memory also depends on the elaboration of processing. The beneficial effects of levels-of-processing are limited to explicit learning; they are not found in implicit learning tasks.

Distinctiveness
- Learning and long-term memory are mostly greater for distinctive stimuli than for non-distinctive ones. The effects of distinctiveness are often separate from those of processing depth.

The testing effect
- A third way to improve learning and long-term memory is to test oneself on the materials studied. Although this is hard to believe for many students, testing yourself is more efficient than studying the contents once more, in particular when the memory test does not follow the learning immediately.

LONG-TERM MEMORY

Learning can be seen as the *encoding* of information in long-term memory. For learning to be effective, the information must not only be encoded but also stay stored in memory and be retrievable at the moment it is needed. As we saw in Chapter 4, Atkinson and Shiffrin (1968) postulated a *single* long-term memory store. Such a view seems unlikely, however, given the existence of explicit and implicit learning and given the huge variety of information stored in long-term memory, including knowledge about the world, about our personal experiences throughout our lifetime, about how to read books, how to perform various skills, and so on. As a result, many researchers assume that there are several long-term memory stores. In what follows, we consider the main long-term memory systems that have been proposed. Figure 5.8 gives a diagram of the distinctions made.

DECLARATIVE VS. NON-DECLARATIVE MEMORY

The most important distinction between different types of long-term memory is that between declarative memory and non-declarative memory. Declarative memory "requires conscious recollection of previous experiences" (Graf & Schacter, 1985, p. 501). It refers to memories that can be "declared" or described. Declarative memory is also sometimes called explicit memory. Declarative memory is what you use when you remember someone's name when you see them, when you remember some fact in psychology, or when you remember how to get to your friend's house.

In contrast, non-declarative memory does *not* involve conscious recollection, and is sometimes referred to as implicit memory. Typically, we obtain evidence of non-declarative memory by observing changes in behavior. For example, consider the following anecdote from Edouard Claparède (1873–1940) reported by him in 1911. He studied a female patient who suffered from amnesia due to chronic alcoholism. She couldn't recognize doctors and nurses she had seen virtually every day over a period of several years, indicating that her declarative memory was extremely poor.

Key terms

Declarative memory:
also known as explicit memory, this is memory that involves conscious recollection of information; see **non-declarative memory**.

Non-declarative memory:
also known as implicit memory, this is memory that doesn't involve conscious recollection of information; see **declarative memory**.

Figure 5.8 Various memory systems distinguished in the traditional multiple-memories view of long-term memory. Semantic memory is discussed in Chapter 6, autobiographical memory in Chapter 7.

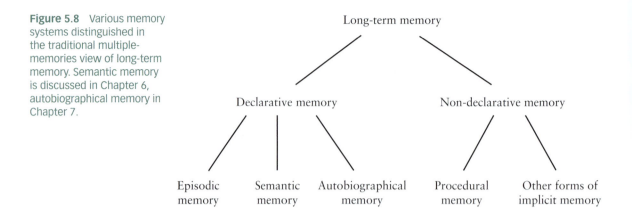

One day Claparède hid a pin in his hand before shaking hands with the patient. The following day she was very sensibly reluctant to shake hands with him. However, she felt very embarrassed because she couldn't explain her reluctance. Her behavior indicated the presence of non-declarative memory of what had happened the previous day even though she had no conscious recollection of it.

As you probably noticed, the distinction between declarative and non-declarative memory resembles the distinction between explicit and implicit learning. Indeed, the discovery of implicit learning in amnesia patients was the origin of the distinction between both memory systems.

Declarative memory

How many types of declarative or explicit memory are there? First, there is *episodic memory*. This is the memory system we use when we remember that we had cereal for breakfast and that we went to the movies yesterday. It is also the memory we need when we are asked to remember words from a list in a psychological experiment, because we must remember which words were in *that specific* list.

Second, there is *semantic memory*. This is the memory system we use when remembering general facts and information, such as the name of the current President of the United States, the number of planets in the solar system, or the meaning of the word "psychology." We remember this information without knowing when and where we learned it. More generally, semantic memory consists of our knowledge of language and of the world.

Third, there is *autobiographical memory*. We use autobiographical memory when we remember personal experiences of importance in our lives. For example, we might think about our first boyfriend/girlfriend or the best holiday of our lives. Autobiographical memory is related to episodic memory, but differs in that it relates to knowledge on the life-long progress of personal goals (Conway, 2001). As such, it goes beyond the time-limited episodes associated with episodic memory. In spite of its importance, autobiographical memory is not discussed in this chapter. Because it is such an important aspect of everyday memory, it is dealt with at length in Chapter 7.

Non-declarative memory

There are at least two varieties of non-declarative memory. First, there is the memory for motor skills, known as **procedural memory** (Foerde & Poldrack,

| Key term

Procedural memory: this is a form of **non-declarative memory** involving learned skills and concerned with "knowing how."

2009). Examples of such skills are tying shoelaces, riding a bike, driving a car, playing a musical instrument, cooking food, and playing a sport.

The implicit learning observed in the mirror drawing of the patient H.M. (Figure 5.4) was an example of encoding in procedural memory. The same is true for the implicit learning observed in the serial reaction time task (Figure 5.1) and in learning to type without looking at the keyboard. Many people also use their procedural memory when they enter their password on a keyboard. This can easily be shown by asking them to enter it on a non-standard keyboard. Then they suddenly have to think harder about what the password is.

However, non-declarative memory is more than procedural memory. Implicit learning not only happens for motor responses. We saw that it also occurs in the word-fragment task (Research Activity 5.1), and in Chapter 2 we described how the perception of a badly organized stimulus is much easier once you have deciphered the stimulus (look back at Figure 2.1; do you still recognize the cowboy?).

The observation that a stimulus is processed more efficiently when the same (or a similar) stimulus has been processed before is called priming. One way to show (and to study) the existence of priming is by means of the word-fragment task, as we saw earlier. Another way is to ask participants to identify briefly presented words. When the presentation time is made short enough, only some words can be identified. Chances of identifying a word are higher, if the word was presented in an unrelated task shortly before (Tulving & Schacter, 1990). In general, priming improves performance without us being aware of it (hence its inclusion in the non-declarative memory).

EPISODIC MEMORY

We use episodic memory to remember past events that have happened to us. Episodic memories generally fulfill what are known as the www criteria – they contain information about *what* happened, *where* it happened, and *when* it happened. Such memories have a strong component of experience (we remember being there when it happened).

You might expect that the episodic memory system would work like a video recorder, providing us with accurate and detailed information about past events. That is *not* the case. As Schacter and Addis (2007, p. 773) pointed out, "Episodic memory is . . . a fundamentally constructive, rather than reproductive process that is prone to various kinds of errors and illusions."

Many people bemoan the limitations of their own memory system and regard it as rather defective. In fact, however, forgetting can be very useful (Schacter, 1999). For example, suppose you remembered all the dates and times of your classes from last year. That information might make it harder for you to remember the dates and times of classes this semester. Much of the time we only need to remember the current situation rather than what used to be the case (Schacter, 1999).

We generally want to access the gist or essence of our past experiences but don't want to remember the trivial details. Consider the Russian Shereshevskii. He was first discovered when working as a journalist. His editor was amazed that he could remember complex briefing instructions without taking any notes.

Shereshevskii had a truly amazing memory and could recall events from the distant past in great detail (Luria, 1968). He was sometimes so overwhelmed

Key terms

Priming:
this is a form of **non-declarative memory** involving facilitated processing of (and response to) a target stimulus when the same or a related stimulus was presented previously.

Episodic memory:
a form of **declarative memory** concerned with personal experiences or episodes occurring in a given place at a given time; see **semantic memory**.

by specific images that he couldn't see the forest for the trees, as when trying to make sense of a prose passage: "Each word calls up images, they collide with one another, and the result is chaos. I can't make anything out of this." The take-home message is that it is a good idea to forget information that is irrelevant to your current life and activities.

There are two other reasons why our episodic memory system is prone to error (Schacter & Addis, 2007). First, it would require an incredible amount of processing to produce a semi-permanent record of all our experiences, because we experience thousands of events every single day. Second, episodic memory is also used to make plans for the future (Szpunar & Radvansky, 2016). This would not be possible if episodic memory were a simple recording device without the power to construct new possibilities (and as a byproduct to reconstruct memories on the basis of incomplete information).

The fact that episodic memory is needed to imagine the future leads to the prediction that individuals with poor episodic memory (e.g., amnesic patients) will have impaired ability to imagine future events. Hassabis et al. (2007) asked amnesic patients and healthy controls to imagine future events (e.g., "Imagine you are lying on a white sandy beach in a beautiful tropical bay"). The amnesic patients produced imaginary experiences consisting of isolated fragments of information lacking the richness and spatial coherence of the experiences imagined by the controls.

On that hypothesis, brain areas important to episodic memory (e.g., the hippocampus) should be activated when individuals imagine future events. Viard et al. (2012) reported a meta-analysis of relevant neuroimaging studies. Most studies observed hippocampal activation when individuals imagined future events. There was greater hippocampal activation when individuals imagined future events in response to personally relevant cues rather than impersonal cues.

Imagining future events not only requires episodic memory; we also need our knowledge of the world. Thus, it is likely that semantic memory is involved in imagining future events as well (Szpunar, 2010). Zeidman and Maguire (2016) further argued that future thinking is built on a model we have of the spatial world around us, which is stored in the hippocampus. This is another reason why the hippocampus is so heavily involved in future thinking.

Recollection vs. familiarity

Episodic knowledge may manifest itself in two ways: either we remember the event as such, including the what-when-where information, or the stimulus looks familiar to us. This distinction can be clarified with the following anecdote. Several years ago the first author walked past a man in Wimbledon, the part of London in which he lives. He was immediately confident he recognized the man. However, he simply couldn't think of the situation in which he had seen the man previously. After some thought (this is the kind of thing academic psychologists think about!), he realized the man was a ticket-office clerk at Wimbledon railway station. Initial recognition based purely on familiarity was replaced by recognition based on recollection.

An effective way of distinguishing between familiarity and recollection is the *remember/know task* (Tulving, 1985; Migo et al., 2012). On this task, participants indicate whether their positive recognition decisions were based on recollection of contextual information (remember responses) or solely on familiarity (know responses).

Recollection is more complex and attention-demanding than familiarity. There have been several studies in which participants' attention during a recognition test was distracted by irrelevant stimuli. Such distraction typically disrupts recollection more than familiarity (see Yonelinas, 2002 for a review). In similar fashion, distraction at the time of learning adversely affects recollection more than familiarity (Yonelinas, 2002).

The binding together of information about stimuli ("what" information) and the context in which they were seen ("where" information) is needed for recollection but not for familiarity (Diana et al., 2007). Where in the brain does this binding occur? According to Diana et al., the hippocampus is of crucial importance. It follows that patients with damage to the hippocampus should have severely impaired recollection but less impaired familiarity judgments.

Skinner and Fernandes (2007) reviewed studies of amnesic patients with and without damage in the hippocampus (including the surrounding medial temporal lobes). The findings are shown in Figure 5.9. As you can see, both brain-damaged groups had comparable levels of recognition performance on measures of familiarity. As predicted, patients with medial temporal lobe and hippocampal damage performed much worse than the other brain-damaged group on measures of recollection. These findings suggest that recollection involves different processes from judgments of familiarity. They are consistent with the notion that the hippocampus is of central importance to recollection.

SEMANTIC MEMORY

What is the capital of France? How many months are there in a year? Who is Beyoncé? Do rats have wings? Is *umplitude* an English word? What is the past tense of the verb *laugh*?

You probably found all those questions relatively easy to answer and answered them quickly. This is possible because we all possess an enormous store of general knowledge that we take for granted. Our organized general knowledge about the world is stored in semantic memory. This type of memory is only mentioned briefly here, as it is covered extensively in Chapter 6.

There are similarities between episodic and semantic memory. Suppose you remember meeting your friend yesterday afternoon at Starbucks. That involves episodic memory, because you are remembering an event at a given time in a given place. However, semantic memory is also involved – some of what you remember depends on your general knowledge about coffee shops, what coffee tastes like, and so on.

Tulving (2002, p. 5) clarified the relationship between episodic and semantic memory:

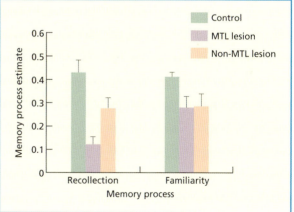

Episodic memory . . . shares many features with semantic memory, out of which it grew . . . but also possesses features that semantic memory does not . . . Episodic memory is a recently evolved, late-developing, and early-deteriorating past-oriented memory system, more vulnerable than other memory systems to neuronal dysfunction.

Figure 5.9 Mean recollection and familiarity estimates for healthy controls, patients with medial temporal lobe (MTL) lesions or brain damage, and patients with non-MTL lesions.
Source: Reprinted from Skinner and Fernandes (2007), with permission from Elsevier.

We can test the notion that episodic memory is more vulnerable than semantic memory by studying patients suffering from amnesia. These patients indeed have greater problems with episodic than with semantic memory (Spiers et al., 2001). The first symptoms are memory failures related to episodic memory (things that happened to the person), and patients usually remain able to understand language and speak up to the last stages of the disease when their episodic and autobiographical memories have almost disappeared.

Section summary

Declarative vs. non-declarative memory
- Declarative or explicit memory involves conscious or deliberate retrieval of events and facts. Episodic, semantic, and autobiographical memory are all forms of declarative memory.
- Non-declarative or implicit memory doesn't involve conscious or deliberate retrieval. Skill learning or procedural memory is a form of non-declarative memory, in which participants become better at performing tasks by simply doing them. Priming is another form in which there is more efficient processing of a repeated stimulus.

Episodic memory
- Episodic memories generally contain information about what happened, where it happened, and when it happened. Episodic memory is constructive rather than reproductive and allows us to imagine possible future events. Recognition can be based on recollection or on familiarity. Recollection (but not familiarity) depends on binding together stimulus and contextual information within the hippocampus at the time of learning.

Semantic memory
- General knowledge is stored in semantic memory. In Chapter 6 we will see that much of the information in semantic memory is in the form of schemas (packets of knowledge).

AMNESIA

In the previous sections we have seen several examples of patients with amnesia and how they informed theories of memory. In this section we discuss some more findings about amnesia. Amnesia is a condition caused by brain damage in which there are severe problems with long-term memory, in particular episodic memory and autobiographical memory. Amnesia is most often caused by closed head injury (a stroke or an accident); another common cause is chronic alcohol abuse. The damage involves the hippocampus and the surrounding medial temporal cortex (Aggleton, 2008; Moscovitch et al., 2006).

If you are a movie fan you are likely to have mistaken ideas about amnesia (Baxendale, 2004). In the movies, serious head injuries typically cause characters to forget the past while still being fully able to engage in new learning. In the real world, however, new learning is often greatly impaired in amnesia patients. In the movies, amnesic individuals sometimes suffer a profound loss of identity or their personality changes completely. In fact, such personality

Key term

Amnesia:
a condition caused by brain damage in which there are serious impairments of long-term memory (especially **episodic memory**).

shifts are extremely rare. Most bizarrely, the rule of thumb in the movies is that the best cure for amnesia caused by severe head injury is to suffer another massive blow to the head. Again, this is not what is recommended in real life!

RETROGRADE AND ANTEROGRADE AMNESIA

Traditionally, a distinction is made between retrograde amnesia and antero-grade amnesia. **Retrograde amnesia** involves impaired memory for events occurring *before* the accident. Retrograde amnesia is often observed when patients have been in a coma. When they awake, they usually have lost memory for the events leading up to the accident.

Manning (2002) described a case study of a 65-year-old patient CH, who had been in a coma for 24 hours after brain surgery. Afterwards she complained about being unable to "fully" remember a variety of past episodes and to find her way to familiar places. Detailed testing showed that CH's intellectual abilities, language, visual perception, visuo-spatial capacities, visual imagery, and executive functions were good and that she had no problems learning new information.

Different results were found when CH was given cue words (e.g., party, friend, book, prize, film) and asked to produce memories based on these words. Each word was given five times to cover four periods before and one after the injury (0–18 years; 19–33 years; 34–49 years; 50–65 years; after the injury). Presentation of words and time periods was randomized. No time limit was set, and CH was encouraged to say as much as possible and to give as many details as possible. CH's husband confirmed the veracity of the patient's recollections. A similar procedure was followed for three control subjects of the same age.

Figure 5.10 shows the results and confirms that CH had a focal retrograde amnesia for the 15 years preceding the injury. Interestingly, the deficiency was limited to autobiographical (episodic) memory. There were no deficits in semantic and non-declarative memory.

Anterograde amnesia is a reduced ability to remember information learned *after* the accident that caused the amnesia.

Because anterograde amnesia affects the learning of new information, most research has focused on this type of memory disorder. We already saw the example of H.M. Another famous example is Clive Wearing, who featured in a television documentary (look on YouTube!). In March 1985 he developed encephalitis (infection of the brain), which destroyed most of the hippocampus and the surrounding cortex. As a result, Clive Wearing can remember practically nothing of his daily activities and can't even remember the names of his children. As with other anterograde amnesia patients, he still can have fluent conversations, knows how to perform daily activities, and can play the piano (he was an accomplished musician before the accident). He also recognizes his wife, who he always is very happy and relieved to see (even if she has been away for only a few minutes).

Key terms

Retrograde amnesia: impaired ability of amnesic patients to remember information and events (i.e., **declarative memory**) from the time period prior to the onset of **amnesia**.

Anterograde amnesia: impaired ability of amnesic patients to learn and remember information acquired after the onset of **amnesia**.

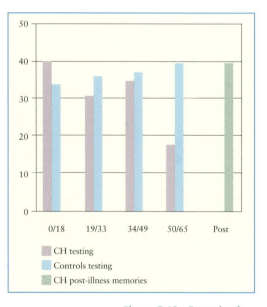

Figure 5.10 Example of focal retrograde amnesia. After a brain injury followed by a coma, a 65-year-old patient CH had diminished autobiographical memories for a time period of 15 years before the injury (i.e., when she was 50 to 65 years old). Source: From Manning (2002). Reprinted with permission from Elsevier.

When Clive Wearing became aware that something was terribly wrong with him, he wept almost non-stop for over a month. One of his recurrent complaints was, "What's it like to have one long night lasting . . . how long? It's like being dead." Clive Wearing is not only robbed of what happened to him since the accident, but he is also completely dependent on others to take care of him, because he cannot make plans of what to do next.

Although we have described anterograde and retrograde amnesia as two separate disorders, it is important to realize that they mostly go together, because learning and memory make use of neighboring brain tissue. Indeed, in general there is a positive correlation between the degree of anterograde and retrograde amnesia in patients (Smith et al., 2013).

WHAT REMAINS INTACT?

So far, we have seen anecdotal evidence in selected patients that non-declarative memory and implicit learning are more spared in amnesia than declarative memory and explicit learning. In some studies the performance of amnesics is even comparable to that of healthy individuals (e.g., Meulemans & Van der Linden, 2003).

Spiers et al. (2001) reviewed 147 cases of anterograde amnesia, most of whom had severe problems with several aspects of long-term memory. However, non-declarative memory was essentially intact in these patients: "None of the cases was reported to . . . be impaired on tasks which involved learning skills or habits, priming, simple classical conditioning and simple category learning" (Spiers et al., 2001, p. 359).

Hamann and Squire (1997) studied an amnesic patient, EP, who seemed to have no explicit memory at all. For example, on a test of recognition memory he was correct on only 52% of trials (chance = 50%) compared to 65% for other amnesic patients and 81% for healthy controls. However, his performance on priming tasks (involving non-declarative memory) was good. EP was given the task of trying to identify briefly presented words and pseudowords. He found it easier to identify those that had been presented previously than those that hadn't. His performance on this priming task was as good as that of healthy controls.

Many of the tasks used to study non-declarative memory and implicit learning (e.g., serial reaction time task) require learning far removed from that occurring in everyday life. What happens when more realistic tasks are used? Anderson et al. (2007) studied car driving in two patients with severe amnesia. The findings suggested that the patients had reasonably intact procedural memory. Their steering, speed control, safety errors, and driving with distraction were all comparable to healthy controls. Because amnesic patients have very poor declarative memory, these findings strengthen the argument that procedural and declarative memory are different.

Cavaco et al. (2004) used five skill-learning tasks requiring skills similar to those needed in the real world. For example, there was a weaving task and a control stick task requiring movements similar to those involved in operating machinery. Amnesic patients showed comparable rates of learning to those of healthy individuals on all five tasks in spite of having impaired declarative memory for the tasks assessed by recall and recognition tests.

WHAT IS IMPAIRED?

The review by Spiers et al. (2001) suggests that amnesic patients have no problems with non-declarative memory. However, they have severe problems with declarative memory, with the ability to form episodic memories being impaired in all cases.

Why is amnesics' episodic memory so poor? An important reason is that amnesics' newly formed episodic memories are very fragile. Dewar et al. (2010) found that 90% of their amnesics recalled nothing of a story presented only 10 minutes earlier if they performed a tone-detection task during the retention interval. However, recall performance was much better if the patients spent the interval quietly in a darkened, empty room. Thus, amnesic patients *can* form new episodic memories, but such memories are very easily disrupted.

The evidence assembled by Spiers et al. (2001) suggests that episodic memory is generally more vulnerable than semantic memory to the effects of brain damage. If so, we might be able to discover amnesic patients with very poor episodic memory but intact semantic memory. Vargha-Khadem et al. (1997) did precisely that. They studied Beth and Jon, both of whom had suffered damage to the hippocampus at an early age before they had had the chance to develop semantic memories. Both of these patients had very poor episodic memory for the day's activities, television programs, and telephone conversations. In spite of this, Beth and Jon both attended ordinary schools, and their levels of speech and language development and their factual knowledge were within the normal range. Vargha-Khadem et al. (2002) carried out a follow-up study on Jon at the age of 20. His semantic memory continued to be much better than his episodic memory.

In spite of patients such as Beth and Jon, many amnesic patients have severe problems with semantic memory as well as episodic memory. Why is that so if semantic memory and episodic memory form fairly separate memory systems? There are two main answers. First, the two memory systems don't function entirely independently of each other. For example, suppose you think of an episodic memory of a sunlit beach on holiday. You need to use semantic memory to understand what is meant by words such as *beach* and *holiday*.

Second, the brain areas involved in the formation of new episodic and semantic memories are very close to each other. Episodic memory (especially recollection) depends heavily on the hippocampus (Diana et al., 2007; Vargha-Khadem et al., 1997). In contrast, semantic memory involves the medial temporal lobe areas adjacent to the hippocampus (Vargha-Khadem et al., 1997). Thus, brain damage sufficient to impair episodic memory will typically also impair semantic memory.

AN ALTERNATIVE SINGLE-SYSTEM VIEW

So far, we have assumed that the best explanation for the performance of amnesics is to make a distinction between declarative memory (explicit memory) and non-declarative memory (implicit memory). That viewpoint has proved very successful and seems to account for most findings.

However, along with the dominant multiple-memories view, a number of authors have defended the idea that what distinguishes between the various memories may not be the type of memory but the processes that must be performed during encoding and retrieval of the information. Explicit memory tests (in particular the free recall test, in which participants have to remember as much as possible from a specific piece of information, without any memory cues) involve conscious, controlled search processes, which are absent in implicit memory tests. In addition, explicit memory tests mostly involve *associations* between stimuli. To remember which words were presented in a particular list, one must make an association between the words and the list (or the study context), which is a completely arbitrary relationship. Such associations are usually not needed in implicit memory tests.

According to the alternative, single-system approach (e.g., Henke, 2010; Reder et al., 2009), there are no different memory systems but amnesic patients find it hard to form associations between two concepts or pieces of information (the *binding hypothesis*).

Suppose we consider amnesics' performance on a procedural memory task that involves forming associations. Amnesics should perform poorly according to the binding hypothesis but should not perform poorly according to the traditional viewpoint. Relevant findings were reported by Ryan et al. (2000). Amnesic patients and healthy individuals were presented with color images of real-world scenes (e.g., a winding road) in three conditions:

1. *Novel scenes*: The scene hadn't been presented before.
2. *Repeated old scenes*: An identical scene had been presented before.
3. *Manipulated old scenes*: The scene had been presented before, but the positions of some objects were altered (e.g., in the original picture two girls were walking on the road, in the manipulated picture the girls were at a different place).

The participants' eye fixations were recorded to assess implicit memory. Two comparisons were critical: (1) between the novel scenes and the repeated scenes, and (2) between the repeated scenes and the manipulated scenes. People typically look less at repeated scenes, because they remember them. Therefore, the first comparison allowed the researchers to see whether the patients with amnesia showed the same implicit memory effect. The second comparison was important, because it involved an arbitrary relationship between a scene and elements in it. Would people with amnesia notice that something in the scene had changed?

As shown in the left part of Figure 5.11, both patients and controls made less fixations to repeated scenes than to novel scenes, indicative of implicit learning. In addition, the healthy controls looked relatively more to the critical region in the manipulated condition than in the other two conditions (the right part of Figure 5.11). However, no such difference was observed for the amnesic patients. This indicates that the normal controls, but not the amnesic patients, remembered something about the relations of the objects in the original scene. These findings support the binding hypothesis.

Another test of the binding hypothesis involves amnesics' performance on an explicit memory task that does not require forming associations. According to the traditional viewpoint, their performance should be poor. In contrast, amnesics' performance should be normal according to the binding hypothesis. Relevant research was reported by Huppert and Piercy (1976). Different pictures were presented on Day 1 and on Day 2. Afterwards, participants were

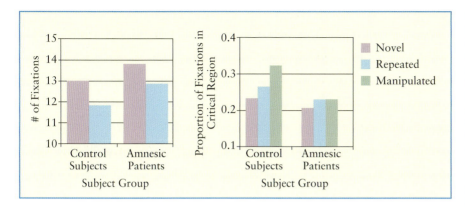

Figure 5.11 Eye movements to novel and repeated scenes in healthy controls and amnesic patients.
The left part shows that both patients and controls looked less at repeated scenes, indicative of learning. The right part shows that controls, but not amnesic patients, paid particular attention to parts of repeated scenes that had been altered. Apparently, the patients had some memory for the scene that had been presented but not for the relations between the elements in the scenes, suggesting that the problems of amnesics have more to do with learning associations between stimuli rather than implicit vs. explicit learning.
Source: Data from Ryan et al. (2000). Reprinted by permission of SAGE Publications.

presented with new pictures and had to indicate whether the pictures looked familiar or not. No prior binding of picture and temporal context was necessary to make such familiarity judgments. The amnesic patients and healthy controls performed comparably well on this task, as predicted by the binding hypothesis.

Huppert and Piercy (1976) also used a recognition-memory test on which participants decided which pictures had been presented on Day 2. Successful performance on this task required binding of picture and temporal context at the time of learning. Healthy controls performed much better than amnesic patients on this task. Thus, amnesic patients were at a great disadvantage when binding was necessary for good memory performance, precisely as predicted by the binding hypothesis (see also the findings of Skinner and Fernandes, 2007, on familiarity vs. recollection, discussed earlier).

In summary, declarative memory tasks require the formation of associations and non-declarative memory tasks often do not. As a result, the findings from most studies are consistent with the traditional viewpoint *and* with the binding hypothesis. When the two theoretical positions make different predictions, a number of findings support the binding hypothesis. When associations need to be formed, amnesic patients perform poorly even on implicit memory tasks (e.g., Ryan et al., 2000). When associations don't need to be formed, amnesic patients perform well even on explicit memory tasks (e.g., Huppert & Piercy, 1976). These findings have been interpreted as evidence for the single-system theory.

According to Cabeza and Moscovitch (2013), neither the hypothesis of multiple memory systems nor the alternative single-system view captures the true nature of human memory. They argued that brain imaging instead points to a *components of processing model*, according to which there are no neatly divided memory systems or processing modes, but a network of numerous brain areas that are recruited in different combinations by memory tasks and that yield complex patterns of associations and dissociations. fMRI evidence suggests that brain regions attributed to one memory system can contribute to tasks associated with other memory systems and that brain regions attributed to the same processing mode can be dissociated from each other. According to Cabeza and Moscovitch (2013), memory processes are supported by transient interactions between multiple brain regions/functions. This is why it is difficult to find neat distinctions between different "types" of memory and/or amnesia.

> ## Section summary
>
> - The study of patients with amnesia has provided a good test-bed for theories of memory.
>
> ### Retrograde vs. anterograde amnesia
> - Retrograde amnesia involves difficulties to remember information from the time before the incident; anterograde amnesia involves difficulties to remember new information after the injury; most patients show both forms with different degrees of severity. Research has focused on anterograde amnesia.
>
> ### What remains intact?
> - Amnesic patients typically have a good ability to acquire numerous new motor skills including weaving and operating machinery. They also show intact performance on priming tasks. It has been argued that amnesic patients have intact non-declarative memory.
>
> ### What is impaired?
> - The greatest impairment in amnesic patients is in the formation of new episodic memories. In addition, they often have problems in forming new semantic memories. Thus, amnesic patients seem to have problems with declarative memory.
>
> ### An alternative single-system view
> - According to the binding hypothesis, amnesics' crucial problem lies in the formation of associations between two concepts or pieces of information. In support, amnesics' declarative memory is often good when associations don't have to be formed. In addition, their non-declarative memory is poor when associations need to be formed.
> - Yet another view is that amnesics differ not because different memory systems are affected or different memory processes in a single system, but because each task involves an interaction of several brain regions, some of which are impaired. Symptoms will differ depending on which component of the network is impaired.

FORGETTING AND MISREMEMBERING

So far in this chapter we have focused on what we remember. However, most of us feel that we have a really poor memory, which can be embarrassing. Many years ago, the British Royal family toured South America. As they left by plane from one airport, a member of the crowd waving them off enthusiastically realized with a sinking feeling he should have been on the plane rather than on the tarmac!

Some evidence that our memories can be poor for important information comes from the study of passwords. In one study (Brown et al., 2004), 31% of American students admitted to having forgotten one or more passwords. Almost half of these students increased the memorability of their passwords by using their own name in password construction, but this may not be the ideal way to have a secure password! However, as we would expect, passwords that are meaningful and familiar are best remembered (Ostojic & Phillips, 2009).

What should we do with our passwords? Brown et al. suggested keeping a record of your passwords in a place to which only you have access (e.g., a safe deposit box or an app). Of course, you then need to remember where you have put your passwords!

THE FORGETTING CURVE

The rate of forgetting is generally fastest shortly after learning and decreases progressively as time goes by. This was first shown by the German psychologist Hermann Ebbinghaus (1885/1913). He carried out extensive studies with himself as the only participant (not a practice to be recommended!). His basic approach involved learning lists of nonsense syllables having little or no meaning (such as kep and zor). At various intervals of time after learning a list, he relearned it. He assessed how much was still remembered by the reduction in the number of trials during relearning compared to original learning (the savings method). Forgetting was very rapid over the first hour after learning but slowed down considerably after that (see Figure 5.12).

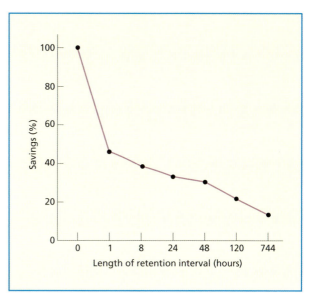

Figure 5.12   Forgetting over time as indexed by reduced savings during relearning.
Source: Data from Ebbinghaus (1885/1913).

As we saw above (Schacter, 1999), forgetting is not something that must be avoided in all situations. Our world is dynamic, and there are frequent changes in the information that is useful to us. For example, it is not useful to remember where you parked your car yesterday, what your schedule of lectures was last semester, or where your friends used to live. What you want to do is to *update* your memory of such information and forget what was previously the case. Fortunately, our memory system is reasonably efficient at doing precisely that.

CONTEXT EFFECTS

When we store away information about an event, we typically also store away information about the context in which that event was experienced. As a result, long-term memory is often better when the context at retrieval is the same as that at the time of learning. More generally, memory is better when the information available at the time of retrieval matches (is the same as) that contained in the memory trace. That is the **encoding specificity principle** put forward by Endel Tulving (e.g., 1979).

Godden and Baddeley (1975) showed the importance of context in a study on deep-sea divers. Divers listened to 40 words on the beach or under 10 feet of water. They were then tested on their ability to recall these words in the same environment or the other one. Recall was considerably better when the environment was the same at test as at learning than when it was different (Figure 5.13).

So far we have considered the importance of context in the form of the *external* environment. However, the *internal* environment is also important. Christopher Miles and Elinor Hardman (1998) wondered whether our internal

Key term

Encoding specificity principle:
the notion that retrieval depends on the *overlap* between the information available at retrieval and the information within the memory trace; memory is best when the overlap is high.

Figure 5.13 Words learned and tested in the same environment are better recalled than those items for which the environmental context varied between study and test.
Source: Data from Godden and Baddeley (1975).

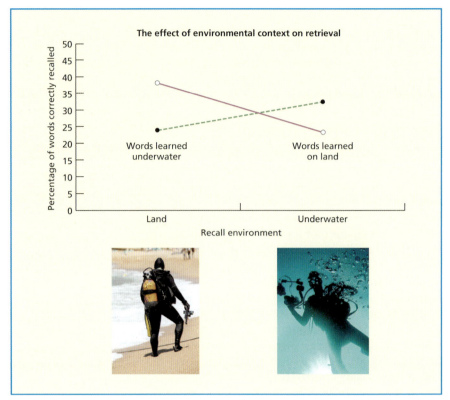

cardiovascular state might influence how much we can remember. Participants learned a list of words while resting at their ease on an exercise bicycle or while pedaling the bicycle vigorously to raise their heart rate to over 120 beats per minute. Word recall was 20% higher when participants were in the same cardiovascular state at retrieval as at learning.

Marian and Kaushanskaya (2007) studied bilingual Mandarin-English speakers. The participants were asked questions such as "Name a statue of someone standing with a raised arm while looking into the distance" in English or in Mandarin. There was a language-dependency effect – participants were more likely to respond "Statue of Liberty" when asked in English but "Statue of Mao" if asked in Mandarin. Thus, the language context influences the information we retrieve.

On the other hand, Koens et al. (2003) were unable to obtain a context effect in a medical exam. Doctor trainees were not better at remembering the details of a case study when they were tested in the hospital room where they had learned about the case study than when they were tested in a classroom. Koens et al. (2003) ventured that context effects have been exaggerated in typical laboratory settings, because:

1. The materials to be studied do not require much insight (e.g., learning a list of unrelated words).
2. There are no intrinsic relations between the context and the stimulus materials to be learned (e.g., learning words on land or under water).

3. The learning materials do not really interest the participants; participants are not motivated much to remember the information.

Saufley et al. (1985) already reported that university students were not at an advantage if they were allowed to take the exam in their usual lecture theater than if they had to take the exam in another, dissimilar room. Smith and Vela (2001) on the basis of a meta-analysis also concluded that environmental, context-dependent memory effects are less probable under conditions in which the immediate environment is likely to be suppressed.

In summary, there is some evidence for context effects in psychological studies in line with the coding specificity principle, but questions have been raised about the applicability of the finding to more realistic circumstances where people are more focused on the contents of the information conveyed than on the surroundings.

INTERFERENCE EFFECTS

If any of your female acquaintances are married, you may have found yourself remembering their maiden name rather than their married name (at least, if you live in a country where brides take on their husband's name upon marriage). Their previous name interferes with (or disrupts) your ability to recall their current name. The notion that interference is important in forgetting goes back to the German psychologist Hugo Münsterberg (1863–1916). Men had pocket watches in those days, and Münsterberg kept his watch in one particular pocket. When he started to keep it in a different pocket for reasons lost in the mists of history, he often fumbled around in confusion when asked for the time.

This story shows the key features of interference theory. Münsterberg had learned an association between the stimulus, "What's the time, Hugo?" and the response of removing the watch from his pocket. Subsequently, the stimulus remained the same but a different response was now associated with it.

Proactive interference

Münsterberg's memory problem is an example of **proactive interference**, in which previous learning disrupts later learning and memory. This type of interference has often been shown in studies on paired-associate learning (see Figure 5.12). Participants initially learn pairs of words on List 1 (e.g., Cat – Dirt). They then learn different pairs of words on List 2 (e.g., Cat – Tree). Finally, they are given the first word (e.g., Cat – ???) and asked to recall the word paired with it on the second list. Memory performance tends to be poor because of interference from the initial associate (i.e., Dirt).

Most research on proactive interference has involved explicit memory. However, proactive interference occurs with implicit memory as well. Lustig and Hasher (2001) used a word-fragment completion task (e.g., A _ L _ _ GY), on which participants wrote down the first appropriate word coming to mind. Participants previously exposed to words almost fitting the fragments (e.g., ANALOGY) showed evidence of proactive interference.

What causes proactive interference? Jacoby et al. (2001) argued there is competition between two responses: the correct one and the incorrect one. As a result, there are two potential reasons why proactive interference occurs: (1)

Key term
Proactive interference: disruption of memory by previous learning (often of similar material); see **retroactive interference**.

Key term
Retroactive interference: disruption of memory for what was learned originally by other learning or processing during the retention interval; see **proactive interference**.

the incorrect response is very strong; or (2) the correct response is very weak. Jacoby et al. found that proactive interference was due much more to the strength of the incorrect response than to the weakness of the correct response.

Bäuml and Kliegl (2013) discussed ways in which the influence of proactive inhibition can be decreased. A first way is simply to tell the participants that they can forget the first list they learned; they will never be tested on this information. The second way is, surprisingly, to test the knowledge of the first list. This too reduces the proactive inhibition of the list (possibly because participants after the test assume they will no longer be questioned about the information in the first list). Finally, according to Bäuml and Kliegl (2013), proactive inhibition also diminishes if the experimenter asks the participants to mentally walk through their childhood home and tell details for about a minute. Apparently, being mentally transported to another place or time between the lists helps to reduce the strengths of the response associated with the first list.

Retroactive interference

There is also retroactive interference, in which later learning disrupts memory for previous learning. This has also been studied using paired-associate learning (see Figure 5.14). In general terms, both proactive and retroactive interference are maximal when two different responses have been associated with the same stimulus (e.g., Cat – Tree and Cat – Dirt) (Underwood & Postman, 1960).

Here is an everyday example of retroactive interference. Suppose you became skillful in carrying out a range of tasks on one computer. After that, you become an expert at performing the same tasks on a different computer with different software. If you went back to your first computer, you might discover that you kept doing things that were correct with the second computer even though they were wrong with the first computer.

Figure 5.14 Methods of testing for proactive and retroactive interference.

		Proactive interference	
Group	**Learn**	**Learn**	**Test**
Experimental	A–B (e.g., Cat–Dirt)	A–C (e.g., Cat–Tree)	A–C (e.g., Cat–Tree)
Control	–	A–C (e.g., Cat–Tree)	A–C (e.g., Cat–Tree)

		Retroactive interference	
Group	**Learn**	**Learn**	**Test**
Experimental	A–B (e.g., Cat–Tree)	A–C (e.g., Cat–Dirt)	A–B (e.g., Cat–Tree)
Control	A–B (e.g., Cat–Tree)	–	A–B (e.g., Cat–Tree)

Note: for both proactive and retroactive interference, the experimental group exhibits interference. On the test, only the first word is supplied, and the participants must provide the second word.

Isurin and McDonald (2001) argued that retroactive interference explains why people forget some of their first language when acquiring a second one. Bilingual participants fluent in two languages were first presented with various pictures and the corresponding words in Russian or Hebrew. Some were then presented with the same pictures and the corresponding words in the other language. Finally, they were tested for recall of the words in the first language. There was substantial retroactive interference – recall of the first-language words became progressively worse the more learning trials there were with the second-language words.

Lustig et al. (2004) argued that retroactive interference in paired-associate learning might occur for two reasons: (1) the correct response is hard to retrieve; or (2) the incorrect response is highly accessible. For example, if participants learn "bed – sheet" on List 1 and "bed – linen" on List 2, they may fail to produce "sheet" on the final test because its strength is weak or because the word "linen" is very strong. Lustig et al. found that retroactive interference was due mainly to the strength of the incorrect response.

Retroactive interference is generally greatest when the new learning resembles previous learning. However, there is some retroactive interference when people expend mental effort during the retention interval even though no new learning is required (Dewar et al., 2007). In Dewar et al.'s experiment, participants learned a list of words and were then exposed to various tasks during the retention interval before list memory was assessed. There was significant retroactive interference even when the intervening task involved detecting differences between pictures or detecting tones. Dewar et al. (2007) concluded that retroactive interference can occur in two ways:

1. Expenditure of mental effort during the retention interval.
2. Learning of material similar to the original learning material.

Interference and real life

There is good evidence that interference is the reason why many people experience difficulties with the multiplication tables. When you come to think of it, learning the multiplications tables is not such a big feat. There are only 100 problems from 0×0 to 9×9. Furthermore, some are these are so easy you don't have to learn them. This is the case for the 0× table and the 1× table (0 times a number = 0; 1 times a number = the number). Of the remaining 8×8 problems, nearly half are each other's mirror image, because $5 \times 4 = 4 \times 5$. So, the actual number of multiplications to be remembered is only 36! Why then do so few people manage to remember these 36 facts, despite intensive training?

The answer lies in an analysis of the errors (Noel et al., 1997). When students are asked how much 4×8 is, they rarely give answers like 30 or 33, even though these are close to the correct answer. The erroneous answers most often given are 24, 28, and 36. When you think of it, you see that these answers belong to the table of 8 ($3 \times 8 = 24$) or to the table of 4 ($4 \times 6 = 24$, $4 \times 7 = 28$, $4 \times 9 = 36$). This means that when we try to find the correct answer to the problem 4×8, we co-activate solutions to nearby problems which interfere with the correct answer. Even worse, Campbell and Thompson (2012) reported that it is more difficult for us to find the solution to 4×8 if before we have solved the problem $4 + 8$. Apparently there is not only interference from the multiplication tables but also from the addition tables. Little surprise then that we find ourselves constantly scratching our heads! When we study hard to finally know by heart how much 7 × 8 is, we suddenly find that we have more difficulty solving the problems 7 × 6, 7 × 7, 7 × 9, 6 × 8, 7 × 8, and 7 + 8 because of increased interference from the problem 7 × 8.

RECALL VS. RECOGNITION

Recognition memory is generally better than recall. For example, we may be unable to recall an acquaintance's name, but if someone mentions their name we instantly recognize it. The reason why recognition is usually better than recall is that there are many more memory cues in recognition questions than in recall questions. These cues help to retrieve the memory trace. For instance, if we are unable to recall an acquaintance's name, often we need not see their full name to recognize it. It is enough to see their first name or even the first letter of their name to suddenly remember the full name. As a result, recognition tests such as yes/no questions or multiple-choice questions may be used to measure what Cantor et al. (2014) called *marginal knowledge*, knowledge that is not available for uncued retrieval but that can be retrieved when given an appropriate memory cue.

CONSOLIDATION

We have considered several factors that play important roles in forgetting. However, we haven't directly addressed the issue of why the rate of forgetting is greatest shortly after learning. The answer may be **consolidation** (Wixted, 2004). Consolidation is a physiological process lasting for a long time (possibly years) that fixes information in long-term memory. A key assumption of consolidation theory is that recently formed memories that are still being consolidated are especially vulnerable to interference and forgetting. In other words, "New memories are clear but fragile and old ones are faded but robust" (Wixted, 2004, p. 265).

According to some versions of consolidation theory (e.g., Eichenbaum, 2001), the process of consolidation involves two major phases. The first phase occurs over a period of hours and centers on the hippocampus. The second phase takes place over a period of time ranging from days to years and involves interactions between the hippocampal region and the neocortex. This phase occurs mostly during sleep (Diekelmann & Born, 2010).

Evidence for consolidation theory comes from the study of brain-damaged patients with retrograde amnesia, in which there is impaired memory for events occurring before the accident. Many of these patients have suffered damage to the hippocampus as the result of an accident. Because the hippocampus is of central importance in the first phase of consolidation, the most recently formed memories should be the ones most impaired in these patients. This pattern has been found in numerous patients with retrograde amnesia (Manns et al., 2003; see also Figure 5.10).

According to consolidation theory, newly formed memories should be more susceptible to retroactive interference from subsequent learning than older ones. The predicted findings have been obtained even when the interfering material is dissimilar to the material learned originally (see the research by Dewar et al., 2007, mentioned earlier). In such cases, there is often more

Key term
Consolidation: a physiological process involved in establishing long-term memories; this process lasts several hours or more, and newly formed memories that are still being consolidated are fragile.

retroactive interference when it is presented *early* in the retention interval (Wixted, 2004).

Finally, consider the effects of alcohol on memory. Individuals who drink excessive amounts of alcohol sometimes suffer from "blackouts." This is an almost total loss of memory for all events occurring while they were conscious but very drunk. These blackouts indicate a failure to consolidate memories formed while intoxicated.

Evaluation

+ Consolidation theory explains why the rate of forgetting decreases over time.

+ Consolidation theory successfully predicts that retrograde amnesia is greater for recently formed memories and that retroactive interference effects are greatest shortly after learning.

+ The theory identifies the brain areas most associated with consolidation.

− Forgetting involves several factors other than consolidation. For example, forgetting is greater when there is little informational overlap between the memory trace and the retrieval environment (encoding specificity principle).

− Consolidation theory deemphasizes the role of *cognitive* processes in forgetting.

− As we will see in the next section, consolidation processes are more complex than was implied by early versions of consolidation theory.

MISREMEMBERING

We saw earlier that it is often useful for us to update our information (e.g., about our lecture schedule) and at the same time to forget previously relevant information. What is involved in this updating process? As discussed earlier, learning leads to a consolidation process in which memory traces are initially very fragile but become decreasingly so over time.

Reconsolidation

Several theorists (e.g., Hardt et al., 2010; Schwabe et al., 2014) have put forward a more complex version of consolidation theory. According to them, *reactivation* of a memory trace that has already been consolidated puts it back into a fragile state. This leads to reconsolidation (a new consolidation process), with the fragility of the memory trace allowing it to be updated and altered.

Reconsolidation is very useful if we want to update our knowledge because what we learned previously is no longer relevant. However, it can cause us to misremember if we subsequently want to recall the information we learned originally. This is how it happens. We learn some information at Time 1. At Time 2, we learn additional information. If the memory traces based on the information learned at Time 1 are activated at Time 2, then those Time 1 memory traces immediately become fragile. As a result, some information learned

Key term

Reconsolidation: this is a new **consolidation** process that occurs when a previously formed memory trace is reactivated; it allows that memory trace to be updated.

at Time 2 will mistakenly become incorporated into the memory traces of the Time 1 information and cause misremembering.

An early study showing the importance of reconsolidation was by Walker et al. (2003). They used a finger-tapping task in which participants remembered a given sequence of responses. Two conditions were very similar in that one sequence was learned initially and then a second sequence was learned 24 hours later. The only difference was that in one condition the participants briefly rehearsed the first sequence before learning the second one.

According to reconsolidation theory, brief rehearsal should have made the memory traces of the first sequence fragile and thus produced errors in memory. That is precisely what happened – long-term memory for the first sequence was much worse when it was briefly rehearsed.

Walker et al. (2003) found that reconsolidation played an important role in motor memory. Hupbach et al. (2007, 2008) showed that reconsolidation is also important in memory for a set of objects. In one condition, participants' memory traces of their Time 1 learning were reactivated by reminding them of that learning just before the new learning at Time 2 (e.g., "Can you describe the general procedure of what you did on Monday?").

When participants were later asked to recall the Time 1 information, they misremembered some of the Time 2 information as having been learned at Time 1. There was much less such misremembering when participants were *not* reminded of their Time 1 learning prior to Time 2 learning. This was because the Time 1 memory traces were less likely to be reactivated in this condition.

Hindsight bias

Hindsight bias occurs when someone provided with accurate information about the outcome of an event mistakenly thinks that they knew it all along. For example, suppose you were asked "How high is the Eiffel tower?" and estimated its height at 650 feet (200 m). You are then told its actual height is 1,063 feet (324 m). You would show hindsight bias if you subsequently claimed you had always known it was about 1,000 feet high.

Hindsight bias depends on various cognitive and motivational factors (see Guilbault et al., 2004, for a review). However, memory distortions play an important role. According to Hardt et al. (2010), providing the correct information about an event (e.g., Eiffel tower is 1,063 feet) *reactivates* the relevant memory trace (e.g., Eiffel tower is 650 feet) and can cause it to be altered during reconsolidation.

If hindsight bias depends on basic physiological processes involved in reconsolidation, it should be hard to eliminate. That is precisely what Pohl and Hell (1996) found in a study using difficult general knowledge questions. Some participants were warned in advance about hindsight bias, but this failed to reduce the size of the bias. Other participants were given individual feedback about the errors in their recall, but this also failed to reduce hindsight bias when they were tested again.

Post-event misinformation effect

Reconsolidation also helps to explain the post-event misinformation effect. This effect (discussed more fully in Chapter 7) occurs when eyewitness memory for an incident is distorted by misleading information presented afterwards.

Key term

Hindsight bias: the tendency for people to exaggerate how accurately they would have predicted some event in advance after they know what actually happened.

For example, Loftus and Zanni (1975) showed people a short video of a car accident. Afterwards, some eyewitnesses were asked, "Did you see the broken headlight?" In fact, there was no broken headlight even though the question implied there was. This misleading question led several eyewitnesses to mistakenly claim they had seen a broken headlight.

According to the reconsolidation account, the presentation of misleading information causes reactivation of the memory traces of the original incident. This makes those memory traces fragile and can lead to some of the misleading information being incorporated into the memory traces. This provides a potential explanation of the post-event misinformation effect, although other factors are also involved (see Chapter 7).

Section summary

The forgetting curve
- The rate of forgetting is generally fastest shortly after learning and then decreases progressively. Forgetting occurs in both explicit and implicit memory tasks.

Context effects
- According to the encoding specificity principle, memory is generally better when the context at retrieval matches that at learning. This context can involve the external environment or internal physiological or emotional state. The context effect may be limited to situations in which the participants have to learn ill-structured information that does not really interest them.

Interference effects
- What we have learned can be forgotten due to previous similar learning (proactive interference) or learning during the retention interval (retroactive interference). Both forms of interference are greatest when the same stimulus is associated with two responses. Proactive and retroactive interference are due more to the strength of incorrect responses than the weakness of correct ones.

Recall vs. recognition
- Recall and recognition are two of the most used measures of explicit memory. Recognition is usually easier than recall, because the recognition question includes more memory cues than the recall question.

Consolidation
- Consolidation is a physiological process involved in the storage of memories. Recently formed memories that are still being consolidated are especially vulnerable to forgetting. Consolidation theory explains why retrograde amnesia is generally greater for recently formed memories. However, its focus is physiological; psychological and cognitive processes are deemphasized.

Misremembering
- Reactivation of a memory trace that has already been consolidated makes it fragile again and leads to reconsolidation. Reconsolidation processes can cause misremembering.

- Reconsolidation probably plays a role in hindsight bias. This occurs when someone mistakenly believes they knew something all along when given the correct answer.
- Reconsolidation may also be partly responsible for the post-event misinformation effect, which occurs when misleading information provided after an event causes distortions in an eyewitness's memory for that event.

Essay questions

1. What are some of the main factors involved in effective learning of information?
2. "Implicit learning is very different from explicit learning." Discuss.
3. Discuss some of the main forms of long-term memory.
4. What can amnesics remember? What can't they remember?
5. Why do we forget?

Further reading

- Baddeley, A., Eysenck, M. W., & Anderson, M. C. (2015). *Memory* (2nd ed.). New York: Psychology Press. This introductory textbook discusses at length all the main areas within memory research.
- Della Sala, S. (2010). *Forgetting*. New York: Psychology Press. The major contemporary approaches to understanding forgetting are discussed in this edited book.
- Foerde, K., & Poldrack, R. A. (2009). Procedural learning in humans. In L. R. Squire (Ed.), *The new encyclopedia of neuroscience* (Vol. 7, pp. 1083–1091). Oxford, UK: Academic Press. This chapter provides a thorough overview of theory and research on procedural learning and memory.
- Reber, P. J. (2013). The neural basis of implicit learning and memory: a review of neuropsychological and neuroimaging research. *Neuropsychologia*, *51*(10), 2026–2042. In this article Reber argues that implicit learning is involved most of the time as we interact with the environment.

REFERENCES

Aggleton, J. P. (2008). Understanding anterograde amnesia: Disconnections and hidden lesions. *Quarterly Journal of Experimental Psychology, 61,* 1441–1471.

Anderson, S. W., Rizzo, M., Skaar, N., Cavaco, S., Dawson, J., & Damasio, H. (2007). Amnesia and driving. *Journal of Clinical and Experimental Neuropsychology, 29,* 1–12.

Atkinson, R. C., & Shiffrin, R. M. (1968). Human memory: A proposed system and its control processes. In K. W. Spence & J. T. Spence (Eds.), *The psychology of learning and motivation* (Vol. 2). London, UK: Academic Press.

Bangert-Drowns, R. L., Kulik, J. A., & Kulik, C. L. C. (1991). Effects of frequent classroom testing. *Journal of Educational Research, 61,* 213–238.

Bäuml, K. H. T., & Kliegl, O. (2013). The critical role of retrieval processes in release from proactive interference. *Journal of Memory and Language, 68*(1), 39–53.

Baxendale, S. (2004). Memories aren't made of this: Amnesia at the movies. *British Medical Journal, 329,* 1480–1483.

Bjork, R. A., & Bjork, E. L. (1992). A new theory of disuse and an old theory of stimulus fluctuation. In A. Healey, S. Kosslyn, & R. Shiffrin (Eds.), *From learning processes to cognitive processes: Essays in honor of William K. Estes* (Vol. 2). Hillsdale, NJ: Lawrence Erlbaum.

Brown, A. S., Bracken, E., Zoccoli, S., & Douglas, K. (2004). Generating and remembering passwords. *Applied Cognitive Psychology, 18,* 641–651.

Cabeza, R., & Moscovitch, M. (2013). Memory systems, processing modes, and components functional neuroimaging evidence. *Perspectives on Psychological Science, 8*(1), 49–55.

Campbell, J. I., & Thompson, V. A. (2012). Retrieval-induced forgetting of arithmetic facts. *Journal of Experimental Psychology: Learning, Memory, and Cognition, 38*(1), 118–129.

Cantor, A. D., Eslick, A. N., Marsh, E. J., Bjork, R. A., & Bjork, E. L. (2014). Multiple-choice tests stabilize access to marginal knowledge. *Memory & Cognition, 43,* 193–205.

Cavaco, S., Anderson, S. W., Allen, J. S., Castro-Caldas, A., & Damasio, H. (2004). The scope of preserved procedural memory in amnesia. *Brain, 127,* 1853–1867.

Challis, B. H., Velichkovsky, B. M., & Craik, F. I. M. (1996). Levels-of-processing effects on a variety of memory tasks: New findings and theoretical implications. *Consciousness and Cognition, 5,* 142–164.

Clark, G. M., Lum, J. A., & Ullman, M. T. (2014). A meta-analysis and meta-regression of serial reaction time task performance in Parkinson's disease. *Neuropsychology, 28*(6), 945–958.

Conway, M. A. (2001). Sensory–perceptual episodic memory and its context: Autobiographical memory. *Philosophical Transactions of the Royal Society B: Biological Sciences, 356*(1413), 1375–1384.

Corkin, S. (2013). *Permanent present tense: The man with no memory, and what he taught the world.* London: Penguin UK.

Craik, F. I. M., & Lockhart, R. S. (1972). Levels of processing: A framework for memory research. *Journal of Verbal Learning and Verbal Behavior, 11,* 671–684.

Craik, F. I. M., & Tulving, E. (1975). Depth of processing and the retention of words in episodic memory. *Journal of Experimental Psychology: General, 104,* 268–294.

D'Hooge, R., & De Deyn, P. P. (2001). Applications of the Morris water maze in the study of learning and memory. *Brain Research Reviews, 36*(1), 60–90.

Dehaene, S., Naccache, L., Cohen, L., Le Bihan, D., Mangin, J., Poline, J., et al. (2001). Cerebral mechanisms of word masking and unconscious repetition priming. *Nature Neuroscience, 4,* 752–758.

Destrebecqz, A., & Cleeremans, A. (2001). Can sequence learning be implicit? New evidence with the process dissociation procedure. *Psychonomic Bulletin & Review, 8*(2), 343–350.

Dewar, M. T., Cowan, N., & Della Sala, S. (2007). Forgetting due to retroactive interference: A fusion of Müller and Pizecker's (1900) early insights into everyday forgetting and recent research on retrograde amnesia. *Cortex, 43,* 616–634.

Dewar, M., Della Sala, S., Beschin, N., & Cowan, N. (2010). Profound retroactive amnesia: What interferes? *Neuropsychology, 24,* 357–367.

Diana, R. A., Yonelinas, A. P., & Ranganath, C. (2007). Imaging recollection and familiarity in the medial temporal lobe: A three-component model. *Trends in Cognitive Sciences, 11,* 379–386.

Diekelmann, S., & Born, J. (2010). The memory function of sleep. *Nature Reviews Neuroscience, 11*(2), 114–126.

Ebbinghaus, H. (1885/1913). *Über das Gedächtnis*. Leipzig, Germany: Dunker [translated by H. Ruyer & C. E. Bussenius]. New York, NY: Teachers College, Columbia University.

Eichenbaum, H. (2001). The hippocampus and declarative memory: Cognitive mechanisms and neural codes. *Behavioral Brain Research, 127*, 199–207.

Eysenck, M. W. (1979). Depth, elaboration, and distinctiveness. In L. S. Cermak & F. I. M. Craik (Eds.), *Levels of processing in human memory*. Hillsdale, NJ: Lawrence Erlbaum.

Eysenck, M. W., & Eysenck, M. C. (1980). Effects of processing depth, distinctiveness, and word frequency on retention. *British Journal of Psychology, 71*, 263–274.

Foerde, K., & Poldrack, R. A. (2009). Procedural learning in humans. In L. R. Squire (Ed.), *The new encyclopedia of neuroscience, Vol. 7* (pp. 1083–1091). Oxford, UK: Academic Press.

Gebauer, G. F., & Mackintosh, N. J. (2007). Psychometric intelligence dissociates implicit and explicit learning. *Journal of Experimental Psychology: Learning, Memory, and Cognition, 33*, 34–54.

Gheysen, F., & Fias, W. (2012). Dissociable neural systems of sequence learning. *Advances in Cognitive Psychology, 8*(2), 73–82.

Godden, D. R., & Baddeley, A. D. (1975). Context dependent memory in two natural environments: On land and under water. *British Journal of Psychology, 66*, 325–331.

Graf, P., & Schacter, D. L. (1985). Implicit and explicit memory for new associations in normal and amnesic subjects. *Journal of Experimental Psychology: Learning, Memory, & Cognition, 11*, 501–518.

Guilbault, R. L., Bryant, F. B., Brockway, J. H., & Posavac, E. J. (2004). A meta-analysis of research on hindsight bias. *Basic and Applied Social Psychology, 26*, 103–117.

Hamann, S. B., & Squire, L. R. (1997). Intact perceptual memory in the absence of conscious memory. *Behavioral Neuroscience, 111*, 850–854.

Hardt, O., Einarsson, E. O., & Nader, K. (2010). A bridge over troubled water: Reconsolidation as a link between cognitive and neuroscientific memory research traditions. *Annual Review of Psychology, 61*, 141–167.

Hassabis, D., Kumaran, D., Vann, S. D., & Maguire, E. A. (2007). Patients with hippocampal amnesia cannot imagine new experiences. *Proceedings of the National Academy of Sciences of the United States of America, 104*, 1726–1731.

Henderson, E. N. (1903). A study of memory for connected trains of thought. *The Psychological Review, Series of Monograph Supplements, V*(6), (Whole No. 23, p. 93). New York: Palgrave Macmillan.

Henke, K. (2010). A model for memory systems based on processing modes rather than consciousness. *Nature Reviews Neuroscience, 11*(7), 523–532.

Howard Jr, J. H., & Howard, D. V. (2013). Aging mind and brain: Is implicit learning spared in healthy aging? *Frontiers in Psychology, 4*(817), 1–6.

Howard, D. V., & Howard, J. H. (1992). Adult age differences in the rate of learning serial patterns: Evidence from direct and indirect tests. *Psychology & Aging, 7*, 232–241.

Hunt, R. R. (2006). The concept of distinctiveness in memory research. In R. R. Hunt & J. E. Worthen (Eds.), *Distinctiveness and memory* (pp. 3–25). New York, NY: Oxford University Press.

Hupbach, A., Gomez, R., Hardt, O., & Nadel, L. (2007). Reconsolidation of episodic memories: A subtle reminder triggers integration of new information. *Learning & Memory, 14*, 47–53.

Hupbach, A., Hardt, O., Gomez, R., & Nadel, L. (2008). The dynamics of memory: Context-dependent updating. *Learning & Memory, 15*, 574–579.

Huppert, F. A., & Piercy, M. (1976). Recognition memory in amnesic patients: Effect of temporal context and familiarity of material. *Cortex, 4,* 3–20.

Isurin, L., & McDonald, J. L. (2001). Retroactive interference from translation equivalents: Implications for first language forgetting. *Memory & Cognition, 29,* 312–319.

Jacoby, L. L., Debner, J. A., & Hay, J. F. (2001). Proactive interference, accessibility bias, and process dissociations: Valid subjective reports of memory. *Journal of Experimental Psychology: Learning, Memory, & Cognition, 27,* 686–700.

Janacsek, K., & Nemeth, D. (2013). Implicit sequence learning and working memory: Correlated or complicated? *Cortex, 49*(8), 2001–2006.

Karpicke, J. D., Butler, A.C., & Roediger III, H. L. (2009). Metacognitive strategies in student learning: Do students practise retrieval when they study on their own? *Memory, 17,* 471–479.

Kaufman, S. B., DeYoung, C. G., Gray, J. R., Jiménez, L., Brown, J., & Mackintosh, N. (2010). Implicit learning as an ability. *Cognition, 116*(3), 321–340.

Kirchhoff, B. A., Schapiro, M. L., & Buckner, R. L. (2005). Orthographic distinctiveness and semantic elaboration provide separate contributions to memory. *Journal of Cognitive Neuroscience, 17,* 1841–1854.

Koens, F., Ten Cate, O. T. J., & Custers, E. J. (2003). Context-dependent memory in a meaningful environment for medical education: In the classroom and at the bedside. *Advances in Health Sciences Education, 8*(2), 155–165.

Lewandowsky, S., & Oberauer, K. (2015). Rehearsal in serial recall: An unworkable solution to the nonexistent problem of decay. *Psychological Review, 122*(4), 674–699.

Loftus, E. F., & Zanni, G. (1975). Eyewitness testimony – Influence of wording of a question. *Bulletin of the Psychonomic Society, 5,* 86–88.

Luria, A. (1968). *The mind of a mnemonist.* New York, NY: Basic Books.

Lustig, C., & Hasher, L. (2001). Implicit memory is not immune to interference. *Psychological Bulletin, 127,* 618–628.

Lustig, C., Konkel, A., & Jacoby, L. L. (2004). Which route to recovery? Controlled retrieval and accessibility bias in retroactive interference. *Psychological Science, 15,* 729–735.

Manning, L. (2002). Focal retrograde amnesia documented with matching anterograde and retrograde procedures. *Neuropsychologia, 40*(1), 28–38.

Manns, J. R., Hopkins, R. O., & Squire, L. R. (2003). Semantic memory and the human hippocampus. *Neuron, 38,* 127–133.

Marian, V., & Kaushanskaya, M. (2007). Language context guides memory content. *Psychonomic Bulletin & Review, 14,* 925–933.

Metcalfe, J., & Kornell, N. (2007). Principles of cognitive science in education: The effects of generation, errors, and feedback. *Psychonomic Bulletin & Review, 14,* 225–229.

Meulemans, T., & Van der Linden, M. (2003). Implicit learning of complex information in amnesia. *Brain and Cognition, 52,* 250–257.

Migo, E. M., Mayes, A. R., & Montaldi, D. (2012). Measuring recollection and familiarity: Improving the remember/know procedure. *Consciousness and Cognition, 21*(3), 1435–1455.

Miles, C., & Hardman, E. (1998). State-dependent memory produced by aerobic exercise. *Ergonomics, 41,* 20–26.

Milner, B. (2005). The medial temporal-lobe amnesic syndrome. *Psychiatric Clinics of North America, 28*(3), 599–611.

Morris, C. D., Bransford, J. D., & Franks, J. J. (1977). Levels of processing versus transfer appropriate processing. *Journal of Verbal Learning and Verbal Behavior, 16,* 519–533.

Moscovitch, M., Nadel, L., Winocur, G., Gilboa, A., & Rosenbaum, R. S. (2006). The cognitive neuroscience of remote episodic, semantic and spatial memory. *Current Opinion in Neurobiology, 16,* 179–190.

Nairne, J. S., Thompson, S. R., & Pandeirada, J. N. (2007). Adaptive memory: Survival processing enhances retention. *Journal of Experimental Psychology: Learning, Memory, and Cognition, 33*(2), 263.

Noël, M. P., Fias, W., & Brysbaert, M. (1997). About the influence of the presentation format on arithmetical-fact retrieval processes. *Cognition, 63*(3), 335–374.

Ostojic, P., & Phillips, J. G. (2009). Memorability of alternative password systems. *International Journal of Pattern Recognition and Artificial Intelligence, 23,* 987–1004.

Pavlov, I. P. (1927). *Conditioned reflexes.* London: Oxford University Press (English translation).

Pohl, R. F., & Hell, W. (1996). No reduction in hindsight bias after complete information and repeated testing. *Organizational Behavior and Human Decision Processes, 67,* 49–58.

Pothos, E. M. (2007). Theories of artificial grammar learning. *Psychological Bulletin, 133*(2), 227–244.

Reber, A. S. (1993). *Implicit learning and tacit knowledge: An essay on the cognitive unconscious.* Oxford, UK: Oxford University Press.

Reder, L. M., Park, H., & Kieffaber, P. D. (2009). Memory systems do not divide on consciousness: Reinterpreting memory in terms of activation and binding. *Psychological Bulletin, 135,* 23–49.

Rescorla, R. A., & Wagner, A. R. (1972). A theory of Pavlovian conditioning: Variations in the effectiveness of reinforcement and nonreinforcement. In A. H. Black & W. F. Prokasy (Eds.), *Classical conditioning II* (pp. 64–99). New York: Appleton-Century-Crofts.

Roediger, H. L. (2008). Relativity of remembering: Why the laws of memory vanished. *Annual Review of Psychology, 59,* 225–254.

Roediger, H. L., & Karpicke, J. D. (2006). Test-enhanced learning: Taking memory tests improves long-term retention. *Psychological Science, 17,* 249–255.

Rogers, T. B., Kuiper, N. A., & Kirker, W. S. (1977). Self-reference and the encoding of personal information. *Journal of Personality and Social Psychology, 35,* 677–688.

Rowland, C. A. (2014). The effect of testing versus restudy on retention: A meta-analytic review of the testing effect. *Psychological Bulletin, 140*(6), 1432–1463.

Ryan, J. D., Althoff, R. R., Whitlow, S., & Cohen, N. J. (2000). Amnesia is a deficit in relational memory. *Psychological Science, 11,* 454–461.

Saufley, W. H., Otaka, S. R., & Bavaresco, J. L. (1985). Context effects: Classroom tests and context independence. *Memory & Cognition, 13*(6), 522–528.

Schacter, D. L. (1999). The seven sins of memory – Insights from psychology and cognitive neuroscience. *American Psychologist, 54,* 182–203.

Schacter, D. L., & Addis, D. R. (2007). The cognitive neuroscience of constructive memory: Remembering the past and imagining the future. *Philosophical Transactions of the Royal Society B: Biological Sciences, 362,* 773–786.

Schwabe, L., Nader, K., & Pruessner, J. C. (2014). Reconsolidation of human memory: Brain mechanisms and clinical relevance. *Biological Psychiatry, 76*(4), 274–280.

Seaman, K. L., Howard, D. V., & Howard, J. H. (2013). Adult age differences in learning on a sequentially cued prediction task. *The Journals of Gerontology Series B: Psychological Sciences and Social Sciences, 69*(5), 686–694.

Shanks, D. R. (2005). Implicit learning. In K. Lamberts & R. Goldstone (Eds.), *Handbook of cognition* (pp. 202–220). London, UK: Sage.

Shanks, D. R. (2010). Learning: From association to cognition. *Annual Review of Psychology, 61,* 273–301.

Shanks, D. R., & St. John, M. F. (1994). Characteristics of dissociable human learning systems. *Behavioral & Brain Sciences*, *17*, 367–394.

Shuell, T. J. (1969). Clustering and organization in free recall. *Psychological Bulletin*, *72*, 353–374.

Skinner, E. I., & Fernandes, M. A. (2007). Neural correlates of recollection and familiarity: A review of neuroimaging and patient data. *Neuropsychologia*, *45*, 2163–2179.

Smith, C. N., Frascino, J. C., Hopkins, R. O., & Squire, L. R. (2013). The nature of anterograde and retrograde memory impairment after damage to the medial temporal lobe. *Neuropsychologia*, *51*(13), 2709–2714.

Smith, S. M., & Vela, E. (2001). Environmental context-dependent memory: A review and meta-analysis. *Psychonomic Bulletin & Review*, *8*(2), 203–220.

Snyder, K. M., Ashitaka, Y., Shimada, H., Ulrich, J. E., & Logan, G. D. (2014). What skilled typists don't know about the QWERTY keyboard. *Attention, Perception, & Psychophysics*, *76*, 162–171.

Spiers, H. J., Maguire, E. A., & Burgess, N. (2001). Hippocampal amnesia. *Neurocase*, *7*, 357–382.

Sun, R., Zhang, X., & Mathews, R. (2009). Capturing human data in a letter-counting task: Accessibility and action-centeredness in representing cognitive skills. *Neural Networks*, *22*, 15–29.

Symons, C. S., & Johnson, B. T. (1997). The self-reference effect in memory: A meta-analysis. *Psychological Bulletin*, *121*, 371–394.

Szpunar, K. K. (2010). Episodic future thought: An emerging concept. *Perspectives on Psychological Science*, *5*, 142–162.

Szpunar, K. K., & Radvansky, G. A. (2016). Cognitive approaches to the study of episodic future thinking. *The Quarterly Journal of Experimental Psychology*, *69*(2), 209–216.

Tulving, E. (1979). Relation between encoding specificity and levels of processing. In L. S. Cermak & F. I. M. Craik (Eds.), *Levels of processing in human memory*. Hillsdale, NJ: Lawrence Erlbaum.

Tulving, E. (1985). Memory and consciousness. *Canadian Psychology*, *26*(1), 1–12.

Tulving, E. (2002). Episodic memory: From mind to brain. *Annual Review of Psychology*, *53*, 1–25.

Tulving, E., & Schacter, D. L. (1990). Priming and human-memory systems. *Science*, *247*, 301–306.

Underwood, B. J., & Postman, L. (1960). Extra-experimental sources of interference in forgetting. *Psychological Review*, *64*, 49–60.

Vargha-Khadem, F., Gadian, D. G., & Mishkin, M. (2002). Dissociations in cognitive memory: The syndrome of developmental amnesia. In A. Baddeley, M. Conway, & J. Aggleton (Eds.), *Episodic memory: New directions in research* (pp. 153–163). New York, NY: Oxford University Press.

Vargha-Khadem, F., Gadian, D. G., Watkins, K. E., Connelly, A., Van Paesschen, W., & Mishkin, M. (1997). Differential effects of early hippocampal pathology on episodic and semantic memory. *Science*, *277*, 376–380.

Viard, A., Desgranges, B., Eustache, F., & Piolino, P. (2012). Factors affecting medial temporal lobe engagement for past and future episodic events: An ALE meta-analysis of neuroimaging studies. *Brain and Cognition*, *80*(1), 111–125.

Vingerhoets, G., Vermeule, E., & Santens, P. (2005). Impaired intentional content learning but spare incidental retention of contextual information in non-demented patients with Parkinson's disease. *Neuropsychologia*, *43*, 675–681.

Walker, M. P., Brakefield, T., Hobson, J. A., & Stickgold, R. (2003). Dissociable stages of human memory consolidation and reconsolidation. *Nature*, *425*, 616–620.

Warrington, E. K., & Weiskrantz, L. (1968). New method of testing long-term retention with special reference to amnesic patients. *Nature, 217,* 972–974.

Wilkinson, L., & Shanks, D. R. (2004). Intentional control and implicit sequence learning. *Journal of Experimental Psychology: Learning, Memory, & Cognition, 30,* 354–369.

Wilkinson, L., Khan, Z., & Jahanshahi, M. (2009). The role of the basal ganglia and its cortical connections in sequence learning: Evidence from implicit and explicit sequence learning in Parkinson's disease. *Neuropsychologia, 47*(12), 2564–2573.

Wixted, J. T. (2004). The psychology and neuroscience of forgetting. *Annual Review of Psychology, 55,* 235–269.

Yang, J., & Li, P. (2012). Brain networks of explicit and implicit learning. *PloS One, 7*(8), e42993.

Yonelinas, A. P. (2002). The nature of recollection and familiarity: A review of 30 years of research. *Journal of Memory and Language, 46,* 441–517.

Zeidman, P., & Maguire, E. A. (2016). Anterior hippocampus: The anatomy of perception, imagination and episodic memory. *Nature Reviews Neuroscience, 17*(3), 173–182.

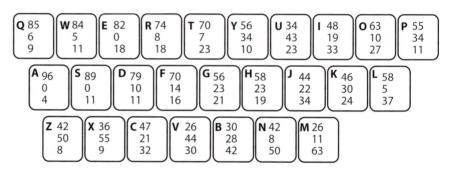

Percentages of experienced typists given an unfilled schematic keyboard (Figure 5.2) who correctly located (top number), omitted (middle number) or misplaced (bottom number) each letter with respect to the standard QWERTY keyboard.
Source: From Snyder et al. (2014). Reprinted with permission of Springer.

Chapter 6

Contents

Knowledge in semantic memory

6

INTRODUCTION

We all possess huge amounts of general knowledge about words and about the world in which we live. You are likely to know the meanings of over 40,000 words (Brysbaert et al., 2016), you know the name of the current pope, that Brussels is the capital of Europe, and so on. This general knowledge is stored in semantic memory (Chapter 5).

It is almost impossible to exaggerate the importance of general knowledge in our everyday lives. For example, your ability to perceive the animal in front of you as a dog or a cat depends on relating sensory information to relevant knowledge in semantic memory.

General knowledge is also important when memorizing information. For example, consider the task of learning a word list consisting of, say, four words belonging to each of six categories (e.g., four-footed animals, girls' names, flowers, vehicles, furniture, and kitchen utensils). Subsequent recall is much higher when the words are presented in their categories rather than in random order (Shuell, 1969). This is because it is much easier to use category knowledge to organize the material during learning and retrieval when the words are presented category by category.

General knowledge is also vital when it comes to making sense of what you read. Consider the following: *Tom was driving along when a tire on his car blew. He arrived home very late*. You would use your general knowledge to work out that the blown tire forced Tom to stop and that he lost time to fix the problem. The same knowledge helps you to decide that the following scenario is much less plausible and, therefore, does not make much sense unless some extraordinary factor is involved: *Tom was eating an apple. He arrived home very late*.

A substantial amount of our general knowledge relates to individual elements, which we will call concepts. For example, we know that cats are smallish animals having four legs, fur, a tail, and so on. However, knowledge of the meanings of individual elements is not enough to interact successfully with the world around us. We also need to store combinations of concepts in semantic memory. As we will see, such integrated packets of information are called schemas.

CONCEPTS

Suppose you phone a friend sitting in their study at home. They tell you they see a lamp, a desk, a printer, a computer, several books, a few photographs, and trees out in the garden. The important point here is that you are able to understand your friend's description even though it isn't very detailed and specific. For example, your friend doesn't point out that the lamp is made of metal and is adjustable, nor do they indicate that the desk is made of light brown wood with a black top. Similarly, you don't assume the lamp is a floor lamp or a table lamp, nor do you assume that the computer is a desktop or a laptop (do you?).

This example suggests we generally focus on the essentials of objects and don't clutter our minds with irrelevant details. To account for this finding, researchers assume that we store knowledge in semantic memory by means of concepts. A **concept** refers to a mental representation of a category of objects, such as a dog, a car, or a bed. A **category** is a set or class of objects that belong together.

FUNCTIONS OF CONCEPTS

Why is so much of our knowledge in semantic memory stored in the form of concepts? The single most important reason is that concepts provide a very *efficient* way of representing our knowledge of the world and the objects in it. Concepts allow us to focus on the *similarities* among objects that resemble each other but are not identical. This enables *communication*. When we have conversations with other people, we constantly use concepts to convey information about ourselves and the world as we understand it.

Another function of concepts is that they permit us to make accurate *predictions* about objects in the world (Heit, 1992). For example, if we categorize an animal as a cat, we can predict it is unlikely to do us any harm. In contrast, if we categorize an animal as a lion, we can predict that it may be dangerous and so take avoiding action.

Key terms

Concept:
a mental representation of a **category** of objects; stored in long-term memory.

Category:
a set or class of objects that belong together (e.g., articles of furniture; four-footed animals).

What would it be like to be unable to categorize your experience? The South American writer Jorge-Luis Borges (1964, pp. 93–94) answered this question when he described the experiences of a fictional man called Funes who found himself in that situation:

> *Funes remembered not only every leaf of every tree of every wood, but also every one of the times he had perceived or imagined it . . . Not only was it difficult for him to comprehend that the symbol dog embraces so many unlike individuals of diverse size and form; it bothered him that the dog at three fourteen (seen from the side) should have the same name as the dog at three fifteen (seen from the front). His own face in the mirror, his own hands, surprised him every time he saw them.*

Contrary to what is believed, deciding whether an object belongs to a category is often open to debate. Consider the concept of a *planet*, which has historically been defined as a large body circling a sun. That definition came under pressure a number of years ago when it became clear that Pluto is smaller and its orbit less circular than those of other objects in our solar system. As a result, Pluto was stripped of its status as a planet and named a dwarf planet, along with a number of other bodies in the Kuiper belt.

CONCEPTS ARE DIFFICULT TO DEFINE

Although we all daily use concepts to think and talk about the world and our role in it, it has proven extremely difficult for psychologists to understand what concepts are (Wills & Pothos, 2012). Which principles are used to delineate concepts?

In this section, we discuss the most important theoretical approaches that have been proposed. First, we will deal with the intuitively appealing idea that concepts are defined by essential features. Then we will discuss the prototype and exemplar approaches. Both approaches have been designed to account for the major categories of concepts and the nature of category membership. Afterwards, we turn to the role of knowledge and experience in the organization of concepts. For example, our knowledge of a concept often includes information about the causal relations among its features or the appropriate action to take with respect to it.

In the Real World 6.1 *Semantic dementia*

It is generally accepted that the general knowledge stored in semantic memory plays a major role in everyday life. This can be demonstrated most clearly by considering individuals lacking such knowledge. Precisely that was done by the Colombian novelist Gabriel García Márquez in his novel *One Hundred Years of Solitude*. The inhabitants of Macondo are struck by the insomnia plague. This gradually causes them to lose information about the meanings and functions of the objects around them, thereby producing a state of despair.

Here is how the central character (José Arcadio Buerdia) responds to this desperate situation:

> The sign that he hung on the neck of the cow was an exemplary proof of the way in which the inhabitants of Macondo were prepared to fight against loss of memory: This is the cow. She must be milked every morning so that she will produce

milk, and the milk must be boiled in order to be mixed with coffee to make coffee and milk.

The fictional account provided by Gabriel García Márquez is amazingly similar to the real-life experiences of brain-damaged patients suffering from semantic dementia (Hodges et al., 2009; Rascovsky et al., 2009). **Semantic dementia** is a condition in which there is widespread loss of knowledge about the meanings of concepts and words (Patterson et al., 2007). This differs from Alzheimer's disease, where problems primarily have to do with episodic memory: Patients still understand the meanings of concepts and words, but don't remember what happened to them. Semantic dementia involves damage to the anterior temporal lobes and other areas are relatively spared initially. As we will see, patients with semantic dementia show substantial loss of meaning across all sensory modalities.

Patients with semantic dementia have problems categorizing objects from pictures, especially when the categorization is relatively difficult. They can categorize pictures at a very general level (e.g., animal; non-living) better than at an intermediate (e.g., dog; cat) or specific level (e.g., Labrador; collie) (Rogers & Patterson, 2007). Thus, patients find it hard to assign detailed meaning to visual objects.

Patients with semantic dementia perform poorly when asked to draw objects (see Figure 6.1; Rascovsky et al., 2009). The patient GW omitted important features from his drawings – his fish lacks fins, one of his birds lacks wings, and the elephant lacks a trunk. These drawings indicate that GW has very limited access to information concerning object meanings.

Patients with semantic dementia also have problems in the auditory modality. They can't identify objects when listening to their characteristic sounds (e.g., a phone ringing; a dog barking; Patterson et al., 2007).

Patients with semantic dementia are also poor at identifying flavors when tasting jelly beans with various flavors such as coffee, coconut, and vanilla (Piwnica-Worms et al., 2010). A 67-year-old female patient (CMR) was found to have reduced empathy (the ability to understand others' feelings). She was also poor at identifying facial emotions (Calabria et al., 2009). These findings indicate the

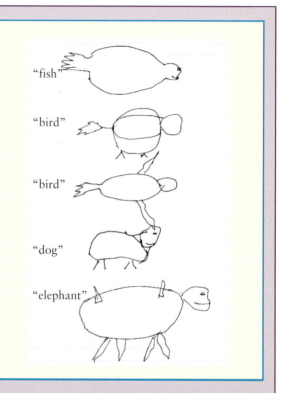

Figure 6.1   Drawings of animals by patient GW show major semantic deficits. Important distinguishing features are missing: the fish lacks fins, the first bird lacks wings, and the elephant has no trunk. Because of the lack of details, all pictures of animals resemble each other excessively.
Source: From Rascovsky et al. (2009), with permission from Oxford University Press.

widespread nature of the loss of meaning experienced by patients with semantic dementia.

What is spared in semantic dementia? Strikingly, patients in the early stages of the disease seem to have almost intact autobiographical memory and episodic memory (concerned with personal experiences) for the preceding 12 months (Matuszewski et al., 2009). This allows them to remember day-to-day events, to honor appointments, and to function in their everyday lives until the disease becomes more severe (Rascovsky et al., 2009). Patients are often good at jigsaw puzzles (which require visuo-spatial abilities) and spend much of their time solving them (Green & Patterson, 2009).

Finally, some aspects of language are spared initially (Kertesz et al., 2010). Patients make very few errors of pronunciation and their speech is grammatical. However, they make subtle grammatical errors (e.g., "That's made me cried a lot": Meteyard & Patterson, 2009). In addition, their speech is often not very meaningful (e.g., frequent use of general, uninformative words such as "thing" and "stuff").

The problems experienced by patients with semantic dementia have various negative consequences. They often exhibit behavioral changes such as lowered emotional mood states, rigid patterns of behavior, and mild obsessions (Green & Patterson, 2009).

Patients with semantic dementia are often especially concerned about the gradual loss of autobiographical memory. One patient (RB) kept a list of where he had lived over the preceding 32 years. He carried this list around with him the whole time to help to preserve his sense of self. He also recorded familiar names together with information on location or occupation (e.g., "Virgil and Lois = were in Yukon").

In sum, the progressive erosion of semantic memory in patients with semantic dementia causes a very wide-ranging loss of meaning. This can lead to behavioral abnormalities and loss of a sense of personal identity. From a theoretical perspective, it is important that early-stage patients can show reasonably intact autobiographical and episodic memory, pronunciation of words, knowledge of grammar, and visuo-spatial processing. The pattern of findings shows clearly those aspects of cognition more or less reliant on semantic memory.

The common feature approach

When someone asks us to explain what *fruit* is, we almost all will start by giving a list of typical (common) features of fruits. These may include: "is edible, grows on trees or is the fruit of a plant, is sweet, is healthy, is juicy, contains seeds, is rich in vitamins, can get rotten, is round" (Hampton, 1979; Storms et al., 2001). Dictionaries follow the same procedure. For instance, the Wordnet dictionary (http://wordnet.princeton.edu/) defines *fruit* as "the ripened reproductive body of a seed plant." According to this definition, three features are essential to define *fruit*: ripe, reproductive body, and seed plant. The other features (juicy, sweet, rich in vitamins, round) are not essential because they are shared with other concepts.

The intuitive idea that concepts are defined by essential, common features was the first theory of concept formation adopted in philosophy and psychology. However, it rapidly ran into trouble, even to such an extent that the philosopher Wittgenstein (1889–1951), after a lifetime of thinking about concepts, despaired of whether it was possible to ever find definitions of concepts. For instance, he wondered whether it was at all possible to find a set of criteria that distinguished the category of all sports from the category of all games. Is chess a sport or a game? And why?

Wittgenstein's problem can easily be illustrated by asking a group of people whether a pumpkin is a fruit or a vegetable (you can also try with a tomato, a cucumber, or a gherkin). McCloskey and Glucksberg (1978) presented the question to 30 people, along with a few other similar questions, such as "Is a stroke a disease?" The authors found that 16 participants said a pumpkin was fruit and 14 said it was a vegetable. A stroke was regarded as a disease by 16 people too, but not by the remainder. More surprisingly, when McCloskey and Glucksberg tested the same people a month later, 11 had changed their minds about *stroke* being a disease, and eight had altered their opinion about *pumpkin* being a fruit!

According to the definition of the Wordnet dictionary (and botanists), pumpkins and tomatoes are types of fruit, even though many people intuitively

| Key term

Semantic dementia: a condition caused by brain damage in which there is initially mainly extensive loss of knowledge about the meanings of words and concepts.

classify them as vegetables (because pumpkins and tomatoes are not sweet and are used in the kitchen on par with vegetables instead of fruits).

The difficulty of classifying pumpkins and tomatoes illustrates that many concepts have **fuzzy boundaries**, gradual transitions with other, related concepts. This makes it hard to find *the* defining features and, if you manage to do so, the resulting definition rarely agrees with spontaneous human thinking. For instance, many children know what fruit is long before they know what "ripe," "reproductive body," and "seed plant" are!

There are considerable individual differences in beliefs about the nature of category membership. Some individuals are convinced that category membership should be all-or-none, whereas others have more flexible beliefs (Simmons & Hampton, 2006). The former individuals are more likely to argue that words on a fuzzy boundary belong to one category or the other as a matter of fact rather than of opinion.

Prototype approach

Because of the difficulties with the common feature approach, the prototype approach was proposed as an alternative (Rosch & Mervis, 1975; Hampton, 2007, 2010). According to this approach, each category has a **prototype**, which is a central description or conceptual core representing the category. Categorization is achieved by comparing new information to the prototypes of known concepts.

What does a prototype look like? The most popular view is that it is a set of characteristic attributes or features in which some attributes are weighted more than others. We can assess prototypes by asking people to indicate those attributes typical of a category. Previously we saw the features defining the prototype of fruit. Features of the bird prototype include: is alive, flies, has feathers, has a beak, has wings, has legs and feet, lays eggs, builds nests, sings, has claws, is lightweight (Hampton, 1979).

Within the prototype approach, an object is a member of a category if there is a good match between its features and those of the prototype. This is called *family resemblance*. Animals that share many features with the bird prototype (e.g., sparrows, robins, tits, finches) are seen as more representative of the concept bird than species with a smaller resemblance (e.g., chickens, swans, penguins). As a result, people are faster to decide that a robin is a bird than that a swan is a bird. This is called the **typicality effect**.

The prototype theory also provides a good explanation for the fuzzy boundaries between categories (Hampton, 2010). The fewer features a stimulus shares with a prototype, the less it will be seen as part of the category and the higher the chances it will share a similar number of features with another category (which is why more people think a whale is a fish rather than a mammal).

The prototype theory also explains why people list features shared by most category members when they are asked to give the features of a category, even when the feature is not shared by all members (Hampton, 2010). For instance, people happily say that birds "can fly," even though ostriches do not fly. So, technically speaking, "can fly" is not a common feature of all birds and, therefore, should not be used according to the common feature approach, as is endearingly illustrated in Wordnet's definition of birds: "warm-blooded egg-laying vertebrates characterized by feathers and forelimbs modified as wings" (in case you ever wondered why dictionaries give convoluted explanations for simple words).

Prototypes exist for abstract concepts as well. Fehr (2004) investigated whether there is a prototype for friendship. She found evidence that there was.

Women and men agreed that self-disclosure, emotional support, and loyalty are all typical features of friendship intimacy and so contribute heavily to the prototype. Shared activities and practical support are less prototypical features. Interestingly, women attached more importance than men to the key features of self-disclosure, emotional support, and loyalty.

Why is it useful for us to form prototypes for the categories we have stored in semantic memory? We have seen that information can belong to different categories depending on the feature focused upon, so that the boundaries of categories are vague and hard to establish. In addition, these boundaries can change when we discover new information, as when someone finds out that *tomato* is technically a fruit rather than a vegetable. What is generally most consistent and unchanging about a category or concept is its conceptual core, which is in essence what a prototype is.

FINDINGS

Impressive evidence for the importance of family resemblances within categories was reported by Rosch and Mervis (1975). They used six categories and asked participants which were the most typical exemplars of each category. Table 6.1 shows the 20 most typical members in decreasing order. Next, a new group of participants was asked to list the attributes of each category member (e.g., car, truck, bus, motorcycle).

Table 6.1 Typicality of items belonging to six categories. Ask a few friends to name all the types of furniture they know or all the types of clothing. See how well their answers agree with the typicality data obtained by Rosch and Mervis (1975). Are the more typical instances named more often and earlier than the less typical ones? Are there any differences with the data collected 50 years ago?

Typicality	Furniture	Fruit	Vehicle	Weapons	Clothing	Vegetables
1	Chair	Orange	Car	Gun	Pants	Peas
2	Sofa	Apple	Truck	Knife	Shirt	Carrots
3	Table	Banana	Bus	Sword	Dress	String beans
4	Dresser	Peach	Motorcycle	Bomb	Skirt	Spinach
5	Desk	Pear	Train	Hand grenade	Jacket	Broccoli
6	Bed	Apricot	Trolley	Spear	Coat	Asparagus
7	Bookcase	Plum	Bicycle	Cannon	Sweater	Corn
8	Footstool	Grape	Airplane	Bow and arrow	Underpants	Cauliflower
9	Lamp	Strawberry	Boat	Club	Socks	Brussels sprouts
10	Piano	Grapefruit	Tractor	Tank	Pajamas	Lettuce
11	Cushion	Pineapple	Cart	Tear gas	Bathing suit	Beets
12	Mirror	Blueberry	Wheelchair	Whip	Shoes	Tomato
13	Rug	Lemon	Tank	Ice pick	Vest	Lima beans
14	Radio	Watermelon	Raft	Fists	Tie	Eggplant
15	Stove	Honeydew	Sled	Rocket	Mittens	Onion
16	Clock	Pomegranate	Horse	Poison	Hat	Potato
17	Picture	Date	Blimp	Scissors	Apron	Yam
18	Closet	Coconut	Skates	Words	Purse	Mushroom
19	Vase	Tomato	Wheelbarrow	Foot	Wristwatch	Pumpkin
20	Telephone	Olive	Elevator	Screwdriver	Necklace	Rice

Source: From Rosch and Mervis (1975). Reprinted with permission from Elsevier.

Most of the attributes of any given category member were shared by at least some of the other members of the same category. This information was used to calculate family resemblance scores for each member. For example, suppose a category member had two attributes, one possessed by 16 category members and the other possessed by 14 category members. That would give a family resemblance score of 16 + 14 = 30.

Rosch and Mervis's (1975) key finding was that typical category members had much higher family resemblance scores than did atypical category members. The correlation between typicality and family resemblance ranged between +.84 (for vegetables) and +.94 (for weapons).

Rosch and Mervis (1975) also considered the numbers of attributes shared by the five most typical and those shared by the five least typical members of each category. We will discuss the findings from the vehicle category, but similar results were obtained with the other categories. The five most typical members of the vehicle category (*car, truck, bus, motorcycle*, and *train*) had 36 attributes in common (e.g., wheels, engine, driver). In contrast, the five least typical members (*horse, blimp, skates, wheelbarrow*, and *elevator*) had only two attributes in common.

LIMITATIONS

Although the prototype theory explains many more findings than the common feature theory, it fails to account for all findings. Barsalou (1985) reported that family resemblance scores did not predict typicality scores for members of goal-derived categories. These are categories in which all category members satisfy a given goal (e.g., birthday presents that make the recipient happy). Typical members of such categories were those best satisfying the goal (e.g., providing pleasure to someone celebrating his/her birthday) rather than sharing attributes with other category members.

The prediction that prototypes represent the features of most members in the category also failed to explain the data reported by Lynch et al. (2000). These authors asked tree experts and novices to provide typicality ratings for trees. According to prototype theory, we would expect that trees of average height should be rated as the best examples. In fact, experts identified very tall, non-weedlike trees as the best examples of trees. In other words, their ratings were determined by the extent to which any given tree corresponded to an *ideal* tree rather than by a tree sharing features with *most* other trees.

The findings from the novices in the study by Lynch et al. (2000) differed considerably from those of the experts, but also failed to support prototype theory. For novices, the most important factor determining the typicality ratings was their familiarity with the tree types. As a result, *maple* and *oak* emerged as the best examples of trees and *ginkgo* and *catalpa* were among the worst, even though they share the same number of features with the prototype of tree.

Finally, not all categories have clear prototypes (think of the concepts *science, criminality, justice, belief*; Hampton, 1981), and people can categorize instances in newly defined categories (e.g., "things to sell at a garage sale" or "people to meet if I were to move to California"). Barsalou (1983) called the latter type of categories "ad hoc categories." Because ad hoc categories are newly formed, they cannot have prototypes yet. Still, people happily provide members for these categories. How is that possible?

Evaluation

+ The prototype approach provides a reasonable account of the typicality ratings found with the members of many categories.

+ It is plausible that summary descriptions (prototypes or conceptual cores) of most categories are stored in semantic memory.

− Prototype approaches are more applicable to some kinds of concepts than to others. For example, some abstract concepts don't seem to have prototypes (Hampton, 1981), and family resemblances fail to predict typicality ratings for the members of goal-derived categories (Barsalou, 1985).

− Concepts are more complex than assumed by the prototype approach. For example, the approach doesn't provide a coherent explanation of effects due to expertise (Lynch et al., 2000).

Exemplar approach

The exemplar approach was proposed to explain some difficulties encountered with the prototype theory (e.g., Rips & Collins, 1993). Instead of there being some abstract description of a category (a central prototype), the exemplar approach assumes that a new entity is categorized by comparing it to exemplars from various categories. Thus, for example, when we see a new type of flying animal and want to decide whether it is a bird or an insect, we would not do so by comparing the new animal to the prototype of a bird and the prototype of an insect, but by comparing the new animal to the birds we are familiar with (tits, robins, finches, pigeons, blackbirds, starlings, sparrows) and to the insects we are familiar with (hoverflies, butterflies, ladybirds, bees, wasps, dragonflies). In addition, we would not compare the new animal to stored prototypes of these animals but to all the memories (instances) of these animals we have acquired throughout our lives.

FINDINGS

Much evidence supporting prototype theories can also be explained by exemplar theories. For example, consider the faster categorization judgments for some category members than for others. When asked, "Is a robin a bird?" you can answer much faster than when asked, "Is a penguin a bird?" Given that you have encountered many robins in the past, there are likely to be more stored instances of robins than penguins. Therefore, a robin instance will be retrieved from memory much faster than a penguin instance, thus giving rise to the difference in judgment times.

According to the exemplar approach, an important factor influencing a category member's typicality is the *frequency* with which it has been encountered. Evidence of this was reported by Novick (2003). The typicality of *airplane* as a vehicle was assessed before the terrorist airplane attack of 9/11 and then at various times after the attack. The huge publicity generated by 9/11 caused an increase in the rated typicality of *airplane* 5 hours and 1 month after the terrorist attack. However, its typicality returned to its pre-attack level 4.5 months after the attack. In similar fashion, it is assumed that a sparrow is a more typical instance of a bird than a penguin because people have stored many more instances of sparrows than of penguins.

Storms et al. (2000) compared the exemplar approach with the prototype approach for common categories such as *furniture, fruit,* and *birds.* Two types of information were collected for concepts belonging to these categories (e.g., finch and ostrich). First, a prototype similarity measure was collected by determining to what extent the concepts shared the features of the prototype. So, participants were asked whether finches and ostriches are alive, fly, have feathers, have a beak, have wings, have legs and feet, lay eggs, build nests, sing, have claws, are lightweight, and so on. The other measure was an exemplar similarity measure. This evaluated the similarity of the concept to the most typical exemplars of the category. So, participants were asked how similar finches and ostriches were to an eagle, a robin, a blue jay, a cardinal, a hawk, a bluebird, and so on (the bird species most frequently mentioned when American students are asked to name bird types). Storms et al. (2000) correlated the prototype similarity measure and the exemplar similarity measure with various dependent variables, such as the typicality rating of the concept or the time needed to decide that the concept belonged to the category. All dependent variables were predicted reasonably well by both the prototype similarity measure and the exemplar similarity measure. However, the exemplar similarity measure consistently outperformed the prototype similarity measure.

LIMITATIONS

The main problem with exemplar-based concepts is that it is not clear how they can be used in everyday life (Binder, 2016; Murphy, 2016). As we have seen, concepts form the core of semantic memory and are combined with each other to understand and store incoming information. How can this be done with exemplar-based concepts that lack any degree of abstraction? For instance, how can we bring organization in concepts? We know for instance that robins are birds, animals, and living things. How is this possible if each of these concepts is entirely exemplar-based?

Another limitation of the exemplar approach is that it works less well with simple concepts than with complex ones (Smith and Minda, 2000). According to Feldman (2003), this is because simple concepts often have a common feature that defines them (e.g., all even numbers are divisible by 2). For these concepts the exemplar approach is not needed. Only when concepts lack clear, defining features do we need the exemplar approach (as we have seen earlier).

A POSSIBLE SOLUTION?

A possible solution to decide between the prototype and the exemplar theory was proposed by Vanpaemel and Storms (2008). They started from the idea that the prototype and exemplar approaches need not be mutually exclusive. The approaches can be considered as the two ends of an abstraction continuum: exemplar theories assume no abstraction at all, whereas prototype theories assume total abstraction. According to Vanpaemel and Storms (2008), a better explanation may be to assume that categories differ in their degree of abstraction (as a result of the category itself or the amount of experience a person has with the category).

Vanpaemel and Storms (2008) applied a new "variable abstraction" model to previously published datasets that had been used in favor of the exemplar theory, and found that the new model outperformed the original exemplar-based models.

Evaluation

(+) When attempts have been made to contrast the predictions of exemplar models with those of prototype models, exemplar models have generally outperformed prototype models (Storms et al., 2000).

(−) Exemplar models tend to be less successful when applied to the learning of simple concepts than to very complex ones (Feldman, 2003; Smith & Minda, 2000).

(−) Most exemplar models assume that every instance of a category we encounter is stored in memory. On that assumption, it is hard to see how we prevent information (and storage) overload. In addition, some level of abstraction seems to be needed if we want to combine concepts to build up general knowledge about the world and our place in it.

(+) A possible solution may be that exemplar models and prototype models are not mutually exclusive, but vary in the degree of abstraction.

Knowledge-based approach

The theories discussed so far fail to provide a full account of the knowledge we have about many concepts. In addition to knowledge of a concept's features, we usually have some understanding of the *relations* among the features. For example, *dangerous* and *sharp* are two features of the concept of a knife. These two features are related in that many people argue that knives are dangerous precisely because they are sharp (Heussen & Hampton, 2007).

Causal relations are especially important. For example, we know a car has a motor, needs fuel, and is self-propelled. However, an object might have all these features and still not be seen as a car. Consider an object in which the motor only caused the windshield wipers to move, the fuel was only used to warm the passengers, and the object moved when the wind caught its sails (Hampton, 2010). The above object differs considerably from the cars with which we are familiar. With such cars, fuel drives the motor, and the motor causes the car to move. In other words, the features are *causally* related to each other.

We can see the importance of causal relations among features in a study by Ahn et al. (2000). Participants were told that members of a given category tend to have three features (e.g., blurred vision; headaches; insomnia). They were also told that blurred vision causes headaches and that headaches cause insomnia. Then participants indicated the likelihood that an item belonged to the category if one feature was absent. The rated likelihood of membership was lowest when the initial cause (i.e., blurred vision) was absent and highest when the final effect (i.e., insomnia) was missing. Thus, people believe that if the cause is missing, it is unlikely that an item is a member of the category.

Another limitation of the theories discussed so far is that concepts are thought of as fixed and inflexible. In fact, how we represent a concept *changes* as a function of the context in which it appears (Barsalou, 2008). For example, when we read the word *frog* in isolation, the phrase "eaten by humans" probably remains inactive in our memory system. However, "eaten by humans" *becomes* active when reading about frogs in a French restaurant. Thus, concepts are unstable or flexible to the extent that the precise concept information activated varies from situation to situation. Yee and Thompson-Schill (2016) argued that the context-dependency of concepts goes so far that there is not even a core representation activated across all possible contexts. For instance, it might be that the feature "animal" is not activated when a *frog* is encountered in the context of a child playing with a fluffy toy frog.

Barsalou (2008, 2009) points out that in everyday life we process concepts mostly in a specific context and *not* in isolation. So, the finding that the nature of the concept depends on the context means that most of the time the concept information activated is partial and subject to change. More generally, the representation of any given concept will vary from situation to situation depending on the individual's current goals and the major characteristics of the situation. Remember our example at the beginning of this chapter of your friend saying to you over the phone that they see a lamp and a desk. The image you formed about the lamp and the desk is likely to be very minimal and influenced by the context (see also Research Activity 6.1).

Research Activity 6.1 *Concept activation and the context*

This Research Activity (based on research reported by Wu and Barsalou, 2009) is best done with a friend. Take each of the words in List A in turn and write down as many properties as you can of each one. Then ask your friend to do the same task for the noun phrases in List B.

List A	List B
Lawn	Rolled-up lawn
Watermelon	Half watermelon
Car	Comfortable car

If you compare the two sets of properties, you will probably find some interesting differences. You probably focused on *external* properties of the concepts (e.g., plant; blades; rind; green and yellow; bonnet; trunk) and omitted some of their *internal* properties (e.g., dirt; soil; pips; red; heater; radio). In contrast, your friend may have shown the opposite pattern, focusing more on internal properties and less on external ones.

What is the meaning of this finding (first reported by Wu and Barsalou, 2009)? It indicates that our processing of concepts often has a *perceptual* quality about it. It is harder to think of object properties that wouldn't be visible if you were actually looking at the object itself.

Wu and Barsalou (2009) further discovered that participants often wrote down properties referring to the background situation rather than the object itself. Indeed, between 25% and 50% of the total properties produced related to the background situation.

You may have found something similar. For example, *lawn* may have led you to write down properties such as *picnic* or *you play on it*, and *car* to write down *highway* or *holiday*. In our everyday lives, we typically perceive objects in a particular situation or context, and this aspect of perception is also found when we process concepts.

THE KNOWLEDGE-BASED ALTERNATIVE
The knowledge-based approach has been proposed to explain why causal relations between features of a concept have a powerful influence over

TARGET "BIRD"   PERCEPTUALLY   PERCEPTUALLY
                     DISSIMILAR   SIMILAR
                     "BIRD"   "DINOSAUR"

Figure 6.2 Drawings of the stimuli used by Gelman and Coley (1990). Two-year-old children first saw a target picture of a typical bird and were told that this animal lives in a nest. Later, they were shown the picture of an atypical, perceptually dissimilar dodo bird and asked whether a dodo lived in a nest or not. They were also shown the picture of a pterodactyl dinosaur, which perceptually resembled the picture of the bird, and were asked whether this dinosaur lived in a nest. The children were more likely to judge that the dodo lived in a nest than the pterodactyl, illustrating that they relied more on their general knowledge of birds to make the categorization than on the perceptual similarity. Source: From Gelman and Coley (1990). Reprinted with permission from the American Psychological Association.

categorization, and why the categorization depends on an individual's current goals and the characteristics of the situation. According to the knowledge-based approach, categories are based on knowledge about causal, functional, or structural properties of things in the world, and the ability to perceive and learn causal patterns is a fundamental prerequisite for category formation. This is already true for infants (Keil et al., 1998; Pauen, 2002).

Gelman and Coley (1990) illustrated knowledge-based categorization in 2-year-old children. The children were first shown a picture of a typical category member (e.g., a bird; see the left panel of Figure 6.2) and given some information ("it lives in a nest"). Then they were shown other pictures and asked whether the things represented on the pictures lived in nests or not. One of these pictures was of a dodo bird, which did not resemble the target picture perceptually; another picture was of a pterodactyl dinosaur, which graphically resembled the original bird picture. Gelman and Coley (1990) wanted to see whether the children were more likely to say that the dodo lived in a nest than the pterodactyl (suggesting knowledge-based categorization) or the other way around (suggesting perception-based categorization). They obtained clear evidence in favor of the first hypothesis.

Because concepts are knowledge-based, Gelman (2009) argued that they allow children to do two things. First, they enable dissimilar objects to be treated alike, as having properties in common (e.g., living in a nest). Second, knowledge-based concepts promote inferences regarding non-obvious features, such as internal parts, functions, and other non-visible aspects.

The knowledge-based account also helps to explain how we can make ad hoc categorizations for situations we have not yet encountered. If we were asked to categorize which objects are worth saving in case of a fire, we are more likely to rely on our general knowledge of the world than on common features, prototypes or exemplars.

Embodied cognition approach

The approaches so far stressed concepts as abstract representations, which are independent of perceptual and motor experiences. However, this is unlikely to be the full picture.

The main reason why concepts must include more than abstract, modality-free information is that it is impossible to know the full meaning of many concepts without having experienced what they stand for. When we think of a "tree," it is next to impossible to fully communicate the meaning of the

concept to someone who does not live in a world with trees. For someone who
never experienced a tree, the concept remains incomplete. This was formulated most eloquently by the philosopher Jackson (1982), who described the
following Mary thought experiment:

*Mary is a brilliant scientist who is, for whatever reason, forced to inves-
tigate the world from a black and white room via a black and white
television monitor. She specializes in the neurophysiology of vision and
acquires, let us suppose, all the physical information there is to obtain
about what goes on when we see ripe tomatoes, or the sky, and use terms
like 'red', 'blue', and so on. She discovers, for example, just which wave-
length combinations from the sky stimulate the retina, and exactly how
this produces via the central nervous system the contraction of the vocal
chords and expulsion of air from the lungs that results in the uttering of
the sentence 'The sky is blue.' . . .*

*What will happen when Mary is released from her black and white
room or is given a color television monitor? Will she learn anything or
not? It seems just obvious that she will learn something about the world
and our visual experience of it. But then it is inescapable that her previous knowledge was incomplete. But she had all the physical information.
Ergo there is more to have than that. . .*

(Jackson, 1982, p. 130)

The fact that the meaning of concepts partly relies on physical interactions
of our body with the surrounding world, is called **embodied cognition**.

Harnad (1990) argued that embodied cognition is also needed for understanding language: We can never understand the meaning of words if each word
is defined entirely in terms of other words. You can easily get a feeling of this
by taking a dictionary of a language you don't know. Each word is defined by
other words, which you can look up as well, but as long as you do not know the
meaning of a single word, it is impossible to start building up an understanding
of the language you are watching. Thus, the meaning of at least some words
must be grounded in non-verbal experiences you have with the world around
you. When children learn the word "apple," they do so by relating the word to
a range of sensory experiences (visual, touch-related, taste-related) and motor
actions (eating, carrying the apple, giving it to mommy, letting it fall).

Vincent-Lamarre et al. (2016) analyzed English dictionaries to find out the
minimum number of experience-grounded words needed to define all other
words in the dictionary. For a dictionary of 100,000 words they observed that
this was possible with a minimal set of some 1,000 seed words. Interestingly,
there was not a single minimal set of experience-grounded words; the same
result could be obtained from various sets of similar size. Thus, each of us
can have learned our language entirely on the basis of a slightly different set
of experience- grounded seed words. As can be expected, the seed words were
acquired earlier, occurred more frequently in the language, and tended to be
more concrete than the other words.

FINDINGS

There are many findings indicating that perceptual and motor information is
incorporated into concepts.

Pecher et al. (2009) reported the involvement of visual perception in sentence comprehension. Participants were asked to read sentences and judge whether they made sense or not. A quarter of the participants saw the sentence "Angela put the toothpaste in her shopping basket." Another quarter saw the sentence "Angela put the toothpaste on her toothbrush." The remaining participants saw two other sentences. After the reading phase, participants got a surprise memory task. They were shown pictures of objects and had to judge whether the objects figured in one of the sentences they had judged before. So, the participants who had seen one of the sentences above had to press "yes" to the picture of a toothpaste tube; the others had to press "no." Importantly, some participants saw a closed tube while others saw an open tube. Participants were significantly more accurate when the picture matched the meaning of the sentence (e.g., an open tube after the sentence "Angela put the toothpaste on her toothbrush") than when it did not (a closed tube after the sentence "Angela put the toothpaste on her toothbrush").

The question whether knowledge in semantic memory consists of more than abstract concepts has received particular attention with respect to visual imagery. Imagine the living room in your parents' house. How many windows does it have? When answering this question, which information from your semantic memory do you use: stored visual images or stored abstract concepts?

Kosslyn (2005) argued that the mechanisms used to generate images involve the same processes as those used to perceive stimuli. This approach is known as the *perceptual anticipation theory*. It assumes there are close similarities between visual imagery and visual perception. In contrast, Pylyshyn (2003) argued that we form visual images on the basis of abstract concept information stored in memory, when we are trying to imagine things. This concept-based theory predicts systematic differences between visual imagery and visual perception.

One element strongly in favor of Kosslyn's perception anticipation theory is the finding that visual imagery activates very much the same areas in the visual cortex as those involved in perception (Kosslyn & Thompson, 2003). Klein et al. (2004), for instance, presented participants with flickering black-and-white, bow-tie-shaped stimuli with a horizontal or a vertical orientation. As expected, there was more activation within early visual cortex in the vertical direction when the stimulus was in the vertical orientation and more in the horizontal direction when it was in the horizontal orientation. More interestingly, the authors also asked the participants to imagine the same bow-tie-shaped stimuli. The same patterns of brain activation were observed when the participants imagined the vertical and the horizontal stimuli. This provides evidence that the processes involved in visual imagery approximate those involved in visual perception. You find more evidence (and also some counter-evidence) in Research Activity 6.2.

Barsalou and Wiemer-Hastings (2005) reported evidence that even our knowledge of abstract things includes experience-based properties. They asked people to list the characteristic properties of various abstract concepts. Many properties referred to imaginable settings or events associated with the concept (e.g., scientists working in a laboratory for *invention*) and others referred to relevant mental states. Vigliocco et al. (2014) argued that many abstract concepts include emotions. According to them, children learn the meaning of concepts such as *love* or *injustice* partly by relying on the feelings associated with them.

Hauk et al. (2004; see also Pulvermüller, 2013) tested the assumption that the motor system is involved when we access concept information. They made use of the fact that tongue, finger, and foot movements produce different patterns of activation along the motor strip of the cerebral cortex. When they presented participants with words such as "lick," "pick," and "kick," the verbs activated parts of the motor strip overlapping with the cortex active when participants performed the actions. Thus, the word "lick" activated a brain area associated with tongue movements.

In sum, the ways we use conceptual knowledge in everyday life often involve the perceptual, motor, and emotional systems. This potentially helps in explaining why concepts show variability and instability from one situation to another. The precise meaning we assign to a concept depends on the situation and on the perceptual and motor processes engaged by the current task.

Research Activity 6.2 *Similarities and differences between perception and visual imagery*

Study the outline of the island depicted in Figure 6.3, so that you will be able to answer some questions from memory.

Your task now is to indicate for each of the following objects whether it was on the island or not. Make sure you keep the figure covered. Which of

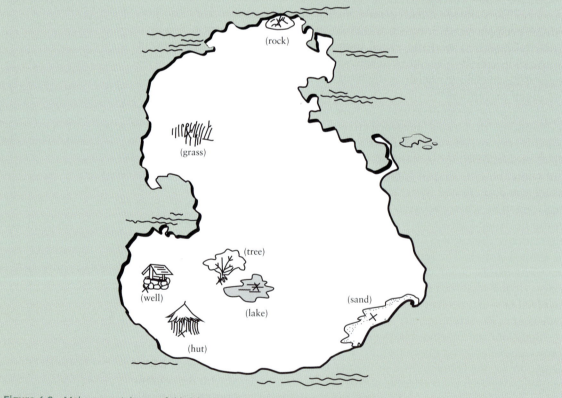

(rock)

(grass)

(tree)

(well)

(lake)

(sand)

(hut)

Figure 6.3 Make a mental map of this island. Make a detailed mental map of the picture. Then cover it and answer the questions in the text.
Source: From Kosslyn et al. (1978). Reprinted with permission from the American Psychological Association.

the following objects was on the island: well, tree, hut, grass, bench?

Did you notice that it took you longer to respond to grass than to tree and hut? Kosslyn et al. (1978) observed that it took the participants longer to respond to objects far away from each other in the picture than to objects close to each other, suggesting that the mental map was very similar to the visual percept.

Pylyshyn (2003) was not impressed by this evidence and pointed to studies showing that mental images differ substantially from visual percepts. Look at Figure 6.4, which contains the outlines of three objects. Start with the object on the left and form a clear image of it. When you have done so, close your eyes, mentally rotate the image by 90 degrees clockwise, and decide what you see. Then repeat this exercise with the other two objects. When you have done that, see what happens when you actually rotate the book through 90 degrees. You should find it easy to identify the objects when you perceive them, even though you probably couldn't when you only imagined rotating them.

Slezak (1991, 1995) carried out research with the stimuli shown in Figure 6.4. No observers reported seeing the objects. This *wasn't* a deficit in memory – participants who sketched the image

Figure 6.4 Memorize these images in your visual memory. Slezak (1991, 1995) asked participants to memorize one of the above images. They then imagined rotating the image 90 degrees clockwise and reported what they saw. None of them reported seeing the figures that can be seen clearly if you rotate the page by 90 degrees clockwise.
Source: Left image from Slezak (1995), center image from Slezak (1991), right image reprinted from Pylyshyn (2003), reprinted with permission from Elsevier and the authors.

from memory and then rotated it saw the new object. According to Pylyshyn (2003), these findings show that our mental images are much poorer than people think. Instead, Pylyshyn argues, when we imagine something we build a new image on the basis of abstract concepts stored in semantic memory. Even if one disagrees with Pylyshyn's interpretation, Figure 6.4 illustrates that the information contained in images can't be used as *flexibly* as visual or perceptual information.

Integration: the hub-and-spoke-model

For a long time, the embodied view was presented in opposition to the abstract models. This need not be the case (Louwerse, 2011). Concepts involve all types of information, including sensory, motor, emotional, functional, and verbal codes. The sensory and motor information helps to acquire a rich meaning of concepts (and is essential to ground the first learned words); the verbal and functional information is needed to detect similarities in concepts differing greatly in perceptual terms, so that we know that *scallops* and *prawns* belong to the same category (*shellfish*) even though they have different shapes, colors, and forms of movement. Also we need some level of abstract to keep coherent concepts across a multitude of situations.

A model proposed to integrate the various ideas is the **hub-and-spoke model** (Rogers et al., 2004; Coutanche & Thompson-Schill, 2015; Lambon Ralph et al., 2017; see Figure 6.5). The "spokes" consist of several modality-specific regions involving sensory, motor, emotional, verbal, and functional processing. In addition, each concept has a "hub" – a modality-independent unified conceptual representation efficiently integrating all our knowledge of any given concept.

The hub-and-spoke model has been developed in particular to explain findings with semantic dementia. As discussed earlier, one of the main problems

Key term

Hub-and-spoke model: model that provides an idea of how abstract concepts can be based on different types of information and on how they can be stable and context-dependent at the same time.

Figure 6.5 The hub-and-spoke model. According to the hub-and-spoke model, concepts consist of central, modality-independent nodes (hubs) that integrate knowledge associated with the verbal, motor, sensory, functional, and emotional information related to concepts. The model is implemented as a connectionist network (left part) and is associated with specific brain areas (right part). The hubs are thought to be situated in the anterior temporal lobes (ATL). This is the part of the brain that is first affected in semantic dementia.
Source: From Lambon Ralph et al. (2017). Reprinted with permission from Macmillan Publishers Ltd.

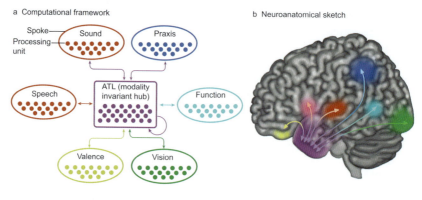

during the initial stages of semantic dementia is the extensive loss of conceptual knowledge (Patterson et al., 2007). The pictures of objects drawn by semantic dementia patients rapidly lose essential features. The patients also lose the ability to name objects when presented with pictures or when given a description of the object (e.g., "What do we call the African animal with black-and-white stripes?"). They can no longer identify objects when listening to their characteristic sounds (e.g., a dog barking). The theory is that in these patients the hub system deteriorates, so that they can no longer combine the various features that make the concepts.

The hub-and-spoke model also provides an explanation of how concepts can be stable and context dependent at the same time. The coherence and stability of concepts is achieved via the hubs, and the contextual variability is made possible by means of the spokes.

Finally, the hub-and-spoke model also attempts to link the various types of information to brain regions (right part of Figure 6.5). It assumes that concepts combine information from very distant brain regions, which is integrated in the anterior temporal lobes. Surprisingly, it does not (yet?) give a big role to the hippocampus, which has been so important in other memory research.

Conclusion

As you will agree with us, the research on how knowledge is encoded and stored in our semantic memory is not the easiest literature to digest. Still, it is the core of our functioning, as illustrated by the grave consequences of semantic dementia.

One reason why the literature is so difficult is that researchers have proposed very different and sometimes conflicting ideas of what may be going on. Instead of seeing the various ideas as mutually exclusive (one or the other), we have noticed that it is better to consider the various approaches as each covering an important aspect of the rich reality of categorization and concept formation.

When the distinction between two categories (concepts) is simple and depends on a single, salient feature, the evidence points to the use of that common feature in the categorization (Feldman, 2003). This will be particularly the case for artificial concepts, where we have full control over the criteria needed for categorization.

Because naturally emerged concepts usually are complex and have fuzzy boundaries, their categorization is more likely to be based on prototypes, certainly when the concept is familiar and open to abstraction.

If the concept is new or ad hoc, we are likely to depend on comparisons with exemplars and on our knowledge of the world.

Finally, the hub-and-spoke model reminds us that not all information related to concepts is abstract, but consists of sensory, motor, and emotion information as well. It further provides an explanation of why concepts can be stable and variable at the same time.

Section summary

Functions of concepts
- Concepts refer to mental representations of categories of objects.
- We need concepts because they provide an efficient way of representing knowledge about the world. They allow us to communicate our knowledge and experience to others and to make predictions about the world.

Semantic dementia
- Brain-damaged patients with semantic dementia suffer a widespread loss of their conceptual knowledge, which seriously disrupts their everyday lives. However, patients in the early stages of semantic dementia have reasonably intact autobiographical and episodic memory, and are often good at jigsaw puzzles.

Common features approach
- The common features approach is the one we intuitively associate with categorization: a category is formed by instances having the same features. As a result, the features define the category. A problem with this approach is that in the real world different features often contradict each other, so that there are fuzzy boundaries between concepts.

Prototype approach
- A prototype is a conceptual core consisting of characteristic features. Prototype theories assume that family resemblance is very important in determining typicality. The theory accounts for the fuzzy boundaries but has problems with goal-derived categories and concepts that do not (yet) seem to have prototypes.

Exemplar approach
- The exemplar approach assumes we store large numbers of examples of categories and that we categorize stimuli by matching them to the stored exemplars. The predictions of the exemplar approach are often more accurate than those of the prototype approach, but the approach does not tell how concepts can be used to build knowledge of the world, and it may require too much storage capacity for category exemplars.

Knowledge-based approach
- Causal relations among a concept's features are important. Those features causally related to other features determine categorization judgments to a greater extent than do other features. Children already use their knowledge of the world to categorize stimuli, rather than the perceptual similarity between the stimuli.

> **Embodied-cognition approach**
> • The embodied-cognition approach stresses that concepts not only consist of verbal information, but also of bodily experiences.
>
> **Integration**
> • The various approaches add different insights to the rich and complex process of categorization and concept formation. As such, they do not exclude each other but illustrate the various ways in which categorization can be achieved and the various types of information that are included.
> • The hub-and-spoke model provides a framework to understand how the various bits of information can be integrated in a coherent system.

ORGANIZATION OF CONCEPTS

A good semantic system requires not only concepts but also an efficient organization of the concepts. For example, it takes about one second to decide that a *sparrow* is a *bird* or to think of a *fruit* starting with *p*. How is this possible?

In this section, we review the various theories that have been proposed about the organization of concepts.

HIERARCHIES OF CONCEPTS

One of the first insights about the organization of concepts started from the observation that concepts can be defined at various levels of generality. Suppose you are shown a photograph of a *chair* and asked what you are looking at. There are various answers you could provide based on information in semantic memory. You might say it is an *item of furniture*, a *chair*, or an *easy chair*. This example suggests that concepts can be organized into hierarchies.

Rosch et al. (1976) argued that a distinction should be made between three levels of concepts: superordinate categories at the top (*item of furniture*), basic-level categories in the middle (*chair*), and subordinate categories at the bottom (*easy chair*).

According to Rosch et al. (1976), people typically deal with objects at the intermediate, basic level. They asked participants to list all the attributes of concepts at each level in the hierarchy. Very few attributes were listed for the superordinate categories because the categories were abstract. Many attributes were listed for the categories at the other two levels. However, very similar attributes were listed for different categories at the lowest level. Thus, basic-level categories seemed to be the most useful – they have the best balance between informativeness and distinctiveness. Informativeness is missing at the highest level of the hierarchy and distinctiveness is missing at the lowest level.

Rosch et al. (1976) also asked participants to name pictures of objects. Basic-level names were used 1,595 times in the course of the experiment. In contrast, subordinate names were used only 14 times, and superordinate names just once.

Subordinate category information is lost first in semantic dementia. The situation is less clear for superordinate information, as sometimes patients have worse performance with living things than with man-made things, which is a superordinate distinction (Lambon Ralph et al., 2017).

Finally, the basic level is the level at which people use similar motor movements for interacting with category members. For example, all chairs can be sat on in roughly the same way, and this differs markedly from how we interact with tables.

Although the three-level hierarchical idea has had much impact, throughout the years many findings have been reported that questioned the view. We review some of them.

Limitations

Tanaka and Taylor (1991) studied the concepts of birdwatchers and dog experts who were shown pictures of birds and dogs. Both groups used basic-level names for the domain they were novice in, but they more often gave subordinate names in their expert domain. Bird experts used subordinate names 74% of the time with birds, and dog experts used subordinate names 40% of the time with dogs. This suggests that there is not a single level of basic categories, but that our level of basic categories depends on our familiarity with the category. After all, we would expect a botanist to refer to the different kinds of plants in a garden rather than simply describing them all as plants.

There is one type of object with which most of us are very familiar – faces. Would we use subordinate categories for this type of stimuli rather than basic-level ones? Anaki and Bentin (2009) presented participants with a category label at the superordinate level (*living being*), at the basic level (*human*), or at the subordinate level (*Barack Obama*) followed by a picture of a familiar face. The participants' task was to decide whether the picture matched the label. As expected, matching occurred faster after the basic level than after the superordinate label, but it was also faster after the subordinate or exemplar label than after the basic label. Thus, familiarity with individual stimuli was more important to explain categorization speed than the level in Rosch et al.'s (1976) hierarchy.

Familiarity may also explain some cultural differences. Coley et al. (1997) and Medin and Atran (2004) compared categorization in members of the Itza culture in Guatemala and American undergraduates. The Itza were more likely than the Americans to categorize plants, animals, and birds at the subordinate level, arguably because of their closer contact with the natural environment. This incidentally is a good reminder of the problem that nearly all the research on humans' use of categories has involved participants from Western, Educated, Industrialized, Rich, and Democratic societies (whom Henrich et al., 2010, called WEIRD people).

Basic-level categories are usually preferred because they have the right mix of informativeness and distinctiveness. However, if the categorization task focuses on perceptual distinctiveness, then it is possible to show a processing advantage for superordinate categories. Prass et al. (2013) gave participants the task of categorizing photographs of objects presented very briefly. Categorization was at the superordinate level (animal or vehicle), the basic level (cat or dog), or the subordinate level (Siamese cat vs. Persian cat). Performance was most accurate and also fastest at the superordinate level and least accurate and slowest at the subordinate level.

There is another problem with Rosch et al.'s (1976) distinction among three levels. Many concepts are part of larger hierarchies. What are the basic, superordinate, and subordinate levels in the hierarchy: living thing, mammal, human, woman, Adele, Adele's face, pictures of Adele's face taken at a particular shoot?

A NETWORK OF CONCEPTS

Collins and Loftus (1975) proposed an alternative view of the organization of the semantic system. According to them, semantic memory is not primarily organized hierarchically but on the basis of semantic relatedness. Concepts form the nodes of a semantic network. Closely related concepts are situated together in the network and linked to each other.

Figure 6.6 Example of a semantic network. Source: From Collins and Loftus (1975). Reprinted with permission from the American Psychological Association.

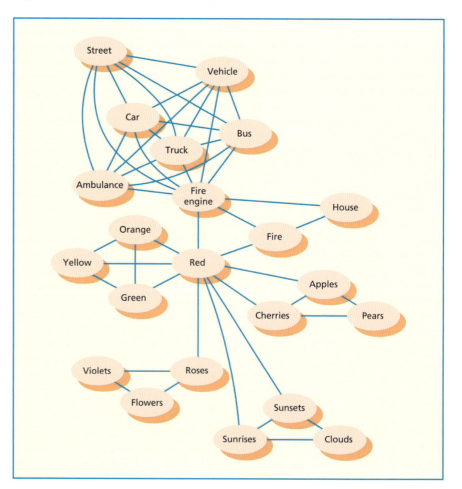

You can see a small part of the organization of semantic memory assumed by Collins and Loftus (1975) in Figure 6.6. An important feature is that the length of the links between two concepts indicates the degree of semantic relatedness between them. Thus, for example, *red* is more closely related to *orange* than it is to *sunsets*.

Assessment of semantic relatedness

A first way to assess the semantic relatedness between words is the word association task. In this task, participants are shown a target word and asked to name the first word (or the first three words) that come to mind. Table 6.2 shows the answers obtained when participants are shown the words *red* and *fire*.

The word association data can be integrated within a network, as shown in Figure 6.7.

Key term

Word association task: task in which participants are asked to mention the first word (or three words) that come to mind upon seeing a target word; used to determine the semantic relatedness between words.

Table 6.2   Associates of the target words *red* and *fire* in decreasing order of times mentioned.

Red	Fire
Color	Hot
Blue	Flame
Blood	Burn
Rose	Heart
Green	Water
Yellow	Red
Bright	Man
White	Truck
Pink	House
Anger	Flames
Dress	Smoke
Angry	Shoot
Lips	Alarm
Lipstick	Hose
Head	Sack
Orange	Wood
Crimson	Warm
Communist	Danger
Hot	Fighter
Scarlet	Place
Sky	Burning
Stop	Escape
Sunset	Axe
Waming	Station
Light	Orange
Face	Ice
Flag	Firefighter
Cardinal	Engine
Carmine	Fly
Coat	Camping

Source: From www.smallworldofwords.org/en/project/home

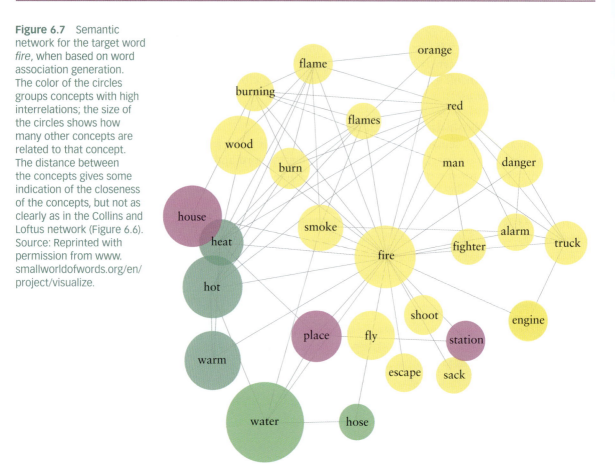

Figure 6.7 Semantic network for the target word *fire*, when based on word association generation. The color of the circles groups concepts with high interrelations; the size of the circles shows how many other concepts are related to that concept. The distance between the concepts gives some indication of the closeness of the concepts, but not as clearly as in the Collins and Loftus network (Figure 6.6). Source: Reprinted with permission from www.smallworldofwords.org/en/project/visualize.

A second way to assess semantic relatedness is to determine feature overlap. As we have seen in the first part of the chapter, concepts are defined by features; according to the prototype and exemplar theory, the semantic distance between concepts depends on the number of features shared.

McRae et al. (2005) asked 725 participants to enumerate the features of 541 concepts. For the concept *knife*, this resulted in the following list: is a cutlery, is a utensil, is a weapon, found in kitchens, has a blade, has a handle, is dangerous, is serrated, is sharp, is shiny, made of metal, made of stainless steel, used by butchers, used for cutting, used for killing, used with forks. By counting the number of overlapping features between concepts, McRae et al. were able to obtain useful estimates of semantic distance.

A final task to determine semantic relatedness is simply to ask participants to rate the distance between two concepts. Gerz et al. (2016), for instance, asked participants to rate the similarity between 3,500 pairs of verbs on a 10-point scale (0 = not related at all, 10 = are synonyms with the same meaning). Table 6.3 shows ratings for the verb *to assume*. These agree reasonably well with the similarity measures obtained in the association task.

Spreading of activation

The semantic distance in a network is important because Collins and Loftus (1975) argued that when a node in the network is activated, there is a

Table 6.3   Rated semantic similarities between the target verb *to assume* and nine other verbs (0 = not related at all, 10 = mean exactly the same).

suppose	9.13
presume	5.81
judge	5.81
think	5.15
adopt	4.32
predict	3.98
believe	2.99
know	2.49
. . .	
tumble	0.5
. . .	

Source: From Gerz et al. (2016).

Key term

Spreading of activation: the notion that activation of a node (corresponding to a concept) in a semantic network causes activation to spread to related nodes, so that the meaning of a concept becomes richer.

spreading of activation to the linked nodes. Whenever a person sees, hears, or thinks about a concept, the appropriate node in semantic memory is activated. This causes activation to spread strongly to closely related concepts and weakly to those more distantly related. For example, activation passes quickly from *fire* to *burn* in the sentence "The casino is on fire," because *fire* and *burn* are closely related semantically (as shown in Figure 6.7). Because of the spreading of activation, the meaning of an activated concept becomes much richer. In Chapter 8 we will see how the semantic priming effect provides evidence for the spreading of activation.

In the Real World 6.2 *Feeding meaning to computers: the use of semantic vectors*

Not only psychologists are interested in the meaning of concepts. Computer scientists are also searching for ways to make computers more intelligent.

A game changer here was the discovery that the meaning of words can be derived to a large extent by analyzing the words (concepts) co-occurring with the target word. Suppose you want to know the meaning of *dinosaur*. One way is to analyze texts in which the word appears and look at the other words in the texts. This approach is known in cognitive psychology as *latent semantic analysis (LSA)*, because it was the name of the first influential computer model implementing the approach (Landauer & Dumais, 1997). Since then, the LSA model has been superseded by better models based on connectionist networks (Mandera et al., 2017).

In Chapter 1, we saw how connectionist networks can be used to capture relationships between layers of information (Figure 1.15). Research has indicated that this can be done for semantic information as well (Mikolov et al., 2013). Figure 6.8 illustrates the process.

The input to the model consists of many texts (usually a few billion words). At each learning step, a target word is predicted on the basis of the surrounding words (in Figure 6.8 this is limited to the word before and the word after the target word *furry*). So, the output of the model is the target word (*furry* in the example), and the input of the model consists of the surrounding words (*black*

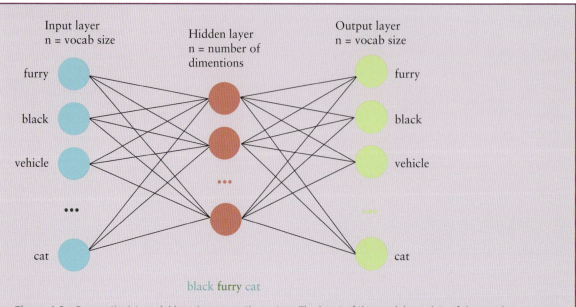

Figure 6.8 Connectionist model learning semantic vectors. The input of the model consists of the words surrounding a target word in a series of texts. The output is the target word to be predicted. The weights between the nodes are changed so that the model better and better predicts the output on the basis of the input. The hidden layer is the semantic vector. It consists of 200–300 nodes. The weights of these nodes encode the meaning of concepts.
Source: From Mandera et al. (2017). Reprinted with permission from Elsevier.

and *cat*). There are input and output nodes for all the words encountered in the texts (usually a few hundred thousand). The hidden layer connecting the input to the output is much smaller and usually consists of 200 to 300 nodes.

For each target word, the weights of the connections are changed so that the surrounding input words better and better predict the output node (remember that collections of texts with a few billion words are fed to the model).

At the end of the learning, each word entered at the input level of the model will activate the hidden nodes to some extent. These 200 to 300 values constitute the semantic vector of the word (a vector is an array of values, in this case the weights of the connections to the nodes in the hidden layer). By comparing the semantic vectors of two words, it is possible to determine the semantic similarity between the words. Table 6.4 shows the words that according to the model are semantically closest to the target word *fire*. By comparing them to the word associates given in Table 6.2, you can see how well the model based on word co-occurrences does.

Semantic vectors do surprisingly well to predict the semantic similarities among words obtained from human data (word association, feature overlap, ratings; Mandera et al., 2017). They can certainly be used as a good approximation of the verbal component in the hub-and-spoke model (Figure 6.5). The fact that the meaning of all words of a language can be captured with vectors of 200 to 300 values furthermore suggests that word meanings may be described reasonably well with a total of only 200 to 300 semantic features (Hollis & Westbury, 2016).

The big advantage of the approach is that the vectors can be calculated for all words of a language (which is almost impossible for the collection of human data). As a result, the approach figures prominently in current attempts to provide computers with meaning-related information of words and texts. The vector similarities can easily be translated to distances in a semantic network.

It will be interesting to see how much impact semantic vectors will have on research in cognitive psychology.

Table 6.4   Semantic similarities to the target word *fire* based on the similarities of the semantic vectors of a connectionist model as illustrated in Figure 6.6 (0 = not similar at all, 1 = completely similar). The lists gives the 20 words with the highest similarities.

burn	0.60
burning	0.59
relight	0.58
douse	0.54
burned	0.52
blazing	0.51
firing	0.50
flame	0.50
ablaze	0.50
smoke	0.50
alight	0.49
hydrant	0.49
extinguish	0.49
flamethrower	0.47
brigade	0.47
kindle	0.47
detonation	0.47
shoot	0.47
fired	0.47
blaze	0.47

Source: From Mandera et al. (2017). Reprinted with permission from Elsevier.

Section summary

Hierarchies of concepts

- According to Rosch et al. (1976), there are hierarchies of concepts consisting of superordinate, basic-level, and subordinate categories. Basic-level categories are generally the most useful because they combine informativeness with distinctiveness. However, the basic level differs as a function of the expertise we have with the concepts, and there are often more than three levels in a hierarchy.

A semantic network

- Collins and Loftus (1975) argued that concepts in semantic memory are organized in terms of semantic relatedness or distance. Activation of a concept causes activation to spread to related concepts. As a result, the meaning of a concept that is activated becomes richer. Psychologists investigate the semantic relatedness by means of association tasks, feature overlap calculations, and semantic rating tasks.

Semantic vectors

- The semantic relatedness of concepts can be estimated surprisingly well on the basis of the concepts co-occurring with a target concept. This has resulted in semantic vectors of 200 to 300 values quite accurately representing the meaning of words. This approach is currently used to feed meaning to computers. It will be interesting to see how well it accounts for the richness of human concepts.

Key term

Proposition:
a configuration of
concepts based on
a limited number of
combination rules and
resulting in a true-false
statement; assumed to
be the unit of storage in
semantic memory.

SCHEMAS AND STEREOTYPES

So far in this chapter we have focused on knowledge (information in memory) stored in the form of concepts. However, much of our knowledge of the world is broader in scope, because concepts are brought in relation to each other, and these relationships are remembered.

FROM CONCEPTS TO PROPOSITIONS

The most worked-out proposals about how concepts are related to each other assume that concepts are combined into propositions (e.g., Anderson, 1983, 1996; Zwaan, 2016). A proposition is a configuration of concepts based on a limited number of combination rules and resulting in a true-or-false statement. Propositions represent information. For instance, if someone tells you that "a rich young professor has bought a beautiful townhouse," you may store the information in the following three propositions:

1. Proposition 1 (action, agent, object): [buy, professor, house]
2. Proposition 2 (is a, agent, status1, status2): [professor, rich, young]
3. Proposition 3 (is a, object, status1, status2): [house, beautiful, town]

A good proposition theory is able to represent all possible meanings with a limited number of relations. In one of the first attempts, Schank (1972) argued that the meaning of all action verbs can be captured by 12 base actions, such as "transfer of property" (give, lend, take), "physical movement from one place to the other" (walk, move, drive), and "intake of food or air" (eat, breathe).

Findings

Evidence that verbal messages are translated into propositions was reported by Sachs (1967). She presented participants with taped messages. One described how a man in Holland invented the telescope, how Galileo was informed about this, and how he started to experiment with a telescope himself. The passage contained the following critical sentence: "He sent a letter about it to Galileo, the great Italian scientist."

Passage administration was interrupted from time to time by a bell. At that moment the participants heard a new sentence and had to indicate whether the sentence had been said in the passage or not. There were two important types of test sentences:

1. In which the meaning of the sentence was changed ("Galileo, the great Italian scientist, sent him a letter about it").
2. In which the same information was given but with a different wording ("A letter about it was sent to Galileo, the great Italian scientist").

The test sentence could appear immediately after the target sentence or 45 seconds later in the passage. Sachs noted how often the participants rightly indicated that none of the above two test sentences had been part of the initial passage. Figure 6.9 shows the results.

Sachs observed that participants were reasonably good at remembering the meaning of the sentence 45 seconds later (i.e., they remembered that the

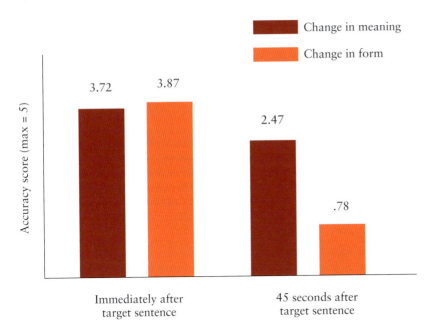

Figure 6.9 Results showing that when we hear a passage, we rapidly forget the specific word order used in the sentences but remember most of the meaning. This finding is taken as evidence that we translate the text into a sequence of propositions to be stored in memory. Source: Based on data described in Sachs (1967).

letter had been sent *to* Galileo and not *by* Galileo). However, they had little memory left of whether the sentence had been in active or passive voice. This finding agrees with the hypothesis that the contents of a message are translated into a series of propositions to be stored in memory. After the translation, the specific words in the sentences and their order are lost. Form information is present immediately after the sentence, arguably because (part of) the sentence is still in working memory (see the Glossary).

COMBINING PROPOSITIONS INTO EVENTS AND SCHEMAS

It is thought that propositions are linked to each other in order to create situation models of what happens around us. According to the event-indexing model (Zwaan & Radvansky, 1998; Zwaan, 2016), this happens on the basis of events that are related to each other on the basis of time, space, entity, causation, and motivation. As each incoming bit of information (e.g., new sentence in a message) is processed, an event representation is formed and integrated with the event representation(s) currently in working memory based on its overlap with those representations on each of the five dimensions. If the event occurs within the same time frame as the events in working memory, there is overlap on the temporal dimension; if the event takes place within the same spatial region there is spatial overlap; and so on. Together the events form our memory of the situation.

It is further assumed that frequent and familiar sequences of propositions become grouped in schemas. A **schema** is a set of related propositions (an event), which forms a packet of typical knowledge about the world, events, or people. For example, try to imagine what is involved in a typical bank robbery. You may well have imagined the robbers were male, with masks over their faces, and that they were carrying guns. These features are found in most people's bank-robbery schemas (Tuckey & Brewer, 2003).

> **Key term**
>
> **Schema:**
> a set of related propositions, which forms a packet of typical knowledge about the world, events, or people.

Schemas

Henderson (1903) and Bartlett (1932) were the first to argue that we use schemas to store and retrieve information from semantic memory. They examined what people remember after hearing or reading a story. Particularly informative were studies in which participants were presented with stories that produced a *conflict* between what was presented and the participants' prior knowledge.

Bartlett (1932) gave English students stories taken from the North American Indian culture. These stories contained strange, mystical elements and plot twists the participants were unfamiliar with (if you are curious, search for "The war of the ghosts" on the internet). Bartlett observed many distortions in the remembered versions of the story, making them more conventional and acceptable from the students' own cultural background. Bartlett used the term rationalization for this type of error.

According to schema theory, information in semantic memory is stored in schemas. The precise information gets lost, in particular when there is some time between receiving the information and being asked about it. Sulin and Dooling (1974) presented half of their participants with a story about Gerald Martin: "Gerald Martin strove to undermine the existing government to satisfy his political ambitions. . . . He became a ruthless, uncontrollable dictator. The ultimate effect of his rule was the downfall of his country" (Sulin & Dooling, 1974, p. 256). The other half of the participants received the same story, but the main actor was called Adolf Hitler. The participants in the latter condition were much more likely than those in the other group to believe incorrectly that they had read the sentence: "He hated the Jews particularly and so persecuted them." The effect was larger after a 1-week retention interval than after a 5-minute retention interval.

Brewer and Treyens (1981) investigated whether schemas also influence incidental learning, given that much of the information we remember during the course of our everyday lives is acquired incidentally rather than intentionally (Chapter 5). Accordingly, they decided to see whether people would show schema-driven memory errors in incidental memory in a naturalistic situation. They asked participants to spend about 35 seconds in a room designed to look like a graduate student's office before the experiment proper took place. The room contained a mixture of schema-consistent objects you would expect to find in a graduate student's office (e.g., desk, calendar, eraser, pencils) and schema-inconsistent objects (e.g., a skull, a toy top). Some schema-consistent objects (e.g., books) were omitted.

Schematic knowledge had both positive and negative influences on subsequent unexpected recall and recognition tests. First, participants recalled more schema-consistent than schema-inconsistent objects for objects that were present. Second, they falsely recalled more schema-consistent objects (e.g., books; filing cabinet) that had not been in the room than schema-inconsistent objects. In a similar study, Lampinen et al. (2001) found that far more schema-consistent objects that hadn't been present were falsely recalled 48 hours after presentation, in line with the prediction that schematic information becomes more important over time.

So far, we have stressed the fact that schemas can lead to memory errors when they deviate from the information to be remembered. However, it is good to keep in mind that most of the time events are in line with our schemas and that under those circumstances schemas are extremely useful because the amount of information we have to store can be reduced. Indeed, Steyvers and Hemmer (2012) provided evidence that, in naturalistic environments, schemas are more often a help than a hindrance to remember what happened. They argued that it is important to use ecologically valid stimuli in memory studies, because the findings of memory studies using unrepresentative stimulus material are unlikely to give insights about the operation of human memory in more natural settings.

Uses of schemas

Schematic knowledge is useful for four main reasons. First, schemas allow us to form *expectations*. In a restaurant, for example, we expect to be shown to a table, to be given a menu, to order food, and so on. If any one of these expectations is violated, we usually take action. For example, if no menu is produced, we catch the eye of the server. Schemas help to make the world more predictable, because our expectations are generally confirmed.

Second, schemas help to prevent cognitive overload. For example, consider stereotypes (schemas involving simplified generalizations about various groups of people). When we meet someone for the first time, we often use stereotypical information (e.g., about their sex, age, nationality, and ethnicity) to assist us in forming an impression of that person. It is simpler (even if potentially misleading) to use such information rather than to engage in detailed cognitive processing of his/her behavior (Macrae & Bodenhausen, 2000).

Evidence that schemas reduce cognitive processing was reported by Macrae et al. (1994). The participants performed two tasks at the same time. One task involved forming impressions of imaginary people when given their names and personality traits, and the other was a comprehension task. Participants who were able to use stereotypical information on the impression formation task performed better on both tasks than those who were not provided with that information. Thus, stereotypes reduced processing demands and led to enhanced performance.

Third, schemas play an important role in reading and listening because they allow us to fill in the gaps in what we read or hear and so enhance our understanding (see Chapter 8). More specifically, they provide the basis for us to draw inferences as we read or listen. Previously, we discussed the inferences made when we read the sentences "Tom was driving along when a tire on his car blew. He arrived home very late." and how these allow us to make sense of the situation described.

Fourth, schematic knowledge can assist us when we perceive visual scenes. Palmer (1975) presented a picture of a scene (e.g., a kitchen) followed by the very brief presentation of the picture of an object. The object was appropriate to the context (e.g., loaf) or inappropriate (e.g., mailbox). There was a further condition in which no contextual scene was presented initially. The probability of identifying the object was greatest when it was appropriate to the context, with activation of schematic knowledge of the scene facilitating visual perception. Performance was worst when the context was inappropriate because activated schematic knowledge was unrelated to the object subsequently presented.

Key term

Stereotypes:
schemas incorporating oversimplified generalizations (often negative) about certain groups.

Executive control processes in retrieving schema information

So far, we have discussed schemas as if they were fixed sequences of propositions and events, activated and used as fixed entities. This is not quite the case, as illustrated by Cosentino et al. (2006). These authors assessed schema memory in two groups of brain-damaged patients by presenting them with short stories about well-known schemas (e.g., about fishing). Some of the stories contained sequencing errors (e.g., dropping fish in a bucket *before* casting the fishing line), whereas others contained meaning errors (e.g., placing a flower on the hook).

Half of the patients had semantic dementia (discussed earlier). The other half had fronto-temporal dementia. This is a type of dementia primarily characterized by deterioration of frontal (and to a lesser extent temporal) brain tissue (Neary & Snowden, 1996). The most pressing problem of these patients is cognitive control. Major symptoms are: disinhibition, impulsivity, inability to sustain simple voluntary acts such as keeping the eyes closed, loss of social awareness and insight, personal neglect, mental rigidity, and inflexibility. The symptoms are in line with the observation that the frontal lobes are essential for so-called executive functions.

Executive functions refer to a set of cognitive skills needed to control and coordinate our cognitive abilities and behaviors. According to Miyake et al. (2000), executive skills can be grouped under three functions:

1. mental set shifting (shifting between tasks, e.g. by deactivating the present goal and activating a new goal),
2. updating and monitoring of working memory representations (needed to achieve the goal),
3. inhibition of irrelevant dominant or prepotent responses (in order not to be distracted from the goal and its achievement).

These skills are needed:

- to activate a goal and keep it active,
- to select the right information and actions to achieve the goal,
- to suppress irrelevant information and actions,
- to take into account the context in which the task must be performed and specific requirements because of the context,
- to detect errors and correct them.

When Cosentino et al. (2006) compared the patients with semantic dementia to those with fronto-temporal dementia, they observed that the semantic dementia patients made as many sequencing errors as semantic ones, but that fronto-temporal dementia patients made twice as many sequencing errors as semantic ones (see Figure 6.10). Thus, the frontal cortex (used for complex cognitive processing) is particularly important for keeping the sequence of events of a schema in the right order. Apparently, the sequence of events in a schema requires active search in memory, for which executive functions are important.

After a review of the literature, Fletcher and Henson (2001) concluded that executive functions in the frontal lobes have three main roles related to long-term memory:

1. updating and maintenance of information activated from memory,
2. selection, manipulation, and monitoring of that information,
3. selection of processes and subgoals.

The importance of control processes in memory retrieval can also be seen in the fact that a number of patients with frontal damage start to confabulate (i.e., tell things that are not true). This is particularly the case when they talk about their autobiographical memory, but it is also seen in retrieval from semantic memory (Burgess & Shallice, 1996; Ghosh et al., 2014).

STEREOTYPES

We saw that stereotypes (simplified generalizations about groups) are a form of schema. To experience how they can influence our thinking and behavior, start with Research Activity 6.3.

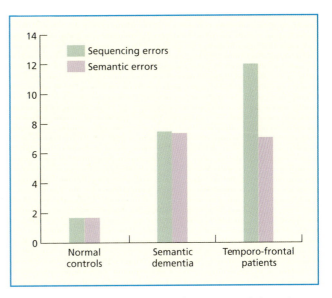

Figure 6.10 Semantic and sequencing errors made by patients with semantic dementia, temporo-frontal patients, and normal controls. The units on the y-axis are the mean number of errors in each condition.
Source: Data from Cosentino et al. (2006).

Research Activity 6.3 *Effects produced by stereotypes*

Read the following passage from Reynolds et al. (2006), and answer the question at the end:

A man and his son were away for a trip. They were driving along the highway when they had a terrible accident. The man was killed outright but the son was alive, although badly injured. The son was rushed to the hospital and was to have an emergency operation. On entering the operating theater, the surgeon looked at the boy and said, "I can't do this operation. This is my son."

How can this be?

If you found the problem difficult, you are in good company. The majority of participants tested by Reynolds et al. (2006) were puzzled as well. *Why?* We tend to have a stereotypical image of surgeons as men. However, some surgeons are female, and the surgeon in the passage was the boy's mother! Thus, stereotypical information can affect our text understanding and interfere with our problem solving.

Stereotypes have been studied extensively in social psychology, because they influence our appreciation of and interactions with people from stereotyped groups. For instance, one of the cues we use in our interactions with others is their accent. It has repeatedly been shown that people with a standard accent are treated with much more friendliness and respect than persons with a non-standard accent (MacFarlane & Stuart-Smith, 2012; Fuertes et al., 2012; Tombs & Rao Hill, 2014; Dragojevic et al., 2016). Apparently a person's accent activates a schema that will be used to encode (and regulate) our interactions with the person.

As illustrated in Research Activity 6.3, schematic information in the form of stereotypes also influences performance on various cognitive activities, including problem solving and language comprehension. More specifically, performance is impaired when there is a conflict between an individual's expectations based on his/her stereotypical schemas and the information presented in the task.

Stereotype stability: context effects

Many people assume that an individual's stereotypical schemas are relatively stable and invariant over time. That assumption may sound reasonable but is actually incorrect. Garcia-Marques et al. (2006) asked participants to select five traits out of 43 that best described various groups (e.g., gypsies; African immigrants). The same participants then repeated the task 2 weeks later. To their surprise, Garcia-Marques et al. found considerable instability over that time period, especially for less typical traits.

Stereotypes are unstable and changeable over time for several reasons. One is that they are much influenced by context. The impact of context on stereotype activation was shown by Casper et al. (2010). On each trial of the experiment, they first presented the participants with a category word denoting a group that is stereotyped, such as Arabs, Italians, or women. After 300 ms, two new stimuli were presented: a target sequence of letters and a context picture. The task of the participants was to decide whether the target letter sequence formed an existing word or not (they could ignore the picture). If the target letter sequence was a word, it was either related to a stereotypical characteristic of the group (Arabs -> terrorist, Italians -> romantic, women -> clumsy) or not (Arabs -> ill, Italians -> ambitious, women -> rich). The context picture provided a situation in which the stereotypical feature made sense (an airport hall for the Arabs, a rose for the Italians, and a badly parked car for the women) or not (a tissue for the Arabs, an expensive car for the Italians, and an overloaded bus for the women).

Casper et al. (2010) observed that participants recognized the target word faster when it was a stereotypical feature of the category group than when it was not. However, the effect was only obtained when the context picture matched the stereotype. So, participants recognized the word *clumsy* faster after seeing the category word *women* than the target word *rich*, but only when the target word was accompanied by a picture of a badly parked car and not when it was accompanied by the picture of an overloaded bus. This suggests that stereotypical traits are not activated automatically upon seeing the category word, but require appropriate contextual information.

Thus, stereotypes (and schemas in general) are much more *flexible* than usually assumed. Remember that we came to the same conclusion with respect to concepts.

Section summary

From concepts to propositions
- Concepts are combined into propositions to store information in our brain. As a result we do not remember stimuli literally, as was shown with auditory passages (Sachs, 1967).

Combining propositions into events and schemas

- Sequences of propositions are combined into events and situations on the basis of time, space, entity, causation, and motivation.
- Familiar sequences of events are stored as schemas in semantic memory. Such schematic knowledge allows us to form expectations, to prevent cognitive overload, and to draw inferences.
- Schematic knowledge is not retrieved as a single entity. In particular, the sequence of events in a schema requires executive functions to be put in place. This can be concluded from the fact that patients with fronto-temporal dementia have problems discovering wrong sequences of actions within a schema.

Stereotypes

- Stereotypes are schemas related to groups of people. Stereotypical information that conflicts with task information can interfere with language comprehension and problem solving. Stereotypes are less stable than usually imagined. This is partly because stereotype activation depends on contextual information.

Essay questions

1. Describe the different ways in which brain damage can lead to problems with semantic memory.
2. What are the main assumptions of the different approaches to concepts? Which of these approaches do you find most convincing, and why?
3. Discuss some of the ways in which the conceptual system is linked to the perceptual and motor systems.
4. What is schematic knowledge? How useful is such knowledge in everyday life?
5. How does the existence of schemas influence our interactions with other people?

Further reading

- Baddeley, A., Eysenck, M.W., & Anderson, M.C. (2015). *Memory* (2nd ed.). Hove, UK: Psychology Press. Chapter 6 in this textbook is devoted to semantic memory and stored knowledge.
- The journal *Psychonomic Bulletin & Review* published a special issue on concepts in August 2016 (Volume 23, Issue 4) with articles from most of the big names in the field. Have a look and prepare yourself for some theoretical clashes. The article of Barsalou (2016) gives his impression of the various contributions and the latest ideas about his influential model of grounded cognition.
- Hampton, J. A. (2010). Concepts in human adults. In D. Mareschal, P. Quinn, & S.E.G. Lea (Eds.), *The making of human concepts* (pp. 293–311). Oxford, UK: Oxford University Press. James Hampton provides a useful overview of theory and research on concepts.
- Patterson, K., Nestor, P. J., & Rogers, T. T. (2007). Where do you know what you know? The representation of semantic knowledge in the human brain. *Nature Reviews Neuroscience, 8*, 976–987. The ways in which our conceptual knowledge is stored in the brain are identified in this important review article.

REFERENCES

Ahn, W. K., Kim, N. S., Lassaline, M. E., & Dennis, M. J. (2000). Causal status as a determinant of feature centrality. *Cognitive Psychology, 41*, 361–416.

Anaki, D., & Bentin, S. (2009). Familiarity effects on categorization levels of faces and objects. *Cognition, 111*, 144–149.

Anderson, J. (1983). *The architecture of cognition*. Cambridge, MA: Harvard University Press.

Anderson, J. R. (1996). ACT: A simple theory of complex cognition. *American Psychologist, 51*(4), 355–365.

Barsalou, L. W. (1983). Ad hoc categories. *Memory & Cognition, 11*(3), 211–227.

Barsalou, L. W. (1985). Ideals, central tendency, and frequency of instantiation as determinants of graded structure in categories. *Journal of Experimental Psychology: Learning, Memory, & Cognition, 11*, 629–654.

Barsalou, L. W. (2008). Grounded cognition. *Annual Review of Psychology, 59*, 617–645.

Barsalou, L. W. (2009). Simulation, situated conceptualization, and prediction. *Philosophical Transactions of the Royal Society B: Biological Sciences, 364*, 1281–1289.

Barsalou, L. W., & Wiemer-Hastings, K. (2005). Situating abstract concepts. In D. Pecher & R. Zwaan (Eds.), *Grounding cognition: The role of perception and action in memory, language, and thought*. New York, NY: Cambridge University Press.

Bartlett, F. C. (1932). *Remembering: An experimental and social study*. Cambridge, UK: Cambridge University Press.

Binder, J. R. (2016). In defense of abstract conceptual representations. *Psychonomic Bulletin and Review, 23*, 1096–1108.

Borges, J. L. (1964). *Labyrinths: Selected stories and other writing*. New York, NY: New Directions.

Brewer, W. F., & Treyens, J. C. (1981). Role of schemata in memory for places. *Cognitive Psychology, 13*, 207–230.

Bruner, J. S., Goodnow, J. J., & Austin, G. A. (1956). *A study of thinking*. New York: John Wiley & Sons, Inc.

Brysbaert, M., Stevens, M., Mandera, P., & Keuleers, E. (2016). How many words do we know? Practical estimates of vocabulary size dependent on word definition, the degree of language input and the participant's age. *Frontiers in Psychology, 7*, 1116.

Burgess, P. W., & Shallice, T. (1996). Confabulation and the control of recollection. *Memory, 4*(4), 359–412.

Calabria, M., Cotelli, M., Adenzato, M., Zanetti, O., & Miniussi, C. (2009). Empathy and emotion recognition in semantic dementia: A case report. *Brain and Cognition, 70*, 247–252.

Casper, C., Rothermund, K., & Wentura, D. (2010). Automatic stereotype activation is context-dependent. *Social Psychology, 41*, 131–136.

Coley, J. D., Medin, D. L., & Atran, S. (1997). Does rank have its privilege? Inductive inferences within folkbiological taxonomies. *Cognition, 64*, 73–112.

Collins, A. M., & Loftus, E. F. (1975). A spreading activation theory of semantic memory. *Psychological Review, 82*, 407–428.

Cosentino, S., Chute, D., Libon, D., Moore, P., & Grossman, M. (2006). How does the brain support script comprehension? A study of executive processes and semantic knowledge in dementia. *Neuropsychology, 20*, 307–318.

Coutanche, M. N., & Thompson-Schill, S. L. (2015). Creating concepts from converging features in human cortex. *Cerebral Cortex, 25*(9), 2584–2593.

Dragojevic, M., Mastro, D., Giles, H., & Sink, A. (2016). Silencing nonstandard speakers: A content analysis of accent portrayals on American primetime television. *Language in Society*, 45(1), 59–85.

Fehr, B. (2004). Intimacy expectations in same-sex friendships: A prototype interaction-pattern model. *Journal of Personality and Social Psychology*, 86, 265–284.

Feldman, J. (2003). The simplicity principle in human concept learning. *Current Directions in Psychological Science*, 12, 227–232.

Fletcher, P. C., & Henson, R. N. A. (2001). Frontal lobes and human memory. *Brain*, 124(5), 849–881.

Fuertes, J. N., Gottdiener, W. H., Martin, H., Gilbert, T. C., & Giles, H. (2012). A meta-analysis of the effects of speakers' accents on interpersonal evaluations. *European Journal of Social Psychology*, 42(1), 120–133.

Garcia-Marques, L., Santos, A. S. C., & Mackie, D. M. (2006). Stereotypes: Static abstractions or dynamic knowledge structures? *Journal of Personality and Social Psychology*, 91, 814–831.

Gelman, S. A. (2009). Learning from others: Children's construction of concepts. *Annual Review of Psychology*, 60, 115–140.

Gelman, S. A., & Coley, J. D. (1990). The importance of knowing a dodo is a bird: Categories and inferences in 2-year-old children. *Developmental Psychology*, 26(5), 796–804.

Gerz, D., Vulić, I., Hill, F., Reichart, R., & Korhonen, A. (2016). *SimVerb-3500: A large-scale evaluation set of verb similarity*. Available at http://people.ds.cam. ac.uk/dsg40/simverb.html (Retrieved October 5, 2017).

Ghosh, V. E., Moscovitch, M., Colella, B. M., & Gilboa, A. (2014). Schema representation in patients with ventromedial PFC lesions. *The Journal of Neuroscience*, 34(36), 12057–12070.

Green, H. A. C., & Patterson, K. (2009). Jigsaws – A preserved ability in semantic dementia. *Neuropsychologia*, 47, 569–576.

Hampton, J. A. (1979). Polymorphous concepts in semantic memory. *Journal of Verbal Learning and Verbal Behavior*, 18(4), 441–461.

Hampton, J. A. (1981). An investigation of the nature of abstract concepts. *Memory & Cognition*, 9, 149–156.

Hampton, J. A. (2007). Typicality, graded membership, and vagueness. *Cognitive Science*, 31, 355–384.

Hampton, J. A. (2010). Concepts in human adults. In D. Mareschal, P. Quinn, & S. E. G. Lea (Eds.), *The making of human concepts* (pp. 293–311). Oxford, UK: Oxford University Press.

Harnad, S. (1990). The symbol grounding problem. *Physica D: Nonlinear Phenomena*, 42, 335–346.

Hauk, O., Johnsrude, I., & Pulvermüller, F. (2004). Somatotopic representation of action words in human motor and premotor cortex. *Neuron*, 41, 301–307.

Heit, E. (1992). Categorization using chains of examples. *Cognitive Psychology*, 24, 341–380.

Henderson, E. N. (1903). A study of memory for connected trains of thought. *The Psychological Review, Series of Monograph Supplements*, V(6), (Whole No. 23, p. 93). New York: Palgrave Macmillan.

Henrich, J., Heine, S. J., & Norenzayan, A. (2010). Beyond WEIRD: Towards a broad-based behavioral science. *Behavioral and Brain Sciences*, 33, 111–135.

Heussen, D., & Hampton, J. A. (2007). 'Emeralds are expensive because they are rare': Plausibility of property explanations. In S. Vosniadou, D. Kayser, & A. Protopapas (Eds.), *Proceedings of Eurocogsci07: The European cognitive science conference* (pp. 101–106). Hove, UK: Psychology Press.

Hodges, J. R., Mitchell, J., Dawson, K., Spillantini, M. G., Xuereb, J. H., McMonagle, P., . . . Patterson, K. (2009). Semantic dementia: Demography, familial factors and survival in a consecutive series of 100 cases. *Brain*, *133*, 300–306.

Hollis, G., & Westbury, C. (2016). The principals of meaning: Extracting semantic dimensions from co-occurrence models of semantics. *Psychonomic Bulletin & Review*, *23*(6), 1744–1756.

Jackson, F. (1982). Epiphenomenal qualia. *The Philosophical Quarterly*, *32*(127), 127–136.

Keil, F. C., Smith, W. C., Simons, D. J., & Levin, D. T. (1998). Two dogmas of conceptual empiricism: Implications for hybrid models of the structure knowledge. *Cognition*, *65*, 103–135.

Kertesz, A., Jesso, S., Harciarek, M., Blair, M., & McMonagle, P. (2010). What is semantic dementia? A cohort study of diagnostic features and clinical boundaries. *Archives of Neurology*, *67*, 483–489.

Klein, L., Dubois, J., Mangin, J.-F., Kherif, F., Flandin, G., Poline, J.-B., et al. (2004). Retinopic organization of visual mental images as revealed by functional magnetic resonance imaging. *Cognitive Brain Research*, *22*, 26–31.

Kosslyn, S. M. (2005). Mental images and the brain. *Cognitive Neuropsychology*, *22*, 333–347.

Kosslyn, S. M., & Thompson, W. L. (2003). When is early visual cortex activated during visual mental imagery? *Psychological Bulletin*, *129*, 723–746.

Lambon Ralph, M. A., Jefferies, E., Patterson, K., & Rogers, T. T. (2017). The neural and computational bases of semantic cognition. *Nature Reviews Neuroscience*, *18*, 42–55.

Lampinen, J. M., Copeland, S. M., & Neuschatz, J. S. (2001). Recollections of things schematic: Room schemas revisited. *Journal of Experimental Psychology: Learning, Memory, & Cognition*, *27*, 1211–1222.

Landauer, T. K., & Dumais, S. T. (1997). A solution to Plato's problem: The latent semantic analysis theory of acquisition, induction, and representation of knowledge. *Psychological Review*, *104*(2), 211–240.

Louwerse, M. M. (2011). Symbol interdependency in symbolic and embodied cognition. *Topics in Cognitive Science*, *3*(2), 273–302.

Lynch, E. B., Coley, J. D., & Medin, D. L. (2000). Tall is typical: Central tendency, ideal dimensions, and graded category structure among tree experts and novices. *Memory & Cognition*, *28*, 41–50.

MacFarlane, A. E., & Stuart-Smith, J. (2012). "One of them sounds sort of Glasgow Uni-ish." Social judgements and fine phonetic variation in Glasgow. *Lingua*, *122*(7), 764–778.

Macrae, C. N., & Bodenhausen, G. V. (2000). Social cognition: Thinking categorically about others. *Annual Review of Psychology*, *51*, 93–120.

Mandera, P., Keuleers, E., & Brysbaert, M. (2017). Explaining human performance in psycholinguistic tasks with models of semantic similarity based on prediction and counting: A review and empirical validation. *Journal of Memory and Language*, *92*, 57–78.

Matuszewski, V., Piolino, P., Belliard, S., de la Sayette, V., Laisney, M., Lalevée, C., et al. (2009). Patterns of autobiographical memory impairment according to disease severity in semantic dementia. *Cortex*, *45*, 456–472.

McCloskey, M. E., & Glucksberg, S. (1978). Natural categories: Well defined or fuzzy sets? *Memory & Cognition*, *26*, 121–134.

McRae, K., Cree, G. S., Seidenberg, M. S., & McNorgan, C. (2005). Semantic feature production norms for a large set of living and nonliving things. *Behavior Research Methods*, *37*(4), 547–559.

Medin, D. L., & Atran, S. (2004). The native mind: Biological categorization and reasoning in development and across cultures. *Psychological Review*, *111*, 960–983.

Meteyard, L., & Patterson, K. (2009). The relation between content and structure in language production: An analysis of speech errors in semantic dementia. *Brain and Language, 110,* 121–134.

Mikolov, T., Chen, K., Corrado, G., & Dean, J. (2013). Efficient estimation of word representations in vector space. *arXiv:1301.3781* [cs]. Retrieved from http://arxiv.org/abs/1301.3781

Miyake, A., Friedman, N. P., Emerson, M. J., Witzki, A. H., Howerter, A., & Wager, T. D. (2000). The unity and diversity of executive functions and their contributions to complex "frontal lobe" tasks: A latent variable analysis. *Cognitive Psychology, 41*(1), 49–100.

Murphy, G. (2016). Is there an exemplar theory of concepts? *Psychonomic Bulletin and Review, 23,* 1035–1042.

Neary, D., & Snowden, J. (1996). Fronto-temporal dementia: nosology, neuropsychology, and neuropathology. *Brain and Cognition, 31*(2), 176–187.

Novick, L. R. (2003). At the forefront of thought: The effect of media exposure on airplane typicality. *Psychonomic Bulletin & Review, 10,* 971–974.

Palmer, S. E. (1975). The effects of contextual scenes on the identification of objects. *Memory & Cognition, 3,* 519–526.

Patterson, K., Nestor, P. J., & Rogers, T. T. (2007). Where do you know what you know? The representation of semantic knowledge in the human brain. *Nature Reviews Neuroscience, 8,* 976–987.

Pauen, S. (2002). Evidence for knowledge-based category discrimination in infancy. *Child Development, 73*(4), 1016–1033.

Pecher, D., van Dantzig, S., Zwaan, R. A., & Zeelenberg, R. (2009). Language comprehenders retain implied shape and orientation of objects. *The Quarterly Journal of Experimental Psychology, 62*(6), 1108–1114.

Piwnica-Worms, K. E., Omar, R., Hailstone, J. C., & Warren, J. D. (2010). Flavor processing in semantic dementia. *Cortex, 46,* 761–768.

Prass, M., Grimsen, C., König, M., & Fahle, M. (2013). Ultra rapid object cagetorisation: Effect of level, animacy and context. *PLOS ONE, 8*(6), e68051.

Pylyshyn, Z. (2003). Return of the mental image: Are there really pictures in the brain? *Trends in Cognitive Sciences, 7*(3), 113–118.

Rascovsky, K., Growdon, M. E., Pardo, I. R., Grossman, S., & Miller, B. L. (2009). The quicksand of forgetfulness: Semantic dementia in *One Hundred Years of Solitude. Brain, 132,* 2609–2616.

Reynolds, D. J., Garnham, A., & Oakhill, J. (2006). Evidence of immediate activation of gender information from a social role name. *Quarterly Journal of Experimental Psychology, 59,* 886–903.

Rips, L. J., & Collins, A. (1993). Categories and resemblance. *Journal of Experimental Psychology: General, 122,* 468–486.

Rogers, T. T., & Patterson, K. (2007). Object categorization: Reversals and explanations of the basic-level advantage. *Journal of Experimental Psychology: General, 136,* 451–469.

Rogers, T. T., Lambon Ralph, M. A., Garrard, P., Bozeat, S., McClelland, J. L., Hodges, J. R., & Patterson, K. (2004). Structure and deterioration of semantic memory: A neuropsychological and computational investigation. *Psychological Review, 111*(1), 205–235.

Rosch, E., & Mervis, C. B. (1975). Family resemblances: Studies in the internal structure of categories. *Cognitive Psychology, 7,* 573–605.

Rosch, E., Mervis, C. B., Gray, W. D., Johnson, D. M., & Boyes-Braem, P. (1976). Basic objects in natural categories. *Cognitive Psychology, 8,* 382–439.

Sachs, J. S. (1967). Recognition memory for syntactic and semantic aspects of connected discourse. *Perception & Psychophysics, 2*(9), 437–442.

Schank, R. C. (1972). Conceptual dependency: A theory of natural language understanding. *Cognitive Psychology, 3*(4), 552–631.

Shuell, T. J. (1969). Clustering and organization in free recall. *Psychological Bulletin*, 72, 353–374.

Simmons, C. L., & Hampton, J. A. (2006). *Essentialist beliefs about basic and superordinate level categories*. Poster presented at the 47th Annual Meeting of the Psychonomic Society, Houston, TX, November.

Slezak, P. (1991). Can images be rotated and inspected? A test of the pictorial medium theory. *Program of the Thirteenth Annual Conference of the Cognitive Science Society*, Chicago, IL, pp. 55–60.

Slezak, P. (1995). The "philosophical" case against visual imagery. In T. Caelli, P. Slezak, & R. Clark (Eds.), *Perspectives in cognitive science: Theories, experiments and foundations* (pp. 237–271). New York, NY: Ablex.

Smith, J. D., & Minda, J. P. (2000). Thirty categorization results in search of a model. *Journal of Experimental Psychology: Learning, Memory, & Cognition*, 26, 3–27.

Steyvers, M., & Hemmer, P. (2012). Reconstruction from memory in naturalistic environments. *Psychology of Learning and Motivation*, 56, 125–144.

Storms, G., De Boeck, P., & Ruts, W. (2000). Prototype and exemplar-based information in natural language categories. *Journal of Memory and Language*, 42, 51–73.

Storms, G., De Boeck, P., & Ruts, W. (2001). Categorization of novel stimuli in well-known natural concepts: A case study. *Psychonomic Bulletin & Review*, 8(2), 377–384.

Sulin, R. A., & Dooling, D. J. (1974). Intrusion of a thematic idea in retention of prose. *Journal of Experimental Psychology*, 103, 255–262.

Tanaka, J. W., & Taylor, M. E. (1991). Object categories and expertise: Is the basic level in the eye of the beholder? *Cognitive Psychology*, 15, 121–149.

Tombs, A., & Rao Hill, S. (2014). The effect of service employees' accent on customer reactions. *European Journal of Marketing*, 48(11/12), 2051–2070.

Tuckey, M. R., & Brewer, N. (2003). How schemas affect eyewitness memory over repeated retrieval attempts. *Applied Cognitive Psychology*, 7, 785–800.

Vanpaemel, W., & Storms, G. (2008). In search of abstraction: The varying abstraction model of categorization. *Psychonomic Bulletin & Review*, 15(4), 732–749.

Vigliocco, G., Kousta, S. T., Della Rosa, P. A., Vinson, D. P., Tettamanti, M., Devlin, J. T., & Cappa, S. F. (2014). The neural representation of abstract words: The role of emotion. *Cerebral Cortex*, 24(7), 1767–1777.

Vincent-Lamarre, P., Massé, A. B., Lopes, M., Lord, M., Marcotte, O., & Harnad, S. (2016). The latent structure of dictionaries. *Topics in Cognitive Science*, 8(3), 625–659.

Wills, A. J., & Pothos, E. M. (2012). On the adequacy of current empirical evaluations of formal models of categorization. *Psychological Bulletin*, 138(1), pp. 102–125. doi: 10.1037/a0025715

Wu, L. L., & Barsalou, L. W. (2009). Perceptual simulation in conceptual combination: Evidence from property generation. *Acta Psychologica*, 132, 173–189.

Yee, E., & Tompson-Schill, S. L. (2016). Putting concepts into context. *Psychonomic Bulletin and Review*, 23, 1015–1027.

Zwaan, R. A. (2016). Situation models, mental simulations, and abstract concepts in discourse comprehension. *Psychonomic Bulletin and Review*, 23, 1028–1034.

Zwaan, R. A., & Radvansky, G. A. (1998). Situation models in language comprehension and memory. *Psychological Bulletin*, 123(2), 162–185.

Chapter 7

Contents

Everyday memory

INTRODUCTION

Over the past 35 years, there has been a rapid increase in research on everyday memory. The study of everyday memory is concerned with the ways we use memory in our daily lives. Everyday memory differs in some important ways from the kinds of memory traditionally studied in the laboratory and discussed in Chapters 4–6. Much of everyday memory relates to our goals and motivations (Cohen, 2008). We can see this most clearly with prospective memory (remembering to carry out intended actions). Most of our intended actions are designed to assist us in achieving our current goals. For example, the authors of this book often form the intention to track down an article or book needed to achieve the goal of completing a chapter in their textbooks.

Learning objectives
After studying Chapter 7, you should be able to: • Define repressed memories, false memories, recovered memories, and flashbulb memories, and explain how autobiographical memory is not always perfect.   • Explain how the cognitive interview addresses limitations of natural eyewitness testimony.   • Explain which features of human memory are illustrated by schema theories.   • Define, compare, and contrast prospective and retrospective memory.

TRADITIONAL MEMORY RESEARCH VS. EVERYDAY MEMORY RESEARCH

What are the main differences between the traditional approach to memory and the one based on everyday memory phenomena? First, everyday memories are often of events that happened a long time ago and have frequently been thought about or rehearsed during that time. As a result, "Naturally occurring memories are very often memories of memories rather than memories of the originally perceived objects and events" (Cohen, 2008, p. 2). In contrast, participants in laboratory studies usually remember information presented shortly beforehand.

Second, learning in most everyday memory research is *incidental* (not deliberate), with people learning information relevant to their goals or interests. In most traditional memory research, however, learning is *intentional*. What individuals learn is determined largely by the instructions they have been given.

Third, *social* factors are often important in everyday memory but are typically absent in traditional memory research. We share everyday memories with friends, relatives, and colleagues; this is not true for the tasks studied in traditional memory research.

Fourth, participants in traditional memory studies are generally motivated to be as *accurate* as possible in their memory performance. In contrast, everyday memory research is typically based on the notion that, "Remembering is a form of purposeful action" (Neisser, 1996, p. 204). This approach involves three assumptions about everyday memory:

1. It is purposeful (i.e., motivated).
2. It has a personal quality about it, meaning it is influenced by the individual's personality and other characteristics.
3. It is influenced by situational demands (e.g., the wish to impress one's audience).

The essence of Neisser's (1996) argument is this: what we remember in everyday life is determined by our personal goals, whereas what we remember in traditional memory research is mostly determined by the experimenter's demands for accuracy. Sometimes we strive for maximal accuracy in our recall in our everyday life (e.g., during an examination), but accuracy is typically *not* our main goal.

Findings

Evidence that the memories we report in everyday life are sometimes deliberately distorted was reported by Marsh and Tversky (2004). Students kept a record of their retelling of personal memories over a period of a month and admitted that 42% were inaccurate.

If what you say about an event is deliberately distorted, does this change your memory and make your subsequent recall inaccurate? Very often the answer is "yes." Dudokovic et al. (2004) asked people to read a story and then recall it three times accurately (as in traditional memory research) or entertainingly (as in the real world). Unsurprisingly, entertaining retellings were more emotional but contained fewer details than accurate retellings.

The participants subsequently tried to recall the story accurately. Those who had previously provided entertaining retellings recalled fewer story events, fewer details, and were less accurate than those who had provided accurate retellings. This is an example of the **saying-is-believing effect** – tailoring a message about an event to suit a given audience causes subsequent inaccuracies in memory for that event.

Further evidence of the saying-is-believing effect was reported by Hellmann et al. (2011). Participants saw a video of a pub brawl involving two men. They then described the brawl to a student whom they had been told believed that person A was (or was not) responsible for what happened. The participants' retelling of the event reflected the student's biased views. Finally, the participants were given an unexpected test of free recall for the crime event. Their recall was systematically influenced by their earlier retelling of the event. Free recall was most distorted in those participants whose retelling of the event had been most biased.

CHAPTER STRUCTURE

In this chapter, we will consider three of the most important topics in everyday memory. First there is autobiographical memory, which is concerned with personal memories about our own lives. It is extremely important because our sense of who we are depends on having an intact autobiographical memory. Much of what it is to be human is lost if someone suffers brain damage that eliminates most (or all) of their personal memories.

Second, we turn to one of the most important applications of memory research in the real world: eyewitness testimony. In thousands of court cases, the defendant was judged guilty or innocent mostly based on eyewitness evidence. As a result, it is vital to know the accuracy (or otherwise) of eyewitnesses' memories of a crime.

Third, we discuss the factors determining whether we remember to carry out intended actions such as buying something at the shops or meeting a friend. This is prospective memory, which is also important in everyday life. Anyone who rarely does what he/she has promised to do (e.g., meet up with friends) is unlikely to succeed socially or at work!

Section summary

- Learning in everyday life differs in four respects from traditional memory research: memories often happened a long time ago, learning was incidental, the memory is shared with other people, and the information learned is relevant to the individual's goals or interests.
- Most everyday remembering is intended for communication purposes rather than strict accuracy. Our goals in everyday remembering can distort the accuracy of subsequent long-term memory (saying-is-believing effect).

Chapter structure
- This chapter deals with three major topics in everyday memory: autobiographical memory, eyewitness testimony, and prospective memory.

AUTOBIOGRAPHICAL MEMORY

We have hundreds of thousands of memories relating to an endless variety of things. However, those relating to the experiences we have had and to people important to us have special significance and form our autobiographical memory (memory for the events of one's own life). *Why* are our autobiographical memories of consuming interest to us? They relate to our major life goals, to our most powerful emotions, and to our personal meanings.

Key term

Autobiographical memory:
a form of **declarative memory** involving memory for personal events across the lifespan.

AUTOBIOGRAPHICAL VS. EPISODIC MEMORY

What is the relationship between autobiographical memory and episodic memory (concerned with events occurring at a given time in a specific place; see Chapter 5)? One important similarity is that both types of memory relate to personally experienced events.

However, there are also several differences between autobiographical and episodic memory. First, autobiographical memory relates to events of personal significance, whereas episodic memory often relates to events of less importance (e.g., was the word "chair" presented in the first list?).

Second, autobiographical memory typically deals with complex memories selected from a huge collection of personal experiences. In contrast, episodic memory is much more limited in scope.

Third, autobiographical memory extends back over years or decades. In contrast, episodic memory (at least for laboratory events) often extends back only for minutes or hours (sometimes days).

Fourth, some brain-damaged patients with little or no episodic memory can nevertheless recall information about themselves (e.g., knowledge about their own personality; Klein & Lax, 2010).

An alternative view (e.g., Andrews-Hanna et al., 2014) is that episodic and autobiographical memory are not two different types of memory but that episodic memory is part of autobiographical memory. Retrieval of episodic elements (what, when, where) and contextual details contribute to the autobiographical experience. However, autobiographical memories in addition require (1) integration of such elements with conceptual knowledge about the self, and (2) reflection on the feelings, emotions, and/or beliefs of one's self or other people involved in the experience. In this view, autobiographical memory is not seen as a different form of memory but contains episodic memory plus two extra components. The alternative view fits within the "components of processing" approach, discussed in Chapter 5. An argument against the alternative view is that many episodic memories have little autobiographical value, as illustrated by the example: "Was the word *chair* present in the first list?"

Research Activity 7.1 *Autobiographical memories and personality*

Recall an event in your life that caused you to experience *happiness*. Write down a brief description of the event as you now remember it. Then do the same for each of the following emotions in turn: *anger; pride; fear; relief;* and *sadness*.

Now go back over your descriptions. Some of your memories may be communal (involving your relationships with other people). They may relate to love and friendship and to the emotions that others caused you to experience. Other memories may be agentic (involving themes of independence, achievement, and personal power). In other words, these are memories in which the associated emotional states are due to *personal* success and failure rather than your relationships with others.

Woike et al. (1999) carried out a very similar study. They argued that our personality influences the kinds of emotional autobiographical memories we recall. They distinguished between two types of personality:

1. *Agentic personality type*, with an emphasis on independence, achievement, and personal power.
2. *Communal personality type*, with an emphasis on interdependence and similarity to others.

Woike et al. (1999) found that students with an agentic personality recalled more autobiographical memories concerned with agency (e.g., success, absence of failure, failure). In contrast, those with a communal personality recalled more memories concerned with communion (e.g., love, friendship, betrayal of trust). When you look back at the autobiographical memories you wrote down, do you feel they reveal your personality?

HOW GOOD IS AUTOBIOGRAPHICAL MEMORY?

If your autobiographical memory is like that of the authors, you probably find that it is good enough for everyday life but short of details when you focus on individual past experiences. Sometimes, entire memories seem to be lost, even ones that seemed important and emotional at the time. This lack of autobiographical detail is not true of everyone. In Chapter 5 we discussed the Russian journalist Shereshevskii, who could remember complex briefing instructions without taking any notes and who could recall events from the distant past in great detail.

Parker, Cahill, and McGaugh (2006) reported another fascinating case of AJ, a woman born in 1965. She has an incredible ability to recall detailed information about almost every day of her life over the past several decades. Parker et al. coined the term *hyperthymestic syndrome* (formed from two Greek words meaning "more than normal" and "remembering") to describe this ability. Currently, researchers seem to prefer the term *highly superior autobiographical memory*. In 2008, AJ published a book (*The Woman Who Can't Forget*) about her life under her real name of Jill Price.

You might think it would be a huge advantage to have access to incredibly detailed information about your own autobiographical memory. However, that isn't how Jill Price sees it: "Most have called it a gift, but I call it a burden. I run my entire life through my head every day and it drives me crazy!!!" (Parker et al., 2006, p. 35). Strangely, her semantic and episodic memories are very ordinary. For example, her ability to recall lists of words is about average, and she finds it very hard to remember which locks fit each of the five keys on her keyring.

What are the secrets of her outstanding autobiographical memory? First, she has obsessional tendencies and spends most of her time thinking about herself and her past. Second, she has poor inhibitory processes and so finds it much harder than most people to switch her personal memories off. Third, Jill Price makes the passage of time seem more concrete by representing it in spatial form (e.g., drawing January in the 11 o'clock position on a circle and working counterclockwise from there). This linkage of time and space is often associated with very good memory (Simner et al., 2009). Fourth, areas of the temporal lobe that store events and dates are larger in Jill Price's brain than most other people's.

LePort et al. (2012) carried out a thorough investigation of 11 individuals having highly superior autobiographical memory. Their findings confirmed the conclusions based on Jill Price. Importantly, LePort et al. (2012) found that individuals with hyperthymestic syndrome showed structural differences from controls in brain regions (e.g., parahippocampal gyrus; anterior insula) associated with an autobiographical memory network.

Another individual with highly superior autobiographical memory is HK, a blind man who was tested when he was 20 years old (Ally et al., 2013).

Long-term memory of emotional material is enhanced by amygdala activation (the amygdala is strongly involved in emotional processing; see Chapter 11), and HK's right amygdala was approximately 20% larger than in most other people. In addition, he had enhanced connectivity between the amygdala and the hippocampus (centrally involved in the formation of long-term memories). It remains to be established whether the structural and functional differences found in individuals with highly superior autobiographical memory partially cause the remarkable autobiographical memory ability or are a consequence of it.

Most people have good autobiographical memories for certain things. Bahrick et al. (1975) made use of photographs from high-school yearbooks dating back many years. Ex-students showed remarkably little forgetting of information about their former classmates at retention intervals up to 25 years. Performance was 90% for recognizing a name as being that of a classmate, for recognizing a classmate's photograph, and for matching a classmate's name to his/her school photograph. Performance remained very high on the last two tests even after almost 50 years, but performance on the name recognition task declined.

Bahrick et al. (2008) asked American ex-college students to recall their academic grades. Distortions in recall occurred shortly after graduation but thereafter remained fairly constant over retention intervals up to 54 years. As you might guess, the great majority of distortions involved inflating the actual grade.

Bahrick (1984) used the term "permastore" to refer to very long-term stable memories. This term was derived from permafrost, the permanently frozen subsoil found in polar regions. It seems probable that the contents of the permastore consist mainly of information that was very well learned in the first place.

FLASHBULB MEMORIES

Whereas many people agree they have a rather poor autobiographical memory, they feel they have excellent memory for dramatic world events (e.g., terrorist attacks, the dramatic death of a much liked and admired person). Such memories have been called **flashbulb memories** by Brown and Kulik (1977).

At first, research seemed to support the introspection that flashbulb memories are exceptional because of their strong emotional involvement. Researchers assumed that flashbulb memories were much more accurate and long-lasting than other memories, because dramatic events activated a special neural mechanism if the events were surprising and had real consequences for the individual. This mechanism "printed" the details of such events permanently in the memory system. Details were stored about the person who supplied the information, the place where the news was heard, the ongoing event when the news was heard, the individual's own emotional state, the emotional state of others, and the consequences of the event for the individual.

Findings

Subsequent research was not able to confirm the initial beliefs, however. Much of this research was related to the 9/11 attack in 2001, when terrorists flew two airplanes into the New York World Trade Center and one into the Pentagon in Washington, D.C., and many people believed this could be the beginning of a new, global war. Immediately after the attack, memory psychologists started to collect memories from participants. This gave an unprecedented insight into the accuracy and longevity of flashbulb memories.

| Key term

Flashbulb memories: vivid and detailed memories of dramatic and significant events.

The most interesting study was run by Talarico and Rubin (2003). They assessed students' memories for the events of September 11 one day afterwards. At the same time, they assessed students' memory for another recent everyday event that students thought was memorable. The students were tested again 7, 42, or 224 days later. This allowed the authors to draw a forgetting curve for both events (Chapter 5). If flashbulb memories are special because of their strong emotional component, the forgetting curve for these memories should be much shallower than the forgetting curve for the matched events.

Talarico and Rubin (2003) came up with two key findings (Figure 7.1). First, the reported vividness of flashbulb memories remained very high over the entire 32-week period, whereas that of the control memories sharply declined.

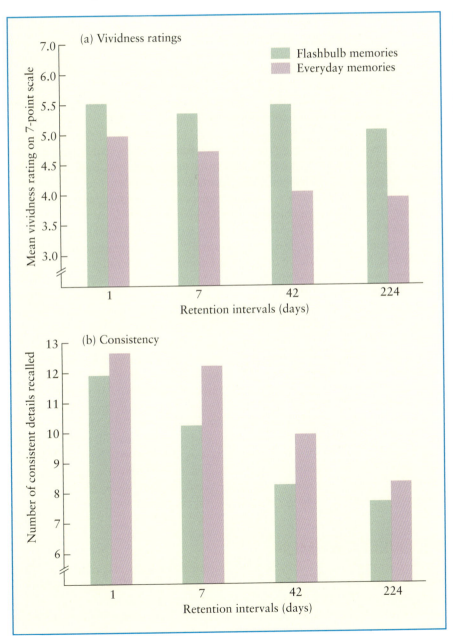

Figure 7.1 (a) Vividness ratings and (b) consistency of memory as a function of type of memory (flashbulb vs. everyday) and length of retention interval.
Source: Data from Talarico and Rubin (2003).

Second, against expectation, flashbulb memories were no more accurate or consistent than the matched everyday memories. As it happened, the reverse was true: students had slightly more detailed and consistent memories for the event they experienced themselves than for 9/11, and both types of memories showed very similar forgetting curves. Thus, there was a major discrepancy between people's beliefs in the strength of their flashbulb memories and the actual accuracy of those memories.

Why do we mistakenly believe our flashbulb memories are exceptionally accurate? The first factor is that flashbulb memories are not formed at once but over a period of several days. According to Weaver and Krug (2004), the best predictor of long-term flashbulb memories for 9/11 was not the memories reported immediately after the event but the memories reported one week later. We are blind to the fact that our memories of dramatic world events are constructed over a period of time rather than being fully formed at once.

We also underestimate the fact that flashbulb memories, just like other memories, become fragile during recall (Chapter 5), so that they can be changed as a function of what we hear at the time of recall. For example, it was found in one study (Coman et al., 2009) that memories for 9/11 could be altered by a single conversation several years later.

On a more positive note, Rimmele et al. (2012) reported that the consistency of flashbulb memories varies across features. They compared participants' memory for 9/11 one week and three years after the event. There was high consistency for remembering the location at which they heard about 9/11 (83%) but lower consistency for informant (70%), ongoing activity (62%), and their own immediate reaction (34%).

Sharot et al. (2007) argued that it may require intense emotional experience to produce genuine flashbulb memories. They compared the memories of individuals close to the World Trade Center (about 2 miles) on 9/11 with those who were somewhat farther away (about 4 ½ miles) three years after the event. The memories of those close to the event were more vivid and involved more activation of the amygdala (emotion) than the memories of those further away. Their memories were also more detailed. These findings point to the importance of the intensity of the emotional reaction to a dramatic event.

In sum, the evidence is mixed concerning the claim that flashbulb memories are special. On the one hand, so-called flashbulb memories are often remembered no better than ordinary memories and show only moderate consistency over time. On the other hand, there is generally good consistency over time for some details (e.g., where the news was heard). Thus, there may be selective enhancement of some kinds of information in flashbulb memories, arguably because this information is very distinctive (Chapter 5). Flashbulb memories also seem to be more detailed and long-lasting if there was an intense emotional experience when they were formed. We will return to this issue in Chapter 11, when we discuss the effects of emotion on memory.

RECOVERED MEMORIES

Another contentious issue in autobiographical memory research is whether memories of what happened to us can be repressed. The idea that very threatening or traumatic memories can be excluded from conscious awareness and pushed into an unconscious, almost inaccessible part of our memory was put forward in the early 20th century by the Austrian psychologist Sigmund Freud. He used the term **repression** to refer to this phenomenon.

At the end of the 20th century, there was much controversy about the possible existence of **recovered memories**. These are traumatic memories (typically of childhood sexual abuse) that had been forgotten for many years but suddenly were remembered in adult life. There were a number of high-profile court cases of claimants accusing relatives of sexual abuse after they had recovered previously suppressed memories. Is it possible that memories can be excluded from conscious memory for some time and later – sometimes – retrieved, as claimed by Freud?

Subsequent research has doubted the existence of recovered memories. Loftus and Davis (2006) argued that many of these so-called recovered memories are **false memories** referring to events and experiences that never actually happened. Some claimed recovered memories are undoubtedly false. For example, some people "remember" having being abducted by space aliens (Clancy et al., 2002). In addition, Loftus and Pickrell (1995) showed that false memories can be implanted rather easily in healthy people. Participants took part in what they thought was a study on the kind of things you may be able to remember from your childhood. Three of the four events had actually happened to the participants (told to the experimenters by the participants' relatives). One of the events had not happened, but could plausibly have occurred (e.g., being lost in a large shopping mall). Participants were given a short description of the events and asked to elaborate on them in writing. Later the participants were interviewed on two occasions. During these interviews participants often told that they remembered the event from their own life. This was the case for 68% of the events that had really happened to them, but also for 29% of the false events!

Lief and Fetkewicz (1995) found that 80% of adult patients who admitted reporting false recovered memories had been treated by therapists who made suggestions that childhood sexual abuse could be the reason of their problems. Arguably, these suggestions could be at the origin of the supposedly recovered memories.

Clancy and McNally (2005/2006; see also McNally & Geraerts, 2009) provided another explanation as to why some adults may have so-called recovered traumatic memories of sexual abuse. In their interviews with victims, they noticed that many victims did not understand what had happened to them when they were a child. Only two of 27 interviewees remembered the experience as terrifying, overwhelming, or traumatic. The other participants remembered it as weird, confusing, or uncomfortable. Moreover, only two people understood the experience as sexual at the time it occurred. However, after recalling their experience during adulthood, and viewing it through the eyes of an adult as sexual abuse, the participants became distressed.

According to Clancy and McNally, recovered memories are not repressed memories or false memories, but memories that got a different, more disturbing meaning as participants grew up and realized what had happened. Because of the new interpretation, the memories became much more powerful than they had been before.

All in all, there is consensus among empirical memory researchers that recovered memories as conceived by Freud do not exist.

Traumatic abuse in childhood does seem to have another effect on memory, however: it leads to impoverished autobiographical memories. People

Key terms

Repression: motivated forgetting of traumatic or other very threatening events.

Recovered memories: childhood traumatic or threatening memories that are remembered many years after the relevant events or experiences.

False memories: apparent **recovered memories** that refer to imagined rather than genuine events or experiences.

Key terms

Childhood amnesia: the inability of adults to recall autobiographical memories from early childhood.

Reminiscence bump: the tendency of older people to recall a disproportionate number of autobiographical memories from the years of adolescence and early adulthood.

who have experienced traumatic abuse report less detailed memories both for positive and negative personal events (Kuyken & Brewin, 1995; Ono et al., 2016). The same is true for individuals with major depression.

MEMORIES ACROSS THE LIFESPAN

Suppose we ask 70-year-olds to recall personal memories suggested by cue words (e.g., nouns referring to common objects, such as house, tree, shop). From which points in their lives would most memories come? Rubin et al. (1986) answered this question by combining findings from several studies. Two findings were of theoretical interest:

- **Childhood amnesia** (or infantile amnesia), shown by the almost total lack of memories from the first three years of life
- **Reminiscence bump**, consisting of a surprisingly large number of memories coming from the years between 10 and 30 (especially between 15 and 25)

Childhood amnesia

Adults report very few autobiographical memories from before the age of 3 and show limited recall for events occurring between the ages of 3 and 6. How can we explain this phenomenon? The most famous (or notorious!) account was provided by Sigmund Freud (1915/1957). He attributed it to repression, with threat-related thoughts and experiences being consigned to the unconscious. This dramatic theory fails to explain why adults cannot remember *positive* and *neutral* events from early childhood.

More recent research suggests that childhood amnesia consists of two stages (Jack & Hayne, 2010; Josselyn & Frankland, 2012). There is *full* amnesia for the first two years of life followed by *partial* amnesia in the remaining preschool years. Two factors are thought to contribute to the absolute amnesia before the age of 2. The first is the observation that very young animals also fail to retain information over long periods of time. Apparently the brain of a newborn is not yet capable of retaining information that can subsequently be retrieved, possibly because the hippocampus is still developing in the first years of life, disrupting previously formed memories (Josselyn & Frankland, 2012). The second factor refers to the fact that children can only form autobiographical memories after they develop a sense that some events have personal significance (Howe & Courage, 1997). This is only possible after the development of the self-concept, which occurs late in the second year of life (as indexed by visual self-recognition in a mirror).

The gradual increase of autobiographical memories between the age of two and six has been attributed to the development of language. According to the social-cultural developmental theory (Fivush & Nelson, 2004; Fivush, 2010), language is important because we use it to communicate our memories. Experiences occurring before children develop language are hard to express in language later on.

Other factors may be involved as well. For example, children's development of semantic memory may be important. There are dramatic changes in children's understanding of the world during the early years, and these changes may limit access to our early autobiographical memories. Yet another factor is that childhood amnesia may be partly due to forgetting over the years. This is particularly a problem because most studies have focused on *adults'* memories from early childhood. Tustin and Hayne (2010) asked children and adolescents to provide early memories. The earliest memories of children between the ages of 5 and 9 were from about 1 ½ years on average, those of adolescents were from 2 ½ years, and those of adults were from just over 3 years. Thus, childhood amnesia may partly depend on forgetting over the years rather than on the encoding issues stressed by other explanations.

| Key term

Life script:
the typical major life events for individuals living within a given society; sample life events are getting married and having children.

Reminiscence bump

Older people asked to recall personal memories mention numerous events from adolescence and early adulthood (the reminiscence bump). Conway et al. (2005) asked older people from America, China, Japan, England, and Bangladesh (2005) to recall autobiographical memories. There was a reminiscence bump in all five cultures.

How can we explain the existence of the reminiscence bump? Rubin and Berntsen's (2003) influential theory is based on the notion of a life script (cultural expectations about the major life events in most people's lives). Examples of such events are falling in love, marriage, and having children. Most of these events are emotionally positive and generally occur between the ages of 15 and 30. According to the theory, the life script guides and organizes the retrieval of autobiographical memories. To test their theory, Bohn and Berntsen (2011) did not ask older people to look back at their life but asked children aged between 10 and 14 to write about their future lives. In these stories 79% of the events were life-script events, which showed a pattern similar to the reminiscence bump.

Further support for life-script theory was reported by Berntsen et al. (2011). Older people were asked to identify the most positive and the most negative event in their lives. Positive events showed a reminiscence bump, but negative ones did not (see Figure 7.2). This finding is consistent with life-script

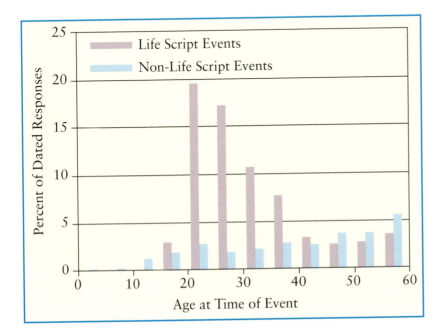

Figure 7.2 Percentage of life-script and non-life-script events remembered by old adults as a function of age at the time of the event. In line with the life-script theory, only life-script events showed a reminiscence bump. Source: From Berntsen et al. (2011). Reprinted with permission from the American Psychological Association.

theory given that the great majority of life-script events are positive. Of the positive events, 68% related to the life script: having children (34%), marriage (22%), college (6%), and falling in love (1%). In contrast, few of the negative events (e.g., someone's death; life-threatening illness) related to the life script. The positive events recalled were also rated as much more central to the participants' life story and identity than the negative ones.

The finding that the reminiscence bump is stronger for positive memories than for negative ones provides support for the life-script theory. Dickson et al. (2011), however, observed that older people show a reminiscence bump not only for very *expected* personal events but also for very *unexpected* personal events, which is less consistent with the notion of a life script guiding retrieval. A possible explanation for the latter observation is that our strongest autobiographical memories tend to be those of direct relevance to our self-identity (Conway, 2005). Most people's self-identity develops substantially during adolescence and early adulthood. The late teens and twenties differ in several ways from the life periods that precede and follow them (e.g., establishment of self-identity; novel or first-time experiences). This aspect is likely to contribute to the reminiscence bump as well. Whatever the explanation of the reminiscence bump, it is clear that your university years will form an important part of your autobiographical memory!

SELF-MEMORY SYSTEM MODEL

Conway and Pleydell-Pearce (2000) put forward a theory of autobiographical memory (further developed by Conway, 2005). They argued that we possess a self-memory system having two major components:

1. *Autobiographical knowledge base* containing personal information at three levels of specificity:
   - *Lifetime periods*: These generally cover substantial periods of time defined by major ongoing situations (e.g., time at high school).
   - *General events*: These include repeated events (e.g., visits to a sports club) and single events (e.g., a holiday in Spain). General events are often related to each other as well as to lifetime periods.
   - *Event-specific knowledge*: This knowledge consists of images, feelings, and other details relating to general events, and spanning time periods from seconds to hours. Knowledge about a specific event is usually organized in the correct temporal order.
2. *Working self*: This is concerned with the self, what it may become in the future, and with the individual's current set of goals. The goals of the working self will influence the kinds of memories stored within the autobiographical knowledge base. They also partly determine which autobiographical memories we recall.

Conway and Pleydell-Pearce (2000) argued that autobiographical memories can be accessed through generative (voluntary) retrieval or direct (involuntary) retrieval. We use generative retrieval when we deliberately construct autobiographical memories by combining the resources of the working self with information contained in the autobiographical knowledge base (e.g., when we try to recall the names of our friends in primary school). In contrast, direct retrieval doesn't involve the working self; autobiographical memories produced by direct retrieval are triggered by specific cues (e.g., hearing the word "gambling" on the radio may produce direct retrieval of a trip to Las Vegas). Generative retrieval is more effortful and involves more active involvement by the rememberer than does direct retrieval.

Conway (2005) developed this theory (see Figure 7.3). The knowledge structures in autobiographical memory are divided into the conceptual self and episodic memories (previously called event-specific knowledge). At the top of the hierarchy, the life story and themes have been added. The life story consists of very general factual and evaluative knowledge we possess about ourselves. Themes refer to major life domains (e.g., work; relationships).

Conway (2005) argued that we want our autobiographical memories to exhibit *coherence* (consistency with our current goals and beliefs) and

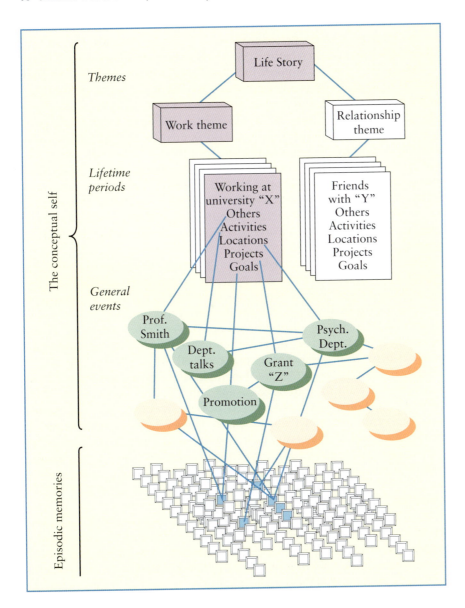

Figure 7.3 The knowledge structures within autobiographical memory, as proposed by Conway (2005).
Source: Reprinted with permission of Elsevier.

correspondence (being accurate). Over time, coherence tends to win out over correspondence.

Findings

Research on patients with retrograde amnesia (widespread forgetting of events preceding brain injury; see Chapter 5) supports the notion of a distinction between the conceptual self and episodic memories. Some patients have great difficulty in recalling episodic memories, but their ability to recall general events and lifetime periods is less impaired (Conway & Pleydell-Pearce, 2000). Rosenbaum et al. (2005) studied an amnesic patient (KC) who had no episodic memories. However, he could access some general autobiographical knowledge about his own life. In addition, several brain-damaged patients with practically no episodic memory can still recall the kind of personality they have. This is the case even in patients with severe deficits in semantic memory as well as episodic memory (Klein & Lax, 2010), showing the resilience of self-knowledge about one's personality.

The model distinguishes between generative or effortful retrieval and direct or spontaneous retrieval. Support for this distinction was reported by Uzer et al. (2012). Participants recalled autobiographical memories when presented with emotion words (e.g., *frustrated*; *amused*) and thought aloud while doing so. Direct retrieval was three times faster than generative retrieval, which is as expected given its automatic nature. Also as predicted, direct retrieval was associated with much less vocalization of effort than generative retrieval.

How different are the autobiographical memories produced via generative and direct retrieval? Memories elicited by direct retrieval are more specific, less significant, and less relevant to the individual's personal identity than those involving generative retrieval (Johannessen & Berntsen, 2010). Thus, as predicted, the individual's working self and goals were more involved in generative than direct retrieval.

Addis et al. (2012) compared patterns of brain activation when autobiographical memories were accessed by direct or generative retrieval. Generative retrieval was associated with more activation in parts of the prefrontal cortex thought to be involved in strategic search for autobiographical information. Other areas (e.g., left hippocampus) were more activated during direct than generative retrieval. These findings confirm there are important differences between direct and generative retrieval.

Conway (2005) argued that autobiographical memories are often inaccurate because we want them to be consistent with the working self's goals. For example, people often claim that aspects of their lives (e.g., the self; marital relationship) are better now than in the past. However, this "improvement" is typically due to misremembering their past selves in a negatively biased way (see Newman and Lindsay, 2009, for a review). Such inaccuracies can enhance our self-image and our social relationships with other people.

Evaluation

The theoretical approach of Conway and Pleydell-Pearce (2000) and Conway (2005) provides a reasonably comprehensive account of autobiographical memory. Several of the major theoretical assumptions (e.g., the hierarchical structure of autobiographical memory; the intimate relationship between autobiographical memory and the self; the importance of goals in autobiographical memory) are well supported. There is also good support for the distinction between generative and direct retrieval.

What are the limitations with the self-memory system model? First, neuroscientific research shows that the retrieval of autobiographical memories involves more brain areas and processes than captured by the model. Second, we need to know more about *how* the working self *interacts* with the autobiographical knowledge base to produce recall of specific autobiographical memories. Third, autobiographical memories vary in the extent to which they contain episodic information (e.g., contextual details) and semantic information (e.g., world knowledge). However, this is not addressed fully within the model.

Evaluation

+ The theoretical approach of Conway and Pleydell-Pearce (2000) and Conway (2005) is a comprehensive one.

+ Several of the theory's assumptions (e.g., the hierarchical structure of autobiographical memory; the intimate relationship between autobiographical memory and the self; the importance of goals in autobiographical memory) are well supported by the evidence.

− The ways in which the working self interacts with the autobiographical knowledge base to produce recall of specific autobiographical memories are not well understood.

− Autobiographical memories vary in the extent to which they contain episodic information (e.g., contextual details) and semantic information (e.g., schema-based information). However, this issue isn't fully addressed within the theory.

Section summary

Autobiographical vs. episodic memory

- There are several differences between autobiographical memory and episodic memory: autobiographical memories have personal significance, typically deal with complex memories, and extend back over years. According to many authors, this suggests that autobiographical and episodic memory are different stores. Not everyone agrees, however. According to the critics, it is better to see episodic memory as a component of autobiographical memory among other components.
- Individuals with an agentic personality regard memories concerned with personal achievement as important, whereas those with a communal personality emphasize memories concerned with love and friendship.

How good are our autobiographical memories?

- Most people have excellent retention of information about their school classmates even several decades later because this information was very well learned. A few obsessional individuals have an exceptional ability to recall detailed information about their lives.

- Most of the time, however, our autobiographical memories are rather poor. They tend to be fragmentary and distorted to give us a good feeling about our current functioning.

Flashbulb memories

- Many people believe their flashbulb memories for dramatic events are more accurate than is actually the case. They underestimate the changes that occur to such memories over the first few days after the event and the impact of discussions about the event with other people.

Recovered memories

- Individuals sometimes claim to have recovered memories of traumatic events that had been forgotten for many years. Research has not been able to find much evidence for the existence of repressed autobiographical memories. There is more evidence for false memories and memories that gained a more disturbing and powerful meaning as the individual grew. Traumatic abuse in childhood can also lead to impoverished memories.

Memories across the lifetime

- We have no memories of what happened in our first 2 years of life and degraded information for what happened between the age of 2 and 6, a phenomenon called childhood amnesia. Several factors are involved, including the impossibility of the very young brain to store and retrieve information over a long period, the absence of a self-concept before the age of 2, the importance of language and semantic memory for detailed autobiographical memories, and forgetting over time.
- Older people recall numerous personal memories from adolescence and early adulthood (the reminiscence bump). There is a much clearer reminiscence bump for positive than for negative memories. These positive memories often relate to events associated with a real sense of personal development and progress forming part of the life script (major life events based on cultural expectations).

Self-memory system model

- The self-memory system consists of hierarchically organized knowledge and the working self. Autobiographical memories can be accessed through voluntary or involuntary retrieval. Voluntary retrieval is influenced by the working self's goals, whereas involuntary retrieval is influenced by the cue given.

EYEWITNESS TESTIMONY

The accuracy (or otherwise) of an individual's memory is sometimes of enormous importance. Suppose you are the only eyewitness to a very serious crime. Subsequently, the person you identify as the murderer on a lineup is found guilty even though there is no other strong evidence. Such cases raise the question: is it safe to rely on eyewitness testimony?

Many people answer "yes" to this question. Simons and Chabris (2011) found that 37% of Americans believe the testimony of a single confident eyewitness should be enough to convict a criminal defendant. DNA testing is relevant to answering this question. These tests can often help to establish whether the convicted person was actually the culprit. Note, however, that such tests generally only indicate a given individual was present at the crime scene.

In the United States, 200 convicted individuals have been shown to be innocent by DNA tests mostly on the basis of mistaken eyewitness identification. Unfortunately, most jurors and judges underestimate problems with eyewitness testimony. Benton et al. (2006) found that judges disagreed with eyewitness experts on 60% of eyewitness issues, and jurors disagreed with the experts on 87% of them!

POST-EVENT MISINFORMATION EFFECT

Why do you think eyewitnesses often make mistakes when recalling a crime they have observed? Perhaps the most obvious explanation is that eyewitnesses often fail to pay attention to the crime and to the criminal (or criminals). After all, the crime they observe typically occurs suddenly and unexpectedly. However, Loftus and Palmer (1974) argued it is *not* only what happens at the time of the crime that matters. According to them, eyewitness memories are fragile and can – surprisingly easily – be distorted by what happens *after* observing the crime, a phenomenon called the post-event misinformation effect.

In their well-known study (Loftus & Palmer, 1974), eyewitnesses were shown a film of a multiple-car accident. After viewing the film, they described what had happened and then answered specific questions. Some were asked, "About how fast were the cars going when they hit each other?" Others were asked the same question but with the word "hit" replaced by "collided," "bumped," "contacted," or "smashed into."

What did Loftus and Palmer (1974) find? Speed estimates were higher (40.8 mph) when the word "smashed" was used, lower with "collided" (39.3), and lower still with "bumped" (38.1) and "hit" (34). One week later, all the eyewitnesses were asked, "Did you see any broken glass?" In fact, there was no broken glass. However, 32% of those previously asked about speed using the verb "smashed" said they had seen broken glass. In contrast, only 14% of eyewitnesses who had been asked using the verb "hit" said they had seen broken glass. Thus, our memory for events is so fragile it can be distorted by changing *one* word in one question!

How worried should we be that eyewitnesses' memory can be systematically distorted by information presented after they observe a crime? In fact, most research has focused on distortions for peripheral or minor details (e.g., presence of broken glass) rather than central features. In one study (Dalton & Daneman, 2006), however, participants were presented with misinformation about both central and peripheral features.

Pairs of eyewitnesses watched a video clip of an action sequence and were told they would discuss it later in detail with each other. The video clip consisted of a 5-minute clip of an escape scene during which one character, a scientist, was chased through the grounds of an industrial laboratory by an assassin who was instructed to retrieve a syringe containing a substance that the scientist was trying to protect.

Key terms

Post-event misinformation effect:
the distorting effect on eyewitness memory of misleading information provided after the crime or other event.

After watching the clip, participants discussed it with the other member of their group. This member was a confederate of the experimenter, who mentioned two central false suggestions, two peripheral small suggestions, along with two central true pieces of information and two peripheral true pieces of information. An example of a false central suggestion was that the scientist avoided hitting a red sports car in the parking lot, whereas in the film clip the scientist had collided with the car. An example of a false peripheral suggestion was that a little boy was holding a balloon and wearing a baseball hat, whereas in the movie the boy wore a hat made out of a clown's balloon.

After the discussion the participants were given a recognition test in which they were asked to read statements and decide whether they were true or false. Participants accepted 93% of the peripheral false suggestions but also 43% of the central false suggestions. The effects were slightly smaller, but still present, when in another experiment the participants did not discuss the film clip alone with the confederate but together with three to five other, naive viewers. In that situation, they accepted 70% of the false peripheral suggestions and 27% of the false central suggestions. The smaller effects were mainly due to the fact that one of the members of the group had protested against the confederate's false information.

SOURCE MISATTRIBUTION

How does misleading post-event information distort what eyewitnesses report? One possibility is **source misattribution** (Johnson et al., 1993). The basic idea is that a memory probe (e.g., a question) activates memory traces overlapping with it in terms of information. Any memory probe may activate memories from various sources. The individual decides on the *source* of any activated memory on the basis of the information it contains. Source misattribution is likely when the memories from two sources resemble each other.

Evidence of source misattribution was reported by Allen and Lindsay (1998). They presented two narrative slideshows describing two events with different people in different settings. However, some details in the two events were similar (e.g., a can of Pepsi vs. a can of Coke). When eyewitnesses recalled the first event, some details from the second event were mistakenly recalled.

Source misattribution is not limited to post-event information; it can also be caused by misleading information presented *before* an event. Lindsay et al. (2004) showed eyewitnesses a video of a museum burglary. On the previous day, they listened to a narrative thematically similar to the video (a palace burglary) or thematically dissimilar (a school field-trip to a palace) to the video. Eyewitnesses made many more errors when recalling information from the video when the narrative was thematically similar. This is potentially important, because eyewitnesses often have relevant past experiences that may distort their memory for a crime.

As you may have noticed, the findings showing that pre- and post-event information can distort eyewitness memory reveal the importance of respectively proactive and retroactive interference in memory retrieval, as discussed in Chapter 5.

REMEMBERING FACES

Information about the culprit's face is very often the most important information that eyewitnesses may or may not remember. We will consider factors determining whether culprits' faces are remembered (see also Chapter 2).

In several countries, there has been a dramatic increase in the number of closed-circuit television (CCTV) cameras. How easy is it to identify someone from CCTV images? Burton et al. (1999) considered this question. They presented people with a target face taken from a CCTV video together with an array of 10 high-quality photographs (see Figure 7.4).

The participants' task in the Burton et al. (1999) study was to select the matching face or to decide the target face wasn't present in the array. When the target face was present, it was selected only 65% of the time. When it wasn't present, 35% of the participants nevertheless claimed that a face in the array matched the target face!

Eyewitnesses sometimes remember a face but fail to remember the precise circumstances in which they saw it. In one study (Ross et al., 1994), eyewitnesses observed an event in which there was a bystander as well as the culprit. Eyewitnesses were three times more likely to select the bystander than someone else they hadn't seen before from a line-up including the bystander but not the culprit. This is known as **unconscious transference** – a face is correctly recognized as having been that of someone seen before but incorrectly judged

Key term

Unconscious transference: the tendency of eyewitnesses to misidentify a familiar (but innocent) face as belonging to the person responsible for a crime.

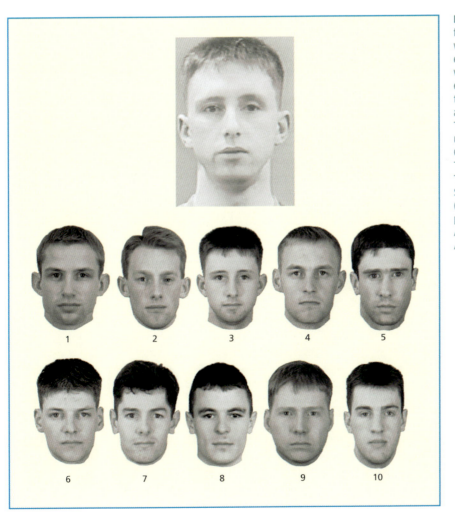

Figure 7.4 Example of full-face neutral target with an array used in the experiments. You may wish to attempt the task of establishing whether or not the target is present in this array and which one it is. The studio and video images used are from the Home Office Police Information Technology Organisation. Target is number 3. Source: From Bruce et al. (1999). Reprinted with permission from the American Psychological Association.

to be responsible for a crime. Ross et al. found that there was no unconscious transference effect when eyewitnesses were informed before seeing the line-up that the bystander and the culprit were not the same person.

Same-race faces are recognized better than cross-race faces – the **cross-race effect**. For example, Behrman and Davey (2001) found from an analysis of 271 actual criminal cases that the suspect was much more likely to be identified when he/she was of the same race as the eyewitness rather than a different race (60% vs. 45%, respectively).

How can we explain the cross-race effect? Expertise is a factor. Eyewitnesses having the most experience with members of another race often show a smaller cross-race effect than others (see review by Shriver et al., 2008). Another factor is that we may process the faces of individuals belonging to groups with which we identify (our ingroup) more thoroughly than those of individuals belonging to groups with which we don't identify (outgroups).

Shriver et al. (2008) showed the importance of ingroup identification in a study among middle-class white students at the University of Miami. They saw photographs of college-aged males in impoverished contexts (e.g., dilapidated housing; rundown public spaces) or in wealthy contexts (e.g., large suburban homes; golf courses). They then received a test of recognition memory.

What did Shriver et al. (2008) find? There was the usual cross-race effect when white and black faces had been seen in wealthy contexts. However, the cross-race effect disappeared when white and black faces had been seen in impoverished contexts. The reason was that the white faces weren't regarded as belonging to the students' ingroup when appearing in an impoverished context.

The other-race effect occurs because we find it hard to *remember* the faces of individuals belonging to different races. However, that is not a complete explanation. Megreya et al. (2011) found that *perceptual* processes are involved as well. British and Egyptian participants were presented with a target face and an array of 10 faces (see Figure 7.5). They had to decide whether the target face was in the array and, if so, to identify it. There were minimal demands on memory because all the photographs remained in view. Megreya

Figure 7.5 Examples of Egyptian (left) and UK (right) face-matching arrays. The task was to decide whether the person shown at the top was present in the array underneath.
Source: From Megreya et al. (2011). © The Experimental Psychology Society, reprinted with permission from Taylor & Francis Ltd (www.tandfonline.com) on behalf of The Experimental Psychology Society.

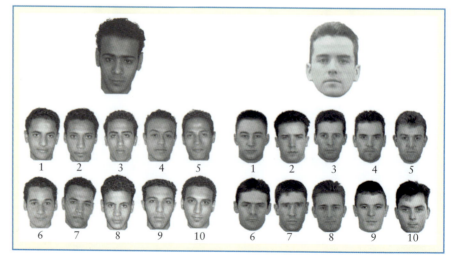

et al. (2011) still found the other-race effect. Correct identifications of the target face when present in the array were 70% for same-race faces versus 64% for other-race faces. When the target face was not present, there was mistaken identification of a non-target face 34% of the time with same-race faces versus 47% of the time with other-race faces.

As we discussed in Chapter 2, the reason why faces are difficult to recognize is that photographs of the same face can show considerable *variability*. This means it is hard for eyewitnesses to make an identification on the basis of a *single* photograph, as typically happens. Jenkins and Burton (2011) argued that the way forward is to *combine* information from multiple photographs of the same face to create an average face. They found that averaged faces were recognized significantly faster than single photographs. Thus, detectives should use pictures of averaged faces (wherever possible) to maximize the ability of eyewitnesses to make accurate identifications.

CONFIRMATION BIAS

Eyewitness testimony can be distorted via **confirmation bias** (i.e., event memory is influenced by the observer's expectations). In one study (Lindholm & Christianson, 1998), Swedish and immigrant students saw a videotaped simulated robbery in which the perpetrator seriously wounded a cashier with a knife. After watching the video, participants were shown color photographs of eight men (four Swedes and four immigrants). Both Swedish and immigrant participants were twice as likely to select an innocent immigrant than an innocent Swede. Immigrants are overrepresented in Swedish crime statistics, and this influenced participants' expectations concerning the likely ethnicity of the criminal.

As we saw in Chapter 6, Bartlett (1932) argued that we possess memory schemas. These schemas (see definition in the Glossary) lead us to form certain expectations and can distort our memory by causing us to reconstruct an event's details based on "what must have been true." Most people's bank-robbery schema includes information that robbers are male, wear disguises and dark clothes, and have a getaway car with a driver (Tuckey & Brewer, 2003a). Tuckey and Brewer showed eyewitnesses a video of a simulated bank robbery followed by a memory test. As predicted by Bartlett's theory, eyewitnesses recalled information relevant to the bank-robbery schema better than irrelevant information (e.g., the color of the getaway car).

Tuckey and Brewer (2003b) focused on eyewitnesses' memory for ambiguous information. Some eyewitnesses saw a video with a robber's head covered by a balaclava (ski mask) so the robber's gender was ambiguous. As predicted, eyewitnesses mostly interpreted the ambiguous information as being consistent with their male bank-robbery schema, also when the robber in the video was female. Thus, participants' recall was systematically distorted by including information from their bank-robbery schema even when it didn't correspond to what they had observed.

VIOLENCE AND ANXIETY

What are the effects of anxiety and violence on the accuracy of eyewitness memory? There is evidence for **weapon focus** – eyewitnesses attend to the criminal's weapon, which reduces their memory for other information. In one

Key terms

Confirmation bias: distortions of memory caused by the influence of expectations concerning what is likely to have happened.

Weapon focus: the finding that eyewitnesses pay so much attention to some crucial aspect of the situation (e.g., the weapon) that they ignore other details.

study, Loftus et al. (1987) asked participants to watch one of two sequences: (1) a person pointing a gun at a cashier and receiving some cash; (2) a person handing a check to the cashier and receiving some cash. The participants looked more at the gun than at the check. As predicted, memory for details unrelated to the gun/check was poorer in the weapon condition.

Pickel (2009) pointed out that people often attend to stimuli that are *unexpected* in a situation (inconsistent with their schema of that situation). This impairs their memory for other stimuli. This led Pickel (2009) to argue that the weapon focus effect will be greater when the presence of a weapon is unexpected. As predicted, there was a stronger weapon focus effect when a criminal carrying a folding knife was female, because it is more unexpected to see a woman with a knife. Also as predicted, the weapon focus effect was greater when a criminal with a knitting needle was male rather than female.

Fawcett et al. (2013) carried out a meta-analysis (see Glossary) of studies on weapon focus. There was a moderate effect on eyewitness memory of weapon focus. Of importance, the size of this effect was similar regardless of whether the event occurred in the laboratory or in the real world.

What are the effects of stress and anxiety on eyewitness memory? Deffenbacher et al. (2004) carried out a meta-analysis. Culprits' faces were identified 54% of the time in low-anxiety or low-stress conditions versus 42% for high-anxiety or high-stress conditions. The average proportion of details recalled correctly was 64% in low-stress conditions and 52% in high-stress conditions. Thus, stress and anxiety generally impair eyewitness memory.

Deffenbacher et al.'s (2004) findings were supported by Valentine and Mesout (2009). Participants encountered somebody in the Horror Labyrinth at the London Dungeon. Their subsequent memory performance for the person encountered was worse among those participants who were experiencing the most anxiety while in the Labyrinth.

Why does stress impair memory? According to Easterbrook's (1959) hypothesis, stress causes a narrowing of attention on central or important stimuli, which causes a reduction in people's ability to remember peripheral details. Yegiyan and Lang (2010) presented people with distressing pictures. As picture stressfulness increased, recognition memory for the central details improved progressively. In contrast, memory for peripheral details was much worse with highly stressful pictures than with moderately stressful ones. Thus, the findings supported Easterbrook's hypothesis.

AGING AND EYEWITNESS TESTIMONY

Older eyewitnesses' memory is less accurate than that of younger adults, and misinformation effects are often much greater on older than younger adults. Jacoby et al. (2005) presented misleading information to younger and older adults. The older adults had a 43% chance of producing false memories on a later recall test compared to only 4% for the younger adults. According to Morcom (2016), a factor contributing to the poorer memories of older people may be that these people fail to adequately monitor their recall to detect errors.

Wright and Stroud (2002) considered differences between younger and older adults identifying the culprits after being presented with crime videos. They found an own-age bias – both groups had more accurate identification when the culprit was of a similar age to themselves.

| Key term

Own-age bias: the tendency for eyewitnesses to identify the culprit more often when he/she is of similar age to the eyewitness.

What causes own-age bias? Harrison and Hole (2009) found it was largely due to the greater *exposure* most people have to people of their own age. Teachers (who spend hours a day exposed to children's faces) showed no evidence of own-age bias – they recognized children's faces as well as those of people of their own age. Wiese et al. (2013) found that young geriatric nurses had no own-age bias either because they recognized old faces much better than did young controls as a result of their experience with older people.

FROM LABORATORY TO COURTROOM

Can we apply findings from laboratory studies to real-life crimes and eyewitnesses? There are several differences. First, eyewitnesses are much more likely to be the victims in real life than in the laboratory. Second, it is much less stressful to watch a video of a violent crime than to experience it in real life. Third, in laboratory research the consequences of an eyewitness making a mistake are trivial, but they can literally be a matter of life or death in an American court of law.

In spite of these differences, there are important similarities. Ihlebaek et al. (2003) used a staged robbery involving two robbers armed with handguns. In the live condition, eyewitnesses were ordered repeatedly to "Stay down." A video taken during the live condition was presented to eyewitnesses in the video condition. Participants in both conditions exaggerated the duration of the event, and they showed similar patterns in terms of what was well and poorly remembered. However, eyewitnesses in the video condition recalled more information.

In a study by Pozzulo et al. (2008), eyewitnesses observed a staged theft live or via video. Identification accuracy of the culprit was comparable in the two conditions. However, eyewitnesses in the live condition reported more stress and arousal.

Tollestrup et al. (1994) analyzed police records concerning identification by eyewitnesses to crimes involving fraud and robbery. Factors found to be important in laboratory studies (e.g., weapon focus; retention interval) were also important in real-life crimes.

In sum, artificial laboratory conditions typically don't distort the findings. If anything, the errors in eyewitness memory obtained under laboratory conditions *underestimate* memory deficiencies for real-life events. Overall, laboratory research provides evidence of genuine relevance to the legal system.

COGNITIVE INTERVIEW

The police want to maximize the amount of information provided by eyewitnesses when interviewed. Psychologists have contributed substantially to achieving that goal by developing the cognitive interview (e.g., Geiselman & Fisher, 1997) based on four retrieval rules:

1. Mental reinstatement of the environment and any personal contact experienced during the crime
2. Encouraging the reporting of *every* detail including minor ones
3. Describing the incident in several different orders (e.g., backwards in time)
4. Reporting the incident from different viewpoints, including those of other eyewitnesses

The cognitive interview increases the information obtained from eyewitnesses. It is effective because it is based on our knowledge of human memory. The first two rules derive from the encoding specificity principle (Tulving, 1979; see Chapter 5). According to this principle, recall depends on the overlap or match between the *context* in which an event is witnessed and that at recall. The third and fourth rules are based on the assumption that memory traces are complex and contain several kinds of information. As a result, crime information can be retrieved using different retrieval routes.

Techniques from the cognitive interview can also be used with suspects. Inexperienced detectives tend to interview suspects with a confrontational style in the hope of obtaining a confession. A problem with this approach is that it has a rather high chance of resulting in a false confession, particularly in vulnerable people (Kassin et al., 2010). The alternative is a more co-operative interviewing style, which consists of inquiry-examining and adding to the existing evidence. The latter style is known as *investigative interviewing*. It has been developed with the assistance of psychologists and is now part of various police training programs, intended to enhance confidence in evidence obtained through police questioning.

Findings

Memon et al. (2010) carried out a meta-analysis comparing the effectiveness of the cognitive interview with the standard police interview. There was a large increase in the number of details correctly recalled by eyewitnesses with the cognitive interview compared to the standard interview. This increase was comparable whether the crime or incident was viewed live or via videotape.

Memon et al. (2010) further found that the beneficial effects of the cognitive interview were reduced when the situation was highly arousing. They were also reduced when there was a long retention interval between the incident and the interview. However, the cognitive interview remained effective even with high arousal and a long retention interval.

The cognitive interview had only one negative effect on eyewitness performance. There was a fairly small but significant increase in recall of incorrect details compared to the standard interview.

Advocates of the cognitive interview often recommend that eyewitnesses recall the event with their eyes closed. Vredeveldt et al. (2011) obtained evidence that this indeed enhances recall. *Why* is eye-closure beneficial? It reduces cognitive load on the eyewitness and reduces distraction.

Does the cognitive interview reduce the adverse effects of misleading information on eyewitness memory? Memon et al. (2009) found it did not when the misleading information was presented *before* the cognitive interview. However, the impact of misleading information on eyewitness memory was reduced when presented *after* the cognitive interview.

Is it essential to use all components of the cognitive interview? The answer appears to be "no." Colomb and Ginet (2012) found mental reinstatement of the situation and reporting all the details both enhanced recall. However, altering the eyewitness's perspective and changing the order in which the information was recalled were less effective. Dando et al. (2011) found that requiring eyewitnesses to recall information in a backward temporal order even *reduced* the number of correct details recalled and *increased* recall errors. This happened because it disrupted the temporal organization of eyewitnesses' memory for the crime.

Evaluation

The cognitive interview has the advantage of having a well-established theoretical and empirical basis. There is compelling evidence that it is an effective method for obtaining as much accurate information as possible from eyewitnesses under most circumstances. Some progress has been made in identifying the components of the cognitive interview that are most responsible for its effectiveness.

What are the limitations with the cognitive interview? First, the small increased amount of incorrect eyewitness recall can lead detectives to misinterpret the evidence.

Second, recreating the context at the time of the incident is a key ingredient in the cognitive interview. However, context reinstatement can result in more false recognitions by increasing the perceived familiarity of non-target faces (Wong & Read, 2011).

Third, the cognitive interview is less effective when the event was stressful than when it was not. It is also less effective when there is a long delay between the event and the interview.

Section summary

- Eyewitness testimony is very important. Sometimes it leads to innocent individuals being wrongly imprisoned, as is indicated by DNA evidence.

Post-event misinformation effect and source misattribution
- Misleading information provided after an event can distort eyewitnesses' memory, especially for minor details.
- The post-event misinformation effect is sometimes due to source misattribution when memories from two sources resemble each other.

Remembering faces
- Face recognition is often poor, especially when the culprit is of a different race or ingroup to the eyewitness. Even when eyewitnesses recognize a face, they may misremember the circumstances in which they saw it originally.

Confirmation bias
- Eyewitnesses' memory can be distorted by their expectations based on schemas stored in long-term memory. For example, eyewitnesses tend to interpret ambiguous information about a bank robbery as being consistent with their bank-robbery schema (e.g., bank robbers are male).

Violence and anxiety
- When the criminal has a weapon, eyewitnesses attend to it (especially when it is unexpected in the context). Weapon focus leads to reduced memory for other information. Stress and anxiety impair memory for culprits' faces and details of the crime scene.

Aging and testimony
- Older eyewitnesses' memory is less accurate than that of young adults.
- Eyewitness identification is usually better for culprits of the same age, due to more exposure to such faces. This is called the own-age bias.

> **Cognitive interview**
> • The cognitive interview is based on the finding that recall depends on the overlap between the recall context and that during an incident. In general, such an interview is more effective than a standard interview.

PROSPECTIVE MEMORY

Think of occasions on which your memory has let you down. Perhaps you remember your mind going blank in the middle of an exam or forgetting someone's name when introducing two people to each other. These are failures of retrospective memory, memory related to remembering events, words, and so on from the past.

PROSPECTIVE MEMORY VS. RETROSPECTIVE MEMORY

Retrospective memory is not the only form of memory we need. Often we must remember to do something in the future. This form of memory is called prospective memory, remembering to carry out intended actions without being instructed to do so. In essence, it is remembering to remember. Failures of prospective memory (absentmindedness when action is required) can be as frustrating and embarrassing as failures of retrospective memory. For example, think of occasions you completely forgot you had arranged to meet a friend.

How different are retrospective memory and prospective memory? People certainly interpret failures of the two types of memory differently. They interpret failures of prospective memory involving promises to another person as indicating poor motivation and reliability (Graf, 2012). In contrast, failures of retrospective memory are attributed to a poor memory. Thus, deficient prospective memory means "flaky person" whereas deficient retrospective memory means "faulty brain" (Graf, 2012).

There are several other differences. First, retrospective memory generally involves remembering *what* we know about something and can be high in informational content (Baddeley et al., 2015). In contrast, prospective memory typically focuses on *when* to do something and has low informational content. This low informational content helps to ensure that non-performance of the prospective memory task is *not* due to retrospective memory failure. Second, prospective memory is more relevant to the plans or goals we form for our daily activities. Third, more external cues are typically available with retrospective memory than prospective memory. Fourth, as Moscovitch (2008, p. 309) pointed out, "Research on prospective memory is about the only major enterprise in memory research in which the problem is not memory itself, but the uses to which memory is put."

Remembering and forgetting often involve prospective *and* retrospective memory. Suppose you agree to buy various goods at the supermarket for yourself and friends with whom you share an apartment. Two things need to happen. First, you must remember your intention to go to the supermarket (prospective memory). Even if you remember to go to the supermarket, you then have to remember what you had agreed to buy (retrospective memory).

Key terms

Retrospective memory: memory for events, words, people, and so on encountered or experienced in the past; see **prospective memory**.

Prospective memory: remembering to carry out some intended action in the absence of any explicit reminder to do so; see **retrospective memory**.

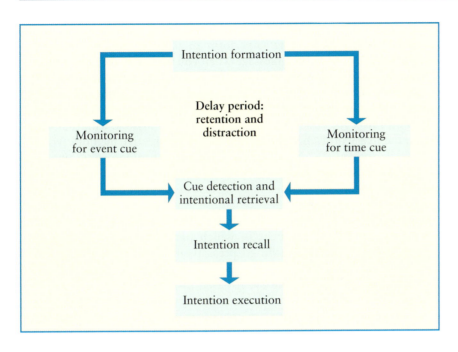

Figure 7.6 A model of the component processes involved in prospective memory. Intention formation is followed by monitoring for event and/or time cues. Successful monitoring leads to cue detection and intention retrieval, intention recall, and intention execution.
Source: From Zogg et al. (2012). Reprinted with permission from Springer.

STAGES IN PROSPECTIVE MEMORY

Prospective memory involves several separate processes or stages, and so there are various ways prospective memory can fail. Zogg et al. (2012) summarized the views of several theorists. According to them, there are five stages in prospective memory (see Figure 7.6):

1. *Intention formation*: At this stage, the individual forms or encodes an intention linked to a specific cue (e.g., "I will talk to my friend when I see him").
2. *Retention interval*: There is a delay between intention formation and intention execution of between minutes and weeks. During that time, there is typically some environmental monitoring for task-relevant cues (e.g., sighting your friend).
3. *Cue detection and intention retrieval*: The individual detects and recognizes the relevant cue; this is followed by self-initiated retrieval of the appropriate intention.
4. *Intention recall*: The individual retrieves the intention from retrospective memory. There may be problems because of the intention's complexity, its relationship to other stored intentions, or the presence of competing intentions.
5. *Intention execution*: This is typically fairly automatic and undemanding.

EVENT-BASED VS. TIME-BASED PROSPECTIVE MEMORY

There is an important distinction between time-based and event-based prospective memory. Time-based prospective memory is assessed by tasks that involve remembering to perform a given action at a particular time (e.g., phone a friend at 8 pm). In contrast, event-based prospective memory is assessed by tasks that involve remembering to perform an action in the appropriate circumstances (e.g., passing on a message when you see someone).

There is much more research on event-based prospective memory. With event-based tasks, researchers can manipulate the precise nature and timing of cues indicating participants should perform the intended action. That provides more control over the conditions of retrieval than is possible with time-based tasks. In the real world, the requirement to use prospective memory typically occurs while individuals are busily involved in performing some unrelated task. The set-up in most laboratory research is similar in that participants are generally engaged in an unrelated ongoing task at the same time as performing a prospective memory task.

Sellen et al. (1997) compared time-based and event-based prospective memory in a work environment in which participants had badges containing buttons. They were told to press their button at a pre-arranged time (time-based task) or when in a pre-specified place (event-based task). Performance was better on the event-based task than the time-based task (52% vs. 33%, respectively). Sellen et al. argued that event-based tasks are easier because the intended actions are more likely to be triggered by external cues. Kim and Mayhorn (2008) supported that argument, finding that event-based prospective memory was superior under laboratory and naturalistic conditions.

Hicks et al. (2005) confirmed that event-based tasks are less demanding than time-based ones. However, both kinds of tasks were more demanding when the task was ill-specified (e.g., detect animal words) than when it was well-specified (e.g., detect the words "nice" and "hit"). A well-specified time-based task was no more demanding than an ill-specified event-based task.

The strategies used on time-based and event-based tasks often differ considerably. An important difference is that the occurrence of the prospective memory cues is typically much more *predictable* on time-based tasks. As a result, people generally engage in only sporadic monitoring of prospective memory cues on time-based tasks, with this monitoring increasing as the occurrence of the cue approaches. In contrast, there is much more evidence of continuous monitoring on event-based tasks because of the unpredictability concerning the occurrence of the cue.

Cona et al. (2012) reported clear-cut differences between event-based and time-based tasks. On the ongoing task, five letters were presented and participants decided whether the second and fourth letters were the same or different. At the same time, they performed an event-based task (detect the letter "B" in the second or fourth position) or a time-based task (respond every 5 minutes). Cona et al. (2012) used event-related potentials (ERPs; see Glossary) to assess the patterns of brain activity on each trial.

What did Cona et al. (2012) find? First, the greater amplitude of the ERPs 130–180 ms after stimulus onset in the event-based condition probably reflected the greater use of attentional resources in that condition (see Figure 7.7). Second, the greater amplitude of the ERPs 400–600 ms after stimulus onset in the event-based condition was probably due to the greater frequency of target checking in that condition. Overall, there was greater processing activity in the event-based condition.

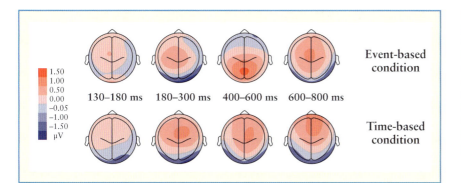

Figure 7.7   Event-related potential (ERP) amplitudes at various post-stimulus intervals in event-based and time-based conditions. Areas exhibiting high ERP amplitudes are shown in dark red.
Source: From Cona et al. (2012). Reprinted with permission from PLOS One.

PROSPECTIVE MEMORY IN REAL LIFE

In this section, prospective memory in various groups of people will be discussed. For the In the Real World box, we consider people (e.g., pilots; air traffic controllers) for whom forgetting of intended actions can easily prove fatal. We also consider people who are regarded as having poor prospective memory.

In the Real World 7.1 *Airplane crashes*

More than 50% of fatal accidents involving aircraft are due to pilot error. Dismukes and Nowinski (2007) studied reports submitted to the Aviation Safety Reporting System (ARAS) relating to incidents and accidents. They uncovered 75 reports in which memory failure was important. In 74 cases, there was a failure of prospective memory, with only one case involving retrospective memory!

Why were there practically no failures of retrospective memory? The main reason is that airline pilots receive lengthy and demanding training. As a result, they have excellent knowledge and memory of all the operations needed to fly a plane.

Here is a concrete example of an airplane crash due to a failure of prospective memory. On August 31, 1988, a Boeing 727 (Flight 1141) was held in a long line awaiting departure from Dallas–Fort Worth airport. The air traffic controller unexpectedly told the crew to move up past the other airplanes to the runway. This caused the crew to forget to set the wing flaps and leading-edge slats to 15° (a failure of prospective memory). As a result, the plane crashed a few thousand feet beyond the end of the runway, leading to several deaths.

Pilots often suffer from failures of prospective memory due to interruptions. Latorella (1998) found that commercial pilots who were interrupted while flying a simulator made 53% more errors than those who weren't interrupted. Of course, interruptions occur frequently in most workplaces. However, such failures can have far more serious consequences for pilots than for most other workers (Loukopoulos et al., 2009).

How can we reduce the negative effects of interruptions on prospective memory? Some answers were provided by Dodhia and Dismukes (2009, Experiment 1), who reported that after an interruption it is important to take a few seconds to re-establish the interrupted task sequence (including the prospective memories). Participants answered blocks of questions, each containing different types of question (e.g., math; vocabulary). Each block was followed by a 2.5-second pause during which the message "uploading the next section" was shown. From time to time, an ongoing block was interrupted by another block of questions. If such an interrupting block was presented, participants were told to return to the interrupted block after completing the interrupting block. To do so, they had to press a key during the 2.5 seconds with the message "uploading the next section."

There were four conditions. In the first, baseline condition, the blocks simply followed upon each other. In this condition, only 48% of the participants resumed the interrupted block after the interruption (see Figure 7.8). In two other conditions, the interruption did not take place at once but was preceded by a 4-second period. In the first of these conditions the screen contained the reminder "Please remember to return to the block that was just interrupted"; in the other condition, the screen was blank. Both conditions resulted in an improvement of prospective memory performance to 65%. Interestingly, there was no difference between the blank screen and the explicit reminder. In the final condition, there was no pause at the beginning of the interruption, but the "uploading time" after the interruption was increased from 2.5 seconds to 8–12 seconds. In this condition, 88% of the participants resumed the interrupted task.

What do the above findings mean? They indicate that it is important for people to have a few seconds at the end of an interruption to recall the intention of returning to the interrupted task. The take-home message is as follows: when interrupted, pause briefly while you develop a new plan to carry out all of your intended actions.

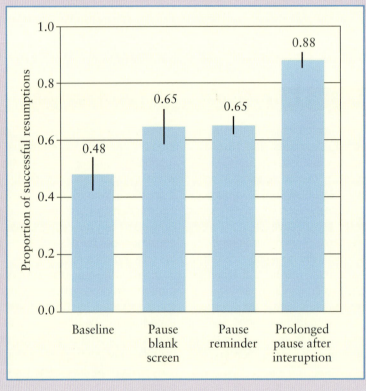

Figure 7.8 Percentages of participants returning to an interrupted task as a function of cuing and pause duration before or after interruption.
Source: Data from Dodhia and Dismukes (2009). Reprinted with permission of John Wiley & Sons.

Obsessive-compulsive disorder and checking behavior

Most patients with obsessive-compulsive disorder have checking compulsions. They check repeatedly that they have locked their front door, that the gas has been turned off, and so on. In spite of this repeated checking, they are uncertain whether they have actually performed their intended actions.

How can we explain checking behavior? Perhaps obsessional individuals have poor *retrospective* memory ability that causes them to forget whether they have recently engaged in checking behavior? In fact, however, most findings indicate compulsive checkers do *not* differ from controls in retrospective memory (Cuttler & Graf, 2009a).

An alternative explanation is that checkers have poor *prospective* memory. Cuttler and Graf (2009b) reported that checkers indeed have impaired performance on event-based and time-based prospective memory tasks.

Another factor may be that checkers differ in meta-memory, knowledge and beliefs about one's own memory. In particular, their confidence in their own prospective memory may be compromised. Cuttler et al. (2013) provided healthy students with fake feedback indicating that their prospective memory performance was poor. This caused diminished confidence in their prospective memory ability and an increased urge to engage in checking behavior.

This evidence suggests that poor prospective memory and low confidence in prospective memory ability lead people to engage in excessive checking. However, it is also possible that excessive checking leads to poor prospective memory and low confidence. Suppose you check several times every day that you have locked your front door. You would obviously remember you have checked it hundreds or thousands of times. However, you might well be unsure about whether you completed your prospective task of checking your front door *today* because of all the competing memories.

Van den Hout and Kindt (2004) asked some (but not all) participants to engage in repeated checking of a virtual gas stove. Those who had checked repeatedly had less vivid and detailed memories of what had happened on the final trial. Linkovski et al. (2013) carried out a similar study. In addition, they assessed participants' level of inhibitory control. They did so because they hypothesized that obsessional patients may have deficient inhibitory control, which leads to intrusive thoughts and memory problems.

What did Linkovski et al. (2013) find? Repeated checking did not impair prospective memory performance itself but did reduce memory vividness and detail and also lowered participants' confidence in their memory. These effects were all much stronger in participants with poor inhibitory control.

In sum, several factors explain why obsessionals engage in compulsive checking. They have poor prospective memory, low confidence in their own memory, and deficient inhibitory control. Their repeated checking further diminishes their confidence in their memory.

IMPROVING PROSPECTIVE MEMORY

The simplest way of improving your prospective memory is to use external memory aids (objects or devices designed to assist memory). There is an enormous number of such memory aids. Examples include diaries, calendars, knotted handkerchiefs, shopping lists, sticky notes, smartphones, and alarm clocks (Herrmann et al., 2006). For example, if the first author of this book has to take some books or papers into work the next day, he typically puts them on top of the desk in his study to ensure that he remembers them.

Another way of improving prospective memory is to take steps to prevent unexpected interruptions from causing you to forget to carry out an intended action. Such interruptions often mean your original plan can't be implemented as anticipated. As a result, it is necessary to take a few seconds to produce a new action plan.

It is especially important to think of the *context* in which an intended action is likely to be carried out when you form the intention. Consider a study by Cook et al. (2005), in which participants were told to make a response after between 6 and 7 minutes had elapsed. In one condition, participants expected this time window to occur during the third phase of the experiment when they were engaged in a specified task. When this expectation about the context in which the intended action was to be performed was true, 71% of the participants performed the prospective memory task correctly. This compared to only 48% in the control condition who had no expectation.

These findings suggest that prospective memory is good when there is a *match* between the information stored initially and that available at the time the intended action should be produced. Matching of stored information and that available at the time of retrieval is also important in retrospective memory (remember the encoding specificity principle from Chapter 5).

Section summary

Introduction
- Prospective memory involves remembering to carry out actions without being instructed to do so. It relates to our plans and goals. Prospective memory focuses on *when* to do something, whereas retrospective memory focuses on remembering *what* we know.

Stages of prospective memory
- Prospective memory involves five stages: intention formation, intention maintenance during the retention interval, intention retrieval upon cue detection, intention recall, and intention execution.

Prospective vs. retrospective memory
- Prospective memory is more related to motivation than to the functioning of the memory system itself, focuses on *when* rather than *what*, is more relevant to our plans and goals, is less often signaled by external cues, and concerns the *uses* to which memory is put.
- Prospective memory tasks mostly involve retrospective memory as well.

Types of prospective memory
- Event-based prospective memory is often better than time-based prospective memory. In addition, it is also often less demanding because more external cues are available. However, the demands of a prospective memory task depend on how well specified the target is as well as on the type of task.

Prospective memory in real life
- Many airplane crashes involve failures of prospective memory. These failures often occur as a result of interruptions.

- Compulsive checkers seems to have poorer prospective memory and also less confidence in their prospective memory.

Improving prospective memory
- Prospective memory can be improved by using external memory aids. It can also be improved by ensuring that contextual information stored at the time an intention is formed matches that likely to be available when the intended action should be performed.

Essay questions

1. Why are some autobiographical memories much easier to recall than others?
2. "Eyewitness testimony is generally inaccurate and prone to error." Discuss.
3. What factors determine whether or not we remember to perform intended actions?

Further reading

- Baddeley, A., Eysenck, M.W., & Anderson, M.C. (2015). *Memory* (2nd ed.). Hove, UK: Psychology Press. This textbook provides detailed coverage of research and theory on all the main topics discussed in this chapter.
- Berntsen, D., & Rubin, D.C. (Eds.) (2012). *Understanding autobiographical memory: Theories and approaches.* Cambridge: Cambridge University Press. This edited volume has interesting contributions by leading memory experts.
- Dismukes, R.K. (2012). Prospective memory in workplace and everyday situations. *Current Directions in Psychological Science*, *21*, 215–220. Dismukes provides a brief introduction to research on prospective memory in the real world.
- Frenda, S.J., Nichols, R.M., & Loftus, E.F. (2011). Current issues and advances in misinformation research. *Current Directions in Psychological Science*, *20*, 20–23. Some of the major factors causing eyewitness testimony to be distorted are discussed in this article by Loftus and her colleagues.
- Prebble, S.C., Addis, D.R., & Tippett, L.J. (2013). Autobiographical memory and sense of self. *Psychological Bulletin*, *139*, 815–840. Prebble and her colleagues provide a framework for understanding the relationship between our autobiographical memory and our sense of self.

REFERENCES

Addis, D. R., Knapp, K., Roberts, R. P., & Schacter, D.L. (2012). Routes to the past: Neural substrates of direct and generative autobiographical memory retrieval. *NeuroImage, 59*, 2908–2922.

Allen, B. P., & Lindsay, D. S. (1998). Amalgamations of memories: Intrusion of information from one event into reports of another. *Applied Cognitive Psychology, 12*, 277–285.

Ally, B. A., Hussey, E. P., & Donahue, M. J. (2013). A case of hyperthymesia: Rethinking the role of the amygdala in autobiographical memory. *Neurocase, 19,* 166–181.

Andrews-Hanna, J. R., Saxe, R., & Yarkoni, T. (2014). Contributions of episodic retrieval and mentalizing to autobiographical thought: evidence from functional neuroimaging, resting-state connectivity, and fMRI meta-analyses. *Neuroimage, 91,* 324–335.

Bahrick, H. P. (1984). Semantic memory content in permastore: Fifty years of memory for Spanish learning in school. *Journal of Experimental Psychology: General, 113,* 1–29.

Bahrick, H. P., Bahrick, P. O., & Wittlinger, R. P. (1975). Fifty years of memory for names and faces: A cross-sectional approach. *Journal of Experimental Psychology: General, 104,* 54–75.

Bahrick, H. P., Hall, L. K., & Da Costa, L. A. (2008). Fifty years of memory of college grades: Accuracy and distortions. *Emotion, 8,* 13–22.

Bartlett, F. C. (1932). *Remembering: An experimental and social study.* Cambridge, UK: Cambridge University Press.

Behrman, B. W., & Davey, S. L. (2001). Eyewitness identification in actual criminal cases: An archival analysis. *Law and Human Behavior, 25,* 475–491.

Benton, T. R., Ross, D. F., Bradshaw, E., Thomas, W. N., & Bradshaw, G.S. (2006). Eyewitness memory is still not common sense: Comparing jurors, judges and law enforcement to eyewitness experts. *Applied Cognitive Psychology, 20,* 115–129.

Berntsen, D., Rubin, D. C., & Siegler, I. C. (2011). Two different versions of life: Emotionally negative and positive life events have different roles in the organisation of life story and identity. *Emotion, 11,* 1190–1201.

Bohn, A., & Berntsen, D. (2011). The reminiscence bump reconsidered: Children's prospective life stories show a bump in young adulthood. *Psychological Science, 22,* 197–202.

Brown, R., & Kulik, J. (1977). Flashbulb memories. *Cognition, 5,* 73–99.

Burton, A. M., Bruce, V., & Hancock, P. J. B. (1999). From pixels to people: A model of familiar face recognition. *Cognitive Science, 23,* 1–31.

Clancy, S. A., & McNally, R. J. (2005/2006). Who needs repression? Normal memory processes can explain "forgetting" of childhood sexual abuse. *Scientific Review of Mental Health Practice, 4,* 66–73.

Clancy, S. A., McNally, R. J., Schacter, D. L., Lenzenweger, M. F., & Pitman, R. K. (2002). Memory distortion in people reporting abduction by aliens. *Journal of Abnormal Psychology, 111,* 455–461.

Cohen, G. (2008). The study of everyday memory. In G. Cohen & M. A. Conway (Eds.), *Memory in the real world* (3rd ed., pp. 1–19). Hove, UK: Psychology Press.

Colomb, C., & Ginet, M. (2012). The cognitive interview for use with adults: An empirical test of an alternative mnemonic and of a partial protocol. *Applied Cognitive Psychology, 26,* 35–47.

Coman, A., Manier, D., & Hirst, W. (2009). Forgetting the unforgettable through conversation: Socially shared retrieval-induced forgetting of September 11 memories. *Psychological Science, 20,* 627–633.

Cona, G., Arcara, G., Tarantino, V., & Bisiacchi, P. S. (2012). Electrophysiological correlates of strategic monitoring in event-based and time-based prospective memory. *PLOS ONE, 7*(2), e31659. doi: 10.1371/journal.pone.003 1659.

Conway, M. A., & Pleydell-Pearce, C. W. (2000). The construction of autobiographical memories in the self-memory system. *Psychological Review, 107,* 261–288.

Conway, M. A., Wang, Q., Hanyu, K., & Haque, S. (2005). A cross-cultural investigation of autobiographical memory. *Journal of Cross-Cultural Psychology, 36,* 739–749.

Cook, G. I., Marsh , R. L., & Hicks, J. L. (2005). Associating a time-based prospective memory task with an expected context can improve or impair intention completion. *Applied Cognitive Psychology, 19,* 345–360.

Cuttler, C., & Graf, P. (2009a). Checking-in on the memory deficit and meta-memory deficit theories of compulsive checking. *Clinical Psychology Review, 29,* 393–409.

Cuttler, C., & Graf, P. (2009b). Sub-clinical compulsive checkers show impaired performance on habitual, event- and timecued episodic prospective memory tasks. *Journal of Anxiety Disorders, 23,* 813–823.

Cuttler, C., Sirois-Delisle, V., Alcolado, G. M., Radomsky, A. S., & Taylor, S. (2013). Diminished confidence in prospective memory causes doubts and urges to check. *Journal of Behavior Therapy and Experimental Psychiatry, 44,* 329–334.

Dalton, A. L., & Daneman, M. (2006). Social suggestibility to central and peripheral misinformation. *Memory, 14,* 486–501.

Dando, C. J., Ormerod, T. C., Wilcock, R., & Milne, R. (2011). When help becomes hindrance: Unexpected errors of omission and commission in eyewitness memory resulting from changes in temporal order at retrieval? *Cognition, 121,* 416–421.

Deffenbacher, K. A., Bornstein, B. H., Penroad, S. D., & McGorty, E. K. (2004). A meta-analytic review of the effects of high stress on eyewitness memory. *Law and Human Behavior, 28,* 687–706.

Dickson, R. A., Pillemer, D. B., & Bruehl, E. C. (2011). The reminiscence bump for salient personal memories: Is a cultural life script required? *Memory & Cognition, 39,* 977–991.

Dismukes, K., & Nowinski, J. (2007). Prospective memory, concurrent task management, and pilot error. In A. Kramer, D. Wiegmann, & A. Kirlik (Eds.), *Attention from theory to practice.* New York, NY: Oxford University Press.

Dodhia, R. M., & Dismukes, R. K. (2009). Interruptions create prospective memory tasks. *Applied Cognitive Psychology, 23,* 73–89.

Dudukovic, N. M., Marsh, E. J., & Tversky, B. (2004). Telling a story or telling it straight: The effects of entertaining versus accurate retellings on memory. *Applied Cognitive Psychology, 18,* 125–143.

Easterbrook, J. A. (1959). The effect of emotion on cue utilization and the organization of behavior. *Psychological Review, 66,* 183–201.

Fawcett, J. M., Russell, E. J., Peace, K. A., & Christie, J. (2013). Of guns and geese: A meta-analytic review of the "weapon focus" literature. *Psychology, Crime & Law, 19,* 35–66.

Fivush, R. (2010). The development of autobiographical memory. *Annual Review of Psychology, 62,* 2–24.

Fivush, R., & Nelson, K. (2004). Culture and language in the emergence of autobiographical memory. *Psychological Science, 15,* 573–577.

Geiselman, R. E., & Fisher, R. P. (1997). Ten years of cognitive interviewing. In D. G. Payne & F. G. Conrad (Eds.), *Intersections in basic and applied memory research.* Mahwah, NJ: Lawrence Erlbaum.

Graf, P. (2012). Prospective memory: Faulty brain, flaky person. *Canadian Psychology, 53,* 7–13.

Harrison, V., & Hole, G.J. (2009). Evidence for a contact-based explanation of the own-age bias in face recognition. *Psychonomic Bulletin & Review, 16,* 264–269.

Hellmann, J. H., Echterhoff, G., Kopietz, R., Niemeier, S., & Memon, A. (2011). Talking about visually perceived events: Communication effects on eyewitness memory. *European Journal of Social Psychology, 41,* 658–671.

Herrmann, D. J., Yoder, C. Y., Gruneberg, M., & Payne, D G. (Eds.). (2006). *Applied cognitive psychology: A textbook.* Mahwah, NJ: Lawrence Erlbaum.

Hicks, J. L., Marsh, R. L., & Cook, G. I. (2005). Task interference in time-based, event-based, and dual intention prospective memory conditions. *Journal of Memory and Language, 53,* 430–444.

Howe, M. L., & Courage, M. L. (1997). The emergence and early development of autobiographical memory. *Psychological Review*, *104*, 499–523.

Ihlebaek, C., Love, T., Eilertsen, D. E., & Magnussen, S. (2003). Memory for a staged criminal event witnessed live and on video. *Memory*, *11*, 310–327.

Jack, F., & Hayne, H. (2010). Childhood amnesia: Empirical evidence for a two-stage phenomenon. *Memory*, *18*, 831–844.

Jenkins, R., & Burton, A. M. (2011). Stable face representations. *Philosophical Transactions of the Royal Society B: Biological Sciences*, *366*, 1671–1683.

Johannessen, K. B., & Berntsen, D. (2010). Current concerns in involuntary and voluntary autobiographical memories. *Consciousness and Cognition*, *19*, 847–860.

Johnson, M. K., Hashtroudi, S., & Lindsay, D. S. (1993). Source monitoring. *Psychological Bulletin*, *114*, 3–28.

Josselyn, S. A., & Frankland, P. W. (2012). Infantile amnesia: A neurogenic hypothesis. *Learning & Memory*, *19*, 423–433.

Kassin, S. M., Drizin, S. A., Grisso, T., Gudjonsson, G. H., Leo, R. A., & Redlich, A. D. (2010). Police-induced confessions: Risk factors and recommendations. *Law and Human Behavior*, *34*(1), 3–38.

Kim, P. Y., & Mayhorn, C. B. (2008). Exploring students' prospective memory inside and outside the lab. *American Journal of Psychology*, *121*, 241–254.

Klein, S. B., & Lax, M. L. (2010). The unanticipated resilience of trait self-knowledge in the face of neural damage. *Memory*, *18*, 918–948.

Kuyken, W., & Brewin, C. R. (1995). Autobiographical memory functioning in depression and reports of early abuse. *Journal of Abnormal Psychology*, *104*(4), 585–591.

Latorella, K. A. (1998). Effects of modality on interrupted flight deck performance: Implications for data link. In *Proceedings of the human factors and ergonomics society 42nd annual meeting* (Vols. 1 and 2, pp. 87–91). Chicago, IL: HFES.

LePort, A. K. R., Mattfield, A. T., Dickinson-Anson, H., Fallon, J. H., Stark, C. E. L., Kruggel, F., Cahill, L., & McGaugh, J. L. (2012). Behavioural and neuroanatomical investigation of highly superior autobiographical memory. *Neurobiology of Learning and Memory*, *98*, 78–92.

Lief, H., & Fetkewicz, J. (1995). Retractors of false memories: The evolution of pseudo-memories. *Journal of Psychiatry & Law*, *23*, 411–436.

Lindholm, T., & Christianson, S.-A. (1998). Intergroup biases and eyewitness testimony. *Journal of Social Psychology*, *138*, 710–723.

Lindsay, D. S., Allen, B. P., Chan, J. C. K., & Dahl, L. C. (2004). Eyewitness suggestibility and source similarity: Intrusions of details from one event into memory reports of another event. *Journal of Memory and Language*, *50*, 96–111.

Linkovski, O., Kalanthroff, E., Henik, A., & Anholt, G. (2013). Did I turn off the stove? Good inhibitory control can protect from influences of repeated checking. *Journal of Behavior Therapy and Experimental Psychiatry*, *44*, 30–36.

Loftus, E. F., & Davis, D. (2006). Recovered memories. *Annual Review of Clinical Psychology*, *2*, 469–498.

Loftus, E. F., & Palmer, J. C. (1974). Reconstruction of automobile destruction: An example of the interaction between language and memory. *Journal of Verbal Learning and Verbal Behavior*, *13*, 585–589.

Loftus, E. F., & Pickrell, J. E. (1995). The formation of false memories. *Psychiatric Annals*, *25*(12), 720–725.

Loftus, E. F., Loftus, G. R., & Messo, J. (1987). Some facts about "weapons focus." *Law and Human Behavior*, *11*, 55–62.

Loukopoulos, L. D., Dismukes, R. K., & Barshi, I. (2009). *The multitasking myth: Handling complexity in real-world operations*. Burlington, VT: Ashgate.

Marsh, E. J., & Tversky, B. (2004). Spinning the stories of our lives. *Applied Cognitive Psychology, 18*, 491–503.

McNally, R. J., & Geraerts, E. (2009). A new solution to the recovered memory debate. *Perspectives on Psychological Science, 4*(2), 126–134.

Megreya, A. M., White, D., & Burton, A. M. (2011). The other-race effect does not rely on memory: Evidence from a matching task. *Quarterly Journal of Experimental Psychology, 64*, 1473–1483.

Memon, A., Meissner, C. A., & Fraser, J. (2010). The cognitive interview: A meta-analytic review and study space analysis of the past 25 years. *Psychology, Public Policy and Law, 16*, 340–372.

Memon, A., Zaragoza, M., Clifford, B. R., & Kidd, L. (2009). Inoculation or antidote? The effects of cognitive interview timing on false memory for forcibly fabricated events. *Law and Human Behavior, 34*, 105–117.

Morcom, A. M. (2016). Mind over memory: Cuing the aging brain. *Current Directions in Psychological Science, 25*, 143–150.

Moscovitch, M. (2008). Commentary: A perspective on prospective memory. In M. Kliegel, M. A. McDaniel, & G. O. Einstein (Eds.), *Prospective memory: Cognitive, neuroscience, developmental, and applied perspectives.* New York, NY: Lawrence Erlbaum.

Newman, E. J., & Lindsay, D.S. (2009). False memories: What the hell are they for? *Applied Cognitive Psychology, 23*, 1105–1121.

Ono, M., Devilly, G. J., & Shum, D. H. (2016). A meta-analytic review of overgeneral memory: The role of trauma history, mood, and the presence of posttraumatic stress disorder. *Psychological Trauma: Theory, Research, Practice, and Policy, 8*(2), 157–164.

Parker, E. S., Cahill, L., & McGaugh, J. L. (2006). A case of unusual autobiographical remembering. *Neurocase, 12*, 35–49.

Pickel, K. L. (2009). The weapon focus effect on memory for female versus male perpetrators. *Memory, 17*, 664–678.

Pozzulo, J. D., Crescini, C., & Panton, T. (2008). Does methodology matter in eyewitness identification research? The effect of live versus video exposure on eyewitness identification of accuracy. *International Journal of Law and Psychiatry, 31*, 430–437.

Rosenbaum, R. S., Köhler, S., Schacter, D. L., Moscovitch, M., Westmacott, R., Black, S. E., et al. (2005). The case of KC: Contributions of a memory-impaired person to memory theory. *Neuropsychologia, 43*, 989–1021.

Rimmele, U., Davachi, L., & Phelps, E. A. (2012). Memory for time and place contributes to enhanced confidence in memories for emotional events. *Emotion, 12*, 834–846.

Ross, D. F., Ceci, S. J., Dunning, D., & Toglia, M. P. (1994). Unconscious transference and mistaken identity: When a witness misidentifies a familiar but innocent person. *Journal of Applied Psychology, 79*, 918–930.

Rubin, D. C., & Berntsen, D. (2003). Life scripts help to maintain autobiographical memories of highly positive, but not negative, events. *Memory & Cognition, 31*, 1–14.

Sellen, A. J., Lowie, G., Harris, J. F., & Wilkins, A. J. (1997). What brings intentions to mind? An *in situ* study of prospective memory. *Memory, 5*, 483–507.

Sharot, T., Martorella, E. A., Delgado, M. R., & Phelps, E. A. (2007). How personal experience modulates the neural circuitry of memories of September 11. *Proceedings of the National Academy of Sciences, 104*, 389–394.

Shriver, E. R., Young, S. G., Hugenberg, K., Bernstein, M. J., & Lanter, J. R. (2008). Class, race, and the face: Social context modulates the cross-race effect in face recognition. *Personality and Social Psychology Bulletin, 34*, 260–274.

Simner, J., Mayo, N., & Spiller, M. J. (2009). A foundation for savantism? Visuo-spatial synesthetes present with cognitive benefits. *Cortex*, *45*, 1246–1260.

Simons, D. J., & Chabris, C.F. (2011). What people believe about how memory works: A representative survey of the US population. *Public Library of Science One*, *6*, e22757.

Talarico, J. M., & Rubin, D. C. (2003). Confidence, not consistency, characterizes flashbulb memories. *Psychological Science*, *14*, 455–461.

Tollestrup, P. A., Turtle, J. W., & Yuille, J. C. (1994). Actual victims and witnesses to robbery and fraud: An archival analysis. In D. F. Ross, J. D. Read, & M. P. Toglia (Eds.), *Adult eyewitness testimony: Current trends and developments*. New York, NY: Wiley.

Tuckey, M. R., & Brewer, N. (2003a). How schemas affect eyewitness memory over repeated retrieval attempts. *Applied Cognitive Psychology*, *7*, 785–800.

Tuckey, M. R., & Brewer, N. (2003b). The influence of schemas, stimulus ambiguity, and interview schedule on eyewitness memory over time. *Journal of Experimental Psychology: Applied*, *9*, 101–118.

Tulving, E. (1979). Relation between encoding specificity and levels of processing. In L. S. Cermak & F. I. M. Craik (Eds.), *Levels of processing in human memory*. Hillsdale, NJ: Lawrence Erlbaum.

Tustin, K., & Hayne, H. (2010). Defining the boundary: Age-related changes in childhood amnesia. *Developmental Psychology*, *46*, 1049–1061.

Uzer, T., Lee, P. J., & Brown, N. R. (2012). On the prevalence of directly retrieved autobiographical memories. *Journal of Experimental Psychology: Learning, Memory, and Cognition*, *38*, 1296–1308.

van den Hout, M., & Kindt, M. (2004). Obsessive–compulsive disorder and the paradoxical effects of perseverative behaviour on experienced uncertainty. *Journal of Behavior Therapy and Experimental Psychiatry*, *35*(2), 165–181.

Valentine, T., & Mesout, J. (2009). Eyewitness identification under stress in the London Dungeon. *Applied Cognitive Psychology*, *23*, 151–161.

Vredeveldt, A., Hitch, G. J., & Baddeley, A. D. (2011). Eyeclosure helps memory by reducing cognitive load and enhancing visualization. *Memory & Cognition*, *39*, 1253–1263.

Wiese, H., Wolff, N., Steffens, M. C., & Schweinberger, S. R. (2013). How experience shapes memory for faces: An eventrelated potential study on the own-age bias. *Biological Psychology*, *94*, 369–379.

Weaver III, C. A., & Krug, K. S. (2004). Consolidation-like effects in flashbulb memories: Evidence from September 11, 2001. *The American Journal of Psychology*, *117*(4), 517–530.

Woike, B., Gershkovich, I., Piorkowski, R., & Polo, L (1999). The role of motives in the content and structure of autobiographical memory. *Journal of Personality and Social Psychology*, *76*, 600–612.

Wong, C. K., & Read, J. D. (2011). Positive and negative effects of physical context reinstatement on eyewitness recall and recognition. *Applied Cognitive Psychology*, *25*, 2–11.

Wright, D. B., & Stroud, J. N. (2002). Age differences in line-up identification accuracy: People are better with their own age. *Law and Human Behavior*, *26*, 641–654.

Yegiyan, N. S., & Lang, A. (2010). Processing central and peripheral detail: How content arousal and emotional tone influence encoding. *Media Psychology*, *13*, 77–99.

Zogg, J. B., Woods, S. P., Sauceda, J. A., Wiebe, J. S., & Simoni, J. M. (2012). The role of prospective memory in medication adherence: A review of an emerging literature. *Journal of Behavioral Medicine*, *35*, 47–62.

Chapter 8

Contents

Language

INTRODUCTION

Our lives would be remarkably limited without language. Our social interactions rely very heavily on language, and a good command of language is vital for all students. As the English writer Samuel Johnson said, language is "the dress of thought." The main reason we are much more knowledgeable than people of previous generations is that knowledge is passed from one generation to the next via language, in particular written language.

Why do we need language? Crystal (1997) identified *eight* functions of language. The first, of course, is communication; the primary function of language is to exchange information with others. In addition, we use language for (2) thinking, (3) social interactions (e.g., "How are you?"), (4) to record information, (5) to express emotion (e.g., "I love you"), (6) to express identity with a group (e.g., singing in church), (7) to attempt to control the environment (e.g., "Hey there!"), and (8) even to pretend to be animals (e.g., saying "Woof! Woof!" when we see a dog or a cat).

An interesting aspect about human language is that it develops into a rich system of possible word combinations (grammar) even in groups with practically no input from an existing language. The clearest case was reported by Senghas et al. (2004). They studied deaf children in Nicaragua after the first special school had been established for them. Very rapidly, these deaf children developed a new system of gestures that expanded into a basic sign language, in which gestures were not only generated but also combined with each other to convey messages (indicating who does what to whom). The sign language passed on to successive groups of children who joined the school. Interestingly, each generation added new combination rules, until they could express all messages they wanted. Because Nicaraguan Sign Language bore very little relation to the language spoken in Nicaragua (Spanish) or to the gestures made by hearing children, it is a genuinely new language owing remarkably little to other languages.

What do these findings mean? They certainly suggest that humans have a strong innate *motivation* to acquire language (including grammatical rules) and to communicate with others. According to Bickerton's (1984) language bioprogram hypothesis, humans have an innate capacity to create a grammar even if they aren't exposed to an existing language. A similar claim was previously made by Chomsky (1965), who argued that the linguistic input to which children are exposed is too limited to explain the speed with which they learn language. Chomsky claimed that humans possess a language acquisition device consisting of innate knowledge of grammatical structure.

Other authors disagree with the idea that humans would have an innate language acquisition device (e.g., Christiansen & Chater, 2008; Samuelson & McMurray, 2017), but it is true that the rapid creation of grammatical rules to combine words into rich messages is unique to humans. Animals can be taught to use words, but they do not spontaneously combine them into sentences (Harley, 2014, pp. 54–67).

Learning objectives

After studying Chapter 8, you should be able to:

- Explain the different stages of speech production.
- Have an idea of the degree of planning made when we produce a spoken utterance.
- Be able to indicate how speech errors give us information of the processes involved in speech production.
- Apply knowledge of top-down and bottom-up processes to the process of speech perception.
- Discuss the evidence for orthographic activation during speech perception.
- Summarize the most important models of auditory word recognition.
- Describe how eye-tracking is used to investigate reading comprehension processes.
- Discuss the evidence for phonological activation during reading.
- Explain how the DRC-model accounts for word reading in English and discuss the limitations of the model.
- Describe dyslexia and its implications for studying in higher education.
- Explain which factors make some words easier to process than others.
- Define parsing, and discuss models that account for how sentence parsing occurs.
- Describe how inferences and pragmatics are needed for discourse understanding.

CHAPTER ORGANIZATION

There are four main language skills: speaking, speech perception, reading, and writing. It is customary to divide the four types of skills into two groups. In the first group we have speaking and writing. These skills are concerned with the *production* of language. In the second group we find reading and speech perception. These skills are concerned with *comprehension* of language in visual and auditory modality. Of the four skills, we will discuss speaking, speech perception, and reading. Writing will not be discussed. If you are interested in this topic, we refer you to Berninger (2012).

The four types of language skills all involve different layers, going from processing isolated words, over sentences, to discourse. So, after a description of what is particular to each language skill, we will discuss what they have in common.

Section summary

Introduction

- Language is used primarily for communication but has several other functions as well.
- Humans are strongly motivated to develop a language, so that even with minimal input they will spontaneously come up with symbols (words, signs) to denote things and – more importantly – grammatical rules to combine the symbols into messages. According to some authors, this is because language is an innate capacity of humans.

SPEAKING

As said before, the most important goal of speakers is to communicate with other people. We will start with the messages we want to convey *ourselves*.

On the face of it (by the sound of it?), speech production is an easy task. It generally seems almost effortless when we chat with friends or acquaintances about the topics of the day. Indeed, we frequently seem to speak without much preparation or planning. We typically speak at a rate of four to five syllables per second or 150–200 words per minute. This speech rate fits the notion that speaking is undemanding of processing resources.

On the other hand, there is evidence that speakers resort to strategies to reduce processing demands, suggesting that speaking does have a non-negligible processing cost. One example is preformulation – this involves reducing processing costs by producing phrases used before. About 70% of our speech consists of word combinations we use repeatedly (Altenberg, 1990). Preformulation is especially common among groups of people (e.g., auctioneers; sports commentators) who need to speak very rapidly. Speaking quickly leads them to repeat many expressions (e.g., "They're off and racing now"; "They're on their way") (Kuiper, 1996).

Another strategy we use to make speech production easier is underspecification, which involves using simplified expressions. Smith (2000) gave an illustration of underspecification: "Wash and core six cooking apples. Put them in an oven." In the second sentence, the word "them" underspecifies the phrase "six cooking apples."

Sometimes speech production takes the form of monolog, in which one person talks to another person. Most of the time, however, it involves dialog or conversation. It could be argued that speech production is harder in interactive dialog than in monolog because speakers have to adjust what they say to fit what the previous speaker just said. However, the opposite is generally the case. Speakers often copy phrases and even sentences they heard when the other person was speaking (Pickering & Garrod, 2004). Thus, the other person's words serve as a prime or prompt. As a result, dialog is often more repetitive than monolog.

There is another way in which monolog is harder than dialog. Speakers delivering a monolog have to generate their own ideas. In contrast, speakers within a dialog typically make extensive use of the ideas communicated by the other person.

Key term

Preformulation: the production by speakers of phrases used frequently before; it is done to reduce the demands of speech production.

Another way in which speakers make use of what they have just heard to make their speaking less effortful is via syntactic priming. Syntactic priming occurs when a previously experienced syntactic structure is repeated. Here is a concrete example. If you have just heard a passive sentence (e.g., "The man was bitten by the dog"), this increases the chances you will produce a passive sentence yourself. This occurs even when you are talking about a different topic. Syntactic priming often occurs in the absence of conscious awareness of copying a previous syntactic structure (Pickering & Ferreira, 2008).

Evidence of syntactic priming was reported by Cleland and Pickering (2003). A confederate of the experimenter described a picture to participants using an adjective – noun order (e.g., "the red sheep") or a noun – relative clause order (e.g., "the sheep that's red"). Participants used the syntactic structure they had heard even when the words in the two sentences were very different. Syntactic priming is common in speech, because the processing demands are reduced when a heard syntactic structure is copied.

STAGES OF SPEECH PRODUCTION

Several levels or stages of processing are involved in speech production. We initially decide what we want to say and finish up by producing a sentence or other utterance. In this chapter, we discuss Gary Dell's (1986) model as an example, although there are other models with slightly different architectures (see, e.g., Levelt et al., 1999; Hickok, 2012). Dell (1986) argued that four levels are involved in speech production (see Figure 8.1).

Initial planning of the message to be communicated is considered at the semantic level. As we have seen in Chapter 7, this involves the activation of concepts and propositions.

At the syntactic level, the grammatical structure of the words in the planned utterance is decided. Nearly all utterances longer than a single word include a verb. In addition, most verbs have a subject (someone or something doing the action) and an object (someone or something acted upon). So, for most sentences, the grammatical structure of the utterance consists of a subject, a verb, and an object, possibly augmented with further elements.

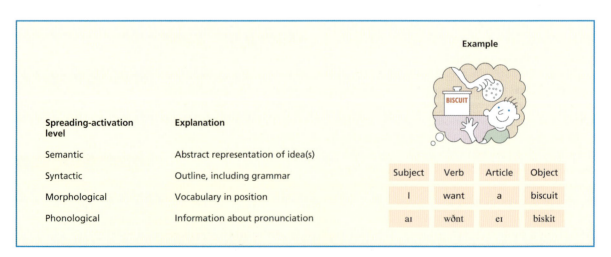

Spreading-activation level	Explanation	Example			
Semantic	Abstract representation of idea(s)				
Syntactic	Outline, including grammar	Subject	Verb	Article	Object
Morphological	Vocabulary in position	I	want	a	biscuit
Phonological	Information about pronunciation	aɪ	wɒnt	eɪ	biskit

Figure 8.1 The sentence "I want a biscuit" broken down into the different stages involved in sentence production.

At the morphological level, the **morphemes** (basic units of meaning) are worked out. Short, monosyllabic words mostly consist of a single morpheme (e.g., "ball"), although this is not always true (e.g., "balls" consists of two morphemes: "ball" + plural). Words with a single morpheme are called mono-morphemic words (from the Ancient Greek word "mono" – single). Longer words often consist of several morphemes. This is the case for compound words ("flowerpot" = "flower" + "pot") and derivations ("recognizable" = "recognize" + "able"). Such words are called polymorphemic (from the Ancient Greek word "poly," meaning many).

At the phonological level, the **phonemes** are added. Phonemes are units of sound in a language that convey meaning. Languages use between 20 and 50 phonemes. British English, for instance, uses 44 phonemes, whereas Spanish uses only 25. Languages with fewer phonemes usually have longer words (Cutler & Bruggeman, 2013). British words, for example, are on average 6.9 phonemes or 2.7 syllables long, whereas Spanish words are on average 8.3 phonemes or 3.5 syllables long.

Importantly, phonemes convey meaning. The spoken word "red" does not have the same meaning as the spoken word "led." So, "r" and "l" are different phonemes. When sound differences do not lead to meaning differences, they are not perceived. For instance, the "p" in "pin" is aspirated, whereas the "p" in "spin" is not (Harley, 2014). If you don't believe this, put your hand before your mouth and say both words. You will feel more air coming out of your mouth when you say "pin" than when you say "spin." The fact that you do not make a difference between an aspirated and an unaspirated "p" is not a problem, unless you start studying Thai. In this language the difference between an aspirated and an unaspirated "p" has the same status as the difference between "r" and "l" in English. Similarly, because many Asian languages do not make a distinction between "r" and "l," these people find it difficult to make the distinction when they learn English (e.g., pronouncing "velocity" as "verocity"). The same is true for the distinction between "t" and "th," which is absent in many languages (so that speakers of these languages pronounce "three" as "tree" and "third" as "turd").

In short, we become very sensitive to sound changes that signal meaning differences in our native language, whereas we find it hard to produce (and notice) sound changes that do not signal meaning differences in our native language. Research suggests that babies initially are sensitive to all possible sound changes, but by the end of their first year tune in to the sound changes in the language they hear around them (Werker & Tees, 1984; Segal et al., 2016).

Figure 8.1 suggests that the processes involved in speech and word production proceed neatly and tidily from the semantic level through the syntactic and morphological levels down to the phonological level. It is certainly true that speakers typically have some idea of what they want to say (semantic level) before working out the words they are going to say. However, as we will see, processes at the different levels frequently *interact* with each other.

TIP-OF-THE-TONGUE STATE

Sometimes we find it hard to move from one level to another. For example, we have all had the experience of having a concept or idea in mind while searching in vain for the right word to describe it. This frustrating situation

> **| Key terms**
>
> **Morpheme:**
> unit of meaning; words consist of one or more morphemes.
>
> **Phoneme:**
> meaningful sound in a spoken language; part of the phonology of a word.

defines the **tip-of-the-tongue state**. Don't despair when you are in the tip-of-the-tongue state. Individuals in that state often guess the first letter of the word correctly as well as the number of syllables (Brown & McNeill, 1966). Indeed, they fairly frequently produce the word itself if they spend a few minutes struggling to retrieve it.

The tip-of-the-tongue state happens when semantic processing is successful but phonological processing is unsuccessful (i.e., we cannot produce the sound of the word). As would be expected, we mostly experience the tip-of-the-tongue state with relatively rare words.

Evidence that problems with accessing phonological information underlie the tip-of-the-tongue state was reported by Harley and Bown (1998). Words sounding unlike nearly all other words (e.g., apron; vineyard) were much more susceptible to the tip-of-the-tongue state than words sounding like several others (e.g., litter; pawn). The unusual phonological forms of words susceptible to the tip-of-the-tongue state make them hard to retrieve.

What can be done to assist individuals in the tip-of-the-tongue state to produce the sought word? One approach is to present them with words sharing the first syllable with the correct word. This has been shown to be effective (Abrams, 2008).

Bilinguals (individuals fluent in two languages) experience the tip-of-the-tongue state more often than monolinguals (individuals fluent in only one language). Why is this? One possibility is that bilinguals' attempts to find a word in one language are disrupted by *interference* from the phonological representations of words in their other language.

In fact, this explanation doesn't account for all the findings. Bilinguals fluent in American Sign Language and English had more tip-of-the-tongue states than monolinguals when searching for English words (Pyers et al., 2009). This couldn't be due to phonological interference because there is no phonological overlap between English and American Sign Language.

Another reason for the overall tendency of bilinguals to experience the tip-of-the-tongue state more than monolinguals is that bilinguals use many words (in either of their two languages) somewhat less frequently than monolinguals. As a result, the connections between meaning and phonological form are less well established (Gollan & Acenas, 2004).

SPEECH PLANNING

To what extent do speakers plan their utterances in advance? One possibility is that planning occurs at the level of the **phrase** (a group of words expressing a single idea, like "a big, blue car," which can be replaced by the word "it"). Another possibility is that it occurs at the level of the **clause** (a part of a sentence containing a subject and a verb, such as "a big, blue car drove away").

Planning at the phrase level was reported by Martin et al. (2004). Participants produced sentences to describe moving pictures. The sentences had a simple initial phrase (e.g., "The ball moves above the tree and the finger") or they had a complex initial phrase (e.g., "The ball and the tree move above the finger"). Speakers took longer to start speaking when using complex initial phrases than when using simple ones, indicating they were planning the initial phrase before speaking. Similar findings were reported by Martin et al. (2010).

The phrase is often important in speakers' advance planning. However, there are two main reasons why there is no simple answer to the question of how much speakers plan in advance:

1. Planning can occur at four different levels (refer back to Figure 8.1). There is often more advance planning at the higher levels (e.g., message planning at the semantic level) than at lower levels (e.g., the sounds of individual words).
2. The amount of planning can vary considerably depending on various factors (e.g., time available for planning; sentence complexity), possibly because there is greater chunking of information at higher levels.

We will consider these two factors in turn.

Planning level

Some support for the notion that the extent of forward planning by speakers varies at different processing levels comes from the study of speech errors (discussed more fully in the next section). Here we will consider two types of speech error: word-exchange errors and sound-exchange errors. Word-exchange errors involve two words changing places. The words exchanged typically come from the same clause but are often some way apart in the sentence (e.g., "My chair seems empty without my room"). The finding that a word (e.g., "chair") can be spoken much earlier than was intended suggests some aspects of planning can be extensive. It may be that the general syntactic structure of an utterance is planned clause-by-clause (Harley, 2014).

Sound-exchange errors (also known as spoonerisms – discussed later) involve two sounds exchanging places (e.g., "She fainted the pence" instead of "She painted the fence"). Such errors typically occur over *short* distances within the sentence (Harley, 2014). This suggests that the sounds of words to be spoken are only planned shortly in advance.

Experimental support for the notion that phonological planning (involving the sounds of words) is less extensive than planning at other stages was reported by Meyer (1996). Speakers produced sentences based on pairs of objects (e.g., "The arrow is next to the bag"). At the same time, they heard an auditory distractor related in sound or meaning to the first or second noun. Meyer (1996) found there was an effect on the time to start speaking when the distractor was related in sound to the first noun but not the second one. Thus, the speakers only retrieved the sound of the *first* noun before starting to speak. In contrast, the time taken to start speaking was longer when the distractor was related in meaning to *either* the first *or* the second noun. This indicates that the meanings of the words to be spoken were planned prior to speaking.

Flexibility in planning

The amount of planning preceding speech is *flexible* and depends on processing demands experienced by speakers. Consider a study by Ferreira and Swets (2002). Participants answered mathematical problems varying in difficulty level. The time taken to start speaking and the length of time spent speaking were recorded. If there was complete planning before speaking, the time taken to start speaking would be longer for more difficult problems than for easier ones, but the time spent speaking wouldn't vary. In contrast, if people started speaking before planning their responses, the time taken to start speaking might be the same for all problems. However, speech duration should be longer with harder problems.

What did Ferreira and Swets (2002) find? Task difficulty affected the time taken to start speaking but *not* the time spent speaking. Thus, participants planned their responses fully before speaking. However, the findings differed when participants had to start producing their answers to mathematical problems very rapidly. In these circumstances, some planning occurred before speaking, with additional planning occurring during speaking. Thus, speakers do as much prior planning as possible in the time available before starting to speak.

Wagner et al. (2010) identified several factors determining the extent of grammatical advance planning. First, individuals who spoke relatively slowly tended to engage in more planning than those who spoke rapidly. Second, speakers engaged in more planning before producing simple sentences (e.g., "The frog is next to the mug") than more complex ones ("The blue frog is next to the blue mug"). Third, there was more planning when speakers were operating under a low cognitive load than when they were burdened with a high cognitive load (e.g., remembering digits for a few seconds).

How can we account for the flexibility of speakers' advance planning? They are faced with a tradeoff between avoiding errors and cognitive demands. If they focus on avoiding errors, the cognitive demands on them will be substantial. On the other hand, if they try to minimize cognitive demands, they will make many errors while speaking. In practice, speakers mostly engage in extensive planning when such planning is not very cognitively demanding (e.g., the sentence to be produced is simple; there is no additional task).

SPEECH ERRORS

Most of the time, people produce speech that is accurate and coherent. However, we are all prone to error. It has been estimated that the average person makes a speech error once every 1,000 words (Vigliocco & Hartsuiker, 2002). In spite of their rarity, speech errors are important. Why is this? In essence, we can use information about the relative frequencies of different kinds of speech error to shed light on the processes underlying speech production.

Why do we make speech errors? There are many reasons. However, the single most important one was identified by Gary Dell (1986). He emphasized the notion of **spreading activation**: Activation or energy spreads from an activated node (e.g., word) to related nodes or words.

According to Dell (1986) and Dell et al. (2008), the processes involved in speech production occur in parallel (at the same time). When we plan an utterance, this leads to activation of several of the sounds and words in the intended sentence before we speak. The crucial assumption is that speech errors occur whenever an incorrect item is more activated than the correct one.

Suppose we intend to say, "You have wasted the whole term." This may lead to activation of all the words and their sounds during the planning process. As a result, we may say something like, "You have tasted the whole worm."

Activation typically extends to words related in meaning to those in the intended sentence. For example, you may intend to say, "Give me a spoon."

Key term
Spreading activation: the notion that activation of a word or node within the brain causes some activation to spread to several related words or nodes.

However, activation of the word "spoon" may lead to activation of the related word "fork," leading you to say, "Give me a fork."

Lexical bias effect

Our speech errors are *not* random in nature. For example, our phonological speech errors generally form words rather than nonwords. The latter are sequences of sounds (or letters) that are easily pronounceable but that do not form existing words (e.g., "nall, bork"). The finding that phonological speech errors form words rather than nonwords is called the lexical bias effect. Informal evidence of this effect was reported by the Reverend William Archibald Spooner. He gave his name to the spoonerism, which occurs when the initial sound or sounds of two or more words are mistakenly switched. Spooner is credited with several memorable spoonerisms (e.g., "You have hissed all my mystery lectures"; "The Lord is a shoving leopard to his flock"). Alas, most of the Rev. Spooner's gems were the result of much painstaking effort.

The most used way of studying the lexical bias effect was introduced by Baars et al. (1975). They presented word pairs in rapid succession, and the participants had to say both words rapidly. All word pairs were of the same sequence, except for the last word pair. An example is:

cool dude
cave dish
key day
kid door
deep cot

Because the last word pair deviated from the rhythm installed by the previous word pairs, participants in Baars et al. (1975) made frequent errors on that pair. With some word pairs, swapping the first letters produced two new words (e.g., "deep cot" could become "keep dot"). This wasn't the case with other word pairs (e.g., "deed cop" could become "keed dop"). The key finding was that people made many more slips consisting of words than of nonwords.

Why does the lexical bias effect occur? Two main explanations have been suggested. First, Dell (1986) and Dell et al. (2008) argued that speakers generally produce the sounds most highly activated at any given moment. These sounds are typically the correct ones. However, occasionally they are not because several phonemes (sounds) and words are activated at the same time. Activation at the word level helps to explain the lexical bias effect. For example, seeing "deep cot" may activate the words "keep" and "dot," and this extra activation can produce an error. In contrast, seeing "deed cop" does *not* activate "keed" or "dop," as these are not available at the word level, and so speakers are unlikely to produce these nonwords.

Second, we may *monitor* our own internal speech before speaking out loud to eliminate any nonwords (Hartsuiker et al., 2005; Levelt et al., 1999). In other words, the monitoring system asks the question, "Is this a word?"

Both explanations possess some validity. Evidence that we engage in self-monitoring of our internal speech was reported by Nooteboom and Quené (2008). They used the technique introduced by Baars et al. (1975) that was discussed earlier. Participants frequently started to produce a spoonerism but

---

Key terms

Nonword:
string of letters or sounds that are pronounceable but that do not form existing words.

Lexical bias effect:
the tendency for speech errors to form words rather than nonwords; see **spoonerism**.

Spoonerism:
a speech error in which the initial sound or sounds of two words (typically close together) are mistakenly switched; an example of **lexical bias**.

then stopped themselves and produced the correct words. For example, they would see "BARN DOOR" and say, "D . . . BARN DOOR."

Mixed-error effect

We have seen that Dell (1986) argues that several different kinds of information are activated at the same time when someone is preparing to speak. All that activation is responsible for many (or even most) speech errors. Consider, for example, the mixed-error effect, which occurs when an incorrect word is both semantically and phonemically related to the correct word.

Dell (1986) quoted the example of someone saying "Let's stop" instead of "Let's start," where the word "stop" is both semantically and phonemically related to the correct word "start." The existence of this effect suggests that the various levels of processing *interact* flexibly with each other. More specifically, the mixed-error effect suggests that semantic and phonological factors can both influence word selection at the same time.

Ferreira and Griffin (2003) provided evidence of the mixed-error effect. In their key condition, participants were presented with an incomplete sentence such as, "I thought that there would still be some cookies left, but there were . . ." followed by picture naming (e.g., of a priest). Participants often produced the wrong word "nun." This was due to the semantic similarity between *priest* and *nun* combined with the phonological identity of *nun* and *none*.

Other speech errors

We will briefly mention some other speech errors. First, there are semantic substitution errors, in which the correct word is replaced by a word of similar meaning. For example, we say "Where is my tennis bat?" instead of "Where is my tennis racket?" In 99% of cases, nouns substitute for nouns and verbs substitute for verbs (Hotopf, 1980).

Second, there are *number-agreement errors*, in which singular verbs are mistakenly used with plural subjects or vice versa. For example, consider the two sentence fragments, "The editor of the history book . . ." and "The editor of the history books . . .". Strictly speaking, the verb should be singular in both cases. However, quite a few people use a plural verb in the second example because of the interfering plural noun "books" (Bock & Cutting, 1992).

Why do we make number-agreement errors? One reason is that we often have insufficient processing resources to avoid such errors. McDonald (2008) asked participants to decide whether various sentences were grammatically correct. This was done with or without an externally imposed cognitive load. Participants with a load found it especially difficult to make accurate decisions concerning subject-verb agreement.

SPREADING ACTIVATION

As we saw earlier, Dell (1986) argued that several kinds of information are activated at the same time when we are planning an utterance. As a result, we are prone to error when an incorrect item is more activated than the correct one. A potential problem with Dell's spreading-activation approach is that it seems to predict that we would make more speech errors than is actually the case. For example, the theory predicts too many errors in situations in which two or more words are activated simultaneously (e.g., Glaser, 1992).

How can chaos be avoided? Dell et al. (2008) argued that through learning we possess a "syntactic traffic cop." It monitors what we intend to say and inhibits any words not belonging to the appropriate syntactical or grammatical category. This syntactic traffic cop explains why we nearly always replace a noun with a noun and a verb with a verb when we make mistakes when speaking.

We might expect that some patients have suffered damage to the syntactic traffic cop and so should make numerous syntactic errors. Supporting evidence was reported by Berndt et al. (1997) in a study on patients with **aphasia** (impaired speech abilities due to brain damage). The patients named pictures and videos of objects (noun targets) and actions (verb targets).

The errors made by some of the patients nearly always involved words belonging to the correct syntactic category. The errors made by other patients were almost randomly distributed across nouns and verbs. It could be argued that the latter patients had an impaired syntactic traffic cop.

Key term

Aphasia:
a condition due to brain damage in which the patient has severely impaired language production abilities.

Individual differences

There are large individual differences in the number and nature of errors made when speaking. Dell et al. (1997) made an important contribution to understanding why these individual differences exist. They argued that most speech errors belong to two categories:

1. *Anticipatory*: Sounds or words are spoken ahead of their time (e.g., "cuff of coffee" instead of "cup of coffee"). These errors mainly reflect inefficient planning.
2. *Perseveratory*: Sounds or words are spoken later than they should have been (e.g., "beef needle" instead of "beef noodle"). These errors reflect a failure to monitor what one is about to say (planning failure).

According to Dell et al. (1997), expert speakers plan ahead more than non-expert ones, and so have increased activation of *future* sounds and words. As a result, a high proportion of the speech errors of expert speakers should be anticipatory. In contrast, non-expert speakers should have relatively few anticipatory errors.

Dell et al. (1997) assessed the effects of practice on the anticipatory proportion (the proportion of total errors [anticipation + perseveration] that is anticipatory). In one study, participants were given extensive practice at saying several tongue twisters (e.g., five frantic fat frogs; thirty-three throbbing thumbs). As expected, the number of errors decreased as a function of practice. However, the anticipatory proportion *increased* from .37 early in practice to .59 at the end of practice, in line with prediction.

Dell et al. (1997) argued that speech errors are most likely when the speaker hasn't formed a coherent speech plan. In such circumstances, there will be relatively few anticipatory errors, and so the anticipatory proportion will be low. Thus, the anticipatory proportion should decrease as the overall error rate (anticipatory + perseverative) increases.

Dell et al. (1997) worked out the overall error rate and the anticipatory proportion for several sets of published data. The anticipatory proportion decreased from about .75 with low overall error rates to about .40 with high overall error rates (see Figure 8.2).

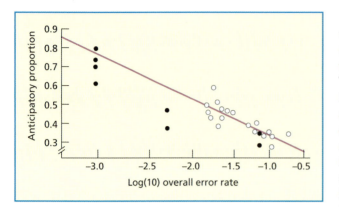

Figure 8.2 The relationship between overall error rate and the anticipatory proportion. Filled circles come from studies reported by Dell et al. (1997) and unfilled circles come from other studies. Source: Adapted from Dell et al. (1997).

Vousden and Maylor (2006) tested the theory by assessing speech errors in 8-year-olds, 11-year-olds, and young adults who said tongue twisters aloud at a slow or fast rate. There were two main findings. First, the anticipatory proportion increased as a function of age. This is predicted by the theory, because older children and young adults have had more practice at producing language. Second, fast speech produced a higher error rate than slow speech and also resulted in a lower anticipatory proportion. This is in agreement with the prediction that a higher overall error rate should be associated with a reduced anticipatory proportion.

Facilitation effects

According to Dell's spreading-activation theory, information about several words is often processed at the same time. This can produce facilitation effects. Support for this prediction was reported by Meyer and Damian (2007). Participants named target pictures while ignoring simultaneously presented distractor pictures. The names of the objects in the two pictures were phonologically related (e.g., dog – doll; ball – wall) or unrelated. Meyer and Damian (2007) found that the naming of target pictures was *faster* when accompanied by phonologically related distractors. This finding indicates that the phonological representations of the distractors were activated at the same time as those of target names.

A facilitation effect is *not* always found. In one study (Janssen et al., 2008), English speakers were presented with colored objects (e.g., *red rake*) and named the color or the object. When the phonological representations of color and object were related (as in the *red rake* example), there was a facilitation effect when the *object* was named, as predicted by Dell. In contrast, there was no facilitation effect when the object color was named, suggesting there was little or no activation of the object name, against Dell's predictions. So, it looks like the words in a phrase are not always activated together. In English, color adjectives are typically processed before object names. So, both words are activated before the object is named. However, the color word can be activated without the accompanying object noun.

These findings suggest the extent of phonological activation depends on word order – phonological activation is often limited to those words essential for the current task. Janssen et al. (2008) obtained further support for this account by carrying out the same experiment on French speakers. In French, the adjective typically *follows* the noun. For example, the French for *red rake* is *rateau rouge*. Accordingly, we would expect the findings to be exactly the opposite of those in English. That is what Janssen et al. found. Thus, activation can be constrained by word order and can be less extensive than assumed by Dell (1986).

In sum, Dell's theoretical approach provides a plausible explanation of many speech errors (e.g., the mixed-error effect; lexical bias effect; semantic substitution errors). It also provides an explanation for the interesting finding that the proportion of speech errors that is anticipatory increases as a function of practice and increasing expertise. Finally, Dell's theoretical approach can account for some facilitation effects. However, it seems that the number of speech errors is often less than would be expected by Dell. In addition, facilitation effects are less extensive than his theory would predict.

> ### Section summary
>
> #### Stages of speech production
> - Speech production involves four levels or stages of processing: message planning level, syntactic level, morphological level, and phonological level. The tip-of-the-tongue state occurs when semantic processing is successful but phonological processing is unsuccessful.
>
> #### Speech planning
> - There is often more advance planning at the semantic and syntactic levels than at the phonological level. The extent of speakers' advance planning is relatively greater when speakers speak slowly, when they aren't performing an additional task at the same time, and when simple sentences are planned. Much of the flexibility in advance planning occurs because there is a tradeoff between avoiding errors in speech and the cognitive load on speakers.
>
> #### Speech errors
> - Speech errors occur when an incorrect item is more activated than the correct one. Our phonological speech errors generally form words rather than nonwords, in part because we monitor our internal speech before speaking out loud. The mixed-error effect, in which an incorrect spoken word is semantically and phonologically related to the correct word, indicates that several kinds of information are activated at the same time. Number-agreement errors are frequent because it is often cognitively demanding to prevent them.
>
> #### Spreading activation
> - Dell's spreading-activation theory seems to predict too many speech errors when several words are activated at the same time. We may have a "syntactic traffic cop" that inhibits words not belonging to the appropriate syntactic category. The proportion of speech errors that is anticipatory rather than perseveratory increases as a function of expertise and practice. Dell's theory predicts phonological facilitation effects which are sometimes (but not always) found.

SPEECH PERCEPTION

Most of us are very good at understanding what other people say to us even when they speak in a strange dialect and/or ungrammatically. In our everyday lives, we take our ability to understand the speech of others for granted. Indeed, in view of the enormous experience we have all had in using the

English language and in listening to other people, speech perception seems easy and straightforward.

In fact, speech perception is much more complex than it appears to be. First, as we have seen earlier, language is spoken rather rapidly, at a rate of about four to five syllables (10 phonemes) per second. Second, speech typically consists of a continuously changing pattern of sound with few periods of silence, making it hard to decide when one word ends and the next begins. Even worse, not all pauses in the speech signal fall between words. Often, the last consonant of one word is added to the next word, a process known as *resyllabification*. So, the words "let us" are pronounced exactly the same as "lettuce," "ice cream" is pronounced like "I scream," and "keep in" is similar to "key pin." This creates a **segmentation** problem, a difficulty to separate out the words from the pattern of speech sounds. In addition, the way any given phoneme is pronounced depends in part on the phonemes preceding and following it. Thus, listeners in addition have to adjust to variations in pronunciation. Finally, much of the time when we listen to someone speaking there is background noise from other people, traffic, and so on. This noise must be filtered out.

On the positive side, long words can often be identified before they are fully pronounced. This is particularly true in constraining contexts. So, when you hear the sentence "They went to an Italian restaurant and ate spaghetti," you are able to identify the words "restaurant" and "spaghetti" at the beginning of the second syllable, because there are no other (likely) words starting with these sounds. This gives the speech recognition system some respite.

MODELS OF SPEECH PERCEPTION

Psychologists try to understand the workings of speech perception (and other cognitive processes) by building computer simulations, known as **computational models**. The ideal is to have these models perform exactly as humans do. When confronted with the input given to humans, they produce the same output as humans.

As we saw in Chapter 1, most computational models make use of connectionist networks. These networks consist of layers of nodes connected to each other (see Figure 1.15). There are two opposing views about what the nodes represent. According to the *localist view*, each node stands for a meaningful unit of information, such as a sound feature, a phoneme, a spoken word, or a meaning unit. As a result, nodes only become active when they correspond to the input. In contrast, the *distributed view* holds that there are no neurons in the brain devoted to specific pieces of information (a particular phoneme or word). According to this view, information is encoded and stored as patterns of activity in many nodes of the network. Each node in a layer is active to some extent upon encountering input, and the specific pattern of activity across the entire layer determines the information presented. In the following, we give an example of each type of model.

The trace model

McClelland and Elman (1986) and McClelland (1991) put forward a localist model of speech perception based on connectionist principles. It is assumed that there are processing units or nodes at three different levels: features of words sounds (e.g., voicing, manner of production), phonemes, and words (see Figure 8.3).

Figure 8.3 illustrates how the TRACE model responds when the spoken input word "sun" is presented. Because spoken words take time to pronounce, all models of speech recognition work with sequential presentation, in which the sounds of a word are divided in time units (as we will see later, this is different from visual word recognition, where it is assumed the entire word is processed at once, with all letters in parallel). The feature layer shows which features are activated at each time unit (rectangle) for the input "sun." First, the so-called fricative unit in the model is active while the "s" is being heard. Next, the back vocal feature is active, while the "u" is processed. Finally, the nasality feature becomes active when the "n" is presented.

As soon as a feature unit becomes active, it forwards its activity to the phoneme level. That is, all phonemes containing a fricative sound (s, z, sh, f, v, . . .) will receive activation as soon as the fricative feature becomes active. Because the s-sound contains other features (it is generated in the front of the mouth and with the front part of the tongue, there is a great deal of noisiness, and there is no complete closure of the vocal tract), these features will become activated as well, and the phoneme "s" will receive more activation than the other phonemes.

When phonemes become active, two things happen. First, activation is forwarded to the words containing that phoneme at that place. So, all words starting with an s-sound will become activated (sun, soup, song, Sunday, . . .). Words starting with the same sounds are called a *cohort*. Second, the phonemes that are activated will inhibit the other phonemes. Because the phoneme "s" is

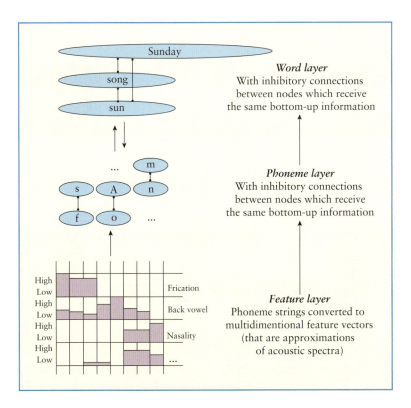

Figure 8.3 The basic TRACE model, showing how activation among the three levels (features, phonemes, and words) is activated. Arrows indicate activation; lines ending in circles mean inhibition. In the example, the word "sun" is presented. See the text for further explanation. Source: From Weber & Scharenborg (2012). Reprinted with permission of John Wiley & Sons.

activated the most, it will inhibit the activity of the other phonemes and will come out as the winner of the competition.

A similar mutual inhibition happens between the various word candidates that are activated. In addition, word candidates receive activation from the successive phonemes activated over time. As a result, the number of activated word candidates in the cohort will rapidly decrease. Whereas the cohort initially included all words starting with an "s" phoneme, after processing the phoneme u, only those words with "s" as the first sound and "u" as the second sound will remain active (the others will be inhibited), and so on.

Finally, words that are active feed their activity level back to the phonemes in them (this is the arrow downward between the word and the phoneme layer in Figure 8.3). This too will increase the activation of the phonemes "s" in the first place and "u" in the second place.

A model like TRACE can account for many findings. For instance, it predicts that when a word is pronounced, other words starting with the same sounds will be co-activated. This was shown beautifully by Allopenna et al. (1998). The authors asked participants to look at stimuli like the one shown in Figure 8.4. On the picture, you can see a beaker, a beetle, a speaker, and a pram (or carriage). Participants were instructed aurally to move one of the pictures with the mouse to one of the shapes (e.g., "put the beaker on the circle"). The eyes of the participants were monitored to see where they were looking.

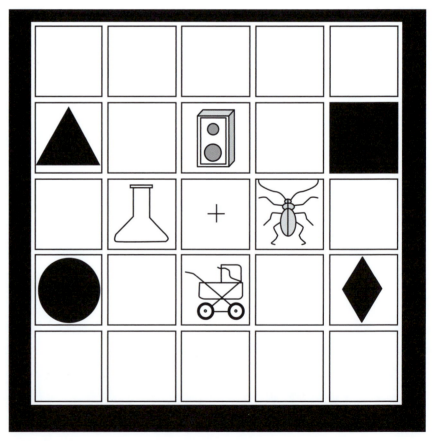

Figure 8.4 Example of the stimuli shown in the study of Allopenna et al. (1998). Source: From Allopenna et al. (1998). Reprinted with permission from Elsevier.

Although the participants always ended up looking at the target (the beaker), they initially often had a peek at one of the other pictures. Crucially, they looked more often to the beetle (starting with the same sounds as beaker) than to the pram (unrelated in sounds). They also looked more often to the speaker (rhyming with the target beaker) than to the pram, but not as often as to the beetle, as shown in Figure 8.5. Both phenomena were predicted by the TRACE model. Interestingly, participants were not aware of the fact that they sometimes looked at the wrong picture before looking at the right one, in line with the observation that many perceptual processes occur outside of awareness (Chapters 2 and 3).

Another prediction of the TRACE model is that it will be easier to detect a phoneme in a word than in a nonword. This is due to the top-down activation from the word layer to the phoneme layer. The input "sun" will strongly activate the word node "sun," which will feed back activation to the phonemes "s," "u," and "n." The same will not happen with the input "suph," as there is no word node matching this input that can be activated. The prediction of the TRACE model that performance should be better in the word condition is called *the word superiority effect*. Mirman et al. (2008) tested the prediction. Listeners detected a target phoneme (/t/ or /k/) in words and nonwords. Words were presented on 80% or 20% of the trials. The argument was that attention to (and activation at) the word level would be greater when most of the auditory stimuli were words. This should increase the word superiority effect.

What did Mirman et al. (2008) find? First, the predicted word superiority effect was found in most conditions (see Figure 8.6). Second, the magnitude

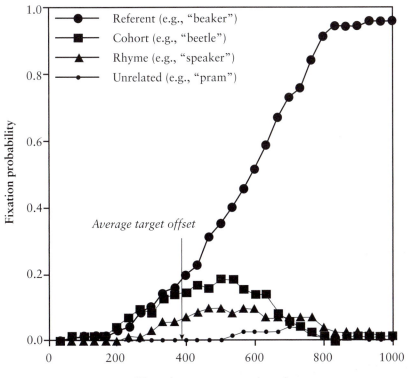

Figure 8.5 Probability of looking at the various pictures in Figure 8.4 upon hearing the target word "beaker". Some 200 ms into the pronunciation of the word "bea-" participants started to look both at the picture of the beaker and the beetle, showing that both word candidates were activated at that point. As more information came in, participants increasingly looked at the intended target word "beaker." Interestingly, towards the end of the words, they also occasionally looked at the speaker, which rhymes with the word beaker. These phenomena were predicted by the TRACE model. Source: From Allopenna et al. (1998). Reprinted with permission from Elsevier.

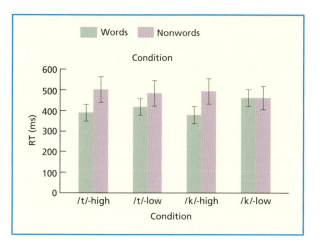

Figure 8.6 Mean reaction times for recognition of /t/ and /k/ phonemes in words and nonwords when words were presented on a high (80%) or low (20%) proportion of trials.
Source: From Mirman et al. (2008). Reprinted with permission of John Wiley & Sons.

of this effect was greater when 80% of the auditory stimuli were words than when only 20% were. These findings provide strong evidence for the involvement of top-down processes in speech perception.

On the other hand, there is evidence that the TRACE model may attach too much importance to top-down processing. McQueen (1991) presented ambiguous phonemes at the end of auditory stimuli. Each ambiguous phoneme could be perceived as completing a word or a nonword. According to the model, top-down effects from the word level should have produced a preference for perceiving the phonemes as completing words. This prediction was confirmed *only* when the stimulus was degraded. So, the top-down influences postulated by the TRACE model do not overrule clear bottom-up information.

The distributed cohort model

As we indicated above, not all researchers believe that localist models like the TRACE model are a truthful simulation of how the brain works. According to them, there is little evidence that there would be a group of neurons specifically devoted to the phoneme "s" or to the spoken word "sun." Rather, the meanings of stimuli are represented by activity patterns of a complete layer of nodes.

Figure 8.7 shows such a model for speech perception, called the *distributed cohort model* (Gaskell & Marslen-Wilson, 1997).

The input layer consisted of 11 nodes representing the speech signal at a particular moment in time (i.e., the activity pattern when a particular sound of the word was pronounced). All nodes of the input layer were connected to a hidden layer of 200 units. At each processing cycle, the hidden layer was copied to a context layer, which fed back to the hidden layer. In this way, the hidden layer received input not only from the current processing cycle but also from the previous processing cycle. This top-down part of the model allowed it to capture systematic transitions in time. The hidden layer fed activation forward to a layer of 50 semantic nodes and three layers of output phonology representing the sounds (phonemes) of the word. The three layers of output phonology represented the three parts of monosyllabic words: the consonants before the vowel (called the *onset* of the word; can be empty), the vowel (called the *nucleus* of the word), and the consonants after the vowel (the *coda*; can also be empty). By using this coding scheme, all monosyllabic words could be represented.

The input to the model consisted of monosyllabic English words. Importantly, the words were attached to each other, with no pauses in-between, to simulate the fact that words in a stream of spoken language are not separated. The model was trained by presenting the continuous sequence of phonetic feature bundles representing incoming speech to the input layer. The output of the network was compared to a second sequence of the same length, which represented the semantics and phonology of the words. The second sequence was used for comparison with the network output, allowing connection weights

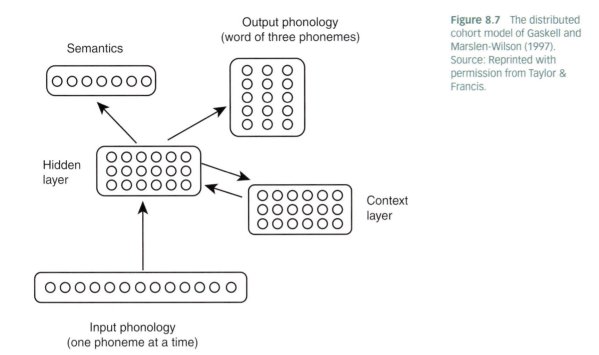

Semantics

Output phonology
(word of three phonemes)

Hidden
layer

Context
layer

Input phonology
(one phoneme at a time)

Figure 8.7 The distributed cohort model of Gaskell and Marslen-Wilson (1997). Source: Reprinted with permission from Taylor & Francis.

to be updated, so that the output of the network gradually approached that of the comparison sequence. During training, the words were presented a few hundred times in various orders.

After training, the model performed very similarly to human observers. In particular, the model showed activation of cohorts (both at the phonological and semantic level) when the onset and the nucleus of the word were presented, and ended up with a unique representation after the coda was presented, even though there were no gaps in the input. The model was also able to decide whether a real word had been presented ("sun") or a non-existing monosyllabic nonword ("suph"). Notice that the model was capable of doing so without explicit top-down effects from the semantic level. The only top-down information came from the context layer that kept a record of the preceding processing step.

Evaluation

➕ The TRACE model and the distributed cohort model provide reasonable accounts of phenomena such as the activation of a cohort of words that fit the input and the word superiority effect in phoneme monitoring.

➕ A significant strength of the TRACE model is its assumption that bottom-up and top-down processes both contribute to spoken word recognition, combined with explicit assumptions about the processes involved.

➕ The TRACE model emphasizes the role of top-down processes. This allows it to account for effects when bottom-up processes are insufficient to deal with limited stimulus information.

- The TRACE model exaggerates the importance of top-down processes to speech perception when the auditory stimulus isn't degraded (e.g., McQueen, 1991). This is not true for the distributed cohort model, which has no top-down influences between words and phonemes.

- Both models only work for a small number of words. In particular, they are limited to monosyllabic words, and they either have no semantic representations (TRACE) or very simplified representations (the distributed cohort model).

REALISTIC LISTENING CONDITIONS

Masking by competing stimuli

Most research on speech perception has involved idealized conditions (Mattys et al., 2009). Listeners are presented with a single, carefully recorded speech signal to which they give their undivided attention. Contrast such listening conditions with those typically found in our everyday lives. We often try to understand what one person is saying while other people are also talking or some of our attention is captured by something else.

Mattys et al. (2009) studied the effects of *imperfect* listening conditions on speech perception. They identified two major ways in which the identification of a spoken word can be made more difficult:

1. *Energetic masking*: Distracting sounds can cause the audibility of the spoken word to be degraded due to blending of their acoustic signals. Here the problem affects bottom-up processing.
2. *Informational masking*: Performing a second task at the same time as trying to identify a spoken word creates cognitive load and makes it harder to use stored knowledge about words (e.g., their meanings). Here the problem affects top-down processing.

The task used by Mattys et al. (2009) involved presenting a phrase (e.g., *mile doption*; *mild option*) and asking participants to decide the identity of a word in the phrase (e.g., *mild* or *mile*). They reported several important findings.

First, energetic masking impaired performance on the word-identification task. Second, informational masking also impaired task performance. These two findings indicate that bottom-up and top-down processes are both important in recognition of spoken words. Third, energetic masking led listeners to place more reliance on salient or conspicuous acoustic detail, whereas informational masking led them to rely more on their knowledge of words and word meanings.

What are the implications of these findings? It has generally been assumed that adverse listening conditions do not affect the processes used by listeners involved in speech perception. However, this assumption is inconsistent with Mattys et al.'s (2009) findings. In fact, listeners respond to adverse listening conditions by altering the balance between bottom-up and top-down processes. Thus, the precise nature of the alteration depends on whether energetic or informational masking is involved.

Activation of orthographic information

Imagine you are listening to spoken words. Would you activate the *spellings* of those words? It seems unlikely that orthography (information about word spellings) is involved in speech perception, and there is no allowance for its involvement in the TRACE model or the distributed cohort model.

In fact, however, orthography does play a role in speech perception. Perre and Ziegler (2008) gave listeners an auditory *lexical decision task* (deciding whether auditory stimuli were words or nonwords). The words varied in the consistency between their phonology or sounds and their orthography or spelling. For instance, -iss is a consistent syllable ending because it is always pronounced the same way (kiss, miss, . . .). In contrast, -int is inconsistent because of the difference in pronunciation between hint and pint.

The spelling consistency should be irrelevant if orthography isn't involved in speech perception. However, listeners performed the lexical decision task more slowly when the words were inconsistent than when they were consistent, suggesting that the phonological representations interacted with the orthographic representations (Perre et al., 2010). Further evidence was reported by Pattamadilok et al. (2008), who observed a rapid difference in the ERP signal (see Glossary) evoked by spoken words with a consistent and inconsistent spelling. Apparently, in proficient readers orthographic codes interact with phonological codes and help in speech perception.

The contribution of lip movements

When we are listening to someone, we generally see their lips moving at the same time. Indeed, many people find it unsettling when they are watching a dubbed television program in which the lip movements do not coincide with the sounds emitted, or when they are watching a television program with the sounds a few seconds out of sync with the lip movements. Does this mean that the lip movements help us understand speech? We know that deaf people make use of visual information in the form of lip-reading to assist them in understanding speech. Is this also true for hearing individuals?

McGurk and MacDonald (1976) prepared a videotape of someone saying "ba" repeatedly. At the same time they changed the sound channel, so that the voice said "ga" instead of "ba." The authors wanted to know which input channel would dominate: the auditory or the visual. Against all predictions, listeners did not report hearing "ga" (visual) or "ba" (auditory), but reported they heard the person in the video saying "da," which was a blending of the visual and auditory information. This combining of visual and auditory information when the two sources of information conflict is called the McGurk effect. It shows that what we hear is an integration of the visual and auditory cues in the speech signal (Marques et al., 2016).

The McGurk effect is influenced by top-down processes based on listeners' expectations. More listeners show the McGurk effect when the crucial word (based on blending the discrepant visual and auditory cues) is consistent with the meaning of the rest of the sentence than when it is not (Windmann, 2004).

Section summary

- Speech perception is complex because of the speed of spoken language, the variable nature of the stimulus input, and the presence of background noise. Speech perception involves the activation of word cohorts fitting word beginnings, which are pruned as more information comes in and only the target word remains.

Computational models

- According to the TRACE model, there are processing units at the level of features, phonemes, and words. The model's emphasis on top-down processes allows it to account for the word superiority effect. However, the model exaggerates the importance of top-down processes and ignores the role played by orthographic information in speech perception.
- The distributed cohort model shows that monosyllabic spoken words can also be processed with distributed representations, in which individual nodes no longer represent meaningful information, but in which information is encoded by activation patterns across a whole layer. This model could simulate human performance without the need of semantic top-down influences.

Realistic listening conditions

- Speech perception usually is extra difficult because (1) there are distracting sounds and (2) the listener is performing another task at the same time. Speech perception is impaired by both of these manipulations. However, the two manipulations have different effects on the precise processing used by listeners.
- In fluent readers, the orthographic representations of written words interact with the speech input to improve auditory perception.
- When we are listening to someone, we are also influenced by their lip movements, as can be concluded from the McGurk effect, the fact that lip movements influence the sounds we hear.

READING

Reading is an important skill because we learn a lot from books and computer screens (as you are doing right now!). It is difficult to imagine that reading only became widespread after the introduction of compulsory education at the beginning of the 20th century. In particular, silent reading seems to be a very recent achievement. Before the 20th century, most people mumbled while they were reading.

Adults without effective reading skills are at a great disadvantage in industrialized cultures. That means that we need to understand the processes involved in reading both to understand our own functioning and to help poor readers. Reading involves several perceptual and other cognitive processes as well as a good knowledge of language and of grammar.

IT'S IN THE EYES

The average reading rate is 200–300 words per minute. This is faster than speech perception, suggesting that the visual layout helps processing. Two aspects are important. First, in most languages (but not in all; Chinese is a prominent exception), words are segmented by spaces. Second, if processing is encountering difficulties, readers can look back at the text they just read. This is different from the auditory signal, which is lost once it has decayed from echoic memory (Chapter 4).

Three factors determine reading speed. First, there are important individual differences. Even among proficient readers, some readers read twice as fast as others and still remember as much from the text. Second, some texts are easier to read than others. This will affect the reading speed. Finally, much depends on the reading purpose. When you are searching for information on the internet or on social media, you skim over many more words per minute than when you are studying a textbook (hopefully!). In the latter case, progress can be lower than 100 words per minute (Klatt & Klatt, 2011).

How can we understand the processes involved in reading? One useful (and unobtrusive) method is to record eye movements during reading. The reader wears a piece of equipment (Figure 8.8) allowing precise assessment of *where* the eyes fixate and *when* they move.

Our eyes seem to move smoothly across the page when we read. In fact, they actually move in rapid jerks (**saccades**), as you can see if you look closely at someone reading. Once a saccade is initiated, its direction can't be changed. The length of each saccade is about eight letters or spaces. Saccades take 20–30 ms to complete and are separated by **fixations**, moments at which the eyes remain still, lasting 200–250 ms. Information is extracted from the text during fixations and not during saccades. There are fairly frequent regressions in which the eyes move backwards in the text, accounting for about 10% of all saccades. At the end of a line, readers make a return sweep to the next line. They are good at that, provided the text column is not too wide.

Readers typically fixate about 80% of content words (nouns, verbs, and adjectives) but only 20% of function words (articles, conjunctions, and pronouns). Words not fixated tend to be common, short, or predictable. In contrast, words fixated for longer than average are generally rare words or words that are unpredictable in the sentence context.

How does the reading system function to produce these effects? A simple view would be that readers fixate on a word until they have processed it adequately, after which they immediately fixate the next word until it has been adequately processed. Alas, there are *two* major problems with this view. First, it takes 85–200 ms to execute an eye-movement program. If readers operated according to the simple view described, they would waste time waiting for their eyes to move to the next word. Second, it is hard to see how readers could skip words – they wouldn't know anything about the next word until they had fixated it.

The E-Z Reader model (Reichle et al., 2013; Reichle, 2015) provides an elegant solution to these problems. A crucial assumption is that the next eye

Key terms

Saccades:
rapid eye movements that are separated by eye fixations.

Fixations:
moments during reading when the eyes remain still and information is picked up from the text; last on average 250 ms.

Figure 8.8 An eye tracker that records and stores information about an observer's eye fixations.
Source: Photo supplied by SR Research Ltd.

movement is programmed after only *part* of the processing of the currently fixated word has occurred. This assumption greatly reduces the time between completion of processing on the current word and eye movement to the next word.

Any spare time is used to start processing the next word. It is harder and more time-consuming to process rare words than common ones, and there is typically less spare time available with rare words. As a result, the fixation time on a word is longer when it is preceded by a rare word. If the processing of the next word is completed rapidly enough (e.g., it is highly predictable in the sentence context), it is skipped.

According to the model, readers can attend to two words (the currently fixated one and the next word) during a single fixation. However, it is a *serial* processing model (i.e., at any given moment only *one* word is processed). Not all researchers agree with the assumption that words are processed serially (one at a time). Engbert et al. (2005) argued that there is parallel processing of the word currently fixated, the previous word, and the next one. Strong support for this view would be found if the processing ease of the next word influenced the processing efficiency of the current word. Although some evidence has been published along these lines (e.g., Barber et al., 2010), it is rather weak and may be due to the fact that sometimes the eyes land on a different word than intended, a result of noise in the eye movement planning and execution (Reichle & Drieghe, 2015).

Evaluation

+ There is reasonable evidence indicating the existence of close connections between eye movements and cognitive processes during reading.

+ The assumptions of the E-Z Reader model have received support from research.

− The model focuses mainly on early and basic processes in reading rather than on higher-level processes (e.g., those involved in integrating information across words).

− The assumption that processing during reading is always serial has been questioned, although the evidence for parallel word processing in reading is modest.

SOUND AS WELL AS VISION?

We have seen that orthography interacts with phonology in spoken word processing. The In the Real World box discusses that young children learning to read are taught to pronounce the words. Does this mean that phonology is involved in reading?

The first bit of evidence that phonology plays a role in reading is the finding that sentences which are difficult to say also take more time to read silently. Tongue-twisters are sentences difficult to pronounce, because they repeat similar sounds (e.g., "A tutor who tooted the flute tried to tutor two tooters to toot"). Hanson et al. (1991) reported that college students needed more time reading such sentences than control sentences, even when the reading was silent. The observation that we rely on phonology when we are reading silently agrees with the fact that people report hearing an inner voice in their head while they are reading. It also suggests that reading relies on the phonological loop in working memory (Chapter 4).

Van Orden (1987) presented more evidence that phonology is involved in visual word recognition. He presented participants with words on a computer screen. The participants had to indicate whether the words referred to a semantic category, such as a type of flower. So, upon seeing the word "rose" the participants would have to indicate yes, and upon seeing the word "nose" they would have to indicate no. Some of the words with no-responses were homophones of category members (i.e., they sounded the same). So, Van Orden used the words "rows" and "knows." He observed that it took participants longer to indicate that "rows" did not belong to the category of flowers than to indicate that "knows" did not belong to the category (the reverse was true when participants were asked to indicate whether the words referred to a body part). The participants also made more errors, erroneously saying that "rows" referred to a type of flower. Van Orden argued that this was because the phonological overlap of the homophones interfered with the participants' processing of the visual words.

A third line of evidence is based on **priming**, the finding that the processing of a stimulus is facilitated when the stimulus is preceded by a related stimulus than when it is preceded by an unrelated stimulus. Rastle and Brysbaert (2006) showed that a target word more rapidly elicits a yes-response in a visual lexical decision task when it was preceded by a homophonic prime than when it was preceded by a control prime. So, participants responded faster yes to the word "clip" when it was preceded by the phonologically identical nonword prime "klip" than when it was preceded by "plip," a control prime that had as many letters in common with the target word but that was not homophonic. Interestingly, the phonological priming effect was also found when the primes were presented so briefly that participants could not consciously detect their presence. Such brief presentation is called *masked priming*, because after a very brief delay (typically some 50 ms) the processing of the prime is masked by the presence of the target.

In sum, there is clear evidence that in adults (as well as in children; Sauval et al., 2017) orthographic and phonological codes interact during reading. This phonological processing occurs rapidly and does not require conscious awareness.

TWO ROUTES FROM ORTHOGRAPHY TO PHONOLOGY

The finding that phonology is involved in reading raises the question of how phonology is activated from written input. Two aspects are involved. First, as we have seen earlier, the spelling of words is not always consistent, certainly not in English. If you know the correct pronunciation of the words "awful, awkward, awning, awl, very, sorry, story, and pastry," you may be forgiven if you wrongly pronounce the word "awry" (which actually sounds like "a rye"). So, some written words can only be pronounced correctly after they have been recognized. Other examples of such words are "pint, aisle, heir, cough, pearl, sew, glove."

At the other end, we are able to pronounce new words we have never seen, such as family names ("Flewell, Trissbart, Rinck"), new words we learn in texts (phoneme, phonology, morpheme), or nonwords made up by researchers ("klip, plip, cruss, trino, trint"). The fact that we are able to pronounce such letter sequences, despite never having encountered them before, means that we can make use of direct letter-sound correspondences.

The DRC-model

A computational model designed to account for the translation of written input into spoken output is the **DRC-model** (dual-route cascaded model; Coltheart et al., 2001). As shown in Figure 8.9, the model has two routes from print to sound. There is a *direct, lexical* route (the left route in the figure), in which we access information about the sound (and meaning) of words from a **mental lexicon** or internal dictionary. Visually presented words activate representations in a mental lexicon, from which all other information (phonology, syntax, semantics) is derived. The DRC-model postulates the existence of an orthographic lexicon for the recognition of written words in addition to a phonological lexicon for the recognition of spoken words. Each lexicon connects to the semantic system, where the meanings of known words are stored. The phonological lexicon operates on principles very similar to the TRACE model (Figure 8.3). The orthographic lexicon operates on the same principles, with the exception that all letter nodes *simultaneously* activate word candidates (and not sequentially as in spoken input). Like most other computational models, the DRC-model is limited to monosyllabic words.

In addition to the direct route, the DRC-model has an *indirect, non-lexical* route (the right route in the figure), in which **graphemes** (basic units of written language) are converted into phonemes by means of a set of grapheme-phoneme conversion rules. The conversion happens sequentially from word beginning to word end, and the resulting phonemes can be converted into spoken sounds. The phonemes also activate lexical entries in the phonological lexicon in a way similar to the one described for the TRACE model. Words activated in the phonological lexicon spread their activation to their corresponding entries in the orthographic lexicon, so that word representations in the orthographic lexicon can receive additional phonology-mediated activation.

Coltheart et al. (2001) assumed that we use both routes when we read aloud. In addition,

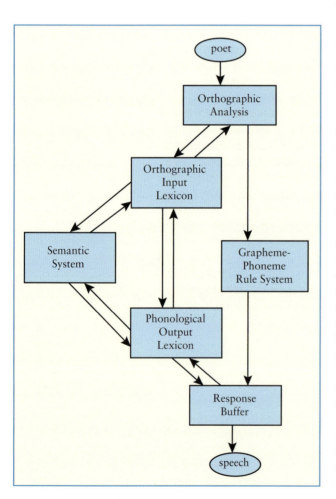

Figure 8.9 The DRC-model of the translation from written input to spoken output.
Source: Based on Coltheart et al. (2001).

they argue that the direct route operates faster than the indirect route, so that this route dominates in naming known words. Alternatively, the indirect route is the only one available for reading new words or nonwords, because these letter sequences do not have an entry in the orthographic lexicon.

Coltheart et al. (2001) further postulated a set of grapheme-phoneme conversion rules. Words that follow the rules are called *regular words*. Their pronunciation is predictable from the letters (e.g., "tint, punt") and the information streams coming from the direct and indirect route converge. Words that do deviate from the grapheme-phoneme conversion rules are called *irregular words*. Their pronunciation is *not* completely predictable from the letters (e.g., "island, yacht"), and there will be a mismatch between the information activated by the direct route and the indirect route. According to Coltheart et al., this mismatch will create a processing cost, so that we require more time to name irregular words than regular words, a processing cost that has been reported in experiments (Coltheart & Rastle, 1994). The model further predicts that different brain areas will be involved in reading irregular words (direct route) and nonwords (indirect route). This distinction has also been documented (Taylor et al., 2013).

Key terms

Grapheme: basic unit of written language that corresponds to a phoneme (e.g., the letter sequence "ph" forms a grapheme because it is pronounced as the phoneme "f") ; a word consists of one or more graphemes.

Phonics approach: a method of teaching young children to read in which they learn to link individual letters and groups of letters to the sounds of the language; see **whole-language approach**.

In the Real World 8.1 *Learning to read*

Children learning to read in the English language face more of a challenge than those learning to read in most other languages. Indeed, it takes them about *three* years to reach a level of mastery of reading aloud that children learning other languages attain in *one* year (Seymour et al., 2003).

Why is English so difficult? Most languages (e.g., Spanish) are characterized by a *consistent* relationship between spelling and sound. As a result, it is easy to predict how an unfamiliar word should be pronounced, and there are few (or no) irregular words. In contrast, there are numerous irregular or exception words in English, including some of the most common words in the language (e.g., "some"; "was").

Children learning most languages are taught primarily by the **phonics approach**. This approach is also much used by children learning English (Share, 2008). The main emphasis is on teaching children how to form connections between letters or groups of letters and the sounds of the spoken language. It also involves learning to blend the sounds of letters together to pronounce unknown words.

When the phonics approach is used to teach children to read, the emphasis is often on pronouncing words grapheme by grapheme. David Share (2008) argued that a major advantage of this approach is that it ensures that children attend to the order and identity of letters when reading. As a result, this approach should improve readers' ability to recognize words and to spell them correctly.

Suppose we ask children to engage in silent reading of words and nonwords while repeatedly saying something meaningless. This would largely prevent them from processing the sounds of the words and nonwords they are reading, and so should disrupt their ability to learn word spellings. Precisely this was found by de Jong et al. (2009) with 7- and 8-year-old children. Their findings suggest that phonological recoding of words occurs during silent reading and is important when learning word spellings.

The phonics approach has been criticized for being too narrow (e.g., Goodman, 1986), because it focuses mostly on allowing readers to pronounce words accurately. In fact, however, readers' main goal is to understand the meaning of what they read, which is the emphasis of the **whole-language approach**. According to Ken Goodman

(1986, p. 39), who is a leading advocate of this approach, "Developing readers must be encouraged to predict and guess as they try to make sense of print." A reader may recognize a given word by taking account of the relevant sentence context. For example, in the sentence, "The captured soldier pleaded for _____," we might guess that the missing word is "mercy."

There is much overlap between the whole-language approach and the whole-word approach. According to the whole-word approach (which used to be called the "look-and-say" approach), readers should focus on relating the entire word to its meaning. In so doing, they shouldn't focus on the way it sounds.

Evidence that semantic knowledge (information about word meanings) is important in learning to read was reported by Nation and Cocksey (2009). They used very consistent words (consisting of letter patterns pronounced the same in all words in which they appear) and exception words having very unusual spelling-sound relationships. The exception words are harder to read.

Those children with good semantic knowledge of words had significantly greater reading accuracy than those with poor semantic knowledge. This was especially the case with the exception words that couldn't be read accurately by relying solely on phonics.

Although top-down, semantic knowledge helps in reading, there is good evidence that the phonics approach is an essential component in teaching children to read in every alphabetical language, including English (Share, 2008). So far as English is concerned, Ehri et al. (2001) reported a meta-analysis (see Glossary) combining the findings from many studies. Phonics instruction led to fairly large improvements in word reading, text comprehension, and spelling. Overall, phonics instruction was more beneficial than whole-word or whole-language instruction in enhancing reading abilities.

The ability to decode or identify individual words is very important when learning to read. However, other skills are also involved. According to the Simple View of Reading (e.g., Kendeou et al., 2009), children's reading comprehension is determined by their *listening* comprehension skills as well as their decoding skills for *written* words. Kendeou et al. (2009) and Hulme et al. (2015) found that both of these skills contributed to children's reading comprehension.

In sum, several kinds of information need to be acquired by young children learning to read. First, they must learn the connections between the letters in words and sounds. Second, they must learn to use context to assist in identifying individual words. Third, they must learn to relate words to their meanings.

The triangle model

You may have noticed that the DRC-model is a localist model, like the TRACE model. In such a model, nodes represent meaningful information. As we discussed earlier, not all researchers agree that neurons encode stimulus-specific information. In their view, information is coded by activation patterns across layers of neurons. A similar model has been proposed for the naming (and recognition) of visually presented words, as shown in Figure 8.10.

According to the triangle model, written words activate orthographic nodes, which forward their information to phonological nodes and semantic nodes. In this model, there are no lexicons with dedicated nodes for orthographic and phonological words. Nor are there rules to translate graphemes to phonemes. All the model does is learn to produce the correct output from the input by adjusting the weights between the nodes in a training phase (similar to what was done in the distributed cohort model).

Words with inconsistent pronunciations (e.g., "pint" vs. "mint, hint") in the triangle model activate the correct phonology, because the phonological nodes receive information not only from the orthographic nodes but also

Key terms

Whole-language approach:
a method of teaching young children to read in which the emphasis is on understanding the meaning of text; it includes using sentence context to guess the identity of unknown words.

Triangle model:
a computational model of how written input is translated into spoken output based on distributed representations; see also the **DRC-model**.

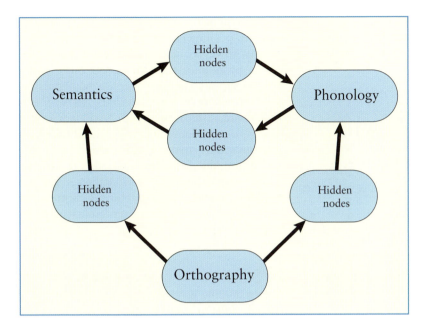

Figure 8.10 The triangle model of the translation from written input to spoken output. Source: From Harm & Seidenberg (2004); see also Monaghan et al. (2017). Reprinted with permission from the American Psychological Association.

from the semantic nodes. So, the letters of "pint" activate not only the nodes involved in the sounds "p," "i," "ai," "n," and "t" at the phonological level, but also the nodes involved in the meaning of the word "pint" at the semantic level. The latter forward information to the phonological level, which makes sure that the phoneme "ai" gets more activation than the phoneme "i."

According to the triangle model, grapheme-phoneme *consistency* (is this sequence of letter always pronounced the same?) is more important than grapheme-phoneme *regularity* (does this sequence of letters produce the correct pronunciation according to a set of rules?). Regularity predicts that regular words will be pronounced equally fast whether or not their spelling is consistent. Thus, the regular word "hint" will be pronounced equally fast as the consistent word "husk," whereas the irregular word "pint" will take longer than the consistent word "puss." Consistency, on the other hand, predicts that it will take longer to pronounce "hint" than "husk," because the former has an inconsistent correspondence between the spelling and the pronunciation, whereas the latter has not. Research has confirmed that the time taken to pronounce words depends more on their consistency than on their regularity (Glushko, 1979).

Another problem with regularity is that a set of rules always contains an element of arbitrariness. For instance, what is the rule-based pronunciation of "-ave": as in "have" or "gave"?

Consistency also affects the reading of nonwords. For example, the word rhyme "-ust" is consistent because it is always pronounced the same in mono-syllabic words, and so the nonword "nust" is easy to pronounce. In contrast, the word rhyme "-ear" is inconsistent because it is pronounced in different ways in different words (e.g., "bear" and "dear"), and so it is not clear how to pronounce the nonword "kear."

According to the dual-route model, nonwords are pronounced using spelling-sound pronunciation rules. As a result, DRC predicts that the nonword

	Total	Below level 1b	level 1b	level 1a
	%	%	%	%
OECD average	18.0	1.3	4.4	12.3
Shanghai - China	2.9	0.1	0.3	2.5
Hong Kong - China	6.8	0.2	1.3	5.3
Korea	7.6	0.4	1.7	5.5
Estonia	9.1	0.2	1.3	7.7
Vietnam	9.4	0.1	1.5	7.8
Ireland	9.6	0.3	1.9	7.5
Japan	9.8	0.6	2.4	6.7
Singapore	9.9	0.5	1.9	7.5
Poland	10.6	0.3	2.1	8.1
Canada	10.9	0.5	2.4	8.0
Finland	11.3	0.7	2.4	8.2
Macao - China	11.5	0.3	2.1	9.0
Switzerland	13.7	0.5	2.9	10.3
Netherlands	14.0	0.9	2.8	10.3
Australia	14.2	0.9	3.1	10.2
Germany	14.5	0.5	3.3	10.7
Denmark	14.6	0.8	3.1	10.7
Belgium	16.1	1.6	4.1	10.4
Norway	16.2	1.7	3.7	10.8
New Zealand	16.3	1.3	4.0	11.0
United Kingdom	16.6	1.5	4.0	11.2
Czech Republic	16.9	0.6	3.5	12.7
Latvia	17.0	0.7	3.7	12.6
Spain	18.3	1.3	4.4	12.6
France	18.9	2.1	4.9	11.9
Austria	19.5	0.8	4.8	13.8
Iceland	21.0	2.3	5.4	13.3
Slovenia	21.1	1.2	4.9	15.0
Luxembourg	22.2	2.0	6.3	13.8
Russian Federation	22.3	1.1	5.2	16.0

Figure 8.11   Percentage of school-going 15-year-olds who have only very basic reading skills.
Source: From OECD, 2016.

"kear" will be pronounced as rhyming with "dear," and the pronunciation requires no extra time. In reality, however, inconsistent nonwords take longer to pronounce than consistent ones, and their pronunciations mimic the various possibilities encountered in words (Glushko, 1979; Zevin & Seidenberg, 2006). So, "kear" will not only take longer to pronounce but will also occasionally be pronounced as rhyming with "bear."

In sum, the processes involved in reading words and nonwords are more *flexible* than is assumed by the DRC-model. This flexibility is captured better by models with distributed representations like the triangle model.

DYSLEXIA

A considerable percentage of people do not acquire enough skills to read fluently. Figure 8.11 shows the percentage of school-going 15-year-olds in different countries who cannot read properly. Level 1b is defined as someone who is just able to find an easy word in a short, simple text or a list of words. Level 1a refers to someone who only manages to recognize the main theme in a simple text on a familiar topic. As can be seen in Figure 8.11, some 18% of the children in industrialized countries do not get beyond level 1a. Learning difficulties and limited mental capacity mean that a significant part of society never learns to read well enough to understand more than the basic message of an easy text. The percentage of non-proficient readers is influenced by the efforts a country is willing to invest in these people and whether or not they are allowed to go to school, as shown by the large differences in prevalence among countries.

Related to low reading proficiency but not completely overlapping is the effort required to learn to read and write. Some individuals must make many more efforts than others to acquire these skills and still do not reach the same performance level. These individuals suffer from developmental dyslexia. Dyslexia refers to persistent problems in learning to read and write, leading to a lower performance level than can be expected on the basis of a person's intelligence and education received (Peterson & Pennington, 2015). The clearest cases of dyslexia are those children who have normal intelligence (as measured with IQ tests and evidenced by school tasks that do not require reading and writing) and a good education (indeed often with considerable remediation efforts), who still struggle to read fluently. In secondary and higher education, these individuals often no longer make errors while reading, but they require considerably more time to read a text.

The main origin of dyslexia is thought to be poor connections between the written word recognition areas in the brain's occipital and temporal cortices and the phonological processing areas in the frontal and the parietal cortices, impeding interactions between phonological and orthographic codes (Figure 8.12). This can be related to the fact that reading is a recent skill, which has to make use of the existing brain machinery, evolved over millenniums for visual object recognition and auditory language processing (Dehaene et al., 2010). Apparently some brain organizations are better equipped to accommodate for the new skill than others. The biological basis of dyslexia is also in line with the finding that dyslexia has a strong hereditary component. A child of parents with dyslexia has 30–50% chances of being dyslexic as well, against 4–7% in the general population (Grigorenko, 2001; Thompson et al., 2015).

Due to improved educational support in primary and secondary education, dyslexia no longer is an insurmountable handicap to entering higher education. As a result, some 5% of the students entering higher education have an assessment of dyslexia. Several studies looked at the cognitive profile of these students (Callens et al., 2012; Swanson & Hsieh, 2009; Warmington et al., 2013). Strengths and weaknesses are expressed as effect sizes. An *effect size* is a standardized measure indicating how large the difference between two groups is. One of these measures is Cohen's d, which has the following interpretation. Differences smaller than d = .4 do not have practical implications; differences of d = .8 or higher have implications at the individual level and must be taken into account both by the person with dyslexia and by educational settings. Figure 8.13 gives a summary of the findings.

Because of the problems students with dyslexia are confronted with, educational settings must provide some compensation. They should give students with dyslexia 25% more time for their exams, allow them to use text-to-speech software, accommodate for the higher number of spelling mistakes (if correct spelling is not a core requirement of the course), and let students use calculators if much arithmetic must be done for the exam (e.g., for an exam in statistics). The students themselves should be aware that they require more time to study and that it is a

Key term

Dyslexia:
persistent problems in learning to read and write, leading to a lower performance level than can be expected on the basis of person's intelligence and education received.

Figure 8.12 Areas and connections involved in reading. Three areas are important in fluent reading. First, there is the occipito-temporal region involved in visual word recognition. Second, there is the temporo-parietal region involved in orthography-phonology translation. And finally, there is the inferior frontal region involved in spoken word representations. Researchers assume that suboptimal communication between these regions, because of deficient white matter tracts between them, may be the origin of dyslexia. In particular, the arcuate fasciculus is thought to be important, which connects all three regions.
Source: From Peterson & Pennington (2015). Reprinted with permission of Annual Review of Psychology, © by Annual Reviews.

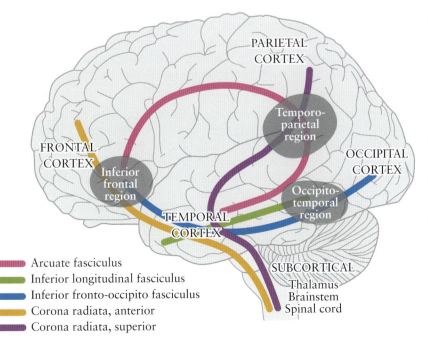

PARIETAL CORTEX

Temporo-parietal region

FRONTAL CORTEX

Inferior frontal region

OCCIPITAL CORTEX

Occipito-temporal region

TEMPORAL CORTEX

SUBCORTICAL
Thalamus
Brainstem
Spinal cord

Arcuate fasciculus
Inferior longitudinal fasciculus
Inferior fronto-occipito fasciculus
Corona radiata, anterior
Corona radiata, superior

Figure 8.13 Challenges faced by students in higher education who have dyslexia. These students have particular problems with spelling accuracy and reading speed. Also arithmetic (e.g., multiplication) is considerably slower. Slower processing is observed in nonverbal tasks as well, although the cost here is reduced to d = .6. Vocabulary is lower and reading comprehension too, but the effects here are limited as well. No differences are seen in reasoning accuracy, auditory perception and being liked by other people. The results are very similar for English and Dutch (a language with a more transparent orthography), suggesting that the findings generalize across languages and educational settings. Source: Based on Callens et al., 2012; Swanson & Hsieh, 2009; Warmington et al., 2013.

Spelling accuracy	2.0
Reading speed	1.8
Arithmetic speed	1.0
Naming speed	1.0
Processing speed	0.6
Vocabulary	0.6
Reading comprehension	0.6
Problem solving, reasoning accuracy	0.1
Auditory perception	0.0
Ratings by third persons	−0.3

good strategy to read aloud their course texts at least once (and ideally record this reading). If needed, they should seek assistance from friends and family if they are not able to read the course aloud without errors (text-to-speech software can help here as well). Finally, it is a good idea for these students to have their reports and theses proofread for spelling errors before submitting them.

Section summary

It's in the eyes

- Average reading rate is 200–300 words per minute. Readers move their eyes in saccades about four times per second. Information is extracted from the text during fixations. The next eye movement is programmed after only partial processing of the currently fixated word. The E-Z Reader model assumes that reading involves only serial processing.

Sound as well as vision?

- There is good evidence that reading involves phonology. This explains why sentences with tongue-twisters are harder to read, why participants find it hard to say that the word "rows" does not refer to a flower, and why words are processed faster after a homophonic prime. The phonological priming effect is also observed when the prime is not consciously visible, suggesting that phonological processing occurs rapidly and automatically.

Two routes from print to sound

- Theories must explain why we are capable of correctly naming both the word "yacht" (pronounced as "yot") and the nonword "fusk." This requires the existence of two routes. According to the DRC-model, one route involves the activation of entries in an orthographic lexicon (needed to explain why we can correctly name words with unclear correspondences between the letters and the sounds) and another route in which graphemes are converted to phonemes (needed to name nonwords). According to the triangle model, a mental lexicon is not needed, if one assumes that known words activate their meaning in addition to the sounds corresponding to the letters.

Learning to read in English

- It is especially hard to learn to read English because there are many inconsistent spelling-sound correspondences. Children often learn to read using the phonics approach. This approach focuses on teaching readers to pronounce words accurately. In contrast, the whole-language and whole-word approaches focus more on understanding the meanings of words. Research indicates that the phonics approach is required as a central part of reading education. In addition to word-decoding skills, listening comprehension skills are important as well.

Dyslexia

- Some individuals find it harder to learn to read and write than their peers of the same intelligence and under the same learning conditions. This condition is called dyslexia. It is to a large extent a biological condition and thought to be due to suboptimal connections between the brain areas responsible for visible word recognition and spoken word representations. Students with dyslexia still have problems with reading and writing in higher education, often despite intensive efforts to remediate the problems.

FROM WORDS TO CONVERSATIONS

In the previous sections we have seen what is typical for the various language modalities: speaking, speech perception, reading. Each skill, of course, also shares a number of common features, which we will discuss now. We make a distinction between word recognition, sentence processing, and discourse understanding.

EASY AND DIFFICULT WORDS

Not all words are equally easy to recognize. Some take longer than others, which says something about the organization of the word recognition system (whether this is seen as a mental lexicon or as connections among layers of orthographic, phonological, and semantic nodes). You can easily experience the differences in word recognition speed by reading aloud the two columns of words in Figure 8.14. Measure the time you need to read each column.

Variables affecting word processing speed

If you responded like the majority of people to the words in Figure 8.14, you found the words of List 2 easier than the words of List 1 (Keuleers et al., 2012). *Why* is this?

A first factor making a difference between the lists is how often you encounter the words in your daily life. Try it out. Give a number from 1 (I've encountered this word almost never) to 5 (I come across this word every day) and see whether the words of List 2 are more frequent than those of List 1. In general, words with a high frequency are easier to process than words with a low frequency, an effect we call the word frequency effect. The **word frequency effect** is a type of practice-makes-perfect effect: you're faster at recognizing words you've processed many times in your life before.

A second factor that makes a difference between the words of List 1 and List 2 is the age at which you acquired the words. Again, try it out. Indicate for each word how old you were (in years) when you learned the word. In all probability

List1	List2
telltale	contact
chummy	yellow
pincer	hungry
pawnshop	welcome
forthright	happy
pageant	closer
dispelled	apple
godly	double
mutter	harvest
pristine	appear
snooty	relax
infringe	angry
toadstool	believe

Figure 8.14 The speed with which we recognize words. Name the words of List 1 and register how much time you need for this. Then name List 2 and again register your time. Were you equally fast for both lists? If not, which list was harder? Did you also experience that List 2 was easier? Why would this be so?
Source: Data from Keuleers et al. (2012).

(if you had a normal youth and if you are a native speaker), you will find that you learned the words of List 2 earlier than those of List 1. This effect is called the **age-of-acquisition effect**: the earlier we learned a word, the easier it is for us to recognize it. Part of the effect is the same as the frequency effect, because early-acquired words are likely to be frequent words, but this is not the complete story. Even infrequent words we learned at a young age are surprisingly easy to recognize. Stadthagen-Gonzalez et al. (2004) reported that British psychology professors rapidly recognized words like "alphabet, banana, daffodil, princess, tiger, strawberry," even though these words did not figure prominently in their academic lives.

A third factor affecting the speed of processing is *word length*: everything else being the same, short words are easier to process than long words. This is most certainly true for auditory word recognition, where long words take longer to be pronounced, but it is also found in visual word recognition, even though all letters are processed in parallel (at least up to a word length of eight to ten letters).

Finally, a fourth factor affecting word processing efficiency is the degree to which the word is connected to the preceding context: related words are easier to process than unrelated words. If we measured your eye movements, we would find that you require less time to read the word "letter" in the sentence "the postman wrote a letter to the mayor" than in the sentence "the actor refused a letter from the mayor." The word "letter" is pre-activated more by the preceding words "write" and "postman" than by the preceding words "refuse" and "artist," and this pre-activation helps in word recognition (see Chapter 6 for the spreading of activation in semantic networks). This means that under adverse listening or reading conditions, we are more likely to recognize words related to the ongoing topic than words introducing a new topic.

Semantic pre-activation can already be shown with word pairs. We are faster to recognize the target word "sand" if immediately before we saw or heard the word "beach" than if we saw or heard the word "bread." Similarly, we are faster at identifying the target word "ride" after the semantically related word "horse" than after the unrelated word "hole." This phenomenon is called **semantic priming**. Interestingly, semantic priming is also observed with masked priming, when the prime word is presented too briefly to be consciously perceptible (Lukatela & Turvey, 1994). This indicates that semantic pre-activation can be an automatic language process and does not require conscious predictions of upcoming words on the basis of elaborated world knowledge.

Morphologically complex words

At the beginning of the chapter we saw that not all words are monomorphemic words representing a single meaning unit. Indeed, one of the strengths of human languages is that new words can be formed by derivation ("undrinkable") and compounding ("flowerpot cleaner"). As a matter of fact, the English

Key terms

Age-of-acquisition effect:
the finding that words learned early in life are easier to process than words learned later in life.

Semantic priming:
the finding that a target word (e.g., "king") is identified faster after a semantically related prime word ("throne") than after an unrelated prime ("torch").

language contains less than 20,000 morphemes, of which only 11,000 are generally known (Brysbaert et al., 2016). On the basis of these morphemes, we generate the hundreds of thousands of word forms we can interpret.

There are two ways in which morphologically complex words can be produced and understood: either they may be present in the mental lexicon or they may be assembled on the spot. If you know what the word "iodization" means, you can derive the meaning of the words "iodize, iodizable, and iodization problem," without having encountered these words or word combinations before.

Authors disagree about how familiar, morphologically complex words are processed. Some authors think all familiar words are stored in the mental lexicon (including the morphologically complex words), whereas other authors argue that only monomorphemic words are included in the lexicon, in order not to overload the system.

Bertram and Hyönä (2003) defend a position in-between the two extremes and propose three principles increasing the chances of a familiar morphologically complex word being part of the mental lexicon. The first is the frequency of the word: high-frequency words (e.g., "beehive") are more likely to be part of the mental lexicon than low-frequency words (e.g., "bee hater"). The second variable is the length of the word: short words (e.g., "drop-out") are more likely to be included in the mental lexicon than long words (e.g., "living room"). Finally, polymorphemic words with meanings that cannot easily be derived from their components (such as "honeymoon, walkie-talkie, belly button") are more likely to be stored in the lexicon than polymorphemic words with transparent meanings (such as "flowerpot, peanut butter, touch screen"). To some extent, the English language helps us to know which morphologically complex words are likely to be assembled, because such words tend to be written as word sequences separated by spaces (bee hater, living room, ice cream man), whereas opaque compounds usually (but not always) are written as single words or with a hyphen in-between. Other languages (e.g., German, Finnish) write all compound words in a single word, often ending up with very long words (icecreamman, longtermmemory).

Incidentally, did you notice that we taught you two new morphologically complex words in this chapter: monomorphemic and polymorphemic? What do you think? Will they become part of your mental lexicon or not? Why?

SENTENCE PARSING: WHO DOES WHAT TO WHOM?

To understand language, it is not enough to know the individual words. We must also be able to interpret how the various words in a sentence relate to each other. Which action is described by the verb? Who is performing the action (i.e., is the subject of the action)? Who or what is receiving the action (i.e., is the object)? And who or what else is involved? Indeed, patients with brain damage have been reported (e.g., Caplan et al., 1996) who had no problems understanding words but who misinterpreted sentences, in particular sentences more complex than the simple subject-verb-object sequence (as in "The teacher ate an apple"). These patients are likely to misinterpret a sentence like "the dog was bitten by the man," because this sentence not only deviates from the preferred word order but also goes against expectations in terms of contents.

Identifying the grammar of a sentence

Understanding how the words are combined within a sentence is known technically as **parsing**. It involves identifying a language's grammar or syntactical structure. The grammar of a language is a set of rules that allow users (1) to generate every possible legal sentence, and (2) not to generate unacceptable sentences. It differentiates between different types of words and puts them in a hierarchy, consisting of phrases (word combinations that express a single idea), clauses (basic sentences describing something doing something), and sentences (combination of one or more clauses). The hierarchy can be described by means of a *tree diagram* describing the relations between the words (Figure 8.15). Speakers need the grammar to construct sentences; listeners require it to parse the message. Listeners do not wait until the end of a sentence before they build a tree diagram; they start building such a diagram as soon as the sentence begins. This happens on the basis of bottom-up information (e.g., an article introduces a noun phrase) and top-down information (sentences nearly always contain a verb phrase describing the action and a noun phrase performing the action).

A challenge for the parser is that sentences are often temporarily ambiguous, so that it is not clear which tree to build, as can be seen in the following example:

- He showed her the baby pictures.
- He showed her baby the pictures.

In these sentences the interpretation of the grammatical role of the word "her" is unclear until the disambiguating information follows. In some sentences the ambiguity is never resolved, and we rely on world knowledge to know which message is meant (i.e., which tree diagram should be built). Here are some examples of such ambiguous sentences. They come from newspaper headlines, which are often ambiguous because they are shortened as much as possible:

- Visiting relatives can be a nuisance.
- Police help murder victims.
- Teenage sex problem is mounting.
- American sentenced to life in Scotland.

Even texts can contain ambiguous parts. Here is an extract from an email one of the authors received: "We have decided on a provisional date and location for the workshop. . . . The workshop topics will be how to deal with difficult students in the morning, and how to make lectures and seminars interesting in the afternoon."

Solving ambiguities

How does the parser make sense of sentences with ambiguities? All researchers agree that we use syntactic or grammatical information plus semantic information about the meanings of the individual words. However, there has been controversy concerning the details.

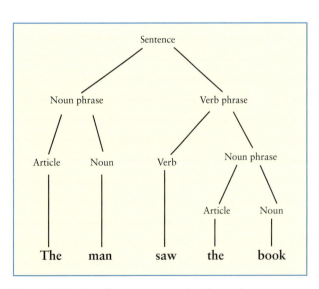

Figure 8.15 Tree diagram representing the parsing output. The words are differentiated in different categories (article, noun, verb), which are put into a hierarchy.

According to the **garden-path theory** (Frazier & Rayner, 1982), only syntactic information is used initially to build a tree diagram, with semantic information being used in a second stage to correct initial misinterpretations. One of the syntactic principles is that the parser prefers to build the simplest possible syntactic tree. This predicts that we will have less problems reading the sentence "The spy saw the cop with binoculars" than the sentence "The spy saw the cop with a revolver." In the latter case, the parser will have to reconfigure the tree diagram upon encountering the disambiguating word "revolver." Figure 8.16 shows that the syntactic tree is simpler for the first sentence than for the second.

Other theorists (e.g., MacDonald et al., 1994; Van Gompel et al., 2005) argue that it is much more a question of "All hands to the pump." In other words, we use *all* sources of information (syntactic, semantic, and world knowledge) from the outset to build the syntactic tree. According to MacDonald et al.'s (1994) **constraint-based theory**, competing analyses of the current sentence are activated simultaneously and are ranked according to activation strength. The syntactic structure receiving most support from the various sources of information is highly activated, with other syntactic structures being less activated. Readers become confused when reading ambiguous sentences if an incorrect syntactic structure is activated more than the correct one.

According to MacDonald et al.'s (1994) theory, one factor influencing the assignment of syntactic structure to a sentence is information included in the words. Take the words "duck" and "play." Both words can be used as a verb or a noun. However, the word "duck" is more often used as a noun than as a verb, whereas "play" is used more often as a verb than as a noun. According to the garden-path theory, this difference in relative frequency should not affect the syntactic tree being built when the parser is processing the sentence beginning "He saw her . . .". Because the tree is simpler if the next word is a noun than a verb, the parser should prefer the noun interpretation as in "he saw her duck and family last week" than the verb interpretation as in "he saw her duck and moan last week." This should be true for the word "play" as well. So, the parser should initially prefer the noun interpretation as in "he saw her play and family last week" than "he saw her play and moan last week." However, this is not what Boland and Blodgett (2001) found: readers experienced fewer problems (revealed by eye movements) with sentences like "he saw her play and moan last week" than with sentences like "he saw her play and family last week," as predicted by the constraint-based theory.

Other studies pitting the garden-path theory against the constraint-based theory have also reported that the parser rapidly takes into account word-based and meaning-based information when identifying the most likely

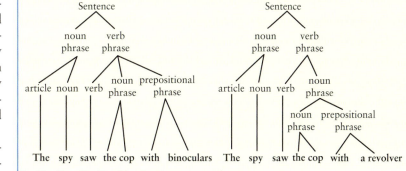

Figure 8.16 Tree diagram illustrating why the parser prefers the left sentence over the right one according to the garden-path theory. When the parser encounters the ambiguous preposition "with," it is simpler to postulate a prepositional phrase attached to the verb phrase than to postulate a new noun phrase consisting of the old noun phrase and a new prepositional phrase.

interpretation (tree diagram) of a sentence. As a result, most researchers currently defend that the constraint-based theory provides the best explanation of how sentences are parsed (e.g., Kuperberg & Jaeger, 2016).

Good-enough representations

For a long time it was assumed that the syntactic trees of sentences were always "complete, detailed, and accurate" (Ferreira et al., 2002, p. 11), at least for language users without brain damage.

There is increasing evidence that this assumption is unduly optimistic (Christianson, 2016; Karimi & Ferreira, 2016). Ferreira (2003) presented sentences auditorily and found that her listeners' sentence representations were often inaccurate. A sentence such as "The mouse was eaten by the cheese" was sometimes misinterpreted as meaning the mouse ate the cheese. The sentence "The man was visited by the woman" was sometimes mistakenly interpreted to mean the man visited the woman.

Why are people so prone to error when processing sentences (especially passive ones)? According to Ferreira (2003), we use heuristics or rules of thumb to simplify the task of understanding sentences. A very common heuristic (the NVN or noun-verb-noun strategy) is to assume that the first noun of a sentence refers to the agent of the action, whereas the second noun refers to the object of the sentence. We use this heuristic because the vast majority of English sentences conform to this pattern.

According to the good-enough hypothesis, our typical comprehension goal is not to make sure we are not misunderstanding sentences but to produce "good enough" representations that will do for everyday purposes. As a result, our sentence processing will often be deficient if we are hearing or reading sentences with rare syntactic structures.

It further follows from the good-enough approach that readers will only process sentences thoroughly if there is a good reason to do so. In line with this prediction, Swets et al. (2008) observed that participants read syntactically ambiguous sentences more slowly only when anticipating detailed comprehension questions about the ambiguity than when expecting superficial comprehension questions unrelated to the ambiguity. In the latter case, the ambiguous sentences were often read *more* rapidly than the non-ambiguous ones, because the participants didn't care about whether they correctly understood all the details of the sentences.

FROM SENTENCES TO CONVERSATION

So far we have focused on the processes involved in understanding individual words and sentences. In real life, however, we are generally presented with discourse (written text or speech at least several sentences in length). The processes involved in making sense of discourse overlap considerably with those involved in making sense of individual sentences. However, processing discourse is more complex. Consider the following two discourse extracts: "Peter was walking on thin ice. He drowned." vs. "Peter was eating a red apple. He drowned." In terms of word difficulty and syntactic structure, both stories are matched. Still, the second is perceived as more difficult than the second. Why?

Inferences based on word knowledge and schemas

Rumelhart and Ortony (1977) used the following text to illustrate what happens when we combine sentences into discourse.

Mary heard the ice cream man coming.
She remembered her pocket money.
She rushed into the house.

Suppose you were to explain this story to an alien landing on Earth, who has just digested an English dictionary and grammar, but who is not yet familiar with our way of life. Then you'd probably have to tell something like this:

An ice cream man is someone who comes around selling ice cream, a substance made of milk, fruit extracts, and sugar that children like very much. Usually, the ice cream man uses some signal such as a melody to announce his arrival. This is what Mary heard. Mary probably is a child. Mary wanted to have an ice cream, but for that you have to pay. Luckily, Mary remembered she had pocket money. This money is usually stored in the house. So, Mary ran into the house to collect her money. Once this is done, Mary is likely to come out of the house and run to the ice cream man to buy ice cream. Usually the ice cream man waits a few moments to give customers time to come and buy ice cream. When a person appears in consecutive sentences, we often replace their full names by pronouns. So, we do not say "Mary heard the ice cream man and Mary ran to the ice cream man," but we say "Mary heard the ice cream man and she ran to him." For this reason, Mary is replaced by the pronoun "she" in the second and third sentence."

Not sure whether the alien would understand everything based on the description so far, but Mary's story shows that we often add a lot of world knowledge to a message when we process it. The implicit addition of world knowledge makes it possible for speakers to keep their messages short and to increase the rate of information transmitted.

In Chapter 6 we saw that world knowledge is packaged in *schemas*, sets of propositions describing things, events, and people. Upon hearing the phrase "ice cream man," we activate the corresponding concept in semantic memory, which in turn activates the schema related to "an ice cream man selling ice cream." This helps us understand the transition from the first to second sentence in the example of Mary, because it allows us to make inferences based on information that is not present in the text. An inference in discourse processing is a logical conclusion derived from information provided in the text and schemas stored in long-term memory.

The fact that we often need inferences to understand the relationship between sentences does not mean that we always make them (Graesser et al., 1994; McKoon & Ratcliff, 1992). Just like we make only good-enough syntactic representations of sentences, we are happy with good-enough representations of stories. We only make the inferences needed to keep the discourse coherent. Occasionally, this can lead to misunderstandings if the speaker and the listener have different ideas of "what is needed."

Key term
Inference: logical conclusion in discourse processing derived from the information given in the discourse and schemas stored in long-term memory.

Calvo (2001) considered the role of individual differences in inference making. He hypothesized that individuals with a high working memory capacity would make more inferences than individuals with low working memory capacity (Chapter 4). Target sentences (e.g., "The pupil studied for an hour approximately") were preceded by a related sentence ("Three days before the examination the pupil went to the library, looked for a separate table and opened his notebook") or an irrelevant control sentence ("The pupil, who was a little tired after finishing his examination, forgot his notebook and left it on a table in the library"). Individuals with high working memory capacity spent less time reading the target sentence when it followed the related sentence rather than the control sentence, suggesting they made an inference connecting both sentences. In contrast, individuals with low working memory capacity did not show a difference in reading speed between the related and the unrelated condition, indicating they were less likely to make inferences in order to better understand the discourse.

The difficulty of understanding discourse without appropriate schemas

Why are schemas important? First, they contain much of the information needed to understand what we hear and read. Second, schemas allow us to form *expectations* (e.g., of the sequence of events in a restaurant). They make the world relatively predictable because our expectations are generally confirmed.

The importance of schemas was illustrated magnificently by Bransford and Johnson (1972). They asked students to read and remember the following text for a subsequent test:

If the balloons popped, the sound wouldn't be able to carry since everything would be too far away from the correct floor. A closed window would also prevent the sound from carrying, since most buildings tend to be well insulated. Since the whole operation depends on a steady flow of electricity, a break in the middle of the wire would also cause problems. Of course, the fellow could shout, but the human voice is not loud enough to carry that far. An additional problem is that a string could break on the instrument. Then there could be no accompaniment to the message. It is clear that the best situation would involve less distance. Then there would be fewer potential problems. With face to face contact, the least number of things could go wrong.

If you found the text difficult to understand, you are like the participants in Bransford and Johnson (1972). Understanding was much better if the participants received the picture shown in Figure 8.17 before reading the text. Then they understood and remembered much more from the text, because they could activate the required background knowledge.

Inexperienced writers (e.g., undergraduate students writing their first reports or their thesis) often underestimate the importance of schemas for the readers. Because they have all the information in their mind during writing, they often forget that the reader may not have access to the same information and as a result may not understand what the text is about. To prevent this from happening, it is usually enough to add a single sentence or title introducing the schema at the beginning of the text, as shown in the Research Activity box, also from Bransford and Johnson (1972).

Research Activity 8.1 *Story comprehension*

Read the following passage taken from Bransford and Johnson (1972, p. 722) and try to make sense of it:

> The procedure is quite simple. First, you arrange items into different groups. Of course one pile may be sufficient depending on how much there is to do. If you have to go somewhere else due to lack of facilities, that is the next step; otherwise, you are pretty well set. It is important not to overdo things. That is, it is better to do too few things at once than too many. In the short run this may not seem important, but complications from doing too much can easily arise. A mistake can be expensive as well. The manipulation of the appropriate mechanisms should be self-explanatory, and we need not dwell on it here. Soon, however, it will become just another fact of life. It is difficult to foresee any end to the necessity for this task in the immediate future, but then one never can tell.

Probably you found it difficult to make sense of the passage. The reason is that you lacked the relevant schema. Now let's add the title "Washing clothes." Now reread the passage, which should be much easier to understand armed with that schematic information.

In their study, Bransford and Johnson (1972) found that participants hearing the passage in the absence of a title rated it as incomprehensible and recalled an average of only 2.8 idea units. In contrast, those supplied beforehand with the title "Washing clothes" found it easier to understand and recalled 5.8 idea units on average. Relevant schema knowledge helped *comprehension* rather than simply acting as a retrieval cue. We know this because participants receiving the title *after* hearing the passage but *before* recall produced only 2.6 idea units on average.

Keep this example in mind when you have to write your next text. Are you giving the reader enough information to know which schema to activate?

Pragmatics

Inferences concern not only the *literal* meaning of sentences but also the meaning *intended* by the speaker or writer. When someone asks you "Could you pass me the salt?" they would be surprised (and possibly offended) if you answered "Yes," even though literally this is a legitimate answer. Similarly, when someone tells you Hitler was a butcher, they may not appreciate it if you told them that technically Hitler was not a butcher, because he never properly learned how to cut meat.

Announcements also often have a different intention than suggested by a literal interpretation of the text, as can be concluded from the following examples. At a university a notice was posted at the entry of the student restaurant saying "Shoes are required to eat in the dining halls." Underneath the notice a student had written "but socks can eat wherever they like." Similarly, in a school a notice was hung above a coat stand, saying: "Only for teachers." Here too a student added "and for coats."

Pragmatics is concerned with practical language and comprehension, especially those aspects going beyond the speaker's literal meaning by taking account of the social context. Thus, pragmatics deals with *intended* rather than *literal* meaning as expressed by speakers and understood by listeners. Cases in which the intended meaning is not the same as the literal meaning include irony, sarcasm, and understatement. For example, we assume that someone who says, "The weather's really great!" when it has been raining nonstop for several days actually thinks the weather is terrible.

There are two ways in which listeners are assisted in the task of deciding on the speaker's intended meaning. First, they often find it easier to understand what the speaker means if they focus on the knowledge and beliefs they

Key term
Pragmatics: in sentence comprehension, using the social context and other information to work out the intended meaning of what is said.

Figure 8.17 Schemas help to understand texts. In the study of Bransford and Johnson (1972), participants had difficulty understanding a text they were asked to read, unless they were shown this picture before starting to read the text.

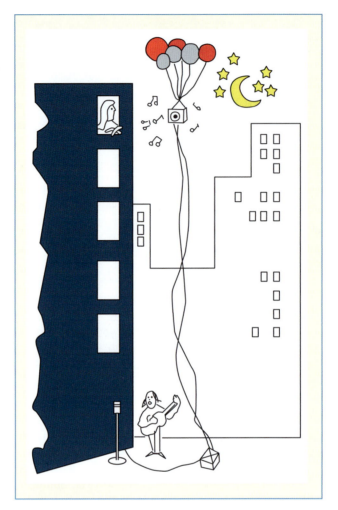

share with the speaker. This is easier when you are familiar with the speaker, meaning that people often struggle with pragmatics when they arrive in a new social environment (when they go to a new school or change work). Then they often experience that the new people they interact with mean something else than the literal meaning of what they say. In particular, irony and sarcasm are difficult to grasp if you are unfamiliar with the speaker (or writer).

Second, when we are listening to a sentence, we can often obtain useful information from the speaker's accompanying gestures. These gestures frequently contain cues about how the message should be understood.

Listeners typically try to work out the speaker's intentions from what he/she has just said. Consider the following example (Holtgraves, 1998, p. 25):

Ken: Did Paula agree to go out with you?
Bob: She's not my type.

Holtgraves found that most people interpreted Bob's reply as meaning that Paula hadn't agreed to go with him, but he wanted to save face.

Suppose Bob gave an indirect reply that didn't seem to involve face saving (e.g., "She's my type"). Listeners took almost 50% longer to comprehend such indirect replies than to comprehend typical indirect replies (e.g., "She's not my type"). This was because it was hard to understand the speaker's motivation with the unexpected indirect reply.

How rapidly do listeners understand the speaker's intention? Holtgraves (2008a) explored this issue. Participants read or listened to part of a conversation (e.g., Bob says to Andy, "I definitely will do it tomorrow"). This was followed by a single word (e.g., "promise"), with participants deciding rapidly whether the word captured the speaker's/writer's intention.

Holtgraves' (2008a) key finding was that participants recognized the speaker's/writer's intention rapidly and automatically. The speaker's intention is also well-remembered (Holtgraves, 2008b). This suggests that listeners regard it as especially important to focus on the speaker's intention or intentions.

Common ground

Pragmatics illustrates that it is often not enough to identify a speaker's literal message correctly. What is important is the shared knowledge and beliefs between speaker and listener. This is called the common ground. A lack of common ground is the reason why you often find it hard to understand what is being said when you overhear a conversation between two people who know each other well, even though you understand all the words they are saying. A lack of common ground is also the reason why ironic and sarcastic message in social media are often misunderstood.

As you may have guessed from what we have seen thus far, listeners are not always motivated to fully work out the common ground between them and the speaker, because it is too effortful. According to Keysar et al. (2000), listeners often use a rapid and non-effortful rule of thumb known as the egocentric heuristic. This involves listeners interpreting what they hear based on their own knowledge rather than on knowledge shared with the speaker.

Keysar et al. (2000) obtained evidence consistent with use of the egocentric heuristic. For example, consider what happened when a listener could see *three* candles of different sizes but a speaker could see only *two*. The speaker (a confederate of the experimenter) said to move the small candle. If the listener used common ground information, he/she would move the smaller of the two candles the speaker could see. However, if the listener used the egocentric heuristic, he/she would consider all three candles, including the candle the speaker couldn't see. In fact, listeners' initial eye movements were often directed to the candle only they could see, and they reached for that object on 20% of trials.

Which listeners are most likely to ignore the common ground? This question was addressed by Brown-Schmidt (2009). Listeners who had deficient inhibitory control were more likely to interpret what the speaker said inappropriately and less likely to make use of common-ground information.

Another group of people who have difficulty using common ground to understand pragmatics are people with autism spectrum disorder (Rapin & Dunn, 2003). Happé (1994) reported that they often gave wrong answers to questions from an IQ test, because they did not take into account the pragmatics of the questions. So, when asked "What should you do when you cut your finger?" they replied "I'd bleed."

Heller et al. (2016) argued that for most people in most situations common ground and egocentric knowledge should not be seen as mutually exclusive, with listeners either using only the egocentric heuristic or only the common ground. The authors provided evidence that both sources of information are typically used but in different proportions depending on the precise details of the task.

Section summary

Word recognition

- Words are easier to produce and recognize when they are frequent, acquired early, short, and primed by the preceding context.

Sentence parsing

- To understand the relations between the words of a sentence, humans build a syntactic tree consisting of a hierarchy of clauses, phrases, and word types. The tree is built online as the sentence is being processed. From time to time, the construction is impeded because of syntactic ambiguities.
- According to the garden-path theory, only the syntactically simplest construction is pursued and needs to be revised if it turns out to be wrong. According to the constraint-based theory, all sources of information (word-related, syntactic, semantic, world knowledge) are used from the outset during sentence comprehension.
- When there is a conflict between the syntactic structure of a sentence and listeners' knowledge of the world, they often favor semantic knowledge at the expense of syntactic structure. More generally, listeners (and readers) are often content with "good enough" representations that are inaccurate.

Discourse understanding

- We use schemas when processing discourse to make inferences about information needed to understand the discourse but not present in the message. Schemas enhance the comprehension and retrieval of discourse. We usually do not make more inferences than needed for good-enough representations. People with high working memory capacity make more inferences than people with low working memory capacity.
- To understand the intended meaning (the pragmatics) of a message, we often have to focus on the speaker's goals rather than on the literal meaning of the message. This requires common ground between the speaker and the listener. Again, we do not always manage to establish common ground (leading to misunderstandings), and there are individual differences in the ability to do so.

Essay questions

1. Which stages are involved when speakers want to say something?
2. To what extent do speakers plan what they are going to say?
3. Describe some of the main speech errors. Why do we make these errors?
4. Describe and evaluate the computational models of spoken word recognition.
5. What sources of information do listeners use to understand what speakers are saying?
6. Describe the eye movements involved in reading.
7. Describe the evidence indicating that phonology is involved in reading and discuss the computational models describing the processes involved. Which model do you prefer and why?

8. What challenges do students with dyslexia face? Can they be overcome?
9. Which words take more time to understand and how can you investigate this?
10. Why is syntax an essential component of language understanding? How is it derived?
11. Why are vocabulary and grammar knowledge not enough to understand language?
12. Are there individual differences in language processing?

Further reading

- Harley, T. A. (2014). *The psychology of language: From data to theory* (4th ed.). Hove, UK: Psychology Press. An excellent textbook with detailed information about the processes involved in visual and auditory language processing.
- Boelte, J., Goldrick, M., & Zwitserlood, P. (2009). *Language production: Sublexical, lexical, and supralexical information*. New York, NY: Psychology Press. Many key issues in language production are addressed fully by leading experts in the area.
- Rayner, K., Pollatsek, A., Ashby, J., & Clifton, C. (2012). *Psychology of reading* (2nd ed.). New York: Psychology Press. An outstanding textbook on reading.
- Gaskell, G. (Ed.). (2007). *Oxford handbook of psycholinguistics*. Oxford, UK: Oxford University Press. Another useful handbook with chapters by leading experts on major topics in language processing.
- Evans, N., & Levinson, S. C. (2009). The myth of language universals: Language diversity and its importance for cognitive science. *Behavioral and Brain Sciences, 32*, 429–448. This article indicates the numerous differences that exist among the world's languages. These differences highlight the limitations in most research, which has focused on English and other major European languages.
- de Groot, A.M.B. (2011). *Language and cognition in bilinguals and multilinguals*. New York: Psychology Press. You may have noticed that our chapter is limited to language processing in the native language. There is a rich literature on language processing in non-native languages, which we could not cover because of size constraints. This book is a good introduction to this literature.

REFERENCES

Abrams, L. (2008). Tip-of-the-tongue states yield language insights: The process of turning thoughts into speech changes with age. *American Scientist, 96*, 234–239.

Allopenna, P. D., Magnuson, J. S., & Tanenhaus, M. K. (1998). Tracking the time course of spoken word recognition using eye movements: Evidence for continuous mapping models. *Journal of Memory and Language, 38*(4), 419–439.

Altenberg, B. (1990). Speech as linear composition. In G. Caie et al. (Eds.), *Proceedings from the fourth nordic conference for English studies*. Copenhagen, Denmark: Copenhagen University Press.

Baars, B. J., Motley, M. T., & MacKay, D. G. (1975). Output editing for lexical status from artificially elicited slips of the tongue. *Journal of Verbal Learning and Verbal Behavior, 14*, 382–391.

Barber, H. A., Donamayor, N., Kutgas, M., & Munte, T. (2010). Parafoveal N400 effect during sentence reading. *Neuroscience Letters, 479*, 152–156.

Berndt, R. S., Mitchum, C. C., Haendiges, A. N., & Sandson, J. (1997). Verb retrieval in aphasia. I. Characterizing single word impairments. *Brain and Language, 56*, 69–106.

Berninger, V. W. (Ed.). (2012). *Past, present, and future contributions of cognitive writing research to cognitive psychology*. New York: Taylor & Francis.

Bertram, R., & Hyönä, J. (2003). The length of a complex word modifies the role of morphological structure: Evidence from eye movements when reading short and long Finnish compounds. *Journal of Memory and Language, 48*(3), 615–634.

Bock, K., & Cutting, J. C. (1992). Regulating mental energy: Performance units in language production. *Journal of Memory and Language, 31*(1), 99–127.

Boland, J. E., & Blodgett, A. (2001). Understanding the constraints on syntactic generation: Lexical bias and discourse congruency effects on eye movements. *Journal of Memory and Language, 45*, 391–411.

Bransford, J. D., & Johnson, M. K. (1972). Contextual prerequisites for understanding. *Journal of Verbal Learning and Verbal Behavior, 11*, 717–726.

Brown, R., & McNeill, D. N. (1966). The "tip of the tongue" phenomenon. *Journal of Verbal Learning and Verbal Behavior, 5*, 325–337.

Brown-Schmidt, S. (2009). The role of executive function in perspective taking during online language comprehension. *Psychonomic Bulletin & Review, 16*, 893–900.

Brysbaert, M., Stevens, M., Mandera, P., & Keuleers, E. (2016). How many words do we know? Practical estimates of vocabulary size dependent on word definition, the degree of language input and the participant's age. *Frontiers in Psychology, 7*, 1116.

Callens, M., Tops, W., & Brysbaert, M. (2012). Cognitive profile of students who enter higher education with an indication of dyslexia. *PLoS One, 7*(6), e38081.

Calvo, M. G. (2001). Working memory and inferences: Evidence from eye fixations during reading. *Memory, 9*, 365–381.

Caplan, D., Hildebrandt, N., & Makris, N. (1996). Location of lesions in stroke patients with deficits in syntactic processing in sentence comprehension. *Brain, 119*(3), 933–949.

Chomsky, N. (1965). *Aspects of the theory of syntax*. Cambridge, MA: MIT Press.

Christiansen, M. H., & Chater, N. (2008). Language as shaped by the brain. *Behavioral and Brain Sciences, 31*, 489–512.

Christianson, K. (2016). When language comprehension goes wrong for the right reasons: Good-enough, underspecified, or shallow language processing. *The Quarterly Journal of Experimental Psychology, 69*(5), 817–828.

Cleland, A. A., & Pickering, M. J. (2003). The use of lexical and syntactic information in language production: Evidence from the priming of noun-phrase structure. *Journal of Memory and Language, 49*, 214–230.

Coltheart, M., & Rastle, K. (1994). Serial processing in reading aloud: Evidence for dual-route models of reading. *Journal of Experimental Psychology: Human Perception and Performance, 20*(6), 1197–1211.

Coltheart, M., Rastle, K., Perry, C., Langdon, R., & Ziegler, J. (2001). DRC: A dual route cascaded model of visual word recognition and reading aloud. *Psychological Review, 108*(1), 204–256.

Crystal, D. (1997). *A dictionary of linguistics and phonetics* (4th ed.). Cambridge, MA: Blackwell.

Cutler, A., & Bruggeman, L. (2013). Vocabulary structure and spoken-word recognition: Evidence from French reveals the source of embedding asymmetry. In *INTERSPEECH 2013: 14th annual conference of the International Speech Communication Association* (pp. 2812–2816). Available at: https://pdfs. semanticscholar.org/7b5d/a80cd0a4acbe3c5b639a37d9dbb00576ccaa.pdf

De Jong, P. F., Bitter, D. J. L., van Setten, M., & Marinus, E. (2009). Does phonological recoding occur during silent reading, and is it necessary for orthographic learning? *Journal of Experimental Child Psychology, 104*, 267–282.

Dehaene, S., Pegado, F., Braga, L. W., Ventura, P., Nunes Filho, G., Jobert, A., . . . Cohen, L. (2010). How learning to read changes the cortical networks for vision and language. *Science, 330*(6009), 1359–1364.

Dell, G. S. (1986). A spreading-activation theory of retrieval in sentence production. *Psychological Review, 93*, 283–321.

Dell, G. S., Burger, L. K., & Svec, W. R. (1997). Language production and serial order: A functional analysis and a model. *Psychological Review, 93*, 283–321.

Dell, G. S., Oppenheim, G. M., & Kittredge, A. K. (2008). Saying the right word at the right time: Syntagmatic and paradigmatic interference in sentence production. *Language and Cognitive Processes, 23*, 583–608.

Ehri, L. C., Nunes, S. R., Willows, D. M., Schuster, B. V., Yaghoub-Zadeh, Z., & Shanahan, T. (2001). Phonemic awareness instruction helps children learn to read: Evidence from the National Reading Panel's meta-analysis. *Reading Research Quarterly, 36*, 250–287.

Engbert, R., Nuthmann, A., Richter, E. M., & Kliegl, R. (2005). SWIFT: A dynamical model of saccade generation during reading. *Psychological Review, 112*, 777–813.

Ferreira, F. (2003). The misinterpretation of noncanonical sentences. *Cognitive Psychology, 47*, 164–203.

Ferreira, F., & Swets, B. (2002). How incremental is language production? Evidence from the production of utterances requiring the computation of arithmetic sums. *Journal of Memory and Language, 46*, 57–84.

Ferreira, F., Bailey, K. G. D., & Ferraro, V. (2002). Good enough representations in language comprehension. *Current Directions in Psychological Science, 11*, 11–15.

Ferreira, V. S., & Griffin, Z. M. (2003). Phonological influences on lexical (mis) selection. *Psychological Science, 14*, 86–90.

Frazier, L., & Rayner, K. (1982). Making and correcting errors in the analysis of structurally ambiguous sentences. *Cognitive Psychology, 14*, 178–210.

Gaskell, M. G., & Marslen-Wilson, W. D. (1997). Integrating form and meaning: A distributed model of speech perception. *Language and Cognitive Processes, 12*(5–6), 613–656.

Glaser, W. R. (1992). Picture naming. *Cognition, 42*, 61–105.

Glushko, R. J. (1979). The organization and activation of orthographic knowledge in reading aloud. *Journal of Experimental Psychology: Human Perception and Performance, 5*, 674–691.

Gollan, T. H., & Acenas, L. A. R. (2004). What is a TOT? Cognate and translation effects on tip-of-the-tongue states in Spanish-English and Tagalog-English bilinguals. *Journal of Experimental Psychology: Learning, Memory, and Cognition, 30*(1), 246–269.

Goodman, K. S. (1986). *What's whole in whole language*. Berkeley, CA: RDR Books.

Graesser, A. C., Singer, M., & Trabasso, T. (1994). Constructing inferences during narrative text comprehension. *Psychological Review, 101*(3), 371–395.

Grigorenko, E. L. (2001). Developmental dyslexia: An update on genes, brains, and environments. *Journal of Child Psychology and Psychiatry, 42*(1), 91–125.

Hanson, V. L., Goodell, E. W., & Perfetti, C. A. (1991). Tongue-twister effects in the silent reading of hearing and deaf college students. *Journal of Memory and Language, 30*(3), 319–330.

Happé, F. G. (1994). Wechsler IQ profile and theory of mind in autism: A research note. *Journal of Child Psychology and Psychiatry, 35*(8), 1461–1471.

Harley, T. A. (2014). *The psychology of language: From data to theory*. New York: Taylor & Francis.

Harley, T. A., & Bown, H. E. (1998). What causes a tip-of-the-tongue state? Evidence for lexical neighborhood effects in speech production. *British Journal of Psychology, 89*, 151–174.

Harm, M. W., & Seidenberg, M. S. (2004). Computing the meanings of words in reading: Cooperative division of labor between visual and phonological processes. *Psychological Review, 111*(3), 662–720.

Hartsuiker, R. J., Corley, M., & Martensen, H. (2005). The lexical bias effect is modulated by context, but the standard monitoring account doesn't fly: Related reply to Baars et al. (1975). *Journal of Memory and Language, 52*, 58–70.

Heller, D., Parisien, C., & Stevenson, S. (2016). Perspective-taking behavior as the probabilistic weighing of multiple domains. *Cognition, 149*, 104–120.

Hickok, G. (2012). Computational neuroanatomy of speech production. *Nature Reviews Neuroscience, 13*(2), 135–145.

Holtgraves, T. (1998). Interpreting indirect replies. *Cognitive Psychology, 37*, 1–27.

Holtgraves, T. (2008a). Automatic intention recognition in conversation processing. *Journal of Memory and Language, 58*, 627–645.

Holtgraves, T. (2008b). Conversation, speech acts, and memory. *Memory & Cognition, 36*, 361–374.

Hotopf, W. H. N. (1980). Slips of the pen. In U. Frith (Ed.), *Cognitive processes in spelling*. London, UK: Academic Press.

Hulme, C., Nash, H. M., Gooch, D., Lervåg, A., & Snowling, M. J. (2015). The foundations of literacy development in children at familial risk of dyslexia. *Psychological Science, 26*(12), 1877–1886.

Janssen, N., Alario, F.-X., & Caramazza, A. (2008). A word-order constraint on phonological activation. *Psychological Science, 19*, 216–220.

Karimi, H., & Ferreira, F. (2016). Good-enough linguistic representations and online cognitive equilibrium in language processing. *The Quarterly Journal of Experimental Psychology, 69*(5), 1013–1040.

Kendeou, P., Savage, R., & van den Broek, P. (2009). Revisiting the simple view of reading. *British Journal of Educational Psychology, 79*, 353–370.

Keuleers, E., Lacey, P., Rastle, K., & Brysbaert, M. (2012). The British Lexicon Project: Lexical decision data for 28,730 monosyllabic and disyllabic English words. *Behavior Research Methods, 44*, 287–304.

Keysar, B., Barr, D. J., Balin, J. A., & Brauner, J. S. (2000). Taking perspectives in conversation: The role of mutual knowledge in comprehension. *Psychological Science, 11*, 32–38.

Klatt, E. C., & Klatt, C. A. (2011). How much is too much reading for medical students? Assigned reading and reading rates at one medical school. *Academic Medicine, 86*(9), 1079–1083.

Kuiper, K. (1996). *Smooth talkers*. Mahwah, NJ: Lawrence Erlbaum.

Kuperberg, G. R., & Jaeger, T. F. (2016). What do we mean by prediction in language comprehension? *Language, Cognition and Neuroscience, 31*(1), 32–59.

Levelt, W. J. M., Roelofs, A., & Meyer, A. S. (1999). A theory of lexical access in speech production. *Behavioral and Brain Sciences, 22*, 1–38.

Lukatela, G., & Turvey, M. T. (1994). Visual lexical access is initially phonological: I. Evidence from associative priming by words, homophones, and pseudohomophones. *Journal of Experimental Psychology: General, 123*(2), 107–128.

MacDonald, M. C., Pearlmutter, N. J., & Seidenberg, M. S. (1994). Lexical nature of syntactic ambiguity resolution. *Psychological Review, 101*, 676–703.

Marques, L. M., Lapenta, O. M., Costa, T. L., & Boggio, P. S. (2016). Multisensory integration processes underlying speech perception as revealed by the McGurk illusion. *Language, Cognition and Neuroscience, 31*, 1115–1129.

Martin, R. C., Crowther, J. E., Knight, M., Tamborello, F. P., & Yang, C. L. (2010). Planning in sentence production: Evidence for the phrase as a default planning scope. *Cognition*, *116*, 177–192.

Martin, R. C., Miller, M., & Vu. H. (2004). Lexical–semantic retention and speech production: Further evidence from normal and brain-damaged participants for a phrasal scope of planning. *Cognitive Neuropsychology*, *21*, 625–644.

Mattys, S. L., Brooks, J., & Cooke, M. (2009). Recognizing speech under a processing load: Dissociating energetic from informational factors. *Cognitive Psychology*, *59*, 203–243.

McClelland, J. L. (1991). Stochastic interactive processes and the effect of context on perception. *Cognitive Psychology*, *23*, 1–44.

McClelland, J. L., & Elman, J. L. (1986). The TRACE model of speech perception. *Cognitive Psychology*, *18*, 1–86.

McDonald, J. L. (2008). Differences in the cognitive demands of word order, plural, and subject – verb agreement constructions. *Psychonomic Bulletin & Review*, *15*, 980–984.

McGurk, H., & MacDonald, J. (1976). Hearing lips and seeing voices. *Nature*, *264*, 746–748.

McKoon, G., & Ratcliff, R. (1992). Inference during reading. *Psychological Review*, *99*, 440–466.

McQueen, J. M. (1991). The influence of the lexicon on phonetic categorization: Stimulus quality in word-final ambiguity. *Journal of Experimental Psychology: Human Perception & Performance*, *17*, 433–443.

Meyer, A. S. (1996). Lexical access in phrase and sentence production: Results from picture–word interference experiments. *Journal of Memory and Language*, *35*, 477–496.

Meyer, A. S., & Damian, M. F. (2007). Activation of distractor names in the picture–picture interference paradigm. *Memory & Cognition*, *35*, 494–503.

Mirman, D., McClelland, J. L., Holt, L. L., & Magnuson, J. S. (2008). Effects of attention on the strength of lexical influences on speech perception: Behavioral experiments and computational mechanisms. *Cognitive Science*, *32*, 398–417.

Monaghan, P., Chang, Y. N., Welbourne, S., & Brysbaert, M. (2017). Exploring the relations between word frequency, language exposure, and bilingualism in a computational model of reading. *Journal of Memory and Language*, *93*, 1–21.

Nation, K., & Cocksey, J. (2009). The relationship between knowing a word and reading it aloud in children's word reading development. *Journal of Experimental Child Psychology*, *103*, 296–308.

Nooteboom, S., & Quené, H. (2008). Self-monitoring and feedback: A new attempt to find the main cause of lexical bias in phonological speech errors. *Journal of Memory and Language*, *58*, 837–861.

OECD (2016). *Low-performing students: Why they fall behind and how to help them succeeed. PISA*. Paris: OECD Publishing. Retrieved November 2, 2016, from www.oecd.org/publications/low-performing-students-9789264250246-en.htm

Pattamadilok, C., Perre, L., Defau, S., & Ziegler, J. C. (2008). On-line orthographic influences on spoken language in a semantic task. *Journal of Cognitive Neuroscience*, *21*(1), 169–179.

Perre, L., & Ziegler, J. C. (2008). On-line activation of orthography in spoken word recognition. *Brain Research*, *1188*, 132–138.

Perre, L., Pattamadilok, C., Montant, M., & Ziegler, J. C. (2010). Orthographic effects in spoken language: On-line activation or phonological restructuring? *Brain Research*, *1275*, 73–80.

Peterson, R. L., & Pennington, B. F. (2015). Developmental dyslexia. *Annual Review of Clinical Psychology, 11,* 283–307.

Pickering, M. J., & Ferreira, V. S. (2008). Structural priming: A critical review. *Psychological Bulletin, 134,* 427–459.

Pickering, M. J., & Garrod, S. (2004). Toward a mechanistic psychology of dialog. *Behavioral and Brain Sciences, 27,* 169–226.

Pyers, J. E., Gollan, T. H., & Emmorey, K. (2009). Biomodal bilinguals reveal the source of tip-of-thetongue states. *Cognition, 112,* 323–329.

Rapin, I., & Dunn, M. (2003). Update on the language disorders of individuals on the autistic spectrum. *Brain and Development, 25*(3), 166–172.

Rastle, K., & Brysbaert, M. (2006). Masked phonological priming effects in English: Are they real? Do they matter? *Cognitive Psychology, 53,* 97–145.

Reichle, E. D. (2015). Computational models of reading: A primer. *Language and Linguistic Compass, 9,* 271–284.

Reichle, E. D., & Drieghe, D. (2015). Using E-Z Reader to examine the consequences of fixation-location measurement error. *Journal of Experimental Psychology Learning Memory and Cognition, 41*(1), 262–270.

Reichle, E. D., Liversedge, S. P., Drieghe, D., Blythe, H. I., Joseph, H. S. S. L., White, S. J., & Rayner, K. (2013). Using E-Z Reader to examine the concurrent development of eye movement control and reading skill. *Developmental Review, 33,* 110–149.

Rumelhart, D. E., & Ortony, A. (1977). The representation of knowledge in memory. In R. C. Anderson, R. J. Spiro, & W. E. Montague (Eds.), *Schooling and the acquisition of knowledge.* Hillsdale, NJ: Lawrence Erlbaum.

Samuelson, L. K., & McMurray, B. (2017). What does it take to learn a word? *Wiley Interdisciplinary Reviews: Cognitive Science, 8,* 1–10.

Sauval, K., Perre, L., Duncan, L. G., Marinus, E., & Casalis, S. (2017). Automatic phonological activation during visual word recognition in bilingual children: A cross-language masked priming study in grades 3 and 5. *Journal of Experimental Child Psychology, 154,* 64–77.

Segal, O., Hejli-Assi, S., & Kishon-Rabin, L. (2016). The effect of listening experience on the discrimination of/ba/and/pa/in Hebrew-learning and Arabic-learning infants. *Infant Behavior and Development, 42,* 86–99.

Senghas, A., Kita, S., & Özyürek, A. (2004). Children creating core properties of language: Evidence from an emerging sign language in Nicaragua. *Science, 305,* 1779–1782.

Seymour, P. H. K., Aro, M., Erskine, J. M., Wimmer, H., Leybaert, J., Elbro, C., et al. (2003). Foundation literacy acquisition in European orthographies. *British Journal of Psychology, 94,* 143–174.

Share, D. L. (2008). On the Anglocentricities of current reading research and practice: The perils of overreliance on an "outlier" orthography. *Psychological Bulletin, 134,* 584–615.

Smith, J. D., & Minda, J. P. (2000). Thirty categorization results in search of a model. *Journal of Experimental Psychology: Learning, Memory, & Cognition, 26,* 3–27.

Stadthagen-Gonzalez, H., Bowers, J. S., & Damian, M. F. (2004). Age-of-acquisition effects in visual word recognition: Evidence from expert vocabularies. *Cognition, 93*(1), B11–B26.

Swanson, H. L., & Hsieh, C. J. (2009). Reading disabilities in adults: A selective meta-analysis of the literature. *Review of Educational Research, 79*(4), 1362–1390.

Swets, B., Desmet, T., Clifton, C., & Ferreira, F. (2008). Underspecification of syntactic ambiguities: Evidence from self-paced reading. *Memory & Cognition, 36,* 201–216.

Taylor, J. S. H., Rastle, K., & Davis, M. H. (2013). Can cognitive models explain brain activation during word and pseudoword reading? A meta-analysis of 36 neuroimaging studies. *Psychological Bulletin*, *139*(4), 766–791.

Thompson, P. A., Hulme, C., Nash, H. M., Gooch, D., Hayiou-Thomas, E., & Snowling, M. J. (2015). Developmental dyslexia: Predicting individual risk. *Journal of Child Psychology and Psychiatry*, *56*(9), 976–987.

Van Gompel, R. P. G., Pickering, M. J., Pearson, J., & Liversedge, S. P. (2005). Evidence against competition during syntactic ambiguity resolution. *Journal of Memory and Language*, *52*, 284–307.

Van Orden, G. C. (1987). A rows is a rose: Spelling, sound and reading. *Memory & Cognition*, *14*, 371–386.

Vigliocco, G., & Hartsuiker, R. J. (2002). The interplay of meaning, sound, and syntax in sentence production. *Psychological Bulletin*, *128*, 442–472.

Vousden, J. L., & Maylor, E. A. (2006). Speech errors across the lifespan. *Language and Cognitive Processes*, *21*, 48–77.

Wagner, V., Jescheniak, J. D., & Schriefers, H. (2010). On the flexibility of grammatical advance planning: Effects of cognitive load on multiple lexical access. *Journal of Experimental Psychology: Learning, Memory, and Cognition*, *36*, 423–440.

Warmington, M., Stothard, S. E., & Snowling, M. J. (2013). Assessing dyslexia in higher education: The York adult assessment battery-revised. *Journal of Research in Special Educational Needs*, *13*(1), 48–56.

Weber, A., & Scharenborg, O. (2012). Models of spoken-word recognition. *Wiley Interdisciplinary Reviews: Cognitive Science*, *3*(3), 387–401.

Werker, J. F., & Tees, R. C. (1984). Cross-language speech perception: Evidence for perceptual reorganization during the first year of life. *Infant Behavior and Development*, *7*(1), 49–63.

Windmann, S. (2004). Effects of sentence context and expectation on the McGurk illusion. *Journal of Memory and Language*, *50*(2), 212–230.

Zevin, J. D., & Seidenberg, M. S. (2006). Simulating consistency effects and individual differences in nonword naming: A comparison of current models. *Journal of Memory and Language*, *54*, 145–160.

Chapter 9

Contents

Problem solving

9

INTRODUCTION

Life presents us with plenty of problems, although thankfully the great majority are fairly trivial ones. We have the problem of working out how to mend our bicycle, how to get hold of a crucial reference for an essay that needs to be handed in on Friday, how to analyze the data from last week's laboratory exercise or practical, and so on.

What do we mean by problem solving? There are three main aspects:

1. It is purposeful (i.e., goal-directed).
2. It involves deliberate or controlled processes and so isn't totally reliant on automatic processes.
3. A problem exists only when the person trying to solve it lacks the relevant knowledge to produce an immediate solution. Thus, a mathematical calculation may be a problem for most of us but not for a professional mathematician.

There are important differences among problems. **Well-defined problems** are ones in which all aspects of the problem are clearly specified, including the initial state or situation, the range of possible moves or strategies, and the goal or solution. The goal is well specified in the sense that it is clear when the goal has been reached. Figure 9.1 shows one of the most famous well-defined problems, called the Tower of Hanoi. Try to solve it (you can also replace Figure 9.1 by three coins of different sizes). Can you solve the problem in seven steps?

| Key terms |

Well-defined problems: problems in which the initial state, the goal, and the methods available for solving them are clearly laid out; see **ill-defined problems**.

Ill-defined problems: problems in which the definition of the problem statement is imprecisely specified; the initial state, goal state, and methods to be used to solve the problem may be unclear; see **well-defined problems**.

Knowledge-rich problems: problems that can only be solved through the use of considerable amounts of relevant prior knowledge; see **knowledge-lean problems**.

Knowledge-lean problems: problems that can be solved without the use of much prior knowledge; most of the necessary information is provided by the problem statement; see **knowledge-rich problems**.

| Learning objectives |

After studying Chapter 9, you should be able to:

- Describe the three main aspects of problem solving.
- Compare and contrast ill-defined and well-defined problems.
- Explain why most laboratory research on problem solving uses well-defined, knowledge-lean problems.
- Define the difference between algorithms and heuristics, give examples of heuristics, and discuss how these are assessed experimentally.

- Define insight, and describe the kinds of problems used in experiments investigating insight.
- Explain what cognitive processes are required by representation change theory in order to solve insight problems.
- Define incubation, and explain how it is used in problem-solving experiments.
- Discuss cognitive advantages (and disadvantages) of having expertise in a particular domain when problem solving within that domain.
- Explain the importance of hypothesis testing and why many people do this in a suboptimal way.

Tower of Hanoi

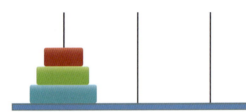

Figure 9.1 The Tower of Hanoi
Your task is to transfer the three disks from rod 1 to rod 3. You can only transfer one disk at a time (the one on the top of a stack) and you are not allowed to place a larger disk on top of a smaller one. The best solution involves seven steps.

Ill-defined problems are underspecified, because it is not clear whether they are solvable, which paths to follow, and whether any given solution is optimal. In all likelihood, you set yourself the goal of passing this academic year. However, there are potentially many strategies you can adopt, and it is hard to know which ones are the most effective, nor whether the end-goal is achievable.

Most problems we are confronted with in life are ill-defined. However, psychologists have focused largely on well-defined problems. Why is this? One important reason is that well-defined problems have a clear solution and a best strategy to reach the solution. This makes it easy to identify the errors and deficiencies in the strategies adopted by human problem solvers.

It is also important to distinguish between knowledge-rich and knowledge-lean problems. **Knowledge-rich problems** can only be solved by those having much relevant specific knowledge. In contrast, **knowledge-lean problems** don't require such knowledge because most of the information needed to solve the problem is contained in the initial problem statement.

Most research on problem solving has involved knowledge-lean problems, in part because this minimizes individual differences in relevant knowledge. However, knowledge-rich problems are very important in the real world. For example, they are the problems faced by scientists when trying to make scientific discoveries. More generally, experts spend most of their working lives dealing with knowledge-rich problems. Expertise is discussed towards the end of the chapter.

In the Real World 9.1 *Monty Hall problem*

We can discuss key issues in solving well-defined problems by considering the notorious Monty Hall problem. It formed a prominent part in a television show by Monty Hall:

Suppose you're on a game show and you're given the choice of three doors. Behind one door is a car, behind the others, goats. You pick a door, say, Number 1. The host (who has full knowledge of what is behind the doors) now opens Door 3. The door he opens has a goat behind it. He then says to you, "Do you want to stay with your initial choice of Door 1 or do you want to switch to Door 2?" Is it to your advantage to switch your choice?

If you decide to stay with your first choice, you are in good company. About 85% of people make that decision (Burns & Wieth, 2004), as did most of those on the TV program. Unfortunately, it is wrong! It seems as if either choice has a 50% chance of being correct. In fact, however, there is a two-thirds chance of being correct if you switch your choice and only one-third if you stay with your initial choice.

Marilyn vos Savant (who was claimed to have the highest IQ in the world: 228) published this problem and its solution in *Parade* magazine in 1990. This triggered thousands of indignant letters

from readers (including nearly 1,000 with PhDs) disagreeing with the correct answer.

It is likely that you furiously disagree with the correct answer. However, you can easily experience its validity yourself. Take three cards. For instance, ace of hearts (car) and jack of spades (goat 1) and jack of clubs (goat 2). Shuffle them and ask a friend to choose a card. Now look at the two remaining cards and take one jack away. Ask your friend whether they want to change. Write down the outcome and play again, until you have convinced yourself and your friend that it is more profitable to change.

Alternatively, consider the analysis of the problem by Krauss and Wang (2003), shown in Figure 9.2. The authors pointed out that there are only three possible arrangements with the Monty Hall problem. You have one chance out of three to pick the car initially.

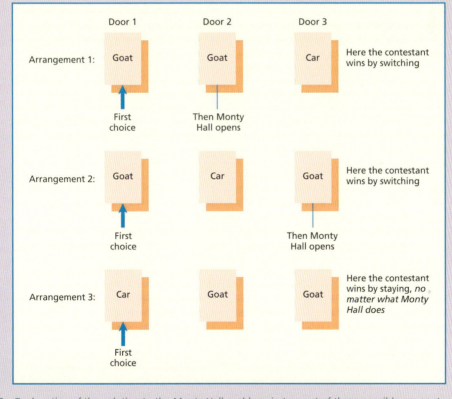

Figure 9.2 Explanation of the solution to the Monty Hall problem: in two out of three possible car-goat arrangements, the contestant wins by switching; therefore she should switch.
Source: From Krauss and Wang, 2003. Reprinted with permission from the American Psychological Association.

The other two-thirds are in the remaining cards. Now the game host tells you that this full probability is located in one card (because they take away a card that is sure to lose). As a result, if you stay, you win only if you initially picked out the car (one chance out of three). If you change, you win whenever you picked a goat (two chances out of three).

Why do most people find the Monty Hall problem so hard? First, the situation is rather ambiguous (even if one strategy is twice as effective as the other). Suppose there were not three doors, but ten. After you choose, eight of the remaining nine doors are opened and you are asked to switch. Probably you would be more willing to switch now! (As you should, because you have 10% chance of winning if you stay, against 90% if you switch.)

Second, people have the illusion that their own choices are better than those of others. Langer (1975) called this the *illusion of control*. In one of the studies described, experimenters sold $1 lottery tickets in offices. Half of the participants could select a lottery ticket from a box, and the other half were simply given a lottery ticket. The next day the experimenters returned to the office and asked whether they could buy the ticket back, as they needed it for someone else. The participants who had been given a ticket were willing to sell it for $1.96 (i.e., nearly double the price they had paid the day before). However, the participants who had selected the ticket from the box required a staggering price of $8.67 before they were willing to sell the ticket, as if the fact that they selected the ticket themselves had magically exploded the chances of winning. Similarly, the Monty Hall problem only works when participants are asked to make the initial choice themselves.

Third, we typically use a heuristic or rule of thumb known as the *uniformity fallacy* (Falk & Lann, 2008). This fallacy involves assuming that all the available options are equally likely and remain equally likely under all conditions. This fallacy leads us to expect that the chances of the remaining door cannot be higher than the one we selected.

Fourth, the Monty Hall problem places substantial demands on the central executive (an attention-like component of working memory, as we have seen in Chapter 4). Participants are even less likely to solve the Monty Hall problem if they perform a demanding task involving the central executive at the same time (8% vs. 22%, according to De Neys & Verschueren, 2006).

Fifth, most people find it hard to think about causality and mistakenly believe that the host's actions are random. Burns and Wieth (2004) made the causal structure of the problem clearer. Suppose a situation in which there are three boxers, one of whom is so good he is certain to win any bout. You select one boxer and then the other two boxers fight each other. The winner of this bout then fights the boxer you selected initially, and you win if you choose the winner of this second bout. You decide whether you want to stay with your initial choice or switch to the winner of the first bout. With this version of the problem, 51% correctly decided to switch versus only 15% with the standard three-door problem. This occurred because it is easy to see that the boxer who won the first bout did so because of skill rather than any random factors.

The fact that so many factors make us humans prefer the wrong strategy explains why the Monty Hall problem is such a counterintuitive problem and why it is hard to convince people of the right strategy. Maybe you keep on doubting even after having read this text?!

Section summary

Introduction
- Problems can be well-defined or ill-defined and knowledge-lean or knowledge-rich. Much laboratory research has focused on well-defined,

> knowledge-lean problems, but many everyday issues we are confronted with are ill-defined, knowledge-rich problems.
>
> **Monty Hall problem**
> - The great majority of people produce the wrong answer to the Monty Hall problem. Why is it so difficult? There are at least five factors that make us prefer the wrong answer. No wonder the misconception is so strong.

PROBLEM-SOLVING STRATEGIES

A major landmark in research on problem solving was the publication in 1972 of a book entitled *Human Problem Solving* by Allen Newell and Herb Simon. Their central insight was that the strategies we use when tackling complex problems take account of our limited ability to process and store information. Newell and Simon assumed we have very limited short-term memory capacity and that complex information processing is typically serial (one process at a time). These assumptions were included in their General Problem Solver (a computer program designed to solve well-defined problems).

How do we cope with our limited processing capacity? Newell and Simon (1972) argued that humans rely on heuristics or rules of thumb, contrary to computers, which are based on algorithms.

ALGORITHMS VS. HEURISTICS

According to Newell and Simon (1972), solving a problem can be compared to finding a path in a maze (Figure 9.3). The path goes from the problem state to the desired goal state. Many attempts to find a path fail because an obstacle is encountered. One, however, works (at least, if a solution exists). Newell and Simon called the maze the problem space. Problem solvers try to find a path in the problem space.

An algorithm is a systematic set of step-by-step operations that covers the entire problem space and guarantees a solution if one exists. It often involves the repetitive application of a rather simple operation. For instance, suppose someone asks you to name a five-letter bird ending on -p. One algorithm would be to generate all five-letter sequences and see which one refers to a bird. Another, more efficient, algorithm would be to start from a list of all bird names and see which one has five letters and ends on -p. Both algorithms are bound to lead to the solution if done systematically.

Algorithms always lead to a solution if the entire problem space is covered. This is also the weakness of algorithms: one must know the problem space to be sure that the algorithm applies to the problem and covers the entire space. As a result, algorithms are efficient for well-defined problems (where the complete problem space is visible), but much less so for ill-defined problems, where

Key terms

Problem space:
model used by Newell and Simon (1972) that compares problem solvers to people trying to find their way in a maze; problem solvers make a mental journey from the initial problem state to the desired goal state via a sequence of intermediate states.

Algorithm:
a systematic set of step-by-step operations that covers the entire problem space and guarantees a solution if one exists; compare **heuristic**.

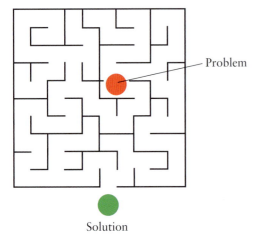

Problem

Solution

Figure 9.3 The problem space model of problem solving
According to the problem space model, problem solving can be compared to finding your way in a maze from the initial problem to the desired goal state (solution).

it is not clear how the problem space looks like. Algorithms work particularly well when a problem can be translated into numbers.

We humans are not good at applying algorithms, because our reasoning is slow and we rapidly get bored of repetitive tasks. Algorithms also require careful planning. Newell and Simon (1972) assumed that most problem solvers engage in only a modest amount of planning because they have limited short-term memory capacity. Another reason may be that planning incurs costs in time and effort, and is often unnecessary because simpler solutions suffice. As a result, we are always on the look-out for simple solutions, shortcuts. Rather than systematically covering the entire problem space, we look for action sequences that rapidly diminish the distance between the problem and the solution.

Most of the time the use of shortcuts works, as reported by Delaney et al. (2004). These authors used water-jar problems in which participants were given problems consisting of three water jars with specified amounts of water, and the participants' task was to end up with a particular amount of water (as illustrated in Figure 9.16 below). For instance, participants were told that Jars A, B, and C contained 25, 5, and 3 liters of water, respectively. Their task was to end up with 14 liters by pouring water from one jar to another. Some participants were told to generate the complete solution before making any moves (planning group), whereas others (control group) were free to adopt whatever strategy they wanted. The control participants showed little evidence of planning, as shown by the fact that they needed more moves than the planning group. So, we have the ability to plan, but often we choose not to do so, because it is too demanding and in the end we get there anyway.

Researchers call the rules of thumb we use **heuristics**. Heuristics are cognitively undemanding and often produce approximately accurate answers. They are based on hunches, intuitions, which themselves are based on experiences and solutions that have worked in the past. Heuristics have the advantage that they don't require extensive information processing. However, from time to time they fail and we get stuck or even come to a wrong solution, as we have seen for the Monty Hall problem.

We discuss some heuristics used in problem solving in the following section.

HEURISTICS USED IN PROBLEM SOLVING

Means-ends analysis

The most important heuristic identified by Newell and Simon (1972) is **means-ends analysis**:

- Note the difference between the current state of the problem and the goal state.
- Form a subgoal to reduce the difference between the current and goal states.
- Select a mental operator that permits attainment of the subgoal.

Means-ends analysis is generally very useful and assists people in their attempts to solve problems. Suppose your washbasin is leaking. Your problem-solving strategy (after having held your finger against the leak a few times) most probably will be to find someone who can fix it or someone who may know someone who can fix it (e.g., your land-lady). These are examples of means-ends analysis.

The means-ends heuristic works when the subgoals are helpful to attain the goal. Sweller and Levine (1982) developed a maze in which this was not the case (Figure 9.4). Participants were blindfolded and asked to put their right index finger on the start of the maze, which consisted of thin strips of hardboard glued to a cardboard backing. Their goal was to find a plastic disk (the finish). Half of the participants were given infor-mation about the position of the goal disk (their left hand was put on it), but the other half was not given the information. As you may expect from the layout of the maze, the participants who were informed about the goal took significantly longer to solve the problem than the participants who were not informed about the goal.

Hill climbing

Another heuristic we use is hill climbing. **Hill climbing** involves a focus on short-term goals (rather than the final goal aimed for). The elements of the situation are listed and changes tried out. The element that leads to the largest improvement is selected.

Someone using this heuristic is like a climber who wants to reach the highest mountain peak in the area. He/she uses the strategy of always mov-ing upwards. This strategy may work, but it is possible the climber will find himself/herself trapped on a hill separated by several valleys from the highest mountain.

The hill-climbing heuristic is a simpler strategy than means-ends analysis and is mostly used when the problem solver has no clear understanding of the structure of a problem. As a result, it more often fails to lead to problem solution than a means-ends analysis (Robertson, 2001).

Progress monitoring

MacGregor et al. (2001) argued that individuals engaged in problem solving also make use of a heuristic known as **progress monitoring**. This involves assess-ing the rate of progress towards the goal. If progress is too slow to solve the problem within a reasonable number of moves, a different strategy is adopted.

Evidence of progress monitoring was reported by MacGregor et al. (2001). Participants were given the nine-dot problem (Figure 9.5). This is a problem in which you have to draw four straight lines connecting all nine dots without lifting your pen off the paper. Try to solve it. If you don't succeed, look at the solution at the end of the chapter for the solution.

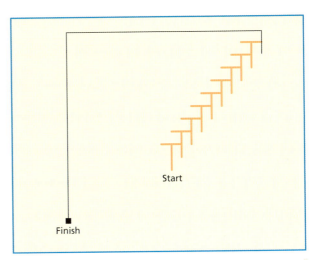

Figure 9.4 The maze used in the study by Sweller and Levine (1982).
Source: Adapted from Sweller and Levine (1982).

Key terms

Hill climbing:
a simple **heuristic** used by problem solvers in which they focus on making moves that will apparently put them closer to the goal or problem solution.

Progress monitoring:
this is a heuristic used in problem solving in which insufficiently rapid progress towards solution leads to the adoption of a different strategy.

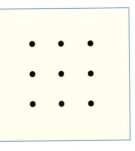

Figure 9.5 The nine-dot problem
Connect all dots by drawing four straight lines without lifting your pen (solution at the end of the chapter).

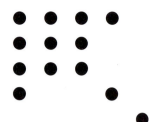

Figure 9.6 The 13-dot problem
Connect all dots by drawing four straight lines without lifting your pen.

The nine-dot problem is one of the most difficult to solve. *Why* is this so? According to MacGregor et al. (2001), the most likely reason is that participants initially make much progress by staying within the square of nine dots. As a result, participants build the expectation that the problem is solvable that way. To test the progress monitoring account, MacGregor et al. (2001) presented participants with the 13-dot problem shown in Figure 9.6. Although this problem has more dots to be crossed, participants found it easier to solve, arguably because progress monitoring did not push them away from the solution.

Availability

Tversky and Kahneman (1974) argued that another heuristic we use is the **availability heuristic**. This heuristic says that we rely on the first solution that comes to mind and that we judge the difficulty of a problem on the basis of how difficult it is to find a first solution.

Relying on the first interpretation that comes to mind usually is a good strategy, certainly if in the past you have solved similar problems successfully. Occasionally, however, it will lead us astray, if the first solution turns out not to work or – worse – results in a misinterpretation that seems to work but in reality does not. For instance, when we are confronted with illness, the availability heuristic tells us to take a cure until the symptoms are gone. Most of the time this works, but it is not a good strategy when you have to take antibiotics against bacteria causing your illness. In that case, it is important to continue taking the antibiotics until all bacteria are killed, so that they cannot build up resistance. Continuing a cure after the symptoms have disappeared goes against the availability heuristic and, therefore, the underlying reason (preventing the disease from reappearing) must be explained extra well by medical doctors.

We also use the availability heuristic to estimate the frequency and the difficulty of a problem. Tversky and Kahneman (1974) gave participants the following problem:

> *The frequency of appearance of letters in the English language was studied. A typical text was selected, and the relative frequency with which various letters of the alphabet appeared in the first and third positions in words was recorded. Words of less than three letters were excluded from the count.*
>
> *You will be given several letters of the alphabet, and you will be asked to judge whether these letters appear more often in the first or in the third position, and to estimate the ratio of the frequency with which they appear in these positions.*
>
> *Consider the letter R. Is R more likely to appear in the first position of a word or in the third position?*

Key term

Availability heuristic: this is a heuristic that makes us use the first solution that comes to mind and that makes us judge the difficulty of a problem on the basis of the ease with which such a first solution is found.

Most participants in Tversky and Kahneman's study thought the letter R is more likely to appear in the first position of a word than in the third, even though in English texts the reverse is true. According to Tversky and Kahneman (1974), this is because we can think more easily of words starting with the letter R than of words that have the letter R in third position. On the basis of the availability, we judge the frequency.

The availability heuristic is also the reason why many people think airplanes are less safe than cars (whereas very much the reverse is true). Most of the time, when the media mention airplanes, it is to report crashes involving tens or hundreds of casualties, making this information highly available in memory.

The availability heuristic further predicts that we will be particularly influenced by recent news, which is still fresh in memory. Kliger and Kudryavtsev (2010), for instance, argued that decisions to buy or sell company shares are influenced not only by how well the company is doing but also by recent events on the market (buying or selling) and recent experiences of the trader (gains or losses). Investors tend to pay extra attention to stocks that have been in the news recently (for whatever reason). Similarly, people's responses to events are especially influenced by the way in which the events have been portrayed in the news recently.

Arguably we also rely on the availability heuristic to estimate the difficulty of a problem. A problem for which a possible solution presents itself easily cannot be a difficult problem. Similarly, a problem for which no immediate solution comes to mind must be a difficult problem. As for the latter, try to solve the equation $X = 75 + (115.46^2 - (4.3 \times 27.5)/88.88) \times 0 \times (558.4 + 112.6)$.

Did you solve the equation? If not, why not? Did you notice we used a classical trick to make a seemingly difficult mathematical equation easy? Because we multiplied a complex term with zero, we can replace the entire part $(115.46^2 - (4.3 \times 27.5)/88.88) \times 0 \times (558.4 + 112.6)$ by zero, so that only $X = 75 + 0$ remains. However, the fact that a problem "looks" complicated makes many people pull out.

Conversely, a problem for which a possible solution comes to mind quickly seems simple. Very few people confronted with the Monty Hall problem perceive it as challenging. They simply "know" the answer (even though it is wrong). In this respect, it is good to know that many people overestimate their degree of knowledge, a phenomenon called the **illusion of knowing** (Glenberg et al., 1982) or the illusion of explanatory depth (Keil, 2012). An easy way to demonstrate the illusion is first to ask participants how well they know the functioning of a particular piece of equipment (e.g., a zipper, a helicopter, a bike) or the viewpoints of a political party, and then to ask them for a full explanation. Afterwards, you give them the opportunity to adjust their initial estimate of knowledge. You will notice that most people find themselves compelled to lower their estimate.

The illusion of knowing could also be the reason why few people perceive psychology as difficult (Keil et al., 2012). Solutions to problems examined by psychologists come easily to mind, even though they are superficial or beside the point. Scharrer et al. (2014) argued that people are particularly prone to the illusion of knowing after reading an easy, comprehensible text on a topic. Then suddenly everything seems clear, even though the knowledge is shallow and the claims in the text may be false. According to Scharrer et al., easy textbooks may do more harm than good, because they give students an illusion of knowing and prevent them from studying the subject deeply or from realizing that the problem's solution requires experts!

Using analogies

Another heuristic to solve problems is making use of analogies or similarities between the current problem and problems solved in the past. As with other heuristics, this is a strategy that often works, but not always and sometimes may lead you astray.

Key term
Illusion of knowing: the conviction people have that they know more about topics than they actually do.

The history of science is full of examples of **analogical problem solving**. For example, the New Zealand physicist Ernest Rutherford used a solar system analogy to understand the structure of the atom. He argued that electrons revolve around the nucleus as the planets revolve around the sun. This analogy helped researchers (and students of physics) to better understand atoms and study them, even though eventually the analogy turned out to be wrong and for a long time hindered scientists to reach a deeper level of understanding.

Similarly, psychologists for a long time used the library analogy to understand memory: memories were acquired, stored, and retrieved like books in a library (e.g., their place in the library could be located by means of indexes). This analogy (or metaphor, as it is sometimes called) helped to understand a new, complex problem and to formulate research questions. At the same time, it hindered progress because it made wrong suggestions (e.g., that a complete memory trace can be read like a book, once it has been located).

How likely are we to make use of a relevant analogy when confronted with a problem? Some findings are discouraging. Gick and Holyoak (1980) used a problem in which a patient with a malignant stomach tumor can only be saved by a special kind of ray. However, a ray strong enough to destroy the tumor will also destroy the healthy tissue, whereas a ray that won't harm healthy tissue will be too weak to destroy the tumor. A further limitation is that the patient cannot be operated on to expose the tumor.

If you are puzzled as to the correct answer (see the end of the chapter), here is an analogy to help you. A general wants to capture a fortress but the roads leading to it are mined, making it impossible for the entire army to march along any one of them. However, the mines were set so that small bodies of men could pass over them safely. The general solved the problem by having his army converge at the same time on the fortress by walking along several different roads.

Gick and Holyoak (1980) found that 80% of people solved the radiation problem when informed that the fortress story was relevant. However, only 40% did so when *not* informed of the story's relevance. These findings indicate that having an analogy in long-term memory is no guarantee it will be used. People must also perceive the *relevance* of the analogy.

Keane (1987) found that participants were more likely to use an analogy if it had superficial similarities to the radiation problem (e.g., a story about a surgeon using rays on a cancer) than if it only had a deep common cause similarity (as in the general-and-fortress story). According to Chen (2002), there are three main types of similarity between problems:

1. *Superficial similarity*: Solution-irrelevant details (e.g., specific objects) are common to the two problems.
2. *Structural similarity*: Causal relations among some of the main components are shared by the two problems.
3. *Procedural similarity*: Procedures or actions for turning the solution principle into concrete operations are common to the two problems.

Superficial similarities are easiest to perceive and, according to Keane (1987), the first we will think of when looking for an analogy, but they can be misleading. Luckily, Dunbar and Blanchette (2001; see also Bearman et al.,

2007) found that participants are less dependent on superficial similarities if they are asked to *generate* analogies rather than perceive them. Then they are more sensitive to structural and procedural similarities. Day and Goldstone (2011) observed that participants are also more perceptive of structural and procedural similarities if they interact with problems rather than only read about them.

Analogies need not involve other problems; they can also involve easier versions of the same problem, as illustrated in Figure 9.7. Sometimes, a difficult problem is easier to solve when we first solved a simple version of it.

As with other heuristics, seeing an analogy most of the time is a blessing for problem solving. Occasionally, however, it can send us on the wrong path, because there is no guarantee for a correct solution, and superficial similarities can be misleading.

Figure 9.7 Which ball is heavier?
You have eight balls with one slightly heavier than the others. You can only find out the difference by using scales. Unfortunately, you are allowed to weigh only twice. Can you find the solution?
If you cannot find the solution, try to find the solution for six balls. Now use this solution as an analogy to solve the problem with eight balls.

Section summary

Problem space model
- According to Newell and Simon (1972), solving a problem can be compared to finding a path in a maze.
- Two strategies can be used to solve a problem: either systematic scanning of the problem space by means of an algorithm or educated guesses that are likely to reduce the distance between the problem and the solution (heuristics).
- Because we have limited short-term memory capacity and our complex information processing is serial, we are more likely to make use of heuristics than of algorithms. Heuristics are cognitively less demanding and in daily life usually lead to the solution, even if not always in an optimal way. Heuristics also work for ill-defined problems.
- Problem solvers often engage in only a modest amount of planning, because such planning is cognitively demanding. They can plan more effectively if encouraged to do so.

Means-ends analysis
- Means-ends analysis is a heuristic that involves forming a subgoal designed to reduce the difference between the current state and the end-goal. It is used even when counterproductive.

Hill climbing
- This heuristic is simpler than means-ends analysis, because it only looks for immediate gain. It is generally used when the problem solver has no clear understanding of the problem structure.

Progress monitoring
- Progress monitoring involves assessing the rate of progress towards the goal. If progress is too slow, the problem solver adopts a different strategy.

Availability

- We mostly go for the solution with the highest availability to us. We also tend to estimate the frequency and the difficulty of problems on the basis of solution availability.
- The availability heuristic makes us sometimes underestimate the difficulty of a problem, because we have a tendency to overestimate our knowledge, in particular when we have read an easy text on the topic (illusion of knowing).

Using analogies

- Individuals solving a current problem can use analogies based on previous problems sharing superficial, structural, or procedural similarities with it. Superficial similarities are easiest to perceive. We are more likely to attend to structural and procedural similarities when we are asked to generate analogies ourselves or if we are allowed to interact with the problem.

DOES INSIGHT EXIST?

The problem space model provides a good metaphor (analogy) for the many times we work out a problem slowly but surely until we reach the solution – what we might call "grind-out-the-answer" problems. For example, solving the problem 758×694 involves several processing operations that must be performed in the correct sequence. Solving this problem feels like moving in the problem space from problem to solution step by step.

Other problems, however, do not feel like gradually finding a path in a maze. For a long time, the solution seems impossible, until suddenly you have an "aha" experience involving a complete, sudden transformation of the problem. Such problems are called **insight** problems.

Insight problems were popular among Gestalt psychologists at the beginning of the 20th century, long before Newell and Simon's (1972) space problem model. Remember from Chapter 2 that Gestalt psychologists emphasized that the whole is more than the sum of the parts. Just like you cannot understand the perception of a melody by studying the individual notes, you cannot understand problem solving by focusing on the individual steps. You must look at the complete problem.

Gestalt psychologists typically referred to Köhler's (1927) work about learning in apes. In one of his studies, Köhler hung a bunch of bananas at the ceiling of a chimpanzee's cage. The ceiling was too high for the chimpanzee to reach, but scattered throughout the cage were boxes that could be used to reach the bananas (Figure 9.8). At first, the chimpanzee tried to reach the bananas by jumping and got very frustrated when this did not work. Then the ape would sit down and seemed to be "thinking," until suddenly he had an "aha" experience and started to stack the boxes.

Figure 9.8 Insight learning in chimpanzee.
Source: Based on Köhler (1927).

INSIGHT VS. NON-INSIGHT PROBLEMS

Insight and non-insight problems are two different types of problems

According to the Gestalt psychologists, solving insight problems differed from solving non-insight (or analytic) problems. The latter was based on *reproductive thinking* (the reuse of previous experiences), whereas insight problems required *productive thinking*, a novel structuring of the problem.

Metcalfe and Wiebe (1987) recorded participants' feeling of "warmth" (closeness to solution) during insight and non-insight problems. Warmth increased progressively during non-insight problems (as expected if they involve a sequence of steps from the problem to the solution). In contrast, the warmth ratings during insight problems remained at the same low level until suddenly increasing dramatically just before the solution was reached.

Insightful solutions to problems seem to "pop into the mind" in a relatively automatic and effortless way. In contrast, deliberate processes involving working memory seem to be required to solve analytic or non-insight problems. Lavric et al. (2000) considered the effects of counting auditory stimuli (requiring the involvement of working memory) on various problems. The counting task impaired performance on analytic problems but not on insight ones, suggesting that working memory is more important for analytic problems than insight ones. In similar fashion, Fleck (2008) found that individual differences in working memory capacity predicted performance on analytic problems but not on insight ones.

Examples of insight problems

To experience insight learning, try solving the following problem. You have 12 black socks and 8 brown socks in your bedroom drawer. It is too dark to see the difference. What is the minimum number of socks you must take with you to the bathroom in order to be sure you have two socks of the same color?

The reason why this is an insight problem is that many people start solving the problem by focusing on the ratio of black vs. brown socks (12 to 8, or 3 to 2), which is not helpful. (Are you among these people?) A much better approach (but one not given explicitly in the problem) is to start from the question "when am I sure to have two socks of the same color?" Then you may realize that as soon as you have three socks, you are sure to have two of the same color (either two brown socks or two black ones). This requires restructuring the problem.

Another example of an insight problem is the mutilated checkerboard (or draught board) in Figure 9.9. The board is initially covered by 32 dominoes occupying two squares each. Then two squares from diagonally opposite corners are removed. Can the remaining 62 squares be filled with 31 dominoes? Think what your answer is before reading on.

Nearly everyone given the problem of the mutilated checkerboard starts by mentally covering squares with dominoes (Kaplan & Simon, 1990). Alas, this strategy is not terribly effective because there are 758,148 possible permutations of the dominoes, as you may have experienced!

The trick is again to reformulate the problem so that it becomes more manageable. If you look carefully, you will see that a domino always covers a white and a black square of the checkerboard. So, you can cover the entire board with dominos if you cut out one white and one black square, but not when you cut out two white squares or two black squares (as in Figure 9.9). Therefore, the 31 dominoes *can't* cover the mutilated board of Figure 9.9.

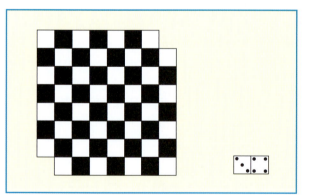

Figure 9.9 The mutilated checkerboard problem A checkerboard can be covered with 32 dominoes if each domino covers two squares. Is it possible to remove two squares from diagonally opposite corners and cover the remaining 62 squares with 31 dominoes? If yes, why? If no, why not?

Insight and non-insight problems have much in common

If one considers insight problems as a separate type of problem, one focuses on the differences between insight and non-insight problems. This risks overlooking the commonalities that exist and the gradual transition from non-insight to insight (Weisberg, 2014).

One way to conceive insight problems within the problem space model is to think of them as problems with a very prominent dead-end path (Öllinger et al., 2014). It is the path our heuristics strongly point to, so that we have a tendency to repeatedly try it out (remember that heuristics are not systematic). Only when we leave the prominent path and try out other, less conspicuous routes are we able to find a solution. According to this view, it is possible to manipulate the dependence on insight by making the dead-end path more or less prominent, or by making the less conspicuous paths more or less visible. This is the approach that led MacGregor et al. (2001) to formulate the 13-dot problem illustrated in Figure 9.6.

In such a view, insight problems are still special because they require a restructuring of the problem space, but they are no longer completely different.

How we think about a problem (the problem representation) is of great importance in problem solving, and insight problems require us to construct more than one problem representation, because the first representation turns out to be wrong. Eventually we form the correct problem representation, which involves a sudden restructuring of the problem.

Brain-imaging techniques have been used to investigate whether insight is associated with a particular pattern of brain activity (Kounios & Beeman, 2014). For example, Bowden et al. (2005) used *remote associate problems*. In these problems, three words are presented (e.g., "card"; "master"; "lamp"), and participants must think of a word that goes with each one to form compound words (solution at the end of the chapter). The participants indicated whether their answers involved insight (i.e., sudden awareness) or not. Bowden et al. (2005) found that the anterior superior temporal gyrus was activated only when solutions involved insight. According to Bowden et al., this area is vital to insight because it is involved in processing general semantic (meaning) relationships.

Activation was stronger in the anterior superior temporal cortex of the right hemisphere than in the same region of the left hemisphere. *Why* is insight more associated with the right than the left hemisphere? According to Bowden and Jung-Beeman (2007), activation of closely connected associations (needed for normal word recognition) occurs mostly in the left hemisphere, but integration of weakly active and distant associations is required for insight, and this happens mostly in the right hemisphere.

Another area associated with insight is the anterior cingulate cortex (located within BA24, BA32, and BA33 of the frontal cortex; see Figure 1.7). This area is involved in the detection of cognitive conflict and the breaking of mindsets. These processes are important for insight given that it involves replacing one way of thinking about a problem with a new and more efficient way.

Previously we saw that insight problems are associated with a subjective experience of a sudden moment of insight "out of nowhere," which makes them special. However, when we look at the underlying processes, a different picture emerges, with a more gradual build-up of knowledge. Ellis et al. (2011) used an anagram task in which four consonants and a vowel were presented. Four of the letters formed a word, and there was an additional distractor consonant (as in K A F M S; solution at the end of the chapter). Ellis et al. (2011) recorded eye movements when the participants were solving the anagrams. On most trials, participants reported they had suddenly solved the anagram (i.e., had insight). However, the eye movements told a different story. During the trial participants spent a gradually decreasing percentage of their time fixating the distractor consonant. Thus, the eye movement data indicated participants were gradually accumulating knowledge relevant to anagram solution even though the participants were unaware of it.

Because of the many commonalities among insight and non-insight problems, researchers currently tend no longer to consider them as two completely separate types of problems, but as problems with more or less clear paths to their solution.

FACILITATING INSIGHT WITH HINTS

If insight is not some type of magical moment but consists of finding the correct problem representation among more attractive but unsuccessful representations, we can expect that hints will help. Indeed, even subtle hints are

effective. For example, consider Maier's (1931) pendulum problem. Participants were brought into a room containing various objects (e.g., a chest, pliers), plus two strings hanging from the ceiling (Figure 9.10).

The task was to tie the two strings together. However, they were too far apart for participants to reach one string while holding the other. The most "insightful" (but rare) solution was to tie the pliers to one string and swing it like a pendulum. Participants could hold one string and catch the other on its upswing.

Thomas and Lleras (2009) used the pendulum problem with occasional exercise breaks in which participants swung their arms up and down or stretched them. Those swinging their arms were more likely to solve the problem (85%) than those stretching their arms (62%), although most were unaware of the relationship between their arm movements and the task. Thus, hints can be effective without conscious awareness of their task relevance.

INCUBATION AND SLEEP

Wallas (1926) argued that **incubation** helps with insight problems. Incubation refers to a stage in which the problem is put aside for some time. According to Wallas, this works because the subconscious mind continues to work towards a solution during the incubation time.

Research on incubation typically involves comparing an experimental group having an incubation period away from an unsolved problem with a control group working continuously. Sio and Ormerod (2009) reported a meta-analysis of these studies. Three findings stood out:

1. Incubation effects were reported in 73% of the studies, but the effects were fairly small.

2. Incubation effects were stronger with creative problems having multiple solutions than with problems having a single solution. Incubation often widens the search for knowledge, which may be more useful with multiple-solution problems.

3. The effects were larger when there was a fairly long preparation time prior to incubation. This may have occurred because an impasse or block in thinking is more likely to develop when preparation time is long.

It is sometimes claimed that "sleeping on a problem" is a very effective form of incubation. Wagner et al. (2004) tested the claim in a study in which participants performed a complex mathematical task and were retested several hours later. The mathematical problems were designed so they could be solved in a much simpler way than the one used initially by nearly all the participants. Of those who slept between training and testing, 59% found the shortcut, compared to only 25% of those who did not.

Why is incubation beneficial? Penaloza and Calvillo (2012) obtained evidence that forgetting misleading information is important. Participants solved insight problems in the presence or absence of misleading clues. One group worked continuously while the other group had a two-minute incubation period. There was a beneficial effect of incubation only when the break allowed misleading information to be forgotten.

In the Real World 9.2 *Constraint relaxation in magic tricks*

Danek et al. (2014) argued that representational change and insight are important in working out how magicians achieve their tricks. Consider a trick in which the magician pours water from a glass into an empty mug. He then turns the mug upside down and a large ice cube drops out (Figure 9.11).

This seems impossible on the basis of reasonable assumptions such as the following: (1) the mug and glass are ordinary objects; (2) it is real water; (3) the mug is empty; and (4) it is a real ice cube.

In fact, the "empty" mug is filled with a white napkin glued to the bottom of the mug and the ice cube. The water is fully absorbed by the napkin, so only the ice cube falls out. When participants were given a verbal cue designed to relax incorrect assumption (3), performance improved significantly.

Figure 9.11 (a) Screenshot from the beginning of the ice cube trick; (b) screenshot from the end of the trick. Source: From Danek et al. (2014). Reprinted with permission from Elsevier.
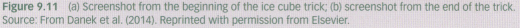

REPRESENTATIONAL CHANGE THEORY

Ohlsson (1992) proposed the representational change theory to understand the processes involved in insight learning. According to the theory, we encounter a block in insight problem solving because we *represent* the problem wrongly. As a result, we need to change the problem representation. This can occur in three ways:

1. *Constraint relaxation*: Inhibitions on what is regarded as permissible are removed.
2. *Re-encoding*: Some aspect of the problem representation is reinterpreted.
3. *Elaboration*: New problem information is added to the representation.

Constraint relaxation is needed to solve the nine-dot problem (Figure 9.5), because participants need to realize that the lines do not have to end within the square of dots.

Knoblich et al. (1999) designed mathematical problems with matchsticks, where constraint relaxation was sometimes crucial for the solution. Figure 9.12 shows two of the problems. Try to solve them. Your task is to replace one matchstick so that each equation becomes valid.

Did you experience problem A as easier than problem B? This is what most people report. In problem A, the usual constraint applies (replace a match so that two numbers change in value). In problem B, however, the constraint that equations primarily involve numbers must be relaxed. Here you have to change the operators: = becomes −, and − becomes =.

What happens when successive problems require the same or a different kind of insight? Öllinger et al. (2008) answered this question using arithmetic problems similar to those of Knoblich et al. (1999). There was facilitation when the *same* kind of insight (e.g., constraint relaxation) was involved over a number of problems. However, there was interference and a slowing of solution times when an insight problem required a different kind of insight from the previous problems.

Reverberi et al. (2005) argued that the lateral frontal cortex is the part of the brain involved in imposing constraints on individuals' processing when they are confronted with an insight problem. Thus, patients with damage to that brain area should *not* impose artificial constraints when solving insight problems, and so might perform better than healthy individuals. That is exactly what they found. Brain-damaged patients solved 82% of the hardest matchstick arithmetic problems compared to only 43% of healthy controls.

Re-encoding, the second representational change strategy, was needed to solve the problem with the socks and the mutilated checkerboard problem of Figure 9.9. Participants had to shift their attention away from the information given in the problem to information derived from the solution. Indeed, sometimes a problem is easier to solve if you start from the solution and work your way back to the problem. This heuristic is particularly relevant when the starting situation has many possible paths, only one of which leads to the solution (e.g., when you want to organize a surprise party for your friend, it is often easier to start from the moment you want to surprise your friend and

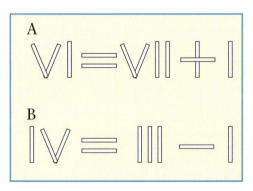

Figure 9.12 Two matchstick problems Move one matchstick to make the equation right. Do not move more than one matchstick (solution at the end of the chapter).
Source: From Knoblich et al. (1999). Reprinted with permission from the American Psychological Association.

to work your way back to how you get everything organized and keep your friend away from the place until the right moment).

The use of *elaboration* was illustrated in a study by Fleck and Weissberg (2013). These authors asked participants to think aloud while solving a series of insight problems. The "classic" impasse – restructuring – insight sequence was found in only a small minority of solutions. The other trials were solved with a variety of methods, ranging from relatively direct application of knowledge, trying out various heuristics, to using new information derived from a failed solution. Many of these methods involved elaboration of the problem. On the basis of their findings, Fleck and Weissberg (2013) concluded that insight problem require much more analysis and elaboration than typically assumed.

Section summary

- Insight involves a sudden transformation of a problem to provide the solution. In this transformation, one problem representation is replaced by another one, resulting in an "aha" experience.

Insight vs. non-insight problems

- The Gestalt psychologists argued that insight problems are completely different from non-insight (analysis) problems. Several findings are in line with this proposal. There is a sudden increase in perceived closeness to solution with insight problems but a more gradual increase with non-insight ones. Brain regions in the temporal and frontal lobes are activated only when solutions involve insight. Individual differences in working memory capacity predict performance on non-insight problems better than on insight ones.
- At the same time, there are many commonalities among insight and non-insight problems, and insight is a gradual process rather than an abrupt transition. Insight can be made more or less easy by providing subtle clues and hints. In addition, there is evidence that insight emerges for some time before the participant becomes consciously aware of it.
- One way to see insight problems is to think of problems with a conspicuous dead-end path in the problem space, which must be overcome. This involves restructuring of the problem. Non-insight problems do not have such a misleading path.

Incubation

- Incubation generally enhances problem solving, especially when there is a long preparation time and the problem has multiple solutions. Incubation seems to work largely via forgetting of unsuccessful strategies. Sleep seems to be a particularly interesting form of incubation.

Representational change theory

- According to representational change theory, changing the problem representation in insight problems can occur through constraint relaxation, re-encoding, or elaboration. Patients with damage to the lateral frontal cortex (involved in imposing constraints on processing) perform better than healthy controls on insight problems.

Key terms

Expertise:
a very high level of thinking and performance in a given domain (e.g., chess) achieved from many years of practice.

Templates:
in perception: forms or patterns in long-term memory that allow us to recognize perceptual input as familiar, meaningful stimuli by matching the input to the forms/patterns stored in memory and selecting the one that fits;

in chess playing: organized abstract structures including information about several chess pieces; these structures (which are larger for chess experts) are useful when players decide on their next move.

HOW USEFUL IS PAST EXPERIENCE?

In general, expertise is good for problem solving, which is why we regularly turn to experts when we encounter a problem. This is particularly true in the real world, where the time available for learning is longer than in a typical psychology experiment, and where the tasks are knowledge-rich rather than knowledge-lean.

EXPERTISE

In everyday life, individuals often spend several years acquiring knowledge and skills in a given area (e.g., psychology; law). The end point of such long-term learning is the development of expertise. Expertise is highly skilled, competent performance in one or more tasks.

The development of expertise helps problem solving because experts have much experience in how to solve numerous problems in their area of expertise. Often, for them a problem no longer needs to be "solved," because they can simply retrieve the solution from memory. Expertise is particularly important for knowledge-rich problems, which require knowledge beyond that presented in the problem itself.

The level of expertise also influences the amount of forward planning. Charness (1981) presented chess players with various chess positions and asked them to think aloud as they planned what to do. A move in chess is defined as a turn by each player, and a ply is a half-move (i.e., one player has a turn). Expert chess players worked out the implications of possible moves about three plies further ahead in the game than non-experts did.

In the remainder of this section, we first continue with chess expertise. There are several advantages to studying chess playing (Gobet et al., 2004). First, the chess Elo ranking system provides a precise assessment of individual players' level of expertise. Second, expert chess players develop specific cognitive skills (e.g., pattern recognition, selective search) that are useful in other areas of expertise. Third, information about chess experts' remarkable memory for chess positions generalizes well to other forms of expertise.

After discussing chess expertise, we turn to medical expertise (especially medical diagnosis). Finally, we consider Ericsson's theoretical approach, according to which deliberate practice is the main requirement for the development of expertise.

Chess-playing expertise

Why are some people much better than others at playing chess? The obvious answer is that they have devoted far more time to *practice* – it takes about 10,000 hours of practice to become a grandmaster. All this practice improves chess-playing ability in several ways. Of special importance, expert chess players have much more detailed information about chess positions stored in long-term memory than do non-experts. According to Gobet (Gobet & Waters, 2003; Gobet & Chass, 2009), much of this information is in the form of templates. Templates are abstract structures containing information relating to about ten pieces. Each template focuses on a particular *pattern*, with a fixed core and a number of variable slots (which allow for flexibility in terms of the pieces involved and their locations).

Gobet and Waters (2003) claimed that expert chess players possess much more template-based information than do non-experts. They can use this information to remember chess positions. Because templates involve up to 15 pieces, each point in time can be represented by three templates at most. As a result, experts' memory for chess positions should be much better than that of non-experts, even though they don't differ in general memory ability (De Groot, 1965). This prediction was supported by Gobet and Clarkson (2004). Interestingly, the difference between strong and weak players was not so much related to the number of templates encoded but to the size of the templates: good players had larger template sizes than bad players.

A second prediction of the template theory is that performance will not be much worse under time pressure. If outstanding chess players owe their excellence mostly to their superior template-based knowledge of chess rather than to their use of slow, strategy-based processing, then the performance of outstanding players should remain high even when making moves under considerable time pressure.

Burns (2004) tested this prediction. He used information about expert chess players' performance in normal competitive games and in blitz chess, in which the entire game has to be completed in five minutes. This is less than 5% of the time available in normal chess. The key finding was that performance in blitz chess was highly associated or correlated with that in normal chess. This suggests that individual differences in chess-playing ability depend highly on template knowledge.

The finding of Burns (2004) does not mean that slow search processes are irrelevant. Van Harreveld et al. (2007) considered the effects of reducing the time available for chess moves. Differences in Elo ratings among players were less predictive of game outcome as the time available decreased. This suggests that slow processes contribute to the level of expertise reached by chess players as well, a conclusion in line with Grabner et al.'s (2007) finding that adult tournament players with high general intelligence have higher chess rankings than those of lower intelligence when the amount of practice is matched (practice was a better predictor of expertise level than intelligence in the study).

Finally, a third prediction of the template theory of chess expertise is that experts will be much better at memorizing board locations of pieces if these fit into templates than if they do not (i.e., if the positions have been randomly allocated). This prediction was confirmed as well, even though experts also tend to remember random positions better than novices, arguably because even random positions and pieces partly overlap with stored templates (Gobet & Waters, 2003).

Medical expertise

The ability of doctors to make rapid and accurate diagnoses is very important, given that medical decision making can be a matter of life or death. There is more research on *visual* specialties such as pathology, radiology, and dermatology than on *technical* specialties such as surgery or anesthesiology, because the former are easier to investigate. In particular, the registration of eye movements allows researchers to go beyond the conscious introspections provided by the participants.

How does the problem solving of medical experts differ from that of novice doctors? An interesting distinction in this respect is that between explicit reasoning and implicit reasoning (Engel, 2008). Explicit reasoning is fairly slow, deliberate, and is associated with conscious awareness. Implicit reasoning, on the other hand, is fast, automatic, and isn't associated with conscious awareness. In particular, expertise in visual specialties involves an increased reliance on fast, automatic processes, followed by a cross-check with slow, deliberate processes if something untoward is noticed (McLaughlin et al., 2008).

The increased use of implicit reasoning can be seen in the eye movements of students with different degrees of practice. Krupinski et al. (2013) carried out a longitudinal study of pathologists viewing breast biopsies at the start of their first, second, third, and fourth years of residency. The findings from one participant are shown in Figure 9.13.

The data of Krupinski et al. (2013) agree with the conclusions Gegenfurtner et al. (2011) drew on the basis of a meta-analysis (see Glossary) across several expertise domains including medicine, sport, and transportation. In all these domains the following differences were found between experts and non-experts: (1) shorter fixations, (2) faster first fixations on task-relevant information, (3) more fixations on task-relevant information, (4) fewer fixations on task-irrelevant areas, and (5) longer eye movements.

According to Gegenfurtner et al. (2011) the changes can be explained by two factors. The first is that the development of expertise is associated with an increasingly efficient and selective allocation of attention. The second factor is that experts can extract information from a wider area than can non-experts within each fixation.

Melo et al. (2012) argued that visual medical experts increasingly process the stimuli of their expertise perceptually (Chapter 2) rather than on the basis of attentional search. That is, they start to see the medical stimuli in the same way as we see familiar scenes. Melo et al. (2012) reported several similarities

Figure 9.13 Learning to diagnose faster
Eye fixations of a pathologist given the same biopsy whole-side image starting in year 1 (a) and ending in year 4 (d). Larger circles indicate longer fixation times.
Source: From Krupinski et al. (2013). Reprinted with permission from Elsevier.

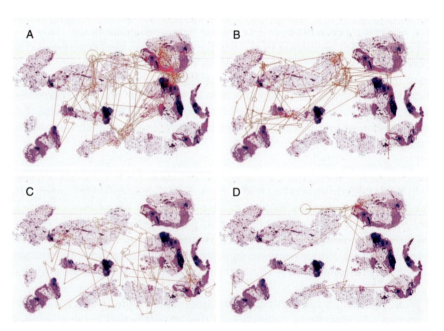

between assessment by experts and scene perception. First, radiology experts needed not much more time to see lesions in chest X-ray images than they needed to name animals (1.33 vs. 1.23 seconds, respectively). In addition, very much the same brain regions were involved in both activities. The only difference was more activity in the frontal lobes during lesion detection, suggesting that diagnosing was more cognitively demanding than naming animals.

The greater reliance on perceptual processes than serial attentional search agrees with the shift from explicit to implicit reasoning, proposed by Engel (2008). It is also in line with an earlier finding of Kulatunga-Moruzi et al. (2004) on skin lesion assessment. In this study the authors found that highly expert dermatologists performed better when they were asked to judge photographs *without* first receiving detailed verbal descriptions of the photographs, whereas less expert participants profited from the verbal descriptions. Arguably, expert dermatologists diagnose skin lesions by rapidly searching for a stored pattern closely resembling the perceived stimulus (the case photograph), and the verbal descriptions interfered with their ability to use that strategy effectively.

DELIBERATE PRACTICE

Expertise requires practice to arise. Ericsson et al. (1993) famously declared that all expertise (not only chess playing) needs 10,000 hours of practice. Ericsson and Ward (2007) provided a theory spelling out what is involved in *effective* practice. They emphasized the importance of deliberate practice. Deliberate practice has four aspects:

1. The task is at an appropriate level of difficulty (not too easy or too hard).
2. The learner is given informative feedback about his/her performance.
3. The learner has adequate chances to repeat the task.
4. The learner has the chance to correct his/her errors.

What exactly happens as a result of prolonged deliberate practice? According to Ericsson and Kintsch (1995), expertise can reduce the negative effects of the limited working memory capacity we have. The authors put forward the notion of **long-term working memory**. This involves the fast transfer of information to and from long-term memory, which enables long-term memory information to support working memory, so that it looks as if the person's working memory capacity has increased (see the impact of chunking in Chapter 4).

Here is an example to show the nature of long-term working memory. Suppose an expert and novice chess player look at the positions of chess pieces on a board. The novice must rely largely on working memory to interpret the information and search for solutions. In contrast, the expert player can use his/her relevant knowledge in long-term memory to interpret the situation and to evaluate the consequences of possible moves. In other words, the expert can offload precious working-memory capacity by making use of long-term memory representations.

A major prediction of the deliberate practice account is that the acquisition of expertise depends more on the amount of deliberate practice than simply on the number of hours devoted to practice. Another prediction (and much

> **Key terms**
>
> **Deliberate practice:**
> a very useful form of practice in which the learner can repeat the task, correct his/her errors, and is given performance feedback.
>
> **Long-term working memory:**
> used by experts to store relevant information rapidly in long-term memory and to access it through retrieval cues in **working memory**.

more controversial) is that deliberate practice is essentially *all* that is needed to develop expert performance. Innate talent or ability is assumed to be of little or no relevance to the development of expertise.

Charness et al. (2005) examined the importance of deliberate practice among tournament-rated chess players. Time spent on serious study alone (deliberate practice), tournament play, and formal instruction all predicted chess-playing performance. However, as predicted, serious deliberate practice was the strongest predictor. Grandmasters had spent an average of 5,000 hours on deliberate practice during their first ten years of playing chess. This was nearly five times as much as the amount of time spent by intermediate players.

On the other hand, Hambrick et al. (2014) reported that the percentage of variance in chess and music performance explained by deliberate practice was only 30% (equivalent to a correlation of r = .55).

More evidence against the monopoly of practice was reported by Campitelli and Gobet (2011). They examined three predictions of the deliberate practice theory:

1. All individuals who engage in massive deliberate practice should achieve very high skills levels.
2. The variability across individuals in the number of hours required to achieve the highest expertise level should be relatively small.
3. Everyone's skill level should benefit comparably from any given amount of deliberate practice.

Campitelli and Gobet (2011) considered the three predictions with reference to chess playing. None was supported. As for the first prediction, there are several chess players who have devoted over 20,000 hours of practice without becoming masters.

With respect to the second prediction, the total numbers of practice hours required to achieve master level varied between 3,000 and 23,600 hours. This indicates the existence of substantial individual differences unaccounted for by deliberate practice theory.

Evidence against the third prediction was reported by Howard (2009). He studied expert chess players in three categories: candidates (the highest level, including elite players who have competed for the right to challenge the world champion); non-candidate grandmasters (elite players but less expert than candidates; intermediate level); and non-grandmasters (lowest level).

For each group, Howard (2009) plotted the players' ratings against the number of games they had played (Figure 9.14). There are two points of interest. First, the strong players learned faster than the weaker players. Second, the ratings of the players showed ceiling effects, such that the lowest group never reached the level of the intermediate group, which in turn remained lower than the level of the top group.

These findings suggest that there are clear differences in natural talent among players and that it is possible early in the career to identify those who eventually can become top players. Top grandmasters are fast learners who keep on practicing.

How can we identify those with high levels of natural talent? When expertise is broad, intelligence is of importance. Gottfredson (1997) reviewed the literature on intelligence and occupational success. The correlation between

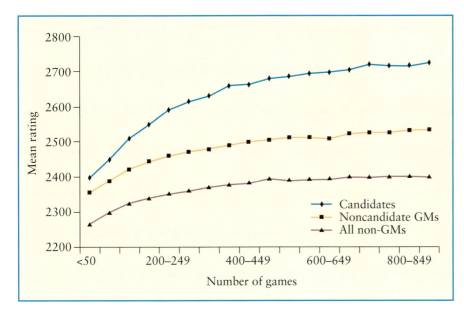

Figure 9.14 Mean chess ratings of candidates, non-candidate grandmasters (GMs), and non-grandmasters as a function of number of games played. Source: From Howard (2009). Copyright © The Psychonomic Society. Reproduced with permission.

intelligence and work performance was +.58 for high-complexity jobs (e.g., accountants, lawyers, doctors). The mean intelligence level of these people was 120–130, which is considerably higher than the population mean of 100 (Mackintosh, 1998). There are very few successful individuals in high-complexity occupations whose IQ is close to the population average of 100. In similar fashion, Grabner et al. (2007) found that none of the chess masters they studied had a verbal IQ below 110 or a non-verbal IQ below 115.

Intelligence is less important when it comes to very specific skills. For example, Ceci and Liker (1986) studied experts at calculating the odds in harness racing. These experts took into account complex interactions of up to seven variables (e.g., track size, each horse's lifetime speed). The experts' IQs ranged from 81 to 128, and there was no correlation between performance and IQ.

Mosing et al. (2014) argued that innate differences in skill could even be the cause of differences in practice rather than the other way around (as defended by Ericsson et al., 1993). The fact that deliberate practice is positively correlated with expert performance does not necessarily mean the former causes the latter (remember that correlation does not mean causation; Chapter 4). For example, individuals with much talent are likely to enjoy early success, and this may motivate them to devote more time to deliberate practice than individuals with less talent. In other words, performance level may influence the amount of practice as well as the amount of practice influencing performance level. For example, there are probably very few individuals willing to devote thousands of hours to practice of a skill when they totally lack any talent for it.

Mosing et al. (2014) reported evidence for their view in a study on music practice and music ability in Swedish twins. Genetic factors played an important role in determining the hours of music practice – this probably occurred because individuals with more innate music talent practiced more. Of importance, there was no difference in music ability between identical or monozygotic twins even when they differed in the amount of music practice they had had. Thus, the relationship between music practice and music ability depended much more on genetic factors than on the causal effects of practice on ability.

Evaluation

+ It is indisputable that extensive practice is essential for the development of expertise.

+ The main factors making practice effective have been identified. They include using tasks of intermediate difficulty, providing performance feedback, and allowing the learner to repeat the task and to correct his/her mistakes.

− The notion that natural talent is unimportant is unconvincing. As Sternberg and Ben-Zeev (2001, p. 302) argued, "Is one to believe that anyone could become a Mozart if only he or she put in the time? . . . or that becoming an Einstein is just a matter of deliberate practice?"

− Knowing that practice is important is not enough. We also need to know more about *why* some individuals decide to devote hundreds or thousands of hours to effortful deliberate practice to achieve high levels of expertise.

FUNCTIONAL FIXEDNESS

So far, we saw plenty of evidence for the beneficial effects of practice and expertise. Does this mean that past experience is *always* useful? Not quite.

Karl Duncker was a student of Köhler, the German Gestalt psychologist we discussed earlier. He developed a series of studies on productive thinking (as he called it), which were translated into English and published after his death (Duncker, 1945). In one of these studies, participants were given a candle, a match box containing matches, some tacks, and several other objects (Figure 9.14). They were asked to attach the candle to a wall by a table so it didn't drip onto the table below. Most participants tried in vain to nail the candle directly to the wall or to glue it to the wall by melting it. (What would you do?)

Only a few participants came up with the correct answer, which is to use the inside of the match box as a candle holder and then to nail it to the wall with the tacks. According to Duncker (1945), his participants "fixated" on the box's function as a container rather than as a platform. Because of their functional fixedness, they failed to solve the problem. From past experience they assumed that the box (or any other given object) had only a limited number of uses. Duncker's account was supported by the finding that more correct solutions were produced when the match box was empty (rather than full) at the start of the experiment. Having the match box empty made it seem less like a container.

There are other ways of improving performance on Duncker's candle problem. Frank and Ramscar (2003) used a condition in which "candle,"

Key term

Functional fixedness: the inflexible focus on the usual function or functions of an object in problem solving.

"book of matches," and "box of tacks" were underlined (in this version the box of the tacks had to be used to attach the candle). The percentage of solutions in the condition with underlined words was more than double the success rate when no words were underlined. *Why* did the simple addition of underlining a few words produce such a large improvement in performance? The underlining led participants to attend more to the objects underlined, and thus focus more directly on the key objects involved in the problem solution.

Duncker's candle problem shows that problem-solving performance can be impaired by functional fixedness caused by past experience accumulated over a long period of time. However, adverse effects of functional fixedness can be found even when individuals have only very limited experience with an object. Ye et al. (2009) asked people to decide whether each of nine objects could be used for a given function (e.g., "packable with" – usable as packing material to pack an egg in a box). Immediately afterwards, they decided whether the same objects could be used for a different function (e.g., play "catch with" over a distance of 15 feet). Some objects (e.g., ski cap; pillow) could be used for both functions. Deciding that one of these objects possessed the first function significantly reduced the probability of detecting that it also possessed the second function. This is a form of short-term functional fixedness.

Figure 9.15   Some of the materials provided for participants who were instructed to mount a candle on a vertical wall in the study by Duncker (1945).

MENTAL SET

Luchins (1942; see also Luchins & Luchins, 1959) published another classic demonstration of how expertise can hinder problem solving. He used water-jar problems. One of the problems was as follows: Jar A can hold 28 quarts of water, Jar B 76 quarts, and Jar C 3 quarts. The task is to end up with exactly 25 quarts in one of the jars. The solution isn't difficult, as we are sure you will agree. Jar A is filled, and then Jar C is filled from it, leaving 25 quarts in Jar A. Not surprisingly, 95% of participants solved it.

Luchins's true demonstration, however, was that only 36% of the participants managed to solve this very simple problem, if immediately before they had solved a series of problems with a different strategy (Figure 9.16).

How can we explain the poor performance on the simple problem of those participants trained on the complex problems? People asked to solve a similar problem repeatedly tend to develop a mental set – a tendency to approach problems in a way that proved successful in the past. Forming a mental set is of value because successive problems often require the same solution strategy and, therefore, can be solved faster and with fewer processing demands by repeating the same strategy (Cherubini & Mazzocco, 2004). However, the resulting mental set may prevent people from seeing the solution to a different problem, even when the new problem is rather simple. In the words of Luchins (1942, p. 1),

Key term

Mental set:
a readiness to think or act in a given way, often because this has been shown to be successful in the past.

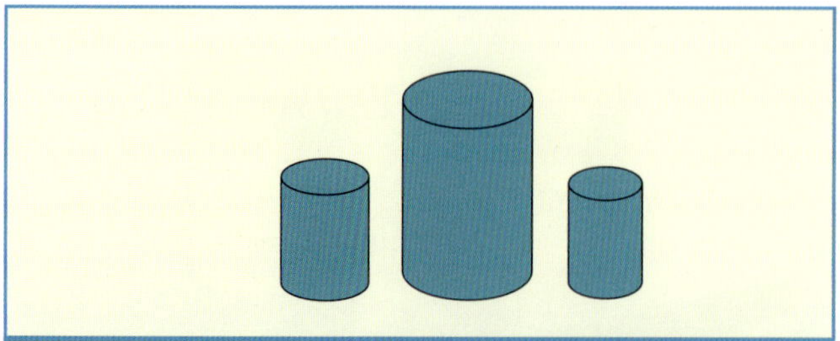

Problem	A	B	C	Target
1	21	127	3	100
2	14	163	25	99
3	18	43	10	5
4	9	42	6	21
5	20	50	4	31
6	28	76	3	25

Figure 9.16   Sequence of water-jar problems used by Luchins (1942) and Luchins and Luchins (1959) to demonstrate the impact of mental set
Participants solved six problems in a row: each line shows how much water the jars A, B, and C contain. The final column gives the target volume to reach. The first five problems require a similar (rather complex) set of operations to be performed. Problem 6 requires a different but simple operation. Only 36% of the participants were able to solve problem 6 after having solved the first five problems.)

"The successive, repetitious use of the same method mechanized many of the subjects – blinded them to the possibility of a more direct and simple procedure."

It is understandable that people given a series of unfamiliar problems make use of a mental set. However, would the same happen to experts given a problem in their area of expertise? Bilalić et al. (2008a) suggested *it does*. They presented expert chess players with a chess problem and told them to find the shortest way to win. The problem could be solved in five moves using a familiar strategy but in only three moves using a less familiar solution. Only 50% of the International Masters and 0% of the Candidate Masters found the shorter solution.

Bilalić et al. (2008b) carried out a similar study designed to clarify why expert chess players often failed to find the shorter solution. After these players found the familiar solution, they reported they had looked hard for a better one. However, their eye movements revealed they were still looking at features of the chessboard position related to the familiar solution. Thus, the direction of attention remained partly under the control of the processes responsible for the initial solution.

WAYS TO COUNTERACT FUNCTIONAL FIXEDNESS AND MENTAL SET

Functional fixedness and mental set hinder problem solving when they highlight a suboptimal (or wrong) solution in the problem space. They are examples of how expertise can be a hindrance and they explain why new, creative solutions sometimes come from novices, who are not yet burdened by existing knowledge.

However, are they unavoidable for experts or are there ways in which expertise can be turned to an advantage even in situations where previous knowledge hurts? After all, experts have more knowledge, which they can apply more flexibly.

Challoner (2009) studied the creation of 1,001 important inventions and the solutions to insight problems. He decided that in almost every case two steps were involved:

1. Find an infrequently noticed or new feature.
2. Form a solution based on that obscure feature.

McCaffrey (2012) argued that both steps can be trained. Functional fixedness, for example, can be reduced by the *generic-parts technique*. The technique works as follows: (1) produce function-free descriptions of each part of a situation, (2) subsequently look at whether the descriptions afford new uses of the parts. After McCaffrey (2012) trained participants in the generic-parts technique, they solved 83% of the insight problems he gave them (e.g., Dunckler's candle problem), compared to only 49% in the control group.

The generic-parts technique is a variant of brainstorming, a method in which participants first generate a wide variety of possible, non-typical solutions and subsequently look at whether some of these ideas can be turned into useful solutions. Brainstorming sessions are typically associated with group gatherings, although Kohn et al. (2011) argued that it may be more efficient to ask the members first to generate their list of ideas on their own before coming together. More ideas are generated in this way.

All in all, knowing that phenomena like functional fixedness and mental set exist need not dissuade us from acquiring expertise. Being aware of their existence can help us to counteract them in fruitful ways.

Key term

Brainstorming: a method of problem solving in which participants generate a wide variety of possible, non-typical solutions and subsequently look at whether some of these ideas can be turned into useful solutions; used when confronted with a block in insight problems, with functional fixedness or with a mental set.

Section summary

Expertise

- Expertise is highly skilled, competent performance in one or more tasks. Experts plan more and have more solutions ready in memory.

Chess-playing expertise

- Chess knowledge is stored in templates, each containing information relating to about ten pieces. Chess experts possess larger templates than do non-experts. In addition, experts make more effective use of slow, strategy-based processes.

Medical expertise

- Medical experts make more use than non-experts of fast, automatic processes when diagnosing, whereas non-experts rely more on slow, deliberate processes. However, experts often cross-check their diagnoses with slow, deliberate processes. Experts' diagnostic performance involves a visual strategy that can be disrupted by detailed verbal descriptions.

Deliberate practice

- It has been claimed that deliberate practice is more effective than other forms of practice and that innate talent is irrelevant to the development of expertise. The evidence indicates that deliberate practice is necessary (but not sufficient) for expertise to develop. Natural talent or ability is also needed.

Functional fixedness and mental set

- Although experience and expertise in general are good, occasionally they lead to problem-solving problems. This is the case when experience with objects prevents us from seeing new uses for these objects (functional fixedness) or when the repeated use of one solution makes us blind to seeing that a new, related problem may require a different type of solution. Techniques like the generic-parts technique or brainstorming can be used to counteract the negative aspects of expertise.

HYPOTHESIS TESTING

Hypothesis testing is an important part of problem solving. A good way to solve problems is to form a potential explanation (hypothesis) and then to test whether it works. If the hypothesis proves to be incorrect, another hypothesis is formed. This continues until the problem is solved. So, studying hypothesis testing may tell us much about how we solve problems.

TWO WAYS TO TEST HYPOTHESES

Verification and Wason's task

There are two ways in which hypotheses can be tested: One we are very familiar with, but which is fallible (like all heuristics), and another that is better but rarely used outside of science. The form of hypothesis testing we are familiar with is that of *verification*. After having formulated a possible solution, we try it out. If it works, we are happy; if it does not work, we continue searching.

Verification for a long time was seen as the critical difference between scientific reasoning and unscientific reasoning: Scientists verified the truth of their explanation, whereas non-scientists didn't bother to test their opinions. Similarly, good problem solvers test the usefulness of their proposals, whereas bad problem solvers give advice without checking it.

Karl Popper (1968) argued, however, that verification is not enough for good understanding. This can be illustrated with a simple task devised by Wason (1960). He told his participants that he had a rule in mind to generate a sequence of three numbers and that the participants' task was to find this rule. One sequence generated by the rule was 2–4–6. The participants were allowed to generate new number sequences (hypotheses) and ask whether these sequences were also valid according to the rule. When the participants felt sure about the rule, they could tell it to the experimenter.

Most participants asked whether sequences such as 4–6–8, 1–3–5, or 22–24–26 also followed the rule (which they all do), before confidently stating that the rule according to them was "add two to the previous number." When told that this was not the rule Wason had in mind, they were allowed to propose further sequences (hypotheses) before formulating the rule again. Participants could now ask, for example, whether the sequences 3–6–9 and 6–12–18 followed the rule (both of which do).

Wason (1960) reported that only 21% of the participants gave the correct rule on the first attempt and that 28% never discovered the rule at all, even after several attempts. Still, the rule was very simple. (Do you have any idea yet? Which sequences would you give to test your idea?) The rule Wason had in mind was: "Form a sequence of three numbers in ascending order of magnitude."

Why did so many participants fail to find the correct explanation? They rapidly formed a possible explanation and exclusively looked for *confirmation* of their explanation. If their idea of the rule was "add two to the previous number," they only asked for the validity of sequences following that rule (which were all true). They rarely formulated sequences to which they would have expected a "no" answer (such as 1–2–3 or 1–3–7 or 11–11–15), even though such sequences are more informative to find the hidden rule.

The tendency of people to only look for information confirming the correctness of their hypotheses is called the **confirmation bias**. As Wason's experiment illustrates, such an exclusive reliance on verification can lead to a misunderstanding of the underlying processes. As the philosopher Bertrand Russell pointed out, a turkey might form the hypothesis, "Each day I am looked after and fed," because this hypothesis has been confirmed every day of its life. However, the generalization provides no *certainty* that the turkey will be fed the next day. Indeed, if the next day is Thanksgiving or Christmas, the hypothesis is likely to be proved false.

Key term

Confirmation bias: in hypothesis testing, seeking evidence that supports one's beliefs.

Falsification

Because verification can lead to misunderstanding, Popper (1968) concluded that *falsification* is a more useful strategy to test hypotheses. Falsification involves repeatedly trying to find evidence against a hypothesis that has been formulated. If the participants in Wason's experiment had used falsification, they would not have asked whether the sequence 4–6–8 followed the rule, but whether sequences like 3–5–6 or 5–5–5 followed the rule. For both of the latter sequences their hypothesis told them that the experimenter would have to answer "no," if the hypothesis "add two to the previous number" was correct. So, if the experimenter said "yes," this was crucial information, because it taught the participants that their hypothesis was wrong and had to be replaced by a new hypothesis, which was in line with all the evidence observed so far. If they followed the falsification approach, they would have discovered that sequences such as 2–3–4 and 2–3–9 followed the rule (indicating that the difference between the numbers needed not be 2, nor had to be of equal size) and that sequences such as 3–3–3 and 25–25–26 did not follow the rule (indicating that the numbers must form an ascending sequence).

More in general, it is good to know that we, humans, have a confirmation bias. We tend to look too much for evidence supporting our beliefs. This arguably is the reason why it took so long before people accepted that smoking is bad for their health. People searching for evidence in favor of smoking can easily find such evidence (e.g., old people smoking, medical doctors smoking, non-smokers dying young). Only those looking for counterevidence ever have to change their mind.

Because people are so prone to the confirmation bias, part of a scientist's education is to learn about the bias and ways to correct for it using falsification. This does not mean that scientific progress involves no verification at all. As it happens, scientists predominantly use verification in the early stages of a new research topic (when they try to understand the topic) and falsification in the later stages (when they have specific hypotheses to test based on the understanding they developed; Manktelow, 2012).

MOTIVATED REASONING

We will see much more about reasoning in Chapter 10. However, one aspect is very relevant for the confirmation bias we have been discussing. It is that much of our reasoning is not neutral but is influenced by our emotions and motivations. As Epley and Gilovich (2016, p. 133) argued:

People generally reason their way to conclusions they favor, with their preferences influencing the way evidence is gathered, arguments are

Key term

Motivated reasoning:
the observation that
people tend to reason
in ways that make the
conclusion they favor
more likely.

processed, and memories of past experience are recalled. Each of these processes can be affected in subtle ways by people's motivations, leading to biased beliefs that feel objective.

This phenomenon is called **motivated reasoning.**

Applied to verification and falsification, people (researchers included!) will be more likely to falsify the hypothesis from someone else than their own hypothesis (Mercier & Sperber, 2011). Similarly, people will think much more critically (scientifically) about a statement they dislike than about a statement that is in line with their beliefs. Mata et al. (2013) illustrated this by giving students comparative information about their own university and a rival university. The students were asked whether they agreed with the conclusion and why. When the own university came out best, the students had a tendency to accept the conclusion, even when the evidence was weak or misleading. In contrast, when the other university looked better, participants were quick to point out deficiencies in the evidence.

Cowley and Byrne (2005) argued that one reason participants perform so badly in Wason's (1960) study is that they are asked to test their own hypothesis. We are loathe to abandon our own hypotheses, whereas we feel much more at ease questioning others' explanations. This prediction was tested by Cowley and Byrne. All participants took part in Wason's task and had to test a hypothesis by asking questions about the validity of number sequences (as explained earlier). Half of the participants were told: "your hypothesis is even numbers ascending by two"; the other half were told "a student, Peter, thinks the hypothesis is even numbers ascending by two." As in Wason (1960), Cowley and Byrne (2005) observed that only 25% of the students asked questions that would falsify their own hypothesis (the rest were verification questions), but the number rose to 62% for those participants who tested Peter's hypothesis.

The take-home message from research on motivated reasoning is that in general it is a good idea to discuss matters with people who disagree with you. Chances are much higher you will spot weaknesses in your approach than if you keep on looking at the evidence yourself or in the company of people agreeing with you.

Section summary

- Hypothesis testing is an important part of problem solving: possible solutions are proposed and subsequently tested.
- Hypothesis testing can be done in two ways: through verification and falsification. Verification is the best known test, certainly when we are testing our own proposals. It leads to a confirmation bias, however, which may prevent us from discovering the true mechanisms.
- A more secure form of hypothesis testing is falsification. Because this form is less intuitive, it has to be taught to scientists.
- Humans are prone to motivated reasoning: they are much more critical about conclusions they dislike than about conclusions they like. They are also more likely to question others' interpretations than their own. Therefore, discussions with disagreeing groups is very informative.

Essay questions

1. Psychologists are asked to make knowledge tests for various situations (e.g., IQ tests, school achievement tests). Which type of problems (well-defined, ill-defined, knowledge-rich, knowledge-lean) would you include and why?
2. Describe and evaluate the usefulness of the main strategies used in problem solving.
3. What is insight? Does it exist?
4. What is involved in deliberate practice? Is it both necessary and sufficient to achieve expert performance?
5. In what circumstances does past experience facilitate or impair problem solving?
6. How can we test hypotheses?
7. In Chapter 1 we saw the limitations of introspection. Discuss which data problem-solving research has added to this literature. Do these data question some of the statements made in Chapter 1?

Further reading

- Ericsson, K. A., Charness, N., Feltovich, P. J., & Hoffman, R. R. (Eds.). (2006). *The Cambridge handbook of expertise and expert performance*. Cambridge, UK: Cambridge University Press. Many of the world's leading authorities discuss theories and research on expertise in this edited volume.
- Hambrick, D.Z., et al. (2014). Deliberate practice: Is that all it takes to become an expert? *Intelligence, 45*, 34–45. The authors show convincingly that deliberate practice is not enough to account for individual differences in expertise.
- Holyoak, K.J., & Morrison, R.G. (Eds.) (2012). *The Oxford handbook of thinking and reasoning*. Oxford: Oxford University Press. Another general handbook about reasoning, with chapters from leading researchers.
- Kounios, J., & Beeman, M. (2014). The cognitive neuroscience of insight. *Annual Review of Psychology, 65*, 71–93. A good review of the cognitive neuroscience approaches to problem solving.
- Weisberg, R.W. (2015). Toward an integrated theory of insight in problem solving. *Thinking & Reasoning, 21*, 5–39. Robert Weisberg provides a useful account of theory and research on insight problems.

Chapter Solutions

Solution to the radiation problem: Many weak rays are sent from different places, and they converge at the point of the tumor. Each individual ray is too weak to cause damage. However, they are added at the point of convergence (tumor), and there they are strong enough to kill the tumor.

Solution to Figure 9.7: Split the eight balls into two groups of three and one of two. Put the first group of three on the left side of the scales and the second group on the right side. If the scales are not in balance, you know which group contains the heavier ball; if the scales are in balance, you know

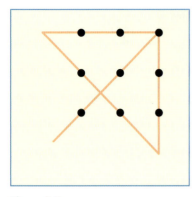

Figure 9.5

the remaining group of two contains the heavier ball. Limit your next weighing to the group with the heavier ball. Put one ball to the left and one to the right. This allows you to find the heavy ball. The split ball version of the problem is much easier, because splitting the group in half puts you in the right direction.

Solution to the remote associate problem: The solution is "post," because you have "postcard, postmaster, and lamppost."

Solution to anagram task: K A F M S make the word MASK if you leave the F out.

Solution to the matchstick problem in Figure 9.11: (a) move a stick from VII to VI, so that VI = VII + I (6 = 7 + 1) becomes VII = VI + I (7 = 6 + 1); (b) move a stick from = to −, so that IV = III − I (4 = 3−1) becomes IV − III = I (4−3 = 1).

REFERENCES

Bearman, C. R., Ball, L. J., & Ormerod, T. C. (2007). The structure and function of spontaneous analogizing in domain-based problem solving. *Thinking & Reasoning, 13*, 273–294.

Bilalić, M., McLeod, P., & Gobet, F. (2008a). Inflexibility of experts: Reality or myth? Quantifying the Einstellung effect in chess masters. *Cognitive Psychology, 56*, 73–102.

Bilalic´, M., McLeod, P., & Gobet, F. (2008b). Why good thoughts block better ones: The mechanism of the pernicious Einstellung (set) effect. *Cognition, 108*, 652–661.

Bowden, E. M., & Jung-Beeman, M. (2007). Methods for investigating the neural components of insight. *Methods, 42*, 87–99.

Bowden, E. M., Jung-Beeman, M., Fleck, J., & Kounios, J. (2005). New approaches to demystifying insight. *Trends in Cognitive Sciences, 9*, 322–328.

Burns, B. D. (2004). The effects of speed on skilled chess performance. *Psychological Science, 15*, 442–447.

Burns, B. D., & Wieth, M. (2004). The collider principle in causal reasoning: Why the Monty Hall dilemma is so hard. *Journal of Experimental Psychology: General, 133*, 434–449.

Campitelli, G., & Gobet, F. (2011). Deliberate practice: Necessary but not sufficient. *Current Directions in Psychological Science, 20*, 280–285.

Ceci, S. J., & Liker, J. K. (1986). A day at the races: A study of IQ, expertise, and cognitive complexity. *Journal of Experimental Psychology: General, 115*, 255–266.

Charness, N. (1981). Search in chess: Age and skill differences. *Journal of Experimental Psychology: Human Perception and Performance, 7*, 467–476.

Charness, N., Tuffiash, M., Krampe, R., Reingold, E., & Vasyukova, E. (2005). The role of deliberate practice in chess expertise. *Applied Cognitive Psychology, 19*, 151–165.

Chen, Z. (2002). Analogical problem solving: A hierarchical analysis of procedural similarity. *Journal of Experimental Psychology: Learning, Memory, & Cognition, 28*, 81–98.

Cherubini, P., & Mazzocco, A. (2004). From models to rules: Mechanization of reasoning as a way to cope with cognitive overloading in combinatorial problems. *Acta Psychologica, 116*, 223–243.

Cowley, M., & Byrne, R. M. J. (2005). Chess masters' hypothesis testing. In *Proceedings of the twenty-sixth annual conference of the cognitive science society* (pp. 250–255). New York, NY: Psychology Press.

Danek, A. H., Fraps, T., von Müller, A., Grothe, B., & Öllinger, M. (2014). Working wonders? Investigating insight with magic tricks. *Cognition*, *130*, 174–185.

De Groot, A. D. (1965). *Thought and choice in chess*. The Hague, The Netherlands: Mouton.

De Neys, W., & Verschueren, N. (2006). Working memory capacity and a notorious brain teaser – The case of the Monty Hall dilemma. *Experimental Psychology*, *53*, 123–131.

Delaney, P. F., Ericsson, K. A., & Knowles, M. E. (2004). Immediate and sustained effects of planning in a problem-solving task. *Journal of Experimental Psychology: Learning, Memory, and Cognition*, *30*, 1219–1234.

Dunbar, K., & Blanchette, I. (2001). The in vivo/in vitro approach to cognition: The case of analogy. *Trends in Cognitive Sciences*, *5*, 334–339.

Duncker, K. (1945). On problem solving. *Psychological Monographs*, *58* (Whole No. 270).

Ellis, J. J., Glaholt, M. G., & Reingold, E. M. (2011). Eye movements reveal solution knowledge prior to insight. *Consciousness and Cognition*, *20*, 768–776.

Engel, P. J. H. (2008). Tacit knowledge and visual expertise in medical diagnostic reasoning: Implications for medical education. *Medical Teacher*, *30*, e184–e188.

Epley, N., & Gilovich, T. (2016). The mechanics of motivated reasoning. *The Journal of Economic Perspectives*, *30*(3), 133–140.

Ericsson, K. A., & Kintsch, W. (1995). Long-term working memory. *Psychological Review*, *102*, 211–245.

Ericsson, K. A., Krampe, R. T., & Tesch-Römer, C. (1993). The role of deliberate practice in the acquisition of expert performance. *Psychological Review*, *100*(3), 363–406.

Ericsson, K. A., & Ward, P. (2007). Capturing the naturally occurring superior performance of experts in the laboratory: Toward a science of expert and exceptional performance. *Current Directions in Psychological Science*, *16*, 346–350.

Falk, R., & Lann, A. (2008). The allure of equality: Uniformity in probabilistic and statistical judgment. *Cognitive Psychology*, *57*, 293–334.

Farah, M. J. (1994). Specialization within visual object recognition: Clues from prosopagnosia and alexia. In M. J. Farah & G. Ratcliff (Eds.), *The neuropsychology of high-level vision: Collected tutorial essays*. Hillsdale, NJ: Lawrence Erlbaum Associates.

Fleck, J. I. (2008). Working memory demands in insight versus analytic problem solving. *European Journal of Cognitive Psychology*, *20*, 139–176.

Fleck, J. I., & Weisberg, R. W. (2013). Insight versus analysis: Evidence for diverse methods in problem solving. *Journal of Cognitive Psychology*, *25*(4), 436–463.

Frank, M. C., & Ramscar, M. (2003). How do presentation and context influence representation for functional fixedness tasks? In *Proceedings of the 25th annual meeting of the cognitive science society* (p. 1345). Mahwah, NJ: Lawrence Erlbaum.

Gegenfurtner, A., Lehtinen, E., & Säljö, R. (2011). Expertise differences in the comprehension of visualisations: A metaanalysis of eye-tracking research in professional domains. *Educational Psychology Review*, *23*, 523–552.

Gick, M. L., & Holyoak, K. J. (1980). Analogical problem solving. *Cognitive Psychology*, *12*, 306–355.

Glenberg, A. M., Wilkinson, A. C., & Epstein, W. (1982). The illusion of knowing: Failure in the self-assessment of comprehension. *Memory & Cognition*, *10*(6), 597–602.

Gobet, F., & Chass, P. (2009). Expertise and intuition: A tale of three theories. *Minds and Machines*, *19*, 151–180.

Gobet, F., & Clarkson, G. (2004). Chunks in expert memory: Evidence for the magical number four . . . or is it two? *Memory*, *12*, 732–747.

Gobet, F., & Waters, A. J. (2003). The role of constraints in expert memory. *Journal of Experimental Psychology: Learning, Memory, and Cognition, 29*, 1082–1094.

Gobet, F., de Voogt, A., & Retschitzki, J. (2004). *Moves in mind: The psychology of board games*. Hove, UK: Psychology Press.

Gottfredson, L. S. (1997). Why g matters: The complexity of everyday life. *Intelligence, 24*, 79–132.

Grabner, R. H., Stern, E., & Neubauer, A. (2007). Individual differences in chess expertise: A psychometric investigation. *Acta Psychologica, 124*, 398–420.

Howard, R. W. (2009). Individual differences in expertise development over decades in a complex intellectual domain. *Memory & Cognition, 37*, 194–209.

Kaplan, G. A., & Simon, H. A. (1990). In search of insight. *Cognitive Psychology, 22*, 374–419.

Keane, M. (1987). On retrieving analogs when solving problems. *Quarterly Journal of Experimental Psychology, 39A*, 29–41.

Keil, F. C. (2012). Running on empty? How folk science gets by with less. *Current Directions in Psychological Science, 21*(5), 329–334.

Kliger, D., & Kudryavtsev, A. (2010). The availability heuristic and investors' reaction to company-specific events. *The Journal of Behavioral Finance, 11*(1), 50–65.

Knoblich, G., Ohlsson, S., Haider, H., & Rhenius, D. (1999). Constraint relaxation and chunk decomposition in insight. *Journal of Experimental Psychology: Learning, Memory, and Cognition, 25*, 1534–1555.

Köhler, W. (1927). *The mentality of apes*. New York: Harcourt Brace.

Kohn, N. W., Paulus, P. B., & Choi, Y. (2011). Building on the ideas of others: An examination of the idea combination process. *Journal of Experimental Social Psychology, 47*(3), 554–561.

Krauss, S., & Wang, X. T. (2003). The psychology of the Monty Hall problem: Discovering psychological mechanisms for solving a tenacious brain teaser. *Journal of Experimental Psychology: General, 132*, 3–22.

Krupinski, E. A., Graham, A. R., & Weinstein, R. S. (2013). Characterising the development of visual search expertise in pathology residents viewing whole slide images. *Human Pathology, 44*, 357–364.

Kulatunga-Moruzi, C., Brooks, L. R., & Norman, G. R. (2004). Using comprehensive feature lists to bias medical diagnosis. *Journal of Experimental Psychology: Learning, Memory, and Cognition, 30*, 563–572.

Langer, E. J. (1975). The illusion of control. *Journal of Personality and Social Psychology, 32*(2), 311–328.

Lavric, A., Forstmeier, S., & Rippon, G. (2000). Differences in working memory involvement in analytical and creative tasks: An ERP study. *NeuroReport, 11*, 1613–1618.

Luchins, A. S. (1942). Mechanization in problem solving: The effect of Einstellung. *Psychological Monographs, 54*, 248.

Luchins, A. S., & Luchins, E. H. (1959). *Rigidity of behavior*. Eugene, OR: University of Oregon.

MacGregor, J. N., Ormerod, T. C., & Chronicle, E. P. (2001). Information processing and insight: A process model of performance on the nine-dot and related problems. *Journal of Experimental Psychology: Learning, Memory, and Cognition, 27*, 176–201.

Mackintosh, N. J. (1998). *IQ and human intelligence*. Oxford, UK: Oxford University Press.

Maier, N. R. F. (1931). Reasoning in humans II: The solution of a problem and its appearance in consciousness. *Journal of Comparative Psychology, 12*, 181–194.

Manktelow, K. (2012). *Thinking and reasoning: An introduction to the psychology of reason, judgment and decision making*. Hove: Psychology Press.

Mata, A., Ferreira, M. B., & Sherman, S. J. (2013). Flexibility in motivated reasoning: Strategic shifts of reasoning modes in covariation judgment. *Social Cognition*, *31*(4), 465.

McCaffrey, T. (2012). Innovation relies on the obscure: A key to overcoming the classic problem of functional fixedness. *Psychological Science*, *23*, 215–218.

McLaughlin, K., Remy, M., & Schmidt, H. G. (2008). Is analytic information processing a feature of expertise in medicine? *Advances in Health Sciences Education*, *13*, 123–128.

Melo, M., Scarpin, D. J., Amaro, E., Passos, R. B. D., Sato, J. R., Friston, K. J., & Price, C. J. (2012). How doctors generate diagnostic hypotheses: A study of radiological diagnosis with functional magnetic resonance imaging. *PLOS ONE*, *6*(12), e28752.

Mercier, H., & Sperber, D. (2011). Why do humans reason? Arguments for an argumentative theory. *Behavioral and Brain Sciences*, *34*(2), 57–74.

Metcalfe, J., & Wiebe, D. (1987). Intuition in insight and noninsight problem solving. *Memory & Cognition*, *15*, 238–246.

Mosing, M. A., Madison, G., Pedersen, N. L., Kuja-Halkola, R., & Ullén, F. (2014). Practice does not make perfect: No causal effect of music practice on music ability. *Psychological Science*, *25*, 1795–1803.

Newell, A., & Simon, H. A. (1972). *Human problem solving*. Englewood Cliffs, NJ: Prentice Hall.

Ohlsson, S. (1992). Information processing explanations of insight and related phenomena. In M. T. Keane & K. J. Gilhooly (Eds.), *Advances in the psychology of thinking*. London, UK: Harvester Wheatsheaf.

Öllinger, M., Jones, G., & Knoblich, G. (2008). Investigating the effect of mental set on insight problem solving. *Experimental Psychology*, *55*, 269–282.

Öllinger, M., Jones, G., & Knoblich, G. (2014). The dynamics of search, impasse, and representational change provide a coherent explanation of difficulty in the nine-dot problem. *Psychological Research*, *78*, 266–275.

Penaloza, A. A., & Calvillo, D. P. (2012). Incubation provides relief from artificial fixation in problem solving. *Creativity Research Journal*, *24*, 338–344.

Popper, K. R. (1968). *The logic of scientific discovery*. London, UK: Hutchinson.

Reverberi, C., Toraldo, A., D'Agostini, S., & Skrap, M. (2005). Better without (lateral) frontal cortex? Insight problems solved by frontal patients. *Brain*, *128*, 2882–2890.

Robertson, S. I. (2001). *Problem solving*. Hove, UK: Psychology Press.

Scharrer, L., Stadtler, M., & Bromme, R. (2014). You'd better ask an expert: Mitigating the comprehensibility effect on laypeople's decisions about science-based knowledge claims. *Applied Cognitive Psychology*, *28*(4), 465–471.

Sio, U. N., & Ormerod, T. C. (2009). Does incubation enhance problem solving? A meta-analysis review. *Psychological Bulletin*, *135*, 94–120.

Sternberg, R. J., & Ben-Zeev, T. (2001). *Complex cognition: The psychology of human thought*. Oxford, UK: Oxford University Press.

Sweller, J., & Levine, M. (1982). Effects of goal specificity on means–ends analysis and learning. *Journal of Experimental Psychology: Learning, Memory, and Cognition*, *8*, 463–474.

Thomas, L. E., & Lleras, A. (2009). Covert shifts of attention function as an implicit aid to insight. *Cognition*, *111*, 168–174.

Tversky, A., & Kahneman, D. (1974). Availability: A heuristic for judging frequency and probability. *Cognitive Psychology*, *5*(2), 207–232.

Van Harreveld, F., Wagenmakers, E. J., & van der Maas, H. L. J. (2007). The effects of time pressure on chess skills: An investigation into fast and slow responses underlying expert performance. *Psychological Research*, *71*, 591–597.

Wagner, U., Gais, S., Haider, H., Verleger, R., & Born, J. (2004). Sleep inspires insight. *Nature, 427*, 352–355.

Wallas, G. (1926). *The art of thought*. London: Cape.

Wason, P. C. (1960). On the failure to eliminate hypotheses in a conceptual task. *Quarterly Journal of Experimental Psychology, 12*, 129–140.

Weisberg, R. W. (2014). Toward an integrated theory of insight in problem solving. *Thinking & Reasoning*. doi:10.1080/13546783.2014.886625.

Ye, L., Cardwell, W., & Mark, L. S. (2009). Perceiving multiple affordances for objects. *Ecological Psychology, 21*, 185–217.

Chapter 10

Contents

Judgment, decision making, and reasoning

10

INTRODUCTION

Thinking takes many forms. In Chapter 9, we focused on problem solving. In this chapter, we consider three more kinds of thinking: judgment; decision making; and reasoning. All are important in everyday life. Let's start with judgment. Judgment involves deciding on the likelihood of various events using whatever information is available. For example, you might use information about your previous examination performance to work out your chance of succeeding in a forthcoming examination. You also make numerous judgments about your friends and acquaintances, perhaps using knowledge of their past behavior to decide how trustworthy, honest, loyal, and so on they are. What matters in judgment is *accuracy*.

Learning objectives

After studying Chapter 10, you should be able to:

- Define and compare judgment and decision making.
- Explain why tasks such as the Wason card selection and the Monty Hall problem illustrate the fact that human decision making and reasoning are not always logical or rational.
- Discuss the experimental evidence that shows how people often ignore base-rate information when making judgments.
- Define, compare, and contrast the representativeness, availability, and recognition heuristics used in judgments and decision making.
- Explain why omission bias, loss-aversion, framing effects, and sunk-cost effects each influence human decision making.

Key term

Judgment:
this involves an assessment of the likelihood of a given event occurring on the basis of incomplete information; it often forms the initial process in **decision making**.

- Define syllogistic reasoning and conditional reasoning, and describe ways these cognitive skills are assessed experimentally.
- Define, compare, and contrast informal reasoning and deductive reasoning.

Key terms

Decision making:
this involves making a selection from various options; full information is often unavailable, so **judgment** is required.

Hindsight bias:
the tendency people have to overestimate the predictability of a decision once they know the outcome.

Decision making involves selecting from among several possibilities. You probably had to decide which university to go to, which courses to study, and so on. The factors involved depend on the precise nature of the decision in question. For example, the processes involved in deciding which career path to follow are much more complex and time-consuming than those involved in deciding whether to buy a can of Coca-Cola or Pepsi!

We generally assess the quality of our decisions in terms of their *consequences* – are we happy with our choice of university or courses? However, this isn't always fair. There is the story of a surgeon saying: "The operation was a success. Unfortunately, the patient died!" This may sound like a sick joke. However, a decision can be good based on the information available when it is made, even if it seems poor later on.

Indeed, one of the problems we have in evaluating the decisions of others is that in the meantime we have information about the consequences. When the outcome is negative, we tend to see the decision as bad; when the outcome is positive, we consider the decision as good. However, at the moment the person was making the decision, nothing was known about the outcome yet. At the moment a broker has to decide whether to sell or to keep shares of a particular company, it is not yet known whether the price of the company will go up or down in the next hours or days. So, when we are asked to evaluate the quality of a decision, we must not look at what happened after the decision but at what information the person had when they made the decision. Our tendency to see a decision as more predictable after we know the outcome is called **hindsight bias**.

Judgment often forms part of the decision-making process. For example, when deciding which car to buy, you might make judgments about how much various cars would cost to run, how reliable they would be, and so on. The link between judgment and decision making explains why both are discussed in the first part of this chapter.

The second part of the chapter is devoted to reasoning, which involves drawing inferences from the knowledge we possess. Much research on reasoning has involved problems based on logic, although we often don't use logic to solve them. The need for such reasoning is surprisingly common in everyday life. For example, suppose your university library has the following rule: "If you fail to return a book by the due date, you will pay a fine." Nancy returns a book a day late. The conclusion, "Nancy has to pay a fine," follows logically.

There are important differences between decision making and reasoning (in particular deductive reasoning). We often make decisions in the absence of full information, and the information we have is sometimes ambiguous. When we make a decision, it may take quite some time before we know whether the decision was a good one or not. In contrast, we have all the information needed to draw the appropriate conclusion in reasoning.

> ## Section summary
>
> - What matters in judgment is accuracy. In contrast, decision quality is generally assessed by its consequences. Judgment often forms part of the decision-making process. Decision making often takes place in the absence of full information, whereas all the information needed to draw the appropriate conclusion is provided in deductive reasoning.

JUDGMENT

Remember that judgment involves estimating the likelihood of various events. We do it all the time; for instance, when we decide to take our raincoat or umbrella with us (because we think it may rain during our trip). As is often the case, psychologists are less interested in the many times judgments go well; rather, they focus on the errors made and the limitations of human judgment.

LIKELIHOOD DEPENDS ON THE AVAILABILITY OF SUPPORTING INFORMATION

We are constantly judging the probability of good and bad things, so that we can increase the likelihood of something good happening to us and decrease the probability of something negative. If we were organisms working on algorithms, the probabilities of the various outcomes would be monitored constantly based on a full analysis of all factors involved and their likelihood. However, as we saw in Chapter 9, our brains are too slow and do not have enough capacity for such full-scale analysis. Therefore, we rely on tricks that work most of the time, so-called heuristics (see Glossary).

In an algorithmic system, probabilities change when causes change. For instance, chances of a terrorist attack increase when a new terrorist movement is formed and voices threats. However, in a heuristic system, probabilities also depend on the way questions are formulated.

Findings

Suppose we ask you: "What is the probability you will die on your next summer holiday?" Your answer might be: "About one chance in a million." Or we may ask you: "What is the probability you will die on your next summer holiday from a disease, a car accident, a plane crash, or any other cause?" Obviously, your answer should be the same for both questions, as no new information has been added in the second question that would change the probabilities. Still, people give higher probabilities in the second scenario than in the first, as can be concluded from a study of Mandel (2005).

Mandel (2005) asked people during the first week of the 2003 Iraq war to assess the risk of a terrorist attack. Some people assessed the risk of at least one terrorist attack over the following 6 months, whereas others assessed the risk of an attack plotted by al-Qaida or by another terrorist organization. The probabilities should be the same in the two conditions. In fact, the mean estimated probability of a terrorist attack was 30% in the first group, but it was 48% in the second group (30% for an al-Qaida attack + 18% for a non-al-Qaida attack).

Redelmeier et al. (1995) reported that experts show the same effect as non-experts. Medical doctors were given a description of a young woman with abdominal pain. Half assessed the probabilities of two specified diagnoses (gastroenteritis or ectopic pregnancy) and of a residual category (everything else). The other half were asked to assess the probabilities of *five* diagnoses (gastroenteritis, ectopic pregnancy, appendicitis, pyelonephritis, pelvic inflammatory disease) and of a residual category (everything else). The key comparison was the subjective probability of all diagnoses other than gastroenteritis and ectopic pregnancy. This probability was 50% when two diagnosis alternatives were given, but 69% when five were given. Thus, the subjective probabilities for gastroenteritis and ectopic pregnancy depended on how the question was formulated.

Judgments can also be influenced by emotion. Lerner et al. (2003) carried out an online study immediately after the terrorist attacks of September 11, 2001. The participants focused on aspects of the attacks that made them afraid, angry, or sad. The key finding was that the estimated probability of future terrorist attacks was higher in fearful participants than in sad or angry ones.

Support theory

Why do people give different judgments when problems are formulated in more or less detail? In their *support theory*, Tversky and Koehler (1994) explained the findings by pointing out that memory limitations prevent people from remembering all the information relevant to making a judgment. As a result, they will focus on the aspects described in the question. This focus will affect their judgment. Similarly, people will be biased toward the aspects they have strong feelings about.

Availability heuristic

Support theory assumes that judgments rely on memory information that is most available at the time of the judgment. This is called the **availability heuristic**, the observation that estimating the frequencies of events is based on how easy or hard it is to retrieve relevant information from long-term memory.

The availability heuristic is well documented. For example, Lichtenstein et al. (1978) asked people to judge the relative likelihood of different causes of death. Causes of death attracting considerable publicity (e.g., murder) were judged more likely than those that don't (e.g., suicide), even when the opposite was actually the case.

Pachur et al. (2012) argued that there are three ways of explaining people's judged probabilities or frequencies of various causes of death. First, people may use an availability heuristic based on their own direct experiences. Second, they may use an availability heuristic based on media coverage of causes of death as well as their own experience (availability by total experience). Third, they may use an *affect heuristic*, which Pachur et al. (2012, p. 316) defined as follows: "Gauge your feeling of dread that Risk A and Risk B, respectively, evoke and infer that risk to be more prevalent in the population for which the dread is higher."

Pachur et al. (2012) found availability based on recall of direct experiences was the best predictor of the judged frequencies of different causes of death. Judged risks were also predicted by the affect heuristic: people gave higher frequency estimates for the risks they dreaded. Availability based on media coverage was the least successful predictor.

Key term

Availability heuristic: a rule of thumb in which the frequency of a given event is estimated (often wrongly) on the basis of how easily relevant information about that event can be accessed in long-term memory.

The availability heuristic can be overridden. Oppenheimer (2004) presented American participants with pairs of names (one famous, one non-famous) and asked them to indicate which surname was more common in the United States. For example, one pair consisted of the names "Bush" and "Stevenson," another pair of "Clinton" and "Woodall" (Clinton was President of the USA from 1993 to 2001, and Bush was President at the time of the study). If participants in Oppenheimer's (2004) study had used the availability heuristic, they would have said "Bush" and "Clinton." In fact, however, only 12% said Bush and 30% Clinton. They were correct to avoid these famous names, because the non-famous names were slightly more common. Why wasn't the availability heuristic used? Participants realized that names such as "Bush" and "Clinton" were familiar because individuals with those names were famous rather than because the names were common ones.

These findings suggest that the participants used deliberate thought to override the availability heuristic. Oppenheimer and Monin (2009) tested this hypothesis by putting participants under cognitive load while they decided which surname was more common. In this condition, the participants could not suppress the availability heuristic, and the famous name was mistakenly selected 80% of the time.

In the Real World 10.1 *Availability heuristic in medical diagnosis*

An example of poor medical decision making triggered by use of the availability heuristic was discussed by Groopman (2007). When Dr. Harrison Alter was working in the Accident and Emergency Department (A&E) at a hospital in Arizona, he saw dozens of patients in a three-week period suffering from viral pneumonia. One day, Blanche Begaye, a Navajo woman, arrived in A&E complaining of having trouble breathing. She had taken a few aspirin and was breathing at almost twice the normal rate.

Dr. Alter diagnosed viral pneumonia even though she did not have the white streaks in her lungs or rhonchi (harsh sounds in the lungs characteristic of that disease). However, her blood had become slightly acidic, which can occur when someone has a major infection. A few minutes later, an internist argued correctly that Blanche Begaye had aspirin toxicity, which occurs when patients overdose on that drug. Dr. Alter used the availability heuristic because he was overly influenced by the numerous recent cases of viral pneumonia, which made that disease spring to mind. He admitted, "She was an absolutely classic case – the rapid breathing, the shift in her blood electrolytes – and I missed it."

BASE-RATE INFORMATION

When we judge the likelihood of an event, it is good to take the base rate into account. The base rate is the generally expected probability of an event or outcome. For instance, suppose it is early morning and you prepare for a day out in Glasgow, Scotland or Phoenix, Arizona. The sun is shining. You wonder whether you should take an umbrella with you, in case it starts raining. In all likelihood, you will ponder the usefulness of an umbrella more in Glasgow (where there are more days with rain than without) than in Phoenix (where it rarely rains more than a few days per month and showers are short). So, you will take the base rate into account – the generally expected probability of rain in Glasgow vs. Phoenix.

Base-rate information can be combined with *individuating information* to improve the judgment. Individuating information is information specific to the situation at hand. For instance, while pondering whether to take an umbrella with you in Glasgow you may take into account that it is springtime and that it hasn't rained in the last two days.

As we will see in the next section, there is good evidence that people often (but not always) underestimate the importance of base-rate information when making a judgment: that is, when deciding whether to take an umbrella with them in Glasgow, they will be more influenced by the fact that it hasn't rained in the last two days than by the knowledge that there are more rainy days than dry days in Glasgow.

Evidence for base-rate neglect

Kahneman and Tversky (1972) reported the first evidence that base-rate information is often ignored. They presented their participants with the following taxi-cab problem.

A cab was involved in a hit-and-run accident at night: two cab companies, the Green and the Blue, operate in the city. You are given the following data:

1. 85% of the cabs in the city are Green and 15% are Blue.
2. A witness identified the cab as a Blue cab. The court tested his ability to identify cabs under the appropriate visibility conditions. When presented with a sample of cabs (half of which were Blue and half of which were Green), the witness made correct identifications in 80% of the cases and erred in 20% of the cases.

Question: What is the probability that the cab involved in the accident was Blue rather than Green?

Kahneman and Tversky (1972) reported that the vast majority of participants thought the correct answer was 80%. So, the participants reasoned that if identification was correct 80% of the time, the same would apply to the situation depicted. The answer would have been correct, if there were as many Blue cabs as Green cabs (i.e., if both companies had 50% of the cabs). Then the following would have been true:

Probability cab is Blue and witness says Blue = .50 × .80 = .40
Probability cab is Blue and witness says Green = .50 × .20 = .10
Probability cab is Green and witness says Green = .50 × .80 = .40
Probability cab is Green and witness says Blue = .50 × .20 = .10
Probability cab is Blue when the witness says Blue = .40 ÷ (.40 + .10) = .80

However, the base rates of Blue and Green cabs are not the same (similar to the base rates of rain in Glasgow vs. Phoenix). When these are taken into account, we get the following numbers:

Probability cab is Blue and witness says Blue = .15 × .80 = .12
Probability cab is Blue and witness says Green = .15 × .20 = .03
Probability cab is Green and witness says Green = .85 × .80 = .68

Probability cab is Green and witness says Blue = .85 × .20 = .17
Probability cab is Blue when the witness says Blue = .12 ÷ (.12 + .17) = .41

So, the chances that the cab in reality is Blue when the witness says Blue is only 41%. That is, the chances that a Green cab was involved in the accident were higher than the chances that a Blue cab was involved, even though the witness thought he had seen a Blue cab! This is equivalent to the chances of rain in Glasgow being higher than those of no rain, even on a day with a bright morning.

Casscells et al. (1978) showed that the neglect of base-rate information is also true for experts. They gave the following problem to staff and students at Harvard Medical School:

> *If a test to detect a disease whose prevalence [occurrence] is 1/1000 has a false positive rate of 5% [chance of indicating the disease is present when it isn't], what is the chance that a person found to have a positive result actually has the disease, assuming that you know nothing about the person's symptoms or signs?*

Forty-five percent of the Harvard medical experts produced the wrong answer of 95%. Only 18% produced the correct answer, which is 2% (you can easily do the calculations on the basis of the above examples).

Representativeness heuristic

The observation that we focus too much on individuating information and neglect base-rate information can also be shown in our interaction with people. Consider the following example (based on Swinkels, 2003):

> *Dr. Swinkels' cousin, Rudy, is a bit on the peculiar side. He has unusual tastes in movies and art, he is married to a performer, and he has tattoos on various parts of his body. He is interested in ropes. In his spare time, Rudy takes yoga classes and likes to collect 78 rpm records. An outgoing and rather boisterous person, he has been known to act on a dare on more than one occasion. What do you think Rudy's occupation most likely is?*
> *(a) lawyer, (b) student, (c) trapeze artist, (d) librarian*

What is your answer? Is it trapeze artist? If so, you've been a victim to base-rate neglect. Why? Only about one in a million people are trapeze artists (how many of them do you know?). On the other hand, about one in ten persons is a student. So, the chances that Rudy is a student are much higher than the chances that Rudy is a trapeze artist, even though the person details (the individuating information) favor the trapeze artist prototype more than the student prototype. In all likelihood, even the chances that Rudy is a lawyer or a librarian are higher than that he is a trapeze artist, as those two professions are much more common as well.

The observation that we pay too much attention to individuating information at the expense of base-rate information is an example of the **representativeness heuristic**, the tendency we have to decide that an object belongs to a given category simply because it appears typical or representative of that category.

Here is another problem for you to consider (from Tversky and Kahneman, 1983):

Key term
Representativeness heuristic: the rule of thumb that an object or individual belongs to a specified category because it is representative (typical) of that category; it is used in **judgment** and produces the wrong answer when it leads the individual to ignore **base-rate** information.

Key term

Conjunction fallacy:
the mistaken assumption
that the probability of
two events occurring
in conjunction or
combination is greater
than one of these
events on its own; most
famously studied with the
Linda problem.

Linda is 31 years old, single, outspoken and very bright. She majored in philosophy. As a student, she was deeply concerned with issues of discrimination and social justice, and also participated in anti-nuclear demonstrations.

Do you think it is more likely that Linda is a bank teller or a feminist bank teller? Most people (including you?) argue that it is more likely that Linda is a feminist bank teller than a bank teller. They do so because they rely on the representativeness heuristic – the description sounds more like that of a feminist bank teller than of a bank teller. However, every single feminist bank teller must necessarily also be a bank teller. Thus, the probability that Linda is a feminist bank teller *must* be less than the probability that she is a bank teller. The mistaken belief that the conjunction or combination of two events (A and B) is more likely than one of the events on its own is the conjunction fallacy.

Evidence that base-rate information is not always ignored in daily life

Lots of studies have shown the existence of base-rate neglect (we report more studies in the following section), which is stunning when you come to think of it, as it is akin to a traveler not making a distinction between Glasgow and Phoenix when deciding on whether an umbrella is a sensible thing to take along.

Krynski and Tenenbaum (2007) argued that familiarity and *causal knowledge* allow us to avoid neglect of base-rate information and make accurate judgments in everyday life. Suppose a friend of yours has a cough. You know a cough can be caused by a common cold or by lung cancer. You use your base-rate knowledge that far more people have colds than lung cancer to decide your friend is suffering from a cold.

To test their hypothesis that causal knowledge helps in judgment problems, Krynski and Tenenbaum (2007) gave some participants the following judgment task closely resembling those used previously to show that people neglect base rates:

The following statistics are known about women at age 60 who participate in a routine mammogram screening, an X-ray of the breast tissue that detects tumors:

- *Approximately 2% of women have breast cancer at the time of screening. Most of them will receive a positive result on the mammogram.*
- *There is a 6% chance that a woman without breast cancer will receive a positive result on the mammogram.*

Suppose a woman at age 60 gets a positive result during a routine mammogram screening. Without knowing any other symptoms, what are the chances she has breast cancer?

As we have seen, the base rate of cancer in the population is often neglected by participants given this task. This was also the case in the study of Krynski and Tenenbaum (2007): only 25% of the participants answered correctly. The authors argued that this may be because breast cancer is the *only* cause of positive mammograms mentioned. Suppose we reworded the problem slightly to indicate there is an alternative cause of positive mammograms. Krynski and Tenenbaum did this by changing the wording of the third paragraph:

There is a 6% chance that a woman without breast cancer will have a dense but harmless cyst that looks like a cancerous tumor and causes a positive result on the mammogram.

Krynski and Tenenbaum (2007) reported that participants given the benign cyst scenario were far more likely to take full account of the base-rate information (44%), arguably because the more extensive *causal* knowledge available to participants given the benign cyst scenario allowed them to more deeply assess the problem.

A second reason why neglect of base-rate information may be less of a problem in daily life than suggested by psychological experiments is that we tend to use base-rate information when we are *motivated* to do so. Suppose you were asked to put some saliva on a strip of paper. If it turned blue, that would mean you had an enzyme deficiency indicating a health problem. However, there was a 1 in 10 probability that the test was misleading. Unfortunately, the paper turns blue.

Ditto et al. (1998) gave their participants this task. Most used the base-rate information (i.e., 1 in 10 probability of misleading result) to argue that the test was inaccurate. In contrast, participants who were told the paper turning blue meant they didn't have a health problem perceived no deficiencies in the test, arguably because they weren't motivated to take account of the base-rate information of misleading results (see motivated cognition in Chapter 9).

Finally, there is evidence that base-rate information in some circumstances can also be *overemphasized*. Consider the following problem (Teigen & Keren, 2007):

Fred travels every day to work on a bus that departs on the hour (i.e., 6:00, 7:00, and 8:00) from the station next to his house.

Based on his long experience, he noticed that, on average, in 1 out of 10 cases the bus departs before schedule, in 8 out of 10 cases it departs 0–10 minutes late, and in 1 out of 10 cases it departs more than 10 minutes late.

Suppose that Fred arrives at the bus stop exactly on time and waits for 10 minutes without the bus coming. What is the probability (chance) that the bus will still arrive?

What is your answer? Teigen and Keren (2007) found the most popular answer (given by 63% of students) was 10%. The second most popular answer (given by 26% of students) was 90–100%. Only 3% said 50%, which is the correct answer!

Why is 50% correct? According to the base-rate information, there is a 10% chance of the bus being early, 80% chance of it arriving 0–10 minutes late, and a 10% chance of it arriving more than 10 minutes late. On this morning, however, it failed to appear in the 0–10 minute time period, so we can eliminate that from consideration. There is an equal probability of the bus being early and more than 10 minutes late. Because the total probability must come to 100%, the probability that the bus will still arrive is 50% (as is the probability that it was early).

Why do most people rely excessively on the base-rate information (10%/80%/10%) with the above problem? One reason is that the base-rate probabilities are easy to calculate, whereas to move beyond those probabilities involves complex calculations. Another reason is that it is not very obvious why Fred standing *passively* at the bus stop for 10 minute has an impact on the probability of the bus arriving more than 10 minutes late.

Teigen and Keren (2007) used a version of the bus problem in which participants were told there was a 10% chance that a bus from company A would arrive first, an 80% chance that a bus from company B would arrive first, and a 10% chance that a bus from company C would arrive first. On a particular day, however, the company B bus drivers were on strike. When the impact of removing the 80% option was made much more obvious in this way, 82% of participants correctly decided there was a 50% chance that the first bus to arrive would belong to company C.

In sum, the notion that people always underestimate the importance and relevance of base-rate information is not true. If base-rate information is easy to calculate, it is sometimes used even when it isn't relevant to a given judgment. At the same time, the research on base-rate neglect shows how careful authorities must be when they communicate about the performance of a test. If they simply give a few percentages of correct and incorrect assessments, they can be sure that many users will misunderstand the figures, even when the users are medical experts (Whiting et al., 2015).

Natural frequency hypothesis

Gigerenzer and Hoffrage (1999) argued that one reason why people perform so badly on base-rate information in psychology studies is that these problems are stated in terms of probabilities rather than frequencies. In everyday life, we encounter examples of a category at different points in time – this is natural sampling. As a result, according to Gigerenzer and Hoffrage's (1999) *natural frequency hypothesis*, we find it easy to work out the frequencies of different kinds of event. However, we have difficulties in dealing with the fractions and percentages used in most laboratory research, which are more abstract than the frequencies of events experienced in everyday life.

It follows from this hypothesis that performance would improve greatly if problems used natural frequencies (i.e., the *numbers* of individuals belonging to different categories). Hoffrage et al. (2000) gave advanced medical students four realistic diagnostic tasks containing base-rate information in a probability or frequency version. The probability version of a cancer screening test read as follows:

> *The probability of colorectal cancer is 0.3%. If a person has colorectal cancer, the probability that the hemoccult test is positive is 50%. If a person does not have colorectal cancer, the probability that he still tests positive is 3%. What is the probability that a person who tests positive actually has colorectal cancer?*

The frequency version of the cancer screening test was the following:

> *Out of every 10,000 people, 30 have colorectal cancer. Of these, 15 will have a positive hemoccult test. Out of the remaining 9,970 people without colorectal cancer, 300 will still test positive. How many of those who test positive actually have colorectal cancer?*

Hoffrage et al. (2000) found that their experts paid little attention to base-rate information in the probability versions. However, the participants performed much better when given the frequency versions (see Figure 10.1).

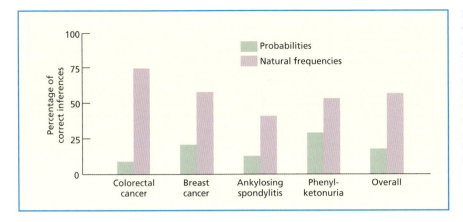

Figure 10.1 Percentage correct inferences by advanced medical students given four realistic diagnostic tasks expressed in probabilities or frequencies.
Source: From Hoffrage et al. (2000). Reprinted with permission from AAAS, Communicating Statistical Information.

Other evidence supporting the natural frequency hypothesis has been published by Garcia-Retamero and Hoffrage (2013) and Brase (2014). Not everyone agrees with the natural frequency hypothesis, however. Evans et al. (2000) pointed out that frequency versions of problems often make the underlying structure much more obvious. When this confounding was avoided, performance was typically no better on frequency versions of problems than on probability versions (later we will see more examples of frequency versions that were not solved very well).

It is further important to distinguish between natural frequencies and the problem protocols used in research. In the problem protocols, participants are simply provided with frequency information and don't have to grapple with the complexities of natural sampling. Fiedler et al. (2000) tested the prediction that frequency sampling increases use of base-rate information. In their problem, there was an 80% chance that a woman with breast cancer would have a positive mammogram compared to 9.6% for a woman without. The base rate of breast cancer in women is 1%. Participants decided whether the woman had breast cancer given a positive mammogram. Participants selected cards from files organized into the categories of women with breast cancer and those without.

Participants' sampling was heavily biased towards women with breast cancer because they mistakenly believed that category was more informative. As a result, the participants produced an average estimate of 63% a woman has breast cancer given a positive mammogram (the correct answer is 7.8%). *Why* was the participants' sampling so biased? They erroneously believed that it was more informative to select women with breast cancer than those without. In this way they exposed themselves heavily to base-rate neglect.

Evaluation

+ Use of natural or objective sampling could enhance the accuracy of many of our judgments.

+ In some studies judgments based on frequency information are superior to those based on probability information.

− Frequency versions of problems typically make the underlying structure easier to grasp. Thus, the improved performance found using frequency formats may occur because this makes the problem clearer rather than because people are naturally equipped to think about frequencies rather than probabilities.

- Sampling behavior in everyday life differs from the neat and tidy frequency data provided in laboratory experiments. As Fiedler et al. (2000) found, the samples selected by participants can provide biased information leading to base-rate neglect.

HEURISTICS ARE OKAY IN GENERAL

In the previous paragraphs, we have seen that psychologists (and information providers!) can easily put people in situations where their judgments are inaccurate because of their reliance on heuristics. Such findings led Glymour (2001, p. 8) to ask the question, "If we're so dumb, how come we're so smart?"

To answer this question, it is good to revisit the reasons why we use heuristics. The main reasons are (1) our brains are not well-equipped to run algorithms (how often did you have to think extra hard about the answers of the problems we explained to you in the previous sections?), and (2) heuristics much of the time provide approximately correct solutions while avoiding the need to think hard (Shah & Oppenheimer, 2008; Todd & Gigerenzer, 2007). As being approximately correct most of the time is good enough in everyday life, this is why our judgment depends so strongly on heuristics.

Another advantage of heuristics is that they can be used almost regardless of the amount of information we have available. In contrast, algorithms are of limited use when information is sparse.

Fast and frugal heuristics

Gigerenzer (e.g., Hafenbrädl et al., 2016) emphasized the importance of fast and frugal heuristics involving rapid processing of relatively little information. They argued we possess an "adaptive toolbox" of several heuristics.

A key fast and frugal heuristic is the *take-the-best heuristic*. This is based on "take the best, ignore the rest." Imagine you have to decide whether Herne or Cologne (two German cities) has the larger population. Suppose you start by assuming the most valid cue to city size is that cities whose names you recognize typically have larger populations than those whose names you don't recognize. Then, you'd indicate Cologne. Now suppose you recognize both names. Then you can think of another valid cue to city size, namely, that cities with cathedrals tend to be larger than those without. If you know that Cologne has a cathedral but are unsure about Herne, you again produce the answer, "Cologne." With each heuristic, the answer is correct, even though you do not know the exact number of inhabitants of Herne and Cologne.

The take-the-best strategy has three components:

1. *Search rule*: Search cues (e.g., name recognition; cathedral) in order of validity.
2. *Stopping rule*: Stop after finding a discriminatory cue (i.e., the cue applies to only one of the possible answers).
3. *Decision rule*: Choose outcome.

The most researched example of the take-the-best strategy is the recognition heuristic. This involves using the knowledge that only one of two objects is recognized when making a judgment. In the previous example, if you recognize the name "Cologne" but not "Herne," you guess (correctly) that Cologne is the larger city.

Evidence that the recognition heuristic is important was reported by Goldstein and Gigerenzer (2002). American students were presented with pairs of German cities and decided which was larger. When only one city name was recognized, participants used the recognition heuristic 90% of the time.

Goldstein and Gigerenzer (2002) also presented American and German students with pairs of American cities and pairs of German cities, and asked them to select the larger city in each pair. The findings were counterintuitive: American and German students performed *less* well on cities in their own country. Students typically recognized both members in the pair with cities in their own country and so couldn't use the recognition heuristic.

It is unsurprising that simple heuristics can be moderately effective. What *is* surprising is that such heuristics sometimes outperform judgments based on much more complex calculations. For example, Wübben and van Wangenheim (2008) considered how managers of clothes shops decide whether customers are active (i.e., likely to buy again) or inactive. The *hiatus heuristic* is a very simple strategy – only customers who have purchased fairly recently are deemed to be active. Another approach is to use a complex model based on all the available information. Wübben and van Wangenheim (2008) observed that the hiatus heuristic correctly categorized 83% of customers, whereas the comparable figure for the complex model was only 75%. This is a less-is-more effect – the approach based on less information was more successful.

Limitations of fast and frugal heuristics

What are the limitations of a theoretical approach that sees heuristics as better for humans than analytic processing? First, the greatest problem was expressed clearly by Evans and Over (2010, p. 174): "The suggestion that we are always better off following intuitions and 'gut feelings' is an extraordinary claim. Why would we have the capacity for logical reasoning if it was of no value to us?"

Second, use of the recognition heuristic is more complex than traditionally assumed. Gigerenzer originally claimed this heuristic was used whenever one out of two objects was recognized. However, people generally also consider *why* they recognize an object and only then decide whether to use the recognition heuristic (Newell, 2011). For example, suppose you decide which of two cities in another country is farther north. It would not make much sense to choose the one you recognize! In fact, people are much more likely to use the recognition heuristic when it is valid than when it is not. Pachur et al. (2012) found in a meta-analysis (see Glossary) that there was a correlation of +0.64 between usage of the recognition heuristic and its validity.

Third, using the take-the-best heuristic is also more complex than suggested by Gigerenzer. This heuristic requires us to organise the various cues hierarchically based on their validity. However, we often do not have sufficient knowledge of cue validities.

Fourth, when the approach is applied to decision making, it de-emphasizes the importance of the decision. Decision making is assumed to stop after finding a single discriminatory cue. This may be fine when you are asked to decide which of two cities is larger, but it may be a bit thin when you have to decide which of two persons you will marry! In the latter case most people want to consider *all* the relevant evidence before making a decision.

Evaluation

➕ People sometimes use fast and frugal heuristics such as the recognition heuristic and the take-the-best strategy to make rapid judgments.

➕ These heuristics can be surprisingly effective in spite of their simplicity, and it is impressive that individuals with little knowledge can sometimes outperform those with greater knowledge.

➕ Familiarity or recognition information can be accessed faster and more automatically than other kinds of information. This encourages its widespread use when individuals are under time or cognitive pressure.

➖ When the decision is important, few people would use fast and frugal heuristics only. For example, most people want to consider *all* the relevant evidence before deciding which of two persons to marry.

➖ We often don't know in advance *which* heuristic will be used in a given situation. As a result, the predictive power of this approach may be limited.

DUAL-PROCESS MODEL

Evans and Over (2010, p. 174) had a point when they argued that people do *not always* use heuristics or rules of thumb when making judgments and decisions. Humans also use careful thinking (now and then). This has led several theorists (e.g., Kahneman, 2003; De Neys, 2012) to propose dual-process models.

According to Kahneman (2003, p. 698), probability judgments depend on processing within two systems:

- *System 1*: This system is intuitive, automatic, and immediate. More specifically, "The operations of System 1 are typically fast, automatic, effortless, associative, implicit [not open to introspection] and often emotionally charged; they are also difficult to control or modify" (Kahneman, 2003). Most heuristics are produced by this system.
- *System 2*: This system is more analytical, controlled, and rule-governed. According to Kahneman (2003), "The operations of System 2 are slower, serial [one at a time], effortful, more likely to be consciously monitored and deliberately controlled; they are also relatively flexible and potentially rule-governed."

What is the relationship between these two systems? Kahneman and Frederick (2005) argued that System 1 rapidly generates intuitive answers to judgment problems. These intuitive answers are then monitored or evaluated by System 2, which may correct the answers. However, we often make little use of System 2: "People who make a casual intuitive judgment normally know little about how their judgment came about" (Kahneman & Frederick, 2005, p. 274).

Findings

De Neys (2006) tested the dual-process model. Participants were presented with the Linda problem (discussed in an earlier section) and another very similar conjunction-fallacy problem. Participants who obtained the correct answers (and so presumably used System 2) took almost 40% longer than those who were incorrect (and so presumably used System 1). This is consistent with the assumption that it takes longer to use System 2.

De Neys (2006) also compared performance on the same problems performed on their own or with a demanding secondary task. Participants performed worse on the problems when accompanied by the secondary task (9.5% correct vs. 17%, respectively). This too is as predicted because System 2 requires use of cognitively demanding processes.

De Neys et al. (2011) tested the dual-process model in an experiment investigating base-rate neglect. The clever manipulation was that they created problems in which there was a conflict between the System 1 and System 2 (*conflict* problems) and problems in which there was no conflict (*no-conflict* problems). An example of a conflict problem is:

> *In a study 1,000 people were tested. Among the participants there were 4 men and 996 women. Jo is a randomly chosen participant of this study.*
>
> *Jo is 23 years old and is finishing a degree in engineering. On Friday nights, Jo likes to go out cruising with friends while listening to loud music and drinking beer.*
>
> *What is most likely?*
> *a. Jo is a man.*
> *b. Jo is a woman.*

This is a conflict version because the individuating information points to a man, whereas the base-rate information points to a woman. In the no-conflict version, the second sentence was replaced by:

> *Among the participants there were 996 men and 4 women. Jo is a randomly chosen participant of this study.*

Heuristic processing based on stereotypes (System 1 processing) would produce the wrong answer (a) in the conflict version, whereas consideration of the base rate (System 2) would produce the correct answer (b). In contrast, in the no-conflict version both System 1 and System 2 pointed to the answer (a), which in this version was the correct answer. Participants also had to indicate how certain they felt about their answer (from 0% to 100%).

As predicted by the dual-process model, performance was much worse with conflict than with no-conflict problems (20% vs. 95%, respectively). However, something interesting was observed in the certainty estimates (Figure 10.2). Even though the participants seemed to neglect the base-rate information, they felt less sure about their answers in conflict problems than in no-conflict problems.

What do De Neys et al.'s (2011) findings mean? On the face of it, they seem inconsistent. On the basis of the participants' answers, there was little evidence they took base-rate information into account. However, the fact that they were less sure on conflict trials than on no-conflict trials

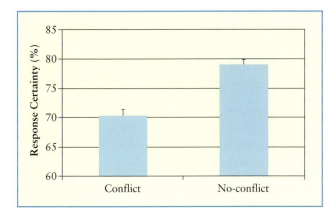

Figure 10.2 Mean certainty with which participants chose the intuitive response alternative for conflict and no-conflict problems. Even though they selected the System 1 response on 80% of the trials with conflict problems, they felt less sure about their choice than in the no-conflict problems.
Source: From De Neys et al. (2011), with permission from *PLOS One*.

indicates that base-rate information had some influence. The most likely explanation is that base-rate information was processed and that participants detected a *conflict* between their intuitive, heuristic-based reasoning and the base-rate information, but at a level below conscious awareness and not strong enough to *inhibit* the wrong System 1 answer.

Other evidence that System 1 and System 2 do not work in a simple sequence was reported by Pennycook and Thompson (2012). They used the following type of problems:

In a study 1,000 people were tested. Among the participants there were 995 nurses and five doctors. Paul is a randomly chosen participant of this study. Paul is 34 years old. He lives in a beautiful home in a posh suburb. He is well spoken and very interested in politics. He invests a lot of time in his career. What is the probability that Paul is a nurse?

Again, the essence of the problem is the conflict between the base-rate information (suggesting Paul is a nurse) and the personality description (which is more consistent with him being a doctor). Use of System 1 processing might lead participants to focus on the personality description using the representativeness heuristic and decide that Paul was a doctor. Interestingly, the participants were asked to answer each problem twice: initially with the first answer that came to mind and then with a more deliberate answer.

On the dual-process theory, people need to use System 2 processing for their answers to reflect base-rate information. That leads to two predictions. First, initial answers should rarely reflect base-rate information but instead should involve the representativeness heuristic. Second, base-rate information should be used much more often in deliberate than initial answers.

Of theoretical importance, neither prediction was supported. Approximately half of the initial answers were based primarily on base-rate information. Of the participants who changed their responses, 30% took more account of base-rate information in their deliberate answer than in their initial one. However, an almost equal number (23%) took *less* account of base-rate information in their deliberate answer.

What is going on here? The assumptions that answers based on base-rate information always involve System 2 processing whereas those based on personality descriptions involve System 1 processing are incorrect. Processing seems to be more *flexible* than these assumptions suggest.

An alternative interpretation

To account for the findings in conflict with Kahneman's dual-process theory, De Neys (2012) suggested the *logical intuition model* (Figure 10.3). In essence, he argued that there is rapid, intuitive processing (System 1), but that this system is not entirely based on heuristic information. It can also do intuitive basic logical processing based on logical and probabilistic principles (e.g., taking into account base-rate information). It is used both when we make judgments and when we reason. The initial processing is followed by deliberate or System 2 processing if a conflict is detected.

What are the advantages of the logical intuition model over Kahneman's dual-process theory? First, heuristic and base-rate information can both be rapidly accessed through intuitive processing, which is consistent with recent evidence (Pennycook & Thompson, 2012). Second, Chun and Kruglanski (2006) observed that easily processed base-rate information is used more often under cognitive load. This is consistent with De Neys' model but not with dual-process theory. Third, it is much easier to understand how conflicts between heuristic and base-rate information are detected rapidly.

On the other hand, the model is silent about the nature of intuitive logical processing and how this relates to explicit logical thinking. How comes that we can have good intuitive logical thinking in the absence of deliberate logical thinking, and how comes that in many laboratory tasks the intuitive logical thinking is not strong enough to affect the response given? These are questions to be answered before the intuitive logical model not only describes the findings but also explains them.

a

Dual-Process Model

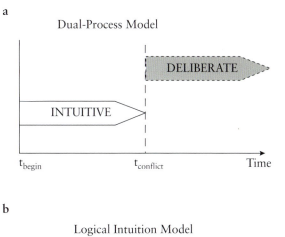

b

Logical Intuition Model

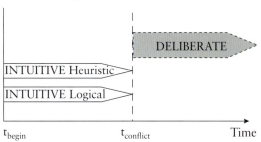

Figure 10.3 The dual-process model vs. the logical intuition model. In the dual-process model, it is assumed that intuitive System 1 thinking precedes deliberate System 2 thinking. In the logical intuition model, System 1 thinking is not entirely based on heuristics but also involves logical thinking. When a conflict is experienced, deliberate thinking is triggered. Source: From De Neys (2012). Reprinted by permission of SAGE Publications

Evaluation

+ There is reasonable evidence for the existence of two different processing systems corresponding to those assumed within the dual-process model.

+ The notion that people's judgments are typically determined by System 1 rather than by System 2 accords with most of the data.

+ The model provides an explanation for individual differences in judgment performance. Individuals making extensive use of System 2 processing perform better than those using only System 1.

− The model is based on the assumption that most people rely almost exclusively on System 1 and so simply ignore base-rate information. In fact, however, most people detect a conflict between their System 1 thinking and base-rate information.

− The logical intuition model provides a better explanation why a conflict is detected, but does not provide much detail about how intuitive logical processing works.

Section summary

- Judgment involves deciding on the likelihood of various events using whatever information is available. What matters is accuracy.

Support theory

- A possible future event seems more likely when it is supported by extra information. This is because people fail to remember all the relevant information when it is not explicitly mentioned.
- The observation that we tend to overestimate the likelihood of information that can easily be retrieved from memory and underestimate the likelihood of information that is hard to retrieve is called the availability heuristic.

Base-rate information

- People often make little or no use of base-rate information when making judgments. This is particularly true when they are reading about information they have no personal experience with and when likelihoods are expressed as probabilities.
- The observation that we pay too much attention to individuating information at the expense of base-rate information is one example of the use of the representativeness heuristic, the tendency we have to decide that an object belongs to a given category simply because it appears typical or representative of that category.
- Ignoring base-rate information can be overcome by deliberate thinking, which is more likely when we question a judgment (motivated reasoning) or when the problem formulation emphasizes the importance of differences in base rate. Judgment also tends to be better when the problems are formulated in frequencies rather than probabilities, although not to the extent predicted by the natural frequency hypothesis.

Heuristics are okay in general

- Laboratory studies have shown situations in which people are easily misguided by their heuristics. However, we rely so heavily on heuristics because in general they are helpful.
- According to Gigerenzer, humans have a toolbox of fast and frugal heuristics that help them survive and cope with demands. Two of these heuristics are the recognition heuristic (what you recognize is more important than what you do not recognize) and the take-the-best heuristic (always go for the option that seems the best and ignore the other options). Not all evidence is in line with this hypothesis, however. It also does not explain why humans ever developed deliberate judgment.

Dual-process model

- According to Kahneman, probability judgments depend on processing within two systems. One system is intuitive and fast, whereas the other is analytical and slow. We often rely almost exclusively on the intuitive system.
- The dual-process model has been examined especially with judgment problems for which the System 1 answer is in conflict with the System 2 answer. This research indicated that people seem to be sensitive to the conflict, even when it is not expressed in their final decisions. The logical intuition model has been proposed as an alternative to account for this finding.

DECISION MAKING

Life is full of decisions. Which movie will I go to see tonight? Would I prefer to go out with Dick or Harry? What career am I going to pursue after university? Who will I share an apartment with next year?

It is often argued that we are fortunate to live at a time when the choices open to us are greater than at any time in history. However, Schwartz (2004, 2009) disagrees, claiming that an explosion of choice burdens decision making. You can see his point in the following anecdote. He was in a shop called The Gap wanting to buy a pair of jeans. "I told them my size, and they asked if I wanted relaxed fit, easy fit, slim fit, boot cut, button-fly, zipper-fly, acid-washed, or stone-washed. And I said, 'I want the kind that used to be the only kind'" (Schwartz, 2004).

In the Real World 10.2 *Omission bias*

People often must decide whether action or inaction is the better way to respond to a given situation. For example, parents have to decide whether to vaccinate their young child against some disease. There is a clear risk in inaction (i.e., not having the child vaccinated) because the child may then develop the disease and possibly die. There is also a risk in action (i.e., having the child vaccinated) because the vaccine may have side-effects.

Ritov and Baron (1990) told participants to assume that their child had 10 chances in 10,000 of dying from flu during an epidemic if he/she wasn't vaccinated. The vaccine was certain to prevent the child from catching flu but had potentially fatal side-effects. Ritov and Baron found that 5 deaths per 10,000 was the average maximum acceptable risk participants were willing to tolerate in order to decide to have their child vaccinated. Thus, people would choose not to have their child vaccinated when the likelihood of the vaccine causing death was much lower than that of the disease against which the vaccine protects!

What was going on in this study? The participants argued they would feel more responsible for the death of their child if it resulted from their own actions rather than their inaction. This is **omission bias**, in which individuals prefer to risk harm from inaction or omission to the harm resulting from action.

Does omission bias in the laboratory predict omission bias in the real world? Evidence that it does was reported by DiBonaventura and Chapman (2008). They assessed omission bias in university staff under laboratory conditions. They also asked them whether they had accepted a free flu vaccine having possible side-effects. Those showing evidence of omission bias in the laboratory were less likely to have been vaccinated than those who didn't exhibit omission bias.

Omission bias is found in medicine. For example, pulmonologists (experts in treating lung disease) were given scenarios involving evaluation of pulmonary embolism and treatment of septic shock (Aberegg et al., 2005). When these experts were given the option of inaction (i.e., doing nothing), they were less likely to select the best management strategy than when this option was unavailable. Thus, these medical experts showed strong evidence of omission bias even when making decisions in their own speciality.

We now turn to gamblers in Las Vegas. Because gamblers by definition have chosen to take risks, we might imagine they wouldn't show omission bias. Nothing could be further from the truth. When people play blackjack, we can categorize their mistakes as passive ones (omission bias) or active ones (being too aggressive). Carlin and Robinson (2009) found that 80% of gamblers' mistakes were passive ones involving omission bias. Gamblers who showed omission bias lost much more money on average than did those avoiding passive mistakes.

How can we explain omission bias? It is generally assumed that the level of anticipated regret is greater when an unwanted outcome has been caused by an individual's own actions. Support for this assumption was reported by Wroe et al. (2005) in a study on MMR vaccinations, which provide protection against measles, mumps, and rubella. Adverse publicity in the UK suggesting that the vaccination might conceivably lead to autism caused thousands of parents to decide not to allow their children to receive it. Many parents argued that the level of anticipated responsibility and regret would potentially be higher if they had their child vaccinated than if they did not.

Not everyone shows omission bias. In one vaccination study (Baron & Ritov, 2004), 58% of the participants showed omission bias, but 22% showed the opposite bias: "action bias." Those susceptible to it use the heuristic, "Don't just sit there. Do something!"

There are cross-cultural differences in omission bias. It is found in more educated and less rural Mayan groups but not in less educated, rural Mayans (Abarbanell & Hauser, 2010). In the latter group there are strong social networks, and action is often regarded as fulfilling one's social obligations.

LOSSES AND GAINS

We all spend much of our time trying to achieve gains (e.g., emotional, financial, at work) while avoiding losses. Thus, we seem to make decisions to maximize the chances of making a gain and minimize the chances of making a loss. However, are we really good at maximizing our gains and minimizing our losses? Make a decision for the following three problems:

Problem 1

> Suppose someone offered you $200 if a tossed coin came up heads and a loss of $100 if it came up tails. Would you take the offer?

Problem 2

> Would you prefer to make a sure gain of $800 or an 85% probability of gaining $1,000 and a 15% probability of gaining nothing?

Problem 3

> Would you prefer to make a sure loss of $800 or an 85% probability of losing $1,000 with a 15% probability of not making any loss?

Loss aversion

The first of the three problems given above was taken from Tversky and Shafir (1992) and the other two come from Kahneman and Tversky (1984). In all three cases, most people did *not* make the best choices.

In Problem 1, the decision with the highest gain is to take the bet, as it provides an average expected gain of $50 per toss. However, typically two-thirds of people refuse to take the bet (did you?).

In Problem 2, the expected value of the second alternative ($850) is greater than that of the first alternative ($800). So, your best choice is the second alternative. Still, in a typical experiment, a majority of participants prefer the first choice with the smaller expected gain (did you?).

In Problem 3, the average expected loss is $800 for the former choice and $850 for the latter one. So, you should go with the former choice (did you?). Again, however, the typical finding is that people prefer the second choice with the larger expected loss!

Kahneman and Tversky accounted for these findings using their *prospect theory* based on two major assumptions:

1. People identify a reference point generally representing their current state.
2. People are much more sensitive to potential losses than to potential gains; this is **loss aversion**.

How does prospect theory account for the findings discussed earlier? If people are much more sensitive to losses than to gains, they should be unwilling to accept bets involving potential losses even though the potential gains outweigh the potential losses. They would also prefer a sure gain to a risky (but potentially greater) gain. Note that prospect theory does *not* predict that people will always seek to avoid risky decisions. Because they are concerned to avoid losses, they will prefer a risky option that includes the possibility of avoiding loss even if the average expected loss of this choice ($850) is larger than that of the sure loss ($800).

The television game show *Deal or No Deal* provides a way of testing prospect theory under real-life conditions involving very large potential gains. In the British version, there are 22 boxes each containing a sum of money between £0.01 and £250,000. Participants initially select one box that will be opened if the game continues to the end. They then choose one box after another.

After every few selections, participants are given the choice between continuing with the game and accepting a cash offer. Towards the end of the game, this decision can become very difficult. For example, Laura Pearce had to decide between a definite cash offer of £44,000 and a 50:50 chance of £3,000 or £250,000. What would you do? Laura Pearce took the gamble and won the top prize of £250,000.

Prospect theory has received some support from analyses of contestants' behavior on *Deal or No Deal*. Brooks et al. (2009) found that most contestants were risk-averse, and there was more risk aversion when the stakes were high. In other words, contestants often accepted the cash offer even though on average the rewards would have been greater by continuing. Males were less risk-aversive than females.

Individual differences (not emphasized within prospect theory) were also important in research by Josephs et al. (1992). They found that individuals high in self-esteem were much more likely to prefer risky gambles than those low in self-esteem. According to Josephs et al., this is because the former group have a strong self-protective system that helps them to maintain self-esteem when confronted by threat or loss.

One reason why people may be loss aversive is that in daily life, we are used to occasional big receipts of money (when we get our monthly wage or pocket money) and constant, small expenses (the things we buy to live). In such an environment, it is a good thing if alarm bells start to ring when a cost exceeds a certain (low) threshold.

In the Real World 10.3 *Risk taking by experts*

Most research on prospect theory is laboratory-based. As a result, there are doubts about the theory's applicability in the real world. In particular, it seems likely experts would have learned how to prevent biases such as loss aversion from influencing their behavior and reducing their income. Here we will briefly consider a few real-world examples.

For professional golfers, birdie (one under par) on a hole is a gain whereas bogey (one over par) is a loss. Loss aversion would lead them to be more cautious when putting for birdie than for par. In the latter case, failure to hole the putt would lead to a bogey and thus a loss.

Pope and Schweitzer (2011) studied over 2.5 million putts made by professional golfers. Par putts were less likely than same-length birdie putts to stop short of the hole (indicative of loss aversion). Pope and Schweitzer found 94% of golfers (including Tiger Woods) showed evidence of loss aversion.

Smith et al. (2009) studied experienced poker players (including many professionals) playing high-stakes poker. The stakes were high – 50% of the players studied won or lost more than $200,000! These expert poker players typically played more aggressively (i.e., betting and raising more often) following a big loss, which is as predicted if players were motivated by loss aversion.

Abdellaoui et al. (2013) studied financial professionals handling an average of 240 million euros each. As prospect theory predicts, they were risk averse for gains and risk seeking for losses on a money-based task. They were also averse to losses, but less so than commonly observed in laboratory studies with students. A substantial minority focused on gains and largely ignored losses.

In sum, even experts whose income depends on accurate decision making show loss aversion. Thus, prospect theory is applicable in the real world. However, there is some evidence (e.g., Abdellaoui et al., 2013) that experts have learned to be less loss averse than non-experts.

Framing effect

Much research has involved the **framing effect**, in which decisions are influenced by irrelevant aspects of the situation. Tversky and Kahneman (1987) used the Asian disease problem. Some participants were told there was likely to be an outbreak of an Asian disease in the United States, and it was likely to kill 600 people. Two programs of actions were proposed:

- Program A would allow 200 people to be saved.
- Program B would have a one-third probability that all 600 people would be saved and a two-thirds probability that none of the 600 would be saved.

When the issue was expressed in this form, 72% of the participants favored Program A. This was the case even though the two programs (if implemented several times) would on average lead to the saving of 200 lives.

Other participants in the study by Tversky and Kahneman (1987) were given the same problem, but this time it was negatively framed. They were told:

- Program A would lead to 400 people dying,
- Program B would have a one-third probability that nobody would die and a two-thirds probability that 600 would die.

Even though the numbers of people who would live and die were the same as in the positive version of the problem, 78% now chose program B.

These findings can be accounted for in terms of loss aversion. With both versions of the problem, the decision made by most participants was designed to avoid definite losses in terms of deaths.

Key term

Framing effect: the finding that decisions are often influenced by aspects of the situation (e.g., precise wording of a problem) that are irrelevant to good decision making.

According to prospect theory, framing effects should only be found when what is at stake has real value for the decision maker. Thus, loss aversion doesn't apply if you don't mind making a loss. Wang et al. (2001) used a life-and-death problem involving 6 billion human lives or 6 billion extraterrestrial lives. There was the usual framing effect when human lives were at stake. However, there was no framing effect when only extraterrestrial lives were involved.

More importantly, Wang (1996) argued that social and moral factors not considered by prospect theory can influence performance on modified versions of the Asian disease problem. Participants chose between definite survival of two-thirds of the patients (the deterministic option) and a one-third probability of all patients surviving and a two-thirds probability of none surviving (the probabilistic option).

In terms of minimizing the number of deaths, the deterministic option in Wang's (1996) version is much superior – on average, it leads to the survival of twice as many patients. However, the probabilistic option seems *fairer* in that all patients share the same fate. Participants strongly preferred the deterministic option when the problem related to six *unknown* patients. However, they preferred the probabilistic option when it related to six *close relatives*, because participants were more concerned about fairness in that condition.

How can we eliminate the framing effect? Almashat et al. (2008) obtained a framing effect using various medical scenarios involving cancer treatments. However, this effect disappeared when participants listed the advantages and disadvantages of each option and justified their decision. Thus, the framing effect is eliminated when individuals think carefully about the available options.

Sunk-cost effect

The sunk-cost effect is "a greater tendency to continue an endeavor once an investment in money, effort, or time has been made" (Arkes & Ayton, 1999, p. 591). The effect is captured by the expression "throwing good money after bad" and involves loss aversion.

Dawes (1988) discussed a study in which participants were told two people had paid a $100 nonrefundable deposit for a weekend at a resort. On the way there, they both became slightly unwell, and felt they would probably have a more pleasurable time at home than at the resort. Should they drive on or turn back? Many participants argued that the two people should drive on to avoid wasting the $100 – this is the sunk-cost effect. This decision involves extra expenditure (money spent at the resort vs. staying at home) and is less preferred than being at home!

Why did many participants make the apparently poor decision to continue with the trip? They thought it would be hard to explain to themselves and other people why they had wasted $100. The importance of being able to justify one's actions may help to explain why children and several animal species (e.g., blackbirds, mice) are much less affected than adult humans by the sunk-cost effect (Arkes & Ayton, 1999). We are much smarter than other species, but they don't feel the need to justify their decisions to other members of the same species.

Key term
Sunk-cost effect: the finding that individuals who have invested effort, time, or money to little avail tend to invest more resources in the hope of justifying the previous investment; it corresponds to "throwing good money after bad."

EMOTIONAL FACTORS

Why are we so sensitive to potential losses? According to Shiv et al. (2005), emotions (e.g., anxiety) make us cautious and risk-averse. That led them to the startling prediction that brain-damaged patients would *outperform* healthy individuals on a gambling task provided the brain damage reduced their emotional experience.

There were three groups of participants in Shiv et al.'s (2005) study. One group consisted of patients with brain damage in areas related to emotion (amygdala, orbitofrontal cortex, and insular or somatosensory cortex). The other groups consisted of patients with brain damage in areas unrelated to emotion and of healthy controls.

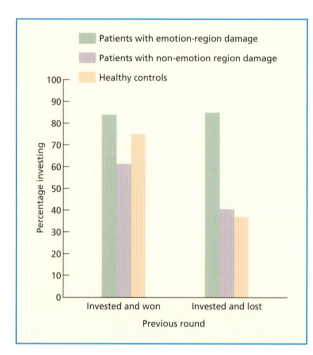

Shiv et al. (2005) initially provided participants with $20. On each of 20 rounds, they decided whether to invest $1. If they did, they lost the $1 if a coin came up heads but won $1.50 if it came up tails. Participants stood to make an average gain of 25 cents per round if they invested compared to simply retaining the $1. Thus, the best strategy to maximize profit was to invest on every single round.

Patients with damage to emotion regions invested in 84% of the rounds compared to only 61% for the other patient group and 58% for the healthy controls. Thus, the patients with restricted emotions performed best. Why was this? Patients with brain damage related to emotion were totally unaffected in their investment decisions by the outcome of the previous round (see Figure 10.4). In contrast, patients with brain damage unrelated to emotion and healthy controls were much less likely to invest following loss on the previous round than following gain.

De Martino et al. (2010) studied loss aversion in two women (SM and AP). Both had suffered severe damage to the amygdala, which is associated with fear. Neither of these women showed evidence of loss aversion. This suggests that loss aversion depends on fear. In the words of De Martino et al. (2010), the amygdala may act as a "cautionary brake."

In sum, emotional states (especially anxiety) lead individuals to become loss-averse. According to Lazarus (1991) this is a good thing, because emotions represent the "wisdom of the ages," providing time-tested responses to recurrent adaptive problems. A similar claim has been made in the *somatic marker hypothesis*, which argues that decision making is a process guided by emotions. Indeed, patients with bilateral lesions in the orbitofrontal cortex, which is critical for emotional experience, develop severe impairments in personal and social decision making, in spite of otherwise largely preserved intellectual abilities (Damasio et al., 1996; Bechara, 2004). Thus, whereas the patients of Shiv et al. (2005) performed better on the experimental betting task (Figure 10.4), they are likely to perform worse on many decisions important for their life.

Figure 10.4   Percentage of rounds in which patients with damage to emotion regions of the brain, patients with damage to other regions of the brain, and healthy controls decided to invest $1 having won or lost on the previous round. The best decision was to always invest. Healthy participants did so only if they had won on the previous rounds. Patients with emotion-region damage always used the best strategy, because their decisions were not influenced by emotions. Source: Data from Shiv et al. (2005).

SOCIAL CONTEXT

Tetlock (2002) pointed out that participants in most laboratory studies on decision making don't feel accountable to others for the decisions they make. In contrast, our decision making in everyday life is strongly influenced by the social and cultural context in which we live. Of particular importance, we often feel the need to *justify* our decisions to other people.

Evidence that the social context is important was reported by Camerer et al. (1997). They examined factors determining how long New York cab drivers decide to work. From a purely economic perspective, the cab driver should work fewer hours when business is slack and longer hours when business is good. In fact, many cab drivers did the opposite. They set themselves a target income for each day and stopped work after reaching it. As a result, they worked unnecessarily long hours when business was poor and missed out on easy money on days when business was good.

If the social context is important, accountability should influence decision making. Precisely that was found by Simonson and Staw (1992) in a study on the sunk-cost effect. Some participants were told their decisions would be shared with other students and instructors (high-accountability condition), whereas others were told their decisions would be confidential (low-accountability condition). Participants in the high-accountability condition were more likely to continue with their previously ineffective course of action and thus showed a stronger sunk-cost effect. This occurred because they experienced a greater need to justify their previous decisions.

Accountability pressures can influence the decisions of experts. In a study by Schwartz et al. (2004), medical experts decided on the appropriate treatment for a patient with osteoarthritis. Their decision making was more biased when they were made accountable for their decision by writing an explanation for it and agreeing to be contacted later to discuss it.

In sum, decision making is influenced by social context. That is even though most relevant research has involved laboratory tasks not making any real demands on social responsibility. There are probably large individual differences in the extent to which people feel the need to justify themselves to others, but little is known about this as yet.

Section summary

- Decision making involves selecting from among several possibilities. The quality is judged on the basis of the consequences.

Omission bias
- Omission bias involves a preference for risking harm from inaction rather than action. It is extremely common and has been found in medical experts and gamblers. It is due to anticipated responsibility and regret. Other individuals use the heuristic, "Don't just sit there. Do something," and show the opposite to omission bias.

Losses and gains
- According to prospect theory, most people show loss aversion – they are much more sensitive to potential losses than to potential gains. The framing

effect (in which decisions are influenced by irrelevant aspects of the situation) and the sunk-cost effect (in which good money is thrown after bad) are consistent with the theory.

Emotional factors

- Our sensitivity to potential losses occurs in part because our emotions (especially fear) make us cautious and risk-averse. People with damage to brain regions involved in emotional processing in general do not make better decisions than healthy people, as could have been expected if decision making were purely cognitive. As a matter of fact, the reverse is true, indicating that emotions are an essential aspect in decision making, as argued by the somatic marker hypothesis. Emotions represent the wisdom of the ages and allow us in general to choose what is good for us and avoid what is bad for us.

Social context

- In the real world, our decision making is influenced by the social context and by our need to justify our decisions to other people. Decision making sometimes becomes more biased when there is increased accountability for decisions.

REASONING

Reasoning involves drawing inferences from the knowledge we possess. A distinction is made between deductive reasoning and inductive reasoning.

Deductive reasoning involves drawing conclusions that are definitely valid (or invalid) provided that other statements (**premises**) are assumed to be true. This is the type of reasoning that mathematicians and logicians love, because it allows them to draw a whole system of valid conclusions from a limited set of premises (also called *axioms*). For a long time, it was considered the only form of science, because if you have valid premises (which were given to humans by their souls), all other knowledge derived from these premises is true as well. Deductive reasoning is something we often do in everyday life as well. For example, I know that Nancy is always punctual on special occasions and that today's party is a special occasion. These two premises allow me to conclude that Nancy will turn up on time.

Inductive reasoning involves drawing general conclusions from a sequence of observations. It is the type of reasoning typically used in modern-day, observation-based scientific research (see also hypothesis testing in Chapter 9). Because there is no guarantee that the conclusion is correct, information based on inductive reasoning was not considered "true" knowledge until the 17th century, when the scientific revolution took place (Brysbaert & Rastle, 2013). Inductive knowledge is something we often use in daily life as well. For instance, you may have noticed that your colleague is always happier on Fridays than on Mondays. From this observation you may draw the conclusion that your colleague likes weekends more than weekdays. The conclusion is not necessarily true (it could also be that your colleague drinks more on Sundays than on Thursdays), but it has a good chance of being true. In addition, it is a hypothesis you can test.

Our focus will be on deductive reasoning. According to philosophers and logicians, this type of reasoning should be based on formal logic, as it is the

Key terms

Deductive reasoning: a form of reasoning in which conclusions can be categorized as valid or invalid given that certain statements or premises are assumed to be true; **conditional reasoning** and syllogistic reasoning are forms of deductive reasoning.

Premises: in **deductive reasoning**, statements that participants are instructed to assume are true.

Inductive reasoning: a form of reasoning in which general conclusions are drawn from a sequence of observations; the conclusions are not necessarily true (like in deductive reasoning), but they can be evaluated via **hypothesis testing**.

only way of reasoning that guarantees truth. However, psychologists rapidly discovered that most people do *not* use logic when presented with a problem in deductive reasoning.

SYLLOGISTIC REASONING

Studies on deductive reasoning often involve syllogisms. A syllogism consists of two premises or statements followed by a conclusion. When presented with a syllogism, you have to decide whether the conclusion is valid in light of the premises. The validity (or otherwise) of the conclusion depends *only* on whether it follows logically from the premises. The truth or falsity of the conclusion in the real world is irrelevant. Thus, for example, the conclusion of the following syllogism is valid even though it is obviously untrue in the real world:

Premises

> Aristotle was a giraffe.
> All giraffes have very long necks.

Conclusion

> Aristotle had a very long neck.

If you assume that both premises are true, then you have to conclude according to rules of logic that the conclusion is also true, even if the conclusion hurts your common sense. Similarly, common-sense conclusions need not be logically valid, even though they sometimes strongly look that way. Have a look at the following syllogism. Is it logically valid according to you?

Premises

> If it rained, the road is wet.
> The road is wet.

Conclusion

> It rained.

If you think this is a valid syllogism, we are sorry to disappoint you. The conclusion does not follow necessarily from the premises, as you can easily see if we slightly change the syllogism.

Premises

> If the fire service practiced, the road is wet.
> The road is wet.

Conclusion

> The fire service practiced.

These problems nicely illustrate an observation made by psychologists. When it comes to reasoning, people seem have two approaches: one that is fast but error-prone and one that is superior but slow and laborious. You can find further examples in Research Activity 10.1.

Research Activity 10.1 *Syllogisms*

Test your powers of deductive reasoning by studying the following syllogisms and deciding which conclusions are valid (these syllogisms are taken from Manktelow, 1999, p. 64). Remember the task involves deciding whether the conclusions follow *logically* from the premises and *not* how sensible the conclusions appear in the real world.

1. *Premises*
   All the athletes are healthy.
   Some healthy people are wealthy.
   Conclusion
   Some of the athletes are wealthy.
2. *Premises*
   All the students are poor.
   No students are stupid.
   Conclusion
   Some poor people are not stupid.
3. *Premises*
   All the men are healthy.
   Some healthy people are women.
   Conclusion
   Some of the men are women.
4. *Premises*
   All the monks are men.
   No monks are women.
   Conclusion
   Some men are not women.

Did you decide that the conclusions to Syllogisms 1 and 2 are valid, whereas those to Syllogisms 3 and 4 are invalid? Hopefully, you didn't! In fact, the conclusions to Syllogisms 2 and 4 are valid, whereas those to Syllogisms 1 and 3 are invalid. Syllogisms 1 and 3 have the same structure. However, it is harder to believe that the conclusion of Syllogism 1 is invalid because it is believable. In similar fashion, Syllogisms 2 and 4 have the same structure, but it is harder to decide that the conclusion to Syllogism 4 is valid because it is less believable.

Most people are affected by the believability of syllogism conclusions. **Belief bias** refers to the tendency to accept believable conclusions and to reject unbelievable ones irrespective of their logical validity or invalidity. Evidence concerning the extent of belief bias was reported by Evans et al. (1983). Explanations for belief bias will be discussed shortly.

CONDITIONAL REASONING

The syllogisms "If it rained . . ." and "If the fire service practiced . . ." are examples of conditional reasoning. **Conditional reasoning** is a form of deductive reasoning in which people decide on the validity of "If . . . then" statements. Again, the conclusion given the premises can be true or false based on principles of logic.

Two of the most important rules of inference in conditional reasoning are *modus ponens* and *modus tollens*, both of which are associated with valid conclusions. Here is an example of *modus ponens*:

Premises

If it is raining, then Nancy gets wet.
It is raining.

Key terms

Belief bias:
in syllogistic reasoning, mistakenly accepting believable conclusions that are invalid and rejecting unbelievable ones that are valid.

Conditional reasoning:
a form of **deductive reasoning** in which an "if . . . then" statement is followed by a conclusion that is logically valid or invalid.

Conclusion

Nancy gets wet.

Here is an example of *modus tollens*:

Premises

If it is raining, then Nancy gets wet.
Nancy does not get wet.

Conclusion

It is not raining.

People consistently perform much better with *modus ponens* than with *modus tollens*. At least part of the reason is that people generally find it harder to deal with negative than with positive information.

An example of a logically false inference in conditional reasoning is *denial of the antecedent*:

Premises

If it is raining, then Nancy gets wet.
It is not raining.

Conclusion

Therefore, Nancy does not get wet.

Many people argue that this conclusion is valid, but it is actually invalid. It does not have to be raining for Nancy to get wet. For example, she may have jumped into a swimming pool.

Another error often made in human reasoning involves *affirmation of the consequent*:

Premises

If Susan is angry, then I am upset.
I am upset.

Conclusion

Therefore, Susan is angry.

Do you accept this conclusion as valid? Many people would, but it is *not* valid according to the rules of logic. The explanation is as follows: I may be upset for some other reason (e.g., I have lost my credit cards).

Other evidence that people have only limited ability to reason logically comes from studies looking at individual differences. De Neys et al. (2005) considered conditional-reasoning performance in individuals high and low in working memory capacity, a dimension closely related to intelligence (see Chapter 4). As predicted, the performance of high-capacity individuals was better than that of low-capacity individuals.

WASON SELECTION TASK

The most studied reasoning task is Wason's selection task, named after the late British psychologist Peter Wason, who designed it. This is the same person who designed the 2–4–6 task, used in research on the confirmation bias and discussed in Chapter 9.

In the Wason selection task, you are shown four cards (see Figure 10.5). There is a rule that applies to these cards: "If there is a vowel on one side, then there is an even number on the other side." Decide which cards you need to turn over to decide if the rule is true. If you aren't familiar with this task, think what your answer would be.

The most common answer by far is to select the A and 2 cards. Alas, if you did the same, you got the answer wrong! In fact, you need to see whether any cards *fail* to obey the rule. From this perspective, the 2 card is irrelevant – if there is a vowel on the other side of it, this only tells us the rule *might* be correct. If there is a consonant, we have also discovered nothing about the validity of the rule.

What is the right answer? It involves selecting the A and 7 cards, an answer given by only 5%–10% of university students (Wason, 1968). The 7 is necessary because it would definitely disprove the rule if it had a vowel on the other side.

Findings

Why do most people perform poorly on the Wason selection task? One reason is that people find it harder to reason with abstract items (e.g., A; 4) than with concrete ones with which they are more familiar. Wason and Shapiro (1971) used four cards (Manchester, Leeds, car, train) and the rule, "Every time I go to Manchester I travel by car" with British students. The task was to select only those cards needing to be turned over to test the rule. The correct answer (i.e., *Manchester*; *train*) was given by 62% of the participants against only 12% given the standard abstract version of the task.

Another reason for poor performance is **matching bias** (the tendency to select cards matching the items named in the rule regardless of whether they are correct). Ball et al. (2003) used the following problems, with the percentage of participants choosing each card in brackets:

Figure 10.5   Rule: If there is a vowel on one side of the card, then there is an even number on the other side. Which cards do you need to turn over to see if the rule is true?

1. Rule: If A then 3
   Cards: A (87%) J (7%) 3 (60%) 7 (3%)
2. Rule: If E then not 5
   Cards: E (83%) L (23%) 2 (13%) 5 (43%)

As you can see, cards matching items in the rule were selected much more often than cards not matching items for both rules. This provides strong evidence for the matching bias. Note that selecting the number "3" in Problem 1 is incorrect, whereas selecting the number "5" in Problem 2 is correct.

How can we improve performance on the Wason selection task? A major reason for poor performance is the failure to try to falsify the rule, and so performance should improve if participants are motivated to disprove the rule. This prediction was tested by Dawson et al. (2002). They gave some participants the rule that individuals high in emotional lability experience an early death. There were four cards referring to individuals. One side indicated whether the person was high or low in emotional lability and the other side indicated whether they experienced an early or a late death. What the participants could see on the tops of the cards was as follows: low emotional lability; high emotional lability; early death; late death.

The correct answer was to select the high emotional lability and late death cards. Of participants low in emotional lability (and so having no powerful reason to disprove the rule), only 9% solved the problem. In contrast, of those participants high in emotional lability, 38% solved the problem because they were highly motivated to disprove the rule.

Munro and Stansbury (2009) replicated these findings. They also discovered that making participants high in emotional lability feel good about themselves reduced their motivation to disprove the rule and impaired their performance.

We can also persuade people to try to disprove the rule by using a deontic rule (e.g., "If there is a p then you *must* do q"). **Deontic rules** are concerned with detection of rule violation (e.g., involving cheating) and so focus participants' attention on the importance of trying to disprove rules.

Sperber and Girotto (2002) gave some participants a deontic version of the selection task. Paolo buys things through the Internet but is concerned he will be cheated. For each order, he fills out a card. On one side of the card, he indicates whether he has received the item ordered, and on the other side he indicates whether he has paid for the items ordered. He places four orders and what is visible on the four cards is as follows: "item paid for," "item not paid for," "item received," and "item not received."

Which cards does Paolo need to turn over to decide whether he has been cheated? Sperber and Girotto found that 68% of their participants made the correct choices (i.e., "item paid for"; "item not received").

In sum, many participants perform poorly on the Wason selection task because they use simple strategies such as matching bias or trying to confirm the rule. Performance improves greatly when steps are taken to increase participants' focus on the possible falsity of the rule and the need to try to disprove it.

THEORIES OF REASONING

Remember that philosophers and logicians assumed that the rules of logic were followed in reasoning. Language is translated in propositions (see Glossary;

Chapter 6), and propositions are combined on the basis of logic. Rapidly, however, psychologists discovered that very few people reason on the basis of propositional logic, because it is cognitively too demanding. In the preceding paragraphs we have seen ample evidence of "non-logic" thinking. How can we explain this?

A first element likely to play a role is that the meanings of words in logic may differ from those in everyday language (Evans, 2002). For example, consider the proposition, "It is raining." In propositional logic, this proposition *must* be true or false. In everyday life, on the other hand, there would be uncertainty if it wasn't really raining but it was so misty you could almost call it raining.

Here is another example. In an "If . . . then" statement, the typical expectation is that the if-part of the statement occurs *before* the then-part (e.g., "If it rains, then I will get wet"). However, our everyday understanding of language can lead to the opposite time order. For example, most people interpret "If the shelf collapsed, then someone put a heavy object on it" as meaning the then-part preceded the if-part (Byrne & Johnson-Laird, 2009).

Another misunderstanding in conditional reasoning is that in traditional logic the proposition "If a, then b" is valid both when "a" is true and untrue. However, the word "if" is ambiguous in natural language, with "If a, then b" sometimes meaning "If and only if a, then b." Here is an example. If someone says to you, "If you mow the lawn, I will give you five dollars," you are likely to interpret it to imply, "If you don't mow the lawn, I won't give you five dollars" (Geis & Zwicky, 1971). However, this interpretation is not consistent with traditional logic. This inconsistency may be a reason why people are so prone to using affirmation of the consequent. The syllogism "If it rained, the street is wet. The street is wet. Thus it rained." is invalid in logic, but the syllogism "If and only if it rained, the street is wet. The street is wet. Thus it rained." is valid.

So, one reason why participants think "illogically" is that they understand the premises differently than assumed by logicians. However, this is not the complete story. There is good evidence that people's reasoning is based on principles other than logic. Many theories have been put forward about the nature of these principles in deductive reasoning (Evans, 2008). In this section, we will consider two of the most important theoretical approaches. First, there is the mental model approach of Johnson-Laird. Second, there is Evans' heuristic-analytic model.

Mental models

Johnson-Laird (e.g., 1983, 2004) assumes that the processes involved in reasoning resemble those involved in language comprehension. *So what?*, you may be thinking. In fact, this assumption has important implications. First, it implies that when we consider a reasoning problem, we don't immediately switch on cognitive processes specialized for logical thinking. Instead, we use processes closely resembling those you are using to understand this paragraph.

Second, when we read some text or engage in reasoning, we typically focus on what the writer is telling us. We focus on what *is* the case rather than on what is *not* the case. More specifically, we construct a **mental model**, which represents a possible state of affairs in the world. For example, a tossed coin has an infinite number of possible trajectories, but there are only two mental

| Key term

Mental model:
used in reasoning, an internal or mental representation of some possible situation or event in the world.

models: heads; tails. Mental models generally represent what is true and ignore what is false – this is known as the **principle of truth**.

Here is a more complex example of a mental model:

Premises

The lamp is on the right of the pad. The book is on the left of the pad. The clock is in front of the book. The vase is in front of the lamp.

Conclusion

The clock is to the left of the vase.

Johnson-Laird (1983) assumed that people use the information contained in the premises (statements assumed to be true) to construct a mental model:

book   pad   lamp
clock   vase

The conclusion that the clock is to the left of the vase clearly follows from the mental model. The fact that it is impossible to construct a mental model consistent with the premises but inconsistent with the conclusion indicates that it is valid.

How do we set about constructing mental models? We use the limited processes of working memory (Glossary; see Chapter 4). If we can't construct a mental model that falsifies the conclusion, then we assume that it is valid.

It is demanding to construct mental models. As a result, we follow the **principle of parsimony** (economy): "individuals tend to construct only a single, simple, and typical model" (Jahn et al., 2007, p. 2076).

How can we test the assumption that the limited capacity of working memory is needed to construct mental models? If the assumption is correct, people should find it harder to solve reasoning problems as the number of mental models consistent with the premises increase. This assumption was confirmed by Copeland and Radvansky (2004). Eighty-six percent of people drew the valid conclusion when the premises only allowed the generation of one mental model. This figure dropped to 39% when two mental models were possible and to 31% with three mental models.

It follows from the theory that syllogistic reasoning should be better in individuals having high working memory capacity than in those with low capacity. That is precisely what Copeland and Radvansky (2004) found.

Jahn et al. (2007) tested the principle of parsimony (the notion that people often construct only a *single* mental model). They presented participants with a series of statements, and the latter decided whether all the statements were consistent with each other. Here is an example:

A table is between the TV and a chair.
The light is on the left of the TV.
The table is next to the light.

Are these statements all consistent with each other? They are consistent, but many individuals in the study by Jahn et al. (2007) said, "no." What they did was to construct a *single* mental model like this:

Key terms

Principle of truth: including what is true but omitting what is false from a mental representation or **mental model**.

Principle of parsimony: in **deductive reasoning**, the tendency to form only one mental model even when additional ones could be constructed.

light TV table chair
[table can't be next to the light]

If they had ignored the principle of parsimony, they would have constructed an alternative mental model in which the statements were all consistent:

chair table light TV

There are large individual differences in reasoning strategies. Bucciarelli and Johnson-Laird (1999) identified the initial strategies used by people given reasoning problems by videotaping them as they evaluated valid and invalid syllogisms. Some participants initially formed a mental model of the first premise, to which they then added information based on the second premise. Others proceeded in the opposite direction, and still others constructed an initial mental model satisfying the conclusion and then tried to show it was wrong.

Evaluation

+ Many reasoning errors occur because people use the principle of parsimony and the principle of truth when they are inappropriate.

+ The notion that reasoning involves similar processes to language comprehension is a powerful one.

+ Reasoning performance is constrained by the limitations of working memory.

− It is not very clear how we decide which pieces of information to include in our mental models.

− The theory doesn't fully explain the existence of large individual differences in reasoning strategies.

Heuristic-analytic theory

Evans (2006) put forward a theory of reasoning differing from mental model theory in two important ways. First, there is more emphasis on the use of world knowledge and the immediate context in reasoning. Second, there is less emphasis on the use of deductive reasoning. According to Evans' heuristic-analytic theory, human reasoning is based on three principles:

1. *Singularity principle*: Only a *single* mental model is considered at any given time.
2. *Relevance principle*: The most *relevant* (i.e., plausible or probable) mental model based on prior knowledge and the current context is considered.
3. *Satisficing principle*: The current mental model is evaluated and accepted if adequate. Use of this principle often leads people to accept conclusions that might be true but are not necessarily so.

What happens in more detail? First, when someone is presented with a reasoning problem, relatively simple heuristic processes use task features, the current goal, and background knowledge to construct a single hypothetical possibility or mental model. Second, time-consuming and effortful analytic processes may or may not intervene to revise or replace this mental model. These analytic processes are most likely to be used by highly intelligent, motivated individuals and when sufficient time is available.

A very useful phenomenon for distinguishing between heuristic and analytic processes is belief bias (discussed earlier in this chapter; see Glossary). This bias occurs when a conclusion that is logically valid but not believable is rejected as invalid, or a conclusion that is logically invalid but believable is accepted as valid. The presence or absence of the effect depends on a conflict between heuristic processes, based on belief, and analytic processes. Belief bias is stronger when only heuristic processes are used than when analytic ones are also used.

Evans' views of reasoning are very similar to the dual-process interpretation of judgment and decision making. The problem is initially taken on with heuristics (and/or intuitive logic), and subsequently analytic processing takes over when the person has enough working memory capacity and motivation and when there is enough time.

Bonnefon et al. (2008) explored individual differences in reasoning. Their main focus was on conditional reasoning involving *modus tollens*, denial of the antecedent, and affirmation of the consequent. They started from a model similar to the dual-process model of judgment. They argued that there are two processing systems individuals might use to solve conditional reasoning problems. System 1 is rapid and fairly automatic, whereas System 2 is slower and more demanding. Bonnefon et al. (2008) identified four major processing strategies on the basis of participants' performance:

1. *Pragmatic strategy* (System 1): This involves processing the problems as they would be processed informally during a conversation. This strategy was associated with numerous errors.
2. *Semantic strategy* (System 1): This involves making use of background knowledge but not of the form of argument in the problem. This strategy was associated with moderate performance.
3. *Inhibitory strategy* (System 2): This involves inhibiting the impact of the pragmatic strategy and background knowledge on performance. This strategy only worked well with some types of problems.
4. *Generative strategy* (System 2): This involves combining the inhibitory strategy with use of abstract analytic processing. This strategy produced consistently good performance on all problems.

Evaluation

+ There is convincing evidence for the distinction between heuristic and analytic processes and for the notion that the latter are more effortful than the former. Phenomena such as belief bias and matching bias indicate the importance of heuristic processes.

+ The general notion that the cognitive processes (e.g., heuristic processes; analytic processes) used by individuals to solve reasoning problems resemble those used in numerous other cognitive tasks is very useful.

+ The notion that thinking (including reasoning) is based on the singularity, relevance, and satisficing principles has received support. Most of the errors people make on reasoning problems can be explained by their adherence to these principles.

+ The theory accounts for some individual differences in performance on reasoning problems. For example, individuals who are high in working memory capacity or intelligence perform better than those low in working memory capacity or intelligence because they are more likely to use analytic processes.

− It is assumed that there are several analytic processes (Evans, 2006). However, it is not clear how individuals decide *which* ones to use.

− The notion that the processes used on reasoning tasks can be neatly categorized as heuristic or analytic is an oversimplification (Keren & Schul, 2009).

INFORMAL REASONING

For a long time, research on reasoning was inspired by propositional logic. Psychologists tested hypotheses derived from logic. However, as more and more research indicated that people reason differently, it became clear that the research inspired by logic was fairly narrow and removed from the informal reasoning of everyday life.

Informal reasoning involves using one's relevant knowledge to argue persuasively in favor of or against some statement. Such reasoning typically has little or nothing to do with logic. We are exposed to numerous informal arguments by our friends and by politicians. You can obtain a clearer idea of the essence of informal reasoning by looking at Research Activity 10.2.

Research Activity 10.2 *Informal reasoning*

Read the following arguments (taken from Ricco, 2007). Decide which of them contain fallacies or errors in reasoning and the nature of those fallacies.

1. The use of soft drugs should be legalized in the United States because a number of our allies in Europe and Asia have legalized them.
2. It's very likely that UFOs (unidentified flying objects) exist because no one has been able to prove that UFOs do not exist.
3. A lack of discipline in adulthood causes students to become criminals in adulthood because it is known that most adult criminals suffered from a lack of discipline in their childhood.
4. We should require every student to study a foreign language because it is important that we provide our students with a quality education.
5. California should have a mandatory seatbelt law because it is needed. Society needs to have laws that require people to wear seatbelts, even if they do not want to wear them.
6. We must stop the movement for a moment of silence in public schools. Because once you allow a moment of silence it soon becomes a moment of teachers leading prayers, and before long, the schools and the government are supporting a specific religion.

In fact, *all* of these arguments are fallacious. Here are the reasons for each argument in turn:

1. Mere fact that others accept or do something is not sufficient reason.
2. Absence of arguments against a claim is not an argument for the claim.
3. Correlation is not necessarily causation.
4. The reason does not appear to have anything to do with the claim.
5. The reason and the claim are the same or too similar.
6. No reasons given as to why one step would lead to another.

Informal vs. deductive reasoning

Informal reasoning is clearly different from deductive reasoning. People's ability to identify fallacies in informal reasoning is only weakly associated with their deductive reasoning performance (Ricco, 2003). This suggests that rather different cognitive processes are involved. On the other hand, individuals who are good at overcoming belief bias (see Glossary) in deductive reasoning often perform well at detecting informal fallacies (Ricco, 2007).

The *content* of an argument is important in informal reasoning (and in everyday life) but is (at least in principle) irrelevant in formal deductive reasoning. For example, consider the two following superficially similar arguments (Hahn & Oaksford, 2007):

1. Ghosts exist because no one has proved they do not.
2. The drug is safe because we have no evidence that it is not.

The implausibility of ghosts existing means that most people find the second argument more persuasive than the first.

A second difference between informal reasoning and deductive reasoning is that *contextual factors* are important in informal reasoning. For example, we are more impressed by arguments on a given topic put forward by an expert than the same arguments proposed by a non-expert (Walton, 2010; see also In the Real World 10.4). Hahn and Oaksford (2007) provided evidence of a different kind of context effect. They used a scenario in which it was argued that a loud noise indicated that a thunderstorm was approaching. Participants were more convinced by that argument when the scenario took place in a woodland campsite than when it took place near an airport.

In the Real World 10.4 *Informal reasoning can be unduly influenced by neuroscience content: "neuroimaging illusion"*

How do we decide whether the explanations of findings given by cognitive psychologists or cognitive neuroscientists are convincing? Perhaps you are most likely to be convinced when there is evidence from functional neuroimaging showing the brain areas that seem to be most involved. Weisberg et al. (2008) addressed this issue in a study on students taking an introductory course in cognitive neuroscience. The students were provided with a mixture of good and bad explanations for various psychological phenomena. Some explanations were accompanied by neuroscience evidence irrelevant to the quality of the explanation. The students indicated how satisfying they found each explanation.

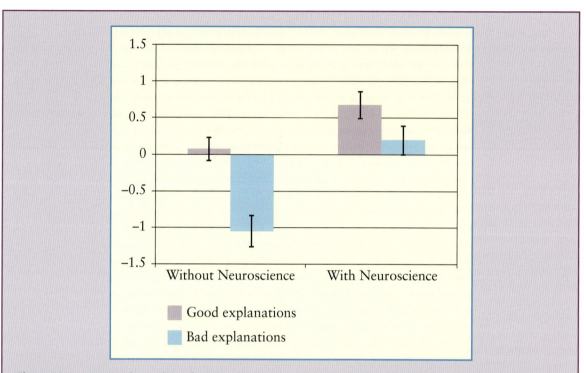

Figure 10.6 Mean student ratings of good and bad explanations of scientific phenomena with and without neuroscience information.
Source: From Weisberg et al. (2008). © Massachusetts Institute of Technology, by permission of the MIT Press.

The students were more impressed by explanations accompanied by neuroscience evidence, especially with bad explanations (see Figure 10.6). This is a clear example of context having a disproportionate impact on informal reasoning. Why were the students so impressed by neuroscience evidence irrelevant to the quality of the explanation? First, neuroscientific findings often seem more "scientific" than purely psychological ones because they involve complex and expensive technology. Second, it is easy to assume information about brain activity provides fairly direct access to information about underlying psychological processes.

In sum, this study provides an illustration of the *neuroimaging illusion*, the observation that people trust neuroimaging findings more than is warranted by the data. The take-home message is that you need to evaluate neuroscientific evidence as carefully as psychological evidence!

A third difference between deductive and informal reasoning is that traditional research on deductive reasoning focuses on *binary logic* – every proposition is assumed to be true or false. In contrast, informal reasoning is all about *probabilities* – we regard most statements or arguments as possibly or probably true rather than certainly true or certainly false.

We can see the importance of these differences by considering fallacies (Hahn & Oaksford, 2014). An example is the *straw man fallacy* in which someone else's views are misrepresented by weakening or distorting them. According to classical logic, such fallacies are totally inadequate forms of argument because they are not supported by logic. However, that position is too extreme if we think in terms of probabilities. As Aikin and Casey (2011) pointed out, one version of the straw man fallacy involves selecting one's opponent's weakest arguments and then trying to demolish them. This version can genuinely reduce the probability that the opponent's position is correct.

Finally, the reasoner's *motives* often differ between deductive reasoning and informal reasoning. People trying to solve deductive reasoning problems are supposed to be motivated to reason as logically and accurately as possible. In contrast, the motives of those engaged in informal reasoning are often very different. According to Mercier and Sperber (2011, p. 57), "The function of informal reasoning is . . . to devise and evaluate arguments intended to persuade. . . . Skilled arguers are not after the truth but after arguments supporting their views." This viewpoint is somewhat narrow. In fact, we also use informal reasoning for thinking generally and for anticipating and planning the future (Evans, 2011).

Motivational factors

If Mercier and Sperber's (2011) view of informal reasoning motivated by persuasion power is right, it follows that people should exhibit myside bias. This is the tendency to evaluate propositions from one's own perspective rather than solely on their merits because this confirms us in the rightness of our views.

Stanovich and West (2007) studied myside bias by presenting contentious (but factually correct) propositions such as the following:

1. College students who drink alcohol while in college are more likely to become alcoholic in later life.
2. The gap in salary between men and women generally disappears when they are employed in the same position.

Students were given the task of rating the accuracy of these propositions.

What did Stanovich and West (2007) find? Students who drank alcohol rated the accuracy of proposition 1 lower than those who didn't. Women rated the accuracy of proposition 2 lower than men. In other words, there was strong myside bias.

Earlier in the chapter we discussed belief bias, which involves accepting believable conclusions that are invalid and rejecting unbelievable conclusions that are valid. Belief bias is regarded as indicative of faulty reasoning within the context of laboratory studies on deductive reasoning. In everyday life, however, the situation is very different (Mercier & Sperber, 2011) – we often *deliberately* strive to confirm our own beliefs in the face of the opposing beliefs of others.

Something else we saw earlier is that the motivation to find support for one's own views can *improve* reasoning performance (see also motivated reasoning in Chapter 9). In the discussion of the Wason selection task, we saw how personal relevance of the rule is of importance. Dawson et al. (2002) found that individuals who were strongly motivated to disprove the rule (because it implied that they would die young) showed more accurate reasoning than did individuals lacking such motivation.

There is yet another way in which motivation can influence informal reasoning. In our everyday lives, we are often influenced by the goals or motives of writers, whereas the writer's goals are ignored on traditional deductive-reasoning tasks. This focus on the writer's goals leads us to draw more *inferences*

Key term

Myside bias:
in informal reasoning, the tendency to evaluate statements in terms of one's own beliefs and behavior rather than on their merits.

than we would with traditional tasks. For example, suppose someone writes, "If the Kyoto accord is ratified, greenhouse gases will be reduced." You would probably infer that the writer favors reducing greenhouse gases, and so believe the Kyoto accord should be ratified (Thompson et al., 2005).

What are the effects on reasoning when people focus on the writer's perspective or goals? Thompson et al. (2005) addressed this issue. Conditional reasoning was superior when participants focused on the writer's perspective than when they didn't. For example, the logically valid *modus ponens* and *modus tollens* inferences (discussed earlier) were accepted more often when participants adopted the writer's perspective. Thus, people can reason more logically than appears from their performance on traditional deductive-reasoning tasks.

Conclusions

In principle, there are several important differences between deductive reasoning and informal reasoning. For example, knowledge of the world is supposed to be completely irrelevant in deductive reasoning but very relevant in informal reasoning. However, the differences are much less marked in practice than in principle. For example, the existence of belief bias in deductive-reasoning tasks means that many people make use of their knowledge of the world even when they have been told not to do so.

There are other ways in which performance on deductive-reasoning tasks resembles that of informal-reasoning tasks more than might have been imagined. Individuals' personal motives often influence informal reasoning but are supposed to be irrelevant of deductive-reasoning tasks. However, personal motivation has been found to influence performance on the Wason selection task (Dawson et al., 2002). Finally, there is much evidence that contextual factors influence informal reasoning. Such factors also influence deductive reasoning (e.g., Byrne, 1989), even though they are strictly irrelevant.

In sum, the processes involved in deductive and informal reasoning resemble each other in many ways. As a result, many findings from studies on informal reasoning are of relevance to research on deductive reasoning. Future research will undoubtedly clarify the similarities and differences between the processing used on the two types of reasoning tasks.

Theory of informal reasoning

Oaksford and Hahn (2004) put forward a theory of informal reasoning (subsequently developed by Hahn & Oaksford, 2007). In this theory, they identified several factors influencing the perceived strength of a conclusion:

1. degree of previous conviction or belief;
2. positive arguments have more impact than negative arguments;
3. strength of the evidence.

Oaksford and Hahn (2004) studied these factors using scenarios such as the following one:

> *Barbara*: Are you taking digesterole for it?
> *Adam*: Yes, why?
> *Barbara*: Well, because I strongly believe that it does have side-effects.

Adam: It does have side-effects.
Barbara: How do you know?
Adam: Because I know of an experiment in which they found side-effects.

This scenario possesses strong prior belief (i.e., "strongly believe"), a positive belief (i.e., it does have side-effects), and weak evidence (i.e., one experiment). There were several variations of this scenario, some of which involved a weak prior belief, negative belief (i.e., does not have side-effects), or 50 experiments rather than one.

Participants decided how strongly Barbara should now believe the conclusion that the drug has side-effects. As predicted, the conclusion was most strongly supported when there was a strong previous belief, positive arguments were put forward, and the supporting evidence was strong.

Section summary

- Reasoning involves drawing inferences from the knowledge we possess. Deductive reasoning involves drawing conclusions that are definitely valid (or invalid) provided that other statements (premises) are assumed to be true. Inductive reasoning involves drawing general conclusions from a sequence of observations. It does not guarantee valid conclusions but generates hypotheses that can be tested. Both forms of reasoning are used in scientific research and daily life to reach conclusions.

Syllogistic reasoning
- A syllogism consists of two premises or statements followed by a conclusion. Syllogistic reasoning is part of deductive reasoning. Many people make errors in syllogistic reasoning because of belief bias. This bias involves focusing on the believability of conclusions rather than on their logical validity.

Conditional reasoning
- Conditional reasoning is a second form of deductive reasoning. Many errors are made in conditional reasoning because most people have a limited ability to think logically and because they are influenced by irrelevant contextual information. Individuals who are high in working memory capacity perform better than those of low capacity.

Wason selection task
- Performance is generally very poor on the Wason selection task because participants rely on simple strategies, such as the matching bias, rather than on logical reasoning. Far more correct answers are produced when deontic rules are used because such rules increase participants' attention to the possibility that the rule is false. Performance is also better when participants are familiar with the contents of the problem and are motivated to disprove the rule.

Theories of reasoning
- According to mental model theory, we construct mental models when reasoning. These models represent what is true and ignore what is false

(principle of truth), even when what is false is relevant to solving the problem. Often only a single mental model is formed even when there are other
possible mental models (principle of parsimony). It is unclear within the
theory how we decide what information to include within a mental model.

- According to heuristic-analytic theory, reasoners use simple heuristic processes to form a mental model. After that, time-consuming analytic processes are sometimes used to revise or replace the initial mental model.

Informal reasoning

- The content of an argument is important in informal reasoning but not in
deductive reasoning. Contextual factors are also more important in informal reasoning. With informal reasoning, people are motivated to try to persuade others of their beliefs and views. Such motivation can produce errors
(e.g., belief bias, myside bias). However, it can also lead people to reason
more logically in some situations. The differences between the processes
involved on informal and deductive-reasoning tasks are larger in principle
than in practice.
- According to Hahn and Oaksford (2007), the perceived strength of a conclusion in informal reasoning depends on three factors: the strength of the
evidence, the degree of prior belief, and whether the arguments are positive or negative. The available evidence supports the theory.

ARE HUMANS RATIONAL?

Research discussed in this chapter and the previous chapter indicates that
human thinking and reasoning are often inadequate. Apparently, many people are not rational in their thinking: we fail to solve fairly simple problems
(Chapter 9); we often ignore base-rate information when making judgments;
90% of people produce the wrong answer on the Wason selection task; and
we are very prone to belief bias in syllogistic reasoning.

These findings reveal a paradox. Most people (but not all!) cope reasonably
well with the problems and challenges of everyday life and yet seem irrational and
illogical when given thinking and reasoning problems in the laboratory. However,
that overstates the differences between everyday life and the laboratory. Our everyday thinking is less rational and effective than we like to believe, and our thinking
and reasoning in the laboratory are less inadequate than is often supposed.

WHY HUMAN REASONING IS NOT LIMITED

There are several reasons why many apparent inadequacies and limitations
of human thinking and reasoning should not be taken at face value. First, it
is often misleading to describe people's use of heuristics as "errors." Heuristics allow us to make rapid, reasonably accurate judgments and decisions. As
Maule and Hodgkinson (2002, p. 71) pointed out:

*Often . . . people have to judge situations or objects that change over
time, making it inappropriate to expend a good deal of time to make a
precise judgment . . . an approximate judgment based on a simpler, less
effortful heuristic may be much more appropriate.*

Second, performance on tasks is often poor because it is unclear which information is important. On many judgment problems, people ignore base-rate information because its relevance is not explicit. When problems are reworded so people can use their intuitive causal knowledge to understand why base-rate information is relevant, their performance is much better (e.g., Krynski & Tenenbaum, 2007).

Third, many so-called errors in human decision making only appear as such when we think of people operating in a social vacuum. As we saw in this chapter, the decisions that people make are often influenced by accountability – the need to justify those decisions to others.

Fourth, "errors" on deductive reasoning problems often mostly reflect the artificiality of such problems. For example, the validity of the conclusions on syllogistic reasoning problems does not depend on whether they are believable or unbelievable. It is hard to think of real-world situations requiring reasoning in which background knowledge is totally irrelevant. Laboratory deductive reasoning tasks are additionally artificial in that conclusions are definitely valid or invalid. In contrast, reasoning in everyday life nearly always involves varying levels of probability rather than certainties.

Thus, performance on many judgment and reasoning tasks underestimates people's ability to think effectively. However, we must beware of the temptation to go further and claim that all our difficulties stem from inadequacies in the problems themselves or because the problems fail to motivate people. Our thinking really is more error-prone than we are aware of.

WHY HUMAN REASONING IS LIMITED

There are several reasons for believing human reasoning is limited. Here we will briefly consider five such reasons.

First, Camerer and Hogarth (1999) reviewed 74 studies concerned with the effects of motivation on thinking and reasoning. The provision of incentives improved performance to some extent but never led to flawless performance, suggesting that motivation alone is not enough for good performance.

Second, poor performance is sometimes due to limitations within the participants rather than the problems themselves. For example, Brase et al. (2006) used a complex judgment task involving use of base-rate information. Students from a leading university were much more likely than those from a second-tier university (40% vs. 19%) to produce the correct answer. Notice again that even the best students performed at a rather low level.

Third, many participants fail to solve problems even when strenuous steps are taken to ensure they fully understand them. For example, Tversky and Kahneman (1983) studied the conjunction fallacy. Participants decided from a description of Linda whether it was more likely she was a feminist bank teller than that she was a bank teller. There was still a strong (although somewhat reduced) conjunction fallacy when the category of bank teller was made explicit: "Linda is a bank teller whether or not she is active in the feminist movement."

Fourth, we would expect experts to interpret problems correctly and avoid cognitive biases in their thinking. In reality, however, medical experts make biased judgments and decisions on topics they are expert in (e.g., Redelmeier et al., 1995; Schwartz et al., 2004).

Figure 10.7 Overconfidence (%) as a function of actual performance (increasing from left to right on the horizontal axis) shown by the blue line. The green line indicates the absence of overconfidence or underconfidence. Each square represents an individual player.
Source: From Simons (2013). Reprinted with permission of Springer.

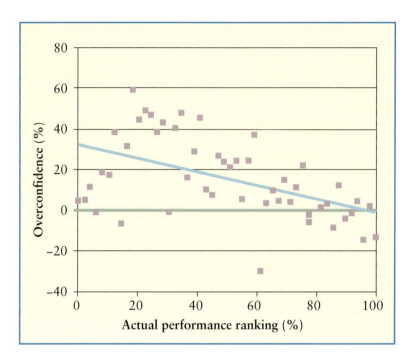

Fifth, there is the **Dunning-Kruger effect**: "those who are incompetent . . . have little insight into their incompetence" (Dunning, 2011, p. 260). Individuals who are largely unaware of their own thinking mistakes are unlikely to show much improvement over time and so continue to exhibit signs of "irrationality."

Why does the Dunning-Kruger effect exist? Evaluating the correctness of one's own responses on cognitively demanding tasks often requires very similar knowledge and expertise to those necessary to produce the correct responses in the first place. The effect can be dramatic. Dunning (2011) considered an experiment of his on the Wason selection task. Some participants used the same correct rule across different versions of this task and so had a success rate of 100%. Other participants used the same incorrect rule consistently, and so had a 0% success rate. Both groups thought they had solved between 80% and 90% of the problems correctly!

Simons (2013) found the Dunning-Kruger effect is unexpectedly robust. Bridge players were given feedback about their performance following each session at a bridge club. In spite of that, weaker players still overestimated their future performance (see Figure 10.7).

WHAT IS RATIONALITY?

Deciding whether humans are rational depends on how we define "rationality." A very popular viewpoint (championed by many traditional researchers) was that rational thought is governed by logic. It follows that deductive reasoning (which seems to require logical thinking) is very relevant for assessing human rationality. Sadly, most people perform relatively poorly on complex deductive reasoning tasks. As a result, humans are not very rational if we define rationality as reasoning according to the rules of logic.

| Key term

Dunning-Kruger effect: the finding that less-skilled individuals overestimate their abilities more than those who are more skilled.

The approach discussed here is an example of *normativism*. Normativism "is the idea that human thinking reflects a normative system [one conforming to norms or standards] against which it should be measured and judged" (Elqayam & Evans, 2011, p. 233). Thus, human thinking is "correct" if it conforms to classical logic but "incorrect" otherwise.

There are serious doubts as to whether logic (and deductive reasoning) provides a suitable normative system against which to evaluate human thinking. Why is that? As Sternberg (2011, p. 270) pointed out, "Few problems of consequence in our lives had a deductive or even any meaningful kind of 'correct' solution. Try to think of three, or even one!"

An alternative (and preferable) approach is that human rationality involves effective use of probabilities rather than logic. This makes sense (and can be regarded as rational) given that we live in a world typically characterized by uncertainty and imprecise information rather than the certainties of logic.

Oaksford and Chater (e.g., 2009) put forward an influential probabilistic approach to human reasoning. The emphasis in this approach is on probability (subjective degree of belief). The central hypothesis is that prior subjective probabilities are modified on the basis of new information to produce posterior subjective probabilities. The theory has received support from research in several areas including informal reasoning.

Bounded rationality

The Nobel Prize winner Herbert Simon devoted much of his research career to the issue of human rationality (Heukelom, 2007). According to Simon (1945, p. 5), behavior is rational, "in so far as it selects alternatives which are conductive to the achievement of the previously selected goals." Such a view is no longer governed by normativism but by *pragmatism* (do our actions allow us to cope with the environment?). In this view, an individual's informal reasoning is rational if it achieves his/her goals, even if it differs from the norms used by the experimenter.

Simon (1957) argued that we possess **bounded rationality**. This means we produce workable solutions to problems in spite of limited processing ability by using various shortcut strategies (heuristics). More specifically, our thinking is "bounded" or constrained by the environment and constraints in the mind (e.g., limited attention, limited short-term memory).

What matters is the degree of fit or match between the mind and the environment. According to Simon (1990, p. 7), "Human rational behavior is shaped like a scissors whose blades are the structure of task environments and the computational capabilities of the actor." If we consider only one of these two blades, we have but a partial understanding of human thinking.

In sum, according to the bounded rationality view many "errors" in human thinking are due to limited processing capacity rather than irrationality. As Stich (1990, p. 27) argued, "It seems simply perverse to judge that subjects are doing a bad job because they are not using a strategy that required a brain the size of a blimp [airship]."

INDIVIDUAL DIFFERENCES: INTELLIGENCE

As we saw earlier, highly intelligent individuals perform better than persons who perform less well in education. Students with high IQs perform better

Key term

Bounded rationality: the hypothesis that people produce workable solutions to problems in spite of limited processing ability by using various shortcut strategies (**heuristics**).

than those with lower IQs on many decision and reasoning tasks, but the effect of intelligence on performance is often modest. Toplak et al. (2011) reported a correlation of +0.32 between cognitive ability and performance across 15 judgment and decision tasks.

How can we explain the limited impact of intelligence on thinking and reasoning? Stanovich (2012) answered this question within his *tripartite model* (see Figure 10.8), which extends previous dual-process models. At the bottom is Type 1 processing (e.g., use of heuristics) within the so-called autonomous mind (which we share with animals). It is rapid and fairly automatic. Above that is Type 2 processing (also called System 2 processing), which is slow and effortful.

Stanovich's (2012) model has two major novel features. First, there are two levels of cognitive control at the higher level. One consists of Type 2 or System 2 processes (the algorithmic mind). The algorithmic mind contains mindware, which consists of "the rules, knowledge, procedures, and strategies that a person can retrieve from memory in order to aid decision making and problem solving" (Stanovich, 2012, p. 355). The algorithmic mind can override the heuristic responses generated by the autonomous mind when these are incorrect. Type 2 processes are only used when the individual realizes they are necessary and has the necessary motivation to initiate them. The other level of control involves the reflective mind, which has access to the individual's goals, beliefs, and general knowledge. It is involved in the decision whether or not to use Type 2 processes.

The model considers the role of individual differences in intelligence as follows. *Fluid intelligence* (which is related to working memory capacity, see

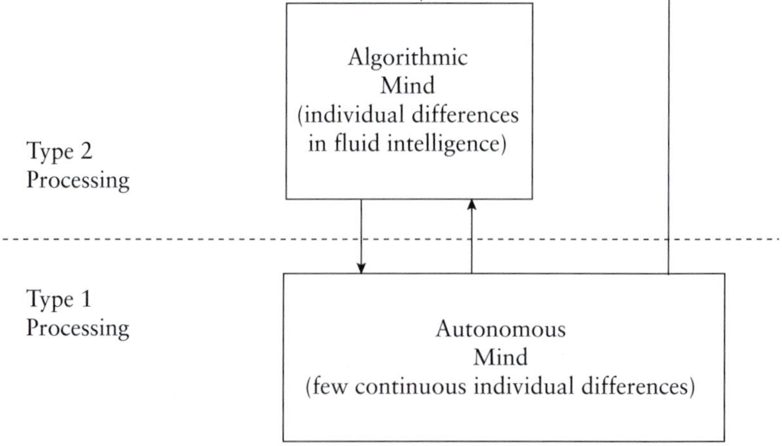

Figure 10.8 Stanovich's tripartite model of reasoning. According to the model, Type 1 processing within the autonomous mind is typically fast and fairly automatic. There are two major forms of Type 2 processing: (1) the algorithmic mind, which contains information about rules, strategies, and procedures; and (2) the reflective mind, which makes use of the individual's goals and beliefs. Individual differences in reasoning are generally much greater with respect to the reflective mind and the algorithmic mind than the autonomous mind.
Source: From Stanovich (2012), with permission from Oxford University Press.

Chapter 4) is of direct relevance to the functioning of the algorithmic mind. Individuals with high levels of fluid intelligence have a greater range of Type 2 processes and can use them more efficiently.

What follows from this tripartite theory? Of greatest importance, there are three different reasons why individuals produce incorrect responses when confronted by problems:

1. They may lack the appropriate mindware within the algorithmic mind to override incorrect heuristic responses.
2. They may have the necessary mindware but have insufficient processing capacity to override incorrect Type 1 processing.
3. They may have the necessary mindware but fail to use it because its use is not triggered by the reflective mind.

These theoretical ideas have direct relevance to the issue of human rationality. Stanovich (2009, p. 35) used the term dysrationalia to refer to "the inability to think and behave rationally despite having adequate intelligence." Why does this occur? Most people (including those with high IQs) are cognitive misers, preferring to solve problems with fast, easy strategies than with more accurate effortful ones.

The tendency to be a cognitive miser (and thus to make limited use of the reflective mind) can be assessed by the *Cognitive Reflection Test* (Frederick, 2005; see Research Activity 10.3). Toplak et al. (2011) found that low scorers on the Cognitive Reflection Test performed relatively poorly on many judgment and reasoning tasks. How are you doing? Let's hope your scores are better after having read this chapter!

Key term

Dysrationalia:
the failure of reasonably intelligent individuals to think and reason in a rational way.

Research Activity 10.3 *Cognitive Reflection Test*

Answer the following three questions to the best of your ability:

1. A bat and a ball cost $1.10 in total. The bat costs $1.00 more than the ball. How much does the ball cost?___ cents
2. If it takes 5 machines 5 minutes to make 5 widgets, how long would it take 100 machines to make 100 widgets?___ minutes
3. In a lake, there is a patch of lily pads. Every day, the patch doubles in size. If it takes 48 days for the patch to cover the entire lake, how long would it take for the patch to cover half the lake?___ days

The correct answers are 5 cents (problem 1), 5 minutes (problem 2), and 47 days (problem 3). Do not worry if you did not get them all right. When this test was administered at Harvard and Princeton Universities, 75% of the participants failed on at least one question and 20% were wrong on every question!

The most common wrong answers on the Cognitive Reflection Test are 10 cents (problem 1), 100 minutes (problem 2), and 24 days (problem 2). These answers strongly suggest people behave like cognitive misers – people who prefer to solve problems with fast, easy strategies (e.g., heuristics) rather than more accurate but more effortful strategies. Consider the first problem. You probably rapidly thought of the answer "10 cents." However, it would follow that the bat cost $1.10, and so the total would be $1.20 rather than $1.10 as required.

Section summary

- The performance of many people on reasoning problems indicates that their reasoning is often inadequate. However, the artificiality of many of the problems used means that human performance on many reasoning problems may underestimate our ability to think rationally. People spend much of their time trying to argue persuasively rather than to seek out the truth, and this motive can lead to errors in tasks on judgment and deductive reasoning.
- At the same time, it cannot be denied that human thinking is limited and that this has negative consequences in life. We are rarely aware of these consequences because we fail to see the flaws in our thinking (the Dunning-Kruger effect). Research in how these flaws can be mediated by better information provision is ongoing.
- When describing human rationality, it is better not to use a normative framework but a pragmatic framework. Within the pragmatic framework, Simon speaks of bounded rationality.

Intelligence and rationality

- Highly intelligent individuals perform better than those of less intelligence on judgment and reasoning tasks, but the effect is often small. According to the tripartite model, intelligent individuals may fail to perform well because they lack the appropriate mindware within the algorithmic mind to override incorrect heuristic responses, or because the algorithmic mind is not triggered by the reflective mind. The latter is due to a lack of motivation (cognitive miserliness).

Essay questions

1. Why do people use heuristics when making judgments? How effective are such heuristics?
2. Describe and evaluate research showing that most people are more sensitive to potential losses than to potential gains.
3. Compare and contrast the mental models and heuristic-analytic approaches to reasoning.
4. What are some of the main features of informal reasoning?
5. How rational is human thinking and reasoning?

Further reading

- Evans, J. S. T. (2008). Dual-processing accounts of reasoning, judgment, and social cognition. *Annual Review of Psychology*, *59*, 255–278. This chapter by Jonathan Evans gives a succinct account of several dual-processing approaches.
- Gigerenzer, G. & Gaissmaier, W. (2011). Heuristic decision making. *Annual Review of Psychology*, 62: 451–82. This chapter provides a comprehensive account of research on the role of heuristics in judgement and decision making.

- Johnson-Laird, P. N. (2006). *How we reason*. Oxford, UK: Oxford University Press. Phil Johnson-Laird provides a comprehensive account of reasoning with an emphasis on his mental model theory.
- Kahneman, D. (2011). *Thinking, fast and slow*. London: Penguin Books. Several chapters in this fascinating book by Danny Kahneman focus on judgement and decision making.
- Manktelow, K. (2012). *Thinking and reasoning: An introduction to the psychology of reason, judgment and decision making*. Hove: Psychology Press. This is a good introduction to the psychology of judgment, decision making, and reasoning.
- Mercier, H., & Sperber, D. (2011). Why do humans reason? Arguments for an argumentative theory. *Behavioral and Brain Sciences*, *34*, 57–74. In this paper, Mercier and Sperber discuss the motives underlying informal reasoning. It provides insights into the reasons why reasoning often appears biased.
- Pachur, T. & Bröder, A. (2013). Judgment: A cognitive processing perspective. *WIREs Cognitive Science*, 4: 665–81. The authors provide a comprehensive account of judgment research and identify the main cognitive processes involved.
- Shah, A. K., & Oppenheimer, D. M. (2008). Heuristics made easy: An effort-reduction framework. *Psychological Bulletin*, *134*, 207–222. The authors make a persuasive case that effort reduction is of central importance with heuristics or rules of thumb.
- Stanovich, K. (2010). *Rationality and the reflective mind*. Oxford: Oxford University Press. Keith Stanovich discusses human rationality at length, including an analysis of the role of intelligence in thinking and reasoning.

REFERENCES

Abarbanell, L., & Hauser, M. D. (2010). Mayan morality: An exploration of permissible harms. *Cognition*, *115*, 207–224.

Abdellaoui, M., Bleichrodt, H., & Kammoun, H. (2013). Do financial professionals behave according to prospect theory? An experimental study. *Theory and Decision*, *74*, 411–429.

Aberegg, S. K., Haponik, E. F., & Terry, P. B. (2005). Omission bias and decision making in pulmonary and critical care medicine. *Chest*, *128*, 1497–1505.

Aikin, S. F., & Casey, J. (2011). Straw men, weak men, and hollow men. *Argumentation*, *25*, 87–105.

Almashat, S., Ayotte, B., Edelstein, B., & Margrett, J. (2008). Framing effect debiasing in medical decision making. *Patient Education and Counseling*, *71*, 102–107.

Arkes, H. R., & Ayton, P. (1999). The sunk cost and Concorde effects: Are humans less rational than lower animals? *Psychological Bulletin*, *125*, 591–600.

Ball, L. J., Lucas, E. J., Miles, J. N. V., & Gale, A. G. (2003). Inspection times and the selection task: What do eye movements reveal about relevance effects? *Quarterly Journal of Experimental Psychology*, *56A*, 1053–1077.

Baron, J., & Ritov, I. (2004). Omission bias, individual differences, and normality. *Organizational Behavior and Human Decision Processes*, *94*, 74–85.

Bechara, A. (2004). The role of emotion in decision-making: Evidence from neurological patients with orbitofrontal damage. *Brain and Cognition*, *55*(1), 30–40.

Bonnefon, J. F., Eid, M., Vautie, S., & Jmel, S. (2008). A mixed Rasch model of dual-process conditional reasoning. *Quarterly Journal of Experimental Psychology*, 61, 809–824.

Brase, G. L. (2014). The power of representation and interpretation: doubling statistical reasoning performance with icons and frequentist interpretations of ambiguous numbers. *Journal of Cognitive Psychology*, 26(1), 81–97.

Brase, G. L., Fiddick, L., & Harries, C. (2006). Participants' recruitment methods and statistical reasoning performance. *Quarterly Journal of Experimental Psychology*, 59, 965–976.

Brooks, R., Faff, R., Mulino, D., & Scheelings, R. (2009). Deal or no deal, that is the question: The impact of increasing stakes and framing effects on decision making under risk. *International Review of Finance*, 9, 27–50.

Brysbaert, M., & Rastle, K. (2013). *Historical and conceptual issues in psychology* (2nd, revised ed.). Harlow: Pearson Education.

Bucciarelli, M., & Johnson-Laird, P. N. (1999). Strategies in syllogistic reasoning. *Cognitive Science*, 23, 247–303.

Byrne, R. M. J. (1989). Suppressing valid inferences with conditionals. *Cognition*, 31, 61–83.

Byrne, R. M. J., & Johnson-Laird, P. N. (2009). "If" and the problems of conditional reasoning. *Trends in Cognitive Sciences*, 13, 282–287.

Camerer, C., Babcock, L., Loewenstein, G., & Thaler, R. (1997). Labor supply of New York cab drivers: One day at a time? *Quarterly Journal of Economics*, CXII, 407–441.

Camerer, C., & Hogarth, R. B. (1999). The effects of financial incentives in experiments: A review and capital-labourproduction framework. *Journal of Risk and Uncertainty*, 19, 7–42.

Carlin, B. I., & Robinson, D. T. (2009). Fear and loathing in Las Vegas: Evidence from blackjack tables. *Judgment and Decision Making*, 4, 385–396.

Casscells, W., Schoenberger, A., & Graboys, T. B. (1978). Interpretation by physicians of clinical laboratory results. *New England Journal of Medicine*, 299, 999–1001.

Chun, W. Y., & Kruglanski, A. W. (2006). The role of task demands and processing resources in the use of base-rate and individuating information. *Journal of Personality and Social Psychology*, 91, 205–217.

Copeland, D. E., & Radvansky, G. A. (2004). Working memory and syllogistic reasoning. *Quarterly Journal of Experimental Psychology*, 57A, 1437–1457.

Damasio, A. R., Everitt, B. J., & Bishop, D. (1996). The somatic marker hypothesis and the possible functions of the prefrontal cortex [and discussion]. *Philosophical Transactions of the Royal Society B: Biological Sciences*, 351(1346), 1413–1420.

Dawes, R. M. (1988). *Rational choice in an uncertain world*. San Diego, CA: Harcourt Brace Jovanovich.

Dawson, E., Gilovich, T., & Regan, D. T. (2002). Motivated reasoning and performance on the Wason selection task. *Personality and Social Psychology Bulletin*, 28, 1379–1387.

De Martino, B., Camerer, C. F., & Adolphs, R. (2010). Amygdala damage eliminates monetary loss aversion. *Proceedings of the National Academy of Sciences of the United States of America*, 107, 3788–3792.

De Neys, W. (2006). Automatic-heuristic and executive-analytic processing during reasoning: Chronometric and dual-task considerations. *Quarterly Journal of Experimental Psychology*, 59, 1070–1100.

De Neys, W., Cromheeke, S., & Osman, M. (2011). Biased but in doubt: Conflict and decision confidence. *PLOS ONE*, 6(1), e15954.

De Neys, W., Schaeken, W., & d'Ydewalle, G. (2005). Working memory everyday conditional reasoning: Retrieval and inhibition of stored counterexamples. *Thinking & Reasoning*, 11, 349–381.

DiBonaventura, M. D., & Chapman, G. B. (2008). Do decision biases predict bad decisions? Omission bias, naturalness bias, and influenza vaccination. *Medical Decision Making*, 28, 532–539.

Ditto, P. H., Scepansky, J. A., Munro, G. D., Apanovitch, A. M., & Lockhart, L. K. (1998). Motivated sensitivity to preference-inconsistent information. *Journal of Personality and Social Psychology*, 75, 53–69.

Dunning, D. (2011). The Dunning Kruger effect: On being ignorant of one's own ignorance. *Advances in Experimental Social Psychology*, 44, 247–296.

Elqayam, S., & Evans, J. St. B. T. (2011). Subtracting "ought" from "is": Descriptivism versus normatism in the study of human thinking. *Behavioral and Brain Sciences*, 34, 233–248.

Evans, J. S. T. (2002). Logic and human reasoning: An assessment of the deduction paradigm. *Psychological Bulletin*, 128, 978–996.

Evans, J. S. T. (2006). The heuristic-analytic theory of reasoning: Extension and evaluation. *Psychonomic Bulletin & Review*, 13, 378–395.

Evans, J. S. T. (2008). Dual-processing accounts of reasoning, judgment, and social cognition. *Annual Review of Psychology*, 59, 255–278.

Evans, J. St. B. T. (2011). Reasoning is for thinking, not just for arguing. *Behavioral and Brain Sciences*, 34, 77–78.

Evans, J. St. B. T., Barston, J. L., & Pollard, P. (1983). On the conflict between logic and belief in syllogistic reasoning. *Memory and Cognition*, 11, 295–306.

Evans, J. St. B. T., Handley, S. J., Perham, N., Over, D. E., & Thompson, V. A. (2000). Frequency versus probability formats in statistical word problems. *Cognition*, 77, 197–213.

Evans, J. St. B. T., & Over, D.E. (2010). Heuristic thinking and human intelligence: A com mentary on Marewski, Gaissmaier and Gigerenzer. *Cognitive Processing, 11*, 171–175.

Fiedler, K., Brinkmann, B., Betsch, T., & Wild, B. (2000). A sampling approach to biases in conditional probability judgments: Beyond base-rate neglect and statistical format. *Journal of Experimental Psychology: General*, 129, 1–20.

Frederick, S. (2005). Cognitive reflection and decision making. *Journal of Economic Perspectives*, 19, 25–42.

Garcia-Retamero, R., & Hoffrage, U. (2013). Visual representation of statistical information improves diagnostic inferences in doctors and their patients. *Social Science & Medicine*, 83, 27–33.

Geis, M., & Zwicky, A. M. (1971). On invited inferences. *Linguistic Inquiry, 2*, 561–566.

Gigerenzer, G., & Hoffrage, U. (1999). Overcoming difficulties in Bayesian reasoning: A reply to Lewis and Keren (1999) and Mellers and McGraw (1999). *Psychological Review, 102*, 684–704.

Glymour, C. (2001). *The mind's arrows: Bayes nets and graphical causal models in psychology*. Cambridge, MA: MIT Press.

Goldstein, D. G., & Gigerenzer, G. (2002). Models of ecological rationality: The recognition heuristic. *Psychological Review, 109*, 75–90.

Groopman, J. (2007). *How doctors think*. New York: Houghton Mifflin.

Hahn, U., & Oaksford, M. (2007). The rationality of informal argumentation: A Bayesian approach to reasoning fallacies. *Psychological Review, 114*, 704–732.

Heukelom, F. (2007). What Simon says. *Tinbergen Institute Discussion Paper*, No. 07–005(1).

Hafenbrädl, S., Waeger, D., Marewski, J. N., & Gigerenzer, G. (2016). Applied decision making with fast-and-frugal heuristics. *Journal of Applied Research in Memory and Cognition*, 5(2), 215–231.

Hoffrage, U., Lindsey, S., Hertwig, R., & Gigerenzer, G. (2000). Communicating statistical information. *Science*, 290, 2261–2262.

Jahn, G., Knauff, M., & Johnson-Laird, P. N. (2007). Preferred mental models in reasoning about spatial relations. *Memory & Cognition*, 35, 2075–2087.

Johnson-Laird, P. N. (1983). *Mental models*. Cambridge, UK: Cambridge University Press.

Johnson-Laird, P. N. (2004). Mental models and reasoning. In J. P. Leighton & R. J. Sternberg (Eds.), *The nature of reasoning*. Cambridge, UK: Cambridge University Press.

Josephs, R. A., Larrick, R. P., Steele, C. M., & Nisbett, R. E. (1992). Protecting the self from the negative consequences of risky decisions. *Journal of Personality and Social Psychology*, 62, 26–37.

Kahneman, D. (2003). A perspective on judgment and choice: Mapping bounded rationality. *American Psychologist*, 58, 697–720.

Kahneman, D., & Frederick, S. (2005). A model of heuristic judgment. In K. J. Holyoak & R. G. Morrison (Eds.), *The Cambridge handbook of thinking and reasoning*. Cambridge, UK: Cambridge University Press.

Kahneman, D., & Tversky, A. (1984). Choices, values and frames. *American Psychologist*, 39, 341–350.

Kahneman, D., & Tversky, A. (1972). Subjective probability: Judgment of representativeness. *Cognitive Psychology*, 3, 430–454.

Keren, G., & Schul, Y. (2009). Two is not always better than one: A critical evaluation of two-system theories. *Perspectives on Psychological Science*, 4, 533–550.

Krynski, T. R., & Tenenbaum, J. B. (2007). The role of causality in judgment under uncertainty. *Journal of Experimental Psychology: General*, 136, 430–450.

Lazarus, R. S. (1991). Progress on a cognitive-motivational-relational theory of emotion. *American Psychologist*, 46(8), 819–834.

Lerner, J. S., Gonzalez, R. M., Small, D. A., & Fischhoff, B. (2003). Effects of fear and anger on perceived risks of terrorism: A national field experiment. *Psychological Science*, 14, 144–150.

Lichtenstein, S., Slovic, P., Fischhoff, B., Layman, M., & Coombs, J. (1978). Judged frequency of lethal events. *Journal of Experimental Psychology: Human Learning and Memory*, 4, 551–578.

Mandel, D. R. (2005). Are risk assessments of a terrorist attack coherent? *Journal of Experimental Psychology: Applied*, 11, 277–288.

Manktelow, K. I. (1999). *Reasoning and thinking*. Hove, UK: Psychology Press.

Maule, A. J., & Hodgkinson, G. P. (2002). Heuristics, biases and strategic decision making. *The Psychologist*, 15, 69–71.

Mercier, H., & Sperber, D. (2011). Why do humans reason? Arguments for an argumentative theory. *Behavioral and Brain Sciences*, 34, 57–111.

Munro, G. D., & Stansbury, J. A. (2009). The dark side of self-affirmation: Confirmation bias and illusory correlation in response to threatening information. *Personality and Social Psychology Bulletin*, 35, 1143–1153.

Newell, B. R. (2011). Recognising the recognition heuristic for what it is (and what it's not). *Judgment and Decision Making*, 6, 409–412.

Oaksford, M., & Chater, N. (2009). Précis of Bayesian rationality: The probabilistic approach to human reasoning. *Behavioral and Brain Sciences*, 32, 69–120.

Oaksford, M., & Hahn, U. (2004). A Bayesian approach to the argument from ignorance. *Canadian Journal of Experimental Psychology*, 58, 75–85.

Oppenheimer, D. M. (2004). Spontaneous discounting of availability in frequency judgment tasks. *Psychological Science*, 15, 100–105.

Oppenheimer, D. M., & Monin, B. (2009). Investigations in spontaneous discounting. *Memory & Cognition*, 37, 608–614.

Pachur, T., Hertwig, R., & Steinmann, F. (2012). How do people judge risks: Availability heuristic, affect heuristic, or both? *Journal of Experimental Psychology: Applied*, 18, 314–330.

Pennycook, G., & Thompson, V. A. (2012). Reasoning with base rates is routine, relatively effortless, and context dependent. *Psychonomic Bulletin & Review, 19,* 528–534.

Pope, D. G., & Schweitzer, M. E. (2011). Is Tiger Woods loss averse? Persistent bias in the face of experience, competition, and high stakes. *American Economic Review, 101,* 129–157.

Redelmeier, C., Koehler, D. J., Liberman, V., & Tversky, A. (1995). Probability judgment in medicine: Discounting unspecified alternatives. *Medical Decision Making, 15,* 227–230.

Ricco, R. B. (2003). The macrostructure of informal arguments: A proposed model and analysis. *Quarterly Journal of Experimental Psychology: Human Experimental Psychology, 56A,* 1021–1051.

Ricco, R. B. (2007). Individual differences in the analysis of informal reasoning fallacies. *Contemporary Educational Psychology, 32,* 459–383.

Ritov, J., & Baron, J. (1990). Reluctance to vaccinate: Omission bias and ambiguity. *Journal of Behavioral Decision Making, 3,* 263–277.

Schwartz, B. (2004). *The paradox of choice: Why more is less.* New York, NY: HarperCollins.

Schwartz, B. (2009). Incentives, choice, education and well-being. *Oxford Review of Education, 35,* 391–403.

Schwartz, J. A., Chapman, G. B., Brewer, N. T., & Bergus, G. B. (2004). The effects of accountability on bias in physician decision making: Going from bad to worse. *Psychonomic Bulletin & Review, 11,* 173–178.

Shah, A. K., & Oppenheimer, D. M. (2008). Heuristics made easy: An effort-reduction framework. *Psychological Bulletin, 134,* 207–222.

Shiv, B., Loewenstein, G., Bechera, A., Damasio, H., & Damasio, A. R. (2005). Investment behavior and the negative side of emotion. *Psychological Science, 16,* 435–439.

Simon, H. A. (1945). Theory of games and economic behaviour. *American Sociological Review, 50,* 558–560.

Simon, H. A. (1957). *Models of man: Social and rational.* New York, NY: Wiley.

Simon, H. A. (1990). Invariants of human behaviour. *Annual Review of Psychology, 41,* 1–19.

Simons, D. J. (2013). Unskilled and optimistic: Overconfident predictions despite calibrated knowledge of relative skill. *Psychonomic Bulletin & Review, 20,* 601–607.

Simonson, I., & Staw, B. M. (1992). De-escalation strategies: A comparison of techniques for reducing commitment to losing courses of action. *Journal of Applied Psychology, 77,* 419–426.

Sperber, D., & Girotto, V. (2002). Use or misuse of the selection task? Rejoinder to Fiddick, Cosmides, and Tooby. *Cognition, 85,* 277–290.

Stanovich, K. E. (2009, November/December). The thinking that IQ tests miss. *Scientific American,* 34–39.

Stanovich, K. E. (2012). On the distinction between rationality and intelligence: Implications for understanding individual differences in reasoning. In K. J. Holyoak & R. G. Morrison (2012). *The Oxford handbook of thinking and reasoning.* Oxford: Oxford University Press.

Stanovich, K. E., & West, R. F. (2007). Natural myside bias is independent of cognitive ability. *Thinking & Reasoning, 13,* 225–247.

Sternberg, R. J. (2011). Understanding reasoning: Let's describe what we really think about. *Behavioral and Brain Sciences, 34,* 269–270.

Stich, S. P. (1990). *The fragmentation of reason.* Cambridge, MA: MIT Press.

Swinkels, A. (2003). An effective exercise for teaching cognitive heuristics. *Teaching of Psychology, 30*(2), 120–122.

Teigen, K. H., & Keren, G. (2007). Waiting for the bus: When base-rates refuse to be neglected. *Cognition, 103,* 337–357.

Tetlock, P.E. (2002). Social functionalist frameworks for judgment and choice: Intuitive politicians, theologians, and prosecutors. *Psychological Review, 109,* 451–471.

Thompson, V. A., Evans, J. St. B. T., & Handley, S. J. (2005). Persuading and dissuading by conditional argument. *Journal of Memory & Language, 53,* 238–257.

Todd, P. M., & Gigerenzer, G. (2007). Environments that make us smart. *Current Directions in Psychological Science, 16,* 167–171.

Toplak, M. E., West, R. F., & Stanovich, K. E. (2011). The Cognitive Reflection Test as a predictor of performance on heuristics-and-biases tasks. *Memory & Cognition, 39,* 1275–1289.

Tversky, A., & Kahneman, D. (1983). Extensional versus intuitive reasoning: The conjunction fallacy in probability judgment. *Psychological Review, 91,* 293–315.

Tversky, A., & Koehler, D. J. (1994). Support theory: A nonextensional representation of subjective probability. *Psychological Review, 101,* 547–567.

Tversky, A., & Shafir, E. (1992). The disjunction effect in choice under uncertainty. *Psychological Science, 3,* 305–309.

Walton, D. (2010). Why fallacies appear to be better arguments than they are. *Informal logic, 30,* 159–184.

Wang, X. T. (1996). Domain-specific rationality in human choices: Violations of utility axioms and social contexts. *Cognition, 60,* 31–63.

Wang, X. T., Simons, F., & Brédart, S. (2001). Social cues and verbal framing in risky choice. *Journal of Behavioral Decision Making, 14,* 1–15.

Wason, P. C. (1968). Reasoning about a rule. *Quarterly Journal of Experimental Psychology, 20,* 63–71.

Wason, P. C., & Shapiro, D. (1971). Natural and contrived experience in reasoning problems. *Quarterly Journal of Experimental Psychology, 23,* 63–71.

Whiting, P. F., Davenport, C., Jameson, C., Burke, M., Sterne, J. A., Hyde, C., & Ben-Shlomo, Y. (2015). How well do health professionals interpret diagnostic information? A systematic review. *BMJ Open, 5*(7), e008155.

Wroe, A. L., Bhan, A., Salkovskis, P., & Bedford, H. (2005). Feeling bad about immunizing our children. *Vaccine, 23,* 1428–1433.

Wübben, M., & van Wangenheim, F. (2008). Instant customer base analysis: Managerial heuristics often "get it right". *Journal of Marketing, 72,* 82–93.

Chapter 11

Contents

Contents

Cognition and emotion

INTRODUCTION

Historically, cognitive psychology was strongly influenced by the computer analogy or metaphor, as can be seen in the emphasis on information-processing models. That approach doesn't lend itself readily to an examination of the relationship between cognition and emotion (especially the effects of emotion on cognition). This is so because it is hard to think of computers as having emotional states.

Most cognitive psychologists ignore the effects of emotion on cognition by trying to ensure their participants are in a relatively neutral emotional state. However, there has been a rapid increase in the number of cognitive psychologists working in the area of cognition and emotion. Examples can be found in research on the perception of faces (Chapter 3), semantic memory (Chapter 6), autobiographical memory (Chapter 7), and decision making (Chapter 10).

At the most general level, two major issues are central to research on cognition and emotion. First, what are the effects of cognitive processes on our emotional experience? Second, what are the effects of emotion on cognition? For example, what are the consequences of feeling anxious for learning and memory?

Learning objectives

After studying Chapter 11, you should be able to:

- Discuss how cognition influences emotion, as well as how emotion influences cognition.
- Discuss the importance of the amygdala in relation to cognition and emotion.
- Explain the process model of emotion regulation, specifically how attention deployment and cognitive change work.
- Define mood-state-dependent memory and discuss its implications for how memories are encoded and retrieved.
- Explain how various emotions (e.g., anxiety, sadness, anger) influence decision making (e.g., risk aversion; risk taking; optimistic judgments).
- Explain how anxiety is related to attentional and interpretive biases and what the findings mean for therapy.

THE STRUCTURE OF EMOTIONS

There has been some controversy concerning the structure of emotions. There are two main schools of thought (Fox, 2008). Some theorists (e.g., Izard, 2007) argue we should adopt a *dimensional* approach. Barrett and Russell (1998; see also Warriner et al., 2013) argued for two basic dimensions of **valence** (negative–positive) and **arousal** (quiet, inactive–excited). However, other theorists prefer a *categorical* approach, according to which there are a small number of basic emotions such as happiness, anger, fear, disgust, and sadness.

The advantage of the categorical approach is that it makes a distinction between negative emotions (Stevenson et al., 2007). A limitation is that the negative emotions are highly intercorrelated (between r = .6 and .8) and that they all correlate negatively with happiness (correlations of about r = -.6), so that the added value of the distinction may be modest. Figure 11.1 shows how words fit into both approaches.

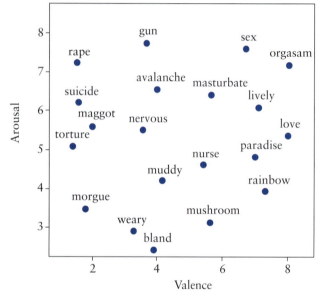

Figure 11.1 Two structures of emotions. The first part of the figure shows the dimensional approach, according to which emotions differ on valence and arousal (rating scale 1–9). The second part of the next page shows the categorical approach, according to which there are five primary emotions (rating scale 1–5). Source: Based on Warriner et al. (2013) and Stevenson et al. (2007).

EMOTION, MOOD, PERSONALITY, AND AFFECT

To investigate the interactions between emotion and cognition, three different lines of research are used. Some researchers focus on emotions, others on moods, and still others on personalities. *How* do they differ? Emotions are the shortest lasting and the most intense. They are usually evoked by a stimulus the person is aware of (e.g., a picture, a memory, an action of another person) and last for a few seconds or minutes. Moods are less intense than emotions, last longer, and often are not (or no longer) tied to a specific event.

Personality differences point to stable differences between people in the degree to which various emotions are experienced (in particular the five basic emotions listed in Figure 11.1: happiness, anger, sadness, fear, and disgust). Some people, for instance, report a high level of anxiety (fear) throughout their life. These people have so-called *trait anxiety* (anxiety as a stable personality feature) rather than *state anxiety* (anxiety provoked by a specific event). Cardiologists make a distinction between Type A and Type B personalities (Friedman & Rosenman, 1959). The first type shows an intense, sustained drive for achievement and is continually involved in competition and deadlines, both at work and in their avocations. They easily get angered. Type B shows the opposite pattern with less ambition, much less arousal, and more positive emotions than negative emotions. Individual differences in personality traits are typically 30%–40% due to genetic factors; the remainder is largely the outcome of learning (e.g., learning to respond with fear, aggression, sadness or indifference to adverse events). Personality differences are stable characteristics, lasting for years rather than seconds to minutes (emotions) or hours to days (moods).

A term sometimes used as a catch-all phrase to refer to emotions, moods, and personality differences is *affect*. Watson and Tellegen (1985) proposed to

Word	Happiness	Anger	Sadness	Fear	Disgust
avalanche	1.23	2.23	2.89	3.88	1.66
bland	1.30	1.46	1.72	1.27	1.80
gun	1.24	3.02	2.88	3.83	2.30
lively	4.16	1.17	1.07	1.07	1.07
love	4.72	1.70	2.16	2.05	1.22
maggot	1.08	2.21	1.59	2.83	4.50
masturbate	2.66	1.35	1.39	1.23	1.96
morgue	1.02	2.15	3.78	3.56	3.17
muddy	2.00	1.84	1.52	1.45	2.55
mushroom	1.85	1.17	1.23	1.58	2.06
nervous	1.30	1.77	2.08	3.41	1.45
nurse	2.48	1.23	1.53	1.82	1.15
orgasm	4.63	1.11	1.09	1.25	1.16
paradise	4.79	1.09	1.09	1.05	1.02
rainbow	4.00	1.08	1.27	1.07	1.14
rape	1.03	4.50	4.33	3.94	4.65
sex	4.55	1.41	1.48	1.73	1.25
suicide	1.01	3.52	4.53	3.73	3.26
torture	1.03	3.96	3.92	4.27	3.92
weary	1.15	1.72	2.73	2.01	1.50

Figure 11.1 Continued

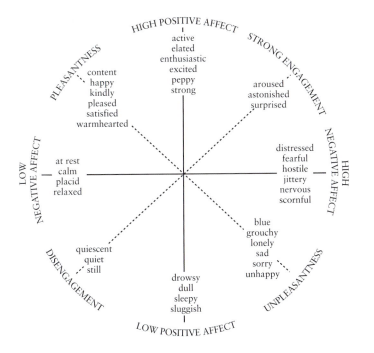

Figure 11.2 The model of Watson and Tellegen (1985) based on independent dimensions of positive and negative affect.
Source: From Watson & Tellegen (1985). Reprinted with permission from the American Psychological Association.

make a distinction between positive and negative affect, which in their view were two separate dimensions (instead of a single bipolar dimension of which positive and negative are each other's opposite). According to Watson and Tellegen (1985), the two dimensions were largely uncorrelated; that is, people scoring high on negative affect could also score high on positive affect, and vice versa. Figure 11.2 shows their model.

Russell and Carroll (1999) took issue with the independence of positive and negative affect and argued that they were each other's opposite: the more positive affect one experiences, the less negative affect there will be, and the other way around. In all likelihood, the truth is somewhere in-between. Gill et al. (2017), for instance, reported correlations around r = -.55 between the degree of positive and negative affect reported by participants. This is different from r = 0 (independence) but also from r = -1.0 (opposites).

Section summary

- There are two possible interactions between emotion and cognition: effects of cognitions on emotions and effects of emotions on cognitions.
- The structure of emotions has been addressed by dimensional and categorical approaches. In the former approach emotions are defined by valence and arousal; in the latter a distinction is made between a small number of basic emotions.
- Emotions are shorter and more intense than moods; they are elicited by stimuli the person is aware of. Moods last longer, are less intense, and are not tied to a specific stimulus. Differences in personality make some people experience some emotions more often and more intensely than other people.
- Affect is sometimes used as a catch-all phrase. Positive and negative affect are to some extent each other's opposite, because they correlate negatively, but they do not completely exclude each other. Some people score relatively high on both affects; others score relatively low on them.

HOW DOES COGNITION INFLUENCE EMOTION?

Cognitive processes clearly influence *when* we experience emotional states and *what* particular emotional state we experience in any given situation. For example, suppose you are walking along and someone knocks into you. If you interpret their action as *deliberate*, you would probably experience anger. However, if you interpret their action as *accidental*, you would probably experience much less emotion. In what follows, we consider how cognitive processes influence our emotional states.

COGNITIVE PROCESSES AND THE BRAIN

How do the workings of the cognitive system influence emotional experience? At the most general level, there are two major possibilities. First, the presentation of an aversive stimulus (e.g., photograph of a mutilated body) or a positive stimulus (e.g., photograph of a scene at a party) might produce emotion through low-level bottom-up processes (see Glossary) involving attention and perception.

Second, emotion might be generated through high-level top-down processes (see Glossary) involving stored emotional knowledge. For example, thinking about some future threatening event (e.g., an important examination) can create a state of high anxiety.

Emotional experience typically depends on both bottom-up and top-down processes (Scherer et al., 2001). Ochsner et al. (2009) used brain imaging to explore these two kinds of processes. In the bottom-up condition, participants were presented with aversive photographs and told to view the images and respond naturally to them. In the top-down condition, participants were told to interpret neutral photographs as if they were aversive.

What did Ochsner et al. (2009) find? The brain areas activated in the bottom-up condition included those in the occipital, temporal, and parietal lobes associated with visual perceptual processing. In addition, and most importantly, there was strong activation of the amygdala. As we saw in Chapter 1, the amygdala is a subcortical structure consisting of two nuclei, buried in the front parts of the temporal lobes (see also Figure 11.3). It is associated with several emotions (especially fear). The level of self-reported negative affect was associated most strongly with activity in the amygdala.

The role of the amygdala in emotion was explored in a direct fashion by Calder et al. (1996) and by Scott et al. (1997) in studies on a woman, DR. She had an operation for epilepsy that had caused extensive damage to the amygdala. When DR described the emotions revealed by various emotional expressions in other people, she was particularly poor at identifying fearful expressions. In another experiment, DR listened to neutral words spoken in

Key term

Amygdala:
subcortical structure particularly important for the detection of danger and other emotion-arousing stimuli.

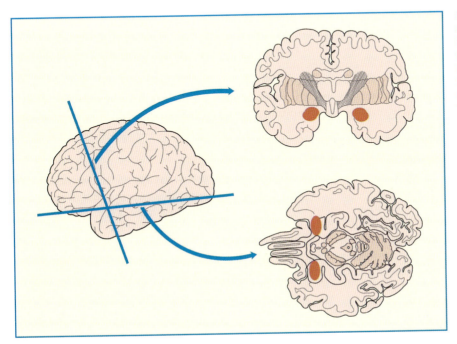

Figure 11.3 Image of the amygdala, a structure that forms part of the limbic system and that is activated in many emotional states. Source: From Ward (2010), with permission from Taylor & Francis.

various emotional tones and tried to identify the relevant emotion. She was very poor at identifying fear and anger. These findings confirm the importance of the amygdala in emotion.

Ochsner et al. (2009) found that the brain areas activated in the top-down condition differed somewhat from those activated in the bottom-up condition. Top-down processing involved the dorsolateral prefrontal cortex and medial prefrontal cortex, areas associated with high-level cognitive processes. The anterior cingulate and amygdala were also activated. The level of self-reported negative affect was associated most with activation of the medial prefrontal cortex, an area involved in producing cognitive representations of stimulus meaning.

These findings might suggest that some brain regions (e.g., prefrontal cortex) engage only in top-down cognitive processing, whereas other brain regions (e.g., amygdala) are mainly involved in bottom-up affective processing. This would be an oversimplification. In fact, emotional experience depends on the activation in an interactive network of brain areas of which the prefrontal cortex and the amygdala are part (Pessoa, 2008; Viviani, 2013).

APPRAISAL APPROACH

Many theorists have argued for the importance of appraisal in determining which emotion we experience in any given situation (Smith & Lazarus, 1993). What is appraisal? It is the evaluation or judgment that we make about situations relevant to our goals, concerns, and well-being, and it typically involves top-down processing.

Cognitive appraisal influences whether we experience guilt or anger in a given situation. Scherer and Ellsworth (2009) identified possible appraisal profiles for major emotions. For example, you experience anger if you blame someone else for the current situation and you appraise the situation as one offering you control and power. In contrast, you experience sadness if you appraise the situation as one permitting very little control or power.

Fontaine et al. (2013) tested the centrality of appraisal to emotion. Participants from 27 countries indicated for various emotion words the probability with which features of appraisal and other components of emotion would apply to someone experiencing each emotion. Emotions were correctly classified solely on the basis of appraisal features in 71% of cases. All other components (e.g., bodily sensations, motor expressions, action tendencies) improved classification accuracy only slightly. These findings suggest appraisal is vitally important in determining emotional states.

From what has been said so far, it might seem that appraisal always involves deliberate, conscious processing. However, most theorists argue that appraisal can also occur automatically without conscious awareness. For example, Smith and Kirby (2001, 2009) distinguished between appraisal based on reasoning (involving deliberate thinking) and appraisal based on activation of memories (involving automatic processes) (see Figure 11.4). Appraisal based on reasoning is slower and more flexible than appraisal based on memory activation.

Findings

Most research in this area has used scenarios in which participants are asked to identify with the central character. The appraisal of any given situation is manipulated across scenarios to observe the effects on emotional experience.

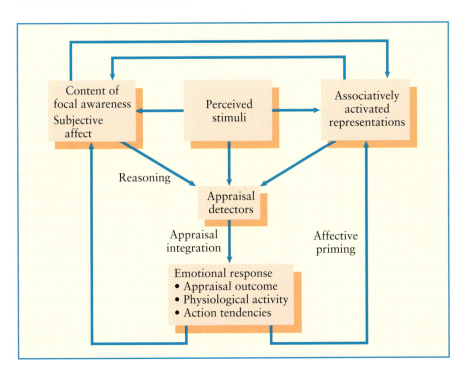

Figure 11.4 Mechanisms involved in the appraisal process. Notice that only one of the components ("Contents of focal awareness/Subjective affect") need to be conscious. The other processes can be automatic, unconscious processes. Source: From Smith and Kirby (2001). Reprinted with permission from Oxford University Press.

One scenario used by Smith and Lazarus (1993) involved a student who had performed poorly in an examination. Participants reported that he would experience anger when he put the blame on the unhelpful teaching assistants. However, guilt was more common when the student blamed himself (e.g., for doing work at the last minute).

Smith and Lazarus's (1993) study involved manipulated situations and appraisals at the same time. As a result, it is often hard to know whether participants' emotional reactions occurred *directly* as a response to situations or *indirectly* as a response to appraisals. Siemer et al. (2007) used a *single* situation in which the experimenter's behavior towards the participants was rude, condescending, and very critical. Afterwards, participants gave emotion ratings on six emotions and five appraisals (e.g., controllability, other-responsibility, self-responsibility). The key finding was that appraisals predicted the intensity of the various emotions. For example, the appraisal of personal control was negatively associated with guilt, shame, and sadness but not anger.

Participants are typically presented with hypothetical scenarios and so experience little genuine emotion. Bennett and Lowe (2008) rectified this by having hospital nurses identify their most stressful work-related incident experienced recently. Anger and frustration were the emotions most strongly experienced. The emotions were predicted reasonably well by the nurses' appraisals of the stressful situations. The exception was sadness, perhaps because it is often used very generally to refer to negative emotional experience.

The appraisal approach can explain some individual differences in emotional reactions to a given situation. In one study (Ceulemans et al., 2012), participants read brief scenarios (e.g., "A friend spreads gossip about you") and indicated the appraisals they would make. Individual differences in the amount of anger triggered by the scenarios depended on two factors: (1) the appraisals activated by each scenario and (2) the specific pattern of appraisal components necessary for the individual to experience anger.

Another example of individual differences concerns the personality dimension of neuroticism. Individuals who are high in neuroticism experience much more negative affect than people who score low. Tong (2010a) identified two reasons for this in a study on four negative emotions: anger, sadness, fear, and guilt. First, those who are high in neuroticism used more negative appraisal styles than did low-neuroticism individuals. Second, the relationships between appraisal and experienced emotion were greater among high-neuroticism individuals.

Other research has indicated that there is no one-to-one mapping between appraisal and emotion. Any given emotion can be produced by several combinations of appraisals. Tong (2010b) considered the negative emotions of anger, sadness, fear, and guilt. Participants repeatedly indicated their negative emotions and their associated appraisals in everyday environments. No single appraisal (or combination of appraisals) was necessary or sufficient for the experience of any of the four emotional states.

According to appraisal theories, appraisals *cause* emotional states rather than emotional states causing appraisals. However, most research has revealed only an association between appraisals and emotions and so doesn't directly address the issue of causality. Some appraisals may occur *after* a given emotion has been experienced and be used to justify that emotion.

To show that appraisal can cause emotional state, we must *manipulate* people's cognitive appraisal when they are confronted with emotional stimuli, and see whether it influences the emotional response. Schartau et al. (2009) used this approach. Participants viewed films of humans and animals experiencing marked distress. Some participants received training in positive

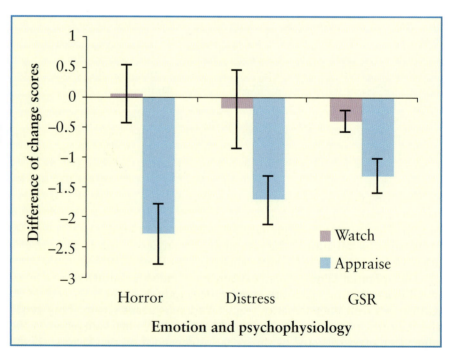

Figure 11.5 Changes in self-reported horror and distress and in galvanic skin response (GSR) between pre-training and post-training for individuals instructed to simply watch the films (watch condition) and those training in positive cognitive appraisal (appraisal condition).
Source: From Schartau et al. (2009). Reprinted with permission from the American Psychological Association.

cognitive appraisal (e.g., "silver lining: there are usually some good aspects to every situation" (p. 19)). This training indeed reduced horror, distress, and physiological arousal as indexed by the galvanic skin response (see Figure 11.5). The latter is a measure of skin conductance, which varies with the state of sweat glands in the skin. Sweating is controlled by the sympathetic nervous system (activated in situations of danger or excitement) and therefore skin conductance is an indication of psychological or physiological arousal.

Evaluation

+ Appraisal is often of great importance in influencing emotional experience.

+ Appraisal processes not only determine whether we experience emotion but also strongly influence which emotion is experienced.

− The links between appraisals and specific emotions are flexible and not especially strong.

− While it is assumed that appraisal causes emotional experience, the causality may sometimes be in the opposite direction. More generally, appraisal and emotional experience often blur into each other.

− The appraisal approach deemphasizes the social context in which most emotion is experienced – emotional experience generally emerges out of *active* social interaction.

NON-CONSCIOUS EMOTIONAL PROCESSING

Suppose you were presented with a picture showing someone who had been seriously injured in a car accident. This would almost certainly trigger a negative emotional state in you. Suppose, however, that the same picture was shown very briefly so that you weren't consciously aware of it. Would you still experience a negative emotional state? As was mentioned earlier, Smith and Kirby (2001) argued that appraisal processes can be automatic and below the level of conscious awareness. They thus predicted that the answer to the question is "yes" – an answer supported by evidence.

Chartrand et al. (2006) presented positive (e.g., music; friends), negative (e.g., war; cancer), or neutral (e.g., building; plant) words repeatedly below the level of conscious awareness. Participants receiving the negative words reported a more negative mood state than those did receiving the positive words.

Öhman and Soares (1994) presented pictures of snakes, spiders, flowers, and mushrooms so rapidly that they couldn't be identified consciously. Some of the participants were spider phobics (intense fear of spiders) and others were snake phobics (intense fear of snakes). The prediction was that pictures *relevant* to the individual's phobia would produce a more negative mood state than those that were irrelevant. That is what they found.

In Chapter 2, we discussed patients with damage to the primary visual cortex, as a result of which they lack conscious visual perception in parts of the visual field. However, they show some ability to respond appropriately to visual stimuli for which they have no conscious awareness (blindsight; see

Glossary). Patients with blindsight have been tested for affective blindsight, in which different emotional stimuli can be discriminated in the absence of conscious perception. Several reports indicate the existence of affective blindsight (Tamietto & de Gelder, 2008, 2010).

Most research on affective blindsight has involved patients with lack of conscious perception in only part of the visual field. As a result, affective blindsight in these patients may have depended in part on the intact parts of their visual processing system. However, Pegna et al. (2005) studied a 52-year-old man who was entirely cortically blind. When he was presented with happy and angry faces he couldn't perceive consciously, he correctly reported the emotion on 59% of trials.

Pegna et al. (2005) also carried out a brain-imaging study in which the patient was presented with angry, happy, fearful, and neutral faces. There was greater activation in the right amygdala with the emotional faces than with neutral faces, with the greatest activation occurring in response to fearful faces. These findings suggest the patient was responding emotionally to the emotional faces.

Jolij and Lamme (2005) set out to show affective blindsight in healthy individuals. They used transcranial magnetic stimulation (TMS; see Glossary) to produce a brief disruption to functioning in the occipital area (involved in visual perception). On each trial, participants were presented with four faces (three neutral and one happy or sad). When the stimulus array was presented very briefly and followed by TMS, participants had no conscious perceptual experience. However, they were reasonably good at detecting the emotional expression. Thus, the participants showed a form of affective blindsight.

In sum, various emotions can be experienced in the absence of conscious awareness of the stimuli that triggered the emotion. It has also been found that different emotional stimuli can be discriminated without conscious awareness. It is unclear whether the underlying automatic processes should be regarded as appraisal processes.

EMOTION REGULATION

So far we have focused on a one-stage approach in which an individual encounters a situation and responds with an emotional experience. This process is *emotion generation*, which involves a spontaneous emotional response to a situation. As we have seen, cognitive appraisal is involved in the emotions that are generated.

In the real world, however, matters are often more complex. For example, someone in authority makes you angry by saying something unpleasant. However, you make strong efforts to inhibit your anger and pretend all is well. Similarly, emergency teams may be confronted with a particularly gruesome scene. Still, they must brace themselves to provide help. This illustrates the two-stage approach in which an initial emotional reaction is followed by attempts to change that emotional reaction.

These examples involve **emotion regulation**. Emotion regulation "requires the activation of a goal to up- or down-regulate either the magnitude or duration of the emotional response" (Gross, 2013, p. 359). Thus, emotion regulation occurs when someone overrides their initial, spontaneous emotional response.

Key term

Emotion regulation: the use of deliberate and effortful processes to change a spontaneous emotional state (usually a negative one) produced by an emotion-generation process.

The distinction between emotion generation and emotion regulation is intuitively appealing and can be studied in the laboratory. In essence, two groups of participants are presented with the same emotional situation. One group is instructed to react naturally (emotion generation). The other group is told to regulate their emotional responses using a specified strategy (emotion regulation). Emotional responding (e.g., self-reported emotion, brain activation) in the two conditions can then be compared.

The distinction between emotion generation and emotion regulation is often blurred, however (Gross et al., 2011). Emotion-generative and emotion-regulatory processes interact and involve overlapping brain systems (Ochsner et al., 2009). Emotion-generative processes are auto-regulatory, meaning they are self-correcting (Kappas, 2011). Emotion-generative processes lead to behavior that changes the situation and thus the emotional response. Therefore, emotion generation is often combined with emotion regulation in the absence of specific instructions. Nevertheless, research evidence shows that emotion regulation differs from emotion generation.

Process model

Gross and Thompson (2007) put forward a process model that allows us to categorize emotion-regulation strategies (see Figure 11.6). It is based on the crucial assumption that emotion-regulation strategies can be used at various points in time. For example, individuals suffering from social anxiety can regulate their emotional state by avoiding potentially stressful social situations (situation selection).

There are several other emotion-regulation strategies that socially anxious individuals can use. For example, they can change social situations by asking a friend to accompany them (situation modification). Alternatively, they can use attentional processes by, for example, focusing on pleasant distracting thoughts (attention deployment).

Socially anxious individuals can also use cognitive reappraisal to reinterpret the current situation as less threatening (cognitive change). For example, socially anxious individuals might tell themselves most people are friendly and will not judge you harshly if you say or do something inappropriate.

Finally, there is response modulation. For example, it is commonly believed it is best to express your angry feelings and so get them "out of your system." Alas, it turns out that expressing anger *increases* rather than decreases angry

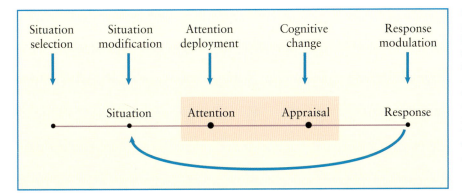

Figure 11.6 A process model of emotion regulation based on five major types of strategy (situation selection; situation modification; attention deployment; cognitive change; and response modulation). Source: From Gross and Thompson (2007). Reprinted with permission from Guilford Press.

feelings (Bushman, 2002), because it facilitates the retrieval of angry thoughts. Another form of response modulation involves suppression of emotional behavior (e.g., hiding your angry feelings).

Most emotion-regulation strategies are used at the attentional deployment stage (e.g., distraction – disengaging attention from emotional processing) or the cognitive change stage (e.g., reappraisal – elaborating emotional information and then changing its meaning). Sheppes et al. (2014) provided evidence that the emotional intensity of an event tends to increase over time if it is not subject to emotion regulation.

Grossman (2015) argued that three stages are involved in starting and stopping emotion regulation. First, there is a stage of identification (deciding whether to regulate). Next, there is a stage of selection (choosing a strategy). Finally, the strategy must be implemented (actually used).

Augustine and Hemenover (2009) carried out a meta-analysis combining the findings from numerous emotion-regulation studies. Distraction and reappraisal were on average the most effective strategies for reducing negative affect.

Distraction

Distraction is less cognitively demanding than reappraisal and can be used early to control negative emotion and so "nip it in the bud." *How* does distraction reduce negative affect? According to Van Dillen and Koole (2007), the working memory system (see Chapter 4) plays a central role. Working memory (involved in the processing and storage of information) has limited capacity. If most of its capacity is devoted to processing distracting stimuli, there is little capacity left to process negative emotional information.

Van Dillen and Koole (2007) tested this working memory hypothesis. Participants were presented with strongly negative, weakly negative, or neutral photographs. After that, they performed an arithmetic task making high or low demands on working memory. Finally, they completed a mood scale. As predicted, participants' mood state following presentation of strongly negative photographs was less negative when they had just performed a task with high working memory demands than one with low demands.

Van Dillen et al. (2009) replicated the findings of Van Dillen and Koole (2007). In addition, they compared brain activity when task demands were high or low. The more demanding task was associated with greater activation in the prefrontal cortex (involved in working memory) but less activity in the amygdala (involved in fear and other negative emotions). Thus, the more demanding task produced more activation within the working memory system. This led to a dampening of negative emotion at the physiological (i.e., amygdala) and experiential (i.e., self-report) levels.

Reappraisal

Reappraisal is more cognitively demanding than distraction, but it has the advantage that re-evaluating emotional information can produce long-lasting benefits. This is important in people who experience debilitating emotions to harmless stimuli, or in professions that are repeatedly confronted with situations eliciting negative emotions.

Sheppes et al. (2014) used the differences between distraction and reappraisal to predict when they are most likely to be used. First, distraction will be used more than reappraisal in high negative intensity situations because it can block emotional information before it intensifies. Second, reappraisal will be used more often with emotional stimuli that are likely to be encountered many times than with those encountered only once. The reason is that the reinterpretation of these stimuli produced by reappraisal serves to reduce their subsequent emotional impact.

In recent years, brain-imaging studies have served to clarify how cognitive reappraisal influences emotional states. Ochsner and Gross (2008) reviewed brain-imaging studies in which the emphasis was on two types of reappraisal strategy:

1. *Reinterpretation*: This involves changing the meaning of the context in which a stimulus is presented (e.g., imagining a picture has been faked).
2. *Distancing*: This involves taking a detached, third-person perspective.

Regardless of which strategy was used, the prefrontal cortex and the anterior cingulate were consistently activated. These brain areas are associated with executive processes that coordinate processing, and so it appears that emotion regulation involves executive processes.

Another general finding was that reappraisal strategies designed to reduce negative emotional reactions to stimuli produced reduced activation in the amygdala (strongly implicated in emotional responding). This is as predicted given that reappraisal reduces self-reported negative emotional experience.

In one study (McRae et al., 2010), participants were presented with very negative pictures. They were instructed to use reappraisal (reinterpret the picture to make themselves feel less negative about it) or distraction (focus on remembering a six-letter string).

Both strategies reduced amygdala activation and negative affect, but reappraisal was more effective in reducing negative affect. Reappraisal was associated with greater increases than distraction in activation within the medial prefrontal cortex and anterior temporal regions (associated with processing affective meaning). Reappraisal was likely more effective than distraction because it was associated with more cognitive control of the individual's emotional state.

Implicit emotion regulation

So far the emphasis has been on deliberate and conscious processes involved in emotion regulation (explicit emotion regulation). Gyurak et al. (2011) argued that implicit emotion regulation is also important. According to their theoretical approach, "Implicit processes are believed to be evoked automatically by the stimulus itself and run to completion without monitoring and can happen without insight and awareness" (p. 401). Implicit emotion regulation need not be a different type of regulation. It can simply be a more practiced, automatic form of explicit regulation (see the distinction between automatic and controlled processes in Chapter 3). Using a given emotion-regulation strategy repeatedly can lead to the development of implicit regulation.

Why is implicit emotion regulation necessary? It would require excessive cognitive resources to use explicit emotion-regulation strategies to deal with every emotional situation we encounter. Koole et al. (2015) argued that implicit processes can help individuals decide whether to engage in emotion regulation and to facilitate strategy selection and execution.

Emotion- and situation-specific strategies

A more critical study about the effectiveness of emotional regulation strategies was published by Webb et al. (2012). They carried out a meta-analysis based on 306 experimental comparisons of different strategies using the process model shown in Figure 11.6. Overall, strategies involving cognitive change (including reappraisal) had a moderate effect on emotion, strategies involving response modulation had a small effect, but strategies involving attentional deployment (including distraction) had a non-significant effect.

Webb et al. (2012) argued that the discouragingly small effects were due to the crudeness of the five categories in Gross and Thompson's (2007) process model. For example, although attentional deployment strategies overall had a non-significant effect, distraction on its own had beneficial effects. With respect to cognitive-change strategies, reappraising the emotional situation was more beneficial than reappraising the emotional response. Related to response modulation, suppressing emotional expression had a moderate effect on emotion but suppressing emotional experience had no effect. In sum, what matters is the *specific* strategy rather than the broad category.

A further qualification of the findings discussed so far is that the effectiveness of any given emotion-regulation strategy seems to vary from situation to situation. For example, consider a study by Troy et al. (2013). They argued that reappraisal would be effective in situations in which stress was uncontrollable. However, it would be ineffective in situations in which stress was controllable, and the optimal strategy would probably be problem-focused coping rather than changing one's emotional state. Troy et al. assessed participants' reappraisal ability, the stressfulness of participants' recent negative life experiences, and the controllability of those recent experiences.

What did Troy et al. (2013) find? Participants with high appraisal ability had *less* depression than those with low ability when high stress was uncontrollable (see Figure 11.7). In contrast, high appraisal ability was associated with *greater* depression when high stress was controllable. Thus, the effectiveness of reappraisal ability depended on the controllability vs. uncontrollability of stressful life events.

The importance of emotion-specific and situation-specific strategies also became clear in a meta-analytic review by Aldao et al. (2010), who assessed the role of various emotion-regulation strategies in changing the symptoms of

Figure 11.7 Mean level of depression as a function of stress severity and cognitive reappraisal ability (high = ———— and low = ------------------) when the situation was low in controllability (left-hand side) and high in controllability (right-hand side).
Source: From Troy et al. (2013). Reprinted by permission of SAGE Publications.

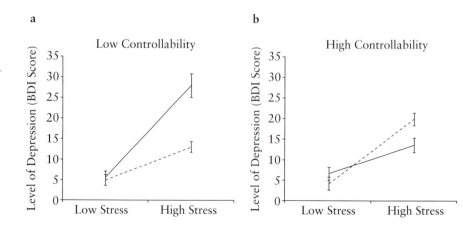

anxiety and depression over time. For these symptoms, acceptance, problem solving, and reappraisal had beneficial effects. In contrast, rumination (obsessive thinking about issues) and avoidance both *increased* the symptoms of anxiety and depression.

In sum, although emotion regulation is important for good functioning, it looks like general theories, such as the one shown in Figure 11.6, are of limited practical value. More important is to assess the usefulness of specific regulation strategies for various problems and in various situations: what is good for one problem in one situation need not be good for another problem or another situation.

Section summary

Cognitive processes and the brain

- Emotional experience depends on bottom-up processes involving the occipital, parietal, and temporal lobes (including the amygdala). It also depends on top-down processes involving the medial and dorsolateral prefrontal cortex, the anterior cingulate, and the amygdala. These brain regions form an interacting network.

Appraisal approach

- Cognitive appraisal processes are involved in determining which emotion is experienced in any given situation. Appraisal often involves deliberate conscious processing but can be automatic. At the same time, the links between appraisal and emotions are flexible, person-dependent, and fairly weak; appraisal and emotional experience often blur into each other.

Non-conscious emotional processing

- Stimuli that can't be consciously perceived can nevertheless trigger emotional experience. Patients with affective blindsight can discriminate among different emotional stimuli presented to parts of the visual field for which they lack conscious awareness. Also, healthy participants can have an emotional experience to a stimulus they did not perceive consciously.

Emotion regulation

- Emotion regulation is the use of deliberate and effortful processes to override the individual's spontaneous emotional reaction, so that our response fits our goals. Regulation is mostly required to contain negative emotional responses.
- According to the process model account, regulation can happen at five different places (situation selection, situation modification, attentional deployment, cognitive change, or response modulation). Research indicates that in particular distraction and cognitive reappraisal are effective. Reappraisal is sometimes more effective than distraction because it involves greater cognitive control of the individual's emotional states.
- When regulation processes are used often, they may become automatic (implicit).
- There are indications that different strategies may be needed for different emotions and in different situations (e.g., depending on the amount of control one has over what happens). There is no "one fits all" recommendation to be made.

HOW DOES EMOTION INFLUENCE COGNITION?

This section is concerned with the effects of emotion on cognition. Our emotional state affects numerous aspects of cognition including perception, attention, interpretation, learning, memory, judgment, decision making, and reasoning (Blanchette & Richards, 2010). Consider driving behavior. Pêcher et al. (2009) used a simulator to study the effects of music on car driving. Sad music had no effect on drivers' ability to keep the car in its lane, but there was a slight reduction in speed. However, happy music had a distracting effect. There was a reduced ability to keep the car in its lane and an 8 mph decrease in speed relative to the neutral music condition.

Many people believe in "road rage," the notion that frustrated drivers become angry and drive dangerously as a consequence. In a study by Stephens and Groeger (2011), drivers performing a simulated driving task were made angry by being trapped behind a slow-moving vehicle. After that, they showed poor decision making by engaging in dangerous overtaking maneuvers and approaching hazards recklessly. Zhang and Chan (2016) carried out a meta-analysis of studies on driving anger and driving behavior. They confirmed Stephens and Groeger's (2011) finding that driving anger is associated with aggressive and risky driving and with driving errors.

Much research on the influence of emotion on cognition involves comparing cognitive processes and performance in groups differing in their mood state. *How* do researchers manipulate mood state? An increasingly popular approach involves asking participants to recall and then write about a personal event in which they experienced a given emotion. For example, Griskevicius et al. (2010) produced feelings of attachment love in some of their participants by telling them to write about a situation "when another person really took care of you and made you feel better."

Another technique was introduced by Velten (1968). Participants read a series of sentences designed to induce increasingly intense feelings of elation or depression. This technique is effective, but it usually produces a blend of several mood states rather than just the desired one (Polivy, 1981). Other techniques include presenting emotionally positive or negative music or movie clips.

Lench et al. (2011) assessed the frequency with which the different techniques have been used to manipulate participants' affect (especially mood state). The most common technique (24% of studies) involved presenting emotional films. Another very popular technique (20% of studies) involved autobiographical recall with participants describing or writing about an intense emotional experience. Other regularly used techniques involve staged real-life situations (15%) and emotional music (7% of studies).

ATTENTION

When we look at the world around us, we have some *flexibility* in the scope of focal attention (see Chapter 3). Some theorists (e.g., Eriksen & St James, 1986) compare visual attention to a zoom lens, in which the attended area can be increased or decreased. This issue is important in enhancing our understanding of attention but is also relevant to long-term memory. What we remember of an event is strongly influenced by what we attended to at the time.

How does affect influence the breadth of attention? An influential answer with reference to negative affect was provided by Easterbrook (1959). He hypothesized that the range of cues processed (i.e., the breadth of attention) decreases as arousal or anxiety increases. This "will reduce the proportion of irrelevant cues employed, and so improve performance. . . . [F]urther reduction in the number of cues employed can only affect relevant cues, and proficiency will fall" (Easterbrook, 1959, p. 193). Thus, high negative affect produces "tunnel vision."

Easterbrook's hypothesis has potential practical importance. For example, it may help us understand eyewitness memory (see Chapter 6) given that eye-witnesses are often highly stressed when they observe a crime. There is also some evidence (e.g., Janelle et al., 1999) that anxious car drivers attend less than non-anxious ones to peripheral information.

What about the effects of *positive* affect on the breadth of attention? According to Fredrickson and Branigan (2005, p. 315), positive emotions "widen the array of percepts, thoughts, and actions presently in mind." Thus, positive affect produces broadening of attention in contrast to the narrowing of attention assumed for negative affect by Easterbrook (1959).

Harmon-Jones et al. (2011) argued that both approaches are limited because they consider only whether the affect is positive or negative (i.e., having the goal of approaching or avoiding a stimulus). The authors claimed we should also consider *motivational intensity*. Positive affect can be produced by listening to pleasant music (low motivational intensity) or by seeing an attractive member of the opposite sex (high motivational intensity). Negative affect can be produced by being exposed to sad situations (low motivational intensity) or by threatening stimuli or situations (high emotional intensity).

What conclusions did Harmon-Jones et al. (2011) draw? They argued that positive and negative affective states of high motivational intensity produce attentional narrowing because this helps people to acquire desirable objects and avoid unpleasant ones. In contrast, there is attentional broadening with positive and negative affective states of low motivational intensity because this leaves people open to encountering new opportunities.

Lee et al. (2014) identified a different way in which emotional states influence visual information processing. Fear is associated with widening of the eyes, whereas disgust is associated with narrowing of the eyes. Eye widening enhances the ability to detect visual stimuli but reduces visual acuity, while eye narrowing has the opposite effect. These effects may be functional: fear facilitates detection and localization of threat, whereas disgust assists in identifying the object triggering disgust (e.g., contaminated food).

MEMORY

Affect influences learning and memory in several ways. We discuss a few findings in the following sections.

Mood congruity

Imagine you are in a negative mood state because you have a serious personal problem. What types of memory would spring to your mind? People generally recall predominantly negative or unpleasant memories in such circumstances. In contrast, we typically recall happy memories when we are in a good mood.

These examples illustrate mood congruity – emotionally toned material is learned and retrieved best when its affective value matches the learner's (or rememberer's) mood state. Mood congruity may help explain why negative mood states in everyday life are sometimes prolonged – the negative mood state makes it easier to learn and to retrieve negative information.

Mood-congruity effects based on mood at the time of learning were studied by Hills et al. (2011). Participants who were induced into a happy mood showed better subsequent recognition memory for happy than for sad faces. In contrast, those induced into a sad mood had slightly (but non-significantly) better recognition memory for sad than for happy faces.

Miranda and Kihlstrom (2005) asked adults to recall childhood and recent autobiographical memories to pleasant, unpleasant, and neutral word cues. They did this in a musically induced happy, sad, or neutral mood. There was mood congruity – the retrieval of happy memories was facilitated when participants were in a happy mood and retrieval of sad memories was enhanced by a sad mood.

In a review article of mood and autobiographical memory, Holland and Kensinger (2010) reported that there was stronger evidence of mood congruity when people were in a positive mood than when they were in a negative mood. Similar findings have been reported in studies of mood congruity with non-autobiographical material (Rusting & DeHart, 2000).

The most plausible explanation for the frequent failure to obtain mood congruity in a negative mood state is that the participants of a study are motivated to change negative feelings into positive ones. The resultant reduction in negative mood state caused by emotion regulation reduces the accessibility of negative memories. Rusting and DeHart (2000) obtained support for this explanation. Participants were presented with positive, negative, and neutral words. Then there was a negative mood induction. Those who claimed to be successful at reducing negative moods showed less evidence of mood congruity than did other participants.

How can we explain mood congruity? The effect can be explained with respect to Tulving's (1979) *encoding specificity principle* (see Chapter 5). According to this principle, memory depends on the overlap between the information available at retrieval and that in the memory trace. This overlap is greater when the to-be-remembered material is congruent with the rememberer's mood state than when it is not. Danker and Anderson (2010, p. 87) discussed an extension of this viewpoint focusing on brain states: "Remembering an episode involves literally returning to the brain state . . . present during that episode."

This assumption was tested by Lewis et al. (2005) in the context of mood congruity. Participants learned positive and negative words and then received a recognition-memory test in a happy or sad mood. There was mood congruity in memory performance. One brain region (the subgenual cingulate) was activated when positive stimuli were presented and was reactivated when participants were in a positive mood at test. In similar fashion, a different brain region (the posteriolateral orbitofrontal cortex) was activated when negative stimuli were presented and was reactivated when participants' mood at test was negative.

Mood-state-dependent memory

A finding related to mood congruity is mood-state-dependent memory. Mood-state-dependent memory is the finding that memory is better when the mood state at retrieval is the same as that at learning than when the two mood states differ. This effect was shown amusingly in the movie *City Lights*. In this movie, Charlie Chaplin saves a drunken millionaire from attempted suicide and is befriended in return. When the millionaire sees Charlie again, he is sober and fails to recognize him. However, when the millionaire becomes drunk again, he catches sight of Charlie, treats him like a long-lost friend, and takes him home with him.

Pamela Kenealy (1997) provided evidence of mood-state-dependent memory. In one study, participants looked at a map and learned a set of instructions concerning a particular route. The next day they were given tests of free recall and cued recall (the cue consisted of the map's visual outline). Context was manipulated by using music to create happy or sad mood states at learning and at test.

As predicted, Kenealy (1997) found that free recall was better when the mood state was the same at learning and at testing than when it differed (see Figure 11.8). This finding resembles those discussed in Chapter 5 showing that memory is better when the context (here mood state) is the same at learning and at retrieval.

However, Kenealy (1997) found no evidence of mood-state-dependent memory (or context) with cued recall. *Why* was this? Eich (1995) argued that mood state exerts less influence when crucial information (the to-be-remembered material or the retrieval cues) is explicitly presented, as happens with cued recall. Eich talked about a "do-it-yourself principle" – memory is most likely to be mood-dependent when *effortful* processing at learning and/ or retrieval is required.

The importance of the "do-it-yourself" principle was shown by Eich and Metcalfe (1989). At the time of learning, participants were assigned to read word pairs (e.g., *river – valley*) or to generate the second word of a pair (e.g., *river – v*). Mood state was manipulated by having continuous music during learning and recall. The mood-state-dependent effect was *four* times greater in the effortful generate condition than in the read condition.

Amygdala involvement

As discussed earlier, the amygdala is involved in the processing of emotional information. It has connections to nearly all cortical regions and facilitates several memory processes. How can we show the role played by the amygdala in emotional learning and memory? An approach that has proved useful involves the study of patients with **Urbach-Wiethe disease**, in which the amygdala and adjacent areas deteriorate because of calcification.

Cahill et al. (1995) studied BP, a patient suffering from Urbach-Wiethe disease. He

Key term

Urbach-Wiethe disease: a disease in which the amygdala and adjacent areas deteriorate; it leads to the impairment of emotional processing and memory for emotional material.

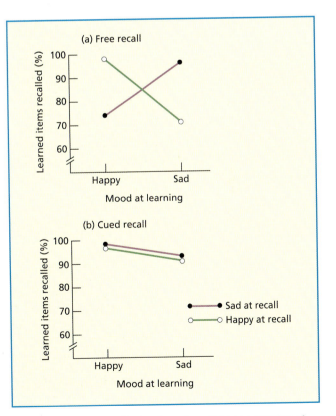

Figure 11.8 Free recall (a) and cued recall (b) as a function of mood state (happy or sad) at learning and at recall (b).
Source: Data from Kenealy (1997).

was told a story, in the middle of which was a very emotional event (a boy is severely injured in a traffic accident). Healthy controls showed much better recall of this emotional event than of the preceding emotionally neutral part of the story one week after learning. In contrast, BP recalled the emotional event *less* well than the preceding part of the story.

The amygdala is involved in memory for positive information as well as negative information. Siebert et al. (2003) compared long-term memory for positive, negative, and neutral pictures in healthy controls and 10 Urbach-Wiethe patients. The patients had poorer recognition memory than the controls for all picture categories, but their memory impairment was greatest for positive pictures and least for neutral ones.

Another approach to assessing the role of the amygdala in memory for emotional material is to use brain-imaging techniques. Individuals with the greatest amygdala activation during the learning of emotional material should have high levels of long-term memory for that material.

Murty et al. (2010) carried out a meta-analysis (see Glossary) of numerous studies and found support for this prediction. More specifically, successful learning of emotional material was associated with enhanced activation in a network of brain areas including the medial temporal lobe memory system as well as the amygdala.

JUDGMENT AND DECISION MAKING

Decision making (discussed in Chapter 10) involves choosing among various options and is something we do every day. These decisions vary from the trivial (e.g., deciding which movie to see tonight) to the enormously important (e.g., deciding whether to get married; deciding which career path to follow).

Judgment is an important component of decision making. It involves assessing the probability of various events occurring and then deciding how we would feel if each one actually happened. The decisions made by those whose judgments about the future are pessimistic would probably differ from those whose judgments are optimistic.

Angie et al. (2011) came to two general conclusions from their review of research in this area. First, major mood states (sadness, anger, fear or anxiety, happiness) have significant (and somewhat different) effects on judgment and decision making. Second, the average effects of mood are greater with respect to decision making than judgment.

In this section, we consider the influence of mood and personality on decision making. An important aspect of decision making is risk taking: are some moods and personality types associated with risk aversion? Common sense might suggest that individuals experiencing negative affect will be pessimistic and risk-averse, whereas those experiencing positive affect will be optimistic and more inclined to take risks. As we will see, however, reality is more complex than that.

Integral vs. incidental emotions

When discussing the influence of emotions on judgment and decision making, we need to distinguish between integral emotions and incidental emotions (Han & Lerner, 2009). *Integral emotions* are triggered by considering the consequences of a decision. For example, gambling a lot of money on a risky project is likely to trigger anxiety. In contrast, *incidental emotions* arise from past events that are totally unrelated to the present decision. For example, hearing you have passed an important examination may influence your subsequent judgments and decisions on other matters.

Most research on emotion and decision making has involved incidental emotions (Lench et al., 2011). For example, participants write about a very emotional experience and then perform a completely unrelated task. However, decision making in the real world very often involves integral emotions (e.g., we make decisions about what to do in order to reduce our sad or depressed state).

In Chapter 10 we saw the somatic marker hypothesis (Damasio, 1994), according to which integral emotions form the basis of good decision making in daily life. According to this hypothesis, automatic bodily arousal responses (somatic markers) are triggered by emotional events and influence decision making. Of key importance is *interoception*, which is the ability to detect subtle bodily changes. Interoception sometimes (but by no means always) involves conscious detection of bodily changes.

Evidence supporting this theoretical approach was reported by Dunn et al. (2010) using a version of the Iowa gambling task (Bechara et al., 1994). Participants chose a card from one of four decks of playing cards. Two decks were profitable (on average, participants would gain money by selecting from them), whereas the other two were unprofitable but had occasional large wins. Decision-making performance on this task improved over time, although the participants had little conscious understanding of how the decks differed. Bodily changes prior to choosing from an unprofitable or a profitable deck were recorded. Finally, participants' interoceptive ability was assessed by their accuracy in counting their own heartbeats.

What did Dunn et al. (2010) find? First, there were significant differences in bodily responses prior to selecting from profitable and unprofitable decks. Participants having the largest differences exhibited superior decision making to those with the smallest differences. Second, individuals who were high in interoceptive ability made much more use of information from their bodily responses than did those low in such ability. Thus, both bodily responses and the perception of these responses influenced decision making.

Anxiety

Of all the negative emotional states, fear or anxiety is most consistently associated with pessimistic judgments about the future. For example, Lerner et al. (2003) carried out an online study very shortly after the 9/11 terrorist attacks. The participants were instructed to focus on aspects of the attacks that made them afraid, angry, or sad. The estimated probability of future terrorist attacks was higher in fearful participants than in sad or angry ones.

Most people have what is known as an **optimism bias**. This bias involves individuals believing they are more likely than other people to experience positive events but less likely to experience negative events. Anxious individuals have less of an optimism bias than other people. Lench and Levine (2005) asked college participants to make judgments of the likelihood of various events happening to them compared to the average college student. Participants who were put into a fearful mood were more pessimistic than those put into a happy or neutral mood.

Key term
Optimism bias: the tendency to exaggerate our chances of experiencing positive events and to minimize our chances of experiencing negative events relative to other people.

Similar findings at the level of personality were reported by Harris et al. (2008). Most individuals perceive others to be more vulnerable than themselves to future risks. However, this tendency was weaker among those high in trait anxiety, a personality dimension related to anxiety susceptibility. This may, at least in part, reflect reality. Individuals with an anxious personality actually experience more negative life events than do those with a non-anxious personality (van Os et al., 2001).

Anxious individuals typically make less risky decisions than do non-anxious ones. Lorian and Grisham (2011) studied risk taking in patients with anxiety disorders who completed the Domain-Specific Risk-Taking Scale. This scale consists of 30 items assessing an individual's likelihood of engaging in risky activities (e.g., "Betting a day's income at the horse races"; "Engaging in unprotected sex"). The anxious patients had lower risk-taking scores than healthy controls.

Raghunathan and Pham (1999) asked participants to decide whether to accept job A (high salary + low job security) or job B (average salary + high job security). Participants in an anxious mood state were less likely than those in a neutral state to choose the high-risk option (job A).

Gambetti and Giusberti (2012) studied real-life financial decision making in individuals having anxious or non-anxious personalities. Anxious participants had made safer or more conservative financial decisions than had non-anxious ones. They were more likely to have put their money into interest-bearing accounts but less likely to have invested large sums of money in stocks, shares, and so on.

Why is anxiety associated with risk aversion? One reason is that anxious individuals are pessimistic about the likelihood of negative future events. Another reason follows from the finding that anxiety is often triggered by high uncertainty and low personal control over a situation (Frijda, 1986). Uncertainty can be minimized by making "safe" decisions.

Anxiety not only leads to risk aversion. It is also associated with impaired decision making. In one study (Preston et al., 2007), participants played the Iowa Gambling Task, which involves learning about the potential gains and losses associated with different decisions. Participants who were made anxious by anticipating that they would have to give a public speech showed slower learning than control participants.

Starcke et al. (2008) used the Game of Dice task, a decision-making task with explicit rules that requires the use of executive processes. Anxious participants (who anticipated giving a public speech) performed worse than control participants.

Why does anxiety impair decision making? Many decision-making tasks involve use of working memory (Baddeley, 1986, 2001; see Chapter 4), especially the attention-like central executive component. There is accumulating evidence that anxiety impairs the efficiency with which the central executive is used when performing complex tasks (Eysenck et al., 2007).

Sadness

Sadness and anxiety are both negative emotional states. However, sadness (which turns into depression when intense) is more strongly associated with an absence of positive affect. As a result, sad individuals experience the environment as relatively unrewarding and so may be especially motivated to obtain rewards even if risks are involved.

Waters (2008) reviewed studies on the effects of mood state on likelihood estimates of health hazards and life events. Those of sad individuals were more pessimistic than those of individuals in a positive mood state. Several studies found sad or depressed individuals have a smaller optimism bias than do non-depressed ones. This has often been referred to as *depressive realism*, meaning sad or depressed individuals are more realistic than other people about the future. However, the name "depressive realism" is problematic, because people with depression do not perform better than people without – on the contrary.

Earlier we discussed a study by Raghunathan and Pham (1999) in which anxious participants tended to choose a low-risk job rather than a high-risk one. Raghunathan and Pham also considered the effects of sadness. Most sad participants differed from anxious ones in selecting the high-risk job (see Figure 11.9). *Why* was this? According to Raghunathan and Pham, sad individuals experience the environment as relatively unrewarding and so are especially motivated to obtain rewards.

Cryder et al. (2008) investigated the misery-is-not-miserly effect – sad individuals will pay more than others to acquire a given commodity. Why does this effect occur? Cryder et al. argued that sad individuals have a diminished sense of self (especially when engaging in self-focus). This increases their motivation to acquire possessions to enhance the self. Sad individuals were willing to pay almost four times as much as those in a neutral mood for a sporty, insulated water bottle. This was particularly true for sad individuals who were high in self-focus.

Lerner et al. (2016) wondered whether sad people would make better financial decisions. They studied the well-known phenomenon that most people are impatient and prefer immediate rewards to larger but later ones. The median participant in a neutral mood regarded receiving $19 today as comparable to receiving $100 in a year. Surprisingly, the median sad participant was even more impatient, regarding $4 today as comparable to $100 in a year!

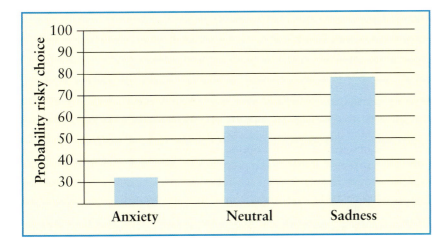

Figure 11.9 Effects of mood manipulation (anxiety, sadness, or neutral) on percentages of people choosing the high-risk job option.
Source: Based on data in Raghunathan and Pham (1999). With permission from Elsevier.

A possible explanation is that sad individuals experienced a need to enhance the self by obtaining an immediate reward, even if this has an economic cost.

Anger

Anger is typically regarded as a negative affect. However, anger can be experienced as relatively pleasant, because it leads individuals to believe that they can control the situation and conquer those whom they dislike (Lerner & Tiedens, 2006). Consider *schadenfreude* (experiencing pleasure at the misfortune of disliked others). Anger increases *schadenfreude* (Hareli & Weiner, 2002), but anger is also associated with negative affect. The events triggering anger are remembered as unpleasant, and it can lead to behavior (e.g., aggression; violence) causing substantial negative affect (Litvak et al., 2010).

In a review mentioned already, Waters (2008) found that anxiety and sadness were both associated with pessimistic judgments about the likelihood of negative events. In striking contrast to these negative moods, anger was associated with relatively *optimistic* judgments. Angry people are more likely than others to experience divorce, to have problems at work, and to have heart disease, but they rate themselves as less at risk (Lerner & Keltner, 2001).

Why is anger associated with optimistic judgments rather than the pessimistic ones associated with other negative mood states? Anger differs from other negative moods in being associated with a sense of *certainty* about what has happened and with perceived *control* over the situation (Litvak et al., 2010). These unique features of anger (especially high perceived control) explain why the effects of anger on judgment differ so much from those of other negative affective states.

We turn now to the effects of anger on decision making. Because angry people perceive themselves to have high control over situations, we might expect them to make riskier decisions than others. There is support for this prediction. Lerner and Keltner (2001) used the Asian disease problem on which most people exhibit risk-averse decision making (see Chapter 10). Fearful participants were risk averse but angry ones were risk seeking. Earlier we discussed a study by Gambetti and Giusberti (2012) in which they found anxious individuals had made less risky real-life financial decisions than those low in anxiety. Gambetti and Giusberti also found individuals with angry personalities had made risker financial decisions (e.g., more likely to have invested money in stocks and shares; more likely to have invested relatively large sums of money) than had non-angry ones.

Research by Kugler et al. (2012) suggests the effects of anger on decision making are more complex than stated so far. First, they replicated the finding that angry participants on their own were much less risk averse than happy or fearful ones on a lottery task involving large real-money payoffs. However, they obtained the opposite findings when participants were in pairs. Each individual chose between a risk-free option in which the outcome did not depend on the other person's choice and a risky option in which it did. Angry participants were much less likely than fearful ones (56% vs. 93%, respectively) to choose the risky option. Angry individuals did not want to lose control of the situation by making the risky choice.

Most people assume anger impairs our ability to think straight. According to the American Ralph Waldo Emerson, anger "blows out the light of reason." This viewpoint was supported by Bright and Goodman-Delahunty

(2006). Mock jurors were asked to read a 20-page, double-spaced summary of a trial involving a defendant charged with his wife's murder. The materials were drawn from a real murder case, and the evidence against the defendant was weak. Some participants were shown gruesome photographs of the murdered woman. They were far more likely to find the husband guilty than those not shown the photographs (41% vs. 9%). The photographs' distorting effect occurred in part because they increased jurors' anger towards the husband.

In a study discussed earlier, Stephens and Groeger (2011) also found that anger impaired decision making using a simulated driving task. More specifically, angry drivers drove in a dangerous and reckless manner.

Why does anger often impair decision making? It can lead to shallow processing based on heuristics (Glossary) rather than systematic or analytic processing (Litvak et al., 2010). Supporting evidence was reported by Coget et al. (2011) in a study of seven film directors. They mostly resorted to intuitive decision making when they were moderately or very angry, whereas moderate anxiety led to analytic processing.

Small and Lerner (2008) presented participants with the fictitious case of Patricia Smith, a young divorced mother with three children. Participants who had been put into an angry mood decided she should receive less welfare assistance than those put into a neutral or sad mood. In another condition, participants were given a second task (cognitive load) to perform at the same time as the decision-making task. This was done to reduce participants' use of systematic or analytic processing on the decision-making task. The added cognitive load did not influence the angry participants' decisions, suggesting they made little use of analytic processing in either condition.

Anger causes judgments as well as decisions to be made using heuristic processing. Ask and Granhag (2007) asked angry or sad police investigators to read the summary of a criminal case and two witness statements. They then judged the witnesses on several measures (e.g., trustworthiness) and stated how likely it was the defendant was guilty. The angry participants processed the case information more superficially than the sad ones (e.g., their judgments were less influenced by the content of the witness statements).

Anger does not always lead to shallow or heuristic processing, however. Moons and Mackie (2008) presented participants in an angry or neutral mood with weak or strong arguments for the position that college students have good financial habits. Angry participants were more persuaded by strong than by weak arguments, indicating that they engaged in analytic or systematic processing. In contrast, participants in a neutral mood were equally persuaded by strong and weak arguments. One explanation may be that anger increases motivated thinking (see Glossary, Chapters 9 and 10).

Positive mood

As discussed earlier, there has been much interest in the optimism bias (the tendency for people to judge they will experience more positive but fewer negative events than others). We would expect optimism bias to be stronger among those in a positive mood than those in a negative or neutral mood.

Lench and Levine (2005) presented participants with several hypothetical positive and negative events. Those in a happy mood showed a stronger optimism bias than did fearful participants. However, they were not more optimistic than participants in a neutral mood.

Research indicates that positive mood states are typically associated with a risk-averse approach to decision making (Blanchette & Richards, 2010). For example, Mustanski (2007) found the prevalence of HIV risk behaviors among gay men is less among those having high levels of positive affect. In one study (Cahir & Thomas, 2010), participants in a positive mood made less risky decisions than those in a neutral mood when betting on hypothetical horse races. Those in a positive mood are probably risk averse because they are motivated to maintain their current happy feeling.

Positive affect is also associated with increased use of heuristic or low-effort processing and decreased use of analytic processing (Griskevicius et al., 2010). De Vries et al. (2012) asked participants on each trial to decide between two gambles: (1) 50% chance of winning 1.20 euro and 50% chance of winning nothing; (2) 50% chance of winning 1.00 euro and 50% chance of winning nothing. Analytic thinking would lead participants to choose the first gamble on every trial. Happy participants were less likely than sad ones to use the analytic process consistently. Instead, happy participants were more likely than sad ones to engage in heuristic processing (e.g., switching gambles if the current one had proved unsuccessful on recent trials).

A surprising aspect of emotion research is that there usually is evidence for several negative emotions (e.g., anxiety, sadness, anger, disgust) but only one broad positive emotion (happiness). According to some authors, this is because negative stimuli are more extreme than positive stimuli (Alves et al., 2017). As a result, negative emotions are more intense and varied. Other authors, however, argue that the lack of differentiation in positive emotions is a result of researcher bias and that it is possible to discern as many as eight positive emotions: awe, amusement, interest, pride, gratitude, joy, love, and contentment (Campos et al., 2013).

Griskevicius et al. (2010) considered the effects of several positive mood states on the ability to assess the persuasiveness of strong and weak arguments. Participants experiencing three positive emotions (anticipatory enthusiasm, amusement, attachment love) exhibited heuristic or shallow processing – they were persuaded by weak arguments. However, two other positive emotions (awe, nurturing love) were associated with less heuristic or shallow processing than a neutral mood state. More research is needed to find out how much a categorical approach to positive affect could add to the prevailing dimensional approach.

Overall conclusions and evaluation

Research on the effects of mood on judgment and decision making has indicated that the effects vary from mood to mood. How can we make sense of this?

Anxiety occurs in threatening situations involving uncertainty and unpredictability. Accordingly, anxious individuals are motivated to reduce anxiety by increasing certainty and predictability, which can be achieved by minimizing risk taking and choosing non-risky options.

Individuals become sad or depressed when they discover a desired goal is unattainable. This leads individuals to abandon the unachievable goal and engage in extensive thinking to find new goals (Andrews & Thomson, 2009). At the same time their decision making becomes less good, likely because they have an increased need for rapid (and risky) reward.

Anger has the function of overcoming some obstacle to an important goal by taking direct and aggressive action. This approach is most likely to be found when individuals feel they have personal control and are thus optimistic the goal can be achieved. This perception of personal control also persuades angry individuals to take risks in order to achieve their goals.

An important function of positive mood states is to maintain the current mood (Oatley & Johnson-Laird, 1987). This leads happy individuals to engage in shallow or heuristic processing and to avoid taking risks that might endanger the positive mood state.

What are the main *limitations* of research in this area? First, most research has involved incidental emotional states of no direct relevance to the judgment or decision-making task. Such research may be relatively uninformative about the effects of integral mood states.

Second, most laboratory research has involved relatively trivial judgments and decisions having no implications outside of the laboratory. It is unsurprising that people use predominantly heuristic processing with such tasks. However, the situation may be different in real life when people in an intense emotional state make major decisions.

Third, many findings have been explained using the distinction between heuristic or shallow processing and analytic or deliberate processing. This distinction is oversimplified and ignores the likelihood that many cognitive processes involve a combination of both types of process (Keren & Schul, 2009).

MORAL DILEMMAS: EMOTION VS. COGNITION

Most research discussed so far has involved *mild* mood manipulations. In the real world, however, strong emotion can be involved when we make complex judgments and decisions, for instance in moral dilemmas, which involve a conflict between moral requirements.

Utilitarian vs. deontological decisions

The *trolley problem* is an example of a moral dilemma. You must decide whether to divert a runaway trolley threatening the lives of five people on to a sidetrack where it will kill only one person (see Figure 11.10). The *footbridge problem* is another example. You must decide whether to push a fat person over a bridge causing the death of the person pushed but saving the lives of five other people farther down the track (see Figure 11.10).

What did you decide? In experimental studies, 90% of participants decide to divert the trolley, but only 10% decide to push the person off the footbridge (Hauser, 2006). Greene et al. (2008) argued that the footbridge problem is an example of a personal moral dilemma because we might directly harm or kill one or more people by our actions. In contrast, the trolley problem is an *impersonal moral dilemma* because the harm that might be done results less directly and immediately from our actions. Most research has focused on personal moral dilemmas.

According to Greene et al. (2008), personal moral dilemmas trigger a strong emotional response. With the footbridge problem, we face a severe conflict. On the one hand, there is a powerful emotional argument not to kill another person. On the other hand, there is a strong cognitive argument that more lives will be saved (five vs. one) if you push the person over the bridge.

Key term
Personal moral dilemma: situation in which we have to make complex judgments and a decision between alternative actions that will harm or kill people; our actions have a direct effect on the well-being of individuals with whom we are interacting in person.

Figure 11.10 Two well-known moral dilemma problems: (a) the trolley problem; and (b) the footbridge problem.

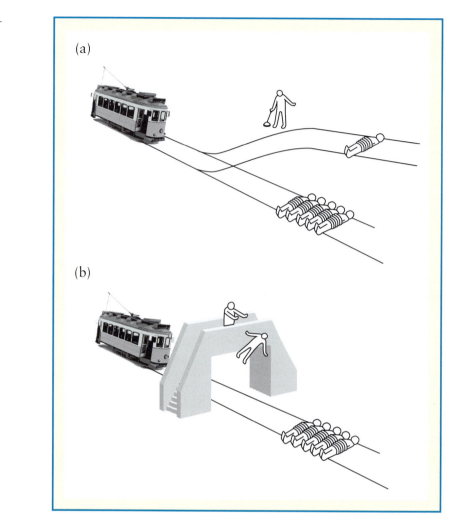

In their dual-process model, Greene et al. (2008) distinguished between two systems: (1) a fast, automatic and affective system; and (2) a slower, effortful, and more "cognitive" system. With personal moral dilemmas, those making decisions based on moral rules or obligations (e.g., do not kill) respond mainly on the basis of the first, affective system. In contrast, those making practical decisions based on saving as many lives as possible use the second, cognitive system. In crude terms, you can use your head or your heart when resolving a moral dilemma. Practical decisions made with the head are called *utilitarian decisions*; emotional decisions based on moral rules or obligations are called *deontological decisions*.

Findings

According to Greene et al.'s (2008) two-process model, utilitarian judgments with personal moral dilemmas typically involve much use of the cognitive system. Suppose participants performed a demanding cognitive task reducing accessibility of cognitive resources while making moral judgments. This task should increase the time taken to make utilitarian judgments (which generally involve much cognitive processing) more than that for deontological judgments. That is precisely what Greene et al. (2008) found.

It is assumed theoretically that deontological judgments depend much more on emotional processing than do utilitarian ones with personal moral dilemmas but not impersonal ones. We can test this assumption by giving an anti-anxiety drug to participants to reduce the impact of emotion on judgments. This was done by Perkins et al. (2013). As predicted, anti-anxiety drugs increased utilitarian judgments (and reduced deontological ones) with personal moral dilemmas but did not affect judgments with impersonal ones.

Interestingly, Costa et al. (2014) reported that bilingual participants also made less deontological decisions when the footbridge problem was presented in the participants' second language than in their native language (Figure 11.11). The authors argued that the finding stemmed from the reduced emotional response elicited by the foreign language, consequently reducing the impact of intuitive emotional concerns. More specifically, the authors suggested that the increased psychological distance of using a foreign language induces extra utilitarianism in moral decisions.

Are utilitarian decisions better than deontological decisions?

We turn now to potential problems with the dual-process model of moral decisions. The model seems to assume that utilitarian decisions are superior to deontological ones. However, Kahane et al. (2015) found utilitarian judgments with various personal moral dilemmas were associated with a somewhat immoral outlook (e.g., psychopathy; less donation of money to charity; poor identification with the whole of humanity).

According to Broeders et al. (2011), the assumption that utilitarian decisions with personal moral dilemmas are based on pragmatic considerations while deontological decisions are based on moral rules is oversimplified. They tested this assumption in a study in which participants were presented

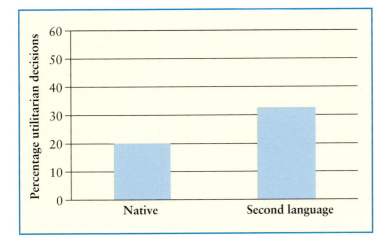

Figure 11.11 Percentage of utilitarian responses to the footbridge problem (throw a man off a bridge to save five lives farther down the track) as a function of whether bilingual participants read the problem in their native language or in their second language.
Source: Based on data in Costa et al. (2014).

with information designed to focus their attention on the moral rules "Do not kill" or "Save lives" prior to the footbridge problem. Participants for whom the rule "Save lives" was more accessible produced more utilitarian decisions than those given the rule "Do not kill." Thus, utilitarian decisions (as well as deontological ones) can be based on moral rules, and the differences between the two types of decisions may be less than generally assumed.

Kahane et al. (2012) pointed out that utilitarian decisions in most previous research were counterintuitive or opposed to common sense. The reason such decisions take longer than deontological decisions could be because they are counterintuitive rather than because they are utilitarian.

We can see what Kahane et al. (2012) meant by considering a personal moral dilemma in which a utilitarian decision is not counterintuitive. Suppose you are a server and a customer you know well tells you he is determined to infect as many people as possible with HIV before he goes to prison in 48 hours. You know he has a very strong allergy to poppy seeds, and so if you put some in his food he would be hospitalized for at least 48 hours. What would you do? In this case, the utilitarian decision (i.e., give him the poppy seeds) is intuitively appealing.

Kahane et al. (2012) studied utilitarian and deontological decisions that were intuitive or counterintuitive. They observed that counterintuitive decisions were experienced as more difficult than intuitive ones regardless of whether those decisions were utilitarian or deontological. Also, the brain responses differed more between intuitive and counterintuitive decisions than between utilitarian and deontological decisions. Thus, the distinction between intuitive and counter-intuitive decisions seems more fundamental than that between utilitarian and deontological ones.

Evaluation

+ Research on moral dilemmas focuses on complex emotional issues of relevance to everyday life.

+ There is much support for the theoretical assumption that people confronting a moral dilemma can use fast affective processes and/or slow cognitive ones.

+ Progress has been made in identifying the brain areas associated with those two types of process based on brain-damaged patients and on neuroimaging studies.

− The assumption that utilitarian decisions are "better" seems dubious given the tendency of individuals with an anti-social personality to prefer such decisions.

− The notion that moral rules are used with deontological decisions but not utilitarian ones is oversimplified. Utilitarian decisions can also be based on moral rules.

− The distinction between utilitarian and deontological decisions may be of less fundamental importance than that between intuitive and counterintuitive decisions.

Section summary

Introduction
- Our emotional state affects numerous aspects of cognition.
- Mood states can be manipulated by asking participants to focus on emotional personal events or by presenting emotional music or movie clips. There are often clear-cut effects of such manipulations.

Attention
- Attention can be broad or narrow in scope. Negative affect narrows the scope; positive affect tends to broaden it. Harman-Jones et al. (2011) disagreed with this conclusion, however, and argued that the decision variable is not positive vs. negative but high vs. low motivational intensity.

Memory
- Emotionally toned information is learned and retrieved best when its affective value is congruent with the learner's or rememberer's current mood state. This is called mood congruity.
- Memory is generally better when the mood state at retrieval is the same as that at learning, especially when effortful processing is needed at learning or retrieval, an observation called mood-state-dependent memory.
- The amygdala plays an important role in enhanced memory for emotional information relative to neutral information.

Judgment and decision making
- Mood states have significant effects on judgment and decision making.
- Decisions often evoke integral emotions as a consequence of the decision to be made. However, decisions can also be influenced by incidental emotions due to past events.
- Anxiety is associated with pessimistic judgments about the future (against the optimism bias). Anxiety is further associated with impaired decision making and avoidance of risk.
- Sadness is also associated with pessimistic judgments about the future, but not with risk aversion. The latter is partly related to a need for immediate reward.
- Anger is associated with optimistic judgments about the future and can lead to impaired decision making based on shallow processing. Some of the differences between the effects of anger and other negative mood states are due to the greater sense of perceived control with anger.
- Positive mood is associated with modestly positive judgments about the future and a risk-averse approach to decision making, which may reflect the motivation to maintain the current mood state.

Moral dilemmas: emotion vs. cognition
- Moral dilemmas create conditions in which strong emotions are opposed to cognition, in particular when the consequences involve people we are personally interacting with. Two much-researched problems are the trolley problem and the footbridge problem.
- A dual-process model is used to interpret the findings and make new predictions. Originally, it was thought that the first process involved deontological (emotional) processing and the second utilitarian (cognitive) processing. However, a better distinction may be between intuitive processing and counterintuitive processing.

ANXIETY AND COGNITIVE BIASES

Millions of people around the world suffer from long-lasting or chronic anxiety. Much research has been based on the assumption that this negative mood state is associated with various effects on cognition (discussed shortly), and that these effects may serve to maintain that negative mood state.

Some research in this area has focused on patients suffering from an anxiety disorder. Other research has involved studying healthy individuals who are high in the personality dimension of trait anxiety (related to the frequency and intensity of the experience of anxiety).

Research on the topic of anxiety is complicated because anxious individuals also tend to have symptoms of depression and vice versa. *Comorbidity* is the term used to indicate a patient has two or more mental disorders at the same time; it is very common in patients with an anxiety disorder or major depressive disorder. Healthy individuals with anxious personalities (high in trait anxiety) also tend to have depressive personalities.

In spite of the overlap between anxiety and depression, there are important differences between them. For example, past losses are associated mainly with depression, whereas future threats are associated more with anxiety. Eysenck et al. (2006) presented participants with scenarios referring to several negative events (e.g., the diagnosis of a serious illness). Each scenario had three versions depending on whether it referred to a past event, a future possible event, or a future probable event. Participants indicated how anxious or depressed each event would make them. Anxiety was associated more with future than past events, whereas the opposite was the case for depression.

There is further support for the above notions if we consider the symptoms of anxiety and depression. Worry about possible future events is a major symptom of several anxiety disorders (Hirsch & Mathews, 2012). Indeed, it is the central symptom of generalized anxiety disorder in which patients have excessive concerns across various domains (e.g., work, interpersonal relationships). In contrast, rumination (which involves dwelling on negative feelings and experiences from the past) is a very common symptom in depressed patients.

Why is it important to study cognitive processes in anxious and depressed people? Patients with clinical anxiety or depression differ from healthy individuals in several ways (e.g., cognitively, behaviorally, physiologically, perhaps biochemically). Therapies differ in terms of which type of symptom is the central focus in treatment (Kring et al., 2012). Within this context, it is of major theoretical importance to establish the interplay between cognitive and emotional factors.

We have already seen that anxiety has several effects on cognitive processing and performance. However, the focus of this section is on two cognitive biases (attentional bias and interpretive bias) claimed to be of particular importance in clinical anxiety. *Why* are these cognitive biases important? A key assumption made by many researchers in this area (e.g., Eysenck, 1997; Williams et al., 1997) is that these biases may increase vulnerability to clinical anxiety and/or serve to maintain an existing anxiety disorder.

ATTENTIONAL BIAS

It seems reasonable to assume that anxious individuals would attend more than non-anxious ones to threat-related words (e.g., stupid; inept). In other words, they show an **attentional bias**, the selective allocation of attention to threat-related stimuli. We might also expect that those with a craving (e.g., for alcohol) would pay particular attention to stimuli related to their craving (e.g., beer; vodka).

Findings

Supporting evidence has been obtained in studies using various modified versions of the Stroop task (see Glossary and Chapter 1). In the *emotional Stroop task* individuals high and low in anxiety are asked to name the color in which words are printed as rapidly as possible. Some of the words are emotionally negative and relevant to anxiety, whereas others are neutral. Anxious individuals, but not healthy controls, take longer to name colors with emotionally negative than neutral words in this task (Bar-Haim et al., 2007).

Attentional bias can also be assessed with the *dot-probe task*. In the original version of this task, two words were presented simultaneously. On critical trials, one word is threat-related and the other is neutral. The allocation of attention is assessed by recording speed of detection of a dot that can replace either word.

Detection times on the dot-probe task are shorter in attended areas. Thus, attentional bias is indicated by a consistent tendency for detection times to be shorter when the dot replaces the threat-related word rather than the neutral one. In some research, threat-related and neutral pictures have been used instead of words because they are likely to trigger a greater emotional response.

Attentional bias has been found in both the emotional Stroop and dot-probe tasks even when the threat stimuli are presented subliminally (below the level of conscious awareness) (Bar-Haim et al., 2007). Further research has indicated that the association goes in both directions: changes in fear and anxiety can lead to changes in attentional bias, but changes in attentional bias can also lead to changes in fear and anxiety. So, the relation between attentional bias and fear and anxiety is best described as a bidirectional, maintaining, or mutually reinforcing relation (Van Bockstaele et al., 2014).

Rudaizky et al. (2014) found high trait anxiety was associated with facilitated attentional *engagement* with negative stimuli and also with slowed attentional *disengagement* from such stimuli. These two biases were uncorrelated with each other. This suggests vulnerability to anxiety depends on *separate* contributions from attentional engagement bias and attentional disengagement bias.

Attentional bias modification

In recent years, there has been an exciting development in research on attentional bias. Suppose that attentional biases help to maintain an individual's high level of anxiety or craving for some substance. It follows that there might be beneficial effects of providing attentional training to reduce (or eliminate) those attentional biases. Such training is called *attentional bias modification*.

How can we reduce attentional biases? We alter the dot-probe task so that the dot *always* (or nearly always) appears in the location in which the neutral word was presented. As a result, individuals learn to avoid allocating attention to the threat word.

MacLeod et al. (2002) argued that attentional training on the dot-probe task can be effective in reducing attentional bias and in improving individuals' well-being. They exposed students who were high in trait anxiety to more than 6,000 training trials on the dot-probe task. The training significantly reduced attentional bias. More importantly, it also led to a significant reduction in the students' trait anxiety scores. In similar fashion, individuals with social anxiety showed less attention bias after training, and they also showed reduced anxiety when engaged in public speaking (Amir et al., 2008).

Meta-analysis has been used to assess the efficiency of attentional bias modification across studies. Mogoase et al. (2014) reported a useful but modest effect size for the treatment of anxiety disorders but not for the treatment of depression or pain. There was also an indication of a useful effect size for substance abuse, but the number of studies was too small to be sure. Finally, there was a modest benefit for healthy participants facing a stressful situation.

In sum, there are reliable individual differences in the extent to which our attention is attracted by various stimuli. This is an important finding because most research on attention has largely ignored individual differences. Of great significance is that training designed to modify attentional bias offers the prospect of benefiting people's lives by reducing conditions such as chronic anxiety and craving. However, the effects are rather modest, and most studies so far have only considered short-term effects. Therefore, attentional bias modification is best seen as a component of a broader therapy, not as a therapy of its own.

INTERPRETIVE BIAS

In our everyday lives, we are often exposed to ambiguous events. For example, does a noise outside in the middle of the night indicate the presence of a burglar or a cat? If someone walks past you without acknowledging your presence, does that mean they dislike you or simply that they failed to notice you?

It has often been assumed that individuals differ considerably in the tendency to interpret such ambiguous situations in a threatening way. More specifically, it has been hypothesized that anxious individuals exhibit interpretive bias – the tendency to interpret ambiguous stimuli and events in a threat-related fashion.

Most research on interpretive bias in anxious individuals has focused on the interpretation of words and sentences (see Research Activity 11.1). However, given that much anxiety occurs in social situations, there are good reasons for also considering interpretive bias with respect to facial expressions. Yoon and Zinbarg (2008) considered the interpretation of neutral facial expressions in individuals high and low in social anxiety. The participants high in social anxiety interpreted neutral faces as negative regardless of whether they anticipated a feared situation (giving a speech). In these participants, interpretive bias was due to their personality. In contrast, the participants low in social anxiety *only* showed interpretive bias when anticipating giving a speech. In these participants, interpretive bias was triggered by being in a situation creating anxiety rather than by their personality.

| Key term

Interpretive bias:
the tendency to interpret ambiguous stimuli and situations in a threatening fashion.

Research Activity 11.1 *Interpretive bias*

Some research on interpretive bias in anxious individuals has focused on the interpretation of **homographs**. These are words having a single spelling but two or more different meanings.

Look at the words in the columns below (taken from Grey & Mathews, 2000). Write down in a word or two the *first* meaning of each word that comes to mind:

beat	nag
tank	maroon
stole	hang
strain	patient

lie   drop
break   throttle

When you have finished, look at the end of the chapter and decide whether each interpretation was closer to the threatening or the neutral one. You might find it interesting to compare your responses to those of a friend.

Much research has considered the effects of anxiety on the interpretation of homographs such as those in the list. Healthy individuals with an anxious personality and patients with anxiety disorders are more likely than other people to produce threatening interpretations (Mathews & MacLeod, 2005).

An important issue concerns the stage of processing at which an interpretive bias occurs in anxious individuals (Blanchette & Richards, 2010). One possibility is that both (or all) meanings of an ambiguous word or sentence are activated initially, with anxious individuals favoring the threatening interpretation at a late stage of processing. Alternatively, anxious individuals may select the threatening interpretation relatively early in processing.

Most research favors the notion that interpretive bias occurs relatively late in processing. Calvo and Castillo (1997) presented ambiguous sentences relating to personal social threat to high-anxious and low-anxious individuals. There was clear evidence of an interpretive bias in high-anxious individuals 1,250 ms after sentence presentation but not at 500 ms. These findings suggest that interpretive bias doesn't occur rapidly and automatically, but rather that it depends on subsequent controlled processes.

Huppert et al. (2007) argued that the interpretation of ambiguous sentences involves successive stages of response generation and response selection. They presented participants with incomplete sentences such as, "As you walk to the podium, you notice your heart racing, which means you are __." Their task was to generate several sentence completions and then to select the one that seemed to fit the sentence the best. Socially anxious individuals (compared to non-anxious ones) showed evidence of interpretive bias at the generation and selection stages.

Key term

Homographs:
words that have a single spelling but at least two different meanings (e.g., maroon; throttle); used to study **interpretive bias**.

In the Real World 11.1 *Anxiety disorders and interpretive bias*

Here we will consider the role of interpretive bias in three of the main anxiety disorders: social phobia; panic disorder; and generalized anxiety disorder.

Social phobia involves extreme fear and avoidance of social situations. Of central importance to social phobia is interpretive bias – social phobics interpret their own social behavior as substantially less adequate than it appears to observers (Rodebaugh et al., 2010).

Patients with panic disorder suffer from panic attacks, but *not* because they have heightened physiological responses to stressful events (Eysenck, 1997). The major reason is that patients with panic disorder are much more likely than other people to have catastrophic misinterpretations of their bodily sensations (Clark, 1986). Austin and Kiropoulos (2008) presented participants with questions such as, "You feel short of breath. Why?" Panic disorder patients gave more harm-related interpretations of such ambiguous internal stimuli than social phobics or healthy controls. They also regarded harm and anxiety outcomes as more catastrophic than did the other groups of participants.

Patients with generalized anxiety disorder exhibit excessive worrying about a wide range of issues. Some of this worrying undoubtedly reflects genuine personal problems, but part is due to an interpretive bias. In a study by Eysenck et al. (1991),

patients with generalized anxiety disorder and healthy controls listened to ambiguous sentences such as the following:

1. At the refugee camp, the weak/week would soon be finished.
2. The doctor examined little Emma's growth.
3. They discussed the priest's convictions.

Only the anxious patients had an interpretive bias for these sentences (i.e., in line with weak, growth as in cancer, and conviction as in being convicted in court).

So far we have seen that there is an *association* between having an anxiety disorder and the presence of an interpretive bias. However, this doesn't clarify whether anxiety disorder leads to interpretive bias and/or vice versa. If interpretive bias plays a role in producing or maintaining anxiety disorder, then therapy designed to reduce or eliminate interpretive bias should reduce anxiety levels, as discussed in the main text.

Cognitive bias modification

If interpretive bias causes anxiety, then modifying the bias should decrease the anxious feelings.

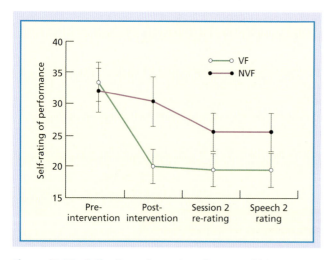

Figure 11.12 Self-ratings of speech performance (high scores are worse) as a function of video feedback intervention (VF) or no video feedback intervention (NVF). Self-ratings of Speech 1 were more positive following video feedback (i.e., post-intervention) and had a positive carry-over effect on Speech 2.
Source: From Rodebaugh et al. (2010). Reprinted with permission from Elsevier.

Rodebaugh et al. (2010) asked social phobics to give two public speeches. After the first one, some social phobics were provided with video feedback of their performance to reduce their interpretive bias for their own social behavior. This feedback reduced their interpretive bias and made them experience less anticipatory anxiety before giving the second speech (see Figure 11.12).

Hayes et al. (2010) trained patients with generalized anxiety disorder to produce non-threatening interpretations of ambiguous homographs and scenarios. This intervention was effective in reducing the interpretive bias and the negative thought intrusions or worry.

Again, meta-analyses have looked at the efficacy of cognitive bias modification therapy across studies. Hallion et al. (2011) reported a big effect size on the interpretations themselves, but only a small effect size on anxiety symptoms. That is, patients interpreted stimuli differently after the training, but they did not feel much better. These findings were replicated in a later meta-analysis by Cristea et al. (2015).

In line with what we discussed for attentional bias, the end conclusion seems to be that interpretive bias modification is a useful technique as part of a wider therapy, but it is not strong enough to tackle anxiety on its own. This again suggests that the interaction between interpretive bias and anxiety is not unidirectional from bias to feeling, but a bidirectional, maintaining, or mutually reinforcing relation, as proposed by Van Bockstaele et al. (2014) for attentional bias. Another reason for the small effect could be that many studies involved only brief interventions and short-term effects. This is different from an intensive cognitive behavior therapy, in which client and therapist work together to address maladaptive thoughts (MacLeod & Mathews, 2012).

Section summary

- Many people around the world suffer from long-lasting or chronic anxiety. They often feel depressed as well (comorbidity). Research has focused on the possible contribution of two cognitive biases: attentional bias and interpretive bias.

Attentional bias
- Anxious individuals show attentional bias on the emotional Stroop and dot-probe tasks.
- Attentional training reduces the bias and the anxiety to some extent, but not enough to use the training as the only element in a therapy.

Interpretive bias
- Anxious individuals exhibit interpretive bias for ambiguous facial expressions, words, and sentences. This interpretive bias depends mainly on later stages of processing.
- Reducing interpretive bias slightly reduces anxiety levels in patients with anxiety disorders and shows that part of the association between anxiety and interpretive bias occurs because interpretive bias increases anxiety. At present, however, the effect is not big enough to warrant a separate therapy based on the technique. It is better to use it as an element in a broader approach.

Essay questions

1. Discuss the role of appraisal in determining which emotion an individual experiences in any given situation.
2. Describe some of the main strategies used in emotion regulation. Which strategies tend to be especially effective?
3. In what ways does mood influence learning and memory?
4. What effects do various mood states have on judgment and decision making?
5. How do emotions influence decisions in moral dilemmas?
6. Discuss the relevance of attentional and interpretive biases for an understanding of the anxiety disorders and depression.

Further reading

- Blanchette, I., & Richards, A. (2010). The influence of affect on higher level cognition: A review of research on interpretation, judgment, decision making and reasoning. *Cognition & Emotion*, *24*, 561–595. Isabelle Blanchette and Anne Richards discuss a wide range of effects of emotion on cognitive processes.
- Fox, E. (2008). *Emotion science*. New York, NY: Palgrave Macmillan. In this excellent book, Elaine Fox discusses at length relationships between cognition and emotion.
- Gross, J.J. (2015). Emotion regulation: Current status and future prospects. *Psychological Inquiry: An International Journal for the Advancement of Psychological Theory*, 26, 1–26. Theory and research on emotion regulation are discussed by a leading expert in the field.
- Lerner, J.S. et al. (2015). Emotion and decision making. *Annual Review of Psychology*, *66*, 799–823. A good review article on emotion and decision making.
- MacLeod, C., & Mathews, A. (2012). Cognitive bias modification approaches to anxiety. *Annual Review of Clinical Psychology*, *8*, 189–217. The role of attentional and interpretive biases in triggering anxiety is discussed at length by Colin MacLeod and Andrew Mathews.
- Robinson, M.D., Watkins, E.R., & Harmon-Jones, E. (Eds.) (2013). *Handbook of cognition and emotion*. New York: Guilford Press. Compendium of research on cognition and emotion with chapters from all the impactful researchers.

Chapter Solution

Interpretation Research Activity: Interpretive bias

Homograph	Threatening interpretation	Neutral interpretation
Beat	hit	drum
Tank	war	reservoir
Stole	theft	clothing
Strain	injure	race
Lie	false statement	be horizontal
Break	smash	holiday
Nag	find fault	horse
Maroon	strand	color
Hang	put to death	put up pictures/hold back
Patient	in a hospital	calm
Drop	cease to associate with	rain
Throttle	strangle	part of an engine

REFERENCES

Alves, H., Koch, A., & Unkelbach, C. (2017). Why good is more alike than bad: Processing implications. *Trends in Cognitive Sciences, 21(2)*, 69–79.

Amir, N., Weber, G., Beard, C., Bomyea, J., & Taylor, C. T. (2008). The effect of a single-session attention modification program on response to a public-speaking challenge in socially anxious individuals. *Journal of Abnormal Psychology*, 117, 860–868.

Augustine, A. A., & Hemenover, S. H. (2009). On the relative merits of affect regulation strategies: A meta-analysis. *Cognition & Emotion, 23,* 1181–1220.

Austin, D., & Kiropoulos, L. (2008). An internet-based investigation of the catastrophic misinterpretation model of panic disorder. *Journal of Anxiety Disorders, 22,* 233–242.

Baddeley, A. (2001). Is working memory still working? *American Psychologist, 56,* 851–864.

Baddeley, A. D. (1986). *Working memory.* Oxford, UK: Clarendon Press.

Bar-Haim, Y., Lamy, D., Pergamin, L., Bakermans-Kronenburg, M. J., & van IJzendoorn, M. H. (2007). Threat-related attentional bias in anxious and nonanxious individuals: A meta-analytic study. *Psychological Bulletin, 133,* 1–24.

Barrett, L. F., & Russell, J. A. (1998). Independence and bipolarity in the structure of current affect. *Journal of Personality and Social Psychology, 74,* 967–984.

Blanchette, I., & Richards, A. (2010). The influence of affect on higher level cognition: A review of research on interpretation, judgment, decision making and reasoning. *Cognition & Emotion, 24,* 561–595.

Bright, D. A., & Goodman-Delahunty, J. (2006). Gruesome evidence and emotion: Anger, blame, and jury decision-making. *Law and Human Behavior, 30,* 183–202.

Bushman, B. J. (2002). Does venting anger feed of extinguish the flame? Catharsis, rumination, distraction, anger, and aggressive responding. *Personality and Social Psychology Bulletin, 28,* 724–731.

Cahill, L., Babinsky, R., Markowitsch, H. J., & McGaugh, J. L. (1995). The amygdala and emotional memory. *Nature, 377,* 295–296.

Calder, A. J., Young, A. W., Rowland, D., Perrett, D. I., Hodges, J. R., & Etcoff, N. L. (1996). Facial emotion recognition after bilateral amygdala damage: Differentially severe impairment of fear. *Cognitive Neuropsychology, 13,* 699–745.

Calvo, M. G., & Castillo, M. D. (1997). Mood-congruent bias in interpretation of ambiguity: Strategic processes and temporary activation. *Quarterly Journal of Experimental Psychology, 50A,* 163–182.

Clark, D. M. (1986). A cognitive approach to panic. *Behaviour Research and Therapy, 24,* 461–470.

Costa, A., Foucart, A., Hayakawa, S., Aparici, M., Apesteguia, J., Heafner, J., & Keysar, B. (2014). Your morals depend on language. *PloS One, 9*(4), e94842.

Cristea, I. A., Kok, R. N., & Cuijpers, P. (2015). Efficacy of cognitive bias modification interventions in anxiety and depression: Meta-analysis. *The British Journal of Psychiatry, 206*(1), 7–16.

Easterbrook, J. A. (1959). The effect of emotion on cue utilization and the organization of behavior. *Psychological Review, 66,* 183–201.

Eich, E. (1995). Searching for mood-dependent memory. *Psychological Science, 6,* 67–75.

Eich, E., & Metcalfe, J. (1989). Mood-dependent memory for internal versus external events. *Journal of Experimental Psychology: Learning, Memory & Cognition, 15,* 443–455.

Eriksen, C. W., & St. James, J. D. (1986). Visual attention within and around the field of focal attention: A zoom lens model. *Perception & Psychophysics, 40,* 225–240.

Eysenck, M. W. (1997). *Anxiety and cognition: A unified theory.* Hove, UK: Psychology Press.

Eysenck, M. W., Derakshan, N., Santos, R., & Calvo, M. G. (2007). Anxiety and cognitive performance: Attentional control theory. *Emotion, 7,* 336–353.

Eysenck, M. W., Mogg, K., May, J., Richards, A., & Mathews, A. (1991). Bias in interpretation of ambiguous sentences related to threat in anxiety. *Journal of Abnormal Psychology, 100,* 144–150.

Fox, E. (2008). *Emotion science.* New York, NY: Palgrave Macmillan.

Friedman, M., & Rosenman, R. H. (1959). Association of specific overt behavior pattern with blood and cardiovascular findings: blood cholesterol level, blood clotting time, incidence of arcus senilis, and clinical coronary artery disease. *Journal of the American Medical Association, 169*(12), 1286–1296.

Frijda, N. H. (1986). *The emotions*. Cambridge, UK: Cambridge University Press.

Gill, N. P., Bos, E. H., Wit, E. C., & de Jonge, P. (2017). The association between positive and negative affect at the inter-and intra-individual level. *Personality and Individual Differences, 105*, 252–256.

Grey, S., & Mathews, A. (2000). Effects of training on interpretation of emotional ambiguity. *Quarterly Journal of Experimental Psychology, 53*, 1143–1162.

Griskevicius, V., Shiota, M. N., & Neufeld, S. L. (2010). Influence of different positive emotions on persuasive processing: A functional evolutionary approach. *Emotion, 10*, 190–206.

Gross, J. J., & Thompson, R. A. (2007). Emotion regulation: Conceptual foundations. In J. J. Gross (Ed.), *Handbook of emotion regulation*. New York, NY: Guilford Press.

Hallion, L. S., & Ruscio, A. M. (2011). A meta-analysis of the effect of cognitive bias modification on anxiety and depression. *Psychological Bulletin, 137*(6), 940–958.

Hareli, S., & Weiner, B. (2002). Dislike and envy as antecedents of pleasure at another's misfortune. *Motivation and Emotion, 26*, 257–277.

Hayes, S., Hirsch, C. R., Krebs, G., & Mathews, A. (2010). The effects of modifying interpretation bias on worry in generalized anxiety disorder. *Behaviour Research and Therapy, 48*, 171–178.

Huppert, J. D., Pasupuleti, R. V., Foa, E. B., & Mathews, A. (2007). Interpretation bias in social anxiety: Response generation, response selection, and self-appraisals. *Behaviour Research and Therapy, 45*, 1505–1515.

Izard, C. E. (2007). Basic emotions, natural kinds, emotion schemas, and a new paradigm. *Perspective in Psychological Science, 2*, 260–280.

Jolij, J., & Lamme, V. A. F. (2005). Repression of unconscious information by conscious processing: Evidence for affective blindsight induced by transcranial magnetic stimulation. *Proceedings of the National Academy of Sciences of the United States of America, 102*, 10747–10751.

Kenealy, P. M. (1997). Mood-state-dependent retrieval: The effects of induced mood on memory reconsidered. *Quarterly Journal of Experimental Psychology, 50A*, 290–317.

Keren, G., & Schul, Y. (2009). Two is not always better than one: A critical evaluation of two-system theories. *Perspectives on Psychological Science, 4*, 533–550.

Koole, S. L., Webb, T. L., & Sheeran, P. L. (2015). Implicit emotion regulation: Feeling better without knowing why. *Current Opinion in Psychology, 3*, 6–10.

Lench, H. C., & Levine, L. J. (2005). Effects of fear on risk and control judgments and memory: Implications for health promotion messages. *Cognition & Emotion, 19*, 1049–1069.

Lerner, J. S., & Keltner, D. (2001). Fear, anger, and risk. *Journal of Personality and Social Psychology, 81*, 146–159.

Lerner, J. S., & Tiedens, L. Z. (2006). Portrait of the angry decision maker: How appraisal tendencies shape anger's influence on cognition. *Journal of Behavioral Decision Making, 19*, 115–137.

Lerner, J. S., Gonzalez, R. M., Small, D. A., & Fischhoff, B. (2003). Effects of fear and anger on perceived risks of terrorism: A national field experiment. *Psychological Science, 14*, 144–150.

Litvak, P. M., Lerner, J. S., Tiedens, L. Z., & Shonk, K. (2010). Fuel in the fire: How anger impacts judgment and decision-making. In M. Potegal, G. Stemmler, & C. Spielberger (Eds.), *International handbook of anger: Constituent and concomitant biological, psychological, and social processes* (pp. 287–310). New York, NY: Springer.

MacLeod, C., & Mathews, A. (2012). Cognitive bias modification approaches to anxiety. *Annual Review of Clinical Psychology, 8*, 189–217.

MacLeod, C., Rutherford, E., Campbell, L., Ebsworthy, G., & Holker, L. (2002). Selective attention and emotional vulnerability: Assessing the causal basis of their association through the experimental manipulation of attentional bias. *Journal of Abnormal Psychology, 111*, 107–123.

Mathews, A., & MacLeod, C. (2005). Cognitive vulnerability to emotional disorders. *Annual Review of Clinical Psychology, 1*, 167–195.

McRae, K., Hughes, B., Chopra, S., Gabrieli, J. D. E., Gross, J. J., & Ochsner, K. N. (2010). Neural systems supporting the control of affective and cognitive conflicts. *Journal of Cognitive Neuroscience, 22*, 248–262.

Miranda, R., & Kihlstrom, J. F. (2005). Mood congruence in childhood and recent autobiographical memory. *Cognition & Emotion, 19*, 981–998.

Mogoaşe, C., David, D., & Koster, E. H. (2014). Clinical efficacy of attentional bias modification procedures: An updated meta-analysis. *Journal of Clinical Psychology, 70*(12), 1133–1157.

Moons, W. G., & Mackie, D. M. (2008). Thinking straight while seeing red: The influence of anger on information processing. *Personality and Social Psychology Bulletin, 33*, 706–721.

Ochsner, K. N., & Gross, J. J. (2008). Cognitive emotion regulation: Insights from social cognitive and affective neuroscience. *Current Directions in Psychological Science, 17*, 153–158.

Ochsner, K. N., Ray, R. R., Hughes, B., McRae, K., Cooper, J. C., Weber, J., et al. (2009). Bottom-up and top-down processes in emotion generation: Common and distinct neural mechanisms. *Psychological Science, 20*, 1322–1331.

Öhman, A., & Soares, J. J. F. (1994). "Unconscious anxiety": Phobic responses to masked stimuli. *Journal of Abnormal Psychology, 103*, 231–240.

Pecher, C., Lemercier, C., & Cellier, J. -M. (2009). Emotions drive attention: Effects on driver's behaviour. *Safety Science, 47*, 1254–1259.

Pegna, A. J., Khateb, A., Lazeyras, F., & Seghier, M. L. (2005). Discriminating emotional faces without primary visual cortices involves the right amygdala. *Nature Neuroscience, 8*, 24–25.

Pessoa, L. (2008). On the relationship between emotion and cognition. *Nature Reviews Neuroscience, 9*, 148–158.

Polivy, J. (1981). On the induction of emotion in the laboratory: Discrete moods or multiple affect states? *Journal of Personality and Social Psychology, 41*, 803–817.

Preston, S. D., Buchanan, T. W., Stansfield, R. B., & Buchanan, A. (2007). Effects of anticipatory stress on decision making in a gambling task. *Behavioral Neuroscience, 121*, 257–263.

Raghunathan, R., & Pham, M. T. (1999). All negative moods are not equal: Motivational influences of anxiety and sadness on decision making. *Organizational Behavior and Human Decision Processes, 79*, 56–77.

Rodebaugh, T. L., Heimberg, R. G., Schultz, L. T., & Blackmore, M. (2010). The moderated effects of video feedback for social anxiety disorders. *Journal of Anxiety Disorders, 24*, 663–671.

Russell, J. A., & Carroll, J. M. (1999). On the bipolarity of positive and negative affect. *Psychological Bulletin, 125*(1), 3–30.

Rusting, C. L., & DeHart, T. (2000). Retrieving positive memories to regulate negative mood: Consequences for mood-congruent memory. *Journal of Personality and Social Psychology, 78*, 737–752.

Scherer, K. R., Schorr, A., & Johnstone, T. (Eds.). (2001). *Appraisal processes in emotion: Theory, methods, research*. Oxford, UK: Oxford University Press.

Schwarzkopf, D. S., Zhang, J. X., & Kourtzi, Z. (2009). Flexible learning of natural statistics in the human brain. *Journal of Neurophysiology, 102,* 1854–1867.

Scott, S. K., Young, A. W., Calder, A. J., Hellawell, D. J., Aggleton, J. P., & Johnson, M. (1997). Impaired auditory recognition of fear and anger following bilateral amygdala lesions. *Nature, 385,* 254–257.

Small, D. A., & Lerner, J. S. (2008). Emotional policy: Personal sadness and anger shape judgments about a welfare case. *Political Psychology, 29,* 149–168.

Smith, C. A., & Kirby, L. D. (2001). Toward delivering on the promise of appraisal theory. In K. R. Scherer, A. Schorr, & T. Johnstone (Eds.), *Appraisal processes in emotion: Theory, methods, research.* Oxford, UK: Oxford University Press.

Smith, C. A., & Lazarus, R. S. (1993). Appraisal components, core relational themes, and the emotions. *Cognition & Emotion, 7,* 233–269.

Starcke, K. W., lf, O. T., Markowitsch, H. J., & Brand, M. (2008). Anticipatory stress influences decision making under explicit risk conditions. *Behavioral Neuroscience, 122,* 1352–1360.

Stevenson, R. A., Mikels, J. A., & James, T. W. (2007). Characterization of the affective norms for English words by discrete emotional categories. *Behavior Research Methods, 39*(4), 1020–1024.

Tamietto, M., & de Gelder, B. (2008). Affective blindsight in the intact brain: Neural interhemispheric summation for unseen fearful expressions. *Neuropsychologia, 46,* 820–828.

Tong, E. M. W. (2010a). The sufficiency and necessity of appraisals for negative emotions. *Cognition & Emotion, 24,* 692–701.

Tong, E. M. W. (2010b). Personality influences in appraisal–emotion relationships: The role of neuroticism. *Journal of Personality, 78,* 393–417.

Tulving, E. (1979). Relation between encoding specificity and levels of processing. In L. S. Cermak & F. I. M. Craik (Eds.), *Levels of processing in human memory.* Hillsdale, NJ: Lawrence Erlbaum.

Van Bockstaele, B., Verschuere, B., Tibboel, H., De Houwer, J., Crombez, G., & Koster, E. H. (2014). A review of current evidence for the causal impact of attentional bias on fear and anxiety. *Psychological Bulletin, 140*(3), 682–721.

Van Dillen, L. F., & Koole, S. L. (2007). Clearing the mind: A working memory model of distraction from negative mood. *Emotion, 7,* 715–723.

Van Dillen, L. F., Heselenfeld, D. J., & Koole, S. L. (2009). Turning down the emotional brain: An fMRI study of the effects of cognitive load on the processing of affective images. *NeuroImage, 45,* 1212–1219.

Velten, E. (1968). A laboratory task for induction of mood states. *Behaviour Research and Therapy, 6,* 473–482.

Viviani, R. (2013). Emotion regulation, attention to emotion, and the ventral attentional network. *Frontiers in Human Neuroscience, 7,* 746. doi: 10.3389/fnhum.2013.00746

Ward, J. (2010). *The student's guide to cognitive neuroscience* (2nd ed.). Hove, UK: Psychology Press.

Warriner, A. B., Kuperman, V., & Brysbaert, M. (2013). Norms of valence, arousal, and dominance for 13,915 English lemmas. *Behavior Research Methods, 45,* 1191–1207.

Waters, E. A. (2008). Feeling good, feeling bad, and feeling at risk: A review of incidental affect's influence on likelihood estimates of health hazards and life events. *Journal of Risk Research, 11,* 569–595.

Watson, D., & Tellegen, A. (1985). Toward a consensual structure of mood. *Psychological Bulletin, 98*(2), 219–235.

Williams, J. M. G., Watts, F. N., MacLeod, C. M., & Mathews, A. (1997). *Cognitive psychology and emotional disorders* (2nd ed.). Chichester, UK: Wiley.

Yoon, K. L., & Zinbarg, R. E. (2008). Interpreting neutral faces as threatening is a default mode for socially anxious individuals. *Journal of Abnormal Psychology*, *117*, 680–685.

Zhang, T. R., & Chan, A. H. S. (2016). The association between driving anger and driving outcomes: A meta-analysis of evidence from the past twenty years. *Accident Analysis and Prevention*, *90*, 50–62.

Glossary

ADHD: a developmental disorder characterized by an attention deficit, hyperactivity, and impulsivity.

affective blindsight: the ability to discriminate among different emotional stimuli in spite of the absence of conscious perception.

age-of-acquisition effect: the finding that words learned early in life are easier to process than words learned later in life.

algorithm: a systematic set of step-by-step operations that covers the entire problem space and guarantees a solution if one exists; compare **heuristic**.

amnesia: a condition caused by brain damage in which there are serious impairments of long-term memory (especially **declarative memory**).

amygdala: subcortical structure that is particularly important for the detection of danger and other emotion-arousing stimuli.

analogical problem solving: a type of problem solving based on detecting analogies or similarities between the current problem and problems solved in the past.

anterograde amnesia: impaired ability of amnesic patients to learn and remember information acquired after the onset of **amnesia**.

Anton's syndrome: a condition in which blind patients mistakenly believe that visual imagery is actually visual perception.

aphasia: a condition due to brain damage in which the patient has severely impaired language abilities.

apperceptive agnosia: a form of visual agnosia in which there is impaired perceptual analysis of familiar objects.

apperceptive aphasia: a condition caused by brain damage in which object recognition is impaired mainly due to deficits in perceptual processing; see **associative aphasia**.

arousal: basic dimension of emotions indicating how much bodily excitation is stirred, going from absent (quiet, inactive) to strong (aroused, excited); see also **valence**.

associative agnosia: a form of visual agnosia in which perceptual processing is fairly normal but there is an impaired ability to derive the meaning of objects from visual input.

associative aphasia: a condition caused by brain damage in which object recognition is impaired mainly due to problems in accessing relevant object knowledge stored in long-term memory; see **apperceptive aphasia**.

attentional bias: the selective allocation of attention to threat-related stimuli when they are presented at the same time as neutral ones.

autobiographical memory: a form of declarative memory involving memory for personal events across the lifespan.

automatic processes: processes that have no capacity limitations, don't require attention, and are very hard to modify once learned; involve parallel processing and usually require extensive practice to acquire; see also **controlled processes**.

availability heuristic: a rule of thumb in which the frequency of a given event is estimated (often wrongly) on the basis of how easily relevant information about that event can be accessed in long-term memory.

base rate: the relative frequency with which an event occurs in the population; it is often ignored (or deemphasized) when individuals make a **judgment**.

behaviorism: an approach to psychology that emphasized a rigorous experimental approach and the role of conditioning in learning.

belief bias: in syllogistic reasoning, mistakenly accepting believable conclusions that are invalid and rejecting unbelievable ones that are valid.

binocular rivalry: when two different visual stimuli are presented one to each eye, only one stimulus is seen; the stimulus that is seen tends to alternate over time.

blindsight: an apparently paradoxical condition often produced by brain damage to the early visual cortex in which there is behavioral evidence of visual perception in the absence of conscious awareness.

body size effect: an extension of the **body swap illusion** in which the size of the body mistakenly perceived to be one's own influences the perceived size of objects in the environment.

body swap illusion: the mistaken perception that part or all of someone else's body is one's own; it occurs when, for example, shaking hands with someone else while seeing what is happening from the viewpoint of the other person.

bottom-up processing: processing that is determined directly by environmental stimuli rather than by the individual's knowledge and expectations.

boundary extension: the finding that internal representations of visual scenes are more complete and extensive than the actual scene; dependent on perceptual **schemas** and expectations.

bounded rationality: the hypothesis that people produce workable solutions to problems in spite of limited processing ability by using various shortcut strategies (**heuristics**).

brainstorming: a method of problem solving in which participants generate a wide variety of possible, non-typical solutions and subsequently look at whether some of these ideas can be turned into useful solutions; used when confronted with a block in insight problems, with functional fixedness, or with a mental set.

categorical perception: the finding that when a sound is intermediate between two **phonemes**, the listener typically perceives one or other of the phonemes.

category: a set or class of objects that belong together (e.g., articles of furniture; four-footed animals).

central executive: the most important component of **working memory**; it is involved in planning and the control of attention and has limited capacity.

change blindness: the failure to detect that a visual stimulus has moved, changed, or been replaced by another stimulus.

change blindness blindness: the tendency of individuals to exaggerate greatly their ability to detect visual changes and so avoid **change blindness**.

Charles Bonnet syndrome: a condition in which individuals with eye disease form vivid and detailed visual hallucinations that are mistaken for visual perception.

child-directed speech: very short and simple utterances based on a limited vocabulary; designed to make it easy for young children to understand what is being communicated.

childhood amnesia: the inability of adults to recall autobiographical memories from early childhood.

chunks: stored units formed from integrating smaller pieces of information.

clause: a group of words within a sentence that contains a subject and a verb; see **phrase**.

coarticulation: the finding that the production of a **phoneme** is influenced by the production of the previous sound and by preparations for the next sound; it provides a useful cue to listeners.

cognitive neuroscience: an approach that aims to understand human cognition by combining information from brain activity and behavior.

cognitive psychology: studies the processes involved in acquiring, storing, and transforming information.

common ground: the shared knowledge and beliefs possessed by a speaker and a listener; its use assists communication.

computational model: a computer program that simulates or mimics the human cognitive processes needed to perform a task.

computational modeling: this involves constructing computer programs that will simulate or mimic some aspects of human cognitive functioning.

concept: a mental representation representing a **category** of objects; stored in long-term memory.

conditional reasoning: a form of **deductive reasoning** in which an "if . . . then" statement is followed by a conclusion that is logically valid or invalid.

confirmation bias: in hypothesis testing, seeking evidence that supports one's beliefs.

conjunction fallacy: the mistaken assumption that the probability of two events occurring in conjunction or combination is greater than one of these events on its own; most famously studied with the Linda problem.

connectionist networks: these consist of units or nodes that are connected in various layers with no direct connection from stimulus to response.

consciousness: information of which we are aware at any given moment; it is associated with perceiving the environment, thinking about events and issues not related to the here-and-now, understanding what other people are thinking, and controlling our actions.

consolidation: a physiological process involved in establishing long-term memories; this process lasts several hours or more, and newly formed memories that are still being consolidated are fragile.

constraint-based theory: theory of sentence parsing, which postulates that syntactic ambiguities are solved by using all available information simultaneously; see also **garden-path theory**.

controlled processes: processes of limited capacity that require attention and can be used flexibly in changing conditions; serial processing is involved; see also automatic processes.

correlation coefficient: statistical measure to indicate how two variables are related; goes from -1.0 to +1.0. Positive values mean that both variables vary in the same direction (when one increases the other increases as well); negative values mean that both variables vary in opposite directions (when one increases the other decreases). The closer the values are to +1.0 or -1.0, the stronger the correlation, the better we can predict one variable on the basis of the other. Values around 0 indicate that the variables are independent; it is not possible to predict one on the basis of the other.

Corsi blocks test: a test with blocks that must be pointed to according to predefined sequences; used to measure the capacity of the visuo-spatial sketchpad.

covert attention: attention to an object in the absence of an eye movement towards it.

cross-modal attention: the coordination of attention across two or more sense modalities (e.g., vision and hearing).

cross-race effect: the finding that recognition memory for same-race faces is more accurate than for other-race faces.

decision making: this involves making a selection from various options; full information is often unavailable and so **judgment** is required.

declarative memory: also known as explicit memory, this is memory that involves conscious recollection of information; see **non-declarative memory.**

deductive reasoning: an approach to reasoning in which conclusions can be categorized as valid or invalid given that certain statements or premises are assumed to be true; **conditional reasoning** and syllogistic reasoning are forms of deductive reasoning.

deliberate practice: a very useful form of practice in which the learner can repeat the task, correct his/her errors, and is given performance feedback.

deontic rules: in reasoning, rules in which the emphasis is on the detection of rule violations.

directed retrospection: a technique used in writing research in which writers categorize the process(es) in which they have just been engaged.

discourse: connected language that is a minimum of several sentences in length; it includes written text and connected speech.

discourse markers: words or phrases used by a speaker (e.g., "oh"; "so") that assist communication even though they are only of indirect relevance to his/her message.

dissociation: as applied to brain-damaged patients, intact performance on one task but severely impaired performance on a different task.

distinctiveness: this characterizes memory traces that are distinct or different from other memory traces stored in long-term memory; it leads to enhanced memory.

distraction: a strategy used in **emotion regulation** in which the individual disengages attention from emotional processing and focuses on neutral information.

divided attention: a situation in which two tasks are performed at the same time; also known as multitasking.

double dissociation: the finding that some individuals (often brain-damaged) have intact performance on one task but poor performance on another task, whereas other individuals exhibit the opposite pattern.

DRC-model: computational model of how written input is translated into spoken output based on localist representations; see also the **triangle model.**

Dunning-Kruger effect: the finding that less-skilled individuals overestimate their abilities more than those who are more skilled.

dysexecutive syndrome: a condition in which damage to the frontal lobes causes impaired functioning of the **central executive** involving deficits in organizing and planning behavior.

dyslexia: persistent problems in learning to read and write, leading to a lower performance level than can be expected on the basis of a person's intelligence and education received.

dysrationalia: the failure of reasonably intelligent individuals to think and reason in a rational way.

ecological validity: the extent to which research findings (especially laboratory ones) can be generalized to the real world.

egocentric heuristic: a rule of thumb in which listeners rely solely on their own knowledge when interpreting what speakers are saying rather than on the **common ground** between them; it can inhibit effective communication.

embodied cognition: the hypothesis that the meaning of concepts depends on the physical interactions of our body with the surrounding world.

emotion regulation: the use of deliberate and effortful processes to change a spontaneous emotional state (usually a negative one) produced by an emotion generation process.

encoding specificity principle: the notion that retrieval depends on the *overlap* between the information available at retrieval and the information within the memory trace; memory is best when the overlap is high.

episodic buffer: a component of working memory that is used to integrate and to store briefly information from the phonological loop, the visuospatial sketchpad, and long-term memory.

episodic memory: a form of declarative memory concerned with personal experiences or episodes occurring in a given place at a given time; see **semantic memory.**

event-based prospective memory: a form of **prospective memory** in which some event (e.g., seeing a grocery store) provides the cue to perform a given action (e.g., buying fruit).

event-related potentials (ERPs): the pattern of electroencephalograph (EEG) activity obtained by averaging the brain responses to the same stimulus (or similar stimuli) presented repeatedly.

executive functions: set of cognitive skills used to control and coordinate cognitive abilities and behaviors.

expertise: a very high level of thinking and performance in a given domain (e.g., chess) achieved from many years of practice.

explicit learning: a form of learning producing long-term memory which involves conscious awareness of what has been learned.

expressive writing: writing in a heartfelt way on a topic of deep personal significance to the writer; it has beneficial effects on emotional states and health.

extinction: a disorder of visual attention in which a stimulus presented to the side opposite the brain damage is not detected when another stimulus is presented at the same time to the same side as the brain damage.

face-in-the-crowd effect: the finding that threatening (especially angry) faces can be detected more rapidly among other faces than can faces with other expressions.

face inversion effect: the finding that faces are much harder to recognize than other objects when presented upside down.

false memories: apparent recovered memories that refer to imagined rather than genuine events or experiences.

figure-ground organization: the division of the visual environment into a figure (having a distinct form) and ground (lacking a distinct form); the contour between figure and ground appears to belong to the figure, which stands out from the ground.

fixations: moments during reading when the eyes remain still and information is picked up from the text; last on average 250 ms.

flashbulb memories: vivid and detailed memories of dramatic and significant events.

focused attention: a situation in which individuals try to attend to only one source of information while ignoring other stimuli; also known as **selective attention**.

framing effect: the finding that decisions are often influenced by aspects of the situation (e.g., precise wording of a problem) that are irrelevant to good decision making.

free will: the notion that we freely or voluntarily choose what to do from a number of possibilities; this notion has been challenged by those who claim that non-conscious processes determine our actions.

Freudian slip: a speech-production error that reveals the speaker's (often unconscious) sexual or other desires.

functional fixedness: the inflexible use of the usual function or functions of an object in problem solving.

functional magnetic resonance imaging (fMRI): a brain-imaging technique based on imaging blood oxygenation using an MRI scanner; it has very good spatial resolution and reasonable temporal resolution.

functional specialization: the assumption (only partially correct) that cognitive functions (e.g., color processing; face processing) occur in specific brain regions.

fusiform face area: an area within the inferotemporal cortex that is associated with face processing; the term is somewhat misleading given that the area is also associated with the processing of other categories of visual objects.

fuzzy boundary: zone of gradual transition that exists between many categories, meaning that for most concepts it is impossible to define them by means of a list of essential features.

garden-path theory: theory of sentence parsing, which postulates that syntactic ambiguities are initially solved on the basis of syntactic principles alone; see also **constraint-based theory**.

geons: basic shapes or components that are combined in object recognition; an abbreviation for "geometric ions" proposed by Biederman.

good-enough hypothesis: hypothesis that people will often misunderstand the details of syntactically complex sentences if they are not motivated to process the sentence in full detail.

grapheme: basic unit of written language that corresponds to a phoneme (e.g., the letter sequence "ph" forms a grapheme because it is pronounced as the phoneme "f"); a word consists of one or more graphemes.

heuristic: rule of thumb that is cognitively undemanding and often produces approximately accurate answers; compare **algorithm**.

hill climbing: a simple **heuristic** used by problem solvers in which they focus on making moves that will apparently put them closer to the goal or problem solution.

hindsight bias: the tendency for people to exaggerate how accurately they would have predicted some event in advance after they know what actually happened.

hippocampus: subcortical structure particularly important for memory encoding and spatial knowledge.

holistic processing: processing that involves *integrating* information from an entire object (especially faces).

homographs: words that have a single spelling but at least two different meanings (e.g., maroon; throttle); used to study **interpretive bias.**

hub-and-spoke model: model that provides an idea of how abstract concepts can be based on different types of information and on how they can be stable and context-dependent at the same time.

hyperthymestic syndrome: an exceptional ability to remember the events of one's own life; in other words, outstanding autobiographical memory.

hypothesis testing: an approach to problem solving based on forming a hypothesis or tentative explanation, which is then subjected to one or more tests.

ill-defined problems: problems in which the definition of the problem statement is imprecisely specified; the initial state, goal state, and methods to be used to solve the problem may be unclear; see **well-defined problems.**

illusion: situation in which a person perceives something other than what is physically presented. This allows researchers to investigate the processes involved in perception.

illusion of knowing: the conviction people have that they know more about topics than they actually do.

illusory conjunction: mistakenly combining features from two different stimuli to perceive an object that isn't present.

implicit learning: a form of learning producing long-term memory in which there is no conscious awareness of what has been learned.

inattentional blindness: the observation that we often fail to notice important objects and

events, especially when we are focused on something else.

incidental learning: learning that takes place without any intent to learn.

incubation: a stage of problem solving in which the problem is put to one side for some time; it is claimed to facilitate problem solving.

inductive reasoning: a form of reasoning in which general conclusions are drawn from a sequence of observations; the conclusions are not necessarily true (like in deductive reasoning), but they can be evaluated via **hypothesis testing.**

inference: logical conclusion in discourse processing derived from the information given in the discourse and schemas stored in long-term memory.

informal reasoning: a form of reasoning that involves arguments based on one's relevant knowledge and experience; it is prone to error and differs from **deductive reasoning** in not being based on logic.

insight: the experience of suddenly realizing how to solve a problem.

intentional learning: learning that is goal directed and motivated by the intention to retain the information learned.

internal lexicon: information about the sounds, spellings, and meanings of words stored in long-term memory; it functions as a dictionary.

interpretive bias: the tendency to interpret ambiguous stimuli and situations in a threatening fashion.

introspection: a careful examination and description of one's own inner mental thoughts and states.

judgment: this involves an assessment of the likelihood of a given event occurring on the basis of incomplete information; it often forms the initial process in **decision making.**

knowledge effect: the tendency of writers to assume (often mistakenly) that those reading what they have written possess the same knowledge.

knowledge-lean problems: problems that can be solved without the use of much prior knowledge; most of the necessary information is provided by the problem statement; see **knowledge-rich problems.**

knowledge-rich problems: problems that can only be solved through the use of considerable amounts of relevant prior knowledge; see **knowledge-lean problems.**

law of Prägnanz: the notion that the simplest possible organization of the visual environment is what is perceived; proposed by the Gestalt psychologists.

lesion: a structural alteration within the brain caused by disease or injury.

levels-of-processing theory: this is the assumption that learning and long-term memory will be better the more deeply the *meaning* of the stimulus materials is processed.

lexical bias effect: the tendency for speech errors to form words rather than nonwords; see **spoonerism.**

lexical decision task: strings of letters are presented, and the task is to decide as rapidly as possible whether each string is a word or a **nonword.**

life script: the typical major life events for individuals living within a given society; sample life events are getting married and having children.

linguistic universals: according to Chomsky, the features (e.g., word order) that are common to virtually all languages; there is controversy concerning the existence of such features.

long-term working memory: used by experts to store relevant information rapidly in long-term memory and to access it through retrieval cues in **working memory.**

loss aversion: the greater sensitivity to potential losses than to potential gains exhibited by most people in decision making.

magneto-encephalography (MEG): a noninvasive brain-scanning technique based on recording the magnetic fields generated by brain activity; it has excellent temporal resolution and reasonably good spatial resolution.

masking: suppression of the processing of a stimulus (e.g., visual; auditory) by presenting a second stimulus (the masking stimulus) very soon afterwards.

matching bias: as applied to the Wason selection task, selection of cards simply because they match those contained within the rule whether they are correct or incorrect.

McGurk effect: when there is a conflict between a spoken **phoneme** and the speaker's lip movements, the sound that is heard combines the auditory and visual information.

means-ends analysis: a **heuristic** for solving problems based on creating a subgoal designed to reduce the difference between the current state of a problem and the end or goal state.

memory span: the number of items (e.g., digits; words) that an individual can recall immediately in the correct order; it is used as a measure of the capacity of short-term memory.

mental lexicon: database containing information about the words known by an individual; it functions as an internal dictionary.

mental model: used in reasoning, an internal or mental representation of some possible situation or event in the world.

mental set: a readiness to think or act in a given way, often because

this has been shown to be successful in the past.

meta-analysis: a form of statistical analysis based on combining the findings from numerous studies on a given issue.

meta-memory: beliefs and knowledge about one's own memory including strategies for learning in memory.

metaphor: an expression in which something or someone is said to mean something it only resembles; for example, someone who is very brave may be described as a "lion in battle."

method of loci: a memory technique in which the items that are to be remembered are associated with various locations that are well known to the learner.

mixed-error effect: a type of speech error where the incorrect word is related in terms of both meaning and sound to the correct one.

mnemonics: these consist of numerous methods or systems that learners can use to enhance their long-term memory for information.

modularity: the assumption that the cognitive system consists of several fairly independent or separate modules or processors, each of which is specialized for a given type of processing (e.g., face processing).

mood congruity: the finding that learning and retrieval are better when the learner's (or rememberer's) mood state is the same as (or congruent with) the affective value of the to-be-remembered material.

mood-state-dependent memory: the finding that memory performance is better when the individual's mood state is the same at learning and retrieval than when it differs.

morphemes: the basic units of meaning; words consist of one or more morphemes.

motivated reasoning: the observation that people tend

to reason in ways that make the conclusion they favor more likely.

multitasking: performing two or more tasks during the same period of time.

myside bias: in informal reasoning, the tendency to evaluate statements in terms of one's own beliefs and behavior rather than on their merits.

neglect: a disorder of visual attention in which stimuli or parts of stimuli presented to the side opposite the brain damage are undetected and not responded to; the condition resembles **extinction** but is more severe.

non-declarative memory: also known as implicit memory, this is memory that doesn't involve conscious recollection of information; see **declarative memory.**

nonwords: strings of letters or sounds that are pronounceable but that do not form existing words.

object superiority effect: the finding that a feature is easier to process when it is part of a meaningful object than when it is part of an unknown form.

omission bias: a preference for risking harm through inaction compared to risking harm through action; it is shown even when the balance of advantage lies in action rather than inaction.

operation span: the maximum number of items (arithmetical questions + words) for which an individual can recall all the last words.

optimism bias: the tendency to exaggerate our chances of experiencing positive events and to minimize our chances of experiencing negative events relative to other people.

orthography: the spelling of written words.

own-age bias: the tendency for eyewitnesses to identify the culprit more often when he/she is of similar age to the eyewitness.

parallel processing: two or more processes occurring simultaneously; see **serial processing.**

parsing: identifying the grammatical structure of sentences that are read or heard.

part-whole effect: the finding that a face part is recognized more easily when presented in the context of a whole face rather than on its own.

pattern recognition: the identification of two-dimensional patterns by matching the input to category information stored in memory; is an essential step in object recognition.

perception: the interpretation and understanding of sensations.

personal moral dilemma: situation in which we have to make complex judgments and a decision between alternative actions that will harm or kill people; our actions have a direct effect on the well-being of individuals with whom we are interacting in person.

phoneme: meaningful sound in a spoken language; part of the phonology of a word.

phonemic restoration effect: the finding that listeners presented with a sentence including a missing **phoneme** use the sentence context to identify it and are not aware that it is missing.

phonics approach: a method of teaching young children to read in which they learn to link individual letters and groups of letters to the sounds of the language; see **whole-language approach.**

phonological dyslexia: a condition in which brain-damaged patients have difficulty in phonological processing; this causes them to find it hard to pronounce unfamiliar words and nonwords (but not familiar words) when reading aloud.

phonological loop: a component of **working memory** in which speech-based information is processed and stored and subvocal articulation occurs.

phonological similarity effect: the finding that immediate recall of word lists in the correct order is impaired when the words sound similar to each other.

phonology: the sounds of words; of importance in reading.

phrase: a group of words within a sentence that expresses a single idea; see **clause.**

positron emission tomography (PET): a brain-scanning technique based on the detection of positrons; it has reasonable spatial resolution but poor temporal resolution.

post-event misinformation effect: the distorting effect on eyewitness memory of misleading information provided after the crime or other event.

pragmatics: in sentence comprehension, using the social context and other information to work out the intended meaning of what is said.

preformulation: the production by speakers of phrases used frequently before; it is done to reduce the demands of speech production.

premises: in deductive reasoning, statements that participants are instructed to assume are true.

priming: facilitated processing of (and response to) a target stimulus because the same or a related stimulus was presented before; see also **repetition priming** and semantic priming.

principle of parsimony: in **deductive reasoning,** the tendency to form only one mental model even when additional ones could be constructed.

principle of truth: including what is true but omitting what is false from a mental representation or **mental model.**

proactive interference: disruption of memory by previous learning (often of similar material); see **retroactive interference.**

problem space: model used by Newell and Simon (1972) that compares problem solvers to people trying to find their way in a maze; problem solvers make a mental journey from the initial problem state to the desired goal state via a sequence of intermediate states.

procedural memory: a form of non-declarative memory involving learned skills and concerned with "knowing how."

progress monitoring: a heuristic used in problem solving in which insufficiently rapid progress towards solution leads to the adoption of a different strategy.

prosodic cues: various aspects of speech (e.g., rhythm; stress) used by speakers to assist communication; used most often by speakers when what they are saying is somewhat ambiguous.

prosopagnosia: a condition mostly caused by brain damage in which there is a severe impairment in face recognition with little or no impairment of object recognition; popularly known as "face blindness."

prospective memory: remembering to carry out some intended action in the absence of any explicit reminder to do so; see **retrospective memory.**

protocol analysis: the study and classification of the verbalizations of participants while performing some task.

prototype: a central description or conceptual core incorporating the major features of a **category,** with some features generally weighted more than others.

psychological refractory period (PRP) effect: the slowing of the response to the second of two stimuli when they are presented close together in time.

rationalization: in Bartlett's theory, the tendency in story recall to produce errors conforming to the cultural expectations of the remember; it is attributed to the influence of **schemas**.

reading span: the greatest number of sentences read for comprehension for which an individual can recall all the final words more than 50% of the time.

reappraisal: a strategy used in **emotion regulation** in which the individual elaborates emotional information from an event prior to changing its meaning.

rebus problems: problems in which there are various verbal and visual cues to a well-known phrase; they are often solved by using **insight**.

recall: retrieving information from long-term memory in the presence or absence of cues.

recency effect: the tendency in free recall for the last few items (typically two or three) to be much more likely to be recalled than those from the middle of the list; this effect has been used to measure the capacity of short-term memory.

recognition heuristic: a rule of thumb in which a **judgment** has to be made between two objects (e.g., which city is larger?); it involves selecting the object that is recognized.

recognition memory: deciding whether a given stimulus was encountered previously in a particular context (e.g., the previous list).

reconsolidation: this is a new **consolidation** process that occurs when a previously formed memory trace is reactivated; it allows that memory trace to be updated.

recovered memories: childhood traumatic or threatening memories that are remembered many years after the relevant events or experiences.

rehearsal: subvocal reiteration of verbal material (e.g., words);

often used in the attempt to increase the amount of information that can be remembered.

reminiscence bump: the tendency of older people to recall a disproportionate number of autobiographical memories from the years of adolescence and early adulthood.

repetition priming: the finding that stimuli are processed more efficiently the second time they are encountered than the first time; see also **priming** and **semantic priming**.

repetitive transcranial magnetic stimulation (rTMS): the administration of transcranial magnetic stimulation several times in rapid succession.

representativeness heuristic: the rule of thumb that an object or individual belongs to a specified category because it is representative (typical) of that category; it is used in **judgment** and produces the wrong answer when it leads the individual to ignore **base-rate information**.

repression: motivated forgetting of traumatic or other very threatening events.

retroactive interference: disruption of memory for what was learned originally by other learning or processing during the retention interval; see **proactive interference**.

retrograde amnesia: impaired ability of amnesic patients to remember information and events (i.e., **declarative memory**) from the time period prior to the onset of **amnesia**.

retrospective memory: memory for events, words, people, and so on encountered or experienced in the past; see **prospective memory**.

rubber hand illusion: the misperception that a rubber hand is one's own; it occurs when the visible rubber hand is

touched at the same time as the individual's own hidden hand.

saccades: rapid eye movements that are separated by eye fixations.

satisficing: in decision making, a **heuristic** that involves selecting the first option that satisfies the individual's minimum requirements; formed from the words "satisfactory" and "sufficing."

saying-is-believing effect: tailoring a message about an event to suit a given audience causes subsequent inaccuracies in memory for that event.

schema: a set of related propositions, which forms a packet of typical knowledge about the world, events, or people.

scripts: another term used for a **schema** of the typical actions associated with certain events (e.g., restaurant meals; football games).

segmentation: dividing the almost continuous sounds of speech into separate words.

selective attention: a situation in which individuals try to attend to only one source of information while ignoring other stimuli; also known as focused attention.

self-reference effect: enhanced long-term memory for information if it is related to the self at the time of learning.

semantic dementia: a condition caused by brain damage in which there is initially mainly extensive loss of knowledge about the meanings of words and concepts.

semantic memory: a form of declarative memory consisting of general knowledge about the world, concepts, language, and so on; see episodic memory.

semantic priming: the finding that a target word (e.g., "king") is identified faster after a semantically related prime word ("throne") than after an unrelated prime ("torch").

sensation: the intake of information by means of receptors and the translation of this information into signals that the brain can process as images, sounds, smells, tastes, and so on.

serial processing: this involves only one process occurring at any given moment; that process is completed before the next one starts; see **parallel processing**.

serial reaction time task: one of the main tasks used to study implicit learning. Participants have to press keys related to a series of lights appearing on a computer screen. Unknown to the participants, the series consists of a complex sequence that is repeated over and over again but that is too difficult to grasp consciously.

shadowing: repeating word for word one auditory message as it is presented while a second auditory message is also presented.

skill learning: see **procedural memory**.

source misattribution: errors in long-term memory that occur when the remember is mistaken about the source or origin of a retrieved memory.

split attention: allocation of attention to two (or more) non-adjacent regions of visual space.

split-brain patients: patients in whom most of the direct links between the two hemispheres have been severed; as a result, they can experience problems in coordinating their processing and behavior.

spoonerism: a speech error in which the initial letter or letters of two words (typically close together) are mistakenly switched; an example of **lexical bias**.

spreading of activation: the notion that activation of a node (corresponding to a concept) in a semantic network causes activation to spread to related nodes, so that the meaning of a concept becomes richer.

stereotypes: schemas incorporating oversimplified generalizations (often negative) about certain groups.

striatum: subcortical structure situated between the cerebral hemispheres and the brainstem that plays a crucial role in implicit learning; is part of the basal ganglia.

Stroop effect: the finding that naming the colors in which words are printed takes longer when the words are conflicting color words (e.g., the word RED printed in green).

subliminal perception: perceptual processing occurring below the level of conscious awareness that can nevertheless influence behavior.

sunk-cost effect: the finding that individuals who have invested effort, time, or money to little avail tend to invest more resources in the hope of justifying the previous investment; it corresponds to "throwing good money after bad."

surface dyslexia: a condition in which brain-damaged patients have difficulty in accessing words in their internal lexicon or dictionary; this causes difficulties in reading irregular words aloud.

syllogism: a type of problem used in studies on **deductive reasoning**; there are two statements or **premises** and a conclusion that may or may not follow logically from the premises.

synesthesia: a sensory experience in which a stimulus in one sense modality (e.g., hearing) evokes an image in a second sense modality (e.g., vision).

syntactic priming: the tendency for the sentences produced by speakers to have the same syntactic structure as sentences they have heard or read shortly beforehand.

templates: *in perception*: forms or patterns in long-term memory that allow us to recognize perceptual input as familiar, meaningful stimuli by matching the input to the forms/patterns stored in memory and selecting the one that fits; *in chess playing*: organized abstract structures including information about several chess pieces; these structures (which are larger for chess experts) are useful when players decide on their next move.

testing effect: the finding that long-term memory is enhanced when some of the learning period is devoted to retrieving the to-be-remembered information.

textisms: the new abbreviations (often involving a mixture of symbols and letters) used when individuals produce text messages.

thalamus: subcortical structure involved in regulating the state of consciousness of the brain.

time-based prospective memory: a form of prospective memory in which time is the cue indicating that a given action needs to be performed.

tip-of-the-tongue state: the frustration experienced by speakers when they have an idea or concept in mind but can't find the appropriate word to express it.

top-down processing: stimulus processing that is determined by expectations, memory, and knowledge rather than directly by the stimulus.

transcranial magnetic stimulation (TMS): a technique in which magnetic pulses briefly disrupt the functioning of a given brain area, thus creating a short-lived **lesion**; when several pulses are given in rapid succession, the technique is known as repetitive transcranial magnetic stimulation (rTMS).

transfer-appropriate processing: the notion that long-term memory will be greatest when the processing at the time of retrieval is very similar to the processing at the time of learning.

triangle model: a computational model of how written input is translated into spoken output based on distributed representations; see also the **DRC-model.**

typicality effect: the finding that the time taken to decide that a category member belongs to a **category** is less for more typical than for less typical members.

unconscious transference: the tendency of eyewitnesses to misidentify a familiar (but innocent) face as belonging to the person responsible for a crime.

unusualness heuristic: a rule of thumb used by scientists in which the emphasis is on unusual or unexpected findings that may lead to the development of new hypotheses and lines of experimentation.

Urbach-Wiethe disease: a disease in which the amygdala and adjacent areas are destroyed; it leads to the impairment of emotional processing and memory for emotional material.

valence: basic dimension of emotions representing the affective component, going from negative (misery) to positive (pleasure); see also **arousal.**

vegetative state: a condition produced by brain damage in which there is wakefulness but an apparent lack of awareness and purposeful behavior.

ventriloquist illusion: the mistaken perception that sounds are coming from their apparent visual source, as in ventriloquism.

verb bias: the finding that some verbs occur more often within one particular syntactic or grammatical structure than within others.

visuo-spatial sketchpad: a component of **working memory** that is used to process visual and spatial information and to store this information briefly.

weapon focus: the finding that eyewitnesses pay so much attention to some crucial aspect of the situation (e.g., the weapon) that they ignore other details.

well-defined problems: problems in which the initial state, the goal, and the methods available for solving them are clearly laid out; see **ill-defined problems.**

whole-language approach: a method of teaching young children to read in which the emphasis is on understanding the meaning of text; it includes using sentence context to guess the identity of unknown words.

word association task: task in which participants are asked to mention the first word (or three words) that come to mind upon seeing a target word; used to determine the semantic relatedness between words.

word-fragment task: a task often used to measure implicit learning, which is not based on motoric responses. Participants get a word fragment and are asked to complete the word. Performance is much better if participants in a previous part of the study saw the words, even when they are not aware of the overlap between both parts of the study.

word frequency effect: the finding that words often occurring in a language are processed more easily than words rarely occurring in the language.

word-length effect: fewer long words than short ones can be recalled immediately after presentation in the correct order.

word superiority effect: the finding that a target letter is detected faster when presented in words than in **nonwords.**

working memory: a system that can store information briefly while other information is processed.

working memory capacity: an assessment of how much information can be processed and stored at the same time; individual differences in this capacity are associated with differences in intelligence and attentional control.

References

Abdellaoui, M., Bleichrodt, H., & Kammoun, H. (2013). Do financial professionals behave according to prospect theory? An experimental study. *Theory and Decision, 74*, 411–429.

Abarbanell, L., & Hauser, M. D. (2010). Mayan morality: An exploration of permissible harms. *Cognition, 115*, 207–224.

Aberegg, S. K., Haponik, E. F., & Terry, P. B. (2005). Omission bias and decision making in pulmonary and critical care medicine. *Chest, 128*, 1497–1505.

Abrams, L. (2008). Tip-of-the-tongue states yield language insights: The process of turning thoughts into speech changes with age. *American Scientist, 96*, 234–239.

Abutalebi, J., & Green, D. W. (2008). Control mechanisms in bilingual language production: Neural evidence from language switching studies. *Language and Cognitive Processes, 23*, 557–582.

Acheson, D. J., Postle, B. R., & MacDonald, M. C. (2010). The interaction of concreteness and phonological similarity in verbal working memory. *Journal of Experimental Psychology: Learning, Memory, and Cognition, 36*, 17–36.

Addis, D. R., Knapp, K., Roberts, R. P., & Schacter, D.L. (2012). Routes to the past: Neural substrates of direct and generative autobiographical memory retrieval. *NeuroImage, 59*, 2908–2922.

Addis, D. R., Wong, A. T., & Schacter, D. L. (2007). Remembering the past and imagining the future: Common and distinct neural substrates during event construction and elaboration. *Neuropsychologia, 45*, 1363–1377.

Aggleton, J. P. (2008). Understanding anterograde amnesia: Disconnections and hidden lesions. *Quarterly Journal of Experimental Psychology, 61*, 1441–1471.

Aguiar, A., Eubig, P. A., & Schantz, S. L. (2010). Attention deficit/hyperactivity disorder: A focused overview for children's environmental health researchers. *Environmental Health Perspectives, 118*(12), 1646–1653.

Ahn, W. K., Kim, N. S., Lassaline, M. E., & Dennis, M. J. (2000). Causal status as a determinant of feature centrality. *Cognitive Psychology, 41*, 361–416.

Aikin, S. F., & Casey, J. (2011). Straw men, weak men, and hollow men. *Argumentation, 25*, 87–105.

Aizenstein, H. J., Stenger, V. A., Cochran, J., Clark, K., Johnson, M., Nebes, R. D., et al. (2004). Regional brain activation during concurrent implicit and explicit sequence learning. *Cerebral Cortex, 14*, 199–208.

Alais, D., & Burr, D. (2004). The ventriloquist effect results from near-optimal bimodal integration. *Current Biology, 14*, 257–262.

Albir, A. H., & Alves, F. (2009). Translation as a cognitive activity. In J. Munday (Ed.), *The Routledge companion to translation studies*. London, UK: Routledge.

Aleman, A., Schutter, D. L. G., Ramsey, N. F., van Honk, J., Kessels, R. P. C., Hoogduin, J. M., et al. (2002). Functional anatomy of top-down visuospatial processing in the human brain: Evidence from rTMS. *Cognitive Brain Research, 14*, 300–302.

Alexander, P. A., Schallert, D. L., & Hare, U. C. (1991). Coming to terms: How researchers in learning and literacy talk about knowledge. *Review of Educational Research, 61*, 315–343.

Allen, B. P., & Lindsay, D. S. (1998). Amalgamations of memories: Intrusion of information from one event into reports of another. *Applied Cognitive Psychology, 12*, 277–285.

Ally, B. A., Hussey, E. P., & Donahue, M. J. (2013). A case of hyperthymesia: Rethinking the role of the amygdala in autobiographical memory. *Neurocase, 19*, 166–181.

Almashat, S., Ayotte, B., Edelstein, B., & Margrett, J. (2008). Framing effect debiasing in medical decision making. *Patient Education and Counseling, 71*, 102–107.

Altenberg, B. (1990). Speech as linear composition. In G. Caie, K. Haastrup, A.L. Jakobsen, J.E. Nielsen, J. Sevaldsen. H. Specht, & A. Zettersten (Eds.), *Proceedings from the fourth nordic conference for English studies*. Copenhagen, Denmark: Copenhagen University Press.

Amir, N., Weber, G., Beard, C., Bomyea, J., & Taylor, C. T. (2008). The effect of a single-session attention modification program on response to a public-speaking challenge in socially anxious individuals. *Journal of Abnormal Psychology, 117*, 860–868.

Anaki, D., & Bentin, S. (2009). Familiarity effects on categorization levels of faces and objects. *Cognition, 111*, 144–149.

Anaki, D., Kaufman, Y., Freedman, M., & Moscovitch, M. (2007). Associative (prosop)agnosia without (apparent) perceptual deficits: A case-study. *Neuropsychologia, 45,* 1658–1671.

Anderson, J. R., Fincham, J. M., Qin, Y., & Stocco, A. (2008). A central circuit of the mind. *Trends in Cognitive Sciences, 12,* 136–143.

Anderson, J. R., & Lebiere, C. (2003). The Newell Test for a theory of cognition. *Behavioral and Brain Sciences, 26,* 587–640.

Anderson, R. C., & Pichert, J. W. (1978). Recall of previously unrecallable information following a shift in perspective. *Journal of Verbal Learning and Verbal Behavior, 17,* 1–12.

Anderson, S. W., Rizzo, M., Skaar, N., Cavaco, S., Dawson, J., & Damasio, H. (2007). Amnesia and driving. *Journal of Clinical and Experimental Neuropsychology, 29,* 1–12.

Andersson, U. (2010). The contribution of working memory capacity to foreign language comprehension in children. *Memory, 18,* 456–472.

Andrés, P. (2003). Frontal cortex as the central executive of working memory: Time to revise our view. *Cortex, 39,* 871–895.

Arkes, H. R., & Ayton, P. (1999). The sunk cost and Concorde effects: Are humans less rational than lower animals? *Psychological Bulletin, 125,* 591–600.

Arnold, J. E. (2008). Reference production: Production-internal and address-oriented processes. *Language and Cognitive Processes, 23,* 495–527.

Atkinson, R. C., & Shiffrin, R. M. (1968). Human memory: A proposed system and its control processes. In K. W. Spence & J. T. Spence (Eds.), *The psychology of learning and motivation* (Vol. 2). London, UK: Academic Press.

Augustine, A. A., & Hemenover, S. H. (2009). On the relative merits of affect regulation strategies: A meta-analysis. *Cognition & Emotion, 23,* 1181–1220.

Austin, D., & Kiropoulos, L. (2008). An internet-based investigation of the catastrophic misinterpretation model of panic disorder. *Journal of Anxiety Disorders, 22,* 233–242.

Awh, E., & Pashler, H. (2000). Evidence for split attentional loci. *Journal of Experimental Psychology: Human Perception and Performance, 26,* 834–846.

Baars, B. J. (1997). Consciousness versus attention, perception, and working memory. *Consciousness and Cognition, 5,* 363–371.

Baars, B. J., & Franklin, S. (2007). An architectural model of conscious and unconscious brain functions: Global Workspace Theory and IDA. *Neural Networks, 20,* 955–961.

Baars, B. J., Motley, M. T., & MacKay, D. G. (1975). Output editing for lexical status from artificially elicited slips of the tongue. *Journal of Verbal Learning and Verbal Behavior, 14,* 382–391.

Baddeley, A. (2001). Is working memory still working? *American Psychologist, 56,* 851–864.

Baddeley, A. D. (1986). *Working memory.* Oxford, UK: Clarendon Press.

Baddeley, A. D. (2000). The episodic buffer: A new component of working memory? *Trends in Cognitive Sciences, 4,* 417–423.

Baddeley, A. D. (2007). *Working memory, thought and action.* Oxford, UK: Oxford University Press.

Baddeley, A. D., & Andrade, J. (2000). Working memory and the vividness of imagery. *Journal of Experimental Psychology: General, 129,* 126–145.

Baddeley, A. D., & Hitch, G. J. (1974). Working memory. In G. H. Bower (Ed.), *Recent advances in learning and motivation* (Vol. 8, pp. 47–89). New York, NY: Academic Press.

Baddeley, A. D., Papagno, C., & Vallar, G. (1988). When long-term learning depends on short-term storage. *Journal of Memory and Language, 27,* 586–595.

Baddeley, A., Eysenck, M. W., & Anderson, M. C. (2009). *Memory.* New York, NY: Psychology Press.

Baddeley, A. D., & Wilson, B. (2002). Prose recall and amnesia: Implications for the structure of working memory. *Neuropsychologia, 40,* 1737–1743.

Bahrick, H. P. (1984). Semantic memory content in permastore: Fifty years of memory for Spanish learning in school. *Journal of Experimental Psychology: General, 113,* 1–29.

Bahrick, H. P., Bahrick, P. O., & Wittlinger, R. P. (1975). Fifty years of memory for names and faces: A cross-sectional approach. *Journal of Experimental Psychology: General, 104,* 54–75.

Bahrick, H. P., Hall, L. K., & Da Costa, L. A. (2008). Fifty years of memory of college grades: Accuracy and distortions. *Emotion, 8,* 13–22.

Ball, L. J., Lucas, E. J., Miles, J. N. V., & Gale, A. G. (2003). Inspection times and the selection task: What do eye movements reveal about relevance effects? *Quarterly Journal of Experimental Psychology, 56A,* 1053–1077.

Bandura, A. (1977). *Social learning theory.* Englewood Cliffs, NJ: Prentice Hall.

Bangert-Drowns, R. L., Kulik, J. A., & Kulik, C. L. C. (1991). Effects of frequent classroom testing. *Journal of Educational Research, 61,* 213–238.

Banks, W. P., & Isham, E. A. (2009). We infer rather than perceive the moment we decided to act. *Psychological Science, 20,* 17–21.

Banks, W. P., & Pockett, S. (2007). Benjamin Libet's work on the neuroscience of free will. In M. Velmans & S. Schinder (Eds.), *Blackwell companion to consciousness* (pp. 657–670). Malden, MA: Blackwell.

Barber, H. A., Donamayor, N., Kutgas, M., & Munte, T. (2010). Parafoveal N400 effect during sentence reading. *Neuroscience Letters, 479,* 152–156.

Bard, E. G., Anderson, A. H., Chen, Y., Nicholson, H. B. V. M., Havard, C., & Dalzel-Job, S. (2007). Let's you do that: Sharing the cognitive burdens of dialog. *Journal of Memory and Language, 57,* 616–641.

Bar-Haim, Y., Lamy, D., Pergamin, L., BakermansKronenburg, M. J., & van IJzendoorn, M. H. (2007). Threat-related attentional bias in anxious and nonanxious individuals: A meta-analytic study. *Psychological Bulletin, 133,* 1–24.

Baron, J., & Ritov, I. (2004). Omission bias, individual differences, and normality. *Organizational Behavior and Human Decision Processes, 94,* 74–85.

Barrett, L. F., & Russell, J. A. (1998). Independence and bipolarity in the structure of current affect. *Journal of Personality and Social Psychology, 74,* 967–984.

Barrett, L. F., Tugade, M. M., & Engle, R. W. (2004). Individual differences in working memory capacity and dual-process theories of the mind. *Psychological Bulletin, 130,* 553–573.

Barsalou, L. W. (1985). Ideals, central tendency, and frequency of instantiation as determinants of graded structure in categories. *Journal of Experimental Psychology: Learning, Memory, & Cognition, 11,* 629–654.

Barsalou, L. W. (2003). Situated simulation in the human conceptual system. *Language & Cognitive Processes, 18,* 513–562.

Barsalou, L. W. (2008). Grounded cognition. *Annual Review of Psychology, 59,* 617–645.

Barsalou, L. W. (2009). Simulation, situated conceptualization, and prediction. *Philosophical Transactions of the Royal Society B: Biological Sciences, 364,* 1281–1289.

Barsalou, L. W., & Wiemer-Hastings, K. (2005). Situating abstract concepts. In D. Pecher & R. Zwaan (Eds.), *Grounding cognition: The role of perception and action in memory, language, and thought.* New York, NY: Cambridge University Press.

Bartlett, F. C. (1932). *Remembering: An experimental and social study.* Cambridge, UK: Cambridge University Press.

Bartolomeo, P. (2002). The relationship between visual perception and visual mental imagery: A reappraisal of the neuropsychological evidence. *Cortex, 38,* 357–378.

Bartolomeo, P. (2008). The neural correlates of visual mental imagery: An ongoing debate. *Cortex, 44,* 107–108.

Bartolomeo, P., & Chokron, S. (2002). Orienting of attention in left unilateral neglect. *Neuroscience and Biobehavioral Reviews, 26,* 217–234.

Barton, J. J. S., Press, D. Z., Keenan, J. P., & O'Connor, M. (2002). Topographic organization of human visual areas in the absence of input from primary cortex. *Journal of Neuroscience, 19,* 3619–2627.

Bauby, J.-D. (1997). *The diving bell and the butterfly.* New York, NY: Knopf.

Bavelas, J., Gerwing, J., Sutton, C., & Prevost, D. (2008). Gesturing on the telephone: Independent effects of dialog and visibility. *Journal of Memory and Language, 58,* 495–520.

Baxendale, S. (2004). Memories aren't made of this: Amnesia at the movies. *British Medical Journal, 329,* 1480–1483.

Baynes, K., & Gazzaniga, M. (2000). Consciousness, introspection, and the split-brain: The two minds/one body problem. In M. S. Gazzaniga (Ed.), *The new cognitive neurosciences.* Cambridge, MA: MIT Press.

Bays, P. M., Singh-Curry, V., Gorgoraptis, N., Driver, J., & Husain, M. (2010). Integration of goal- and stimulus-related visual signals revealed by damage to human parietal cortex. *Journal of Neuroscience, 30,* 5968–5978.

Bearman, C. R., Ball, L. J., & Ormerod, T. C. (2007). The structure and function of spontaneous analogizing in domain-based problem solving. *Thinking & Reasoning, 13,* 273–294.

Beck, M. R., Levin, D. T., & Angelone, B. (2007). Change blindness blindness: Beliefs about the roles of intention and scene complexity in change blindness. *Consciousness and Cognition, 16,* 31–51.

Behrman, B. W., & Davey, S. L. (2001). Eyewitness identification in actual criminal cases: An archival analysis. *Law and Human Behavior, 25,* 475–491.

Benton, T. R., Ross, D. F., Bradshaw, E., Thomas, W. N., & Bradshaw, G.S. (2006). Eyewitness memory is still not common sense: Comparing jurors, judges and law enforcement to eyewitness experts. *Applied Cognitive Psychology, 20,* 115–129.

Bereiter, C., Burtis, P. J., & Scardamalia, M. (1988). Cognitive operations in constructing main points in written composition. *Journal of Memory and Language, 27,* 261–278.

Bereiter, C., & Scardamalia, M. (1987). *The psychology of written composition*. Hillsdale, NJ: Lawrence Erlbaum.

Berman, M. G., Jonides, J., & Lewis, R. L. (2009). In search of decay in verbal short-term memory. *Journal of Experimental Psychology: Learning, Memory, & Cognition, 35*, 317–333.

Berndsen, M., & Manstead, A. S. R. (2007). On the relationship between responsibility and guilt: Antecedent appraisal or elaborated appraisal? *European Journal of Social Psychology, 37*, 774–792.

Berndt, R. S., Mitchum, C. C., Haendiges, A. N., & Sandson, J. (1997). Verb retrieval in aphasia. I. Characterizing single word impairments. *Brain and Language, 56*, 69–106.

Berntsen, D. (1998). Voluntary and involuntary access to autobiographical memory. *Memory, 6*, 113–141.

Berntsen, D. (2010). The unbidden past: Involuntary autobiographical memories as a basic mode of remembering. *Current Directions in Psychological Science, 19*, 138–142.

Berntsen, D., & Hall, N. M. (2004). The episodic nature of involuntary autobiographical memories. *Memory & Cognition, 32*, 789–803.

Berntsen, D., & Rubin, D. C. (2002). Emotionally charged autobiographical memories across the life span: The recall of happy, sad, traumatic and involuntary memories. *Psychology and Ageing, 17*, 636–652.

Berntsen, D., Rubin, D. C., & Siegler, I. C. (2011). Two different versions of life: Emotionally negative and positive life events have different roles in the organisation of life story and identity. *Emotion, 11*, 1190–1201.

Bickerton, D. (1984). The language bioprogram hypothesis. *Behavioral and Brain Sciences, 7*, 173–221.

Biederman, I. (1987). Recognition-by-components: A theory of human image understanding. *Psychological Review, 94*, 115–147.

Biederman, I., & Gerhardstein, P. C. (1993). Recognizing depth-rotated objects: Evidence for 3-D viewpoint invariance. *Journal of Experimental Psychology: Human Perception & Performance, 19*, 1162–1182.

Bilalış, M., McLeod, P., & Gobet, F. (2008a). Inflexibility of experts: Reality or myth? Quantifying the Einstellung effect in chess masters. *Cognitive Psychology, 56*, 73–102.

Bilalić, M., McLeod, P., & Gobet, F. (2008b). Why good thoughts block better ones: The mechanism of the pernicious Einstellung (set) effect. *Cognition, 108*, 652–661.

Bjork, R. A., & Bjork, E. L. (1992). A new theory of disuse and an old theory of stimulus fluctuation. In A. Healey, S. Kosslyn, & R. Shiffrin (Eds.), *From learning processes to cognitive processes: Essays in honor of William K. Estes* (Vol. 2). Hillsdale, NJ: Lawrence Erlbaum.

Blanchette, I., & Richards, A. (2010). The influence of affect on higher level cognition: A review of research on interpretation, judgment, decision making and reasoning. *Cognition & Emotion, 24*, 561–595.

Blanchette, I., Richards, A., Melnyk, L., & Lavda, A. (2007). Reasoning about emotional contents following shocking terrorist attacks: A tale of three cities. *Journal of Experimental Psychology: Applied, 13*, 47–56.

Blandón-Gitlin, I., Przdek, K., Lindsay, D. S., & Hagen, L. (2009). Criteria-based content analysis of true and suggested accounts of events. *Applied Cognitive Psychology, 23*, 901–917.

Bleckley, M. K., Durso, F. T., Crutchfield, J. M., Engle, R. W., & Khanna, M. M. (2003). Individual differences in working memory capacity predict visual attention allocation. *Psychonomic Bulletin & Review, 10*, 884–889.

Bohn, A., & Berntsen, D. (2011). The reminiscence bump reconsidered: Children's prospective life stories show a bump in young adulthood. *Psychological Science, 22*, 197–202.

Boland, J. E., & Blodgett, A. (2001). Understanding the constraints on syntactic generation: Lexical bias and discourse congruency effects on eye movements. *Journal of Memory and Language, 45*, 391–411.

Bolden, G. B. (2006). Little words that matter: Discourse markers "so" and "oh" and the doing of other-attentiveness in social interaction. *Journal of Communication, 56*, 661–688.

Bolden, G. B. (2009). Implementing incipient actions: The discourse marker "so" in English conversation. *Journal of Pragmatics, 41*, 974–998.

Bolognini, N., & Ro, T. (2010). Transcranial magnetic stimulation: Disrupting neural activity to alter and assess brain function. *Journal of Neuroscience, 30*, 9647–9650.

Boly, M., Phillips, C., Tschibanda, L., Vanhaudenhuyse, A., Schabus, M., Dange-Vu, T. T., et al. (2008). Intrinsic brain activity in altered states of consciousness: How conscious is the default mode of brain function? *Annals of the New York Academy of Sciences, 1129*, 119–129.

Bond, C. F., & DePaulo, B. M. (2008). Individual differences in judging deception: Accuracy and bias. *Psychological Bulletin, 134*, 477–492.

Bonnefon, J. F., Eid, M., Vautie, S., & Jmel, S. (2008). A mixed Rasch model of dual-process conditional reasoning. *Quarterly Journal of Experimental Psychology, 61*, 809–824.

Borges, J. L. (1964). *Labyrinths: Selected stories and other writing.* New York, NY: New Directions.

Borst, G., & Kosslyn, S. M. (2008). Visual mental imagery and visual perception: Structural equivalence revealed by scanning processes. *Memory & Cognition, 36*, 849–862.

Bourdais, C., & Pecheux, M.-G. (2009). Categorizing in 13- and 16-month-old infants: A comparison of two methods. *Année Psychologique, 109*, 3–27.

Bowden, E. M., & Beeman, M. J. (1998). Getting the right idea: Semantic activation in the right hemisphere may help solve insight problems. *Psychological Science, 9*, 435–440.

Bowden, E. M., & Jung-Beeman, M. (2007). Methods for investigating the neural components of insight. *Methods, 42*, 87–99.

Bowden, E. M., Jung-Beeman, M., Fleck, J., & Kounios, J. (2005). New approaches to demystifying insight. *Trends in Cognitive Sciences, 9*, 322–328.

Bower, G. H. (1973). How to . . . uh . . . remember! *Psychology Today, 7*, 63–70.

Bower, G. H., Black, J. B., & Turner, T. J. (1979). Scripts in memory for text. *Cognitive Psychology, 11*, 177–220.

Bower, G. H., & Clark, M. C. (1969). Narrative stories as mediators for serial learning. *Psychonomic Science, 14*, 181–182.

Bowers, J. S. (2002). Challenging the widespread assumption that connectionism and distributed representations go hand-in-hand. *Cognitive Psychology, 45*, 413–445.

Bowers, J. S. (2009). On the biological plausibility of grandmother cells: Implications for neural network theories of psychology and neuroscience. *Psychological Review, 116*, 220–251.

Brandt, K. R., Gardiner, J. M., Vargha-Khadem, F., Baddeley, A. D., & Mishkin, M. (2006). Using semantic memory to boost "episodic" recall in a case of developmental amnesia. *NeuroReport, 17*, 1057–1060.

Bransford, J. D., Barclay, J. R., & Franks, J. J. (1972). Sentence memory: A constructive versus interpretive approach. *Cognitive Psychology, 3*, 193–209.

Bransford, J. D., Franks, J. J., Morris, C. D., & Stein, B. S. (1979). Some general constraints on learning and memory research. In L. S. Cermak & F. I. M. Craik (Eds.), *Levels of processing in human memory.* Hillsdale, NJ: Lawrence Erlbaum.

Bransford, J. D., & Johnson, M. K. (1972). Contextual prerequisites for understanding. *Journal of Verbal Learning and Verbal Behavior, 11*, 717–726.

Brase, G. L., Fiddick, L., & Harries, C. (2006). Participants' recruitment methods and statistical reasoning performance. *Quarterly Journal of Experimental Psychology, 59*, 965–976.

Brass, M., & Haggard, P. (2008). The what, when, and whether model of intentional action. *The Neuroscientist, 14*, 319–325.

Brédart, S., Brennen, T., Delchambre, M., McNeill, A., & Burton, A. M. (2005). Naming very familiar people: When retrieving names is faster than retrieving semantic biographical information. *British Journal of Psychology, 96*, 205–214.

Brennan, S. E. (1990). *Seeking and providing evidence for mutual understanding.* PhD dissertation, Department of Psychology, Stanford University, Stanford, CA.

Brewer, W. F., & Treyens, J. C. (1981). Role of schemata in memory for places. *Cognitive Psychology, 13*, 207–230.

Bright, D. A., & Goodman-Delahunty, J. (2006). Gruesome evidence and emotion: Anger, blame, and jury decision-making. *Law and Human Behavior, 30*, 183–202.

Broadbent, D. E. (1958). *Perception and communication.* Oxford, UK: Pergamon.

Brooks, R., Faff, R., Mulino, D., & Scheelings, R. (2009). Deal or no deal, that is the question: The impact of increasing stakes and framing effects on decision making under risk. *International Review of Finance, 9*, 27–50.

Brown, A. S., Bracken, E., Zoccoli, S., & Douglas, K. (2004). Generating and remembering passwords. *Applied Cognitive Psychology, 18*, 641–651.

Brown, R. G., Jahanshahi, M., Limousin-Dowsey, P., Thomas, D., Quinn, N., & Rothwell, J. C. (2003). Pallidotomy and incidental sequence learning in Parkinson's disease. *NeuroReport, 14*, 1–4.

Brown, R., & Kulik, J. (1977). Flashbulb memories. *Cognition, 5*, 73–99.

Brown, R., & McNeill, D. N. (1966). The "tip of the tongue" phenomenon. *Journal of Verbal Learning and Verbal Behavior, 5*, 325–337.

Brown-Schmidt, S. (2009). The role of executive function in perspective taking during online language comprehension. *Psychonomic Bulletin & Review, 16*, 893–900.

Bruce, K. R., & Pihl, R. P. (1997). Forget drinking to forget: Enhanced consolidation of emotionally charged memory by alcohol. *Experimental and Clinical Psychopharmacology, 5*, 242–250.

Bruce, V., Henderson, Z., Greenwood, K., Hancock, P., Burton, A. M., & Miller, P. (1999). Verification of face identities from images captured on video. *Journal of Experimental Psychology: Applied, 5,* 339–360.

Bruce, V., & Young, A. W. (1986). Understanding face recognition. *British Journal of Psychology, 77,* 305–327.

Bruner, J. S., Goodnow, J. J., & Austin, G. A. (1956). *A study of thinking.* New York, NY: Wiley.

Bruner, J. S., & Postman, L. (1949). On the perception of incongruity: A paradigm. *Journal of Personality, 18,* 206–223.

Bruno, N., Bernadis, P., & Gentilucci, M. (2008). Visually guided pointing, the Müller-Lyer illusion, and the functional interpretation of the dorsal–ventral split: Conclusions from 33 independent studies. *Neuroscience and Biobehavioral Reviews, 32,* 423–437.

Brunyé, T. T., & Taylor, H. A. (2008a). Extended experience benefits spatial mental model development with route but not survey descriptions. *Acta Psychologica, 127,* 340–354.

Brunyé, T. T., & Taylor, H. A. (2008b). Working memory in developing and applying mental models from spatial descriptions. *Journal of Memory and Language, 58,* 701–729.

Bryan, W. L., & Harter, N. (1897). Studies in the physiology and psychology of the telegraphic language. *Psychological Review, 4,* 27–53.

Bryan, W. L., & Harter, N. (1899). Studies on the telegraphic language. The acquisition of a hierarchy of habits. *Psychological Review, 6,* 345–375.

Bub, D. N., Masson, M. E. J., & Cree, G. S. (2008). Evocation of functional and volumetric gestural knowledge by objects and words. *Cognition, 106,* 27–58.

Bucciarelli, M., & Johnson-Laird, P. N. (1999). Strategies in syllogistic reasoning. *Cognitive Science, 23,* 247–303.

Bulbrook, M. E. (1932). An experimental inquiry into the existence and nature of "insight". *American Journal of Psychology, 44,* 409–453.

Burke, D., Taubert, J., & Higman, T. (2007). Are face representations viewpoint dependent? A stereo advantage for generalizing across different views of faces. *Vision Research, 47,* 2164–2169.

Burns, B. D. (2004). The effects of speed on skilled chess performance. *Psychological Science, 15,* 442–447.

Burns, B. D., & Wieth, M. (2004). The collider principle in causal reasoning: Why the Monty Hall dilemma is so hard. *Journal of Experimental Psychology: General, 133,* 434–449.

Burton, A. M., Bruce, V., & Hancock, P. J. B. (1999). From pixels to people: A model of familiar face recognition. *Cognitive Science, 23,* 1–31.

Bushman, B. J. (2002). Does venting anger feed of extinguish the flame? Catharsis, rumination, distraction, anger, and aggressive responding. *Personality and Social Psychology Bulletin, 28,* 724–731.

Byrne, R. M. J. (1989). Suppressing valid inferences with conditionals. *Cognition, 31,* 61–83.

Byrne, R. M. J., & Johnson-Laird, P. N. (2009). "If" and the problems of conditional reasoning. *Trends in Cognitive Sciences, 13,* 282–287.

Caccappolo-van Vliet, E., Miozzo, M., & Stern, Y. (2004). Phonological dyslexia: A test case for reading models. *Psychological Science, 15,* 583–590.

Cahill, L., Babinsky, R., Markowitsch, H. J., & McGaugh, J. L. (1995). The amygdala and emotional memory. *Nature, 377,* 295–296.

Cahir, C., & Thomas, K. (2010). Asymmetric effects of positive and negative affect on decision making. *Psychological Reports, 106,* 193–204.

Caird, J. K., Willness, C. R., Steel, P., & Scialfa, C. (2008). A meta-analysis of the effects of cell phones on driver performance. *Accident Analysis and Prevention, 40,* 1282–1293.

Calabria, M., Cotelli, M., Adenzato, M., Zanetti, O., & Miniussi, C. (2009). Empathy and emotion recognition in semantic dementia: A case report. *Brain and Cognition, 70,* 247–252.

Calder, A. J., Young, A. W., Rowland, D., Perrett, D. I., Hodges, J. R., & Etcoff, N. L. (1996). Facial emotion recognition after bilateral amygdala damage: Differentially severe impairment of fear. *Cognitive Neuropsychology, 13,* 699–745.

Calvo, M. G. (2001). Working memory and inferences: Evidence from eye fixations during reading. *Memory, 9,* 365–381.

Calvo, M. G., & Castillo, M. D. (1997). Mood-congruent bias in interpretation of ambiguity: Strategic processes and temporary activation. *Quarterly Journal of Experimental Psychology, 50A,* 163–182.

Calvo, M. G., Castillo, M. D., & Schmalhof, F. (2006). Strategic influence on the time course of predictive inferences in reading. *Memory & Cognition, 34,* 68–77.

Calvo, M. G., & Eysenck, M. W. (1996). Phonological working memory and reading in test anxiety. *Memory, 4,* 289–305.

Calvo, M. G., & Marrero, H. (2009). Visual search of emotional faces: The role of affective content and featural distinctiveness. *Cognition & Emotion, 23,* 782–806.

Camerer, C., Babcock, L., Loewenstein, G., & Thaler, R. (1997). Labor supply of New York cab drivers: One day at a time? *Quarterly Journal of Economics, CXII*, 407–441.

Camerer, C., & Hogarth, R. B. (1999). The effects of financial incentives in experiments: A review and capital-labourproduction framework. *Journal of Risk and Uncertainty, 19*, 7–42.

Campitelli, G., & Gobet, F. (2011). Deliberate practice: Necessary but not sufficient. *Current Directions in Psychological Science, 20*, 280–285.

Cappla, S. F. (2008). Imaging studies of semantic memory. *Current Opinion in Neurology, 21*, 669–675.

Caramazza, A., & Coltheart, M. (2006). Cognitive neuropsychology twenty years on. *Cognitive Neuropsychology, 23*, 3–12.

Carlesimo, G. A., Marfia, G. A., Loasses, A., & Caltagirone, C. (1996). Perceptual and conceptual components in implicit and explicit stem completion. *Neuropsychologia, 34*, 785–792.

Carlin, B. I., & Robinson, D. T. (2009). Fear and loathing in Las Vegas: Evidence from blackjack tables. *Judgment and Decision Making, 4*, 385–396.

Carr, T. H., Davidson, B. J., & Hawkins, H. L. (1978). Perceptual flexibility in word recognition – Strategies affect orthographic computation but not lexical access. *Journal of Experimental Psychology: Human Perception and Performance, 4*, 674–690.

Casper, C., Rothermund, K., & Wentura, D. (2010). Automatic stereotype activation is context-dependent. *Social Psychology, 41*, 131–136.

Casscells, W., Schoenberger, A., & Graboys, T. B. (1978). Interpretation by physicians of clinical laboratory results. *New England Journal of Medicine, 299*, 999–1001.

Cavaco, S., Anderson, S. W., Allen, J. S., CastroCaldas, A., & Damasio, H. (2004). The scope of preserved procedural memory in amnesia. *Brain, 127*, 1853–1867.

Cavenett, T., & Nixon, R. D. V. (2006). The effect of arousal on memory for emotionally-relevant information: A study of skydivers. *Behaviour Research and Therapy, 44*, 1461–1469.

Ceci, S. J., & Liker, J. K. (1986). A day at the races: A study of IQ, expertise, and cognitive complexity. *Journal of Experimental Psychology: General, 115*, 255–266.

Centofanti, A. T., & Reece, J. (2006). The cognitive interview and its effect on misleading postevent information. *Psychology, Crime & Law, 12*, 669–683.

Chaigneau, S. E., Barsalou, L. W., & Zamani, M. (2009). Situational information contributes to object categorization and inference. *Acta Psychologica, 130*, 81–94.

Challis, B. H., Velichkovsky, B. M., & Craik, F. I. M. (1996). Levels-of-processing effects on a variety of memory tasks: New findings and theoretical implications. *Consciousness and Cognition, 5*, 142–164.

Chamberlain, E. (2003). Review of "Behavioral assessment of the dysexecutive syndrome (BADS)". *Journal of Occupational Psychology, 5*, 33–37.

Channon, S., & Baker, J. (1994). Reasoning strategies in depression: Effects of depressed mood on a syllogism task. *Personality and Individual Differences, 17*, 707–711.

Charlton, D., Fraser-Mackenzie, P. A. F., & Dror, I. E. (2010). Emotional experiences and motivating factors associated with fingerprint analysis. *Journal of Forensic Sciences, 55*, 385–393.

Charness, N. (1981). Search in chess: Age and skill differences. *Journal of Experimental Psychology: Human Perception and Performance, 7*, 467–476.

Charness, N., Tuffiash, M., Krampe, R., Reingold, E., & Vasyukova, E. (2005). The role of deliberate practice in chess expertise. *Applied Cognitive Psychology, 19*, 151–165.

Chartrand, T. L., van Baaren, R. B., & Bargh, J. A. (2006). Linking automatic evaluation to mood and information-processing style: Consequences for experienced affect, impression formation, and stereotyping. *Journal of Experimental Psychology: General, 135*, 7–77.

Chen, Y. W., Chen, C. Y., Lin, C. P., Chou, K. H., & Decety, J. (2010). Love hurts: An fMRI study. *NeuroImage, 51*, 923–929.

Chen, Z. (2002). Analogical problem solving: A hierarchical analysis of procedural similarity. *Journal of Experimental Psychology: Learning, Memory, & Cognition, 28*, 81–98.

Chen, Z., & Cowan, N. (2009). Core verbal working memory capacity: The limit in words retained without covert articulation. *Quarterly Journal of Experimental Psychology, 62*, 1420–1429.

Chen, Z. Y., Cowell, P. E., Varley, R., & Wang, Y.-C. (2009). A cross-language study of verbal and visuospatial working memory span. *Journal of Clinical and Experimental Neuropsychology, 31*, 385–391.

Chen, Z., & Klahr, D. (1999). All other things being equal: Children's acquisition of the control of variables strategy. *Child Development, 70*, 1098–1120.

Chenoweth, N. A., & Hayes, J. R. (2003). The inner voice in writing. *Written Communication, 20*, 99–118.

Cherney, I. D. (2008). Mom, let me play more computer games: They improve my mental rotation skills. *Sex Roles, 59,* 776–786.

Cherry, E. C. (1953). Some experiments on the recognition of speech with one and two ears. *Journal of the Acoustical Society of America, 25,* 975–979.

Cherubini, P., Castelvecchio, E., & Cherubini, A. M. (2005). Generation of hypotheses in Wason's 2–4–6 task: An information theory approach. *Quarterly Journal of Experimental Psychology Section A – Human Experimental Psychology, 58,* 309–332.

Cherubini, P., & Mazzocco, A. (2004). From models to rules: Mechanization of reasoning as a way to cope with cognitive overloading in combinatorial problems. *Acta Psychologica, 116,* 223–243.

Chiappe, D. L., & Chiappe, P. (2007). The role of working memory in metaphor production and comprehension. *Journal of Memory and Language, 56,* 172–188.

Cho, S., Holyoak, K. J., & Cannon, T. D. (2007). Analogical reasoning in working memory: Resources shared among relational information, interference resolution, and maintenance. *Memory & Cognition, 35,* 1445–1455.

Chokron, S., Bartolomeo, P., & Sieroff, E. (2008). Unilateral spatial neglect: 30 years of research, discoveries, hope, and (especially) questions. *Revue Neurologique, 164,* S134–S142.

Chokron, S., Dupierrix, E., Tabert, M., & Bartolomeo, P. (2007). Experimental remission of unilateral spatial neglect. *Neuropsychologia, 45,* 3127–3148.

Chomsky, N. (1965). *Aspects of the theory of syntax.* Cambridge, MA: MIT Press.

Chomsky, N. (1986). *Knowledge of language: Its nature, origin, and use.* Westport, CT: Praeger.

Christiansen, M. H., & Chater, N. (2008). Language as shaped by the brain. *Behavioral and Brain Sciences, 31,* 489–512.

Christianson, K., Luke, S. G., & Ferreira, F. (2010). Effects of plausibility on structural priming. *Journal of Experimental Psychology: Learning, Memory, & Cognition, 36,* 538–544.

Christoffels, I. K. (2006). Listening while talking: The retention of prose under articulatory suppression in relation to simultaneous interpreting. *European Journal of Cognitive Psychology, 18,* 206–220.

Christoffels, I. K., de Groot, A. M. B., & Kroll, J. F. (2006). Memory and language skills in simultaneous interpreters: The role of expertise and language proficiency. *Journal of Memory and Language, 54,* 324–345.

Chrysikou, E. G., & Weisberg, R. W. (2005). Following the wrong footsteps: Fixation effects of pictorial examples in a design problem-solving task. *Journal of Experimental Psychology: Learning, Memory, and Cognition, 31,* 1134–1148.

Chun, W. Y., & Kruglanski, A. W. (2006). The role of task demands and processing resources in the use of base-rate and individuating information. *Journal of Personality and Social Psychology, 91,* 205–217.

Cister, J. M., & Koster, E. H. W. (2010). Mechanisms of attentional biases towards threat in anxiety disorders: An integrative review. *Clinical Psychology Review, 30,* 203–216.

Clancy, S. A., & McNally, R. J. (2005 /2006). Who needs repression? Normal memory processes can explain "forgetting" of childhood sexual abuse. *Scientific Review of Mental Health Practice, 4,* 66–73.

Clancy, S. A., McNally, R. J., Schacter, D. L., Lenzenweger, M. F., & Pitman, R. K. (2002). Memory distortion in people reporting abduction by aliens. *Journal of Abnormal Psychology, 111,* 455–461.

Clark, D. M. (1986). A cognitive approach to panic. *Behaviour Research and Therapy, 24,* 461–470.

Clark, H. H., & Krych, M. A. (2004). Speaking while monitoring addressees for understanding. *Journal of Memory and Language, 50,* 62–81.

Cleary, M., & Pisoni, D. B. (2001). Speech perception and spoken word recognition: Research and theory. In E. B. Goldstein (Ed.), *Blackwell handbook of perception* (pp. 499–534). Malden, MA: Blackwell.

Cleland, A. A., & Pickering, M. J. (2003). The use of lexical and syntactic information in language production: Evidence from the priming of noun-phrase structure. *Journal of Memory and Language, 49,* 214–230.

Cleland, A. A., & Pickering, M. J. (2006). Do writing and speaking employ the same syntactic representations? *Journal of Memory and Language, 54,* 185–198.

Coch, D., Sanders, L. D., & Neville, H. J. (2005). An event-related potential study of selective auditory attention in children and adults. *Journal of Cognitive Neuroscience, 17,* 606–622.

Cohen, G. (2008). The study of everyday memory. In G. Cohen & M. A. Conway (Eds.), *Memory in the real world* (3rd ed., pp. 1–19). Hove, UK: Psychology Press.

Cole, S. A. (2005). More than zero: Accounting for error in latent fingerprinting identification. *Journal of Criminal Law & Criminology, 95,* 985–1078.

Coleman, M. R., Davis, M. H., Rodd, J. M., Robson, T., Ali, A., Owen, A. M., & Pickard, J. D. (2009). Towards the routine use of brain imaging to aid the clinical diagnosis of disorders of consciousness. *Brain, 132,* 2541–2552.

Coley, J. D., Medin, D. L., & Atran, S. (1997). Does rank have its privilege? Inductive inferences within folkbiological taxonomies. *Cognition, 64*, 73–112.

Collins, A. M., & Loftus, E. F. (1975). A spreading activation theory of semantic memory. *Psychological Review, 82*, 407–428.

Colman, A. M. (2001). *Oxford dictionary of psychology*. Oxford, UK: Oxford University Press.

Colomb, C., & Ginet, M. (2012). The cognitive interview for use with adults: An empirical test of an alternative mnemonic and of a partial protocol. *Applied Cognitive Psychology, 26*, 35–47.

Coltheart, M. (2001). *Assumptions and methods in cognitive neuropsychology*. Hove, UK: Psychology Press.

Coltheart, M., Rastle, K., Perry, C., Langdon, R., & Ziegler, J. (2001). The DRC model: A model of visual word recognition and reading aloud. *Psychological Review, 108*, 204–258.

Colvin, M. K., & Gazzaniga, M. S. (2007). Split-brain cases. In M. Velmans & S. Schneider (Eds.), *The Blackwell companion to consciousness*. Oxford, UK: Blackwell.

Coman, A., Manier, D., & Hirst, W. (2009). Forgetting the unforgettable through conversation: Socially shared retrieval-induced forgetting of September 11 memories. *Psychological Science, 20*, 627–633.

Cona, G., Arcara, G., Tarantino, V., & Bisiacchi, P. S. (2012). Electrophysiological correlates of strategic monitoring in event-based and time-based prospective memory. *PLOS ONE, 7*(2), e31659. doi:10.1371/journal.pone.003 1659.

Conway, A. R. A., Kane, M. J., & Engle, R. W. (2003). Working memory capacity and its relation to general intelligence. *Trends in Cognitive Sciences, 7*, 547–552.

Conway, M. A. (2001). Sensory–perceptual episodic memory and its context: Autobiographical memory. *Philosophical Transactions of the Royal Society B: Biological Sciences, 356*(1413), 1375–1384.

Conway, M. A. (2005). Memory and the self. *Journal of Memory and Language, 53*, 594–628.

Conway, M. A., & Pleydell-Pearce, C. W. (2000). The construction of autobiographical memories in the self-memory system. *Psychological Review, 107*, 261–288.

Conway, M. A., Wang, Q., Hanyu, K., & Haque, S. (2005). A cross-cultural investigation of autobiographical memory. *Journal of Cross-Cultural Psychology, 36*, 739–749.

Cook, G. I., Marsh, R. L., & Hicks, J. L. (2005). Associating a time-based prospective memory task with an expected context can improve or impair intention completion. *Applied Cognitive Psychology, 19*, 345–360.

Cooke, R., Peel, E., Shaw, R. L., & Senior, C. (2007). The neuroimaging research process from the participants' perspective. *International Journal of Psychophysiology, 63*, 152–158.

Copeland, D. E., & Radvansky, G. A. (2004). Working memory and syllogistic reasoning. *Quarterly Journal of Experimental Psychology, 57A*, 1437–1457.

Corbetta, M., Patel, G., & Shulman, G. L. (2008). The re-orienting system of the human brain: From environment to theory of mind. *Neuron, 58*, 306–324.

Corbetta, M., & Shulman, G. L. (2002). Control of goal directed and stimulus-driven attention in the brain. *Nature Reviews Neuroscience, 3*, 201–215.

Corbetta, M., & Shulman, G.L. (2011). Spatial neglect and attention networks. *Annual Review of Neuroscience, 34*, 569–599.

Cosentino, S., Chute, D., Libon, D., Moore, P., & Grossman, M. (2006). How does the brain support script comprehension? A study of executive processes and semantic knowledge in dementia. *Neuropsychology, 20*, 307–318.

Cowan, N. (2000). The magical number 4 in short-term memory: A reconsideration of mental storage capacity. *Behavioral and Brain Sciences, 24*, 87–185.

Cowan, N., Elliott, E. M., Saults, J. S., Morey, C. C., Mattox, S., Hismjatullina, A., & Conway, A. R. A. (2005). On the capacity of attention: Its estimation and its role in working memory and cognitive aptitudes. *Cognitive Psychology, 51*, 42–100.

Cowey, A. (2010). The blindsight saga. *Experimental Brain Research, 200*, 3–24.

Cowley, M., & Byrne, R. M. J. (2005). Chess masters' hypothesis testing. In *Proceedings of the twenty-sixth annual conference of the cognitive science society* (pp. 250–255). New York, NY: Psychology Press.

Craik, F. I. M., & Lockhart, R. S. (1972). Levels of processing: A framework for memory research. *Journal of Verbal Learning and Verbal Behavior, 11*, 671–684.

Craik, F. I. M., & Tulving, E. (1975). Depth of processing and the retention of words in episodic memory. *Journal of Experimental Psychology: General, 104*, 268–294.

Craik, F. I. M., & Watkins, M. J. (1973). The role of rehearsal in short-term memory. *Journal of Verbal Learning and Verbal Behavior, 12*(6), 599–607.

Crawford, J. R., Smith, G., Maylor, E. A., Della Sala, S., & Logie, R. H. (2003). The Prospective and Retrospective Memory Questionnaire (PRMQ): Normative data and latent structure in a large nonclinical sample. *Memory, 11*, 261–275.

Cree, G. S., & McRae, K. (2003). Analyzing the factors underlying the structure and computation of the meaning of chipmunk, cherry, chisel, cheese, and cello (and many other such concrete nouns). *Journal of Experimental Psychology: General, 132*, 163–201.

Creem, S. H., & Proffitt, D. R. (2001). Grasping objects by their handles: A necessary interaction between cognition and action. *Journal of Experimental Psychology: Human Perception & Performance, 27*, 218–228.

Crystal, D. (1997). *A dictionary of linguistics and phonetics* (4th ed.). Cambridge, MA: Blackwell.

Crystal, D. (2008). *Txtng: The Gr8 Db8*. New York, NY: Oxford University Press.

Cunningham, J. B., & MacGregor, J. N. (2008). Training insightful problem solving: Effects of realistic and puzzle-like contexts. *Creativity Research Journal, 20*, 291–296.

Cunningham, W. A., Preacher, K. J., & Banaji, M. R. (2001). Implicit attitude measures: Consistency, stability, and convergent validity. *Psychological Science, 12*, 163–170.

Cutler, A., & Butterfield, S. (1992). Rhythmic cues to speech segmentation: Evidence from juncture misperception. *Journal of Memory and Language, 31*, 218–236.

Cuttler, C., & Graf, P. (2009a). Checking-in on the memory deficit and meta-memory deficit theories of compulsive checking. *Clinical Psychology Review, 29*, 393–409.

Cuttler, C., & Graf, P. (2009b). Sub-clinical compulsive checkers show impaired performance on habitual, event- and timecued episodic prospective memory tasks. *Journal of Anxiety Disorders, 23*, 813–823.

Cuttler, C., Sirois-Delisle, V., Alcolado, G. M., Radomsky, A. S., & Taylor, S. (2013). Diminished confidence in prospective memory causes doubts and urges to check. *Journal of Behavior Therapy and Experimental Psychiatry, 44*, 329–334.

Dahan, D. (2010). The time course of interpretation in speech comprehension. *Current Directions in Psychological Science, 19*, 121–126.

Dalrymple, K. A., Kingstone, A., & Handy, T. C. (2009). Event-related potential evidence for a dual-locus model of global/local processing. *Cognitive Neuropsychology, 26*, 456–470.

Dalton, A. L., & Daneman, M. (2006). Social suggestibility to central and peripheral misinformation. *Memory, 14*, 486–501.

Danckert, J., & Ferber, S. (2006). Revisiting unilateral neglect. *Neuropsychologia, 44*, 987–1006.

Danckert, J., & Rossetti, Y. (2005). Blindsight in action: What can the different subtypes of blindsight tell us about the control of visually guided actions? *Neuroscience and Biobehavioral Reviews, 29*, 1035–1046.

Dando, C. J., Ormerod, T. C., Wilcock, R., & Milne, R. (2011). When help becomes hindrance: Unexpected errors of omission and commission in eyewitness memory resulting from changes in temporal order at retrieval? *Cognition, 121*, 416–421.

Danek, A. H., Fraps, T., von Müller, A., Grothe, B., & Öllinger, M. (2014). Working wonders? Investigating insight with magic tricks. *Cognition, 130*, 174–185.

Daneman, M., & Carpenter, P. A. (1980). Individual differences in working memory and reading. *Journal of Verbal Learning and Verbal Behavior, 19*, 450–466.

Daneman, M., & Merikle, P. M. (1996). Working memory and language comprehension: A meta-analysis. *Psychonomic Bulletin & Review, 3*, 422–433.

Darling, S., & Havelka, J. (2010). Visuo-spatial bootstrapping: Evidence for binding of verbal and spatial information in working memory. *Quarterly Journal of Experimental Psychology, 63*, 239–245.

Davis, J. P., & Valentine, T. (2009). CCTV on trial: Matching video images with the defendant in the dock. *Applied Cognitive Psychology, 23*, 482–505.

Dawes, R. M. (1988). *Rational choice in an uncertain world*. San Diego, CA: Harcourt Brace Jovanovich.

Dawson, E., Gilovich, T., & Regan, D. T. (2002). Motivated reasoning and performance on the Wason selection task. *Personality and Social Psychology Bulletin, 28*, 1379–1387.

De Beni, R., & Moè, A. (2003). Imagery and rehearsal as study strategies for written or orally presented passages. *Psychonomic Bulletin & Review, 10*, 975–980.

De Beni, R., Moè, A., & Cornoldi, C. (1997). Learning from texts or lectures: Loci mnemonics can interfere with reading but not with listening. *European Journal of Cognitive Psychology, 9*, 401–415.

De Groot, A. D. (1965). *Thought and choice in chess*. The Hague, The Netherlands: Mouton.

De Jong, P. F., Bitter, D. J. L., van Setten, M., & Marinus, E. (2009). Does phonological recoding occur during silent reading, and is it necessary for orthographic learning? *Journal of Experimental Child Psychology, 104*, 267–282.

De Martino, B., Camerer, C. F., & Adolphs, R. (2010). Amygdala damage eliminates monetary loss aversion. *Proceedings of the National Academy of Sciences of the United States of America, 107*, 3788–3792.

De Houwer, J., Teige-Mocigemba, S., Spruyta, A., & Moors, A. (2009). Implicit measures: A normative analysis and review. *Psychological Bulletin, 135*, 347–368.

De Neys, W. (2006). Automatic-heuristic and executive-analytic processing during reasoning: Chronometric and dual-task considerations. *Quarterly Journal of Experimental Psychology, 59,* 1070–1100.

De Neys, W., Cromheeke, S., & Osman, M. (2011). Biased but in doubt: Conflict and decision confidence. *PLOS ONE, 6*(1), e15954.

De Neys, W., & Glumicic, T. (2008). Conflict monitoring in dual process theories of thinking. *Cognition, 106,* 1248–1299.

De Neys, W., Schaeken, W., & d'Ydewalle, G. (2005). Working memory everyday conditional reasoning: Retrieval and inhibition of stored counterexamples. *Thinking & Reasoning, 11,* 349–381.

De Neys, W., Vartanian, O., & Goel, V. (2008). Smarter than we think: When our brains detect that we are biased. *Psychological Science, 19,* 483–489.

De Neys, W., & Verschueren, N. (2006). Working memory capacity and a notorious brain teaser – The case of the Monty Hall dilemma. *Experimental Psychology, 53,* 123–131.

De Paulo, B. M., Lindsay, J. J., Malone, B. E., Muhlenbruck, L., Charlton, K., & Cooper, H. (2003). Cues to deception. *Psychological Bulletin, 129,* 74–118.

De Vries, M., Holland, R. W., & Witteman, C. L. M. (2008). In the winning mood: Affect in the Iowa gambling task. *Judgment and Decision Making, 3,* 42–50.

Dean, I., Harper, N. S., & McAlpine, D. (2005). Neural population coding of sound level adapts to stimulus characteristics. *Nature Neuroscience, 8,* 1684–1689.

Deffenbacher, K. A., Bornstein, B. H., Penroad, S. D., & McGorty, E. K. (2004). A meta-analytic review of the effects of high stress on eyewitness memory. *Law and Human Behavior, 28,* 687–706.

Dehaene, S., Naccache, L., Cohen, L., Le Bihan, D., Mangin, J., Poline, J., et al. (2001). Cerebral mechanisms of word masking and unconscious repetition priming. *Nature Neuroscience, 4,* 752–758.

Dehaene, S., Changeux, J. P., Naccache, L., Sackur, J., & Sergent, C. (2006). Conscious, preconscious, and subliminal processing: A testable taxonomy. *Trends in Cognitive Sciences, 10,* 204–211.

Del Cul, A., Dehaene, S., Reyes, P., Bravo, E., & Slachevsky, A. (2009). Causal role of prefrontal cortex in the threshold for access to consciousness. *Brain, 132,* 2531–2540.

Delaney, P. F., Ericsson, K. A., & Knowles, M. E. (2004). Immediate and sustained effects of planning in a problem-solving task. *Journal of Experimental Psychology: Learning, Memory, and Cognition, 30,* 1219–1234.

Dell, G. S. (1986). A spreading-activation theory of retrieval in sentence production. *Psychological Review, 93,* 283–321.

Dell, G. S., Burger, L. K., & Svec, W. R. (1997). Language production and serial order: A functional analysis and a model. *Psychological Review, 93,* 283–321.

Dell, G. S., Oppenheim, G. M., & Kittredge, A. K. (2008). Saying the right word at the right time: Syntagmatic and paradigmatic interference in sentence production. *Language and Cognitive Processes, 23,* 583–608.

DeLucia, P. R., & Hochberg, J. (1991). Geometrical illusions in solid objects under ordinary viewing conditions. *Perception & Psychophysics, 50,* 547–554.

Delvenne, J. F., Seron, X., Coyette, F., & Rossion, B. (2004). Evidence for perceptual deficits in associative visual (prosop)agnosia: A single-case study. *Neuropsychologia, 42,* 597–612.

Derakshan, N., & Eysenck, M. W. (1998). Working-memory capacity in high trait-anxious and repressor groups. *Cognition & Emotion, 12,* 697–713.

Destrebecqz, A., Peigneux, P., Laureys, S., Degueldre, C., Del Fiorem, G., Aerts, J., et al. (2005). The neural correlates of implicit and explicit sequence learning: Interacting networks revealed by the process dissociation procedure. *Learning and Memory, 12,* 480–490.

Deutsch, J. A., & Deutsch, D. (1963). Attention: Some theoretical considerations. *Psychological Review, 93,* 283–321.

Dewar, M. T., Cowan, N., & Della Sala, S. (2007). Forgetting due to retroactive interference: A fusion of Müller and Pizecker's (1900) early insights into everyday forgetting and recent research on retrograde amnesia. *Cortex, 43,* 616–634.

Dewar, M., Della Sala, S., Beschin, N., & Cowan, N. (2010). Profound retroactive amnesia: What interferes? *Neuropsychology, 24,* 357–367.

Diana, R. A., Yonelinas, A. P., & Ranganath, C. (2007). Imaging recollection and familiarity in the medial temporal lobe: A three-component model. *Trends in Cognitive Sciences, 11,* 379–386.

DiBonaventura, M. D., & Chapman, G. B. (2008). Do decision biases predict bad decisions? Omission bias, naturalness bias, and influenza vaccination. *Medical Decision Making, 28,* 532–539.

Dickson, R. A., Pillemer, D. B., & Bruehl, E. C. (2011). The reminiscence bump for salient personal memories: Is a cultural life script required? *Memory & Cognition, 39,* 977–991.

Dismukes, K., & Nowinski, J. (2007). Prospective memory, concurrent task management, and pilot error. In A. Kramer, D. Wiegmann, & A. Kirlik

(Eds.), *Attention from theory to practice*. New York, NY: Oxford University Press.

Ditto, P. H., Scepansky, J. A., Munro, G. D., Apanovitch, A. M., & Lockhart, L. K. (1998). Motivated sensitivity to preference-inconsistent information. *Journal of Personality and Social Psychology*, 75, 53–69.

Dodhia, R. M., & Dismukes, R. K. (2009). Interruptions create prospective memory tasks. *Applied Cognitive Psychology*, 23, 73–89.

Dorman, M. F., Raphael, L. J., & Liberman, A. M. (1979). Some experiments in the sound of silence in phonetic perception. *Journal of the Acoustical Society of America*, 65, 1518–1532.

Downing, P. E., Chan, A. W. Y., Peelen, M. V., Dodds, C. M., & Kanwisher, N. (2006). Domain specificity in visual cortex. *Cerebral Cortex*, 16, 1453–1461.

Drews, F. A., Pasupathi, M., & Strayer, D. L. (2008). Passenger and cell phone conversations in simulated driving. *Journal of Experimental Psychology: Applied*, 14, 392–400.

Driver, J., & Vuilleumier, P. (2001). Perceptual awareness and its loss in unilateral neglect and extinction. *Cognition*, 79, 39–88.

Dror, I. E., Charlton, D., & Péron, A. E. (2006). Contextual information renders experts vulnerable to making erroneous identifications. *Forensic Science International*, 156, 74–78.

Dror, I. E., & Mnookin, J. L. (2010). The use of technology in human expert domains: Challenges and risks arising from the use of automated fingerprint identification systems in forensic science. *Law, Probability and Risk*, 9, 47–67.

Dror, I. E., & Rosenthal, R. (2008). Meta-analytically quantifying the reliability and bias ability of forensic experts. *Journal of Forensic Sciences*, 53, 900–903.

Duchaine, B. (2006). Prosopagnosia as an impairment to face-specific mechanisms: Elimination of the alternative hypotheses in a developmental case. *Cognitive Neuropsychology*, 23, 714–747.

Duchaine, B., & Nakayama, K. (2006). Developmental prosopagnosia: A window to context-specific face processing. *Current Opinion in Neurobiology*, 16, 166–173.

Dudukovic, N. M., Marsh, E. J., & Tversky, B. (2004). Telling a story or telling it straight: The effects of entertaining versus accurate retellings on memory. *Applied Cognitive Psychology*, 18, 125–143.

Dumay, N., Frauenfelder, U. H., & Content, A. (2002). The role of the syllable in lexical segmentation in French: Word-spotting data. *Brain and Language*, 81, 144–161.

Dunbar, K. (1993). Concept discovery in a scientific domain. *Cognitive Science*, 17, 397–434.

Dunbar, K., & Blanchette, I. (2001). The in vivo/in vitro approach to cognition: The case of analogy. *Trends in Cognitive Sciences*, 5, 334–339.

Duncan, J., & Humphreys, G. W. (1989). A resemblance theory of visual search. *Psychological Review*, 96, 433–458.

Duncan, J., & Humphreys, G. W. (1992). Beyond the search surface: Visual search and attentional engagement. *Journal of Experimental Psychology: Human Perception & Performance*, 18, 578–588.

Duncker, K. (1945). On problem solving. *Psychological Monographs*, 58 (Whole No. 270).

Dunning, D. (2011). The Dunning Kruger effect: On being ignorant of one's own ignorance. *Advances in Experimental Social Psychology*, 44, 247–296.

Eagly, A. H. (2001). Social role theory of sex differences and similarities. In J. Worrell (Ed.), *Encyclopedia of women and gender* (pp. 1069–1078). San Diego, CA: Academic Press.

Easterbrook, J. A. (1959). The effect of emotion on cue utilization and the organization of behavior. *Psychological Review*, 66, 183–201.

Ebbinghaus, H. (1885/1913). *Über das Gedächtnis*. Leipzig, Germany: Dunker [translated by H. Ruyer & C. E. Bussenius]. New York, NY: Teachers College, Columbia University.

Echterhoff, G., Higgins, E. T., Kopietz, R., & Groll, S. (2008). How communication goals determine when audience tuning biases memory. *Journal of Experimental Psychology: General*, 137, 3–21.

Egly, R., Driver, J., & Rafal, R. D. (1994). Shifting visual attention between objects and locations: Evidence from normal and parietal lesion subjects. *Journal of Experimental Psychology: General*, 123, 161–177.

Ehinger, K. A., Hidalgo-Sotelo, B., Torralba, A., & Oliva, A. (2009). Modelling search for people in 900 scenes: A combined source model of eye guidance. *Visual Cognition*, 17, 945–978.

Ehri, L. C., Nunes, S. R., Willows, D. M., Schuster, B. V., Yaghoub-Zadeh, Z., & Shanahan, T. (2001). Phonemic awareness instruction helps children learn to read: Evidence from the National Reading Panel's meta-analysis. *Reading Research Quarterly*, 36, 250–287.

Eich, E. (1995). Searching for mood-dependent memory. *Psychological Science*, 6, 67–75.

Eich, E., & Metcalfe, J. (1989). Mood-dependent memory for internal versus external events. *Journal of Experimental Psychology: Learning, Memory & Cognition*, 15, 443–455.

Eichenbaum, H. (2001). The hippocampus and declarative memory: Cognitive mechanisms and neural codes. *Behavioral Brain Research*, 127, 199–207.

Einstein, G. O., & McDaniel, M. A. (2005). Prospective memory: Multiple retrieval processes. *Current Directions in Psychological Science, 14*, 286–290.

Elder, J. H., & Goldberg, R. M. (2002). Ecological statistics of Gestalt laws for the perceptual organization of contours. *Journal of Vision, 2*, 324–353.

Ellis, J. A., & Cohen, G. (2008). Memory for intentions, actions, and plans. In G. Cohen & M. A. Conway (Eds.), *Memory in the real world* (pp. 141–172). Hove, UK: Psychology Press.

Ellis, J. J., Glaholt, M. G., & Reingold, E. M. (2011). Eye movements reveal solution knowledge prior to insight. *Consciousness and Cognition, 20*, 768–776.

Elqayam, S., & Evans, J. St. B. T. (2011). Subtracting "ought" from "is": Descriptivism versus normatism in the study of human thinking. *Behavioral and Brain Sciences, 34*, 233–248.

Engbert, R., Nuthmann, A., Richter, E. M., & Kliegl, R. (2005). SWIFT: A dynamical model of saccade generation during reading. *Psychological Review, 112*, 777–813.

Engel, H. (2007). *The man who forgot how to read.* Toronto, Canada: Harper Collins.

Engel, P. J. H. (2008). Tacit knowledge and visual expertise in medical diagnostic reasoning: Implications for medical education. *Medical Teacher, 30*, e184–e188.

Engelhardt, P. E., Bailey, K. G. D., & Ferreira, F. (2006). Do speakers and listeners observe the Gricean maxim of quantity? *Journal of Memory and Language, 54*, 554–573.

Ericsson, K. A. (1988). Analysis of memory performance in terms of memory skill. In R. J. Sternberg (Ed.), *Advances in the psychology of human intelligence* (Vol. 4, pp. 137–179). Hillsdale, NJ: Lawrence Erlbaum.

Ericsson, K. A., & Chase, W. G. (1982). Exceptional memory. *American Scientist, 70*, 607–615.

Ericsson, K. A., Delaney, P. F., Weaver, G., & Mahadevan, R. (2004). Uncovering the structure of a memorist's superior "basic" memory capacity. *Cognitive Psychology, 49*, 191–237.

Ericsson, K. A., & Kintsch, W. (1995). Long-term working memory. *Psychological Review, 102*, 211–245.

Ericsson, K. A., & Ward, P. (2007). Capturing the naturally occurring superior performance of experts in the laboratory: Toward a science of expert and exceptional performance. *Current Directions in Psychological Science, 16*, 346–350.

Eriksen, C. W., & St. James, J. D. (1986). Visual attention within and around the field of focal attention: A zoom lens model. *Perception & Psychophysics, 40*, 225–240.

Eriksson, J., Larsson, A., Ahlström, K. R., & Nyberg, L. (2006). Similar frontal and distinct posterior cortical regions mediate visual and auditory perceptual awareness. *Cerebral Cortex, 17*, 760–765.

Ervin-Tripp, S. (1979). Children's verbal turntaking. In E. Ochs & B. B. Schieffelin (Eds.), *Developmental pragmatics* (pp. 391–414). New York, NY: Academic Press.

Evans, J. S. T. (2002). Logic and human reasoning: An assessment of the deduction paradigm. *Psychological Bulletin, 128*, 978–996.

Evans, J. S. T. (2006). The heuristic-analytic theory of reasoning: Extension and evaluation. *Psychonomic Bulletin & Review, 13*, 378–395.

Evans, J. S. T. (2008). Dual-processing accounts of reasoning, judgment, and social cognition. *Annual Review of Psychology, 59*, 255–278.

Evans, J. St. B. T. (2011). Reasoning is for thinking, not just for arguing. *Behavioral and Brain Sciences, 34*, 77–78.

Evans, J. St. B. T., Barston, J. L., & Pollard, P. (1983). On the conflict between logic and belief in syllogistic reasoning. *Memory and Cognition, 11*, 295–306.

Evans, J. St. B. T., Handley, S. J., Perham, N., Over, D. E., & Thompson, V. A. (2000). Frequency versus probability formats in statistical word problems. *Cognition, 77*, 197–213.

Evans, J. St. B. T., & Over, D.E. (2010). Heuristic thinking and human intelligence: A com mentary on Marewski, Gaissmaier and Gigerenzer. *Cognitive Processing, 11*, 171–175.

Evans, N., & Levinson, S. C. (2009). The myth of language universals: Language diversity and its importance for cognitive science. *Behavioral and Brain Sciences, 32*, 429–448.

Eysenck, M. W. (1979). Depth, elaboration, and distinctiveness. In L. S. Cermak & F. I. M. Craik (Eds.), *Levels of processing in human memory.* Hillsdale, NJ: Lawrence Erlbaum.

Eysenck, M. W. (1997). *Anxiety and cognition: A unified theory.* Hove, UK: Psychology Press.

Eysenck, M. W., Derakshan, N., Santos, R., & Calvo, M. G. (2007). Anxiety and cognitive performance: Attentional control theory. *Emotion, 7*, 336–353.

Eysenck, M. W., & Eysenck, M. C. (1980). Effects of processing depth, distinctiveness, and word frequency on retention. *British Journal of Psychology, 71*, 263–274.

Eysenck, M. W., Mogg, K., May, J., Richards, A., & Mathews, A. (1991). Bias in interpretation of ambiguous sentences related to threat in anxiety. *Journal of Abnormal Psychology, 100*, 144–150.

Fadardi, J. S., & Cox, W. M. (2009). Reversing the sequence: Reducing alcohol consumption by overcoming alcohol attentional bias. *Drug and Alcohol Dependence, 101*, 137–145.

Fadiga, L., Craighero, L., Buccino, G., & Rizzolatti, G. (2002). Speech listening specifically modulates the excitability of tongue muscles: A TMS study. *European Journal of Neuroscience, 15*, 399–402.

Faigley, L., & Witte, S. (1983). Analyzing revision. *College Composition and Communication, 32*, 400–414.

Falk, R., & Lann, A. (2008). The allure of equality: Uniformity in probabilistic and statistical judgment. *Cognitive Psychology, 57*, 293–334. Farah, M. J. (1994). Specialization within visual object recognition: Clues from prosopagnosia and alexia. In M. J. Farah & G. Ratcliff (Eds.), *The neuropsychology of high-level vision: Collected tutorial essays*. Hillsdale, NJ: Lawrence Erlbaum Associates.

Farah, M. J., & McClelland, J. L. (1991). A computational model of semantic memory impairment: Modality-specificity and emergent category-specificity. *Journal of Experimental Psychology: General, 120*, 339–357.

Farber, H. S. (2005). Is tomorrow another day? The labor supply of New York City cabdrivers. *Journal of Political Economics, 113*, 46–82.

Farivar, R. (2009). Dorsal–ventral integration in object recognition. *Brain Research Reviews, 62*, 144–153.

Farrell, S. (2010). Dissociating conditional recency in immediate and delayed free recall: A challenge for unitary models of recency. *Journal of Experimental Psychology: Learning, Memory & Cognition, 36*, 324–347.

Fawcett, J. M., Russell, E. J., Peace, K. A., & Christie, J. (2013). Of guns and geese: A meta-analytic review of the "weapon focus" literature. *Psychology, Crime & Law, 19*, 35–66.

Fehr, B. (2004). Intimacy expectations in same-sex friendships: A prototype interaction-pattern model. *Journal of Personality and Social Psychology, 86*, 265–284.

Feldman, J. (2003). The simplicity principle in human concept learning. *Current Directions in Psychological Science, 12*, 227–232.

Feldon, D. F. (2010). Do psychology researchers tell it like it is? A microgenetic analysis of research strategies and self-report accuracy along a continuum. *Instructional Science, 38*, 395–415.

Fellows, L. K., Heberlein, A. S., Morales, D. A., Shivde, G., Waller, S., & Wu, D. H. (2005). Method matters: An empirical study of impact in cognitive

neuroscience. *Journal of Cognitive Neuroscience, 17*, 850–858.

Ferreira, F. (2003). The misinterpretation of noncanonical sentences. *Cognitive Psychology, 47*, 164–203.

Ferreira, F., Bailey, K. G. D., & Ferraro, V. (2002). Good enough representations in language comprehension. *Current Directions in Psychological Science, 11*, 11–15.

Ferreira, F., & Swets, B. (2002). How incremental is language production? Evidence from the production of utterances requiring the computation of arithmetic sums. *Journal of Memory and Language, 46*, 57–84.

Ferreira, V. S. (2008). Ambiguity, accessibility, and a division of labor for communicative success. *Psychology of Learning and Motivation, 49*, 209–246.

Ferreira, V. S., & Griffin, Z. M. (2003). Phonological influences on lexical (mis)selection. *Psychological Science, 14*, 86–90.

Ferreira, V. S., Slevc, L. R., & Rogers, E. S. (2005). How do speakers avoid ambiguous linguistic expressions? *Cognition, 96*, 263–284.

Fery, P., & Morais, J. (2003). A case study of visual agnosia without perceptual processing or structural descriptions' impairment. *Cognitive Neuropsychology, 20*, 595–618.

Fessler, D. M. T., Pillsworth, E. G., & Flamson, T. J. (2004). Angry men and disgusted women: An evolutionary approach to the influence of emotions on risk taking. *Organizational Behavior and Human Decision Processes, 95*, 107–123.

ffytche, D. H., Howard, R. J., Brammer, M. J., David, A., Woodruff, P., & Williams, S. (1998). The anatomy of conscious vision: An fMRI study of visual hallucinations. *Nature Neuroscience, 1*, 738–742.

Fiedler, K. (1988). The dependence of the conjunction fallacy on subtle linguistic factors. *Psychological Research, 50*, 123–129.

Fiedler, K., Brinkmann, B., Betsch, T., & Wild, B. (2000). A sampling approach to biases in conditional probability judgments: Beyond base-rate neglect and statistical format. *Journal of Experimental Psychology: General, 129*, 1–20.

Field, M., Munafo, M. R., & Franken, I. H. A. (2009). A meta-analytic investigation of the relationship between attentional bias and subjective craving in substance abuse. *Psychological Bulletin, 135*, 590–607.

Fields, A. W., & Shelton, A. L. (2006). Individual skill differences and large-scale environmental learning. *Journal of Experimental Psychology: Learning, Memory, and Cognition, 32*, 506–515.

Fivush, R. (2010). The development of autobiographical memory. *Annual Review of Psychology, 62*, 2–24.

Fivush, R., & Nelson, K. (2004). Culture and language in the emergence of autobiographical memory. *Psychological Science, 15*, 573–577.

Fleck, J. I. (2008). Working memory demands in insight versus analytic problem solving. *European Journal of Cognitive Psychology, 20*, 139–176.

Floro, M., & Miles, M. (2001). *Time use and overlapping activities – Evidence from Australia* (SPRC Discussion Paper No. 93). Sydney, Australia: Social Policy Research Center.

Foerde, K., & Poldrack, R. A. (2009). Procedural learning in humans. In L. R. Squire (Ed.), *The new encyclopedia of neuroscience, Vol. 7* (pp. 1083–1091). Oxford, UK: Academic Press.

Foley, M. A., Foley, H. J., & Korenman, L. M. (2002). Adapting a memory framework (source monitoring) to the study of closure processes. *Memory & Cognition, 30*, 412–422.

Foley, M. A., Foley, H. J., Scheye, R., & Bonacci, A. M. (2007). Remembering more than meets the eye: A study of memory confusions about incomplete visual information. *Memory, 15*, 616–633.

Folk, C. L., Remington, R. W., & Johnston, J. C. (1992). Involuntary covert orienting is contingent on attentional control settings. *Journal of Experimental Psychology: Human Perception and Performance, 18*, 1030–1044.

Forster, S., & Lavie, N. (2008). Failures to ignore entirely irrelevant distractors: The role of load. *Journal of Experimental Psychology: Applied, 14*, 73–83.

Forster, S., & Lavie, N. (2009). Harnessing the wandering mind: The role of perceptual load. *Cognition, 111*, 345–355.

Fortin, M., Voss, P., Lord, C., Lassande, M., Pruessner, J., Saint-Arnour, D., et al. (2008). Wayfinding in the blind: Large hippocampal volume and supranormal spatial navigation. *Brain, 131*, 2995–3005.

Foster, D. H., & Gilson, S. J. (2002). Recognizing novel three-dimensional objects by summing signals from parts and views. *Proceedings of the Royal Society of London B: Biological Sciences, 257*, 115–121.

Foulsham, T., B arton, J. J. S., Kingstone, A., Dewhurst, R., & Underwood, G. (2009). Fixation and saliency during search of natural scenes: The case of visual agnosia. *Neuropsychologia, 47*, 1994–2003.

Fox, E. (2008). *Emotion science*. New York, NY: Palgrave Macmillan.

Fox Tree, J. E. (2007). Folk notions of 'um' and 'uh', 'you know', and 'like'. *Text & Talk, 27*, 297–314.

Frank, M. C., & Ramscar, M. (2003). How do presentation and context influence representation for functional fixedness tasks? In *Proceedings of the 25th annual meeting of the cognitive science society* (p. 1345). Mahwah, NJ: Lawrence Erlbaum.

Frattaroli, J. (2006). Experimental disclosure and its moderators: A meta-analysis. *Psychological Bulletin, 132*, 823–865.

Frazier, L., & Rayner, K. (1982). Making and correcting errors in the analysis of structurally ambiguous sentences. *Cognitive Psychology, 14*, 178–210.

Frederick, S. (2005). Cognitive reflection and decision making. *Journal of Economic Perspectives, 19*, 25–42.

Freud, S. (1925 /1961). A note upon the "mystic writing pad." In J. Strachey (Ed.), *Standard edition of the collected works of Sigmund Freud, Vol. 19*. London: Hogarth Press. (Original work published 1925.)

Frick-Horbury, D., & Guttentag, R. E. (1998). The effects of restricting hand gesture production on lexical retrieval and free recall. *American Journal of Psychology, 111*, 43–62.

Friedman, A., Spetch, M. L., & Ferrey, A. (2005). Recognition by humans and pigeons of novel views of 3-D objects and their photographs. *Journal of Experimental Psychology: General, 134*, 149–162.

Friedman, N. P., & Miyake, A. (2004). The relations among inhibition and interference control functions: A latent variable analysis. *Journal of Experimental Psychology: General, 133*, 101–135.

Friedman-Hill, S. R., Robertson, L. C., & Treisman, A. (1995). Parietal contributions to visual feature binding: Evidence from a patient with bilateral lesions. *Science, 269*, 853–855.

Frijda, N. H. (1986). *The emotions*. Cambridge, UK: Cambridge University Press.

Frischen, A., Eastwood, J. D., & Smilek, D. (2008). Visual search for faces with emotional expressions. *Psychological Bulletin, 134*, 662–676.

Fuchs, A. H., & Milar, K. J. (2003). Psychology as a science. In D. F. Freedheim (Ed.), *Handbook of psychology (Vol. 1: The history of psychology)* (pp. 1–26). Hoboken, NJ: Wiley.

Fuller, J. M. (2003). The influence of speaker roles on discourse marker use. *Journal of Pragmatics, 35*, 23–45.

Fuselsang, J. A., Stein, C. B., Green, A. E., & Dunbar, K. N. (2004). Theory and data interactions of the scientific mind: Evidence from the molecular and the cognitive laboratory. *Canadian Journal of Experimental Psychology, 58*, 86–95.

Gable, P., & Harmon-Jones, E. (2010). The blues broaden but the nasty narrows: Attentional consequences of negative affects low and high in motivational intensity. *Psychological Science, 21*, 211–215.

Gainotti, G. (2000). What the locus of brain lesion tells us about the nature of the cognitive defect underlying category-specific disorders: A review. *Cortex, 36,* 539–559.

Galantucci, B., F o wler, C. A., & Turvey, M. T. (2006). The motor theory of speech perception reviewed. *Psychonomic Bulletin & Review, 13,* 361–377.

Galotti, K. M. (2002). *Making decisions that matter: How people face important life choices.* Mahwah, NJ: Lawrence Erlbaum.

Galotti, K. M. (2007). Decision structuring in important real-life choices. *Psychological Science, 18,* 320–325.

Galotti, K. M., & Tinkelenberg, C. E. (2009). Real-life decision making: Parents choosing a first-grade placement. *American Journal of Psychology, 122,* 455–468.

Galpin, A., Underwood, G., & Crundall, D. (2009). Change blindness in driving scenes. *Transportation Research Part F: Traffic Psychology and Behavior, 12,* 179–185.

Galton, F. (1983). *Enquiries into human faculty and its development.* London: J. M. Dent & Co.

Ganis, G., Thompson, W. L., & Kosslyn, S. M. (2004). Brain areas underlying visual mental imagery and visual perception: An fMRI study. *Cognitive Brain Research, 20,* 226–241.

Ganong, W. F. (1980). Phonetic categorization in auditory word perception. *Journal of Experimental Psychology: Human Perception & Performance, 6,* 110–125.

Garcia-Marques, L., Santos, A. S. C., & Mackie, D. M. (2006). Stereotypes: Static abstractions or dynamic knowledge structures? *Journal of Personality and Social Psychology, 91,* 814–831.

Garnsey, S. M., Pearlmutter, N. J., Myers, E., & Lotocky, M. A. (1997). The contributions of verb bias and plausibility to the comprehension of temporarily ambiguous sentences. *Journal of Memory and Language, 37,* 58–93.

Gaskell, M. G., & Marslen-Wilson, W. D. (1997). Integrating form and meaning: A distributed model of speech perception. *Language and Cognitive Processes, 12*(5–6), 613–656.

Gathercole, S. E., & Baddeley, A. D. (1993). Phonological working memory: A critical building-block for reading development and vocabulary acquisition. *European Journal of Psychology of Education, 8,* 259–272.

Gauthier, I., & Tarr, M. J. (2002). Unraveling mechanisms for expert object recognition: Bridging brain activity and behavior. *Journal of Experimental Psychology: Human Perception and Performance, 28,* 431–446.

Gazzaniga, M. S. (1992). *Nature's mind.* London, UK: Basic Books.

Gazzaniga, M. S., Ivry, R. B., & Mangun, G. R. (2009). *Cognitive neuroscience: The biology of the mind* (2nd ed.). New York, NY: W. W. Norton.

Gazzaniga, M. S., & Ledoux, J. E. (1978). *The integrated mind.* New York, NY: Plenum Press.

Gebauer, G. F., & Mackintosh, N. J. (2007). Psychometric intelligence dissociates implicit and explicit learning. *Journal of Experimental Psychology: Learning, Memory, and Cognition, 33,* 34–54.

Gegenfurtner, A., Lehtinen, E., & Säljö, R. (2011). Expertise differences in the comprehension of visualisations: A metaanalysis of eye-tracking research in professional domains. *Educational Psychology Review, 23,* 523–552.

Geis, M., & Zwicky, A. M. (1971). On invited inferences. *Linguistic Inquiry, 2,* 561–566.

Geiselman, R. E., & Fisher, R. P. (1997). Ten years of cognitive interviewing. In D. G. Payne & F. G. Conrad (Eds.), *Intersections in basic and applied memory research.* Mahwah, NJ: Lawrence Erlbaum.

Geraerts, E., Schooler, J. W., Merckelbach, H., Jelicic, M., Hunter, B. J. A., & Ambadar, Z. (2007). Corroborating continuous and discontinuous memories of childhood sexual abuse. *Psychological Science, 18,* 564–568.

Geraerts, E., Lindsay, D. S., Merckelbach, H., Jelicic, M., Raymaekers, L., & Arnold, M. M. (2009). Cognitive mechanisms underlying recovered memory experiences of childhood sexual abuse. *Psychological Science, 20,* 92–98.

Gerwing, J., & Allison, M. (2009). The relationship between verbal and gestural contributions in conversation: A comparison of three methods. *Gesture, 9,* 312–336.

Geyer, T., von Mühlenen, A., & Müller, H. J. (2007). What do eye movements reveal about the role of memory in visual search? *Quarterly Journal of Experimental Psychology, 60,* 924–935.

Gick, M. L., & Holyoak, K. J. (1980). Analogical problem solving. *Cognitive Psychology, 12,* 306–355.

Gigerenzer, G., & Hoffrage, U. (1999). Overcoming difficulties in Bayesian reasoning: A reply to Lewis and Keren (1999) and Mellers and McGraw (1999). *Psychological Review, 102,* 684–704.

Ginet, M., & Verkampt, F. (2007). The cognitive interview: Is its benefit affected by the level of witness emotion? *Memory, 15,* 450–464.

Glanzer, M., & Cunitz, A. R. (1966). Two storage mechanisms in free recall. *Journal of Verbal Learning and Verbal Behavior, 5,* 351–360.

Glaser, W. R. (1992). Picture naming. *Cognition, 42,* 61–105.

Glenberg, A. M., Smith, S. M., & Green, C. (1977). Type I rehearsal: Maintenance and more. *Journal of Verbal Learning and Verbal Behavior, 16,* 339–352.

Glück, J., & Bluck, S. (2007). Looking back across the life span: A life story account of the reminiscence bump. *Memory & Cognition, 35,* 1928–1939.

Glushko, R. J. (1979). The organization and activation of orthographic knowledge in reading aloud. *Journal of Experimental Psychology: Human Perception and Performance, 5,* 674–691.

Glymour, C. (2001). *The mind's arrows: Bayes nets and graphical causal models in psychology.* Cambridge, MA: MIT Press.

Gobet, F., & Chass, P. (2009). Expertise and intuition: A tale of three theories. *Minds and Machines, 19,* 151–180.

Gobet, F., & Clarkson, G. (2004). Chunks in expert memory: Evidence for the magical number four . . . or is it two? *Memory, 12,* 732–747.

Gobet, F., de Voogt, A., & Retschitzki, J. (2004). *Moves in mind: The psychology of board games.* Hove, UK: Psychology Press.

Gobet, F., & Waters, A. J. (2003). The role of constraints in expert memory. *Journal of Experimental Psychology: Learning, Memory, and Cognition, 29,* 1082–1094.

Godden, D. R., & Baddeley, A. D. (1975). Context dependent memory in two natural environments: On land and under water. *British Journal of Psychology, 66,* 325–331.

Goldberg, A., Russell, M., & Cook, A. (2003). The effect of computers on student writing: A meta-analysis of studies from 1992 to 2002. *Journal of Technology, Learning, and Assessment, 2,* 1–52.

Goldenburg, G., Müllbacher, W., & Nowak, A. (1995). Imagery without perception: A case study of anosognosia for cortical blindness. *Neuropsychologia, 33,* 1373–1382.

Goldstein, D. G., & Gigerenzer, G. (2002). Models of ecological rationality: The recognition heuristic. *Psychological Review, 109,* 75–90.

Golumbic, E. Z., Cogan, G. B., Schroeder, C. E., & Poeppel, D. (2013). Visual input enhances selective speech envelope tracking in auditory cortex at a "cocktail party". *Journal of Neuroscience, 33,* 1417–1426.

Gomulicki, B. R. (1956). Recall as an abstractive process. *Acta Psychologica, 12,* 77–94.

Goodman, K. S. (1986). *What's whole in whole language.* Berkeley, CA: RDR Books.

Gorman, M. E. (1995). Hypothesis testing. In S. E. Newstead & J. S. T. Evans (Eds.), *Perspectives on thinking and reasoning: Essays in honor of Peter Wason.* Hove, UK: Lawrence Erlbaum.

Gotlib, I. H., & Joormann, J. (2010). Cognition and depression: Current status and future directions. *Annual Review of Clinical Psychology, 6,* 285–312.

Gottfredson, L. S. (1997). Why g matters? The complexities of everyday life. *Intelligence, 24,* 79–132.

Grabner, R. H., Stern, E., & Neubauer, A. (2007). Individual differences in chess expertise: A psychometric investigation. *Acta Psychologica, 124,* 398–420.

Graf, P. (2012). Prospective memory: Faulty brain, flaky person. *Canadian Psychology, 53,* 7–13.

Graf, P., & Schacter, D. L. (1985). Implicit and explicit memory for new associations in normal and amnesic subjects. *Journal of Experimental Psychology: Learning, Memory, & Cognition, 11,* 501–518.

Grainger, J., & Jacobs, A. M. (2005). Pseudoword context effects on letter perception: The role of word misperception. *European Journal of Cognitive Psychology, 17,* 289–318.

Gray, J. A., & Wedderburn, A. A. (1960). Grouping strategies with simultaneous stimuli. *Quarterly Journal of Experimental Psychology, 12,* 180–184.

Green, H. A. C., & Patterson, K. (2009). Jigsaws – A preserved ability in semantic dementia. *Neuropsychologia, 47,* 569–576.

Green, K. P., Kuhl, P. K., Melzoff, A. M., & Stevens, E. B. (1991). Integrating speech information across talkers, gender, and sensory modality: Female faces and male voices in the McGurk effect. *Perception & Psychophysics, 50,* 524–536.

Greenberg, J. H. (1963). *Some universals of grammar with particular reference to the order of meaningful elements.* Cambridge, MA: MIT Press.

Greene, J., & Cohen, J. (2004). For the law, neuroscience changes nothing and everything. *Philosophical Transactions of the Royal Society London B: Biological Sciences, 359,* 1775–1785.

Greenwald, A. G. (2003). On doing two things at once: III. Confirmation of perfect timesharing when simultaneous tasks are ideomotor compatible. *Journal of Experimental Psychology: Human Perception and Performance, 29,* 859–868.

Gregory, R. L. (1973). The confounded eye. In R. L. Gregory & E. H. Gombrich (Eds.), *Illusion in nature and art.* London, UK: Duckworth.

Grey, S., & Mathews, A. (2000). Effects of training on interpretation of emotional ambiguity. *Quarterly Journal of Experimental Psychology, 53,* 1143–1162.

Grice, H. P. (1967). Logic and conversation. In P. Cole & J. L. Morgan (Eds.), *Studies in syntax* (Vol. III). New York, NY: Seminar Press.

Grill-Spector, K., & Kanwisher, N. (2005). Visual recognition: As soon as you know it is there, you know what it is. *Psychological Science, 16,* 152–160.

Grill-Spector, K., Sayres, R., & Ress, D. (2006). High-resolution imaging reveals highly selective nonface clusters in the fusiform face area. *Nature Neuroscience, 9,* 1177–1185.

Griskevicius, V., Shiota, M. N., & Neufeld, S. L. (2010). Influence of different positive emotions on persuasive processing: A functional evolutionary approach. *Emotion, 10,* 190–206.

Groopman, J. (2007). *How doctors think.* New York: Houghton Mifflin.

Gross, J. J., & Thompson, R. A. (2007). Emotion regulation: Conceptual foundations. In J. J. Gross (Ed.), *Handbook of emotion regulation.* New York, NY: Guilford Press.

Grossberg, S. (2003). Resonant neural dynamics of speech perception. *Journal of Phonetics, 31,* 423–445.

Guerin, B. (2003). Language use as social strategy: A review and an analytic framework for the social sciences. *Review of General Psychology, 7,* 251–298.

Guilbault, R. L., Bryant, F. B., Brockway, J. H., & Posavac, E. J. (2004). A meta-analysis of research on hindsight bias. *Basic and Applied Social Psychology, 26,* 103–117.

Gupta, P., & Cohen, N. J. (2002). Theoretical and computational analysis of skill learning, repetition priming, and procedural memory. *Psychological Review, 109,* 401–448.

Güss, C. D., Tuason, M. T., & Gerhard, C. (2010). Cross-national comparisons of complex problem-solving strategies in two microworlds. *Cognitive Science, 34,* 489–520.

Güss, C. D., & Wiley, B. (2007). Metacognition of problem-solving strategies in Brazil, India, and the United States. *Journal of Cognition and Culture, 7,* 1–25.

Gutschalk, A., Micheyl, C., & Oxenham, A. J. (2008). Neural correlates of auditory perceptual awareness under informational masking. *PLoS Biology, 6,* 1156–1165.

Hagoort, P., & van Berkum, J. (2007). Beyond the sentence given. *Philosophical Transactions of the Royal Society of London B: Biological Sciences, 362,* 801–811.

Hahn, U., & Oaksford, M. (2007). The rationality of informal argumentation: A Bayesian approach to reasoning fallacies. *Psychological Review, 114,* 704–732.

Hafenbrädl, S., Waeger, D., Marewski, J. N., & Gigerenzer, G. (2016). Applied decision making with fast-and-frugal heuristics. *Journal of Applied Research in Memory and Cognition, 5*(2), 215–231.

Hamann, S. B., & Squire, L. R. (1997). Intact perceptual memory in the absence of conscious memory. *Behavioral Neuroscience, 111,* 850–854.

Hampton, J. A. (1981). An investigation of the nature of abstract concepts. *Memory & Cognition, 9,* 149–156.

Hampton, J. A. (2007). Typicality, graded membership, and vagueness. *Cognitive Science, 31,* 355–384.

Hampton, J. A. (2010). Concepts in human adults. In D. Mareschal, P. Quinn, & S. E. G. Lea (Eds.), *The making of human concepts* (pp. 293–311). Oxford, UK: Oxford University Press.

Hampton, J. A., Storms, G., Simmons, C. L., & Heussen, D. (2009). Feature integration in natural language concepts. *Memory & Cognition, 37,* 1150–1163.

Hancock, J. T. (2007). Digital deception: Why, where and how people lie online. In A. N. Joinson, K. McKenna, T. Postmes, & U. Reips (Eds.), *The Oxford handbook of internet psychology* (pp. 287–331). Cambridge, UK: Cambridge University Press.

Hannon, B., & Daneman, M. (2007). Prospective memory: The relative effects of encoding, retrieval, and the match between encoding and retrieval. *Memory, 15,* 572–604.

Hansen, C. H., & Hansen, R. D. (1988). Finding the face in the crowd – An anger superiority effect. *Journal of Personality and Social Psychology, 54,* 917–924.

Hardt, O., Einarsson, E. O., & Nader, K. (2010). A bridge over troubled water: Reconsolidation as a link between cognitive and neuroscientific memory research traditions. *Annual Review of Psychology, 61,* 141–167.

Hareli, S., & Weiner, B. (2002). Dislike and envy as antecedents of pleasure at another's misfortune. *Motivation and Emotion, 26,* 257–277.

Harley, T. A. (2008). *The psychology of language: From data to theory* (3rd ed.). Hove, UK: Psychology Press.

Harley, T. A., & Bown, H. E. (1998). What causes a tip-of-the-tongue state? Evidence for lexical neighborhood effects in speech production. *British Journal of Psychology, 89,* 151–174.

Harm, M. W., & Seidenberg, M. S. (2001). Are there orthographic impairments in phonological dyslexia? *Cognitive Neuropsychology, 18,* 71–92.

Harnsberger, J. D., Hollien, H., Martin, C. A., & Hollien, K. A. (2009). Stress and deception in speech: Evaluating layered voice analysis. *Journal of Forensic Sciences, 54,* 642–650.

Harris, I. M., & Miniussi, C. (2003). Parietal lobe contribution to mental rotation demonstrated with rTMS. *Journal of Cognitive Neuroscience, 15,* 315–323.

Harrison, V., & Hole, G.J. (2009). Evidence for a contact-based explanation of the own-age bias in face recognition. *Psychonomic Bulletin & Review, 16,* 264–269.

Hartley, J., Sotto, E., & Pennebaker, J. (2003). Speaking versus typing: A case-study of using voice-recognition software on academic correspondence. *British Journal of Educational Technology, 34,* 5–16.

Hartsuiker, R. J., Corley, M., & Martensen, H. (2005). The lexical bias effect is modulated by context, but the standard monitoring account doesn't fly: Related reply to Baars et al. (1975). *Journal of Memory and Language, 52,* 58–70.

Harvey, L. O. (1986). Visual memory: What is remembered? In F. Klix & H. Hagendorf (Eds.), *Human memory and cognitive capabilities.* The Hague, The Netherlands: Elsevier.

Haskell, T. R., & MacDonald, M. C. (2003). Conflicting cues and competition in subject – verb agreement. *Journal of Memory and Language, 48,* 760–778.

Hassabis, D., Kumaran, D., Vann, S. D., & Maguire, E. A. (2007). Patients with hippocampal amnesia cannot imagine new experiences. *Proceedings of the National Academy of Sciences of the United States of America, 104,* 1726–1731.

Hastie, R. (2001). Problems for judgment and decision making. *Annual Review of Psychology, 52,* 653–683.

Hauk, O., Johnsrude, I., & Pulvermüller, F. (2004). Somatotopic representation of action words in human motor and premotor cortex. *Neuron, 41,* 301–307.

Havelka, J., & Rastle, K. (2005). The assembly of phonology from print is serial and subject to strategic control: Evidence from Serbian. *Journal of Experimental Psychology: Learning, Memory, and Cognition, 31,* 148–158.

Hayes, J. R., & Bajzek, D. (2008). Understanding and reducing the knowledge effect: Implications for writers. *Written Communication, 23,* 135–149.

Hayes, J. R., & Chenoweth, N. A. (2006). Is working memory involved in the transcribing and editing of texts? *Written Communication, 23,* 135–149.

Hayes, J. R., & Flower, L. S. (1986). Writing research and the writer. *American Psychologist, 41,* 1106–1113.

Hayes, S., Hirsch, C. R., Krebs, G., & Mathews, A. (2010). The effects of modifying interpretation bias on worry in generalized anxiety disorder. *Behaviour Research and Therapy, 48,* 171–178.

Hayes, J. R., Flower, L. S., Schriver, K., Stratman, J., & Carey, L. (1985). *Cognitive processes in revision* (Technical Report No. 12). Pittsburgh, PA: Carnegie Mellon University.

Hayward, W. G. (2003). After the viewpoint debate: Where next in object recognition? *Trends in Cognitive Sciences, 7,* 425–427.

Heit, E. (1992). Categorization using chains of examples. *Cognitive Psychology, 24,* 341–380.

Henderson, J. M., & Hollingworth, A. (1999). High-level scene perception. *Annual Review of Psychology, 50,* 243–271.

Henrich, J., Heine, S. J., & Norenzayan, A. (2010). Beyond WEIRD: Towards a broad-based behavioral science. *Behavioral and Brain Sciences, 33,* 111–135.

Herrmann, D. J., Yoder, C. Y., Gruneberg, M., & Payne, D G. (Eds.). (2006). *Applied cognitive psychology: A textbook.* Mahwah, NJ: Lawrence Erlbaum.

Herron, J. E., & Wilding, E. L. (2006). Brain and behavioral indices of retrieval model. *NeuroImage, 32,* 863–870.

Herschler, O., & Hochstein, S. (2009). The importance of being expert: Top-down attentional control in visual search with photographs. *Attention, Perception & Psychophysics, 71,* 1478–1486.

Hertwig, R., Pachur, T., & Kurzenhäuser, S. (2005). Judgments of risk frequencies: Tests of possible cognitive mechanisms. *Journal of Experimental Psychology: Learning, Memory, and Cognition, 31,* 621–642.

Heukelom, F. (2007). What Simon says. *Tinbergen Institute Discussion Paper,* No. 07–005(1).

Heussen, D., & Hampton, J. A. (2007). 'Emeralds are expensive because they are rare': Plausibility of property explanations. In S. Vosniadou, D. Kayser, & A. Protopapas (Eds.), *Proceedings of Eurocogsci07: The European cognitive science conference* (pp. 101–106). Hove, UK: Psychology Press.

Hicks, J. L., Marsh, R. L., & Cook, G. I. (2005). Task interference in time-based, event-based, and dual intention prospective memory conditions. *Journal of Memory and Language, 53,* 430–444.

Highley, J. R., Esiri, M. M., McDonald, B., CortinaBorja, M., Herron, B. M., & Crow, T. J. (1999). The size and fiber composition of the corpus callosum with respect to gender and schizophrenia: A postmortem study. *Brain, 122,* 99–110.

Hill, N. M., & Schneider, W. (2006). Brain changes in the development of expertise: Neuroanatomical and neurophysiological evidence about skill-based adaptations. In K. A. Ericsson, P. J. Feltovich, & R. R. Hoffman (Eds.), *The Cambridge handbook of expertise and expert performance*. Cambridge, UK: Cambridge University Press.

Hirst, W., Phelps, E. A., Buckner, R. L., Budson, A. E, Cuc, A., Gabrieli, J. D. E., et al. (2009). Long-term memory for the terrorist attack of September 11: Flashbulb memories, event memories, and the factors that influence their retention. *Journal of Experimental Psychology: General, 138*, 161–176.

Hobbs, S., & Burman, J. T. (2009). Is the 'cognitive revolution' a myth? *The Psychologist, 22*, 812–814.

Hoffrage, U., Lindsey, S., Hertwig, R., & Gigerenzer, G. (2000). Communicating statistical information. *Science, 290*, 2261–2262.

Hohwy, J., & Paton, B. (2010). Explaining away the body: Experiences of supernaturally caused touch and touch on non-hand objects within the rubber hand illusion. *PLoS One, 5*, e9416.

Hollingworth, A., & Henderson, J. M. (2002). Accurate visual memory for previously attended objects in natural scenes. *Journal of Experimental Psychology: Human Perception & Performance, 28*, 113–136.

Holliway, D. R., & McCutcheon, D. (2004). Audience perspective in young writers' composing and revising. In L. Allal, L. Chanquoy, & P. Largy (Eds.), *Revision of written language: Cognitive and instructional processes* (pp. 87–101). New York, NY: Kluwer.

Holtgraves, T. (1998). Interpreting indirect replies. *Cognitive Psychology, 37*, 1–27.

Holtgraves, T. (2008a). Automatic intention recognition in conversation processing. *Journal of Memory and Language, 58*, 627–645.

Holtgraves, T. (2008b). Conversation, speech acts, and memory. *Memory & Cognition, 36*, 361–374.

Horton, W. S., & Keysar, B. (1996). When do speakers take into account common ground? *Cognition, 59*, 91–117.

Hotopf, W. H. N. (1980). Slips of the pen. In U. Frith (Ed.), *Cognitive processes in spelling*. London, UK: Academic Press.

Howard, D., & Howard, J. H. (1992). Adult age differences in the rate of learning serial patterns: Evidence from direct and indirect tests. *Psychology & Aging, 7*, 232–241.

Howard, R. W. (2009). Individual differences in expertise development over decades in a complex intellectual domain. *Memory & Cognition, 37*, 194–209.

Howe, M. L., & Courage, M. L. (1997). The emergence and early development of autobiographical memory. *Psychological Review, 104*, 499–523.

Hsiao, J. H. W., & Cottrell, G. (2008). Two fixations suffice in face recognition. *Psychological Science, 19*, 998–1006.

Hubel, D. H., & Wiesel, T. N. (1962). Receptive fields, binocular interaction and functional architecture in the cat's visual cortex. *Journal of Physiology, 160*, 106–154.

Hubel, D. H., & Wiesel, T. N. (1979). Brain mechanisms of vision. *Scientific American, 249*, 150–162.

Humphreys, G. W., Avidan, G., & Behrmann, M. (2007). A detailed investigation of facial expression processing in congenital prosopagnosia as compared to acquired prosopagnosia. *Experimental Brain Research, 176*, 356–373.

Humphreys, G. W., & Riddoch, M. J. (1987). *To see but not to see: A case study of visual agnosia*. Hove, UK: Psychology Press.

Humphreys, G. W., Riddoch, M. J., & Quinlan, P. T. (1985). Interactive processes in perceptual organization: Evidence from visual agnosia. In M. I. Posner & O. S. M. Morin (Eds.), *Attention and performance* (Vol. XI). Hillsdale, NJ: Lawrence Erlbaum.

Hunt, R. R. (2006). The concept of distinctiveness in memory research. In R. R. Hunt & J. E. Worthen (Eds.), *Distinctiveness and memory* (pp. 3–25). New York, NY: Oxford University Press.

Hunt, R. R., & Smith, R. E. (1996). Accessing the particular from the general: The power of distinctiveness in the context of organization. *Memory & Cognition, 24*, 217–225.

Hunter, I. M. L. (2004). James, William. In R. L. Gregory (Ed.), *The Oxford companion to the mind* (2nd ed., pp. 610–612). New York, NY: Oxford University Press.

Hupbach, A., Gomez, R., Hardt, O., & Nadel, L. (2007). Reconsolidation of episodic memories: A subtle reminder triggers integration of new information. *Learning & Memory, 14*, 47–53.

Hupbach, A., Gomez, R., & Nadel, L. (2009). Episodic memory reconsolidation: Updating or source confusion? *Memory, 17*, 502–510.

Hupbach, A., Hardt, O., Gomez, R., & Nadel, L. (2008). The dynamics of memory: Context-dependent updating. *Learning & Memory, 15*, 574–579.

Huppert, F. A., & Piercy, M. (1976). Recognition memory in amnesic patients: Effect of temporal context and familiarity of material. *Cortex, 4*, 3–20.

Huppert, J. D., Pasupuleti, R. V., Foa, E. B., & Mathews, A. (2007). Interpretation bias in social anxiety: Response generation, response selection, and self-appraisals. *Behaviour Research and Therapy, 45*, 1505–1515.

Husain, F. T., Fromm, S. J., Pursley, R. H., Hosey, L. A., Braun, A. R., & Horwitz, B. (2006). Neural bases of categorization of simple speech and nonspeech sounds. *Human Brain Mapping, 27,* 636–651.

Hyde, J. S. (2005). The gender similarities hypothesis. *American Psychologist, 60,* 581–592.

Hyde, K. L., Lerch, J., Norton, A., Forgeard, M., Winner, E., Evans, A. C., et al. (2009). Musical training shapes structural brain development. *Journal of Neuroscience, 29,* 3019–3025.

Hyman, I., Boss, S., Wise, B., McKenzie, K., & Caggiano, J. (2009). Did you see the unicycling clown? Inattentional blindness while walking and talking on a cell phone. *Applied Cognitive Psychology, 24,* 597–607.

Ihlebaek, C., Love, T., Eilertsen, D. E., & Magnussen, S. (2003). Memory for a staged criminal event witnessed live and on video. *Memory, 11,* 310–327.

Intraub, H. (2010). Rethinking scene perception: A multisource model. *Psychology of learning and motivation: Advances in research and theory, 52,* 231–264.

Intraub, H., Daviels, K. K., Horowitz, T. S., & Wolfe, J. M. (2008). Looking at scenes while searching for numbers: Dividing attention multiplies space. *Perception & Psychophysics, 70,* 1337–1349.

Intraub, H., & Dickinson, C. A. (2008). False memory 1/20th of a second later: What the early onset of boundary extension reveals about perception. *Psychological Science, 19,* 1007–1014.

Intraub, H., Gottesman, C. V., & Bills, A. J. (1998). Effects of perceiving and imagining scenes on memory for pictures. *Journal of Experimental Psychology: Learning, Memory & Cognition, 24,* 186–201.

Isen, A. M., Nygren, T. E., & Ashby, F. G. (1988). Influence of positive affect on the subjective utility of gains and losses – It is just not worth the risk. *Journal of Personality and Social Psychology, 55,* 710–717.

Ison, M. J., & Quiroga, R. Q. (2008). Selectivity and invariance for visual object recognition. *Frontiers in Bioscience, 13,* 4889–4903.

Isurin, L., & McDonald, J. L. (2001). Retroactive interference from translation equivalents: Implications for first language forgetting. *Memory & Cognition, 29,* 312–319.

Izard, C. E. (2007). Basic emotions, natural kinds, emotion schemas, and a new paradigm. *Perspective in Psychological Science, 2,* 260–280.

Jack, F., & Hayne, H. (2010). Childhood amnesia: Empirical evidence for a two-stage phenomenon. *Memory, 18,* 831–844.

Jacobs, J. (1887). Experiments in "prehension". *Mind, 12,* 75–79.

Jacobs, N., & Garnham, A. (2007). The role of conversational hand gestures in a narrative task. *Journal of Memory and Language, 56,* 291–303.

Jacoby, L. L., Debner, J. A., & Hay, J. F. (2001). Proactive interference, accessibility bias, and process dissociations: Valid subjective reports of memory. *Journal of Experimental Psychology: Learning, Memory, & Cognition, 27,* 686–700.

Jahn, G., Knauff, M., & Johnson-Laird, P. N. (2007). Preferred mental models in reasoning about spatial relations. *Memory & Cognition, 35,* 2075–2087.

Jain, A. K., & Duin, R. P. W. (2004). Pattern recognition. In R. L. Gregory (Ed.), *The Oxford companion to the mind* (pp. 698–703). New York, NY: Oxford University Press.

Jain, A. K., Feng, J. J., & Nandakumar, K. (2010). Fingerprint matching. *Computer, 43,* 36–44.

James, W. (1890). *Principles of psychology.* New York, NY: Holt.

Janssen, N., Alario, F.-X., & Caramazza, A. (2008). A word-order constraint on phonological activation. *Psychological Science, 19,* 216–220.

Janssen, S. M. J., & Murre, J. M. J. (2008). Reminiscence bump in autobiographical memory: Unexplained by novelty, emotionality, valence or importance of personal events. *Quarterly Journal of Experimental Psychology, 61,* 1847–1860.

Jared, D., Levy, B. A., & Rayner, K. (1999). The role of phonology in the activation of word meanings during reading: Evidence from proof-reading and eye movements. *Journal of Experimental Psychology: General, 128,* 219–264.

Jenkins, R., & Burton, A. M. (2011). Stable face representations. *Philosophical Transactions of the Royal Society B: Biological Sciences, 366,* 1671–1683.

Jiang, Y., Costello, P., Fang, F., Huang, M., & He, S. (2006). A gender- and sexual orientation-dependent spatial attentional effect of invisible images. *Proceedings of the National Academy of Sciences of the United States of America, 103,* 17048–17052.

Johannessen, K. B., & Berntsen, D. (2010). Current concerns in involuntary and voluntary autobiographical memories. *Consciousness and Cognition, 19,* 847–860.

Johnson, M. K., Hashtroudi, S., & Lindsay, D. S. (1993). Source monitoring. *Psychological Bulletin, 114,* 3–28.

Johnson-Laird, P. N. (1983). *Mental models.* Cambridge, UK: Cambridge University Press.

Johnson-Laird, P. N. (2004). Mental models and reasoning. In J. P. Leighton & R. J. Sternberg (Eds.), *The nature of reasoning.* Cambridge, UK: Cambridge University Press.

Johnson-Laird, P. N., Mancini, F., & Gangemi, A. (2006). A hyper-emotion theory of psychological illnesses. *Psychological Review, 113,* 822–841.

Jolij, J., & Lamme, V. A. F. (2005). Repression of unconscious information by conscious processing: Evidence for affective blindsight induced by transcranial magnetic stimulation. *Proceedings of the National Academy of Sciences of the United States of America, 102,* 10747–10751.

Jones, L. L. (2010). Pure mediated priming: A retrospective semantic matching model. *Journal of Experimental Psychology: Learning, Memory, & Cognition, 36,* 135–146.

Jonides, M. G., Lewis, R. L., Nee, D. E., Lustig, C. A., Berman, M. G., & Moore, K. S. (2008). The mind and brain of short-term memory. *Annual Review of Psychology, 59,* 193–224.

Josephs, R. A., Larrick, R. P., Steele, C. M., & Nisbett, R. E. (1992). Protecting the self from the negative consequences of risky decisions. *Journal of Personality and Social Psychology, 62,* 26–37.

Junghaenel, D. U., Smith, J. M., & Santner, L. (2008). Linguistic dimensions of psychopathology: A quantitative analysis. *Journal of Social and Clinical Psychology, 27,* 36–55.

Just, M. A., & Carpenter, P. A. (1992). A capacity theory of comprehension. *Psychological Review, 114,* 678–703.

Juth, P., Lundqvist, D., Karlsson, A., & Öhman, A. (2005). Looking for faces and friends: Perceptual and emotional factors when finding a face in the crowd. *Emotion, 5,* 379–395.

Kahneman, D. (2003). A perspective on judgment and choice: Mapping bounded rationality. *American Psychologist, 58,* 697–720.

Kahneman, D., & Frederick, S. (2005). A model of heuristic judgment. In K. J. Holyoak & R. G. Morrison (Eds.), *The Cambridge handbook of thinking and reasoning.* Cambridge, UK: Cambridge University Press.

Kahneman, D., & Tversky, A. (1984). Choices, values and frames. *American Psychologist, 39,* 341–350.

Kahneman, D., & Tversky, A. (1972). Subjective probability: Judgment of representa tive ness. *Cognitive Psychology, 3,* 430–454.

Kalakoski, V., & Saariluoma, P. (2001). Taxi drivers' exceptional memory of street names. *Memory & Cognition, 29,* 634–638.

Kaliski, S. Z. (2009). 'My brain made me do it!' – How neuroscience may change the insanity defense. *South African Journal of Psychiatry, 15,* 4–6.

Kane, M. J., & Engle, R. W. (2003). Working-memory capacity and the control of attention: The contribution of goal neglect, response competition, and task set to Stroop interference. *Journal of Experimental Psychology: General, 132,* 47–70.

Kanwisher, N., & Yovel, G. (2006). The fusiform face area: A cortical region specialized for the perception of faces. *Philosophical Transactions of the Royal Society B: Biological Sciences, 361,* 2109–2128.

Kaplan, G. A., & Simon, H. A. (1990). In search of insight. *Cognitive Psychology, 22,* 374–419.

Karpicke, J. D., Butler, A.C., & Roediger III, H. L. (2009). Metacognitive strategies in student learning: Do students practise retrieval when they study on their own? *Memory, 17,* 471–479.

Kaufer, D., Hayes, J. R., & Flower, L. S. (1986). Composing written sentences. *Research in the Teaching of English, 20,* 121–140.

Kaup, B., Yaxley, R. H., Madden, C. J., Zwaan, R. A., & Lüdtke, J. (2007). Experiential simulations of negated text information. *Quarterly Journal of Experimental Psychology, 60,* 976–990.

Kay, K. N., Naselaris, T., Prenger, R. J., & Gallant, J. L. (2008). Identifying natural images from human brain activity. *Nature, 452,* 352–355.

Keane, M. (1987). On retrieving analogs when solving problems. *Quarterly Journal of Experimental Psychology, 39A,* 29–41.

Kellogg, R. T. (1988). Attentional overload and writing performance: Effects of rough draft and outline strategies. *Journal of Experimental Psychology: Learning, Memory, & Cognition, 14,* 355–365.

Kellogg, R. T. (1994). *The psychology of writing.* Oxford, UK: Oxford University Press.

Kellogg, R. T. (2001a). Long-term working memory in text production. *Memory & Cognition, 29,* 43–52.

Kellogg, R. T. (2001b). Competition for working memory among writing processes. *American Journal of Psychology, 114,* 175–191.

Kellogg, R. T. (2008). Training writing skills: A cognitive developmental perspective. *Journal of Writing Research, 1,* 1–26.

Kellogg, R. T., & Mueller, S. (1993). Performance amplification and process restructuring in computer-based writing. *International Journal of Man – Machine Studies, 39,* 33–49.

Kellogg, R. T., Olive, T., & Piolat, A. (2007). Verbal, visual, and spatial working memory in written language production. *Acta Psychologica, 124,* 382–397.

Kelly, S. D., Barr, D. J., Church, R. B., & Lynch, K. (1999). Offering a hand to pragmatic understanding: The role of speech and gesture in comprehension and memory. *Journal of Memory and Language, 40,* 577–592.

Kelly, S. D., Creigh, P., & Bartolotti, J. (2010a). Integrating speech and iconic gestures in a Stroop-like task: Evidence for automatic processing. *Journal of Cognitive Neuroscience, 22*, 683–694.

Kelly, S. D., Ozyurek, A., & Maris, E. (2010b). Two sides of the same coin: Speech and gesture mutually interact to enhance comprehension. *Psychological Science, 21*, 260–267.

Kelly, S. W. (2003). A consensus in implicit learning? *Quarterly Journal of Experimental Psychology, 56A*, 1389–1391.

Kemp, R., Towell, N., & Pike, G. (1997). When seeing should not be believing: Photographs, credit cards and fraud. *Applied Cognitive Psychology, 11*, 211–222.

Kendeou, P., Savage, R., & van den Broek, P. (2009). Revisiting the simple view of reading. *British Journal of Educational Psychology, 79*, 353–370.

Kenealy, P. M. (1997). Mood-state-dependent retrieval: The effects of induced mood on memory reconsidered. *Quarterly Journal of Experimental Psychology, 50A*, 290–317.

Keppel, G., & Underwood, B. J. (1962). Proactive inhibition in short-term retention of single items. *Journal of Verbal Learning and Verbal Behavior, 1*, 153–161.

Keren, G., & Schul, Y. (2009). Two is not always better than one: A critical evaluation of two-system theories. *Perspectives on Psychological Science, 4*, 533–550.

Kertesz, A., Jesso, S., Harciarek, M., Blair, M., & McMonagle, P. (2010). What is semantic dementia? A cohort study of diagnostic features and clinical boundaries. *Archives of Neurology, 67*, 483–489.

Key, W. B. (1980). *The clam-plate orgy: And other subliminals the media use to manipulate your behavior.* Englewood Cliffs, NJ: Prentice Hall.

Keysar, B., Barr, D. J., Balin, J. A., & Brauner, J. S. (2000). Taking perspectives in conversation: The role of mutual knowledge in comprehension. *Psychological Science, 11*, 32–38.

Keysar, B., & Henly, A. S. (2002). Speakers' overestimation of their effectiveness. *Psychological Science, 13*, 207–212.

Khetrapal, N. (2010). Load theory of selective attention and the role of perceptual load: Is it time for revision? *European Journal of Cognitive Psychology, 22*, 149–156.

Kim, P. Y., & Mayhorn, C. B. (2008). Exploring students' prospective memory inside and outside the lab. *American Journal of Psychology, 121*, 241–254.

King, W. R., & Dunn, T. M. (2010). Detecting deception in field settings: A review and critique of the criminal justice and psychological literatures. *Policing: An International Journal of Police Strategies & Management, 33*, 305–320.

Kintsch, W. (2000). Metaphor comprehension: A computational theory. *Psychonomic Bulletin & Review, 7*, 257–266.

Kirchhoff, B. A., Schapiro, M. L., & Buckner, R. L. (2005). Orthographic distinctiveness and semantic elaboration provide separate contributions to memory. *Journal of Cognitive Neuroscience, 17*, 1841–1854.

Klahr, D., & Dunbar, K. (1988). Dual-space search during scientific reasoning. *Cognitive Science, 12*, 1–48.

Klahr, D., & Simon, H. A. (2001). What have psychologists (and others) discovered about the process of scientific discovery? *Current Directions in Psychological Science, 10*, 75–79.

Klauer, K. C., & Zhao, Z. (2004). Double dissociations in visual and spatial short-term memory. *Journal of Experimental Psychology: General, 133*, 355–381.

Klein, L., Dubois, J., Mangin, J.-F., Kherif, F., Flandin, G., Poline, J.-B., et al. (2004). Retinopic organization of visual mental images as revealed by functional magnetic resonance imaging. *Cognitive Brain Research, 22*, 26–31.

Klein, S. B., & Kihlstrom, J. F. (1986). Elaboration, organization, and the self-reference effect in memory. *Journal of Experimental Psychology: General, 115*, 26–38.

Klein, S. B., & Lax, M. L. (2010). The unanticipated resilience of trait self-knowledge in the face of neural damage. *Memory, 18*, 918–948.

Knoblich, G., Ohlsson, S., Haider, H., & Rhenius, D. (1999). Constraint relaxation and chunk decomposition in insight. *Journal of Experimental Psychology: Learning, Memory, and Cognition, 25*, 1534–1555.

Knowlton, B. J., & Foerde, K. (2008). Neural representations of nondeclarative memories. *Current Directions in Psychological Science, 17*, 107–111.

Koch, C., & Tsuchiya, N. (2007). Attention and consciousness: Two distinct brain processes. *Trends in Cognitive Sciences, 11*, 16–22.

Koehler, J. J. (1996). The base rate fallacy reconsidered: Descriptive, normative, and methodological challenges. *Behavioral & Brain Sciences, 19*, 1–17.

Koenigsberg, H. W., Fan, J., Ochsner, K. N., Liu, X., Guise, K., Pizzarello, S., et al. (2010). Neural correlates of using distancing to regulate emotional responses to social situations. *Neuropsychologia, 48*, 1813–1822.

Köhnken, G., Milne, R., Memon, A., & Bull, R. (1999). The cognitive interview: A meta-analysis. *Psychology of Crime Law, 5*, 3–27.

Kolko, J. D. (2009). The effects of mobile phones and hands-free laws on traffic fatalities. *Berkeley*

Electronic Journal of Economic Analysis & Policy, 9, No. 10.

Koller, S. M., Drury, C. G., & Schwaninger, A. (2009). Change of search time and non-search time in X-ray baggage screening due to training. *Ergonomics, 52*, 644–656.

Kondo, Y., Suzuki, M., Mugikura, S., Abe, N., Takahashi, S., Iijima, T., et al. (2004). Changes in brain activation associated with use of a memory strategy: A functional MRI study. *NeuroImage, 15*, 1154–1163.

Koole, S. (2009). The psychology of emotion regulation: An integrative review. *Cognition & Emotion, 23*, 4–41.

Kornilova, L. N. (1997). Vestibular function and sensory interaction in altered gravity. *Advances in Space Biological Medicine, 6*, 275–313.

Kosslyn, S. M. (1994). *Image and brain: The resolution of the imagery debate*. Cambridge, MA: MIT Press.

Kosslyn, S. M. (2004). Mental imagery: Depictive accounts. In R. L. Gregory (Ed.), *The Oxford companion to the mind* (pp. 585–587). New York, NY: Oxford University Press.

Kosslyn, S. M. (2005). Mental images and the brain. *Cognitive Neuropsychology, 22*, 333–347.

Kosslyn, S. M., Pascual-Leone, A., Felician, O., Camposano, S., Keenan, J. P., Thompson, W. L., et al. (1999). The role of Area 17 in visual imagery: Convergent evidence from PET and rTMS. *Science, 284*, 167–170.

Kosslyn, S. M., & Thompson, W. L. (2003). When is early visual cortex activated during visual mental imagery? *Psychological Bulletin, 129*, 723–746.

Koster, E. H. W., Baert, S., Bockstaele, M., & De Raedt, R. (2010). Attentional retraining procedures: Manipulating early or late components of attentional bias? *Emotion, 10*, 230–236.

Kraljic, T., & Brennan, S. E. (2005). Prosodic disambiguation of syntactic structure: For the speaker or for the addressee? *Cognitive Psychology, 50*, 194–231.

Krauss, S., & Wang, X. T. (2003). The psychology of the Monty Hall problem: Discovering psychological mechanisms for solving a tenacious brain teaser. *Journal of Experimental Psychology: General, 132*, 3–22.

Kreiner, H., Sturt, P., & Garrod, S. (2008). Processing definitional and stereotypical gender in reference resolution: Evidence from eye-movements. *Journal of Memory and Language, 58*, 239–261.

Króliczak, G., Heard, P., Goodale, M. A., & Gregory, R. L. (2006). Dissociation of perception and action unmasked by the hollow-face illusion. *Brain Research, 1080*, 9–16.

Krupinski, E. A., Graham, A. R., & Weinstein, R. S. (2013). Characterising the development of visual search expertise in pathology residents viewing whole slide images. *Human Pathology, 44*, 357–364.

Krupinsky, E. A., Tillack, A. A., Richter, L., Henderson, J. T., Bhattacharyya, A. K., Scott, K. M, et al. (2006). Eye-movement study and human performance using telepathology and differences with experience. *Human Pathology, 37*, 1543–1556.

Krynski, T. R., & Tenenbaum, J. B. (2007). The role of causality in judgment under uncertainty. *Journal of Experimental Psychology: General, 136*, 430–450.

Kubovy, M., & van den Berg, M. (2008). The whole is greater than the sum of its parts: A probabilistic model of grouping by proximity and similarity in regular patterns. *Psychological Review, 115*, 131–154.

Kuefner, D., Jacques, C., Prieto, E. A., & Rossion, B. (2010). Electrophysiological correlates of the composite face illusion: Disentangling perceptual and decisional components of holistic face processing in the human brain. *Brain and Cognition, 74*, 225–238.

Kuiper, K. (1996). *Smooth talkers*. Mahwah, NJ: Lawrence Erlbaum.

Kulatunga-Moruzi, C., Brooks, L. R., & Norman, G. R. (2004). Using comprehensive feature lists to bias medical diagnosis. *Journal of Experimental Psychology: Learning, Memory, and Cognition, 30*, 563–572.

Kulkarni, D., & Simon, H. A. (1988). The processes of scientific discovery – The strategy of experimentation. *Cognitive Science, 12*, 139–175.

Kunar, M. A., Carter, R., Cohen, M., & Horowitz, T. S. (2008). Telephone conversation impairs sustained visual attention via a central bottleneck. *Psychonomic Bulletin & Review, 15*, 1135–1140.

Kundel, H. L., Nodine, C. F., Conant, E. F., & Weinstein, S. P. (2007). Holistic component of image perception in mammogram interpretation: Gaze-tracking study. *Radiology, 242*, 396–402.

Kuppens, P., van Mechelen, I., Smits, D. J. M., & De Broeck, P. (2003). The appraisal basis of anger: Specificity, necessity and sufficiency of components. *Emotion, 3*, 254–269.

Kurt, S., Deutscher, A., Crook, J. M., Ohl, F. W., Budinger, E., Moeller, C. K., et al. (2008). Auditory cortical contrast enhancing by global winner-take-all inhibitory interactions. *PLoS One, 3*, e1735.

Kurtz, K. J., & Loewenstein, J. (2007). Converging on a new role for analogy in problem solving and retrieval: When two problems are better than one. *Memory & Cognition, 35*, 334–341.

Kvavilashvili, L., & Fisher, L. (2007). Is time-based prospective remembering mediated by self-initiated rehearsals? Role of incidental cues, ongoing activity. age, and motivation. *Journal of Experimental Psychology: General, 136*, 112–132.

LaBar, K. S., & Cabeza, R. (2006). Cognitive neuroscience of emotional memory. *Nature Reviews Neuroscience, 7*, 54–64.

Lamme, V. A. F. (2003). Why visual attention and awareness are different. *Trends in Cognitive Sciences, 7*, 12–18.

Lampinen, J. M., Copeland, S. M., & Neuschatz, J. S. (2001). Recollections of things schematic: Room schemas revisited. *Journal of Experimental Psychology: Learning, Memory, & Cognition, 27*, 1211–1222.

Lamy, D., Salti, M., & Bar-Haim, Y. (2009). Neural correlates of subjective awareness and unconscious processing: An ERP study. *Journal of Cognitive Neuroscience, 21*, 1435–1446.

Landman, R., Spekreijse, H., & Lamme, V. A. F. (2003). Large capacity storage of integrated objects before change blindness. *Vision Research, 43*, 149–164.

Langenburg, G., Champod, C., & Wertheim, P. (2009). Testing for potential contextual bias during the verification stage of the ACE-V methodology when conducting fingerprint comparisons. *Journal of Forensic Sciences, 54*, 571–582.

Larsen, J. D., Baddeley, A., & Andrade, J. (2000). Phonological similarity and the irrelevant speech effect: Implications for models of short-term memory. *Memory, 8*, 145–157.

Latorella, K. A. (1998). Effects of modality on interrupted flight deck performance: Implications for data link. In *Proceedings of the human factors and ergonomics society 42nd annual meeting* (Vols. 1 and 2, pp. 87–91). Chicago, IL: HFES.

Lavric, A., Forstmeier, S., & Rippon, G. (2000). Differences in working memory involvement in analytical and creative tasks: An ERP study. *NeuroReport, 11*, 1613–1618.

Leahey, T. H. (1992). The mythical revolutions of American psychology. *American Psychologist, 47*, 308–318.

Leahey, T. H. (2003). Cognition and learning. In D. F. Freedheim (Ed.), *Handbook of psychology, Vol. 1: The history of psychology* (pp. 109–133). Hoboken, NJ: Wiley.

Lee, A. C. H., Graham, K. S., Simons, J. S., Hodges, J. R., Owen, A. M., & Patterson, K. (2002). Regional brain activations differ for semantic features but not for categories. *NeuroReport, 13*, 1497–1501.

Lehle, C., Steinhauser, M., & Hubner, R. (2009). Serial or parallel processing in dual tasks: what is more effortful? *Psychophysiology, 46*, 502–509.

Lench, H. C., & Levine, L. J. (2005). Effects of fear on risk and control judgments and memory: Implications for health promotion messages. *Cognition & Emotion, 19*, 1049–1069.

Lenton, A. P., & Stewart, A. (2008). Changing her ways: The number of options and mate-standard strength impact mate choice strategy and satisfaction. *Judgment and Decision Making Journal, 3*, 501–511.

LePort, A. K. R., Mattfield, A. T., Dickinson-Anson, H., Fallon, J. H., Stark, C. E. L., Kruggel, F., Cahill, L., & McGaugh, J. L. (2012). Behavioural and neuroanatomical investigation of highly superior autobiographical memory. *Neurobiology of Learning and Memory, 98*, 78–92.

Lerner, J. S., Goldberg, J. H., & Tetlock, P. E. (1998). Sober second thought: The effects of accountability, anger, and authoritarianism on attributions of responsibility. *Personality and Social Psychology Bulletin, 24*, 563–574.

Lerner, J. S., Gonzalez, R. M., Small, D. A., & Fischhoff, B. (2003). Effects of fear and anger on perceived risks of terrorism: A national field experiment. *Psychological Science, 14*, 144–150.

Lerner, J. S., & Keltner, D. (2001). Fear, anger, and risk. *Journal of Personality and Social Psychology, 81*, 146–159.

Lerner, J. S., & Tiedens, L. Z. (2006). Portrait of the angry decision maker: How appraisal tendencies shape anger's influence on cognition. *Journal of Behavioral Decision Making, 19*, 115–137.

Lescroart, M. D., Biederman, I., Yue, X. M., & Davidoff, J. (2010). A cross-cultural study of the representation of shape: Sensitivity to generalized cone dimensions. *Visual Cognition, 18*, 50–66.

Levelt, W. J. M., Roelofs, A., & Meyer, A. S. (1999). A theory of lexical access in speech production. *Behavioral and Brain Sciences, 22*, 1–38.

Levin, D. T., Drivdahl, S. B., Momen, N., & Beck, M. R. (2002). False predictions about the detectability of visual changes: The role of beliefs about attention, memory, and the continuity of attended objects in causing change blindness blindness. *Consciousness and Cognition, 11*, 507–527.

Levin, D. T., & Simons, D. J. (1997). Failure to detect changes to attended objects in motion pictures. *Psychonomic Bulletin and Review, 4*, 501–506.

Levine, L. J., & Edelstein, R. S. (2009). Emotion and memory narrowing: A review and goal-relevance approach. *Cognition & Emotion, 23*, 833–875.

Levine, M. (1971). Hypothesis theory and nonlearning despite ideal S – R reinforcement contingencies. *Psychological Review, 78*, 130–140.

Levy, C. M., & Ransdell, S. E. (1995). Is writing as difficult as it seems? *Memory & Cognition, 23*, 767–779.

Levy, D. M., & Ransdell, S. E. (2001). Writing with concurrent memory loads. In T. Oliver & C. M. Levy (Eds.), *Contemporary tools and techniques for studying writing*. Dordrecht, The Netherlands: Kluwer Academic Publishers.

Levy, J., Pashler, H., & Boer, E. (2006). Central interference in driving: Is there any stopping the psychological refractory period? *Psychological Science, 17*, 228–235.

Liberman, A. M., Cooper, F. S., Shankweiler, D. S., & Studdert-Kennedy, M. (1967). Perception of the speech code. *Psychological Review, 74*, 431–461.

Libet, B., Gleason, C. A., Wright, E. W., & Pearl, D. K. (1983). Time of conscious intention to act in relation to onset of cerebral activity (readiness potential): The unconscious initiation of a freely voluntary act. *Brain, 106*, 623–642.

Lichtenstein, S., Slovic, P., Fischhoff, B., Layman, M., & Coombs, J. (1978). Judged frequency of lethal events. *Journal of Experimental Psychology: Human Learning and Memory, 4*, 551–578.

Lief, H., & Fetkewicz, J. (1995). Retractors of false memories: The evolution of pseudo-memories. *Journal of Psychiatry & Law, 23*, 411–436.

Lin, L. (2009). Breadth-biased versus focused cognitive control in media multitasking behaviors. *Proceedings of the National Association of Sciences of the United States of America, 106*, 15521–15522.

Lindholm, T., & Christianson, S.-A. (1998). Intergroup biases and eyewitness testimony. *Journal of Social Psychology, 138*, 710–723.

Lindsay, D. S., Allen, B. P., Chan, J. C. K., & Dahl, L. C. (2004). Eyewitness suggestibility and source similarity: Intrusions of details from one event into memory reports of another event. *Journal of Memory and Language, 50*, 96–111.

Linkovski, O., Kalanthroff, E., Henik, A., & Anholt, G. (2013). Did I turn off the stove? Good inhibitory control can protect from influences of repeated checking. *Journal of Behavior Therapy and Experimental Psychiatry, 44*, 30–36.

Lippa, R. A., Collaer, M. L., & Peters, M. (2010). Sex differences in mental rotation and line angle judgments are positively associated with gender equality and economic development across 53 nations. *Archives of Sexual Behavior, 39*, 990–997.

Litvak, P. M., Lerner, J. S., Tiedens, L. Z., & Shonk, K. (2010). Fuel in the fire: How anger impacts judgment and decision-making. In M. Potegal, G. Stemmler, & C. Spielberger (Eds.), *International handbook of anger: Constituent and concomitant biological, psychological, and social processes* (pp. 287–310). New York, NY: Springer.

Liu, L., Uttal, D., & Newcomb, N. (2008). *A meta-analysis of training effects on spatial skills: What works, for whom, why and for how long?* Paper presented at the Conference on Research Training in Spatial Intelligence, Evanston, IL.

Locke, S., & Kellar, L. (1973). Categorical perception in a nonlinguistic mode. *Cortex, 9*, 355–369.

Loftus, E. F., & Davis, D. (2006). Recovered memories. *Annual Review of Clinical Psychology, 2*, 469–498.

Loftus, E. F., Loftus, G. R., & Messo, J. (1987). Some facts about "weapons focus". *Law and Human Behavior, 11*, 55–62.

Loftus, E. F., & Palmer, J. C. (1974). Reconstruction of automobile destruction: An example of the interaction between language and memory. *Journal of Verbal Learning and Verbal Behavior, 13*, 585–589.

Loftus, E. F., & Zanni, G. (1975). Eyewitness testimony – Influence of wording of a question. *Bulletin of the Psychonomic Society, 5*, 86–88.

Logie, R. H. (1999). State of the art: Working memory. *The Psychologist, 12*, 174–178.

Logie, R. H., Baddeley, A. D., Mane, A., Donchin, E., & Sheptak, R. (1989). Working memory and the analysis of a complex skill by secondary task methodology. *Acta Psychologica, 71*, 53–87.

Logie, R. H., Del Sala, S., Wynn, V., & Baddeley, A. D. (2000). Visual similarity effects in immediate verbal serial recall. *The Quarterly Journal of Experimental Psychology: Section A, 53*(3), 626–646.

Logie, R. H., & Della Sala, S. (2005). *Disorders of visuo-spatial working memory*. New York, NY: Cambridge University Press.

Logie, R. H., & van der Meulen, M. (2009). Fragmenting and integrating visuo-spatial working memory. In J. R. Brockmole (Ed.), *Representing the visual world in memory*. Hove, UK: Psychology Press.

Loukopoulos, L. D., Dismukes, R. K., & Barshi, I. (2009). *The multitasking myth: Handling complexity in real-world operations*. Burlington, VT: Ashgate.

Loverock, D. S. (2007). Object superiority as a function of object coherence and task difficulty. *American Journal of Psychology, 120*, 565–591.

Luchins, A. S. (1942). Mechanization in problem solving: The effect of Einstellung. *Psychological Monographs, 54*, 248.

Luchins, A. S., & Luchins, E. H. (1959). *Rigidity of behavior*. Eugene, OR: University of Oregon.

Luria, A. (1968). *The mind of a mnemonist*. New York, NY: Basic Books.

Lustig, C., & Hasher, L. (2001). Implicit memory is not immune to interference. *Psychological Bulletin, 127*, 618–628.

Lustig, C., Konkel, A., & Jacoby, L. L. (2004). Which route to recovery? Controlled retrieval and accessibility bias in retroactive interference. *Psychological Science, 15,* 729–735.

Lynch, E. B., Coley, J. D., & Medin, D. L. (2000). Tall is typical: Central tendency, ideal dimensions, and graded category structure among tree experts and novices. *Memory & Cognition, 28,* 41–50.

MacDonald, A. W., Cohen, J. D., Stenger, V. A., & Carter, C. S. (2000). Dissociating the role of the dorsolateral prefrontal cortex and anterior cingulate cortex in cognitive control. *Science, 288,* 1835–1838.

MacDonald, M. C., Pearlmutter, N. J., & Seidenberg, M. S. (1994). Lexical nature of syntactic ambiguity resolution. *Psychological Review, 101,* 676–703.

MacGregor, J. N., & Cunningham, J. B. (2008). Rebus puzzles as insight problems. *Behavior Research Methods, 40,* 263–268.

MacGregor, J. N., & Cunningham, J. B. (2009). The effects of number and level of restructuring in insight problem solving. *Journal of Problem Solving, 2,* 130–141.

MacGregor, J. N., Ormerod, T. C., & Chronicle, E. P. (2001). Information processing and insight: A process model of performance on the nine-dot and related problems. *Journal of Experimental Psychology: Learning, Memory, and Cognition, 27,* 176–201.

Mack, M. L., Gauthier, I., Sadr, J., & Palmeri, T. J. (2008). Object detection and basic-level categorization: Sometimes you know it is there before you know what it is. *Psychonomic Bulletin & Review, 15,* 28–35.

Mackintosh, N. J. (1998). *IQ and human intelligence.* Oxford, UK: Oxford University Press.

MacLeod, C. M. (2005). The Stroop task in cognitive research. In A. Wenzel & D. C. Rubin (Eds.), *Cognitive methods and their application to clinical research* (pp. 17–40). Washington, DC: American Psychological Association.

MacLeod, C., Rutherford, E., Campbell, L., Ebsworthy, G., & Holker, L. (2002). Selective attention and emotional vulnerability: Assessing the causal basis of their association through the experimental manipulation of attentional bias. *Journal of Abnormal Psychology, 111,* 107–123.

Macpherson, R., & Stanovich, K. E. (2007). Cognitive ability, thinking dispositions, and instructional set as predictors of critical thinking. *Learning and Individual Differences, 17,* 115–127.

Macrae, C. N., & Bodenhausen, G. V. (2000). Social cognition: Thinking categorically about others. *Annual Review of Psychology, 51,* 93–120.

Macrae, C. N., Milne, A. B., & Bodenhausen, G. V. (1994). Stereotypes as energy-saving devices: A peak inside the cognitive toolbox. *Journal of Personality and Social Psychology, 66,* 37–47.

Maguire, E. A., Nannery, R., & Spiers, H. J. (2006). Navigation around London by a taxi driver with bilateral hippocampal lesions. *Brain, 129,* 2894–2907.

Maier, N. R. F. (1931). Reasoning in humans II: The solution of a problem and its appearance in consciousness. *Journal of Comparative Psychology, 12,* 181–194.

Mandel, D. R. (2005). Are risk assessments of a terrorist attack coherent? *Journal of Experimental Psychology: Applied, 11,* 277–288.

Maner, J. K., Richey, J. A., Cromer, K., Mallott, M., Lejuez, C. W., Joiner, T. E., et al. (2007). Dispositional anxiety and risk-avoidant decision-making. *Personality and Individual Differences, 42,* 665–675.

Manktelow, K. I. (1999). *Reasoning and thinking.* Hove, UK: Psychology Press.

Mann, S. A., Vrij, A., Fisher, R. P., & Robinson, M. (2008). See no lies, hear no lies: Differences in discrimination accuracy and response bias when watching or listening to police suspect interviews. *Applied Cognitive Psychology, 22,* 1062–1071.

Manns, J. R., Hopkins, R. O., & Squire, L. R. (2003). Semantic memory and the human hippocampus. *Neuron, 38,* 127–133.

Marian, V., & Kaushanskaya, M. (2007). Language context guides memory content. *Psychonomic Bulletin & Review, 14,* 925–933.

Marozeau, J., Innes-Brown, H., Grayden, D. B., Burkitt, A. N., & Blamey, P. J. (2010). The effect of visual cues on auditory stream segregation in musicians and non-musicians. *Public Library of Science One, 5,* e11297.

Marsh, E. J. (2007). Retelling is not the same as recalling – Implications for memory. *Current Directions in Psychological Science, 16,* 16–20.

Marsh, E. J., & Tversky, B. (2004). Spinning the stories of our lives. *Applied Cognitive Psychology, 18,* 491–503.

Martin, A., & Caramazza, A. (2003). Neuropsychological and neuroimaging perspectives on conceptual knowledge: An introduction. *Cognitive Neuropsychology, 20,* 195–221.

Martin, A., & Chao, L. L. (2001). Semantic memory and the brain: Structure and processes. *Current Opinion in Neurobiology, 11,* 194–201.

Martin, R. C., Crowther, J. E., Knight, M., Tamborello, F. P., & Yang, C. L. (2010). Planning in sentence production: Evidence for the phrase as a default planning scope. *Cognition, 116,* 177–192.

Martin, R. C., Miller, M., & Vu. H. (2004). Lexical–semantic retention and speech production: Further evidence from normal and brain-damaged participants for a phrasal scope of planning. *Cognitive Neuropsychology, 21,* 625–644.

Martinez, A., Anllo-Vento, L., Sereno, M. I., Frank, L. R., Buxton, R. B., Dubowitz, D. J., et al. (1999). Involvement of striate and extrastriate visual cortical areas in spatial attention. *Nature Neuroscience, 4,* 364–369.

Marzi, C. A., Smania, N., Martini, M. C., Gambina, G., Tomelleri, G., Palamara, A., et al. (1996). Implicit redundant-targets effect in visual extinction. *Neuropsychologia, 34,* 9–22.

Marzi, C. A., Girelli, M., Natale, E., & Miniussi, C. (2001). What exactly is extinguished in unilateral visual extinction? *Neuropsychologia, 39,* 1354–1366.

Massen, C., & Vaterrodt-Plünnecke, B. (2006). The role of proactive interference in mnemonic techniques. *Memory, 14,* 189–196.

Massen, C., Vaterrodt-Plünnecke, B., Krings, L., & Hilbig, B. E. (2009). Effects of instruction on learners' ability to generate an effective pathway in the method of loci. *Memory, 17,* 724–731.

Mather, G. (2009). *Foundations of sensation and perception* (2nd ed.). New York: Psychology Press.

Mathews, A., & MacLeod, C. (2005). Cognitive vulnerability to emotional disorders. *Annual Review of Clinical Psychology, 1,* 167–195.

Matlin, M. W. (2009). *Cognitive psychology: International student version* (7th ed.). New York, NY: Wiley.

Mattys, S. L., Brooks, J., & Cooke, M. (2009). Recognizing speech under a processing load: Dissociating energetic from informational factors. *Cognitive Psychology, 59,* 203–243.

Mattys, S. L., & Liss, J. M. (2008). On building models of spoken-word recognition: When there is as much to learn from natural "oddities" as artificial normality. *Perception & Psychophysics, 70,* 1235–1242.

Mattys, S. L., White, L., & Melhorn, J. F. (2005). Integration of multiple speech segmentation cues: A hierarchical framework. *Journal of Experimental Psychology: General, 134,* 477–500.

Matuszewski, V., Piolino, P., Belliard, S., de la Sayette, V., Laisney, M., Lalevée, C., et al. (2009). Patterns of autobiographical memory impairment according to disease severity in semantic dementia. *Cortex, 45,* 456–472.

Maule, A. J., & Hodgkinson, G. P. (2002). Heuristics, biases and strategic decision making. *The Psychologist, 15,* 69–71.

Maylor, E. A., & Logie, R. H. (2010). A large-scale comparison of prospective and retrospective memory development from childhood to middle age. *Quarterly Journal of Experimental Psychology, 63,* 442–451.

Mazzone, M., & Lalumera, E. (2010). Concepts: Stored or created? *Minds and Machines, 20,* 47–68.

McCaffrey, T. (2012). Innovation relies on the obscure: A key to solving the classic problem of functional fixedness. *Psychological Science, 23,* 215–218.

McCarley, J. S., Kramer, A. F., Wickens, C. D., & Boot, W. R. (2004). Visual skills in airport-security screening. *Psychological Science, 15,* 302–306.

McCarthy, R. A., Kopelman, M. D., & Warrington, E. K. (2005). Remembering and forgetting of semantic knowledge in amnesia: A 16-year follow-up investigation of RFR. *Neuropsychologia, 43,* 356–372.

McCarthy, R. A., & Warrington, E. K. (1984). A two-route model of speech production. *Brain, 107,* 463–485.

McCauley, C., & Stitt, C. L. (1978). An individual and quantitative measure of stereotypes. *Journal of Personality and Social Psychology, 36,* 929–940.

McClelland, J. L. (1991). Stochastic interactive processes and the effect of context on perception. *Cognitive Psychology, 23,* 1–44.

McClelland, J. L., & Elman, J. L. (1986). The TRACE model of speech perception. *Cognitive Psychology, 18,* 1–86.

McClelland, J. L., Rumelhart, D. E., & The PDP Research Group. (1986). *Parallel distributed processing: Vol. 2. Psychological and biological models.* Cambridge, MA: MIT Press.

McCloskey, M. E., & Glucksberg, S. (1978). Natural categories: Well defined or fuzzy sets? *Memory & Cognition, 26,* 121–134.

McDonald, J. L. (2008). Differences in the cognitive demands of word order, plural, and subject – verb agreement constructions. *Psychonomic Bulletin & Review, 15,* 980–984.

McEvoy, S. P., Stevenson, M. R., & Woodward, M. (2007). The contribution of passengers versus mobile use to motor vehicle crashes resulting in hospital attendance. *Accident Analysis and Prevention, 39,* 1170–1176.

McGlone, M. S., & Manfredi, D. (2001). Topic – vehicle interaction in metaphor comprehension. *Memory & Cognition, 29,* 1209–1219.

McGugin, R. W., & Gauthier, I. (2010). Perceptual expertise with objects predicts another hallmark of face perception. *Journal of Vision, 10* (4), Article No. 15.

McGurk, H., & MacDonald, J. (1976). Hearing lips and seeing voices. *Nature, 264,* 746–748.

McKone, E., Kanwisher, N., & Duchaine, B. C. (2007). Can generic expertise explain special processing for faces? *Trends in Cognitive Sciences*, 11, 8–15.

McKoon, G., & Ratcliff, R. (1992). Inference during reading. *Psychological Review*, 99, 440–466.

McLaughlin, K., Remy, M., & Schmidt, H. G. (2008). Is analytic information processing a feature of expertise in medicine? *Advances in Health Sciences Education*, 13, 123–128.

McMurray, B., Dennhardt, J. L., & Struck-Marcell, A. (2008). Context effects on musical chord categorization: Different forms of top-down feedback in speech and music? *Cognitive Science*, 32, 893–920.

McNally, R. J., & Geraerts, E. (2009). A new solution to the recovered memory debate. *Perspectives on Psychological Science*, 4, 126–134.

McNamara, D. S., & Magliano, J. (2009). Toward a comprehensive model of comprehension. *Psychology of Learning and Motivation*, 51, 297–384.

McNamara, T. P. (1992). Priming and constraints it places on theories of memory and retrieval. *Psychological Review*, 99, 650–662.

McPherson, F. (2004). *The memory key: Unlock the secrets to remembering*. New York, NY: Barnes & Noble.

McQueen, J. M. (1991). The influence of the lexicon on phonetic categorization: Stimulus quality in word-final ambiguity. *Journal of Experimental Psychology: Human Perception & Performance*, 17, 433–443.

McRae, K., Hughes, B., Chopra, S., Gabrieli, J. D. E., Gross, J. J., & Ochsner, K. N. (2010). Neural systems supporting the control of affective and cognitive conflicts. *Journal of Cognitive Neuroscience*, 22, 248–262.

McWilliam, L., Schepman, A., & Rodway, P. (2009). The linguistic status of text message abbreviations: An exploration using a Stroop task. *Computers in Human Behavior*, 25, 970–974.

Medin, D. L., & Atran, S. (2004). The native mind: Biological categorization and reasoning in development and across cultures. *Psychological Review*, 111, 960–983.

Megreya, A. M., White, D., & Burton, A. M. (2011). The other-race effect does not rely on memory: Evidence from a matching task. *Quarterly Journal of Experimental Psychology*, 64, 1473–1483.

Meister, I. G., Wilson, S. M., Delieck, C., Wu, A. D., & Iacobini, M. (2007). The essential role of premotor cortex in speech perception. *Current Biology*, 17, 1692–1696.

Melo, M., Scarpin, D. J., Amaro, E., Passos, R. B. D., Sato, J. R., Friston, K. J., & Price, C. J. (2012). How doctors generate diagnostic hypotheses: A study of radiological diagnosis with functional magnetic resonance imaging. *PLOS ONE*, 6(12), e28752.

Memon, A., Meissner, C. A., & Fraser, J. (2010). The cognitive interview: A meta-analytic review and study space analysis of the past 25 years. *Psychology, Public Policy and Law*, 16, 340–372.

Memon, A., Zaragoza, M., Clifford, B. R., & Kidd, L. (2009). Inoculation or antidote? The effects of cognitive interview timing on false memory for forcibly fabricated events. *Law and Human Behavior*, 34, 105–117.

Menchaca-Brandan, M. A., Liu, A. M., Oman, C. M., & Natapoff, A. (2007). Influence of perspective-taking and mental rotation abilities in space teleoperation. *Proceedings of the 2007 ACM Conference on human–robot interaction*. Washington, DC, March 9–11, pp. 271–278.

Menneer, T., Cave, K. R., & Donnelly, N. (2009). The cost of search for multiple targets: Effects of practice and target similarity. *Journal of Experimental Psychology: Applied*, 15, 125–139.

Mercier, H., & Sperber, D. (2011). Why do humans reason? Arguments for an argumentative theory. *Behavioral and Brain Sciences*, 34, 57–111.

Merikle, P. M., Smilek, D., & Eastwood, J. D. (2001). Perception without awareness: Perspectives from cognitive psychology. *Cognition*, 79, 115–134.

Metcalfe, J., & Kornell, N. (2007). Principles of cognitive science in education: The effects of generation, errors, and feedback. *Psychonomic Bulletin & Review*, 14, 225–229.

Metcalfe, J., & Wiebe, D. (1987). Intuition in insight and noninsight problem solving. *Memory & Cognition*, 15, 238–246.

Meteyard, L., & Patterson, K. (2009). The relation between content and structure in language production: An analysis of speech errors in semantic dementia. *Brain and Language*, 110, 121–134.

Meulemans, T., & Van der Linden, M. (2003). Implicit learning of complex information in amnesia. *Brain and Cognition*, 52, 250–257.

Meyer, A. S. (1996). Lexical access in phrase and sentence production: Results from picture–word interference experiments. *Journal of Memory and Language*, 35, 477–496.

Meyer, A. S., & Damian, M. F. (2007). Activation of distractor names in the picture–picture interference paradigm. *Memory & Cognition*, 35, 494–503.

Meyer, D. E., & Schvaneveldt, R. W. (1976). Meaning, memory structure, and mental processes. *Science*, 192, 27–33.

Miles, C., & Hardman, E. (1998). State-dependent memory produced by aerobic exercise. *Ergonomics*, 41, 20–26.

Miller, G. A. (1956). The magical number seven, plus or minus two: Some limits on our capacity for processing information. *Psychological Review*, *63*, 81–97.

Milner, A. D., & Goodale, M. A. (1998). The visual brain in action. *Psyche*, *4*, 1–14.

Milner, A. D., & Goodale, M. A. (2008). Two visual systems re-viewed. *Neuropsychologia*, *46*, 774–785.

Miranda, R., & Kihlstrom, J. F. (2005). Mood congruence in childhood and recent autobiographical memory. *Cognition & Emotion*, *19*, 981–998.

Mirman, D., McClelland, J. L., Holt, L. L., & Magnuson, J. S. (2008). Effects of attention on the strength of lexical influences on speech perception: Behavioral experiments and computational mechanisms. *Cognitive Science*, *32*, 398–417.

Mitchell, D. B. (2006). Nonconscious priming after 17 years. *Psychological Science*, *17*, 925–929.

Mitchell, K. J., Johnson, M. K., & Mather, M. (2003). Monitoring and suggestibility to misinformation: Adult age-related differences. *Applied Cognitive Psychology*, *17*, 107–119.

Mitterer, H., & de Ruiter, J. P. (2008). Recalibrating color categories using world knowledge. *Psychological Science*, *19*, 629–634.

Miyake, A., Friedman, N. P., Emerson, M. J., Witzki, A. H., Howerter, A., & Wager, T. (2000). The unity and diversity of executive functions and their contributions to complex "frontal lobe" tasks: A latent variable analysis. *Cognitive Psychology*, *41*, 49–100.

Moè, A. (2009). Are males always better than females in mental rotation? Exploring a gender belief explanation. *Learning and Individual Differences*, *19*, 21–27.

Mol, L., Krahmer, E., Maes, A., & Swerts, M. (2009). The communicative import of gestures: Evidence from a comparative analysis of human – human and human – machine interactions. *Gesture*, *9*, 97–126.

Molholm, S., Martinez, A., Shpanker, M., & Foxe, J. J. (2007). Object-based attention is multisensory: Co-activation of an object's representations in ignored sensory modalities. *European Journal of Neuroscience*, *26*, 499–509.

Moons, W. G., & Mackie, D. M. (2008). Thinking straight while seeing red: The influence of anger on information processing. *Personality and Social Psychology Bulletin*, *33*, 706–721.

Moors, A., & de Houwer, J. (2006). Automaticity: A theoretical and conceptual analysis. *Psychological Bulletin*, *132*, 297–326.

Morawetz, C., Holz, P., Baudewig, J., Treue, S., & Dechent, P. (2007). Split of attentional resources in human visual cortex. *Visual Neuroscience*, *24*, 817–826.

Moray, N. (1959). Attention in dichotic listening: Affective cues and the influence of instructions. *Quarterly Journal of Experimental Psychology*, *11*, 56–60.

Moro, V., Berlucchi, G., Lerch, J., Tomaiuolo, F., & Aglioti, S. M. (2008). Selective deficit of mental visual imagery with intact primary visual cortex and visual perception. *Cortex*, *44*, 109–118.

Morris, C. D., Bransford, J. D., & Franks, J. J. (1977). Levels of processing versus transfer appropriate processing. *Journal of Verbal Learning and Verbal Behavior*, *16*, 519–533.

Morris, P. E., Fritz, C. O., Jackson, L., Nichol, E., & Roberts, E. (2005). Strategies for learning proper names: Expanding retrieval practice, meaning and imagery. *Applied Cognitive Psychology*, *19*, 779–798.

Morris, P. E., Jones, S., & Hampson, P. (1978). An imagery mnemonic for the learning of people's names. *British Journal of Psychology*, *69*, 335–336.

Morris, P. E., & Reid, R. L. (1970). Repeated use of mnemonic imagery. *Psychonomic Science*, *20*, 337–338.

Morrison, R. G., Holyoak, K. J., & Truong, B. (2001). Working-memory modularity in analogical reasoning. In J. D. Moore & K. Stenning (Eds.), *Proceedings of the twenty-third annual conference of the cognitive science society*. Mahwah, NJ: Lawrence Erlbaum.

Moscovitch, M. (2008). Commentary: A perspective on prospective memory. In M. Kliegel, M. A. McDaniel, & G. O. Einstein (Eds.), *Prospective memory: Cognitive, neuroscience, developmental, and applied perspectives*. New York, NY: Lawrence Erlbaum.

Moscovitch, M., Nadel, L., Winocur, G., Gilboa, A., & Rosenbaum, R. S. (2006). The cognitive neuroscience of remote episodic, semantic and spatial memory. *Current Opinion in Neurobiology*, *16*, 179–190.

Moscovitch, M., Winocur, G., & Behrmann, M. (1997). What is special about face recognition? Nineteen experiments on a person with visual object agnosia but normal face recognition. *Journal of Cognitive Neuroscience*, *9*, 555–604.

Motley, M. T. (1980). Verification of "Freudian slips" and semantic prearticulatory editing via laboratory-induced spoonerisms. In V. A. Fromkin (Ed.), *Errors in linguistic performance: Slips of the tongue, ear, pen, and hand*. New York, NY: Academic Press.

Mottaghy, F. M. (2006). Interfering with working memory in humans. *Neuroscience*, *139*, 85–90.

Möttönen, R., & Watkins, K. E. (2009). Motor representations of articulators contribute to categorical perception of speech sounds. *Journal of Neuroscience, 29*, 9819–9825.

Moulton, S. T., & Kosslyn, S. M. (2009). Imagining predictions: Mental imagery as mental emulation. *Philosophical Transactions of the Royal Society B: Biological Sciences, 364*, 1273–1280.

Mueller, S. T., Seymour, T. L., Kieras, D. E., & Meyer, D. E. (2003). Theoretical implications of articulatory duration, phonological similarity, and phonological complexity in verbal working memory. *Journal of Experimental Psychology: Learning, Memory & Cognition, 29*, 1353–1380.

Müller, N. G., Bartelt, O. A., Donner, T. H., Villringer, A., & Brandt, S. A. (2003). A physiological correlate of the "zoom lens" of visual attention. *Journal of Neuroscience, 23*, 3561–2565.

Munro, G. D., & Stansbury, J. A. (2009). The dark side of self-affirmation: Confirmation bias and illusory correlation in response to threatening information. *Personality and Social Psychology Bulletin, 35*, 1143–1153.

Münsterberg, H. (1908). *On the witness stand: Essays on psychology and crime*. New York: Doubleday.

Murphy, G., & Kovach, J. K. (1972). *Historical introduction to modern psychology*. London, UK: Routledge & Kegan Paul.

Murray, J. D., & Burke, K. A. (2003). Activation and encoding of predictive inferences: The role of reading skill. *Discourse Processes, 35*, 81–102.

Murty, V. P., Ritchey, M., Adcock, R. A., & LaBar, K. S. (2010). fMRI studies of successful emotional memory encoding: A quantitative meta-analysis. *Neuropsychologia, 48*, 3459–3469.

Mustanski, B. (2007). The influence of state and trait affect on HIV risk behaviors: A daily diary study of MSM. *Health Psychology, 26*, 618–626.

Muter, P. (1978). Recognition failure of recallable words in semantic memory. *Memory & Cognition, 6*, 9–12.

Naccache, L., Blandin, E., & Dehaene, S. (2002). Unconscious masked priming depends on temporal attention. *Psychological Science, 13*, 416–424.

Nadel, L., & Moscovitch, M. (1997). Memory consolidation, retrograde amnesia and the hippocampal complex. *Current Opinion in Neurobiology, 7*, 217–227.

Nahmias, E. (2005). Agency, authorship, and illusion. *Consciousness and Cognition, 14*, 771–785.

Nairne, J. S. (2002). The myth of the encoding – retrieval match. *Memory, 10*, 389–395.

Nairne, J. S., Whiteman, H. L., & Kelley, M. R. (1999). Short-term forgetting of order under conditions of reduced interference. *Quarterly Journal of Experimental Psychology, 52A*, 241–251.

Nation, K., & Cocksey, J. (2009). The relationship between knowing a word and reading it aloud in children's word reading development. *Journal of Experimental Child Psychology, 103*, 296–308.

Navon, D. (1977). Forest before trees: The precedence of global features in visual perception. *Cognitive Psychology, 9*, 353–383.

Neisser, U. (1964). Visual search. *Scientific American, 210*, 94–102.

Newell, A., Shaw, J. C., & Simon, H. A. (1958). Elements of a theory of human problem solving. *Psychological Review, 65*, 151–166.

Newell, B. R. (2011). Recognising the recognition heuristic for what it is (and what it's not). *Judgment and Decision Making, 6*, 409–412.

Newell, A., & Simon, H. A. (1972). *Human problem solving*. Englewood Cliffs, NJ: Prentice Hall.

Newman, M. L., Groom, C. J., Handelman, L. D., & Pennebaker, J. W. (2008). Gender differences in language use: An analysis of 14,000 text samples. *Discourse Processes, 45*, 211–236.

Newman, E. J., & Lindsay, D.S. (2009). False memories: What the hell are they for? *Applied Cognitive Psychology, 23*, 1105–1121.

Newman, M. L., Pennebaker, J. W., Berry, D. S., & Richards, J. M. (2003). Lying words: Predicting deception from linguistic styles. *Personality and Social Psychology Bulletin, 29*, 665–675.

Nieuwland, M. S., & van Berkum, J. J. A. (2006). When peanuts fall in love: N400 evidence for the power of discourse. *Journal of Cognitive Neuroscience, 18*, 1098–1111.

Nijboer, T. C. W., McIntosh, R. D., Nys, G. M. S., Dijkerman, H. C., & Milner, A. D. (2008). Prism adaptation improves voluntary but not automatic orienting in neglect. *NeuroReport, 19*, 293–298.

Nisbett, R. E., & Wilson, T. D. (1977). Telling more than we can know: Verbal reports on mental processes. *Psychological Review, 84*, 231–259.

Noice, H., & Noice, T. (2007). The non-literal enactment effect: Filling in the blanks. *Discourse Processes, 44*, 73–89.

Nolan, M. S. (2010). *Fundamentals of air traffic control* (5th ed.). Florence, KY: Delmar Cengage Learning.

Nooteboom, S., & Quené, H. (2008). Self-monitoring and feedback: A new attempt to find the main cause of lexical bias in phonological speech errors. *Journal of Memory and Language, 58*, 837–861.

Norman, G. (2005). Research in clinical reasoning: Past history and current trends. *Medical Education, 39*, 418–427.

Norris, D., McQueen, J. M., Cutler, A., & Butterfield, S. (1997). The possible-word constraint in the segmentation of continuous speech. *Cognitive Psychology, 34*, 191–243.

Nosek, B. A., Greenwald, A. G., & Banaji, M. R. (2005). Understanding and using the Implicit Association Test: II. Method variables and construct validity. *Personality and Social Psychology Bulletin, 31*, 166–180.

Nosek, B. A., & Hansen, J. J. (2008). Personalizing the Implicit Association Test increases explicit evaluation of target concepts. *European Journal of Psychological Assessment, 24*, 226–236.

Nosek, B. A., Smyth, F. L., Sriram, N., Lindner, N. M., Devos, T., Ayala, A., et al. (2009). National differences in gender-science stereotypes in science and math achievement. *Proceedings of the National Association of Sciences of the United States of America, 106*, 10593–10597.

Novick, L. R. (2003). At the forefront of thought: The effect of media exposure on airplane typicality. *Psychonomic Bulletin & Review, 10*, 971–974.

Novick, L. R., & Sherman, S. J. (2003). On the nature of insight solutions: Evidence from skill differences in anagram solution. *Quarterly Journal of Experimental Psychology, 56A*, 351–382.

Oaksford, M., & Chater, N. (2009). Précis of Bayesian rationality: The probabilistic approach to human reasoning. *Behavioral and Brain Sciences, 32*, 69–120.

Oaksford, M., & Hahn, U. (2004). A Bayesian approach to the argument from ignorance. *Canadian Journal of Experimental Psychology, 58*, 75–85.

Oatley, K., & Djikic, M. (2008). Writing as thinking. *Review of General Psychology, 12*, 9–27.

Obleser, J., Scott, S. K., & Eulitz, C. (2006). Now you hear it, now you don't: Transient traces of consonants and their nonspeech analogs in the human brain. *Cerebral Cortex, 16*, 1069–1076.

O'Brien, E. J., Cook, A. E., & Guerand, S. (2010). Accessibility of outdated information. *Journal of Experimental Psychology: Learning, Memory, & Cognition, 36*, 979–991.

Ochsner, K. N., & Gross, J. J. (2005). The cognitive control of emotion. *Trends in Cognitive Sciences, 9*, 242–249.

Ochsner, K. N., & Gross, J. J. (2008). Cognitive emotion regulation: Insights from social cognitive and affective neuroscience. *Current Directions in Psychological Science, 17*, 153–158.

Ochsner, K. N., Ray, R. R., Hughes, B., McRae, K., Cooper, J. C., Weber, J., et al. (2009). Bottom-up and top-down processes in emotion generation: Common and distinct neural mechanisms. *Psychological Science, 20*, 1322–1331.

O'Craven, K., Downing, P., & Kanwisher, N. (1999). fMRI evidence for objects as the units of attentional selection. *Nature, 401*, 584–587.

Ohlsson, S. (1992). Information processing explanations of insight and related phenomena. In M. T. Keane & K. J. Gilhooly (Eds.), *Advances in the psychology of thinking*. London, UK: Harvester Wheatsheaf.

Öhman, A., & Soares, J. J. F. (1994). "Unconscious anxiety": Phobic responses to masked stimuli. *Journal of Abnormal Psychology, 103*, 231–240.

Olive, T. (2004). Working memory in writing: Empirical evidence from the dual-task technique. *European Psychologist, 9*, 32–42.

Olive, T., Alves, R. A., & Castro, S. L. (2009). Cognitive processes in writing during pause and execution periods. *European Journal of Cognitive Psychology, 21*, 758–785.

Olive, T., & Kellogg, R. T. (2002). Concurrent activation of high- and low-level production processes in written composition. *Memory & Cognition, 30*, 594–600.

Olive, T., & Piolat, A. (2002). Suppressing visual feedback in written composition: Effects on processing demands and coordination of the writing process. *International Journal of Psychology, 37*, 209–218.

Öllinger, M., Jones, G., & Knoblich, G. (2008). Investigating the effect of mental set on insight problem solving. *Experimental Psychology, 55*, 269–282.

Ophir, E., Nass, C., & Wagner, A. D. (2009). Cognitive control in media multitaskers. *Proceedings of the National Association of Sciences, 106*, 15583–15587.

Oppenheimer, D. M. (2003). Not so fast! (and not so frugal!). Rethinking the recognition heuristic. *Cognition, 90*, B1–B9.

Oppenheimer, D. M. (2004). Spontaneous discounting of availability in frequency judgment tasks. *Psychological Science, 15*, 100–105.

Oppenheimer, D. M., & Monin, B. (2009). Investigations in spontaneous discounting. *Memory & Cognition, 37*, 608–614.

Orban, P., Peigneux, P., Lungu, O., Albouy, G., Breton, E., Laberenne, F., et al. (2010). The multifaceted nature of the relationship between performance and brain activity in motor sequence learning. *NeuroImage, 49*, 694–702.

Ostojic, P., & Phillips, J. G. (2009). Memorability of alternative password systems. *International Journal of Pattern Recognition and Artificial Intelligence, 23*, 987–1004.

Overgaard, M., Fehl, K., Mouridsen, K., Bergholt, B., & Cleermans, K. (2008). Seeing without seeing? Degraded conscious vision in a blindsight patient. *PLoS One, 3,* e3028.

Owen, A. M., Coleman, M. R., Boly, M., Davis, M. H., Laureys, S., & Pickard, J. D. (2006). Detecting awareness in the vegetative state. *Science, 313,* 1402.

Pacheco-Cobos, L., Rosetti, M., Cuatianquiz, C., & Hudson, R. (2010). Sex differences in mushroom gathering: Men expend more energy to obtain equivalent benefits. *Evolution and Human Behavior, 31,* 289–297.

Pachur, T., & Hertwig, R. (2006). On the psychology of the recognition heuristic: Retrieval primacy as a key determinant of its use. *Journal of Experimental Psychology: Learning, Memory, & Cognition, 32,* 983–1002.

Pachur, T., Hertwig, R., & Steinmann, F. (2012). How do people judge risks: Availability heuristic, affect heuristic, or both? *Journal of Experimental Psychology: Applied, 18,* 314–330.

Palmer, S. E. (1975). The effects of contextual scenes on the identification of objects. *Memory & Cognition, 3,* 519–526.

Papagno, C., Valentine, T., & Baddeley, A. D. (1991). Phonological short-term memory and foreign language vocabulary learning. *Journal of Memory and Language, 30,* 331–347.

Parker, E. S., Cahill, L., & McGaugh, J. L. (2006). A case of unusual autobiographical remembering. *Neurocase, 12,* 35–49.

Parkin, A. J. (2001). The structure and mechanisms of memory. In B. Rapp (Ed.). *The handbook of cognitive neuropsychology: What deficits reveal about the human mind.* Hove, UK: Psychology Press.

Parkinson, B. (2001). Putting appraisal in context. In K. R. Scherer, A. Schorr, & T. Johnstone (Eds.), *Appraisal processes in emotion: Theory, methods, research.* Oxford, UK: Oxford University Press.

Parkinson, B. (2007). Getting from situations to emotions: Appraisal and other routes. *Emotion, 7,* 21–25.

Parton, A., Mulhotra, P., & Husain, M. (2004). Hemispatial neglect. *Journal of Neurology, Neurosurgery and Psychiatry, 75,* 13–21.

Pashler, H. (1993). Dual-task interference and elementary mental mechanisms. In D. E. Meyer & S. Kornblum (Eds.), *Attention and performance* (Vol. XIV). London, UK: MIT Press.

Patterson, K., Nestor, P. J., & Rogers, T. T. (2007). Where do you know what you know? The representation of semantic knowledge in the human brain. *Nature Reviews Neuroscience, 8,* 976–987.

Paulus, M., Lindemann, O., & Bekkering, H. (2009). Motor simulation in verbal knowledge acquisition. *Quarterly Journal of Experimental Psychology, 62,* 2298–3305.

Payne, J. (1976). Task complexity and contingent processing in decision making: An information search and protocol analysis. *Organizational Behavior and Human Performance, 16,* 366–387.

Pearson, J., Clifford, C. W. G., & Tong, F. (2008). The functional impact of mental imagery on conscious perception. *Current Biology, 18,* 982–986.

Pecher, C., Lemercier, C., & Cellier, J. -M. (2009). Emotions drive attention: Effects on driver's behaviour. *Safety Science, 47,* 1254–1259.

Pegna, A. J., Khateb, A., Lazeyras, F., & Seghier, M. L. (2005). Discriminating emotional faces without primary visual cortices involves the right amygdala. *Nature Neuroscience, 8,* 24–25.

Peissig, J. J., & Tarr, M. J. (2007). Visual object recognition: Do we know more now than we did 20 years ago? *Annual Review of Psychology, 58,* 75–96.

Penaloza, A. A., & Calvillo, D. P. (2012). Incubation provides relief from artificial fixation in problem solving. *Creativity Research Journal, 24,* 338–344.

Pennebaker, J. W. (1993). Putting stress into words: Health, linguistic, and therapeutic implications. *Behaviour Research and Therapy, 31,* 539–548.

Pennycook, G., & Thompson, V. A. (2012). Reasoning with base rates is routine, relatively effortless, and context dependent. *Psychonomic Bulletin & Review, 19,* 528–534.

Peretz, I., & Coltheart, M. (2003). Modularity of music processing. *Nature Neuroscience, 6,* 688–691.

Perfect, T. J., Wagstaff, G. F., Morre, D., Andrews, B., Cleveland, V., Newcombe, S., et al. (2008). How can we help witnesses to remember more? It's an (eyes) open and shut case. *Law and Human Behavior, 32,* 314–324.

Perre, L., Pattamadilok, C., Montant, M., & Ziegler, J. C. (2010). Orthographic effects in spoken language: On-line activation or phonological restructuring? *Brain Research, 1275,* 73–80.

Perre, L., & Ziegler, J. C. (2008). On-line activation of orthography in spoken word recognition. *Brain Research, 1188,* 132–138.

Perry, C., Ziegler, J. C., & Zorzi, M. (2007). Nested incremental modeling in the development of computational theories: The CDP+ model of reading aloud. *Psychological Review, 114,* 273–315.

Persaud, N., & Cowey, A. (2008). Blindsight is unlike normal conscious vision: Evidence from an exclusion task. *Consciousness and Cognition, 17,* 1050–1055.

Persaud, N., & McLeod, P. (2008). Wagering demonstrates subconscious processing in a binary exclusion task. *Consciousness and Cognition, 17,* 565–575.

Pessiglione, M., Schmidt, L., Draganski, B., Kalisch, R., Lau, H., Dolan, R. J., & Frith, C. D. (2007). How the brain translates money into force: A neuroimaging study of subliminal motivation. *Science, 316,* 904–906.

Pessoa, L. (2008). On the relationship between emotion and cognition. *Nature Reviews Neuroscience, 9,* 148–158.

Peters, D. P. (1988). Eyewitness memory in a natural setting. In M. M. Gruneberg, P. E. Morris, & R. N. Sykes (Eds.), *Practical aspects of memory: Current research and issues: Vol. 1. Memory in everyday life.* Chichester, UK: Wiley.

Peterson, L. R., & Peterson, M. J. (1959). Short-term retention of individual verbal items. *Journal of Experimental Psychology, 58,* 193–198.

Petkova, V. I., & Ehrsson, H. H. (2008). If I were you: Perceptual illusion of body swapping. *PLoS One, 3,* e3832.

Pezdek, K. (2003). Event memory and autobiographical memory for the events of September 11, 2001. *Applied Cognitive Psychology, 17,* 1033–1045.

Philipp, A. M., Gade, M., & Koch, I. (2007). Inhibitory processes in language switching: Evidence from switching language-defined response sets. *European Journal of Cognitive Psychology, 19,* 395–416.

Pickel, K. L. (2009). The weapon focus effect on memory for female versus male perpetrators. *Memory, 17,* 664–678.

Pickering, M. J., & Ferreira, V. S. (2008). Structural priming: A critical review. *Psychological Bulletin, 134,* 427–459.

Pickering, M. J., & Garrod, S. (2004). Toward a mechanistic psychology of dialog. *Behavioral and Brain Sciences, 27,* 169–226.

Pickford, R. W., & Gregory, R. L. (2004). Bartlett, Sir Frederic Charles. In R. L. Gregory (Ed.), *The Oxford companion to the mind* (2nd ed., pp. 86–87). New York, NY: Oxford University Press.

Pinker, S. (1984). *Language learnability and language development.* Cambridge, MA: Harvard University Press.

Pinker, S. (1997). *How the mind works.* New York, NY: W. W. Norton.

Pinkham, A. E., Griffin, M., Baron, R., Sasson, N. J., & Gur, R. C. (2010). The face in the crowd effect: Anger superiority when using real faces and multiple identities. *Emotion, 10,* 141–146.

Pisoni, D. B., & Tash, J. (1974). Reaction times to comparisons within and across phonetic categories. *Perception & Psychophysics, 15,* 285–290.

Piwnica-Worms, K. E., Omar, R., Hailstone, J. C., & Warren, J. D. (2010). Flavor processing in semantic dementia. *Cortex, 46,* 761–768.

Plaut, D. C., McClelland, J. L., Seidenberg, M. S., & Patterson, K. (1996). Understanding normal and impaired word reading: Computational principles in quasi-regular domains. *Psychological Review, 103,* 56–115.

Plester, B., Wood, C., & Joshi, P. (2009). Exploring the relationship between children's knowledge of text message abbreviations and school literacy outcomes. *British Journal of Developmental Psychology, 27,* 145–161.

Pohl, R. F., & Hell, W. (1996). No reduction in hindsight bias after complete information and repeated testing. *Organizational Behavior and Human Decision Processes, 67,* 49–58.

Poldrack, R. A., & Gabrieli, J. D. E. (2001). Characterizing the neural mechanisms of skill learning and repetition priming: Evidence from mirror reading. *Brain, 124,* 67–82.

Polivy, J. (1981). On the induction of emotion in the laboratory: Discrete moods or multiple affect states? *Journal of Personality and Social Psychology, 41,* 803–817.

Polka, L., Rvachew, S., & Molnar, M. (2008). Speech perception by 6- to 8-month-olds in the presence of distracting sounds. *Infancy, 13,* 421–439.

Pollatsek, A., Reichle, E. D., & Rayner, K. (2006). Tests of the E-Z Reader model: Exploring the interface between cognition and eye-movement control. *Cognitive Psychology, 52,* 1–56.

Poole, B. J., & Kane, M. J. (2009). Working memory capacity predicts the executive control of visual search among distractors: The influences of sustained and selective attention. *Quarterly Journal of Experimental Psychology, 62,* 1430–1454.

Pope, D. G., & Schweitzer, M. E. (2011). Is Tiger Woods loss averse? Persistent bias in the face of experience, competition, and high stakes. *American Economic Review, 101,* 129–157.

Popper, K. R. (1968). *The logic of scientific discovery.* London, UK: Hutchinson.

Porter, S., & ten Brinke, L. (2010). The truth about lies: What works in detecting high-stakes deception? *Legal and Criminological Psychology, 15,* 57–75.

Posner, M. I. (1980). Orienting of attention: The VIIth Sir Frederic Bartlett lecture. *Quarterly Journal of Experimental Psychology, 32A,* 3–25.

Power, M., & Dalgleish, T. (2008). *Cognition and emotion: From order to disorder* (2nd ed.). New York, NY: Psychology Press.

Pozzulo, J. D., Crescini, C., & Panton, T. (2008). Does methodology matter in eyewitness identification research? The effect of live versus video exposure on eyewitness identification of accuracy. *International Journal of Law and Psychiatry*, 31, 430–437.

Prass, M., Grimsen, C., König, M., & Fahle, M. (2013). Ultra rapid object cagetorisation: Effect of level, animacy and context. *PLOS ONE*, 8(6), e68051.

Prat, C. S., Keller, T. A., & Just, M. A. (2007). Individual differences in sentence comprehension: A functional magnetic resonance imaging investigation of syntactic and lexical processing demands. *Journal of Cognitive Neuroscience*, 19, 1950–1963.

Preston, S. D., Buchanan, T. W., Stansfield, R. B., & Buchanan, A. (2007). Effects of anticipatory stress on decision making in a gambling task. *Behavioral Neuroscience*, 121, 257–263.

Price, J. (2008). *The woman who can't forget: A memoir.* New York, NY: Free Press.

Prince, S. E., Tsukiura, T., & Cabeza, R. (2007). Distinguishing the neural correlates of episodic memory encoding and semantic memory retrieval. *Psychological Science*, 18, 144–151.

Pyers, J. E., Gollan, T. H., & Emmorey, K. (2009). Biomodal bilinguals reveal the source of tip-of-thetongue states. *Cognition*, 112, 323–329.

Pylyshyn, Z. W. (2002). Mental imagery: In search of a theory. *Behavioral and Brain Sciences*, 25, 157–238.

Pylyshyn, Z. (2003). Return of the mental image: Are there really pictures in the brain? *Trends in Cognitive Sciences*, 7, 113–118.

Quinlan, P. T. (2003). Visual feature integration theory: Past, present, and future. *Psychological Bulletin*, 129, 643–673.

Quinlan, P. T., & Wilton, R. N. (1998). Grouping by proximity or similarity? Competition between the Gestalt principles in vision. *Perception*, 27, 417–430.

Quiroga, R. Q., Reddy, L., Kreiman, G., Koch, C., & Fried, I. (2005). Invariant visual representation by single neurons in the human brain. *Nature*, 435, 1102–1107.

Raghunathan, R., & Pham, M. T. (1999). All negative moods are not equal: Motivational influences of anxiety and sadness on decision making. *Organizational Behavior and Human Decision Processes*, 79, 56–77.

Raichle, M. E., & Snyder, A. Z. (2007). A default model of brain function: A brief history of an evolving idea. *NeuroImage*, 37, 1083–1090.

Raizada, R. D. S., & Poldrack, R. A. (2007). Selective amplification of stimulus differences during categorical processing of speech. *Neuron*, 56, 726–740.

Ramsey, J. D., Hanson, S. J., Hanson, C., Halchenko, Y. O., Pokdrack, R. A., & Glymour, C. (2010). Six problems for causal inference from fMRI. *NeuroImage*, 49, 1545–1558.

Rapp, D. N., & Kendeou, P. (2009). Noticing and revising discrepancies as texts unfold. *Discourse Processes*, 46, 1–24.

Rascovsky, K., Growdon, M. E., Pardo, I. R., Grossman, S., & Miller, B. L. (2009). The quicksand of forgetfulness: Semantic dementia in *One Hundred Years of Solitude. Brain*, 132, 2609–2616.

Rasmussen, A. S., & Berntsen, D. (2009). The possible functions of involuntary autobiographical memories. *Applied Cognitive Psychology*, 23, 1137–1152.

Rastle, K., & Brysbaert, M. (2006). Masked phonological priming effects in English: Are they real? Do they matter? *Cognitive Psychology*, 53, 97–145.

Rayner, K., Li, X. S., & Pollatsek, A. (2007). Extending the E-Z model of eye-movement control to Chinese readers. *Cognitive Science*, 31, 1021–1033.

Raz, A., Packard, M. G., Alexander, G. M., Buhle, J. T., Zhu, G. M., Yu, S., & Peterson, B. S. (2009). A slice of pi: An exploratory neuroimaging study of digit encoding and retrieval in a superior memorist. *Neurocase*, 15, 361–372.

Reali, F., & Christiansen, M. H. (2005). Uncovering the richness of the stimulus: Structure dependence and indirect statistical evidence. *Cognitive Science*, 29, 1007–1028.

Reber, A. S. (1993). *Implicit learning and tacit knowledge: An essay on the cognitive unconscious.* Oxford, UK: Oxford University Press.

Recanzone, G. H., & Sutter, M. L. (2008). The biological basis of audition. *Annual Review of Psychology*, 59, 119–142.

Reddy, L., Tsuchiya, N., & Serre, T. (2010). Reading the mind's eye: Decoding category information during mental imagery. *NeuroImage*, 50, 818–825.

Redelmeier, C., Koehler, D. J., Liberman, V., & Tversky, A. (1995). Probability judgment in medicine: Discounting unspecified alternatives. *Medical Decision Making*, 15, 227–230.

Redelmeier, D. A., & Tibshirani, R. J. (1997). Association between cellular-telephone calls and motor vehicle collisions. *New England Journal of Medicine*, 336, 453–458.

Reder, L. M., Park, H., & Kieffaber, P. D. (2009). Memory systems do not divide on consciousness: Reinterpreting memory in terms of activation and binding. *Psychological Bulletin*, 135, 23–49.

Rees, G. (2007). Neural correlates of the contents of visual awareness in humans. *Philosophical Transactions of the Royal Society B: Biological Sciences*, 362, 877–886.

Reese, C. M., & Cherry, K. E. (2002). The effects of age, ability, and memory monitoring on prospective memory task performance. *Aging, Neuropsychology, and Cognition*, 9, 98–113.

Rehder, B., & Kim, S. (2009). Classification as diagnostic reasoning. *Memory & Cognition, 37,* 715–729.

Reicher, G. M. (1969). Perceptual recognition as a function of meaningfulness of stimulus material. *Journal of Experimental Psychology, 81,* 274–280.

Reichle, E. D., Rayner, K., & Pollatsek, A. (2003). The E-Z Reader model of eye-movement control in reading: Comparisons to other models. *Behavioral and Brain Sciences, 26,* 445–526.

Rensink, R. A. (2002). Change detection. *Annual Review of Psychology, 53,* 245–277.

Rensink, R. A., O'Regan, J. K., & Clark, J. J. (1997). To see or not to see: The need for attention to perceive changes in scenes. *Psychological Science, 8,* 368–373.

Repovš, G., & Baddeley, A. (2006). The multicomponent model of working memory: Explorations in experimental cognitive psychology. *Neuroscience, 139,* 5–21.

Reverberi, C., Toraldo, A., D'Agostini, S., & Skrap, M. (2005). Better without (lateral) frontal cortex? Insight problems solved by frontal patients. *Brain, 128,* 2882–2890.

Reynolds, D. J., Garnham, A., & Oakhill, J. (2006). Evidence of immediate activation of gender information from a social role name. *Quarterly Journal of Experimental Psychology, 59,* 886–903.

Ricco, R. B. (2003). The macrostructure of informal arguments: A proposed model and analysis. *Quarterly Journal of Experimental Psychology: Human Experimental Psychology, 56A,* 1021–1051.

Ricco, R. B. (2007). Individual differences in the analysis of informal reasoning fallacies. *Contemporary Educational Psychology, 32,* 459–383.

Richter, T., & Späth, P. (2006). Recognition is used as one cue among others in judgment and decision making. *Journal of Experimental Psychology: Learning, Memory, & Cognition, 32,* 150–162.

Ricker, T. J., & Cowan, N. (2010). Loss of visual working memory within seconds: The combined use of refreshable and non-refreshable features. *Journal of Experimental Psychology: Learning, Memory, and Cognition, 36*(6), 1355–1368.

Riddoch, G. (1917). Dissociations of visual perception due to occipital injuries, with especial reference to appreciation of movement. *Brain, 40,* 15–57.

Riddoch, M. J., & Humphreys, G. W. (2001). Object recognition. In B. Rapp (Ed.), *The handbook of cognitive neuropsychology: What deficits reveal about the human mind.* Hove, UK: Psychology Press.

Riddoch, M. J., Humphreys, G. W., Akhtar, N., Allen, H., Bracewell, R. M., & Scholfield, A. J. (2008).

A tale of two agnosias: Distinctions between form and integrative agnosia. *Cognitive Neuropsychology, 25,* 56–92.

Rinck, M., & Weber, U. (2003). Who, when and where: An experimental test of the event-indexing model. *Memory & Cognition, 31,* 1284–1292.

Rinne, J. O., Tommola, J., Laine, M., Krause, B. J., Schmidt, D., Kaasinen, V., et al. (2000). The translating brain: Cerebral activation patterns during simultaneous interpreting. *Neuroscience Letters, 294,* 85–88.

Rips, L. J., & Collins, A. (1993). Categories and resemblance. *Journal of Experimental Psychology: General, 122,* 468–486.

Rips, L. J., Shoben, E. J., & Smith, E. E. (1973). Semantic distance and the verification of semantic relations. *Journal of Verbal Learning and Verbal Behavior, 12,* 1–20.

Ritov, J., & Baron, J. (1990). Reluctance to vaccinate: Omission bias and ambiguity. *Journal of Behavioral Decision Making, 3,* 263–277.

Rizzi, C., Piras, F., & Marangolo, P. (2010). Top-down projections to the primary visual areas necessary for object recognition: A case study. *Vision Research, 50,* 1074–1085.

Robbins, T., Anderson, E, Barker, D., Bradley, A., Fearneyhough, C., Henson, R., et al. (1996). Working memory in chess. *Memory and Cognition, 24,* 83–93.

Robertson, S. I. (2001). *Problem solving.* Hove, UK: Psychology Press.

Robinson, B. L., & McAlpine, D. (2009). Gain control mechanisms in the auditory pathway. *Current Opinion in Neurobiology, 19,* 402–407.

Rodebaugh, T. L., Heimberg, R. G., Schultz, L. T., & Blackmore, M. (2010). The moderated effects of video feedback for social anxiety disorders. *Journal of Anxiety Disorders, 24,* 663–671.

Roediger, H. L. (2008). Relativity of remembering: Why the laws of memory vanished. *Annual Review of Psychology, 59,* 225–254.

Roediger, H. L., & Karpicke, J. D. (2006). Test-enhanced learning: Taking memory tests improves long-term retention. *Psychological Science, 17,* 249–255.

Rogers, T. B., Kuiper, N. A., & Kirker, W. S. (1977). Self-reference and the encoding of personal information. *Journal of Personality and Social Psychology, 35,* 677–688.

Rogers, T. T., & McClelland, J. L. (2005). A parallel distributed processing approach to semantic cognition: Applications to conceptual development. *Carnegie Mellon Symposia on Cognition, 32,* 335–387.

Rogers, T. T., & Patterson, K. (2007). Object categorization: Reversals and explanations of the basic-level advantage. *Journal of Experimental Psychology: General, 136,* 451–469.

Rosch, E., & Mervis, C. B. (1975). Family resemblances: Studies in the internal structure of categories. *Cognitive Psychology, 7,* 573–605.

Rosch, E., Mervis, C. B., Gray, W. D., Johnson, D. M., & Boyes-Braem, P. (1976). Basic objects in natural categories. *Cognitive Psychology, 8,* 382–439.

Rosen, L. D., Chang, J., Erwin, L., Carrier, L. M., & Cheever, N. A. (2010). The relationship between "textisms" and formal and informal writing among young adults. *Communication Research, 37,* 420–440.

Rosenbaum, R. S., Köhler, S., Schacter, D. L., Moscovitch, M., Westmacott, R., Black, S. E., et al. (2005). The case of KC: Contributions of a memory-impaired person to memory theory. *Neuropsychologia, 43,* 989–1021.

Rosenblum, L. D. (2008). Speech perception as a multimodal phenomenon. *Current Directions in Psychological Science, 17,* 405–409.

Rosenholtz, R., Huang, J., Raj, A., Balas, B. J., & Ilie, L. (2012a). A summary statistic representation in peripheral vision explains visual search. *Journal of Vision, 12*(4), 1–17.

Rosenholtz, R., Huang, J., & Ehinger, K. A. (2012b). Rethinking the role of top-down attention in vision: Effects attributable to a lossy representation in peripheral vision. *Frontiers in Psychology, 3*: 13.

Rosielle, L. J., & Scaggs, W. J. (2008). What if they knocked down the library and nobody noticed? The failure to detect large changes to familiar scenes. *Memory, 16,* 115–124.

Ross, D. F., Ceci, S. J., Dunning, D., & Toglia, M. P. (1994). Unconscious transference and mistaken identity: When a witness misidentifies a familiar but innocent person. *Journal of Applied Psychology, 79,* 918–930.

Rossetti, Y., Rode, G., Pisella, L., Boisson, D., & Perenin, M. T. (1998). Prism adaptation to a rightward optical deviation rehabilitates left hemispatial neglect. *Nature, 395,* 166–169.

Rothermund, K., Voss, A., & Wentura, D. (2008). Counter-regulation in affective attentional biases: A basic mechanism that warrants flexibility in emotion and motivation. *Emotion, 8,* 34–46.

Roussey, J. Y., & Piolat, A. (2008). Critical reading effort during text revision. *European Journal of Cognitive Psychology, 20,* 765–792.

Royden, C. S., Wolfe, J. M., & Klempen, N. (2001). Visual search asymmetries in motion and optic flow fields. *Perception & Psychophysics, 63,* 436–444.

Rubin, D. C., & Berntsen, D. (2003). Life scripts help to maintain autobiographical memories of highly positive, but not negative, events. *Memory & Cognition, 31,* 1–14.

Rubin, D. C., Berntsen, D., & Hutson, M. (2009). The normative and the personal life: Individual differences in life scripts and life story events among US and Danish undergraduates. *Memory, 17,* 54–68.

Rubin, D. C., Rahhal, T. A., & Poon, L. W. (1998). Things learned in early childhood are remembered best. *Memory & Cognition, 26,* 3–19.

Rubinstein, J. S., Meyer, D. E., & Evans, J. E. (2001). Executive control of cognitive processes in task switching. *Journal of Experimental Psychology: Human Perception and Performance, 27,* 763–797.

Ruchkin, D. S., Berndt, R. S., Johnson, R., Grafman, J., Ritter, W., & Canoune, H. L. (1999). Lexical contributions to retention of verbal information in working memory. *Journal of Memory and Language, 41,* 345–364.

Rumelhart, D. E., McClelland, J. L., & the PDP Research Group (1986). *Parallel distributed processing, Vol. 1: Foundations.* Cambridge, MA: MIT Press.

Rumelhart, D. E., & Ortony, A. (1977). The representation of knowledge in memory. In R. C. Anderson, R. J. Spiro, & W. E. Montague (Eds.), *Schooling and the acquisition of knowledge.* Hillsdale, NJ: Lawrence Erlbuam.

Russell, B., Perkins, J., & Grinnell, H. (2008). Interviewees' overuse of the word "like" and hesitations: Effects in simulated hiring decisions. *Psychological Reports, 102,* 111–118.

Russell, M. (1999). Testing on computers: A follow-up study comparing performance on computer and on paper. *Educational Policy Analysis Archives, 7*(20), 1–47.

Russell, R., Duchaine, B., & Nakayama, K. (2009). Super-recognizers: People with extraordinary face recognition ability. *Psychonomic Bulletin & Review, 16,* 252–257.

Rusting, C. L., & DeHart, T. (2000). Retrieving positive memories to regulate negative mood: Consequences for mood-congruent memory. *Journal of Personality and Social Psychology, 78,* 737–752.

Ryan, J. D., Althoff, R. R., Whitlow, S., & Cohen, N. J. (2000). Amnesia is a deficit in relational memory. *Psychological Science, 11,* 454–461.

Sacks, H., Schegloff, E. A., & Jefferson, G. (1974). A simplest systematics for the organization of turn-taking in conversation. *Language, 50,* 696–735.

Sanchez, C. A., & Wiley, J. (2006). An examination of the seductive details effect in terms of working memory capacity. *Memory & Cognition, 34*, 344–355.

Santhouse, A. M., Howard, R. J., & ffytche, D. H. (2000). Visual hallucinatory syndromes and the anatomy of the visual brain. *Brain, 123*, 2055–2064.

Sato, H., & Matsushima, K. (2006). Effects of audience awareness on procedural text writing. *Psychological Reports, 99*, 51–73.

Schacter, D. L. (1999). The seven sins of memory – Insights from psychology and cognitive neuroscience. *American Psychologist, 54*, 182–203.

Schacter, D. L., & Addis, D. R. (2007). The cognitive neuroscience of constructive memory: Remembering the past and imagining the future. *Philosophical Transactions of the Royal Society B: Biological Sciences, 362*, 773–786.

Schacter, D. L., Wig, G. S., & Stevens, W. D. (2007). Reductions in cortical activity during priming. *Current Opinion in Neurobiology, 17*, 171–176.

Schenk, T., & McIntosh, R. D. (2010). Do we have independent visual streams for perception and action? *Cognitive Neuroscience, 1*, 52–62.

Scherer, K. R., Schorr, A., & Johnstone, T. (Eds.). (2001). *Appraisal processes in emotion: Theory, methods, research*. Oxford, UK: Oxford University Press.

Schneider, W., & Shiffrin, R. M. (1977). Controlled and automatic human information processing: I. Detection, search, and attention. *Psychological Review, 84*, 1–66.

Schriver, K. (1984). *Revised computer documentation for comprehension: Ten lessons in protocol-aided revision* (Technical Report No. 14). Pittsburgh, PA: Carnegie Mellon University.

Schumacher, E. H., Seymour, T. L., Glass, J. M., Fencsik, D. E., Lauber, E. J., Kieras, D. E., et al. (2001). Virtually perfect time sharing in dual-task performance: Uncorking the central cognitive bottleneck. *Psychological Science, 12*, 101–108.

Schunn, C. D., & Klahr, D. (1996). The problem of problem spaces: When and how to go beyond a 2-space model of scientific discovery. *Proceedings of the Eighteenth Annual Conference of the Cognitive Science Society*, San Diego, CA, pp. 25–26.

Schwartz, B. (2004). *The paradox of choice: Why more is less*. New York, NY: HarperCollins.

Schwartz, B. (2009). Incentives, choice, education and well-being. *Oxford Review of Education, 35*, 391–403.

Schwartz, B. L., & Hashtroudi, S. (1991). Priming is independent of skill learning. *Journal of Experimental Psychology: Learning, Memory, & Cognition, 17*, 1177–1187.

Schwartz, J. A., Chapman, G. B., Brewer, N. T., & Bergus, G. B. (2004). The effects of accountability on bias in physician decision making: Going from bad to worse. *Psychonomic Bulletin & Review, 11*, 173–178.

Schwarzkopf, D. S., Zhang, J. X., & Kourtzi, Z. (2009). Flexible learning of natural statistics in the human brain. *Journal of Neurophysiology, 102*, 1854–1867.

Scott, S. K., Young, A. W., Calder, A. J., Hellawell, D. J., Aggleton, J. P., & Johnson, M. (1997). Impaired auditory recognition of fear and anger following bilateral amygdala lesions. *Nature, 385*, 254–257.

Scullin, M. K., McDaniel, M. A., Shelton, J. T., & Lee, J. H. (2010). Focal/nonfocal cue effects in prospective memory: Monitoring difficulty or different retrieval processes? *Journal of Experimental Psychology: Learning, Memory, and Cognition, 36*, 736–749.

Seghier, M. L., Lee, H. L., Schofield, T., Ellis, C. L., & Price, C. J. (2008). Inter-subject variability in the use of two different neuronal networks for reading aloud familiar words. *NeuroImage, 42*, 1226–1236.

Sejnowski, T. J., & Rosenberg, C. R. (1987). Parallel networks that learn to pronounce English text. *Complex Systems, 1*, 145–168.

Sekuler, R., & Blake, R. (2002). *Perception* (4th ed.). New York, NY: McGraw-Hill.

Sellen, A. J., Lowie, G., Harris, J. F., & Wilkins, A. J. (1997). What brings intentions to mind? An *in situ* study of prospective memory. *Memory, 5*, 483–507.

Senghas, A., Kita, S., & Özyürek, A. (2004). Children creating core properties of language: Evidence from an emerging sign language in Nicaragua. *Science, 305*, 1779–1782.

Seo, M.-G., & Barrett, L. F. (2007). Being emotional during decision making: Good or bad? An empirical investigation. *Academy of Management Journal, 50*, 923–940.

Seymour, P. H. K., Aro, M., Erskine, J. M., Wimmer, H., Leybaert, J., Elbro, C., et al. (2003). Foundation literacy acquisition in European orthographies. *British Journal of Psychology, 94*, 143–174.

Shah, A. K., & Oppenheimer, D. M. (2008). Heuristics made easy: An effort-reduction framework. *Psychological Bulletin, 134*, 207–222.

Shallice, T., & Warrington, E. K. (1970). Independent functioning of verbal memory stores: A neuropsychological study. *Quarterly Journal of Experimental Psychology, 22*, 261–273.

Shallice, T., & Warrington, E. K. (1974). The dissociation between long-term retention of meaningful sounds and verbal material. *Neuropsychologia, 12*, 553–555.

Shanks, D. R. (2005). Implicit learning. In K. Lamberts & R. Goldstone (Eds.), *Handbook of cognition* (pp. 202–220). London, UK: Sage.

Shanks, D. R., & St. John, M. F. (1994). Characteristics of dissociable human learning systems. *Behavioral & Brain Sciences, 17,* 367–394.

Share, D. L. (2008). On the Anglocentricities of current reading research and practice: The perils of overreliance on an "outlier" orthography. *Psychological Bulletin, 134,* 584–615.

Sharpe, D. (1997). Of apples and oranges, file drawers and garbage: Why validity issues in meta-analysis will not go away. *Clinical Psychology Review, 17,* 881–901.

Shen, W., Olive, J., & Jones, D. (2008). Two protocols comparing human and machine phonetic discrimination performance in conversational speech. *Interspeech,* 1630–1633.

Shepard, R. N., & Metzler, J. (1971). Mental rotation of three-dimensional objects. *Science, 171,* 701–703.

Sheth, B. R., Sandkühler, S., & Bhattacharya, J. (2009). Posterior beta and anterior gamma oscillations predict cognitive insight. *Journal of Cognitive Neuroscience, 21,* 1269–1279.

Shiffrin, R. M., & Schneider, W. (1977). Controlled and automatic human information processing: II. Perceptual learning, automatic attending, and a general theory. *Psychological Review, 84,* 127–190.

Shiv, B., Loewenstein, G., Bechera, A., Damasio, H., & Damasio, A. R. (2005). Investment behavior and the negative side of emotion. *Psychological Science, 16,* 435–439.

Shrager, Y., Levy, D. A., Hopkins, R. O., & Squire, L. R. (2008). Working memory and the organization of brain systems. *Journal of Neuroscience, 28,* 4818–4822.

Shriver, E. R., Young, S. G., Hugenberg, K., Bernstein, M. J., & Lanter, J. R. (2008). Class, race, and the face: Social context modulates the cross-race effect in face recognition. *Personality and Social Psychology Bulletin, 34,* 260–274.

Shuell, T. J. (1969). Clustering and organization in free recall. *Psychological Bulletin, 72,* 353–374.

Sides, A., Osherson, D., Bonini, N., & Viale, R. (2002). On the reality of the conjunction fallacy. *Memory & Cognition, 30,* 191–198.

Siebert, M., Markowitsch, H. J., & Bartel, P. (2003). Amygdala, affect and cognition: Evidence from 10 patients with Urbach-Wiethe disease. *Brain, 126,* 2627–2637.

Siemer, M., & Reisenzein, R. (2007). The process of emotion inference. *Emotion, 7,* 1–20.

Silvanto, J. (2008). A re-evaluation of blindsight and the role of striate cortex (V1) in visual awareness. *Neuropsychologia, 46,* 2869–2871.

Silverman, I., Choi, J., & Peters, M. (2007). The hunter-gatherer theory of sex differences in spatial abilities: Data from 40 countries. *Archives of Sexual Behavior, 36,* 261–268.

Simmons, C. L., & Hampton, J. A. (2006). *Essentialist beliefs about basic and superordinate level categories.* Poster presented at the 47th Annual Meeting of the Psychonomic Society, Houston, TX, November.

Simner, J., Mayo, N., & Spiller, M. J. (2009). A foundation for savantism? Visuo-spatial synesthetes present with cognitive benefits. *Cortex, 45,* 1246–1260.

Simon, D., Krawczyk, D. C., & Holyoak, K. J. (2004). Construction of preferences by constraint satisfaction. *Psychological Science, 15,* 331–336.

Simon, H. A. (1945). Theory of games and economic behaviour. *American Sociological Review, 50,* 558–560.

Simon, H. A. (1957). *Models of man: Social and rational.* New York, NY: Wiley.

Simon, H. A. (1966). Scientific discovery and the psychology of problem solving. In H. A. Simon (Ed.), *Mind and cosmos: Essays in contemporary science and philosophy.* Pittsburgh, PA: University of Pittsburgh Press.

Simon, H. A. (1974). How big is a chunk? *Science, 183,* 482–488.

Simon, H. A. (1978). Rationality as a process and product of thought. *American Economic Association, 68,* 1–16.

Simon, H. A. (1990). Invariants of human behaviour. *Annual Review of Psychology, 41,* 1–19.

Simons, D. J. (2013). Unskilled and optimistic: Overconfident predictions despite calibrated knowledge of relative skill. *Psychonomic Bulletin & Review, 20,* 601–607.

Simons, D. J., & Chabris, F. (1999). Gorillas in our midst: Sustained inattentional blindness for dynamic events. *Perception, 28,* 1059–1074.

Simons, D. J., & Chabris, C.F. (2011). What people believe about how memory works: A representative survey of the US population. *Public Library of Science One, 6,* e22757.

Simons, D. J., & Levin, D. T. (1998). Failure to detect changes to people during a real-world interaction. *Psychonomic Bulletin & Review, 5,* 644–649.

Simons, D. J., & Rensink, R. A. (2005). Change blindness: Past, present, and future. *Trends in Cognitive Sciences, 9,* 16–20.

Simonson, I., & Staw, B. M. (1992). De-escalation strategies: A comparison of techniques for reducing commitment to losing courses of action. *Journal of Applied Psychology, 77,* 419–426.

Simonton, D. K. (2008). Scientific talent, training, and performance: Intellect, personality, and genetic endowment. *Review of General Psychology, 12,* 28–46.

Sio, U. N., & Ormerod, T. C. (2009). Does incubation enhance problem solving? A meta-analysis review. *Psychological Bulletin, 135,* 94–120.

Skinner, E. I., & Fernandes, M. A. (2007). Neural correlates of recollection and familiarity: A review of neuroimaging and patient data. *Neuropsychologia, 45,* 2163–2179.

Slatcher, R. B., & Pennebaker, J. W. (2006). How do I love thee? Let me count the words: The social effects of expressive writing. *Psychological Science, 17,* 660–664.

Slepian, M. L., Weisbuch, M., Rutchick, A. M., Newman, L. S., & Ambady, N. (2010). Shedding light on insight: Priming bright ideas. *Journal of Experimental Social Psychology, 46,* 696–700.

Slezak, P. (1991). Can images be rotated and inspected? A test of the pictorial medium theory. *Program of the Thirteenth Annual Conference of the Cognitive Science Society,* Chicago, IL, pp. 55–60.

Slezak, P. (1995). The "philosophical" case against visual imagery. In T. Caelli, P. Slezak, & R. Clark (Eds.), *Perspectives in cognitive science: Theories, experiments and foundations* (pp. 237–271). New York, NY: Ablex.

Sloboda, J. A., Davidson, J. W., Howe, M. J. A., & Moore, D. G. (1996). The role of practice in the development of performing musicians. *British Journal of Psychology, 87,* 287–309.

Small, D. A., & Lerner, J. S. (2008). Emotional policy: Personal sadness and anger shape judgments about a welfare case. *Political Psychology, 29,* 149–168.

Smania, N., Martini, M. C., Gambina, G., Tomelleri, G., Palamara, A., Natale, E., et al. (1998). The spatial distribution of visual attention in hemineglect and extinction patients. *Brain, 121,* 1759–1770.

Smith, C. A., & Kirby, L. D. (2001). Toward delivering on the promise of appraisal theory. In K. R. Scherer, A. Schorr, & T. Johnstone (Eds.), *Appraisal processes in emotion: Theory, methods, research.* Oxford, UK: Oxford University Press.

Smith, C. A., & Lazarus, R. S. (1993). Appraisal components, core relational themes, and the emotions. *Cognition & Emotion, 7,* 233–269.

Smith, E. E., & Jonides, J. (1997). Working memory: A view from neuroimaging. *Cognitive Psychology, 33,* 5–42.

Smith, J. D., & Minda, J. P. (2000). Thirty categorization results in search of a model. *Journal of Experimental Psychology: Learning, Memory, & Cognition, 26,* 3–27.

Smith, M. (2000). Conceptual structures in language production. In L. Wheeldon (Ed.), *Aspects of language production.* Hove, UK: Psychology Press.

Smith, R. E. (2003). The cost of remembering to remember in event-based prospective memory: Investigating the capacity demands of delayed intention performance. *Journal of Experimental Psychology: Learning, Memory, and Cognition, 29,* 347–361.

Smith, R. E., & Bayen, U. J. (2005). The effects of working memory resource availability on prospective memory: A formal modeling approach. *Experimental Psychology, 52,* 243–256.

Smith, R. E., & Hunt, R. R. (2000). The effects of distinctiveness require reinstatement of organization: The importance of intentional memory instructions. *Journal of Memory and Language, 43,* 431–446.

Smith, R. E., Hunt, R. R., McVay, J. C., & McConnell, M. D. (2007). The cost of event-based prospective memory: Salient target events. *Journal of Experimental Psychology: Learning, Memory, and Cognition, 33,* 734–746.

Snedeker, J., & Trueswell, J. (2003). Using prosody to avoid ambiguity: Effects of speaker awareness and referential context. *Journal of Memory and Language, 48,* 103–130.

Soon, C. S., Brass, M., Heinze, H. J., & Haynes, J. D. (2008). Unconscious determinants of free decisions in the human brain. *Nature Neuroscience, 10,* 257–261.

Sorqvist, P. (2010). High working memory capacity attenuates the deviation effect but not the duplex-mechanism account of auditory distraction. *Memory & Cognition, 38,* 651–658.

Spelke, E. S., Hirst, W. C., & Neisser, U. (1976). Skills of divided attention. *Cognition, 4,* 215–230.

Spence, I., Yu, J. J., Feng, J., & Marshman, J. (2009). Women match men when learning a spatial skill. *Journal of Experimental Psychology: Learning, Memory and Cognition, 35,* 1097–1103.

Sperber, D., & Girotto, V. (2002). Use or misuse of the selection task? Rejoinder to Fiddick, Cosmides, and Tooby. *Cognition, 85,* 277–290.

Sperling, G. (1960). The information that is available in brief visual presentations. *Psychological Monographs, 74*(498), 1–29.

Spiers, H. J., Maguire, E. A., & Burgess, N. (2001). Hippocampal amnesia. *Neurocase, 7,* 357–382.

Spinney, L. (2010). The fine print. *Nature, 464,* 344–346.

Spivey, M. J., Tanenhaus, M. K., Eberhard, K. M., & Sedivy, J. C. (2002). Eye movements and spoken language comprehension: Effects of visual context on syntactic ambiguity resolution. *Cognitive Psychology*, 45, 447–481.

Stanovich, K. E. (2009, November/December). The thinking that IQ tests miss. *Scientific American*, 34–39.

Stanovich, K.E. (2012). On the distinction between rationality and intelligence: Implications for understanding individual differences in reasoning. In K. J. Holyoak & R. G. Morrison (Eds.). *The Oxford handbook of thinking and reasoning*. Oxford: Oxford University Press.

Stanovich, K. E., & West, R. F. (2007). Natural myside bias is independent of cognitive ability. *Thinking & Reasoning*, 13, 225–247.

Stanovich, K. E., West, R. F., & Toplak, M. E. (2011). Individual differences as essential components of heuristics and biases research. In K. Manktelow, D. Over, & S. Elqayam (Eds.), *The science of reason: A Festschrift for Jonathan St. B. T. Evans*. Hove, UK: Psychology Press.

Starcke, K. W., lf, O. T., Markowitsch, H. J., & Brand, M. (2008). Anticipatory stress influences decision making under explicit risk conditions. *Behavioral Neuroscience*, 122, 1352–1360.

Steller, M., & Köhnken, G. (1989). Critera-based content analysis. In D. C. Raskin (Ed.), *Psychological methods in criminal investigation and evidence* (pp. 217–245). New York, NY: Springer-Verlag.

Sternberg, R. J. (2011). Understanding reasoning: Let's describe what we really think about. *Behavioral and Brain Sciences*, 34, 269–270.

Sternberg, R. J., & Ben-Zeev, T. (2001). *Complex cognition: The psychology of human thought*. Oxford, UK: Oxford University Press.

Stich, S. P. (1990). *The fragmentation of reason*. Cambridge, MA: MIT Press.

Stirman, S. W., & Pennebaker, J. W. (2001). Word use in the poetry of suicidal and nonsuicidal poets. *Psychosomatic Medicine*, 63, 517–522.

Storms, G., De Boeck, P., & Ruts, W. (2000). Prototype and exemplar-based information in natural language categories. *Journal of Memory and Language*, 42, 51–73.

Stottinger, E., Soder, K., Pfusterschmied, J., Wagner, H., & Perner, J. (2010). Division of labor within the visual system: Fact or fiction?. Which kind of evidence is appropriate to clarify this debate? *Experimental Brain Research*, 202, 79–88.

Strayer, D. L., & Drews, F. A. (2007). Cell-phone induced driver distraction. *Current Directions in Psychological Science*, 16, 128–131.

Stroop, J. R. (1935). Studies of interference in serial verbal reactions. *Journal of Experimental Psychology: General*, 106, 404–426.

Stuss, D. T., & Alexander, M. P. (2007). Is there a dysexecutive syndrome? *Philosophical Transactions of the Royal Society B: Biological Sciences*, 362, 901–1015.

Subramaniam, K., Kounios, J., Parrish, T. B., & Jung-Beeman, M. (2009). A brain mechanism for facilitation of insight by positive affect. *Journal of Cognitive Neuroscience*, 21, 415–432.

Sulin, R. A., & Dooling, D. J. (1974). Intrusion of a thematic idea in retention of prose. *Journal of Experimental Psychology*, 103, 255–262.

Sun, R., Zhang, X., & Mathews, R. (2009). Capturing human data in a letter-counting task: Accessibility and action-centeredness in representing cognitive skills. *Neural Networks*, 22, 15–29.

Svenson, O., Salo, I., & Lindholm, T. (2009). Post-decision consolidation and distortion of facts. *Judgment and Decision Making*, 4, 397–407.

Sweller, J., & Levine, M. (1982). Effects of goal specificity on means–ends analysis and learning. *Journal of Experimental Psychology: Learning, Memory, and Cognition*, 8, 463–474.

Swets, B., Desmet, T., Clifton, C., & Ferreira, F. (2008). Underspecification of syntactic ambiguities: Evidence from self-paced reading. *Memory & Cognition*, 36, 201–216.

Symons, C. S., & Johnson, B. T. (1997). The self-reference effect in memory: A meta-analysis. *Psychological Bulletin*, 121, 371–394.

Szpunar, K. K. (2010). Episodic future thought: An emerging concept. *Perspectives on Psychological Science*, 5, 142–162.

Szpunar, K. K., & Radvansky, G. A. (2016). Cognitive approaches to the study of episodic future thinking. *The Quarterly Journal of Experimental Psychology*, 69(2), 209–216.

Takahashi, M., Shimizu, H., Saito, S., & Tomayori, H. (2006). One percent ability and ninety-nine percent perspiration: A study of a Japanese memorist. *Journal of Experimental Psychology: Learning, Memory, & Cognition*, 32, 1195–1200.

Talarico, J. M., & Rubin, D. C. (2003). Confidence, not consistency, characterizes flashbulb memories. *Psychological Science*, 14, 455–461.

Talarico, J. M., & Rubin, D. C. (2009). Flashbulb memories result from ordinary memory processes and extraordinary event characteristics. In O. Luminet & A. Curci (Eds.), *Flashbulb memories: New issues and new perspectives* (pp. 79–97). New York, NY: Psychology Press.

Talmi, D., Hurlemann, R., Patin, A., & Dolan, R. J. (2010). Framing effect following bilateral amygdala lesion. *Neuropsychologia*, *48*, 1823–1827.

Tamietto, M., & de Gelder, B. (2008). Affective blindsight in the intact brain: Neural interhemispheric summation for unseen fearful expressions. *Neuropsychologia*, *46*, 820–828.

Tanaka, J. W., & Taylor, M. E. (1991). Object categories and expertise: Is the basic level in the eye of the beholder? *Cognitive Psychology*, *15*, 121–149.

Tanenhaus, M. K., Spivey-Knowlton, M. J., Eberhard, K. M., & Sedivy, J. C. (1995). Integration of visual and linguistic information in spoken language comprehension. *Science*, *268*, 1632–1634.

Tarr, M. J., & Bülthoff, H. H. (1995). Is human object recognition better described by geon structural descriptions or by multiple views? Comment on Biederman and Gerhardstein (1993). *Journal of Experimental Psychology: Human Perception & Performance*, *21*, 1494–1505.

Tarr, M. J., Williams, P., Hayward, W. G., & Gauthier, I. (1998). Three-dimensional object recognition is viewpoint-dependent. *Nature Neuroscience*, *1*, 195–206.

Taubert, J., & Alais, D. (2009). The composite illusion requires composite face stimuli to be biologically plausible. *Vision Research*, *49*, 1877–1885.

Teigen, K. H., & Keren, G. (2007). Waiting for the bus: When base-rates refuse to be neglected. *Cognition*, *103*, 337–357.

Terlecki, M. S., & Newcombe, N. S. (2005). How important is the digital divide? The relation of computer and videogame usage to gender differences in mental rotation ability. *Sex Roles*, *53*, 433–441.

Tetlock, P.E. (2002). Social functionalist frameworks for judgment and choice: Intuitive politicians, theologians, and prosecutors. *Psychological Review*, *109*, 451–471.

Thagard, P. (1998). Explaining disease: Correlations, causes, and mechanisms. *Minds and Machines*, *8*, 61–78.

Thagard, P. (2005). How to be a successful scientist. In M. E. Gorman, R. D. Tweney, D. C. Gooding & A. P. Kincannon (Eds.), *Scientific and technological thinking* (pp. 159–171). Mawah, NJ: Lawrence Erlbaum.

Thimm, M., Fink, G. R., Küst, J., Karbe, H., Willmes, K., & Sturm, W. (2009). Recovery from hemineglect: Differential neurobiological effects of optokinetic stimulation and alertness training. *Cortex*, *45*, 850–862.

Thomas, L. E., & Lleras, A. (2009). Covert shifts of attention function as an implicit aid to insight. *Cognition*, *111*, 168–174.

Thompson, C. P., Cowan, T., Frieman, J., Mahadevan, R. S., Vogl, R. J., & Frieman, R. J. (1991). Rajan – A study of a memorist. *Journal of Memory and Language*, *30*, 702–724.

Thompson, M. B., Tangen, J. M. & McCarthy, D. J. (2014). Human matching performance of genuine crime scene latent fingerprints. *Law and Human Behavior*, *38*, 84–93.

Thompson, V. A., Evans, J. St. B. T., & Handley, S. J. (2005). Persuading and dissuading by conditional argument. *Journal of Memory & Language*, *53*, 238–257.

Thompson, W. L., Slotnick, S. D., Burrage, M. S., & Kosslyn, S. M. (2009). Two forms of spatial imagery: Neuroimaging evidence. *Psychological Science*, *20*, 1245–1253.

Thornton, T. L., & Gilden, D. L. (2007). Parallel and serial processes in visual search. *Psychological Review*, *114*, 71–103.

Todd, N. P. M., Lee, C. S., & O'Boyle, D. J. (2006). A sensorimotor theory of speech perception: Implications for learning, organization, and recognition. In S. Greenberg & W. A. Ainsworth (Eds.), *Listening to speech: An auditory perspective* (pp. 351–373). Mahwah, NJ: Lawrence Erlbaum.

Todd, P. M., & Gigerenzer, G. (2007). Environments that make us smart. *Current Directions in Psychological Science*, *16*, 167–171.

Tollestrup, P. A., Turtle, J. W., & Yuille, J. C. (1994). Actual victims and witnesses to robbery and fraud: An archival analysis. In D. F. Ross, J. D. Read, & M. P. Toglia (Eds.), *Adult eyewitness testimony: Current trends and developments*. New York, NY: Wiley.

Tolman, E. C. (1948). Cognitive maps in rats and men. *Psychological Review*, *55*, 189–208.

Tomasino, B., Borroni, P., Isaja, A., & Rumiati, R. I. (2005). The role of the primary motor cortex in mental rotation: A TMS study. *Cognitive Neuropsychology*, *22*, 348–363.

Tomasino, B., Weiss, P. H., & Fink, G. R. (2010). To move or not to move: Imperatives modulate action-related verb processing in the motor system. *Neuroscience*, *169*, 246–258.

Toms, M., Morris, N., & Foley, P. (1994). Characteristics of visual interference with visuospatial working memory. *British Journal of Psychology*, *85*, 131–144.

Tong, E. M. W. (2010a). The sufficiency and necessity of appraisals for negative emotions. *Cognition & Emotion*, *24*, 692–701.

Tong, E. M. W. (2010b). Personality influences in appraisal–emotion relationships: The role of neuroticism. *Journal of Personality*, *78*, 393–417.

Toplak, M. E., West, R. F., & Stanovich, K. E. (2011). The Cognitive Reflection Test as a predictor of performance on heuristics-and-biases tasks. *Memory & Cognition*, *39*, 1275–1289.

Treisman, A. M. (1960). Contextual cues in selective attention. *Quarterly Journal of Experimental Psychology*, *12*, 242–248.

Treisman, A. M. (1964). Verbal cues, language, and meaning in selective attention. *American Journal of Psychology, 77*, 206–219.

Treisman, A. M., & Gelade, G. (1980). A feature integration theory of attention. *Cognitive Psychology, 12*, 97–136.

Treisman, A. M., & Riley, J. G. A. (1969). Is selective attention selective perception or selective response? A further test. *Journal of Experimental Psychology, 79*, 27–34.

Trickett, S. B., & Trafton, J. G. (2007). "What if. . . ": The use of conceptual simulations in scientific reasoning. *Cognitive Science, 31*, 843–875.

Troiani, V., Price, E. T., & Schultz, R. T. (2014). Unseen fearful faces promote amygdala guidance of attention. *Social, Cognitive, and Affective Neuroscience, 9*, 133–140.

Trout, J. D. (2001). The biological basis of speech: What to infer from talking to the animals. *Psychological Review, 108*, 523–549.

Tuckey, M. R., & Brewer, N. (2003a). How schemas affect eyewitness memory over repeated retrieval attempts. *Applied Cognitive Psychology, 7*, 785–800.

Tuckey, M. R., & Brewer, N. (2003b). The influence of schemas, stimulus ambiguity, and interview schedule on eyewitness memory over time. *Journal of Experimental Psychology: Applied, 9*, 101–118.

Tuffiash, M., Roring, R. W., & Ericsson, K. A. (2007). Expert performance in Scrabble: Implications for the study of the structure and acquisition of complex skills. *Journal of Experimental Psychology: Applied, 13*, 124–134.

Tulving, E. (1979). Relation between encoding specificity and levels of processing. In L. S. Cermak & F. I. M. Craik (Eds.), *Levels of processing in human memory*. Hillsdale, NJ: Lawrence Erlbaum.

Tulving, E. (1985). How many memory systems are there? *American Psychologist, 40*, 385–398.

Tulving, E. (2002). Episodic memory: From mind to brain. *Annual Review of Psychology, 53*, 1–25.

Tulving, E., & Schacter, D. L. (1990). Priming and human-memory systems. *Science, 247*, 301–306.

Tulving, E., Schacter, D. L., & Stark, H. A. (1982). Priming effects in word-fragment completion are independent of recognition memory. *Journal of Experimental Psychology: Learning, Memory, & Cognition, 17*, 595–617.

Turner, M. L., & Engle, R. W. (1989). Is working memory capacity task dependent? *Journal of Memory and Language, 28*, 127–154.

Tustin, K., & Hayne, H. (2010). Defining the boundary: Age-related changes in childhood amnesia. *Developmental Psychology, 46*, 1049–1061.

Tversky, A. (1972). Elimination by aspects: A theory of choice. *Psychological Review, 79*, 281–299.

Tversky, A., & Kahneman, D. (1983). Extensional versus intuitive reasoning: The conjunction fallacy in probability judgment. *Psychological Review, 91*, 293–315.

Tversky, A., & Kahneman, D. (1987). Rational choice and the framing of decisions. In R. Hogarth & M. Reder (Eds.), *Rational choice: The contrast between economics and psychology*. Chicago, IL: University of Chicago Press.

Tversky, A., & Koehler, D. J. (1994). Support theory: A nonextensional representation of subjective probability. *Psychological Review, 101*, 547–567.

Tversky, A., & Shafir, E. (1992). The disjunction effect in choice under uncertainty. *Psychological Science, 3*, 305–309.

Tweney, R. D., & Chitwood, S. C. (1995). Scientific reasoning. In S. Newstead & J. S. T. Evans (Eds.), *Perspectives on thinking and reasoning: Essays in honor of Peter Wason* (pp. 241–260). Hove, UK: Lawrence Erlbaum.

Uddin, L. Q., Rayman, J., & Zaidel, E. (2005). Split-brain reveals separate but equal self-recognition in the two cerebral hemispheres. *Consciousness and Cognition, 14*, 633–640.

Underwood, B. J., & Postman, L. (1960). Extra-experimental sources of interference in forgetting. *Psychological Review, 64*, 49–60.

Underwood, G. (1974). Moray vs. the rest: The effect of extended shadowing practice. *Quarterly Journal of Experimental Psychology, 26*, 368–372.

Unsworth, N. (2010). Interference control, working memory capacity, and cognitive abilities: A latent variable analysis. *Intelligence, 38*, 255–267.

Unsworth, N., Redick, T. S., Lakey, C. E., & Young, D. L. (2010a). Lapses in sustained attention and their relation to executive control and fluid abilities: An individual differences investigation. *Intelligence, 38*, 111–122.

Unsworth, N., Schrock, J. C., & Engle, R. W. (2004). Working memory capacity and the antisaccade task: Individual differences in voluntary saccade control. *Journal of Experimental Psychology: Learning, Memory and Cognition, 30*, 1302–1321.

Unsworth, N., & Spillers, G. J. (2010). Working memory capacity: Attention control, secondary memory, or both? A direct test of the dual-component model. *Journal of Memory and Language, 62*, 392–406.

Unsworth, N., Spillers, G. J., & Brewer, G. A. (2010b). The contributions of primary and secondary memory to working memory capacity: An individual differences analysis of immediate free recall. *Journal of Experimental Psychology: Learning, Memory & Cognition, 36*, 240–247.

Uttl, B. (2008). Transparent meta-analysis of prospective memory and aging. *PLoS One, 3*, e1568.

Uzer, T., Lee, P. J., & Brown, N. R. (2012). On the prevalence of directly retrieved autobiographical memories. *Journal of Experimental Psychology: Learning, Memory, and Cognition, 38*, 1296–1308.

Valentine, E. R. (1992). *Conceptual issues in psychology* (2nd ed.). London, UK: Routledge.

Valentine, T., & Mesout, J. (2009). Eyewitness identification under stress in the London Dungeon. *Applied Cognitive Psychology, 23*, 151–161.

Vallée-Tourangeau, F., & Payton, T. (2008). Graphical representation fosters discovery in the 2–4–6 task. *Quarterly Journal of Experimental Psychology, 61*, 625–640.

Van der Hoort, B., Guterstam, A., & Ehrsson, H. (2011). Being Barbie: The size of one's own body determines the perceived size of the world. *PLoS One, 6*(5), e20195.

Van Boxtel, J. J. A., Tsuchiya, N., & Koch, C. (2010). Opposing effects of attention and consciousness on afterimages. *Proceedings of the National Academy of Sciences of the United States of America, 107*, 8883–8888.

van den Hout, M., & Kindt, M. (2004). Obsessive–compulsive disorder and the paradoxical effects of perseverative behaviour on experienced uncertainty. *Journal of Behavior Therapy and Experimental Psychiatry, 35*(2), 165–181.

Van Dillen, L. F., & Koole, S. L. (2007). Clearing the mind: A working memory model of distraction from negative mood. *Emotion, 7*, 715–723.

Van Dillen, L. F., Heselenfeld, D. J., & Koole, S. L. (2009). Turning down the emotional brain: An fMRI study of the effects of cognitive load on the processing of affective images. *NeuroImage, 45*, 1212–1219.

Van Gompel, R. P. G., Pickering, M. J., Pearson, J., & Liversedge, S. P. (2005). Evidence against competition during syntactic ambiguity resolution. *Journal of Memory and Language, 52*, 284–307.

Van Harreveld, F., Wagenmakers, E. J., & van der Maas, H. L. J. (2007). The effects of time pressure on chess skills: An investigation into fast and slow responses underlying expert performance. *Psychological Research, 71*, 591–597.

Van Orden, G. C. (1987). A rows is a rose: Spelling, sound and reading. *Memory & Cognition, 14*, 371–386.

Vandenberghe, M., Schmidt, N., Fery, P., & Cleeremans, A. (2006). Can amnesic patients learn without awareness? New evidence comparing deterministic and probabilistic sequence learning. *Neuropsychologia, 44*, 1629–1641.

Vanderberg, R., & Swanson, H. L. (2007). Which components of working memory are important in the writing process? *Reading and Writing, 20*, 721–752.

Van Dillen, L. F., Heselenfeld, D. J., & Koole, S. L. (2009). Turning down the emotional brain: An fMRI study of the effects of cognitive load on the processing of affective images. *NeuroImage, 45*, 1212–1219.

Vargha-Khadem, F., Gadian, D. G., & Mishkin, M. (2002). Dissociations in cognitive memory: The syndrome of developmental amnesia. In A. Baddeley, M. Conway, & J. Aggleton (Eds.), *Episodic memory: New directions in research* (pp. 153–163). New York, NY: Oxford University Press.

Vargha-Khadem, F., Gadian, D. G., Watkins, K. E., Connelly, A., Van Paesschen, W., & Mishkin, M. (1997). Differential effects of early hippocampal pathology on episodic and semantic memory. *Science, 277*, 376–380.

Velten, E. (1968). A laboratory task for induction of mood states. *Behaviour Research and Therapy, 6*, 473–482.

Viggiano, M. P., Giovannelli, F., Borgheresi, A., Feurra, M., Berardi, N., Pizzorusso, T., et al. (2008). Disruption of the prefrontal cortex by rTMS produces a category-specific enhancement of the reaction times during visual object identification. *Neuropsychologia, 46*, 2725–2731.

Vigliocco, G., & Hartsuiker, R. J. (2002). The interplay of meaning, sound, and syntax in sentence production. *Psychological Bulletin, 128*, 442–472.

Vingerhoets, G., Vermeule, E., & Santens, P. (2005). Impaired intentional content learning but spare incidental retention of contextual information in non-demented patients with Parkinson's disease. *Neuropsychologia, 43*, 675–681.

Vogel, E. K., Woodman, G. F., & Luck, S. J. (2001). Storage of features, conjunctions, and objects in visual working memory. *Journal of Experimental Psychology: Human Perception and Performance, 27*, 92–114.

Voss, J. L., Reber, P. J., Mesulam, M. M., Parrish, T. B., & Paller, K. A. (2008). Familiarity and conceptual priming engage distinct cortical networks. *Cerebral Cortex, 18*, 1712–1719.

Vousden, J. L., & Maylor, E. A. (2006). Speech errors across the lifespan. *Language and Cognitive Processes, 21*, 48–77.

Vredeveldt, A., Hitch, G. J., & Baddeley, A. D. (2011). Eyeclosure helps memory by reducing cognitive load and enhancing visualization. *Memory & Cognition, 39*, 1253–1263.

Vrij, A. (2008). Nonverbal dominance versus verbal accuracy in lie detection: A plea to change police practice. *Criminal Justice and Behavior, 35*, 1323–1336.

Vrij, A., Mann, S. A., Fisher, R. P., Leal, S., Milne, R., & Bull, R. (2008). Increasing cognitive load to facilitate lie detection: The benefit of recalling an event in reverse order. *Law and Human Behavior, 32*, 253–265.

Vroling, M. S., & de Jong, P. J. (2009). Deductive reasoning and social anxiety: Evidence for a fear-confirming belief bias. *Cognitive Therapy & Research, 33,* 633–644.

Vuilleumier, P., Schwartz, S., Clark, K., Husain, M., & Driver, J. (2002). Testing memory for unseen visual stimuli in patients with extinction and spatial neglect. *Journal of Cognitive Neuroscience, 14,* 875–886.

Vuilleumier, P., Schwartz, S., Verdon, V., Maravita, A., Hutton, C., Husain, M., et al. (2008). Abnormal attentional modulation of retinotopic cortex in parietal patients with spatial neglect. *Current Biology, 18,* 1525–1529.

Vul, E., & Pashler, H. (2007). Incubation benefits only after people have been misdirected. *Memory & Cognition, 35,* 701–710.

Wagner, U., Gais, S., Haider, H., Verleger, R., & Born, J. (2004). Sleep inspires insight. *Nature, 427,* 352–355.

Wagner, V., Jescheniak, J. D., & Schriefers, H. (2010). On the flexibility of grammatical advance planning: Effects of cognitive load on multiple lexical access. *Journal of Experimental Psychology: Learning, Memory, and Cognition, 36,* 423–440.

Walker, M. P., Brakefield, T., Hobson, J. A., & Stickgold, R. (2003). Dissociable stages of human memory consolidation and reconsolidation. *Nature, 425,* 616–620.

Wallas, G. (1926). *The art of thought.* London: Cape.

Walton, D. (2010). Why fallacies appear to be better arguments than they are. *Informal logic, 30,* 159–184.

Wang, A. Y., & Thomas, M. H. (2000). Looking for long-term mnemonic effects on serial recall: The legacy of Simonides. *American Journal of Psychology, 113,* 331–340.

Wang, X. T. (1996). Domain-specific rationality in human choices: Violations of utility axioms and social contexts. *Cognition, 60,* 31–63.

Wang, X. T., Simons, F., & Brédart, S. (2001). Social cues and verbal framing in risky choice. *Journal of Behavioral Decision Making, 14,* 1–15.

Ward, J. (2010). *The student's guide to cognitive neuroscience* (2nd ed.). Hove, UK: Psychology Press.

Warmington, M., Stothard, S. E., & Snowling, M. J. (2013). Assessing dyslexia in higher education: The York adult assessment battery-revised. *Journal of Research in Special Educational Needs, 13*(1), 48–56.

Warren, R. M. (2006). The relation of speech perception to the perception of nonverbal auditory patterns. In S. Greenberg & W. A. Ainsworth (Eds.), *Listening to speech: An auditory perspective* (pp. 333–349). Mahwah, NJ: Lawrence Erlbaum.

Warren, R. M., & Warren, R. P. (1970). Auditory illusions and confusions. *Scientific American, 223,* 30–36.

Wason, P. C. (1960). On the failure to eliminate hypotheses in a conceptual task. *Quarterly Journal of Experimental Psychology, 12,* 129–140.

Wason, P. C. (1968). Reasoning about a rule. *Quarterly Journal of Experimental Psychology, 20,* 63–71.

Wason, P. C., & Shapiro, D. (1971). Natural and contrived experience in reasoning problems. *Quarterly Journal of Experimental Psychology, 23,* 63–71.

Waters, E. A. (2008). Feeling good, feeling bad, and feeling at risk: A review of incidental affect's influence on likelihood estimates of health hazards and life events. *Journal of Risk Research, 11,* 569–595.

Watson, D., & Clark, L. A. (1992). Affects separable and inseparable: On the hierarchical arrangement of the negative affects. *Journal of Personality and Social Psychology, 62,* 489–505.

Watson, D., & Tellegen, A. (1985). Toward a consensual structure of mood. *Psychological Bulletin, 98,* 219–235.

Watson, J. B. (1913). Psychology as the behaviorist views it. *Psychological Review, 20,* 158–177.

Watson, J. M., & Strayer, D. L. (2010). Supertaskers: Profiles in extraordinary multitasking ability. *Psychonomic Bulletin & Review, 17,* 479–485.

Weaver III, C. A., & Krug, K. S. (2004). Consolidation-like effects in flashbulb memories: Evidence from September 11, 2001. *The American Journal of Psychology, 117*(4), 517–530.

Wegner, D. M. (2003). The mind's best trick: How we experience conscious will. *Trends in Cognitive Sciences, 7,* 65–69.

Wegner, D. M., & Wheatley, T. (1999). Apparent mental causation: Sources of the experience of will. *American Psychologist, 54,* 480–492.

Weinman, J., Ebrecht, M., Scott, S., Walburn, J., & Dyson, M. (2008). Enhanced wound healing after emotional disclosure intervention. *British Journal of Health Psychology, 13,* 95–102.

Weisberg, R. W. (2014). Toward an integrated theory of insight in problem solving. *Thinking & Reasoning.* doi:10.1080/13546783.2014.886625.

Weiskrantz, L. (1980). Varieties of residual experience. *Quarterly Journal of Experimental Psychology, 32,* 365–386.

Weiskrantz, L. (2004). Blindsight. In R. L. Gregory (Ed.), *Oxford companion to the mind.* Oxford, UK: Oxford University Press.

Weiskrantz, L., Warrington, E. K., Sanders, M. D., & Marshall, J. (1974). Visual capacity in the hemianopic field following a restricted occipital ablation. *Brain, 97,* 709–728.

Weisstein, N., & Harris, C. S. (1974). Visual detection of line segments – Object superiority effect. *Science, 186,* 752–755.

Weisstein, N., & Wong, E. (1986). Figure – ground organization and the spatial and temporal responses of the visual system. In E. C. Schwab & H. C. Nusbaum (Eds.), *Pattern recognition by humans and machines* (Vol. 2). New York, NY: Academic Press.

Wentura, D., Voss, A., & Rothermund, K. (2009). Playing TETRIS for science: Counter-regulatory affective processing in a motivationally "hot" context. *Acta Psychologica, 131,* 171–177.

Werker, J. F., & Tees, R. C. (1992). The organization and reorganization of human speech perception. *Annual Review of Neuroscience, 15,* 377–402.

Wheeler, M. A., Stuss, D. T., & Tulving, E. (1997). Toward a theory of episodic memory: The frontal lobes and autonoetic consciousness. *Psychological Bulletin, 121,* 331–354.

White, P. A. (2009). Property transmission: An explanatory account of the role of similarity information in causal inference. *Psychological Bulletin, 135,* 774–793.

Whithaus, C., Harrison, S., & Midyette, J. (2008). Keyboarding compared with handwriting on a high-stakes assessment: Student choice of composing medium, raters' perceptions and text quality. *Assessing Writing, 13,* 4–25.

Wiese, H., Wolff, N., Steffens, M. C., & Schweinberger, S. R. (2013). How experience shapes memory for faces: An eventrelated potential study on the own-age bias. *Biological Psychology, 94,* 369–379.

Wilding, J., & Valentine, E. (1994). Memory champions. *British Journal of Psychology, 85,* 231–244.

Wilkinson, L., & Jahanshahi, M. (2007). The striatum and probabilistic implicit sequence learning. *Brain Research, 1137,* 117–130.

Wilkinson, L., Khan, Z., & Jahanshahi, M. (2009). The role of the basal ganglia and its cortical connections in sequence learning: Evidence from implicit and explicit learning in Parkinson's disease. *Neuropsychologia, 47,* 2564–2573.

Wilkinson, L., & Shanks, D. R. (2004). Intentional control and implicit sequence learning. *Journal of Experimental Psychology: Learning, Memory, & Cognition, 30,* 354–369.

Williams, J. M. G., Watts, F. N., MacLeod, C. M., & Mathews, A. (1997). *Cognitive psychology and emotional disorders* (2nd ed.). Chichester, UK: Wiley.

Wilmer, J. B., Germine, L., Chabris, C. F., Chatterjee, G., Williams, M., Loken, E., et al. (2010). Human face recognition ability is specific and highly heritable. *Proceedings of the National Academy of Sciences of the United States of America, 107,* 5238–5241.

Winningham, R. G., Hyman, L. E., Jr., & Dinnel, D. L. (2000). Flashbulb memories? The effects of when the initial memory report was obtained. *Memory, 8,* 209–216.

Winograd, E., & Soloway, R. M. (1986). On forgetting the locations of things stored in special places. *Journal of Experimental Psychology: General, 115,* 366–372.

Wixted, J. T. (2004). The psychology and neuroscience of forgetting. *Annual Review of Psychology, 55,* 235–269.

Woike, B., Gershkovich, I., Piorkowski, R., & Polo, L (1999). The role of motives in the content and structure of autobiographical memory. *Journal of Personality and Social Psychology, 76,* 600–612.

Wolfe, J. M. (2007). Guided search 4.0: Current progress with a model of visual search. In W. Gray (Ed.), *Integrated models of cognitive systems* (pp. 99–119). New York, NY: Oxford University Press.

Wolfe, J. M., Horowitz, T. S., Van-Wert, M. J., Kenner, N M., Place, S. S., & Kibbi, N. (2007). Low target prevalence is a stubborn source of errors in visual search tasks. *Journal of Experimental Psychology: General, 136,* 623–6638.

Wong, C. K., & Read, J. D. (2011). Positive and negative effects of physical context reinstatement on eyewitness recall and recognition. *Applied Cognitive Psychology, 25,* 2–11.

Woollett, K., & Maguire, E. A. (2009). Navigational expertise may compromise anterograde associative memory. *Neuropsychologia, 44,* 1088–1095.

Woollett, K., Spiers, H. J., & Maguire, E. A. (2009). Talent in the taxi: A model system for exploring expertise. *Philosophical Transactions of the Royal Society B: Biological Sciences, 364,* 1407–1416.

Wright, D. B., & Loftus, E. F. (2008). Eyewitness memory. In G. Cohen & M. A. Conway (Eds.), *Memory in the real world* (3rd ed.). Hove, UK: Psychology Press.

Wright, D. B., & Stroud, J. N. (2002). Age differences in line-up identification accuracy: People are better with their own age. *Law and Human Behavior, 26,* 641–654.

Wright, G. (1984). *Behavioral decision theory.* Harmondsworth, UK: Penguin.

Wroe, A. L., Bhan, A., Salkovskis, P., & Bedford, H. (2005). Feeling bad about immunizing our children. *Vaccine, 23,* 1428–1433.

Wu, L. L., & Barsalou, L. W. (2009). Perceptual simulation in conceptual combination: Evidence from property generation. *Acta Psychologica, 132,* 173–189.

Wübben, M., & van Wangenheim, F. (2008). Instant customer base analysis: Managerial heuristics often "get it right". *Journal of Marketing, 72,* 82–93.

Xu, Y., & Chun, M. M. (2009). Selecting and perceiving multiple visual objects. *Trends in Cognitive Sciences, 13,* 167–174.

Yantis, S. (2008). The neural basis of selective attention: Cortical sources and targets of attentional modulation. *Current Directions in Psychological Science, 17,* 86–90.

Yates, M. (2005). Phonological neighbors speed visual word processing: Evidence from multiple tasks. *Journal of Experimental Psychology: Human Perception and Performance, 34,* 1599–1606.

Yates, M., Friend, J., & Ploetz, D. M. (2008). Phonological neighbors influence word naming through the least supported phoneme. *Journal of Experimental Psychology: Human Perception and Performance, 21,* 996–1014.

Ye, L., Cardwell, W., & Mark, L. S. (2009). Perceiving multiple affordances for objects. *Ecological Psychology, 21,* 185–217.

Yegiyan, N. S., & Lang, A. (2010). Processing central and peripheral detail: How content arousal and emotional tone influence encoding. *Media Psychology, 13,* 77–99.

Yonelinas, A. P. (2002). The nature of recollection and familiarity: A review of 30 years of research. *Journal of Memory and Language, 46,* 441–517.

Yoon, K. L., & Zinbarg, R. E. (2008). Interpreting neutral faces as threatening is a default mode for socially anxious individuals. *Journal of Abnormal Psychology, 117,* 680–685.

Young, A. W., Hay, D. C., & Ellis, A. W. (1985). The faces that launched a thousand slips: Everyday difficulties and errors in recognizing people. *British Journal of Psychology, 76,* 495–523.

Young, A. W., Hellawell, D., & Hay, D. C. (1987). Configurational information in face perception. *Perception, 16,* 747–759.

Young, A. W., Newcombe, F., de Haan, E. H. F., Small, M., & Hay, D. C. (1993). Face perception after brain injury: Selective impairments affecting identity and expression. *Brain, 116,* 941–959.

Zacks, J. M. (2008). Neuroimaging studies of mental rotation: A meta-analysis and review. *Journal of Cognitive Neuroscience, 20,* 1–19.

Zago, S., Corti, S., Bersano, A., Baron, P., Conti, G., Ballabio, E., et al. (2010). A cortically blind patient with preserved visual imagery. *Cognitive and Behavioral Neurology, 23,* 44–48.

Zangwill, O. L. (2004). Ebbinghaus. In R. L. Gregory (Ed.), *The Oxford companion to the mind* (2nd ed., p. 276). New York, NY: Oxford University Press.

Zanon, M., Busan, P., Monti, F., Pizzolato, G., & Battaglini, P. P. (2010). Cortical connections between dorsal and ventral visual streams in humans: Evidence by TNS/EEG co-registration. *Brain Topography, 22,* 307–317.

Zeki, S., & Romaya, J. P. (2010). The brain reaction to viewing faces of opposite- and same-sex romantic partners. *PLoS One, 5,* e15802.

Zelko, H., Zammar, G. R., Ferreira, A. P. B., Phadtare, A., Shah, J., & Pietrobon, R. (2010). Selection mechanisms underlying high impact biomedical research – a qualitative analysis and causal model. *PLoS One, 5,* e10535.

Zevin, J. D., & Seidenberg, M. S. (2006). Simulating consistency effects and individual differences in nonword naming: A comparison of current models. *Journal of Memory and Language, 54,* 145–160.

Zhou, X. L., Ye, Z., Cheung, H., & Chen, H. -C. (2009). Processing the Chinese language: An introduction. *Language and Cognitive Processes, 24,* 929–946.

Ziemann, U. (2010). TMS in cognitive neuroscience: Virtual lesion and beyond. *Cortex, 46,* 124–127.

Zimmer, H. D. (2008). Visual and spatial working memory: From boxes to networks. *Neuroscience and Biobehavioral Reviews, 32,* 1373–1395.

Zogg, J. B., Woods, S. P., Sauceda, J. A., Wiebe, J. S., & Simoni, J. M. (2012). The role of prospective memory in medication adherence: A review of an emerging literature. *Journal of Behavioral Medicine, 35,* 47–62.

Zwaan, R. A. (1994). Effects of genre expectations on text comprehension. *Journal of Experimental Psychology: Learning, Memory, & Cognition, 20,* 920–933.

Zwaan, R. A. (2009). Mental simulation in language comprehension and social cognition. *European Journal of Social Psychology, 39,* 1142–1150.

Zwaan, R. A., & Madden, C. J. (2004). Updating situation models. *Journal of Experimental Psychology: Learning, Memory, and Cognition, 30,* 283–288.

Zwaan, R. A., & van Oostendorp, U. (1993). Do readers construct spatial representations in naturalistic story comprehension? *Discourse Processes, 16,* 125–143.

Zwaan, R. A., & Radvansky, G. A. (1998). Situation models in language comprehension and memory. *Psychological Bulletin, 123,* 162–185.

Zwaan, R. A., Stanfield, R. A., & Yaxley, R. H. (2002). Language comprehenders mentally represent the shapes of objects. *Psychological Science, 13,* 168–171.

Name index

Subject index

Note: Italicized page numbers indicate a figure on the corresponding page. Page numbers in bold indicate a table on the corresponding page.

Related Titles

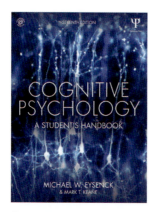

Cognitive Psychology,
7th Edition
By Michael W. Eysenck

Pbk ISBN: 9781848724167
Hbk ISBN: 9781848724150

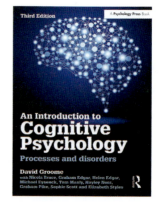

An Introduction to Cognitive Psychology,
3rd Edition
By David Groome

Pbk ISBN: 9781848720923
Hbk ISBN: 9781848720916

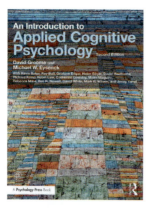

An Introduction to Applied Cognitive Psychology,
2nd Edition
By David Groome and Michael W. Eysenck

Pbk ISBN: 9781138840133
Hbk ISBN: 9781138840126

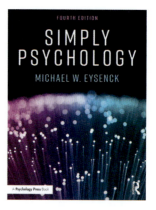

Simply Psychology,
4th Edition
By Michael W. Eysenck

Pbk ISBN: 9781138698963
Hbk ISBN: 9781138698956

www.routledge.com